FREEDOM
REDISCOVERED

FREEDOM REDISCOVERED

*Discovering freedom
as Jesus intended*

Dave (Daividh) Wilkinson

Published by Weerona Publishing Pty Ltd
PO Box 1125, Bairnsdale, Victoria 3875, Australia
https://www.weeronap.com

First published 2024 by Weerona Publishing

Copyright © 2024 by Weerona Publishing

All rights reserved. No part of this book may be reproduced or transmitted by any person or entity in any form or by any means, electronic or mechanical, including photocopying, recording, scanning or by or on any information storage and retrieval system or otherwise, without the express prior written permission of Weerona Publishing, except for brief quotations for critique/review as permitted by fair use / fair dealing and similar copyright legislation.

The author and publisher have taken care in the preparation of this book, but make no expressed or implied warranty of any kind and assume no responsibility for errors or omissions. No liability is assumed for incidental or consequential damages in connection with or arising out of the use of information contained herein.

Edited by Bronwyn Forman
Cover design by Communique Graphics
Cover photo Dreamstime.com
Internal design and typesetting by Communique Graphics
Printed and bound by IngramSpark

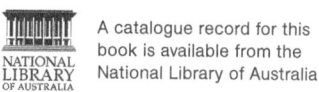 A catalogue record for this book is available from the National Library of Australia

ISBN, print ed. 9781763522701

ISBN, ePub ed. 9781763522718

TABLE OF CONTENTS

AUTHOR'S NOTES v
The challenge of church "traditions" v
Who is this book for? v
To help you read this book vi
The creation of this book vii

SECTION 1: COURAGEOUSLY CHECK THE FOUNDATIONS 1
    Chapter 1: Ask questions of yourself 5
    Chapter 2: Ask questions of the church leaders 27
    Chapter 3: Be an agent of change 61
    Chapter 4: What "church" is not!!! 67
    Chapter 5: So what should "church" look like? 85

SECTION 2: NO MORE "HOLY MEN" 103
    Chapter 6: The issue of professionalism 107
    Chapter 7: The issue of control 137
    Chapter 8: Control of the individual exemplified 163
    Chapter 9: The subtle dangers of "hierarchies" 177
    Chapter 10: Stop supporting the hierarchy 183

SECTION 3: NO MORE CONFORMITY 189
    Chapter 11: Blatant expectations on conformity 193
    Chapter 12: Suppression through "accountability" 199
    Chapter 13: Brazen opposition to individuality? 211
    Chapter 14: Why we need individuals 219

SECTION 4: NO MORE INSTITUTIONALIZED MINISTRY 225
    Chapter 15: Exposing ministry institutionalization 227
    Chapter 16: Church-growth "ministry" 235
    Chapter 17: Ministry without institutions 243

SECTION 5: NO MORE "HOLY HUDDLES" 265
    Chapter 18: The myths of "fellowship" 267

SECTION 6: EXPECT OPPOSITION 279
    Chapter 19: Analysis of persecution, resistance 281
    Chapter 20: Honorable but misguided reasons for resistance ... 289
    Chapter 21: Dishonorable reasons for resistance to your freedom ... 305

SECTION 7: FIRST AID FOR THE DEAD? 313
    Chapter 22: Can't we find some use for local churches? 315
    Chapter 23: What about "home churches" as an alternative? 325
    Chapter 24: We need more than a facelift 329

SECTION 8: SIGNPOSTS TO A BETTER WAY 337
    Chapter 25: Natural fellowship 341
    Chapter 26: Freedom from structures 345
    Chapter 27: A case study of an "organization" that isn't 349
    Chapter 28: You say, "but what if we find a 'good' leader?" 369
    Chapter 29: A line in the sand – stop playing 'follow the leader' 385
    Chapter 30: Individuality as God intended 399
    Chapter 31: Ministry set free 421
    Chapter 32: Identifying the freedom principles 433
    Chapter 33: Applying the freedom principles 459

SECTION 9: CHECK OUT THE PLANK IN YOUR OWN EYE 465
    Chapter 34: You may need to change 467
    Chapter 35: Check out your relationship with God 471
    Chapter 36: Check out your relationship with others 481
    Chapter 37: Check out yourself 495
    Chapter 38: High aims balanced with grace 505

SECTION 10: LAUNCH OUT IN FREEDOM 515
    Chapter 39: Boldness in the face of misunderstanding 517
    Chapter 40: Timid feelings, brave actions 525
    Chapter 41: Discern God's current call on your life 545
    Chapter 42: Beware the comfort of the familiar 567
    Chapter 43: Relating to old-school clergy who want to join you 571
    Chapter 44: Now it's over to you 579

SECTION 11: FINALLY: DON'T GO BACK TO EGYPT 587
    Chapter 45: Money can trap you 589
    Chapter 46: Success can trap you 599
    Chapter 47: "Change" can trap you 609
    Chapter 48: "Getting organized" can trap you 619
    Chapter 49: Avoid the path to leadership 639

ACKNOWLEDGMENTS 647
AFTERWORD 648
BIBLIOGRAPHY 650

AUTHOR'S NOTES

The challenge of church traditions

There are practices within churches that perhaps are more a reflection of habit than a reflection of the life of Christ. As a trivial example, perhaps you were taught to pray kneeling beside your bed with eyes closed and hands clasped? That's an example of "tradition", especially when you consider that Jesus sometimes prayed with His eyes open and lifted towards the heavens.

Perhaps it really doesn't matter if you pray with your eyes open or closed. I would like to think that God is more concerned with whether you pray or not than He is concerned by styles that are more a reflection of your traditions. But are some traditions of greater consequence? Should we protect and carry forward some traditions? Or are some of the traditions that you follow past their use-by date, if indeed they were ever meant to be?

Even if our routines are comfortable, what if they are missing the mark? Human nature sometimes resists change, even if it makes sense to head in a new direction. This book may challenge some of your beliefs, perhaps even leading to some practices you have followed for a life-time being put at risk.

Honestly questioning church practices can be painful. It can also be refreshing, leading to a liberty in Christ you may never have believed possible. It may be lonely if those who are close to you choose to part company with you, and stick with their own routines. Worse, in some controlling groups, you may be shunned, with members instructed to disassociate from you. But even if your price for freedom includes being misunderstood, wouldn't you still want liberty ahead of slavery?

And the real crunch is this: What if *Jesus* wants you to abandon the comfort of your current ways, even if you don't want to change?

Who is this book for?

There are some who perhaps have a general uneasiness about church. For them, something feels wrong, but they may struggle to pinpoint issues.

Then there are those who have been so badly hurt by churches they not only throw away church attendance, but throw away their Christian faith. This is understandable, especially if church leaders have insisted that attendance is essential for them to continue in their Christian walk.

A similar situation arises when those that might otherwise have considered Christ's claims don't go further, based on the assumption that if they do become Christians, they will have to attend churches, pay tithes, agree to the church club rules, and more.

There are probably many other types of people who may benefit from embracing the freedom message in this book, but one type is of great concern to me. It can be identified by those who can't, or won't, ask questions. In the worst-case scenario, they belong to a group whose leaders disparage, or outright condemn, questioning. Some leaders go so far as to ban reading of books that they haven't sanctioned. In these cases, the followers of such controlling leaders will never get to hear this freedom message if not gently introduced to it by friends and family – possibly you.

Then after folk have left abusive and controlling groups, this book may help provide a perspective on their past, and future, journey.

To help you read this book

I will try to keep this section short, but I suggest it may help establish a framework for the rest of the book.

Terms like "Clergy" and "Laity"

Words like "clergy" and "laity" mean different things in different groups. In some circles, the differences between clergy and laity are important. Others hold the view that we are all the same in the Body of Christ—they feel that there should be no clergy/laity distinction.

So rather than get into a dispute from the outset, can I please suggest a simple way forward? I will usually try and avoid the term "clergy" and instead refer to "church leaders". In some circles, these people might be distinguished by a formal title or some office or recognized role. For others, "church leader" may simply be an informal title for those who are looked to when decisions have to be made. Perhaps they are simply respected "elders" within a group.

So, then we are left with the term, "laity". Some dictionaries seem to be a little imprecise as to what constitutes the "laity", giving the impression that they are simply defined as those who are not "clergy". If we take this position, then those members of the Body of Christ who are not recognized as leaders are therefore the laity.

Terms like "local churches", the "Church" and the "Body of Christ"

There is more than a little ambiguity on the term "church". Some of the various meanings and their consequences are addressed later in this book, but for now I would like to define "churches" with a lowercase "c" as local gatherings of people, often in a formal building, but sometimes in homes or some less formal setting. I would also like to define the "Church" (singular, and often written with an upper-case "C") as the "Body of Christ" comprised of all Christians, across time.

Referring to God

Many traditional writers use upper case when referring to God ("He" not "he", and "Him" not "him", and so on). Others just use lower case. This book has many quotes, so both styles are found. But what style do I use? If I go for the modern style, I may offend those who feel it is not showing God due reverence. And if I use the old style, many readers may feel I am reflecting an out-of-date style. Given that I probably can't win, I went for the old style.

Bible references

Lastly, you might be expecting huge volumes of quotes from the Bible, and may wonder why there really aren't many.

An important reason for incorporating less Scripture than some might expect was a conscious choice to avoid "proof-texting". You may know the practice, even if not by that name. A person firstly establishes the beliefs they hold to be true, then as an afterthought find convenient Bible verses to "prove" they're right. One of the key messages in this book is the need for each of us to individually take responsibility for checking things out. So instead of quoting chapter and verse to support my research, can I please suggest that if you find this book challenging, you join me in going directly to God and seeking His guidance? I think that's much better than me trying to prove my conclusions by using selective parts of the Bible.

The creation of this book

This book started out as a personal, informal piece of research for my own purposes as I grappled with some perplexing questions. To that end, many quotations were collected from numerous sources where I felt they fell squarely within the subject matter, and themselves could be open to direct critical analysis as part of my critique. The collection of direct quotations is in contrast to formal tertiary-level research theses where the referenced material is rephrased and summarized in the researcher's own words. In this formative stage, direct quotations were chosen to lessen the likelihood of wrongful interpretation by me as I deliberated on the emerging themes.

Many of the authors I have quoted seemed to place different emphases on certain points of view, or even appeared to hold opposing views. Consequently, while retaining it for personal research purposes, I consciously performed critical review of the material. I added comments, and in some cases I expressed negative criticism of the views of certain authors. The purpose of the reshaped document was to try, objectively and honestly, to consider the underlying ideas behind the collection of material, and to work towards reaching a fair judgment that would shape my personal strategy for applying the lessons learned.

As the document began to take a more definite shape, I concluded that I wished that someone had years ago published just such a book to help me find my way. It would have saved me a lot of heartache and effort over a period spanning more than a decade. It is my sincere desire that my findings be shared for the benefit of the wider public, especially fellow seekers-of-truth.

The direct quotations that helped shape my thinking have been deliberately retained to assist you, the reader, to reach your own conclusions. All reasonable effort has been made to faithfully transcribe the original wording, to accurately give due credit to the source (with attribution included against each individual quote in addition to a list of referenced sources at the back of the book), to ensure the information within this book was correct at time of publication, and to rightly reflect the context and truth of the original. Apologies are given for any failures in reaching these goals, and the reader is strongly encouraged to acquire the original works for their own evaluation. One of the key messages in this book is that of support for the right of each individual to freely think about and challenge the views of others. In the spirit of this freedom, I encourage you to challenge what I have written!

Finally, I want to clarify my attitude to authors whose opinions I have critiqued and reviewed. A large number I have applauded for their views. For some, I have given mixed feedback, and for a small number I have provided negative criticism based on the quotations I have used. I want to be absolutely clear that, even for the latter group, I am not wishing to be seen as implying any shortcomings of character in the individual. I am simply trying to express a view that suggests I have a difference of opinion on what I understand to be their position as expressed in their writings.

I suspect that some of the authors, and possibly you, too, may disagree with my views. Russell Ackoff, in his wonderful book *Ackoff's Fables*, encourages vigorous but respectful debate. I hope my contribution is seen in this light.

SECTION 1:

COURAGEOUSLY CHECK THE FOUNDATIONS

Setting the scene: A myriad of opinions on "church"

Have you noticed the great divergence on opinions about "church"?

Some claim a church should be as big as possible—a mega-church—so that it is able to have a much more powerful, visible impact. Others prefer a smaller, more personal church. Or even smaller again—a home church.

There are also differences of opinion on leadership style. Should a church be led by one man at the top, worldwide? Or one man at the top in your local church (the senior pastor or equivalent)? Or led by a city-wide confederation of churches? Some suggest a different model such as a team of leaders representing the five gifts (apostle, prophet, evangelist, pastor, and teacher). Others suggest we've tried leaders with the last four gifts—teachers at the top after the Reformation, evangelists in the spotlight during the mission years, etc. So now it's time to try "apostolic" leaders. Or let's get more democratic and let the people vote for the leadership team, who in turn choose the pastor. Or get really drastic and have a church with no (apparent) leaders. Or any one of a dozen or more models!

Perhaps we've got all these models because we haven't gone back to the "New Testament" church model. But what if our interpretation of the New Testament model is flawed or the model itself has elements that reflect the human weaknesses of imperfect disciples, and is not the model of Christ Himself?

I have traveled a long journey, seeking answers to such questions. Along the way, I sought God to give me the pieces of a jigsaw puzzle that would eventually form a clearer picture. This book is the assembled collection of such jigsaw pieces, referencing authors from around the world and across a number of centuries. The resultant picture from the assembled jigsaw puzzle may come as a surprise to you, as it did me. But please join me in believing for a Body of Christ where all the members are active in service and are personally relating directly to God Himself.

If you have struggled to know how you should play your part in God's universal Church (the Body of Christ) and how the local expression of "church" fits in, you are not alone. Even great thinkers such as Philip Yancey have also grappled for years with similar issues. His book, *Soul Survivor* is subtitled, *How My Faith Survived the Church*. For him, it was a

> "... lifelong process of separating church from God."

(Yancey, 2001: 43)

Are you willing to be an agent for change?

The "church" of Jesus' day was originally structured according to the direct commands of God through Moses. But traditions of men had slipped in, and Jesus took a bold stand against them. Many in His day saw His actions as opposing the very foundations of what God had established. In contrast to the rejection from the peers of Jesus, we can look back now and admire His courage in challenging the traditions and laws introduced by men.

But in our own time, like the Jews of Jesus' day, we can get defensive of any criticism of "church", feeling it is threatening the institution Jesus established, and not seeing that our church leaders have also introduced "traditions of men". And, just as it was difficult for Jesus and His followers to swim against the tide of tradition, we are going to need men and women with the courage to question, challenge, and oppose introduced errors. Are you willing to be one of those brave people, no matter what the cost? Erwin McManus' delightfully challenging book, appropriately titled *The Barbarian Way*, states:

> *"If you are a follower of Christ and you have allowed yourself to be domesticated, you have lost the power of who you are and who God intends for you to be. You were not created to be normal. God's desire for you is not compliance and conformity. You have been baptized by Spirit and fire. Asleep within you is a barbarian, a savage to all who love the prim and proper. You must go to the primal place and enter the presence of the Most High God, for there you will be changed by His presence. Let Him unleash the untamed faith within you."*
>
> (McManus, 2005: 82)
>
> *"Live or die, succeed or fail, barbarians must pursue and attempt such dreams and visions. The barbarian spirit dreams great dreams and finds the courage to live them."*
>
> (McManus, 2005: 100)

Michael Brown (in *Revolution in the Church*) is likewise challenging:

> *"Will we be true pioneers, following our scriptural convictions and the clear leading of the Spirit, even if others call us crazy? D. L. Moody was known as 'Crazy Moody' early in his Christian work, whereas today his highly respected name is associated with a Bible institute, a Christian magazine, a publishing organization and other Kingdom works. We cannot have all the success first! If we do, it is unlikely that we have fully carried the cross.*
>
> *But this should not strike us as odd. If things are as bad as I believe they are, and as many others insist they are, why should it surprise us if, at least for a time, success and numbers are against us? (Even if we do have great numbers and much blessing, we still do not measure success the way the world does.) Why should it surprise us that we must swim against the tide?"*
>
> (Brown, 2002: 202)

CHAPTER 1:
ASK QUESTIONS OF YOURSELF

The need for questioning your own beliefs

If you suspect you may have cancer, one of many possible reactions is to run to a doctor to seek clarification as to whether or not your suspicions are correct. Another is to simply hope it's not really cancer. For many people, the choice is a struggle. One argument states a visit to the doctor may save your life through early diagnosis and treatment. But there can be opposing thoughts and feelings. Maybe it's not *really* anything serious, so why get everyone upset.

Sometimes denial seems a more attractive option than facing reality. Maybe the church systems are not as healthy as they should be, but we may be tempted to hope it's not really so. Yet, since one of God's names is "Truth", we should be able to evaluate the health of churches without feeling guilty. More than that, perhaps it's part of being Christ-like to always seek the truth, even if the news at first is bad.

Many will recognize that churches today have problems. Perhaps the most ironic of problems is the existence of churches that believe they have nothing wrong with them! The fact that members of hundreds of different denominations each think they are "right" should be sufficient to challenge that argument.

Going to the doctor to seek diagnosis for suspected cancer is surely not fun, and I realize that a truthful appraisal of the state of health of our churches may be no more exciting. Yet it is essential.

However, objectivity in questioning may prove difficult. Yancey believes:

> "... *Christians tend to create subcultures, reading their own books, listening to their own music, educating their children in their own schools. Little cross-fertilisation takes place between that subculture and the wider, secular culture."*
>
> (Yancey, 2001: 225)

Michael Phillips' novel *Mercy and Eagleflight* presents a young lady who was raised in a God-fearing family, went to Bible school, and headed out as an evangelist, only to find that she was unsure of what *she* believed, in contrast to the pat answers she could give others based on what she had been *taught* to believe. She chose to question, even though the experience was painful:

"Even in the midst of what might have seemed like faith-destroying questions and bitterly painful revelations of her own superficial life till now [she] actually felt a sense of strength slowly growing inside.

She was thinking – thinking for herself ...

If it meant that she had to plunge down to the bottom of her being to find out what she wasn't made of and what she hadn't been and what she didn't believe in order then to climb back out and discover who she was and what she was made of and what she did believe ... then she would do it! ...

[Praying to God she said,] 'I want to believe, God. Maybe I don't yet. I don't know – but I want to. If that's something I need to repent of and ask your forgiveness for, talking like I believed when all I was doing was saying everything I'd been taught, then I am sorry.'

... uncluttered by teaching and church, by books and ideas, by parents and brothers and sisters – she had at last met her Father face-to-face in the deepest regions of her heart."

(Phillips, 1996: 138-9, 142, 143)

This need for honest questioning, and the freedom to doubt, is reinforced by Yancey:

"The books of memoirs-in-process continued to flow as he [Buechner] kept probing his past and his present, mining for grace.

If you tell me Christian commitment is a kind of thing that has happened to you once and for all like some kind of spiritual plastic surgery, I say ... you're either pulling the wool over your own eyes or trying to pull it over mine. Every morning you should wake up in your beds and ask yourself: 'Can I believe it all again today?' No, better still, don't ask it till after you've read The New York Times, till after you've studied that daily record of the world's brokenness and corruption, which should always stand side by side with your Bible. Then ask yourself if you can believe in the Gospel of Jesus Christ again for that particular day. If your answer's always Yes, then you probably don't know what believing means. At least five times out of ten the answer should be No because the No is as important as the Yes, maybe more so. The No is what proves you're human in case you should ever doubt it. And then if some morning the answer happens to be really Yes, it should be a Yes that's choked with confession and tears and ... great laughter.

(From The Return of Ansel Gibbs)"

(Yancey, 2001: 252)

ASK QUESTIONS OF YOURSELF

Randall Arthur, in his novel *Wisdom Hunter*, presents the dangers of not questioning, and the honor in truthful questioning:

> *"I have discovered that my thinking was naïve during the duration of my ministry, and this has left me feeling completely humiliated. In retrospect, I must shamefully admit that I blindly believed everything my older peers and my right-wing Bible college and seminary professors fed me. I never honestly questioned the validity of anything they said. Why was I so gullible?*
>
> *The more I've thought about it, the more I've realized that at least one reason for my gullibility was the fact that I was never asked, encouraged, or taught to learn by the process of questioning, disagreeing, challenging, or thinking. Rather I was left to assume (whether intentionally or unintentionally I still am not sure) that all my teachers were masters of their subjects and could neither teach nor believe anything wrong. Consequently I learned by being programmed like a computer. I was not taught how to think. I was taught what to think. As a result I became a pathetic little parrot who all his life simply repeats what he hears.*
>
> *Convinced that I was preaching the inflexible truth, I expected all my followers to blindly believe what I was passing down to them. I carried out a pastoral crusade of 'Believe exactly the way I believe or be damned.' The real tragedy is that my peers, thousands of them, were of the same mold, and still are.*
>
> *My heart now shudders. Like the Catholic hierarchy of old, we indirectly asked our followers to blindly believe us, and then socially punished them in the name of 'church discipline' if they did not.*
>
> *I now understand that to blindly believe any teaching is treacherously wrong. The Pharisees blindly believed the manmade and traditional teachings of their forefathers, equated them with the Scriptures, and guarded them with tenacity. Jesus told them that their blind adherence to those impotent teachings, and their insistence upon revering them, made their worship of God utterly vain (Mark 7:1-13).*
>
> *Instead of blindly believing, we must honestly question every so-called Christian teaching. We must do it to weed out the irrelevant and wasteful manmade teachings from that which truly has eternal value. In Acts 17:10-11, the Bereans even tested Paul's teaching against the Scriptures, and were considered noble for their wise approach."*
>
> (Arthur, 1991: 131-133)

Sometimes we can act defensively when we encounter views different to those we have held for a long time. Jamie Buckingham, in his delightful collection of tales, *The Last Word*, was struck by the words of a visitor to his local church, Bruce Morgan, who said,

> "There is something too strong about truth for the human palate to receive all at once."
>
> (Buckingham, 1978: 113)

His thoughtful response to these words of another was:

> "... truth always demands change. In fact, a full dose will actually put to death the old nature of man. Therefore, rather than accept pure truth we choose to water it down, stone our prophets, or even believe an outright lie if it makes things easier."
>
> (Buckingham, 1978: 113)

A quick look at the flaws in "church" history

Michael Frost and Alan Hirsch (in *The Shaping Of Things To Come*) describe institutionalized religion based around local churches:

> "Christendom is marked by the following characteristics:
>
> 1. Its mode of engagement is attractional ['come to us' rather than going to where people are] ...
>
> 2. A shift of focus to dedicated, sacred buildings or places of worship ...
>
> 3. The emergence of an institutionally recognized, professional clergy class ...
>   This had the effect of creating two classes of Christians: the clergy and the laity. ...
>
> 4. ... the institutionalization of grace in the form of sacraments administered by an institutionally licensed priesthood. ..."
>
> (Frost & Hirsch, 2003: 226-227)

One serious "blind-spot" of many is their desire to deny problems that have occurred throughout history, both as part of Christendom, and also within its roots of Judaism. Yet George Santayana, in *Reason in Common Sense* p.284), 1905, warned, "*Those who cannot remember the past are condemned to repeat it.*" Christians who refuse to acknowledge flaws in their inheritance are also at risk of perpetuating the errors. A very brief recognition of Christendom's history follows, starting with its Old Testament foundations. We must accept the reality of our past, and then be willing to question our present state.

If we use the term "church" to represent a gathering of God's people, we might refer to the institution that lay at the heart of Jewish practices as the "Old Testament church". God founded this institution. However, some of the traditions that followed later were not necessarily a direct reflection of God's plan. Things had become so bad that some of the Old Testament prophets brazenly proclaimed warnings against the way that things had turned out. For example, in *All Nations in God's Purpose*, Cornell Goerner refers to the book of Malachi and notes that there was:

> "... sham and hypocrisy in worship services ..."
>
> (Goerner, 1979: 76)

He then notes God's response, where God calls for someone with the courage and conviction to slam shut the doors of His own temple to prevent the continuance of the useless pretense:

"Oh that there were one among you who would shut the gates, that you might not uselessly kindle fire on My altar!"

Malachi, quoted in Goerner (1979: 76)

One could argue that some, if not most of the "church leaders" of Jesus' day, were still missing the message from Malachi. Jesus, like many prophets before Him, spoke out against traditions that man had added to God's laws. A quick look at the New Testament will reveal stories of Jesus' outspoken criticism of the practices of His day. Yet when Jesus confronted the leaders of His day, he was strongly opposed by them.

Many in the Christian churches of today can readily accept that there were weaknesses in the Jewish temple system of Jesus' day. Some who accept that today's Christian church practices are also flawed call us to return to the standards of the New Testament church. But were the New Testament leaders without fault? The Christian faith is founded on Christ's claims of perfection, but not on claims that the disciples / apostles were perfect.

In his classic book, *What's So Amazing about Grace?* Yancey suggests that Jesus' own disciples did not understand His style of leadership, even after Pentecost. Yancey points out that Jesus set a new standard of grace. For example:

> *"[Jesus] touched ... those suffering from leprosy [and] ... let a woman of ill repute wash his feet with her hair [and] ... dined with tax collectors–one even joined his inner circle of the Twelve–and was notoriously lax about the rules of ritual cleanness and Sabbath observance.*
>
> *Moreover, Jesus deliberately crossed into Gentile territory and got involved with Gentiles."*

(Yancey, 1997: 152)

Yet, in spite of these examples, and the in-filling of the Holy Spirit, the apostles still showed they were ordinary human beings, capable of mistakes, especially in the realm of falling back into the traditions from which Jesus showed freedom. For example:

> *"When Peter, under duress, finally agreed to visit the house of a Roman centurion, he introduced himself by saying, 'You are well aware that it is against our law for a Jew to associate with a Gentile or visit him.' He made such a concession only after losing the argument with God on the rooftop."*

(Yancey, 1997: 151-152)

Another area where early church practices did not align with Jesus' teaching was in the area of giving. Jesus said not to let one's left hand know what their right hand gave, and that God rewards those who give in secret (Matthew 6: 3-4). Acts 2: 45 records that people followed His directive to give to the needy, possibly in secret, but by Acts 4: 35 (and the subsequent story of Ananias and Sapphira), money given to the needy was given openly to the disciples, who then distributed it. It certainly was not anonymous.

Perhaps even more damning was the apostles' failure to obey Christ's clear directive to "go" into all the world. In his article titled *The Hidden Message of 'Acts'*, Don Richardson appears to paint a critical picture of the apostles and the Jerusalem church as they, by-and-large, initially failed to obey Christ's clear command to share the news across the varied cultures of the known world.

> *"How amazing! There were now at least 15 men generally recognized [by the Jerusalem church] as apostles since Matthias, James the Lord's brother and Saul and Barnabas joined the original 11. And yet, out of the 15 only two are 'commissioned' [by this central church] to evangelize the estimated 900 million Gentiles in the world at that time. The other 13 are convinced that they are all needed to evangelize only about three million Jews, among whom there were already tens of thousands of witnessing believers! Their unashamed willingness to let Paul and Barnabas take on the entire Gentile world boggles my mind."*
>
> (Richardson, 1981: 96)

Richardson goes on to state that, after 25% of the book of Acts had unfolded, they

> *"... were not even making plans to obey the rest of Jesus' last command [to go into the rest of the world]!"*
>
> (Richardson, 1981: 90)

There may be errors we can detect in New Testament church practices, but they pale in comparison to the atrocities committed in Jesus' name by the church institutions over the following centuries and millennia. Jesus had the power to have killed His enemies, but didn't, yet many bloody wars under the banner of Christianity were of a mixed religious and political nature and resulted in the brutal killing of those perceived as being the Church's enemies.

Some of these wars were held against those seen as being outside of Christianity, but there were also many wars within Christendom. Perhaps the clearest has been the wars between those with allegiance to the Catholic Church, and Protestants.

On the one hand, Protestants are often offended by the continuing claims by the Catholic Church on the Pope's infallibility. In an extract from Benson Bobrick's *Wide as the Waters: The Story of the English Bible and the Revolution It Inspired*, Brown quotes Pope Gregory VII as follows:

> *"The pope can be judged by no one; the Roman church has never erred and never will err till the end of time; the Roman church was founded by Christ alone; the pope alone can depose and restore bishops; he alone can make new laws, set up new bishoprics, and divide old ones; he alone can translate [i.e. transfer] bishops; he alone can call general councils and authorize canon law; he alone can revise his judgments [in case he got them wrong the first time]; his legates, even though in inferior orders, have precedence over all bishops; an appeal to the papal courts inhibits judgment by all inferior courts; a duly ordained pope is undoubtedly made a saint by the merits of St. Peter."*
>
> (Brown, 2002: 101)

Of course, Protestants may at times find fault with the Catholic Church. But Martin Luther, the founder of Protestantism, was also flawed – for example, he had an intense hatred of the Jews – a view that Hitler used to justify his own actions. Brown (2002) notes that:

> "Nazi soldiers followed Luther's counsel to a tee, setting the synagogues on fire and smashing the windows of Jewish places of business, among other humiliating and even murderous acts."

(Brown, 2002: 168)

Yancey summarizes Christian church history in one damning sentence:

> "... by and large the history of European Christianity is the record of a church that relies on wealth, power, prestige and even coercion and war to advance its cause."

(Yancey, 2001: 157)

Faults existed in the past, but perhaps the churches of today are OK?

It is one thing to recognize mistakes in the "church" over past history. But it is so easy and so dangerous to assume that we have learned from the past mistakes and now are basically "OK". But are we, really? Because if we are not, those outside of the faith that Jesus died for may reject His message because of us!

Bob Girard's book, *Brethren, Hang Loose*, was written decades ago, but has many timely warnings. He gives us an introduction to the problems of "church" as he had experienced it. His view might shock many by its boldness:

> "I hated [the church's] smallness of vision, its suspicion and jealousy of the few men who succeeded in really reaching people, its fear of anything fresh and new, its bondage to clichés, its stuff-shirted spiritual pride, its power politics (which it always tried to hide behind a façade of piety), its endless reports of nothing happening, its press releases that glossed over its failures.
>
> I deplored its total unwillingness to change. Its unwillingness to be honest about its own failures and sins. Its utter inability to drop a method or a practice or a program that was not working to try to find a better way.
>
> I despised the red tape, the unwieldy, super-slow movement of its governmental bodies. I was convinced that if the Holy Spirit did want to do something different or dynamic – He'd lose heart trying to get through all the committees and boards that would have to approve it!"

(Girard, 1972: 21-22)

Charles Sheldon's novel, *In His Steps*, is a classic from a past era (republished in a more modern language in the quotations below). It also paints a critical image of how the churches are seen by many men as

> "... only great piles of costly stone and upholstered furniture and ... the minister as a luxurious idler ..."
>
> (Sheldon, 1984: 199).

Wolfgang Simson, quoted by Brown, goes on and seems to present a cynical view of churches:

> "The image of much of contemporary Christianity could be summarized as holy people coming regularly to a holy place on a holy day at a holy hour to participate in a holy ritual led by a holy man dressed in holy clothes for a holy fee."
>
> (Wolfgang Simson in *Houses that Changed the World*, quoted in Brown, 2002: 50)

Frost and Hirsch suggest the traditions that have led us to today's situation have left us largely bankrupt!

> "We start by confessing a great (and increasing) sense of personal disquiet about the spiritual health and viability of the Western spiritual and theological tradition. It is a tradition that has carried us to this point in history and left us more than a little spiritually bankrupt and with no real success in the grand mission of God."
>
> (Frost & Hirsch, 2003: 116)

The quotations above come from books presenting reasoned arguments about the state of many churches. But even some novels seem to carry sharp criticisms of churches. In *The Visit*, Adrian Plass tells a story where Jesus drops by to visit a local church. Some readers may object theologically to Plass' novel where Jesus' next bodily appearance involves Him quietly dropping by in some English church. However, I encourage you to put aside any such technical objection and instead consider the message behind Plass' novel. I think you might find it instructive:

> "Our church used to be very okay. We did all the things that churches do just about as well as they could be done, and we talked about our founder [Jesus] with much reverence and proper gratitude. We said how much we would have liked to meet him when he was around and how much we looked forward to seeing him at some remote time in the future.
>
> The unexpected news that he was going to pay us an extended visit now, in the present, was, to say the least, very disturbing. Confident statements about 'the faith' tended to dry up. People who usually seemed reasonably cheerful looked rather worried. Many of those who had been troubled appeared to brighten considerably.
>
> A man who had always said that 'atonement was a peculiarly Jewish idea' became extremely thoughtful. Someone who had published a pamphlet entitled 'The Real Meaning of the Resurrection Myth' joined the mid-week prayer group and developed an open mind. Desperate folk just counted the days.
>
> Each of us, I suppose, reacted to the news in our own way, but I think the thing we had in common was a feeling that the game (albeit a very sincere and meaningful game for some) was over. No more pretending when he came. He would know. ...

[Jesus then arrived.] I'd got a copy of the programme in my hand, but when I pulled myself together enough to move towards him, he stood up, turned round and looked at me, and I just couldn't give it to him. I can't describe the look he gave me. It made me want to cry and hit him. That sounds ridiculous, doesn't it, but he made me feel like an idiot, and I admit I felt oddly ashamed as well. …

[Jesus, accompanied by a number of the church members, headed towards the back of the church building before the 'proper' service had started.] I followed them to the door and I actually managed to catch hold of [Jesus'] coat sleeve. 'Excuse me,' I said, 'I thought we were all going to be together for the service.'

'Of course,' he said and smiled. 'Please come with us.'

I just didn't know what to do.

'But we usually have the service in church.'

'Wouldn't you rather be with me?' he said.

Well, I would have really, but I didn't know where he was going to go. I thought he was going to fit in with us, and he seemed so … haphazard.

'Where are you going?' I asked.

He looked up and down the road (here's another thing you won't believe), pointed across the street and said, 'What's that pub like?'

I said, 'It's a bit rough really,' and anyway, I knew for a fact that two or three of the people with him wouldn't go into a pub on principle. At least I thought I knew, because they all trailed in there after him; young fellows, maiden aunts, old men – the lot."

(Plass, 1999: 3, 7, 9)

Jesus often told stories that carried a very punchy message. Randall Arthur's story *Jordan's Crossing* also hits hard. It is the story of a minister who runs a very effective local church, with the emphasis on "runs"—he is most definitely in control. Then a series of events force him to take stock, and the book is absolutely cutting, and probably very threatening to some, just as Jesus' words were to the religious leaders 2000 years earlier. One excerpt follows here, with more extracts later.

"… The American church, generally speaking, possesses very little openness, honesty, and realism … … people normally enter the doors of their church behind a smiling mask and a locked-up heart. They sit front-to-back. Allowed by American tradition to be only spectators, they listen to one-man sermons. And then they go home. Very seldom, if ever, do they touch hearts with one another in a below-the-surface, meaningful, serious, edifying, and productive manner.

On any given Sunday, when millions of believers meet throughout this country, there is a very large percentage of those people who are struggling so intensely in their lives that they feel as if they're dying on the inside. They're struggling with their marriages, they're struggling with faith, they're struggling with addictions, they're struggling with unhealthy fears – the list goes on and on. These people look around in church, see everybody else smiling, and conclude that everybody else is healthy – emotionally, socially, and spiritually.

And because there is virtually no forum or atmosphere for openness and honesty, nearly all of these hurting people, like individual islands detached from the rest of the body of Christ, sit in their pews month after month, year after year, and struggle alone and in secret until they become so pained, disillusioned, depressed, and hopeless that they break. At that point, many of them leave the church. Many of them leave their places of ministry. Many of them leave their marriages. Some of them even commit suicide. …

Unfortunately, … realistic sharing is unknown in most of our American churches, and I believe there are two primary reasons for this.

Number one: Pastors do not breed honesty. As much or more so than anybody else, they hide behind their smiling masks, trying to always project an image of invincibility and impregnability, trying to play the role of perpetual conqueror and victor. They've been trained, both directly and indirectly, to do that. Bible colleges and seminaries teach them to keep a dis-tance from their flock, to not let anyone get close enough to see their humanness, lest their people lose respect for them. …

Our society compounds that directive by putting these men high on a pedestal and refusing to let them be human. The expectations and pressures placed on them by the general public drive them to hide their weaknesses.

But the truth is, everyone in ministry—every pastor, every missionary, every evangelist, every theology professor, every high-profile leader, every low-profile leader—has struggles in life just like every other believer. These people struggle with their marriages, they struggle with their tempers, they struggle with financial temptations, they struggle with lust, they struggle with addictions, they struggle with faith. Some struggle more intensely than others, and some struggle more frequently than others. But they all struggle.

I know, my friends—I am one of them.

If ministers will start taking off their masks … and being honest with people, then they will start breeding honesty. They will start breathing realism into the church. …

The second reason why there is so little openness and honesty … is because our Christian communities in America have become masters at verbally condemning and physically abandoning those whose major weaknesses and struggles are revealed. Instead of creating an environment of honesty in which these people can find it easy to get help at the beginning of their struggles, we force them to hide their weaknesses— right up until the very moment they break or fall. At that point, we feel lied to, betrayed, and deceived. We then broadcast their sins over the radio, print articles about them in the Christian periodicals, and spread the bad news through the gossip grapevines. We treat them as if they were impudent Satanists, usually driving them to complete estrangement from the organized church."

(Arthur, 1993: 137-140)

Arthur's observations on the church institution resonated with me. Although his book is just fiction, it got me thinking that it does in fact reflect the reality of many of my own experiences. He expressed the situation well, helping me to gain greater clarity.

Let's look at *Blood & Fire*, Roy Hattersley's scholarly review of aspects of actual church history for one Protestant institution. It focuses on the formative years of the Salvation Army but, in passing, Hattersley also comments on another of the more traditional churches, and comes to the conclusion:

> "The Church of England [of the 19th century] had failed to come to terms [with] – indeed in some ways refused even to acknowledge – the Industrial Revolution. Its organisation was still built around the rural parishes. Country parsons – remote from towns – ran their godly race in deserted villages while nearby incumbents of urban living wrestled to save thousands of souls from the new temptations of factory life. Often the task, being too great for them to accomplish, was not even attempted. … Instead the Church retreated into its traditional territory and, reinforced by tithes and pew rents, became more and more the preserve of the country gentry and old middle classes with the clergy alienated from the new industrial poor."

(Hattersley, 2000: 202-203)

While the Church of England largely failed to meet the needs of the masses, the emerging Salvation Army at that time stepped forward to fill this void. But today? While acknowledging much community support for the Salvation Army's social care work, one has to question the relevance today of its uniforms and tambourines!

Girard summarizes his personal experience with another out-of-touch local church:

> "… the church as I knew it and its leaders were smugly, self-righteously satisfied to be seeking to reach a generation that had died before the airplane was invented."

(Girard, 1972: 21)

Melody Green and David Hazard's challenging book, *No Compromise*, suggests that the traditions exhibited by many "spiritual" Christians alienate them from the rest of the human race! When she and her husband Keith had their first encounter with a "Jesus Freak", their reaction was:

> "Something about Kathy made us totally uncomfortable. You couldn't have a normal conversation with her. She'd say things like, 'Oh, we're out of milk, praise God,' or 'It's a beautiful day, praise the Lord.' Every other sentence was punctuated with some religious exclamation. It gave me the creeps. We never wanted to walk around uttering mindless phrases like she did. We were content just to call ourselves followers of Jesus and leave it at that. We didn't want to become alienated from the human race!"

(Green & Hazard, 1989: 92)

In his book, *Bacon Sandwiches and Salvation*, Adrian Plass provides an alternative dictionary definition that provides a cynical view (but, I sadly suspect, an accurate one) of how many would see church practices:

> *"Pantomime: event that is completely different from a church service. In a pantomime lots of slightly nervous people sitting in rows are asked to do rather silly things, call out childish responses, join in with a number of banal songs and suspend their disbelief in characters whose manner on stage is significantly different from the way they would behave in real life. Whereas, in church . . . er . . . never mind."*

(Plass, 2007: 142)

Another issue with today's churches relates to unethical behavior and its acceptance by the masses. Unfortunately, this is not a new phenomenon. Thousands of years ago, Micah talked (in Micah 2:11) of how people would welcome a dishonest person who prophesied good news. It did not matter that the prophesy was lies!

Many local churches of our day breach their own standards of behavior, and even break the laws of the land. Even if we take the view that there are "little sins" like so-called white lies and "big sins" like sexual misconduct (and the view that there are different levels of sin must be challenged), the local church leaders can be found guilty at many points along the scale. For example, some of you may have encountered cases where local church leaders used funds for purposes other than indicated, and presented distortions of the truth to protect their reputation, and the followers are expected to cover over the leader's failings. The Bible repeatedly condemns lying. And lying just to protect the image of any church leader, his or her local church, or the denomination as a whole, is despicable.

The quotation below cites one specific example, but is in no way intended to point the finger solely at the denomination concerned. Rather, it is intended to simply highlight the existence of problems within church organizations, as these issues can be found across a diversity of denominations. Denominations aside, Michael Reagan's autobiography, *Twice Adopted*, very effectively exposes the reality of these problems. He noted that a US Conference of Bishops reported:

> *"... some 4,450 priests were accused of sexual abuse by more than 11,000 victims."*

(Reagan, 2004: 146)

Reagan then quotes a Massachusetts Attorney General who said,

> *"The mistreatment of children was so massive and so prolonged that it borders on the unbelievable. ... The choice was very clear, between protecting children and protecting the church. They made the wrong choice.*
>
> *... For decades, cardinals, bishops, and others in positions of authority within the archdiocese chose to protect the image and reputation of their institution rather than the safety and well-being of children."*

(Reagan, 2004: 147)

Another example of abuse of power can relate to the "rules". Again on many points along a continuum, leaders are not averse to reshaping the framework under which they operate. As the Protestants may be quick to point out, papal laws issued by one Pope can be refined by subsequent Popes. But again the Protestant ranks are not without cases of rewriting the rule book. Hattersley tells a story of Booth, founder of the Salvation Army, when he rewrote its constitution:

> *"Booth had already limited the authority of both the Christian Mission's Committee and Conference by proposing, without the slightest consultation, changes to the constitution which increased his personal power."*
>
> (Hattersley, 2000: 221-222)

These are fairly visible examples of actions by those representing Christendom. More subtle, but I suspect of significant concern to God, is when local churches compromise the standards of our direct relationship with Him. For example, Gary Gilley (in *This Little Church Went to Market*) expresses alarm at how what should be pure worship of God can turn into crass entertainment:

> *"... when I am being entertained in either a secular or ecclesiastical setting, and know I am being entertained, it is of little consequence. ... It is not wrong to be entertained as a Christian; it is wrong to confuse it with, or allow it to replace true worship and biblical instruction. ... The desire increasingly being uttered, by a self-fulfilment seeking generation, is the desire to experience or feel the presence of God (not to be confused with a genuine passion to know and worship a most holy God). ... I often ask people who are caught up in this 'experiencing God' current, 'Exactly what does God's presence feel like?' After a fumbling attempt to explain, my next question is, 'How do you know that what you felt is God and not the devil, or your own imagination or last night's pizza?' ... [More importantly] the 'feeling the presence of God' stampede is actually a form of entertainment with a thin layer of worship draped over it. ... [A] number of Christians ... now choose a church on the basis of musical styles and other superficial features, rather than on the ground of whether truth is being taught and God is being honoured. ... Many will endure outright heresies to enjoy a pleasant experience or to 'feel the presence of God', even if that presence is generated by mood-altering methods more akin to manipulation than worship. ... Entertainment gratifies the viewer emotionally. Whether it pleases God may be quite a secondary matter. Error can inspire. It can make people feel good, though it displeases and angers God."*
>
> (Gilley, 2005: 79-81)

The church of today is riddled with problems. For one thing, Christianity is often materialistic. Yancey says:

> *"The Christian message that gets widest exposure in the Western world today follows the cultural mainstream. It offers the appeal, 'God has something good in store for you', and holds out the promise of self-fulfilment. Jesus' statements about finding oneself by losing one's self are conveniently overlooked. In the US a success-based*

theology may work out plausibly well, if only because the resources of the nation are so large. But such a theology has little to say to Christians in China or Indonesia or Iran, where Christian faith compounds suffering."

(Yancey, 2001: 153)

"We talked about the perception of Christianity by the average educated Indian. Those who have been to America come back impressed with all the churches. They tell stories about the television ministers and how much money they collect from supporters. They tell of Christian leaders meeting with the president and of politicians themselves claiming to be born-again. Western spiritual leaders tend to be middle-class and well-groomed, not the austere holy men they are accustomed to in India. ... Reflecting on Christianity, these Indians speak of its power and success. They rarely talk about Jesus' life or the principles he laid down."

(Yancey, 2001: 169)

Yancey's concern about the message coming out of local churches is summed up in a quotation from Gandhi:

" 'The church did not make a favourable impression on me,' he remembers, citing dull sermons and a congregation who 'appeared rather to be worldly-minded, people going to church for recreation and in conformity to custom'. "

(Yancey, 2001: 166)

So even though we've only skimmed across the surface, looking at a few issues, it's enough to warn us that, unless we shape up, we will fail to be the salt and light we are expected to be.

So you think *your* church is 'not too bad'?

Perhaps you can accept that there have been problems with leaders in religious institutions over the years, whether they were found within the temple system of the Old Testament, or some expression of "church" since. And perhaps you can accept that there are still problems today in churches *other* people attend. But what about *your* local church? Could you even contemplate that it may have problems, or are you defensive of even the possibility that your beloved leader may be heading in the wrong direction, and taking you along with him or her?

Perhaps your defense is that "God is clearly blessing us". Jim Cymbala (in *Fresh Wind, Fresh Fire*) warns that many local churches make the assumption that

"Whatever 'works' is the way to go. If a technique gets the building filled and the bills paid, it must be blessed by God. Visible results are the proof that a strategy is heaven-ordained. Such thinking is due for a rude awakening when we stand before the Lord."

(Cymbala, 1997: 164)

A more subtle danger is to give verbal support to the possibility of error within your fellowship ("Of course, we might not be perfect ..."), but in practice to only check with those you (perhaps unconsciously) know will agree with what you are doing. In his novel, *Dawn of Liberty* (#4 in *The Secret of the Rose* series), Michael Phillips portrays a conference with a number of different views being expressed by speakers, but people attending sessions according to their pre-conceived ideas:

> "… it wouldn't surprise me if the only people there listening were the ones who already believed along similar lines.
>
> … people go to hear what confirms positions they already have, more than to be exposed to new ideas.
>
> … Christians rarely mix it up. For this thing to work there needs to be cross-pollination of ideas and methods and personalities, not just staying within one's own little clique."
>
> (Phillips, 1995: 163)

This insular attitude is natural, but unhealthy. We need, as individuals, to consciously move outside of our comfort zone and fellowship with others from different backgrounds. But there is another danger. It comes in the form of local church leadership who openly brag that their way is right, or more subtly apply pressure to those who try to look beyond their all-encompassing wisdom. If you want to find out how it works, just go one Sunday to another church that perhaps a good neighbor attends, and see what reaction you get the following Sunday from your own church.

Frost and Hirsch warn of people who will oppose those who dare to challenge the status quo:

> "Those who call for radical change are often told to stop rocking the boat. The greatest silencing of the call for change often comes from leaders of large churches. They seem to be unaware of or untouched by any effects of significant social change. We have both been told more than once by large-church pastors that the church isn't doing so badly at all."
>
> (Frost & Hirsch, 2003: 147)

David Oliver and James Thwaites, in their excellent book, *Church that Works*, suggest that teaching in 'parables', as Jesus did, is very powerful. However, they point out that the 'parables' generated from within the local churches are typically about the churches themselves rather than ministry outside of the churches, in the world.

> "However, even though parables are used as a teaching technique in the church as construct [i.e. the local church], the main parable communicated ends up being the church itself. Most stories told tend to be about what the pastor is thinking, feeling and doing. They are more often than not about conferences, church ministries, moves of God in other churches and so on. These parables, so powerful in communicating truth, are told in a church building. They are about the church as construct, and they usually centre on the life and deeds of the church minister. It's hardly surprising that we have so effectively trained the saints to see the church gathered as the key container for the divine person and purpose on earth."
>
> (Oliver & Thwaites, 2001: 129)

In summary, you might not see the problems within your local assembly because you are being taught about the successes of the local church, not a wider view.

So what are some of the symptoms of illness to look out for?

Some are hesitant to be seen as criticizing anything to do with churches. But there are problems, and if we don't face them, the secular media is sure to do it on our behalf! For example, newspapers have run articles proclaiming that priests use nuns for safe (i.e. AIDS-free) sex–this scandal was acknowledged by Pope Francis in 2019. And the world-wide press has had a field day with the immoral exploits of some of those who had been perceived by many to have been world-renowned leaders.

Let's face it. There are real problems, and the sooner we face them honestly and openly, the better. So what are some of the symptoms of unhealthy churches?

We start by looking at the dangers of traditions. After recounting Peter's struggle to obey God's clear command to reach out to Cornelius (a Gentile), Juan Ortiz (in *Disciple*) comments,

> *"The power of tradition is awesome. God cannot do many things He would like to do because of our bondage. We are scandalized every time He wants us to change a little."*
>
> (Ortiz, 1975: 123)

He then goes on to argue that we need to be willing to change traditions:

> *"When God began to renew us, there were some traditions that had to be changed."*
>
> (Ortiz, 1975: 125)

Some churches suffer from unwillingness to change traditions; Cymbala argues that some churches suffer from an opposite evil, namely the need to be constantly changing:

> *"Carol and I returned ... sad and depressed. How tragic that young ministers were feverishly writing down all these exotic teachings in the vain hope of igniting their struggling churches back home with techniques and teachings nowhere found in Scripture."*
>
> (Cymbala, 1997: 107)

Cymbala also talks of the dangers of the new holy trinity "A-B-C" i.e. attendance, buildings and cash. He goes on to say,

> *"The apostles ... aimed for a piercing of the heart, for conviction of sin. They had not the faintest intention of asking, 'What do people want to hear? How can we draw more people to church on Sunday?' That was the last thing in their minds. Such an approach would have been foreign to the whole New Testament. ... ... Instead of trying to bring men and women to Christ in the biblical way, we are consumed with the unbiblical concept of 'church growth.'"*
>
> (Cymbala, 1997: 124)

Cymbala then issues a warning that might surprise some – the dangers of single-mindedly and uncritically chasing after leaders whose teaching is seen to reflect 'good doctrine':

> *"Let me make a bold statement: Christianity is not predominantly a teaching religion. We have been almost overrun these days by the cult of the speaker. The person who can stand up and expound correct doctrine is viewed as essential; without such a talent the church would not know what to do."*
>
> (Cymbala, 1997: 150)

Last but not least, we should be concerned if we see the "ministry" being left to the "professional" church leaders, and the laity in any way restricted in their personal Christian walk. It is serious when the laity simply do not rise to Jesus' challenge for ministry. Worse still are the churches that actually hold the people back from exercising their ministry:

> *"If this dislocation of Christ from creation continues [by boxing Him into centralized 'church'], then the fullness we were redeemed to inherit will remain a long way off. Our world will remain cloaked in dense darkness, and the church's journey to cultural oblivion as the salt that lost its savour will continue unabated. Some may fear losing the clarity, comfort and apparent unity of a Sunday meeting, but what is at stake is so much larger than that. We so need a vision of the creation-encompassing Son of the living God at this time."*
>
> (Oliver & Thwaites, 2001: 159)

> *"How great the need to release the many ministry gifts from congregation minding to [instead] serve the church as fullness."*
>
> (Oliver & Thwaites, 2001: 160)

In addition to the problems of traditions, there are a number of other problems that may be found within local church structures. The first mentioned below relates to the governmental structures. My interpretation of Ortiz is that he argues that hierarchical structures (led by the official church leaders) and democratic structures (led by the people) both have weaknesses:

> *"… the Protestant churches reacted [to the hierarchical structures of the Catholic Church] and decided to be democratic. That was good for a time; it brought the so-called laymen back into the work of the church. They had to think once again, to vote, to work.*
>
> *But it was not the cure. …*
>
> *The majority is not always right. …*
>
> *… [We] are going to have a lot of trouble with democracy. I'm not arguing for an episcopal form of government, but neither can I support a democratic form of government."*
>
> (Ortiz, 1975: 126-127)

The next structural weakness identified by Ortiz relates to the use of special titles for church leaders, starting with the formally ordained clergy.

> "We are so upside down today that we give unworthy slaves a diploma that reads, 'Reverend.' Once I was in a meeting where someone was introduced with great fanfare. The organ played and the spotlights came on as someone announced, 'And now, the great servant of God, --.'
>
> If he was great, he was not a servant. And if he was a servant, he was not great."

(Ortiz, 1975: 39)

Ortiz claims to apply this standard to himself.

> "In this new [discipleship] structure, I'm not a Reverend anymore; I'm just Johnny."

(Ortiz, 1975: 115)

This principle is also applied more widely, for example, to cell group leaders.

> "The leader of the cell has no title. Since God has begun to renew us, we have been very careful about titles. We haven't yet laid hands on anyone to name him a deacon, an elder, or whatever."

(Ortiz, 1975: 136)

Finally, we note Ortiz' comments on the concept of church "membership":

> "What is a church member today? Nearly every local church has three requirements:
>
> (1) The person must attend the meetings.
>
> (2) The person must give his money.
>
> (3) The person must live a life of good character.
>
> If he does those three, he is considered a good church member. He's like a good club member; he attends the club, pays his dues, and tries not to embarrass the club."

(Ortiz, 1975: 105)

... and last but not least, abusive churches

Some churches are generally classified as being cults, and some others as being less extreme but still having some cult-like behavior. To whatever level any given church may exhibit such behavior, we should be concerned. And a warning: if a church has cult-like aspects, you can be almost 100% guaranteed that any similarities to cults will be denied by both the leaders and by their loyal followers. Chris Elkins' autobiography, *Heavenly Deception*, gives an insider's view of one group many considered to be a cult. He warns that if you, the reader, are involved in a church with such traits, you may not even be aware:

> "... people ... fail to see the 'process' that creates the 'product' – that slow, almost

imperceptible shifting of values, allegiances, and authority that transforms a person, even a Christian, into a member of a cult."

(Elkins, 1980: 14)

It follows that we need a more objective measuring stick than asking those involved, or maybe even trying to judge our own situation. The former *Free Indeed* website communicated unhealthy and abusive behavior in some churches and offered the following helpful perspective:

"ARE YOU INVOLVED IN A SPIRITUALLY ABUSIVE CHURCH?

Spiritual abuse is the misuse of power, position, and authority - it occurs in Christian Churches where a leader, or the leaders of an organisation, use their status as spiritual overseers to exercise an unhealthy and excessive, often harmful, control over the lives of their members. Most of these Churches are 'aberrant' in that they have separated themselves from mainstream and orthodox Christianity, have little or no denominational accountability, and tend to emphasise one aspect of faith, spiritual experience, or doctrine over all others.

Spiritually abusive Churches can be easily spotted ... [by] those whose eyes are open (or beginning to open). Many, or often all, of the following signs will be present.

1. *Controlling leadership*
   Submission to the leader and his / her teachings, or those endorsed by him / her, is emphasised and either explicitly or implicitly demanded. The leader 'helps' members make decisions about all aspects of life, well beyond matters of faith and morals - such as courtship and relationships, employment, recreation activities, and dress. The leader usually does this by seeking 'God's will' on the matter in question.

2. *Special access to God*
   The leader claims a special closeness to God that results in him / her frequently 'hearing from God' and discerning 'God's will'. Often the leader claims a special gift or title - such as Prophet or Apostle, and likes to be referred to by a title (such as Father, Papa, or Teacher).

3. *Elitism*
   The aberrant Church claims to be 'unique' or to have a special 'calling' that sets it apart from all other Christian Churches and gives it a mandate to be 'different'. Unusual and non-Biblical phenomena are explained away because 'we are on the cutting edge' of what God is doing.

4. *Lack of accountability*
   Unlike mainstream and traditional Churches, the group and its leader are not accountable to a denominational overseer or Bishop. If they are part of a denomination or movement, they often leave it or have threatened to do so.

5. *No dissent*
   The group does not encourage questions. To speak out or question the leadership is to have 'a rebellious spirit' and to 'speak against the oversight'. The leader may

advise against reading certain books, speaking to certain people, and be suspicious or wary of other Christian Churches and especially of theological colleges. All of these are denounced as 'un-spiritual', 'worldly' or 'in error'. Opposition to the group is redefined as 'persecution' or 'a Satanic attack'.

6. *There is an emphasis on spiritual experience*
   Aberrant groups give an exalted place to spiritual manifestations and phenomena (even bizarre ones). The leader receives all of his 'direction' and 'guidance' in this way (not from studying the Scriptures or Christian theology) and cannot therefore be questioned. Using one's mind is frowned upon as 'un-spiritual'.

7. *Young adults are targeted*
   Aberrant groups intentionally target and recruit new members from the 18-25 age group. People at this age are impressionable, often seeking spiritual answers, and are more likely to respond to the lure of a loving and accepting community.

8. *Scripture twisting*
   Aberrant groups treat the Bible as a 'rule book'. Scripture is not set in its cultural and historical context and then applied on its own terms. Usually the leader or preacher will begin with a proposition and then quote Scriptural references from all parts of the Bible which, out of context, seem to substantiate the starting proposition ('proof-texting'). In aberrant and abusive Churches the leader has usually had no formal training but 'relies on the Holy Spirit'.

9. *Traumatic departure*
   It is hard to leave an abusive Church. There will be a very long list of ex-members each with a 'painful exit' story to tell. Often ex-members are depressed, experience marriage or relationship problems, and may be dealing with lifestyle issues. Many find it very hard to resume Christian fellowship. This is used by the abusive leader as 'evidence' of 'God's judgment' and as a warning as to what might happen to existing members if they leave.

If you recognise one or more of the above characteristics then you need to know that THINGS ARE NOT RIGHT. You have probably already begun to sense this yourself. Normal Churches do not control the lives of their congregation."

(Free Indeed, 2000)

We looked above at cult-like behavior in some churches, but how healthy are "normal" churches? Philip Baker, in Weird Christians I Have Met, notes traits in many churches that are uncomfortably similar to the characteristics used above to identify cults:

"The truth that other churches and believers who love God as passionately as [oneself] can experience Him in different ways, is totally incomprehensible to [some].

When this attitude takes hold of an entire church, it can lead to isolationism: Where people begin to withdraw from everyone who might challenge them or speak into their lives. Such a withdrawal is often total: withdrawal from those of different persuasions within the Christian church; withdrawal from those who don't know Christ because they fear contamination; withdrawal from friends and relatives; withdrawal from being a part of this world coupled with a refusal to keep up-to-date with what is happening in the community, the country, indeed the whole of civilisation. Choosing, instead, to just read the Bible and pray.

Although this sounds very noble it quickly produces a fortress mentality within the believer. Everything is 'us and them'. Whatever is outside the group is seen as evil, and whatever is within is right."

(Baker, 1997: 33)

The previous *Free Indeed* quote ended by saying that "normal" churches don't control. By normal, we often mean "usual", or "typical". In contrast, when a doctor says some diagnostic results are normal, we hope he means "healthy". If most people in a given population are overweight and a survey says my weight is normal within my culture (i.e. typical), I'm actually less healthy than I should be, but if my doctor says my weight is normal when aligned with expectations of the medical profession, that's good news.

So, taking the above perspective, I hope we would agree that *healthy* churches "*do not control the lives of their congregation*" at all. But do *typical* churches control? The *Free Indeed* website warned that dangerous behavior may be found in less extreme churches:

"So many people are 'captive' in churches which are not as over-the-edge, but are just as deadly ..."

(in Free Indeed (2000) message board, #4, dated 2 Sept, 2000)

Oliver and Thwaites go further, warning that the simple act of putting "church" first is cult-like:

"Church programmes, meetings and activities are not to be a parasite, sucking into themselves all the most able, most qualified and most spiritual. ...

My fear ... is that, in reality, by our words and by our priorities, we [leaders] want our working men and women to see like we see, to feel like we feel, and to speak like we speak. Commitment then, is not from us to them and on their behalf, but in reality, from them to us. That it so close to being a cult that it is shocking.

We say the church is not a building, and we say the church is not meetings. But look, for a moment, at the language of our commitment courses. We ask for a tithe – commitment to a doctrine and a commitment to all the meetings. The language tells us what to really believe."

(Oliver & Thwaites, 2001: 208-209)

There are some forms of church structures where even personal decisions by individuals cannot be made without the approval of the leadership, where the leaders will not tolerate attempts at correction, and where these leaders may imply (or even explicitly claim) to be infallible. These are symptoms of more extreme forms of abuse. However, David Henke's *Watchman* website warns that spiritual abuse:

> *"... can occur under virtually any organizational structure, but 'top down' hierarchical structures are especially well suited to systemic spiritual abuse."*
>
> (Henke, 2000)

Sometimes these power-based structures are clearly visible in the actions of leaders and in the rules of the constitution, but sometimes they are well hidden. One dangerous attempt at masking the control structures of leaders comes in the form of blatant and pious exhibitions of humility. It can range from some highly orchestrated show of humility such as public displays of kissing the feet of those deemed to be lesser people, through to what appears to me to be self-contradictory and illogical claims by church leaders that they are nothing more than the "first among equals". Presumably in good faith, Frank Tillapaugh, in *Unleashing the Church*, nonetheless uses this phrase:

> *"... there will always be a first among equals, but the stress does not have to be on first; it can be on equal.*
>
> *... At present, I have the role of first among equals. I am the oldest, have been on the church staff the longest, and have given the most direction to the overall ministry."*
>
> (Tillapaugh, 1982: 103-104)

If you, the reader, are in regular interaction with a local church, I hope the warning is clear —there may be aspects of your local church traditions that are not healthy, even if they are hard to detect.

CHAPTER 2:
ASK QUESTIONS OF THE CHURCH LEADERS

To question, or not to question, that is the question!

It's not uncommon for the masses to accept without question. Chrissie Foster, in her heart-wrenching book *Hell on the Way to Heaven*, describes the pain inflicted on her family at the hands of sexually abusive church leadership. She also describes the inbuilt suppression of questioning experienced in her particular church, which she maintains is a form of spiritual abuse. I have chosen to alter Chrissie's quotations slightly to suppress the identity of her particular denomination because I am sadly convinced that such domination by leadership can occur across a variety of denominations.

This part of her story starts after she relocated her daughter Aimee to a different school. The representatives of her previous church-based school had frowned on questioning; the new one was starkly different:

> "[The new school] hosted a 'Policy on Drugs' meeting ... At question time, the parents, in an orderly fashion and a matter-of-fact way, demanded explanations. ...
>
> The questions were put forcefully. I sat there cringing at the serious tone of these parents' voices and their demands. ... Over and over I thought to myself: 'We're going to get into trouble.' I felt a big invisible hand was going to come out of nowhere, and slap us for asking these questions and speaking to a teacher in this way. Then suddenly I realised what I was thinking and how I was feeling. I was scared. It was my [church] conditioning.
>
> No big hand was going to hit me.
>
> What a dominant presence the Church had been all my life – and I had only just

realised it! It was there all along. But it was so ingrained I didn't even know it was intimidating me. The seeds had been planted so early; they were beyond thought and remained unquestioned. In all the [church] school and church meetings I had ever attended we were never allowed the freedom of speech that these [parents from another denomination] knew well and took for granted.

I had received a lifetime of ... training to be silent. From [the church services], where we were never asked our opinions or allowed to speak – except to recite the words printed in prayer books – through to church or school meetings as an adult, silence and obedience were expected. We went there to listen and be told what to do. If we didn't like what we heard we would speak in disgruntled tones quietly after the meeting and then obey anyway. I was not used to a meeting where you could argue the agenda and demand explanations from a teacher, or whoever was in charge, no matter what the subject. It was an eye-opener and made me realise just how brainwashed and dominated we had all been in the [church] system."

(Foster & Kennedy, 2010: 239-240)

Brown presents a summarized history of the role of religious leaders (priests) in the Old Testament. He then notes that Jesus introduced a radical change that

"... made all believers holy priests ..."

(Brown, 2002: 51)

He immediately points out that this change was quickly lost, and comments that

"... for a thousand years or more, it seems that no one thought to question [the false separation of church leaders from those who are 'followers' i.e. the laity]".

(Brown, 2002: 51)

Thomas Lindsay's biography, *Martin Luther: The Man Who Started the Reformation*, appears to reinforce this view of lack of motivation on behalf of the laity to question the role of the church leaders. He suggests that life in that era was centered on the family and that the typical family of that day:

"... had little in common with the ecclesiastical system and professional theology which it <u>accepted without question</u>." [Emphasis mine]

(Lindsay, 1996: 19)

Still worse than the failure of the laity to ask questions, was the proactive suppression by the church leaders of any questions the laity did dare to ask.

"... [the laity] are told to conform and submit without questioning anything, without searching the Scriptures for themselves and, above all, without discussion of any kind."

(Brown, 2002: 104)

Instead of searching the Scriptures for ourselves, church attendees are expected to ingest what is served up to them, without complaint or question. Max Lucado, in *When God Whispers Your Name*, exposes the unacceptability of this approach in a rather confronting manner:

> *"Imagine you are selecting your food from a cafeteria line. You pick your salad, you choose your entrée, but when you get to the vegetables, you see a pan of something that turns your stomach.*
>
> *'Yuck! What's that?' you ask, pointing.*
>
> *'Oh, you don't want to know,' replies a slightly embarrassed server.*
>
> *'Yes, I do.'*
>
> *'Well, if you must. It's a pan of pre-chewed food.'*
>
> *'What?'*
>
> *'Pre-chewed food. Some people prefer to swallow what others have chewed.'*
>
> *Repulsive? You bet. But widespread. More so than you might imagine. Not with cafeteria food, but with God's Word.*
>
> *Such Christians mean well. They listen well. But they discern little. They are content to swallow whatever they are told. No wonder they've stopped growing."*
>
> (Lucado, 1994: 137)

History reveals that many people let their religious leaders proceed unquestioned and unchallenged. It also records that there are those rare individuals who are willing to confront.

The Old Testament prophets were outspoken in their criticisms. Likewise, Jesus confronted the religious leaders of His day, referring to them as whitewashed tombs (clean on the outside but stinking inside), as hypocrites, and as snakes.

Note Martin Luther's stinging words about church leaders, who he claimed:

> "… surpass all that is most sordid and most disgusting in their avarice and impiety."
>
> (Lindsay, 1996: 84).

Luther then went on to say of them:

> "There is a buying and a selling, … cheating and lying, robbing and stealing, debauchery and villainy, and all kinds of contempt of God that Antichrist could not reign worse."
>
> (Lindsay, 1996: 88)

We need to ask questions. Isaiah Berlin, quoted in Jonathan Sacks inspiring work, *The Dignity of Difference*, notes the dangers of belief in one person or one group having the monopoly on all truth.

> "Few things have done more harm than the belief on the part of individuals and groups (or tribes or states or nations or churches) that he or she or they are in sole possession of the truth … It is a terrible and dangerous arrogance to believe that you alone are right: have a magical eye which sees the truth: and that others cannot be right if they disagree. This makes one certain that there is one goal and only one for

one's nation or church or the whole of humanity, and that it is worth any amount of suffering (particularly on the part of other people) if only the goal is attained – 'through an ocean of blood to the Kingdom of Love' (or something like this) said Robespierre: and Hitler, Lenin, Stalin and I daresay leaders in the religious wars of Christian v. Muslim or Catholics v. Protestants sincerely believed this: the belief that there is one and only one true answer to the central questions which have agonized mankind and that one has it oneself – or one's Leader has it – was responsible for the oceans of blood: But no Kingdom of Love sprang from it – or could ..."

(Isaiah Berlin, 2002: 345 – quoted in Sacks, 2003: 63)

Yancey was raised in a fundamentalist church that taught, amongst other things, hatred for Afro-American people and a very strict code of conduct. Yancey was ostracized by others, and made the brunt of jokes, because of his different beliefs. He looks back with pain on his earlier support for such a church:

"Later, when I realised that church had taught me lies as well as truth, I felt lost, homeless, adrift. For what had I sacrificed my pride and prepared for martyrdom? A religion of racists, anti-intellectuals and social misfits?"

(Yancey, 2001: 266)

One may wonder how such behavior may be found in churches that proclaim to represent Jesus. Arthur suggests that they can be passed unchallenged from generation to generation:

"It is clear to me now that many beliefs in the Christian community are held to be valuable not because there is any inherent biblical value in them, but simply because the former generation held them to be valuable."

(Arthur, 1991: 134)

This absence of challenge to long-held beliefs may have many causes. One identified by Yancey is a lack of rigor in truthfully evaluating our principles:

"What bothered me most, as I reflect, was the lack of scholarship by Christians – as if they felt that by leaning on a theological principle they didn't have to be very accurate with the facts."

(Yancey, 2001: 189)

Arthur's character, Jason, identifies another reason for unchallenged beliefs—those who would challenge errors are driven out, while those that are willing to 'follow-the-leader' are retained:

"I realize now that my attitude [as a pastor] was the cause of countless and uncalled-for offenses. The number of people who left my ministry because of it was almost equal to the number of people who joined it for other reasons. For the first time I now understand that those who could not tolerate my attitude, and thus decided to leave, were people who had more potential for dynamic Christian growth than those who stayed. The ones who stayed were the simple-minded 'yes' people. The ones who left

were the 'thinkers,' the people whose active, creative, and hungry minds were being suffocated by my style of leadership."

(Arthur, 1991: 130-131)

Jason learned by observing of his own resistance to challenge. Not only was he now open to others challenging him, he had a liberty in challenging others. He progressed to a position where he declared he would never unquestioningly adopt any teaching:

"I've learned that questioning is good, and that not one dogma, theory, or interpretation should be exempted from its demolishing attempt.

Truth, I've discovered, will not be destroyed by questioning or scrutiny. It will always stand unbeatable. Questioning only confirms truth and makes it visibly stronger; it never crumbles it.

On the other hand, the manmade distortions of truth— those that we sometimes hold to be so valuable, and use as a criteria for fellowship, and are even sometimes willing to die for—will fall apart under such honest questioning. And anything that is destroyed by honest questioning is obviously spurious and deserves to be junked. By crumbling and falling apart, it proves to be vain.

From this day forward I will never again blindly believe anything. I will honestly question everything first. Likewise, if I ever, in any situation, try to share my beliefs with others, I will neither ask nor expect them to blindly believe me. I will encourage them to honestly question and challenge everything I say.

One who learns through the process of honest questioning, objective thinking, and respectful challenging is more apt to know in the end what is really true."

(Arthur, 1991: 133-134)

A history of gagging by many church leaders

We have noted some of those individuals who bravely asked challenging questions. But how did the leaders react to their challenges? The simple answer—poorly.

They killed several Old Testament prophets, and they killed Jesus. And centuries later, when Martin Luther also asked questions that riled the hierarchy, they wanted him killed too. Luther observed that the common people accepted theology without question. He lived in a time when many of the common people strove to live righteous lives, and taught their children such principles as God's grace. But their beliefs were typically based on the unchallenged teachings of their church leaders.

In contrast to the people's blind faith in their church leaders, Luther saw it as his inalienable right to refuse to believe what was unbelievable, or to follow or be controlled by customs that were no more than religious tradition and empty hypocrisy:

"No man was a more distinguished exponent of the rights of the individual human soul ... but this inalienable right was for him the incapacity to believe incredibilities,

to adopt solemn shams, or to live under the rule of religious falsehoods."

(Lindsay, 1996: 14)

Luther's belief in his right to question the authorities led him into open conflict with church leaders. Lindsay tells of the evil practice within the Catholic Church of the so-called Indulgences. By buying indulgence tickets, the purchaser could gain forgiveness from sin, and the church could gain additional income!

"So far as the common people were concerned, this Indulgence meant that on the payment of certain specified sums of money, spiritual privileges, including the forgiveness of sins, could be obtained by the purchasers. The Pope proclaimed this Indulgence to be a great boon, and as such the majority of the common people received it. They were encouraged to look upon it in this light by most of the clergy, and by all who wished to stand well with the higher ecclesiastical powers.

... [But many opponents felt] that their poor territories were being drained of money to enrich the papal court ..."

(Lindsay, 1996: 49)

In Martin Luther's day, the crass use of Indulgences to protect financial interests was highlighted in relation to the mining of a material known as "alum". Mining of this material, unless under the control of (and hence to the benefit of) the Catholic Church, was deemed to be a sin of great significance. While it appears that other more 'minor' sins such as marital unfaithfulness and even murder could be wiped off the record by the purchase of appropriate Indulgences, importing alum from countries outside the church's control was one of a few sins so great they could not be overcome by purchasing indulgences. And the reason? New mines had been found, and:

"The Holy See made haste to work its newly found treasures, and in order to secure the whole profit to itself, it made it a sin to import any alum into Europe. The money to be obtained from the Indulgence was not to be allowed to interfere with the papal revenue from its alum mines; and so the importation of alum was declared to be a sin unpardonable by any Indulgence."

(Lindsay, 1996: 52)

Martin Luther was so opposed to the Indulgences that he went to print and

"... nailed his Ninety-five Theses to the door of the church."

(Lindsay, 1996: 58)

It has been noted that the official church tried to kill Luther. They were more successful with another who expressed similar views to those of Luther.

"John Wessel had openly protested against that earlier Indulgence, and had died in the prison of a Dominican monastery in consequence."

(Lindsay, 1996: 49)

ASK QUESTIONS OF THE CHURCH LEADERS

Luther's dangerous questioning occurred centuries ago, and was spectacularly resisted. In contrast to this suppression of questioning, Charles Sheldon wrote in the late nineteenth century of a preacher who was willing to be totally changed by the respectful but direct criticisms of a visiting tramp who takes over one of his services. In a modernized republication of his classic novel, *In His Steps*, the tramp throws out the challenge:

> *"I'm not an ordinary tramp, though I don't know of any teaching of Jesus that makes one kind of tramp less worth saving than another. Do you? …*
>
> *I don't expect you people can prevent everyone from dying of starvation, lack of proper nourishment, and tenement air, but what does following Jesus mean? I understand that Christian people own a good many of the tenements. A member of a church was the owner of the one where my wife died. I have wondered if following Jesus all the way was true in his case. I heard some people singing at a church prayer meeting the other night,*
>
> > *All for Jesus, all for Jesus;*
> > *All my being's ransomed powers;*
> > *All my thoughts and all my doings,*
> > *All my days and all my hours;*
>
> *I kept wondering as I sat on the steps outside just what they meant by it. It seems to me that there's an awful lot of trouble in the world that somehow wouldn't exist if all the people who sing such songs went and lived them out. I suppose I don't understand. But what would Jesus do? Is that what you mean by following in His steps?"*
>
> (Sheldon, 1984: 16-18).

And the preacher's response to a tramp walking into his church and asking difficult questions?

> *"… all the while [the tramp] was speaking the minister leaned over the pulpit, his face growing more white and sad every moment. But he made no movement to stop him …"*
>
> (Sheldon, 1984: 16).

Not only was the preacher willing to listen to those who asked questions of him, he also willingly took the risk of being outspokenly critical of hypocrites in his church, with no favor being shown to those of social standing or wealth (Sheldon, 1984: 73).

The openness in exchange of views was not limited to the church walls. The story tells of a regular meeting held for the poor of the city. It was characterized by free discussion at the end of the more formal sermon:

> *"… any man in the hall was at liberty to ask questions, to speak out his feelings or declare his convictions."*
>
> (Sheldon, 1984: 234)

... with order provided via a chair-person and a 3-minute limit, due to the number present. This author of a Christian novel openly admitted to the disparaging views held by those outside of Christendom, presented by characters making claims such as:

> "... church people ... [are] just as selfish and greedy for money and worldly success as anybody."
>
> (Sheldon, 1984: 235)

and

> "... I don't look for any reform worth anything to come out of the churches."
>
> (Sheldon, 1984: 237)

Sheldon then went on to ask:

> "Was the church so far from the Master, then, that the people no longer found Him there? Was it true that the church had lost its power ...?
>
> Was it really true that big city churches, as a rule, would refuse to walk in Jesus' steps and sacrifice for His sake?"
>
> (Sheldon, 1984: 240)

We, too, need to be sufficiently courageous to ask the tough questions. Girard held a principle that:

> "... those whom I serve certainly have every right to question both what I do and what I preach."
>
> (Girard, 1972:67)

Sheldon's novel suggested that the pastor would accept being challenged. Similarly, Girard's statements express a refreshing openness. But how would those in *your* church circles react to being challenged?

Do church leaders still suppress questioning today?

It is clear that many church leaders in the past have suppressed questioning. But do the church leaders of today still practice suppression?

There are those who demonstrate both freedom in themselves to ask probing questions, and freedom for others to question them. I knew a colorful and fearless pastor from the 1900s, named Walter Betts. Dallas Clarnette's biography of Betts, *50 Years On Fire For God: The Story of Walter Betts*, recounts several examples of his willingness to speak out on issues. For example, during his training for ordination, Betts showed no hesitancy in opposing the views of his lecturers:

> "Frequently during lectures Walter Betts would rise to his feet protesting, 'Professor, I couldn't preach that!'"
>
> (Clarnette, 1967: 24)

ASK QUESTIONS OF THE CHURCH LEADERS

Later, he showed the same readiness to oppose the hierarchy within his denomination:

> "Often Mr. Betts spoke up in Conference and Synod. He was not backward in contending for the faith, and in publicly asking questions of certain Christian leaders whose ministry seemed to cast doubts upon the Word of God."
>
> (Clarnette, 1967: 31)

It is noteworthy that, while Betts vocally opposed the views of some, he attempted to do so in a Christ-like manner:

> "While Walter Betts has never hesitated to speak in defence of the truth, which also necessitates mentioning names, he has always sought to speak in love."
>
> (Clarnette, 1967: 32)

However, the real question is not whether some church leaders are willing to speak out, but rather, are they willing to let the laity speak where they might disagree. Some who are willing to speak out boldly are in fact the least likely to show grace in letting others communicate opposing views. Betts was different. Firstly, he showed a degree of tolerance to other church leaders, within quite extensive bounds:

> "… while his theological sympathies are definitely within the Wesleyan tradition, yet over the years his pulpits have always been open to men of all traditions and churches, so long as they have honoured the Lord Jesus Christ, the Holy Spirit and the Word of God."
>
> (Clarnette, 1967: 32)

Perhaps even more tellingly, he was a supporter of the views of the laity. Clarnette, commenting on Betts' lonely stance in representing and supporting laity's opposition to trends within his denomination's softening views on morality, stated that he:

> "… commended Mr. Betts for 'refusing to trim his sails to the wind.' 'For years the Church has stifled lay criticism of its changed policy.'"
>
> (Clarnette, 1967: 61)

In contrast to those who encourage questioning, attempts to suppress debate appear to be more clearly visible in some groups. The Seventh Day Adventist church espouses "*unwavering positiveness toward Church leadership*" as a virtue:

> "ASI and its members will be known for their unswerving honesty in business principles and practices, unflagging participation in the various ministries of the Church, unwavering positiveness toward Church leadership, unhesitating provision for the needs of others, and untiring focus on the Christ they represent in the marketplace"
>
> (http://www.tagnet.org/asi/mission.html - 26/12/1999)

Elkins comments on the Moonies, and their leaders' shaping of "truth" based on questionable (but unquestioned) suppositions. He defines what he has labelled "*heavenly deception*" as the

"... policy of using falsehood to achieve, supposedly, goodness [and the] practice of employing lies for the sake of heaven."

(Elkins, 1980: 14)

Many would perhaps accept that practices of suppression do occur today in some of the fringe groups associated more or less with Christianity. But does the practice of suppression also occur within so-called "mainstream" churches?

Some personal, direct observations of various attempts to gag follow. They occurred within these mainstream denominations—generally considered as conventional, traditional and trustworthy churches.

- At a conference, the leader established conference rules at the outset, including a total ban on questions, under the guise of not being able to afford diversions from the massive amount of material that had to be covered. Further, attempts by conference participants at seeking answers to questions *after* the conference closure were met with a blanket ban on discussion as it was seen as criticism of a "man of God".

- A group of leaders at a particular local church chose to resign. Each was motivated by disquiet with the more senior leadership, and each reached this decision independently. The senior pastor banned them from talking to each other or to other church members–this was purportedly out of concern that other people might start questioning why all these people were unhappy and had taken the radical step of resigning.

- When the world-wide media published criticism of the unwholesome activities of a high-profile televangelist, a local church leader instructed his followers not to join in the criticisms, as the subject of their criticism was a "representative of God" and should be respected, totally independent of the offenses he had committed.

- As a pre-cursor to announcing the resignation of a member of the pastoral team, the senior pastor presented an entire sermon on the need to protect fellow members of the Body of Christ by not questioning their actions. Further, the congregation was warned against criticizing the church leaders—any who did would be, in his view, guilty of criticizing the God whom the leaders represent.

- The senior pastor of a church stated that if church members are in good relationship with God, they wouldn't criticize church leaders. He followed this statement with the application of this philosophy by claiming that any who criticize him therefore cannot be in relationship with God.

These may be viewed by some as isolated cases of gagging. However, Jamie Buckingham, himself a pastor, was willing to make critical comments in his book *Where Eagles Soar*, in this case relating in general terms to denominational programs that are

"... rumbling along in the ruts of yesteryear ..."

(Buckingham, 1980: 64)

He also notes how a pastor can be

"... asleep behind the wheel of his stalled church ..."

(Buckingham, 1980: 64)

He then goes on to warn how some of these pastors react to someone in their congregation who makes a life-changing discovery and shares it with others, commenting that

"many leaders prefer to chain the offender ... or if he persists, run over him."

(Buckingham, 1980: 64)

Some misguided reasons given for suppression of questioning

It appears that not only fringe cults but also mainline denominations are indeed capable of gagging those who would question their actions. But why does this occur?

Stacy Rinehart's highly recommended book, *Upside Down: The Paradox of Servant Leadership*, quotes Howard Snyder's *Signs of the Spirit: How God Reshapes the Church* as pointing out that any organization may classify views differing from their own as being evil:

"Institutions become repositories of vested interests, providing power and security not easily given up, for those who wield institutional power. ... Institutions divide people up according to institutional power and status. Generally, institutions make it very clear just where everyone fits – what your place is, and how it compares to those above or below. ... Institutions define reality in their terms. Right becomes, by definition, what the institution wants, and evil is to oppose the institution."

(Snyder, 1989, in Rinehart, 1998: 49)

The following sections describe some of the ways organizational leaders have argued against this "evil" of opposition to their position.

False belief that leaders have all the answers

In a novel, Arthur's prime character, Jason, appears to express the view that some seminaries, and the church leaders they produce, assume they have got all the answers:

"[A pastor confesses,] 'Ever since I graduated from seminary, and even before, I've held to a theology that put God in a box. My beliefs have never allowed God to work outside of my narrow-minded perception of him. It's like this: I've acted as if God gave my seminary and Bible college professors a neat little package of instructions about himself, a package they then passed on to me so I could pass it on to you. And I did – dogmatically, all these years. But I'm discovering that inside that little package is nothing more than pointless matters that strip God of his mystery and his bigness.

It tries to make God completely predictable. That package allows God no flexibility – and it allows us no flexibility. It puts every possible aspect of life into one of only two categories: spotless white or sinful black. And of course I've always known the correct category for everything.

'*I thought I had God all figured out. I knew how he was supposed to act and react in any and every situation. I knew exactly what he believed on every subject from the Second Coming to hair length and clothing styles, of all things.*

'*But suddenly I'm realizing that while I've pretended to know all the answers, the Bible plainly states that in this life we only see through a glass darkly, and we only know in part. So I can't kid myself any longer. I can't assume I know the mind of God about every facet of life.*

… [A church member countered,] '*But you're supposed to know the mind of God! You're the pastor!*' "

(Arthur, 1991: 116-117)

Jason continues:

"*All my Christian life I was taught, both directly and indirectly, both professionally and nonprofessionally, that a preacher should be an authority, and that he should clearly, and forcefully if necessary, display the attitude of an authority.* '*No one,*' *I was told,* '*should ever develop the idea that the preacher is weak or doesn't know the answers.*' "

(Arthur, 1991: 130)

Jason counters this position, warning that such an attitude stunts growth and learning:

"*If you have all the answers, there's nothing more to learn. You know it all. You become an authority with an authoritarian attitude … … It didn't destroy my ability to learn from others, but it did destroy my willingness to learn, especially when other people challenged my beliefs or convictions.*"

(Arthur, 1991: 117-118)

Jason then warns of an even greater danger, namely that the traditions we defend by suppression of questioning may be based more on the traditions of men rather than God's leading:

"*… it's normal for Christians to be given a packaged Christianity. Every aspect is tightly defined and outlined. And there's no admission of the possibility of errors in the way it's all put together. It's practically unforgivable for a thinking Christian to tamper with that packaged shape. Yet it's a form of Christianity shaped mostly by the mere preferences of men.*"

(Arthur, 1991: 227)

Alcoholics Anonymous (in *Alcoholics Anonymous Comes of Age*) goes one step further, warning not only of those who assume they have all the answers, but also warning of the opposite, namely individuals that feel they do not need to know the answers because their leaders already have them, and the individuals therefore stop personally searching:

> *"The assumption that one has all the answers, and the contrary, that one needs to know no answers, but just to follow [your group's teaching], are two indicators of trouble. In both cases open-mindedness is notably absent."*
>
> (AAWS, 1957: 249)

Buckingham recounts a personal story where a visitor sitting at the back of his local church raised his hand during the service. Using a pre-arranged signal for any "disturbance", Buckingham directed deacons to deal with this person. He later wrote:

> *"... I sometimes wonder if he was a prophet sent from God. Or an angel. Even so, it made little difference, for we had no place in the order of worship for messages from God which emanated from the congregation. Even from prophets. Or angels."*
>
> (Buckingham, 1980: 99)

False belief that criticism of local churches equals criticism of the very body of Christ

In Charles Sheldon's novel, *Jesus is Here*, consideration is given as to how Jesus would act if He were to return and speak to the local churches of today. In Jesus' day, He had spoken fearlessly against the wrongs of the Jewish religious practices, even though they were originally based on directions from God Himself. Yet Sheldon portrays a Jesus who is unwilling to speak against errors in today's churches, or at least against individuals who fell short of the mark:

> *" 'Didn't [Jesus] say anything about the hypocrites in the church? ... [And the reply was,] He did not condemn anyone.' "*
>
> (Sheldon, 1999: 36)

In another part of the story, one person explained Jesus' words concerning local churches:

> *"... not a word of censure, fault finding, calling attention to the pitiful weaknesses of us preachers and our poor little discipleship."*
>
> (Sheldon, 1999: 74)

And finally, a newspaper reported that

> *"[Jesus] does not scourge the church nor call attention to its weaknesses. He speaks with transcendent power of its mighty history, its unparalleled achievements, its sacrificial martyrdom."*
>
> (Sheldon, 1999: 175)

So, as a principle, it appears that Sheldon opposes criticism of local churches. At first glance, it also appears that Watchman Nee holds a similar view. In his book, *Changed into His Likeness*, he appears to strongly attack those who, in his view, demonstrate ignorance or arrogance through expressing their own opinions to criticize "the Church". He pictures these individuals as being a pile of rebellious stones rather than stones built into their proper place in the Church (the Body of Christ). He states:

> *"May God have mercy on us when we dare to think that the Church of God is wrong and we are right. <u>It is not just His people that we are repudiating in doing so,</u> **but God himself**, who pleases to reveal Himself among them." [Emphasis mine]*
>
> (Nee, 1967: 41)

While Nee opposes those who would criticize the Church, it seems at first glance that he is allowed to do just that. For example, he criticizes the Catholic Church, stating it:

> *"... is a false house, based on a wrong principle of authority and built largely of dead bricks and not of living stones."*
>
> (Nee, 1967: 40)

He then swings his fire against certain Protestant churches for having:

> *"... many living stones, but they are individual and not united. Liberty of conscience is its specialty. There is much splendid material, but it is not built into a house."*
>
> (Nee, 1967: 40)

Independent of whether or not we agree with Nee's criticisms of the Catholic Church or of those churches who align with certain Protestant traditions, my point is that Nee appears to be a critic of aspects of these churches, and yet criticizes others on the basis that they express criticism. So is Nee hypocritical in his stance?

Nee's answer to such a question may, perhaps, be found in his definition of "church". He states that:

> *"There is much in the world that goes by the name of the house of God. The great historic Churches and denominations all claim that title."*
>
> (Nee, 1967: 39-40)

He contrasts this with the true Body (the Church with a capital "C"), not run by man-imposed principles but consisting naturally when Christians take up the cross and, without fleshly strength, fit into God's house (not a building) …

> *"... as living stones, just the right size and shape for the place He has for us."*
>
> (Nee, 1967: 41)

So according to Nee, it appears we can't criticize the "Body of Christ" but we can criticize specific institutional expressions of "church". Much more is said shortly on what "church" really is. Independent of whether we judge his definition to be correct, for now it may be enough to understand that Nee claims that there are right and wrong ways to voice criticism, and by example he feels free to criticize denominational churches but opposes those who criticize *the* Church.

In his article, *The Church in God's Plan*, Howard Snyder takes a similar stance. Firstly, he has a similar definition for the universal Church. He states that:

> *"The Bible says the Church is nothing less than the body of Christ."*
>
> (Snyder, 1977: 118)

… and is made up of

> "… the people of God which God has been forming and through which he has been acting down through history."
>
> (Snyder, 1977: 118)

This is not to be confused with local churches. With this clear understanding, Snyder claims:

> "… the Church is an indispensable part of the gospel … [and] to adopt what might be called an 'anti-church stance' would be to dilute the very gospel itself and at the same time to demonstrate a misunderstanding of what the Bible means by 'the church.'"
>
> (Snyder, 1977: 118)

Almost without exception, Snyder's article refers to the universal Body of Christ as "Church" with an upper case 'C'. In the above quotations, however, he appears to attack an "anti-church stance", using lower case for "church". Whether consciously or otherwise, to me, this has the danger of moving from a position of warning against attacks on *the* Body of Christ, to a position where church leaders use such phrases to condemn those who would attack their local church.

From the references quoted, Henke seems to cut through what some see as nobler goals to avoid criticism of the Church, and, in my opinion, attacks *any "religious system"* that cannot cope with questioning, or even open dissent, and warns how some unhealthy groups may attempt to make the dissenting party wonder if they are losing their faith in God:

> "… [When] the religious system is not based on the truth it cannot allow questions, dissent, or open discussions about issues. The person who dissents becomes the problem rather than the issue he raised. The truth about any issue is settled and handed down from the top of the hierarchy. Questioning anything is considered a challenge to authority. Thinking for oneself is suppressed by pointing out that it leads to doubts. This is portrayed as unbelief in God and His anointed leaders. Thus the follower controls his own thoughts by fear of doubting God."
>
> (Henke, 2000)

We can and should feel free to critique local churches. Church leaders who oppose questioning of their local church on the basis that we must not criticize the Body of Christ have completely misunderstood the distinction.

False belief in the need for unquestioning submission to authority

There are movements within Christendom that implicitly, or even explicitly, equate submission to church leaders with submission to God. Henke comments:

> "The assumption is that God operates among His people through a hierarchy, or 'chain of command.' In this abusive system unconditional submission is often called a 'covering,' or 'umbrella of protection' which will provide some spiritual blessing to those

who fully submit. Followers may be told that God will bless their submission even if the leadership is wrong. It is not their place to judge or correct the leadership – God will see to that."

(Henke, 2000)

Brown looks at the same problem but from a different perspective, namely the labeling of people as rebels when they do follow God but don't follow the church leaders:

"... when ... sincere children of God try to follow the leading of His Spirit and walk in obedience to Him – which sometimes means differing with their leaders – they are called rebellious. What a travesty! Listening to the voice of Jesus, the Shepherd of the flock, is called rebellion by one of His undershepherds (who is a sheep himself). Thus obedience to God is viewed as disobedience to leadership, while submission to the authority of Jesus is branded resistance to church authority, and a healthy fear of the Lord is labeled pride and independence."

(Brown, 2002: 103)

Going further, Brown explains how Bunyan opposed the established church and the state laws that reflected the churches' thinking, and then asks:

"Why, then, was it right for [Bunyan] to refuse to bow to the unbiblical practices of the Church of his day, following his conscience and the Word of God, while it is wrong for someone to do the same today? Why do we consider him righteous for the stand he took while the authorities of his day called him rebellious?"

(Brown, 2002: 156)

Brown then classifies such suppression of questioning, and the labeling as "rebels" those who *do* question, as abuse by the leadership:

"Where does the New Testament ever require mindless submission and robot-like compliance to authorities within the Body? Who said that disagreement with a church leader constituted rebellion? ... What verse in the Bible states that it is wrong to raise fair and honest questions, with a meek and gracious spirit, to Christian leaders? How can this possibly be called rebellion? Yet it is, in churches across the land, leaving a path of bloodied, battered and bruised believers – the result of abusive spiritual authority."

(Brown, 2002: 102-103)

And last but not least, questioning misguidedly seen as a breach of loyalty

We have looked at several reasons church leaders give for suppressing questioning, but perhaps the most dangerous of these is the attitude by some church leaders that any questioning demonstrates a lack of loyalty to them.

The Fundamentalist Church of Latter Day Saints (FLDS) is a church that many might consider to be a cult. According to Wall's book, the FLDS actively encourages polygamy, rewarding its obedient males with multiple wives. It had one supreme leader, the "prophet" (who at the time of assembly of these notes was serving time in jail for crimes related to rape and child sexual assault). As recounted in Elissa Wall's heartbreaking autobiography, *Stolen Innocence*, this same "prophet" reinforced his authority by claiming:

> "The work of God is a benevolent dictatorship. It is not a democracy."
>
> (Wall, 2008: 285)

Wall recounts how, as a fourteen-year-old girl within the FLDS church, she was ordered to marry a person she despised – her first cousin. When she appealed against the directive the man who later became the "prophet" stated,

> "Your problem is that you are questioning [your husband] and the priesthood itself … And when you question the priesthood and your [husband, the] priesthood head, you are questioning God."
>
> (Wall, 2008: 250)

Later, when Wall began to break free from the enslavement of the group, she expressed her opinion as to why the leadership so actively suppressed questioning.

> "It's hard because once you question one thing, you start to question everything."
>
> (Wall, 2008: 304)

We take from Wall's account that they don't want their domination threatened in any way, including intelligent and sincere questioning by thoughtful church members.

Chris Elkins tells of his personal experiences in the Unification Church, known by many as the Moonies. According to Elkins' account, the leaders were planning a strategy that involved him. He asked a number of questions, such as what he would need to do, what the project entailed, how big it was, etc. The leader's responses included:

> "Chris, do you have to ask these questions? You're a member of the Church …
> You need to accept the will of … [Rev. Moon]. You're questioning it."
>
> (Elkins, 1980: 103)

As Elkins continued to seek for answers, the leaders were concerned they may be losing him from their ranks, and planned to send him on an intensive training program. He knew the results by observation of others who had been subjected to the same training; he knew how he would come out:

> "Not necessarily brainwashed, but totally dependent. I would be like a child, willing to let others make my decisions and would have a childlike, unquestioning loyalty. I wouldn't necessarily get my doubts about the Church resolved as much as I would finally bury my doubts under layers of indoctrination. Children are controlled because they are dependent. The same applies to a member of the Unification Church."
>
> (Elkins, 1980: 132)

An earlier extract noted the following traits in abusive churches that could also be observed in some more mainstream churches:

"Submission to the leader and his / her teachings, or those endorsed by him / her, is emphasised and either explicitly or implicitly demanded. The leader 'helps' members make decisions about all aspects of life, well beyond matters of faith and morals - such as courtship and relationships, employment, recreation activities, and dress. The leader usually does this by seeking 'God's will' on the matter in question."

(Free Indeed, 2000)

Noting the above, we may question whether William Booth, the founder of the Salvation Army, exhibited some abusive aspects of behavior in his leadership.

Before we launch into further analysis, I wish to share that I personally respect the Salvation Army for its various areas of care shown to the disadvantaged in society. From the outset, their organization demonstrated cared for the poor and vulnerable.

I was keen to read Hattersley's book *Blood and Fire*. It provided a deep and well-researched history of not only the Salvation Army as an organization, but importantly provides insight into William (and Catherine) Booth, the founders. A critique of Hattersley's book revealed a perspective on topics such as:

- William Booth's style of leadership.

- How the original structure of the Salvation Army impacted individual freedom. For example, he most certainly was involved in the personal decisions of his followers, as Hattersley explains:

"[William Booth] took it for granted that he should exercise a parent's discipline over the officers under his command – as concerned in their private lives as he was about the way in which they discharged their public duties."

(Hattersley, 2000: 282)

Not only did Booth intrude into the private lives of his followers, he also apparently expected total, unquestioning obedience from them:

"The nature of their commitments – to the Mission and to its leader – made them susceptible to discipline, and the commander-in-chief had always expected his subordinates to accept orders without argument or question."

(Hattersley, 2000: 229)

Further, based on Hattersley's account, Booth's strict expectations on church members were no less harsh for his own children:

"All [Booth's] children had been taught the importance of discipline... They had been brought up to accept his authority without thought or question and to obey his orders no matter how uncongenial they might be."

(Hattersley, 2000: 407)

But it was perhaps in the area of demanding loyalty that William Booth exhibited the most disturbing attitudes:

> "[William Booth was] a General first and a father afterwards ... [and had] no children outside the Salvation Army."
>
> (Hattersley, 2000: 420)

This attitude was highlighted after William Booth received a letter from his own daughter, Kate, who had supported her husband in his choice to leave the Salvation Army. Booth's diary recorded receipt of:

> "... a letter from Mrs Clibborn full of assertions of her great love for myself ..."
>
> (Hattersley, 2000: 421)

Hattersley comments:

> "The entry reads as if [William Booth] did not want to remember that 'Mrs Clibborn' was his daughter. ... he was incapable of realising ... that she loved her husband more than she loved the Salvation Army."
>
> (Hattersley, 2000: 421)

Booth's apparent rejection of any children who did not follow his orders was not limited to a passive attitude (as cutting as that was), but Hattersley noted that this would extend his rejection to even excluding them from family funerals:

> "[There was a] train crash ... in which Emma Booth-Tucker died. Her brother and sister – who had defected from the Army – were excluded from the New York memorial service."
>
> (Hattersley, 2000: Comments on photographs following p. 328)

As we can see, William Booth personally demanded loyalty from his children. As the leadership was about to be handed over to the chosen successor, the favored son, the expectation of loyalty was also passed on to the next generation. As Catherine Booth (William's wife) was dying, she exhibited the same attitude when she:

> "... spoke to each of her children individually and made each one swear eternal fidelity to the Army and to [her son] Bramwell who, by then, was accepted as his father's successor."
>
> (Hattersley, 2000: 337)

Booth's demands extended into the family lives of his followers. For example, it divided families where parents disagreed with the practices of the Salvation Army. Hattersley provides quotes from one parent, the Reverend Mr Samuel Charlesworth, whose daughter was seen as having been "lured" by the Salvation Army. Hattersley notes that:

> "[Charlesworth's] letter could have been written by any one of a thousand distraught parents who, down the years, have seen their children infatuated by religious movements which, to more conventional thinkers, appear to be dangerous sects ..."
>
> (Hattersley, 2000: 298)

Hattersley then quotes Charlesworth as saying

> *"... I fear that the Army's influence has a direct tendency to wean from home associates and interests under the idea that the work is paramount in importance to all other pursuits and obligations and even to the known wishes of parents."*
>
> (Hattersley, 2000: 299)

As a side note, some readers may be tempted to spring to Booth's defense based on the perspective that God has the right to direct His followers, even if His wishes may conflict with those of parents. However, we must recognize that there is a difference between God making demands and a denominational leader making demands. More on that later!

Finally, the demands for loyalty to Booth's denominational church and to himself extended even to church loyalty being ahead of loyalty to one's spouse. For example, the Salvation Army had Articles of Marriage:

> *"... which all soldiers were required to accept before the General would agree to preside at their wedding. The articles included the promises 'never to allow our marriage to lessen in any way our devotion to God and the Army' and 'to regard and arrange our home as a Salvation Army officer's (or soldier's) home.'"*
>
> (Hattersley, 2000: 281)

One example of the impacts of this misguided loyalty is portrayed below:

> *"... the General did not accept [Tucker's] services ... until Tucker has proved himself to be worthy. ... Tucker ..., much to his wife's horror ... resigned from the Indian Civil Service as a token of his absolute sincerity."*
>
> (Hattersley, 2000: 290)

Even one of Booth's own children lashed out:

> *"How can you demand I turn my back on my husband. I love him with all my heart and all my soul. What is there in the rules of the Salvation Army that takes precedence over the conviction between a man and his wife and demands the renunciation of the vows and faithfulness of marriage?"*
>
> (Hattersley, 2000: 420)

Demands for loyalty have been noted in fringe groups many would classify as cults, and also in the Salvation Army, which many might see as being more mainstream. But are the demands for loyalty present on a more wide-spread basis? Brown seems to hint they are:

> *"We have seen our share of Hare Krishna devotees chanting on street corners, or sleep-deprived young people selling flowers eighteen hours a day, or sweet-talking cult members knocking on our doors, eager to share their faith but incapable of thinking for themselves. We don't want to become like that!*
>
> *And for good reason. God does not brainwash His children. He does not lobotomize us when we get saved and remove our capacity to think. He does not immobilize*

our minds and reduce us to robotic obedience. He does not call us to abusive and destructive acts, such as beating our bodies or mutilating ourselves in some bizarre attempt to subdue the flesh. And He certainly does not call us to submit every part of our lives – down to our innermost, secret thoughts – to the whims and demands of an earthly leader. All these things are characteristic of cults, bringing people into bondage and captivity. That is not the Jesus way. Jesus sets the captives free."

(Brown, 2002: 69)

Rinehart is even more direct. He explains that church leaders often assume God's direction and blessing if they can point to measurable, numerical "success". He warns that such people typically go even further and imply that:

"... others should swear blind loyalty to the institution or move on. And the leader perceives any questioning of the vision or integrity of the ministry as a direct threat."

(Rinehart, 1998: 53)

... and that ...

"... the need for control will insist on defining ministry in terms of loyalty to a particular group and to programs directly attached to the institution. It simply can't allow for freedom and diversity in people or programs."

(Rinehart, 1998: 54-55)

Oliver & Thwaites also see demands for loyalty as a general problem within churches:

"For too long, church life has been about loyalty to leaders, to their visions and rights over the people and the process."

(Oliver & Thwaites, 2001: 110)

Rinehart concludes:

"Submission [in the Bible] ... is not a situation of blind kowtowing to a leader's authority."

(Rinehart, 1998: 111)

Hattersley noted several behaviors by Booth that would clearly ring warning bells to many. But expectations to 'follow the leader' can be much more subtle. One frequently observed expectation set by church leaders relates to dress codes. In George MacDonald's novel, *The Poet and the Pauper: The Shepherd's Castle*, Donal is a poor shepherd whose shoes were in need of repair. Donal was certainly not constrained by expectations of church leaders as to what was appropriate clothing for church attendance, and states:

"I'm not that particular about going to church. But if I did want to go, I wouldn't fancy the Lord affronted with me for the bare feet he himself made."

(MacDonald, 1983(b): 20)

The attitudes and hypocrisy of leaders in enforcing codes for appearance were noted by Philip Yancey in his book, *The Jesus I Never Knew*:

> *"It dawned on me that virtually all portrayals of Jesus, including the ... Jesus of my Bible college, showed him wearing a mustache and beard, both of which were strictly banned from the Bible college."*
>
> (Yancey, 1995: 14)

I have personally been instructed by a senior pastor as to what he considered appropriate dress code for footwear, pants, shirts and the like. Based on the way he treated me, I suspect that if Jesus turned up wearing plain, black, laced shoes and neatly pressed slacks, the pastor would have been happy with Jesus' standard, but if Jesus wore leather sandals and a cloak, my guess is that He would have been turned away, or at least not allowed Him to "minister"!

Tanya Levin's autobiography, *People in Glass Houses*, also notes the dress standard expectations foisted on others. She tells the story of one of the largest and best known churches in her country, Australia. She notes not only the issue of setting standards for acceptability, but also on the reaction by senior leadership to those who dare to not conform, especially without asking permission.

> *"[At the Hillsong church, Australia,] nearly all the pastors in my teenage years had moustaches. [Years later I returned and met with Brian Houston, the senior pastor] ... and gone was Brian's broom. It was replaced with a ponytail, just like all the other pastors. ... [But one pastor subsequently broke ranks. He] later told me that he woke up one morning and said, 'I'm thirty-seven and I have a ponytail.' He cut it off, but suffered a verbal thrashing for 'attempting to change the church's image without permission'."*
>
> (Levin, 2007: 98-99, 100)

Some use phrases for leaders such as "God's anointed", with an inference that they are to receive special respect and loyalty. Brown takes a strong position, warning that our respect should be for the common person, not the religious leaders:

> *"The context of Psalm 105:15 ['Don't touch my anointed ones'] has to do with God warning the heathen nations not to touch the patriarchs – Abraham, Isaac and Jacob. If it is applied to us today, it should be applied as a warning to the world not to touch God's people, all of whom are the Lord's anointed. One could even argue that this verse can be used as a warning to abusive leaders: Don't touch God's anointed – meaning His sheep!"*
>
> (Brown, 2002: 215)

Reaction by controlling leaders

We need to be set free from church leaders' demands for loyalty. Instead, our loyalty must be to God. But what might we expect as a reaction when we move towards such freedom? Hattersley's stories of William Booth certainly give us an idea of how some might react. Other writers also seem to suggest that negative responses from those leaders who see themselves as God's representatives on earth are in fact common.

Yancey personally experienced rejection by church leaders when he questioned them:

> "*As a struggling Christian I had received rejection from the church itself: they wanted me to conform and not quibble, to believe and not question.*"

(Yancey, 2001: 268)

Yancey's rejection was not just limited to rejection by the church leaders, but also by other Christian organizations which also could not cope with questioning:

> "*... the Bible college I attended ... tended to punish, rather than reward, intellectual curiosity; one teacher admitted he deliberately lowered my grades in order to teach me humility. 'The greatest barrier to the Holy Spirit is sophistication,' he used to warn his classes.*
>
> *... [Yancey contrasts this narrow-minded suppression of questioning with others who] kindled hope that somewhere Christians existed who loosed rather than restrained their minds, who combined sophisticated taste with a humility that did not demean others and, above all, who experienced life with God as a source of joy and not repression.*"

(Yancey, 2001: 41)

Brown classifies suppression of questioning by church leaders as a form of abuse of authority:

> "*At times leaders will hatch their own carnal plan (often under financial pressure) rather than do things God's way, seeking to enforce it by means of their position as leaders, even pressuring the flock for funds in order to make their plan work. 'Remember,' they say, 'we are your leaders, appointed by God, so you must give yourselves wholeheartedly to our vision' – but everyone with eyes to see can recognize that they are acting in the flesh. Yet no one is allowed to question them or disagree, since they are the anointed leaders. Anyone who does question them is in rebellion against the Lord. What a misuse of authority this is!*"

(Brown, 2002: 118)

Rinehart expresses a similar concern:

> "*A vision that depends upon the continued presence and positional power of its propagators is not authored by God. Visionaries operating in the flesh promote messages like these:*
>
> - *'If you're not getting my vision, you're not listening to God, or you are spiritually immature and inferior.'*
> - *'This is the only true spiritual vision around here. If you have another vision, we will be unequally yoked.'*
> - *'You must remember that you are extensions of the senior pastor [or other position] and are therefore responsible for achieving his vision.'*

- *'You must follow my vision and strategy – it's been proven to work.'* "

(Rinehart, 1998: 57)

Geoff Bullock is a musician with international recognition, and was also part of the pastoral team at Hillsong. In the mid-nineties Bullock chose to move on for personal reasons:

"As the Hillsong conference expanded in the late eighties, so did Geoff's responsibilities and pressures. He and his wife, Janine, were expected to spend infinite hours away from their children to run the music department. International interest in the music grew and so did Geoff's profile. The couple travelled extensively with the Praise and Worship team, and personally with their old friends Brian and Bobbie. Despite the bright lights and the glory, his music career at its peak, Geoff was finding less satisfaction and spirituality in what he was doing.

After the most successful conference yet, Hillsong '95, Geoff went to Brian and told him he was leaving. It was time, he felt, spiritually, to pursue other interests."

(Levin, 2007: 243)

Geoff was not attacking Hillsong; he simply felt that for him and his family the time had come to move on. Yet based on the response of Hillsong, according to Levin, I get the impression that they saw him as a traitor, and their reaction comes across to me as vindictive.

"Hillsong did everything in its power to prevent his future success. Due to speak at a bible college occasion soon after leaving, he received a phone call with a sudden apology. Hillsong had informed the bible college that any association with Geoff Bullock meant no further association with Hillsong. Christian magazines were told the same thing. Piles of the CD Geoff was about to release were found dumped at a tip in Blacktown, not far from Hillsong headquarters."

(Levin, 2007: 243)

Bobbie Houston, the senior pastor's wife, linked Geoff's departure with a series of subsequent disruptions, stating:

"We experienced ... stinking thinking, people throwing in the towel, disloyalty in our team ..., devil induced confusion, opposition and a fine thread of 'cancerous attitude' ..."

(Levin, 2007: 244)

Finally, according to Levin, one Hillsong board member later admitted to Geoff,

"We tried to destroy you ..."

(Levin, 2007: 244)

And while Geoff Bullock has been able to continue to make a contribution to his beloved Christian music ministry, he has been scarred by the way Hillsong reacted to his departure:

"The nightmares remain one of the most intrusive spillovers from the old days. Three or four times a week he dreams about Hillsong events, being humiliated by Brian's demands, being screamed at, berated and bullied along the way. His psyche is deeply affected. He is very aware that he, too, became a bully. Years later, Geoff has tried to make amends to many people he treated ruthlessly in order to avoid punishment from above."

(Levin, 2007: 244)

Gagging must be opposed

When we encounter those who suppress our questioning, there are two aspects to consider in our personal responses to such attempts at gagging.

The first is our own willingness and responsibility to continue to personally question, even if our questions are not welcome. Rick Levine, Christopher Locke, Doc Searls and David Weinberger wrote a confronting book, *The Cluetrain Manifesto*, aimed at challenging many of the positions held by big corporations. While their message is targeted at the business world rather than church organizations, I suspect that many of the issues span both types of "organization". They state:

> *"If you wish to be useful, never take a course that will silence you. Refuse to learn anything that implies collusion, whether it be a clerkship or a curacy, a legal fee or a post in a university. Retain the power of speech no matter what other power you may lose. If you can take this course, and in so far as you take it, you will bless this country. In so far as you depart from this course you become dampers, mutes, and hooded executioners.*
>
> *As a practical matter a mere failure to speak out upon occasions where no opinion is asked or expected of you, and when the utterance of an uncalled-for suspicion is odious, will often hold you to a concurrence in palpable iniquity. Try to raise a voice that will be heard from here to Albany and watch what comes forward to shut off the sound. It is not a German sergeant, nor a Russian officer of the precinct. It is a note from a friend of your father's offering you a place in his office. This is your warning from the secret police."*

(John Jay Chapman in Levine, Locke, Searls and Weinberger, 2000: 44-45)

Secondly, it is one thing to personally find the freedom to ask questions, even if they are unwelcome. There is a challenge, however, to go further—to actively oppose those who try to suppress questioning, and to stand by those who are more timid than you and feel controlled by those who attempt to gag questioning. Are we willing to accept a responsibility to speak out against the whole culture of gagging, especially on behalf of those who may be more timid?

I commence an analysis of the need for active opposition to those who would suppress others by looking at the damage done by gagging as it occurs in secular business:

> *"Just about all the concessions we make to work in a well-run, non-disturbing, secure, predictably successful, managed environment have to do with giving up our voice."*
>
> (Levine, Locke, Searls and Weinberger, 2000: 42)

Rinehart notes that a lack of openness to questioning is also present within church leadership:

> *"... [leaders] fail to ask [themselves] the hard questions. [Their] spiritual position in the community of faith becomes the curtain behind which [their] egos grow unchecked. The younger ones in the faith dare not question [them] – the spiritual elders. And [they] grow more and more skilled at covering up [their] insecurities."*
>
> (Rinehart, 1998: 23)

He then goes on to warn that, while such attitudes exist within the business community as well as within local churches, they are more dangerous within churches:

> *"In the church, the playing field is never level if the leader sets himself up as the one who speaks for God. Who would dare question 'God'? At least the business world doesn't add that spiritual confusion."*
>
> (Rinehart, 1998: 34)

Richard Foster's delightfully balanced book on the thorny topics of *Money, Sex and Power* also sends out a warning, namely that suppression of questioning can lead to unchecked errors that are more a reflection of the demonic than of God:

> *"Power can be an extremely destructive thing in any context, but in the service of religion it is downright diabolical. Religious power can destroy in a way that no other power can. Power corrupts, and absolute power corrupts absolutely; and this is especially true in religion. Those who are a law unto themselves and at the same time take on a mantle of piety are particularly corruptible. When we are convinced that what we are doing is identical with the kingdom of God, anyone who opposes us must be wrong. When we are convinced that we always use our power to good ends, we believe we can never do wrong. But when this mentality possesses us, we are taking the power of God and using it to our own ends. ...*
>
> *What we must see is the wrongness of those who think they are always right. Jesus Christ alone is always right. The rest of us must recognise our own foibles and frailties and seek to learn from the correction of others. If we do not, power can take us down the path of the demonic."*
>
> (Foster, 1985: 578, 579)

Confrontation

Earlier, we considered how some church leaders may suppress questioning, albeit perhaps from misguided motives. A more ugly reason is that some feel that open questioning may lessen their control. This in fact may be true, but it does not in the slightest excuse gagging just so they can remain unchallenged in their positions of authority.

Thomas Petzinger, Jr., in his foreword to *The Cluetrain Manifesto*, notes this ability of open communication to destroy unwanted institutions. In discussing the consequence of global communication, facilitated now by Internet-enabled conversations, the authors perceive that open communication:

> "... tears down power structures and senseless bureaucracies ..."
>
> (Levine, Locke, Searls and Weinberger, 2000: iv)

But the fear of the effects of questioning also appears within churches. Elkins describes how church leadership in the local church he attended believed that a particular newcomer to the church needed to be shielded from those who might question the organization:

> "She already thinks that we are terrific. She is easily influenced by others though, and we need to keep her away from a couple of the more negative people."
>
> (Elkins, 1980: 116)

While Elkins' experience was within a group that many may classify as a cult, similar attitudes have been observed in mainline churches e.g. where remaining members are ordered not to have dealings with certain people, especially those who had left. While you might be unlikely to classify your local church as a cult, you may be willing to accept that suppression of open questioning is a cult-like behavior. But let us not be misled – any gagging of discussion by those seen to be "in authority" in a local church is an abuse of their power.

Brown tells a story of controlling leadership that is hypothetical, but that he sadly recognizes as being all too real:

> "Let me give you an all-too-typical example that will help illustrate just how destructive this controlling ministry mentality really is.
>
> Let's say the pastor of a large, non-charismatic congregation begins to preach on the need for revival in the Church. Several months later, after much corporate prayer, God begins to pour out His Spirit on the hungry flock, and hundreds of lives are transformed. But the outpouring proves too intense for the pastor and his board, so they decide to shut down what God is doing and go back to their old, traditional ways.
>
> Not surprisingly, many in the church are unhappy, feeling that the Spirit has been quenched and a move of God thwarted. But when they seek to bring their concerns to the leadership—not in a harsh, combative way, but in a determined effort to seek and speak the truth rather than gossip about their leaders behind their backs—they are told that they just do not understand. In fact, they are told that they are operating in spiritual pride (although in the past they have been singled out as models of humility), that they have a problem with authority (although their record of service through the years has been exemplary) and that the recent outpouring served to reveal some junk in their own lives (although during the outpouring they were asked to testify to the great work the Spirit had accomplished in their lives). What in the world is going on?

But the story is not yet over for these hurting Christians. After months of deep inner conflict, much painful soul-searching and even bouts of self-condemnation ('Maybe I really am rebellious. Maybe I do have a problem with pride. Was I really touched by the Spirit? Maybe it was all just emotionalism.'), they feel they should leave the church and join another local assembly that affirms the gifts and power of the Spirit. So they lovingly inform the leadership of their decision, asking to be released with blessing and thanking the leaders for everything they have done through the years. And what are they told in response? They are told they are in rebellion!

Soon enough, perhaps the very next Sunday, ominous threats are sounded from the pulpit, warning the startled hearers about 'the rebellion,' urging the congregants not to join this insidious, undermining movement, and reminding them of what God did to Korah and his followers when they tried to rebel against Moses: The earth opened its mouth and swallowed them up. So beware!

The pastor is now pulling out some of his vintage messages from Numbers and Deuteronomy in which the rebellious Israelites dared to disobey Moses, the servant of the Lord, falling in the wilderness as a result. It is time to warn the flock!

'Safety will only be found in staying here under the covering of the mother church. This is the place of protection. This is the place of security. Outside these walls lurk all kinds of deceptive spirits. Doctrinal purity and true church order are found here. And remember what happened to Miriam and Aaron when they dared to grumble about some of the decisions made by Moses: God rebuked them audibly, and Miriam was smitten with leprosy.

'And not only are you in danger; you are also being ungrateful and disloyal. After all, I'm the one who performed your weddings and conducted your families' funeral services. I was there for you during your times of trouble. My staff and my leaders have poured themselves out for you, putting you first, sacrificing time and energy and money, living godly and holy lives—all for you!

'How then can you question those whom God has placed in authority over you? We love you and care for you, and the drastic measures we are taking today are being taken only for you. Just as a parent can't explain everything to a child, we can't explain everything to you. Just trust us, search your heart for a rebellious attitude and support your leadership now. This message is for you.'

Perhaps in the midst of these sermons, some prophetic utterances come forth, echoing the words of Psalm 105:15, 'Touch not My anointed, and do My prophets no harm,' with direct application to the present situation: 'Don't you dare express any disagreement with these anointed servants of the Lord. God will not be happy with that!'

What makes this story so sad is that it is not exaggerated. To the contrary, it is common, especially in evangelical circles (and possibly in Pentecostal and charismatic churches in particular, since one dare not question the charismatic leader). Yet such practices are both manipulative and abusive, using fear and guilt to dominate and control the flock.

How contrary this is to the shepherd's heart, and how utterly destructive and cruel, since it is shepherds who are wounding and mistreating the trusting sheep. Yet it has happened thousands of times. All this is contrary to the Word of God, as Scripture nowhere gives leaders this kind of authority over their people."

(Brown, 2002: 105-107)

I read the above, and began to consider its contents. Could this sort of behavior actually occur, let alone be more widespread than we would like? I sat down, and looked at the past experiences I had personally encountered. I also recollected the stories told to me by others. I could only conclude that Brown's articulate hypothetical could easily have been actual records from past behavior some of "God's anointed".

So how should we react when we observe such controlling behavior? Whether it is pleasant or not, we must be willing to confront the abuser. But before we look at the arguments for confrontation, we need to be cautious of our attitudes. Bill, a co-founder of Alcoholics Anonymous, in *As Bill Sees It* shows that we must neither choose to ignore problems in others, nor should we act in a manner motivated from our own wrong attitudes:

"Most surely, there can be no trust where there is no love, nor can there be real love where distrust holds its malign sway.

But does trust require that we be blind to other people's motives or, indeed, to our own? Not at all; this would be folly. Most certainly, we should assess the capacity for harm as well as the capability for good in every person that we would trust. Such a private inventory can reveal the degree of confidence we should extend in any given situation.

However, this inventory needs to be taken in a spirit of understanding and love. Nothing can so much bias our judgment as the negative emotions of suspicion, jealousy, or anger."

(Bill, 1967: 144)

In *Jesus—Safe, Tender, Extreme*, Adrian Plass shares his fury at leaders who damage those they lead, and speaks honestly of his own struggles to retain the right attitude to those leaders:

"You know, there is not much genuine rage in me nowadays, but I maintain a small store to draw from when necessary, and I suspect that the Holy Spirit tops it up periodically. In my view there is not enough appropriate anger in the church today. A significant portion of this intense fury of mine is reserved for teachers and preachers who seem to specialise in bewildering and bamboozling the children of the kingdom. I am sure you know the ones I mean.

For a start they only have problems in the past, never in the present. They ignore Jesus' teaching about cost and offer conversion as though it were like one of those store cards, one small, effortless prayer as a deposit and after that you can take as much as you want without paying. They teach that Christianity is not about formulae and then make sure that you have learned that principle word for word.

Most important, ... their teaching says that although change is essential, you and I can't do it, only God can do it, and then when you and I find that nothing happens and we haven't changed and we can't do it, they raise a censorial eyebrow and announce that it must be our fault. Most of us would rather be thrown back into the waters from which they fished us than flop helplessly around in the pathetically limited confines of their suffocating, strangling nets.

Do you think I sound judgemental? Ah, well, what you have to understand is that it's prophetic rather than personal. That's my excuse. Thank goodness God loves them. I don't, and therefore I must. I would like to shower them with damp and clammy texts, like emptying a barrel of eels over their heads, if it weren't for the fact that I know how pointless and annoying it is because they have so often done the same to me."

(Plass, 2006: 221-222)

Having an attitude that allows for forgiveness towards those who control others does not mean we do not confront this behavior. Sometimes we may be called to confront specific church leaders. In the context of a congregation seeking spiritual growth, Buckingham describes a pastor who is:

"... reluctant to move, fearful of any kind of movement which might rock the boat ... [and who is] emotionally insecure – and afraid to admit it ..."

(Buckingham, 1980: 100)

Buckingham, as a pastor himself, states:

"Speaking from personal experience, I know [such a minister] must be confronted. Not once, but hundreds of times if necessary, by the sheep of the flock who are determined to move to higher pastures. However, the confrontations must always be in love, never with the threat of rejection. At the same time ... sheep are priests also and therefore as responsible to God as the shepherd ..."

(Buckingham, 1980: 100-101)

Green and Hazard tell a colorful story of one such confrontation, opposing a minister over his deception on the offering for Keith Green's ministry. According to them, the pastor had spoken to the attendees in such a way as to convey a message that everything given by them would be passed on to Keith. Instead, he seemingly held back some of the money for himself, under the guise of "covering costs". For Keith, the issue was not how much he personally received, but rather how the people had been misled by the pastor's deception. And Keith confronted him!

"One night, Keith did a concert in a church that probably held a few hundred people. At the end, the pastor stood and encouraged everyone to give generously, because it was all going to be given to Keith. 'Let's bless him back for the great time of ministry!'

> *About half-an-hour later, we wandered out to [our vehicle] and opened up the envelope we'd been given. We were stunned by the amount inside. We obviously hadn't received all that was given. Keith didn't know what to do.*
>
> *At first Keith said, 'I'll just let it go. I'm not going to make a big deal out of this.' But after a few minutes, he realized he couldn't drive off without talking to the pastor. It wasn't just the money – it was the principle. Keith felt he should be given the whole offering because that's what people were told. Everyone gave with that in mind.*
>
> *When Keith told me he was going to go back in and talk to the pastor, I nearly died. I probably wouldn't have gone, because I'd be afraid to look like I was just being greedy. But Keith was determined.*
>
> *'We always take all of our expenses out of the offering,' the pastor said, in reply to Keith's enquiry.*
>
> *'Then you should have told everyone that was going to happen when you took the offering. Then it would have been fine.'*
>
> *'Well, no one's complained before …'*
>
> *Keith stood firm. 'I just don't think it's right. Everyone was told the offering was going to be given to me, and that's who they thought they were giving to.'*
>
> *I could tell he felt awkward, knowing he was probably being misunderstood. 'I'm not trying to be greedy – but I feel the givers were misled, whether it was intentional or not,' he concluded."*
>
> (Green & Hazard, 1989: 168-169)

Obviously, confrontation does not always have a pleasant outcome. But Buckingham learned we must not fear the outcome, but just speak out when challenged to do so. He was an invited guest at a large public meeting where he felt he had a confrontational message that God wanted spoken out. Out of fear he held back, and missed the opportunity to bring a much-needed challenge. Afterwards, he

> *"… made a fresh commitment to God. From that time on, if God told me to say something, I would do it. Better to be criticized by man than to disappoint God."*
>
> (Buckingham, 1980: 165)

How important is it to confront? After quoting Howard Snyder's claim that religious institutions have abused their power by defining as evil those who oppose them, Rinehart goes on to say:

> "Such inappropriate vestiges of power must be confronted today as vigorously as Jesus confronted the Pharisees."
>
> (Rinehart, 1998: 49)

Green sets an example for us to consider. His ministry delivered an unflinching series of body blows to local churches, not out of bitterness or revenge, but out of a deep desire to wake the churches from their slumber:

> *"Keith's idea was to shake Christians awake from the comfortable 'slumber' we'd seen.*
>
> *... I got to thinking about all the people that give God one day a week. How would you like it if your wife gave you one day a week? 'Well dear, I'm here for the weekly visit.' People like to visit God from ten to eleven on Sunday mornings ... '*
>
> *... 'Do you know the rich young ruler would be accepted in any church today? But Jesus wouldn't accept him ... Why? Because he had an idol in his life ...'*
>
> *... You can't get to heaven by being a nice guy. You might end up to be the nicest guy in hell!' "*
>
> (Green & Hazard, 1989: 187, 191, 193-194, 195)

Keith tackled the Catholic Church for making it too hard to know God personally. Then he tackled the Protestant churches for making it too easy and cheap to know God. He summarized his series of articles with these words:

> *"Don't you see what fools we are? We preach a man-made, plastic gospel. We get people to 'come forward' to the altar by bringing psychological pressures that have nothing to do with God. We 'lead them' in a prayer that they are not yet convinced they need to say. And then to top it all off, we give them 'counselling' ... telling them it is a sin to doubt that they're saved!*
>
> *Beloved family, the world around us is going to hell. Not because of communism, television, drugs, sex, alcohol, or the devil himself. It is because of the Church!"*
>
> (Green & Hazard, 1989: 277)

Finding freedom

Some seem to think that anything produced by non-Christians is to be avoided, whether it is music, literature, films or whatever. Hudson Taylor, the founder of the China Inland Mission, had the freedom to be enriched from wider sources, as is recounted by Howard Taylor (the son of Hudson Taylor) and his wife, Geraldine, in the biography *Hudson Taylor In Early Years – The Growth of a Soul*:

> *"The classics he gave as much time to as possible, and he seems always to have had some useful book on hand dealing with history, biography, or natural science."*
>
> (Taylor & Taylor, 1911: 221)

One aspect of freedom noted above is to learn from the expression of the views of others. Another aspect of freedom is to be able to personally express your views, unhindered by the objections of others. Yancey noted this choice for personal freedom in Buechner's writing:

> *"Out of consideration for his mother, who jealously guarded family secrets, Buechner did not write directly of his father's suicide for decades, though scenes of suicide haunt his novels. His mother reacted with fury to one such scene, and could barely speak to*

> *him for days. Finally Buechner decided that he had as much right to tell his father's story as his mother had not to tell her husband's story, and his memoirs began to probe the family tragedy."*

(Yancey, 2001: 249)

Similarly, through his novel's central character, Arthur challenges us all to not just agree to such freedom in our thinking, but to live it:

> *"… whatever you do, wherever you go, never let anyone persuade you to accept a Christianity that's packaged by man, no matter how attractively it's wrapped."*

(Arthur, 1991: 227-228)

Many years ago I moved to a different town, and attended a church whose practices were quite different to those of my earlier experiences. I quite naturally asked a number of questions. At first, the senior pastor seemed eager to answer. However, after a bit of time had passed, and perhaps as the questions probed more deeply, he resisted. His less-than-subtle communication to me was that when I had matured and learned to trust him, I would stop questioning his practices. Little did he realize that his attempt to gag me and keep me compliant with the "party line" actually rang alarm bells that all was not well, and was a factor in me actually probing even more deeply, albeit without interaction with him.

I encourage you to also think for yourself, to ask questions, and to seek answers beyond the confines of your heritage. Ask questions boldly, and refuse to be suppressed by those who would rather you remain silent.

CHAPTER 3:
BE AN AGENT OF CHANGE

In the setting of the business world, Searls and Weinberger have a message to the 'establishment':

> "... listen to what your market says you are. If it's not to your liking, think long and hard before assuming that the market is wrong, composed of a lot of people who just are too dumb or blind to understand the Inner You. ... If you don't like what you're hearing, the ... task is not to change the market's idea of who you are but actually to change who you are."
>
> (Levine, Locke, Searls and Weinberger, 2000: 101)

We can perhaps gain real insight by applying their cutting critique to the world of "churches". Church leaders should listen to the laity, and if they don't like what's being said about them, then maybe they need to change instead of writing off the critics.

It takes courage to be willing to ask of yourself questions that may shake your personal foundations. But having received answers to your own questions, there is another step of courage required. You may need to apply those answers in a manner that may change your life and the way you see 'church'. You may need to truthfully and consistently align your new direction with those answers.

It also takes courage to ask questions of others, especially when their response may be negative towards you—a reaction for daring to rattle their cage.

Ackoff summarizes this move from discovery of truth to its personal application as follows:

> "Progress begins with grasping the truth about ourselves, however unpleasant it may be. Unfortunately, few things are more difficult than this. Perhaps the only thing that is more difficult is to change ourselves in ways indicated by that truth once it is perceived."
>
> (Ackoff, 1991: 221)

Oliver and Thwaites suggest we really have very little option but to change:

> *"We have hit the wall in so many areas as the church. We are not shining anywhere near the light we need to overcome the darkness. We are not salting the earth; we are being trodden underfoot by the social and economic systems of fallen humanity. We are not leavening the lump that is our world; we are growing stale inside our church buildings and our church meetings. God, by his Spirit, has been stirring up the wells of the eternal within his sons and daughters in these past years. He has been moving to refresh and revive a church that has grown tired. He is raising up people to declare the power and place of all of the saints' work in life. Alongside this, he is bringing into focus the things that have held us back from seeing his church as we should. He is giving us an opportunity to look again and see his church as he intended it to be seen. He is releasing the name church from the buildings, the meetings and the programmes that have held it to themselves, and he is liberating it to name all of the life and all of the works of the saints. Let's take the name church and be the body of Christ, the fullness of him who fills all in all."*
>
> (Oliver & Thwaites, 2001: 59)

It may well be a lonely journey. As Frost and Hirsch warn, many others will not see a need for change:

> *"… the urgency of the day requires a significant shift from the predominant image of 'church.' It is not too harsh a judgment to say that most people in the Western church simply cannot see beyond the Christendom mode they know so well. … It's not uncommon in churches to hear leaders claiming that the way it is now is the way they've always done it."*
>
> (Frost & Hirsch, 2003: 146-147)

Conversely, some may agree with a need for change, but in fact are seeking nothing more than a return to old, and mistaken, ways:

> *"Many of the new Protestant church movements of recent years are simply variations on the old Christendom mode. Whether they place their emphasis on new worship styles, expressions of the Holy Spirit's power, evangelism to seekers, or Bible teaching, these so-called new movements still operate out of the fallacious assumption that the church belongs firmly in the town square, that is, at the heart of Western culture. And if they begin with this mistaken belief about their position in Western society, all their church planting, all their reproduction will simply mirror this misapprehension."*
>
> (Frost & Hirsch, 2003: 17)

One impediment to change is an unwillingness to consider something new if the old way is comfortable and predictable, and perceived to have had some measure of "success":

> *"Edward de Bono … notes that 'If there is a known and successful cure for an illness, the patient would much prefer the doctor to use this cure rather than seek to design a better one. Yet there may be much better cures. How are they ever to be developed*

if at each moment the traditional treatment [is] preferred? It is little wonder that the judgment mode of the last millennium restricts us to past successes ... Design is at best a risky process but without design there is no progress."

(Frost & Hirsch, 2003: 185-186)

C. Peter Wagner, in his article *The Fourth Dimension of Missions: Strategy*, describes one scenario where much effort was wasted because participants would not discard useless structures:

"Missionaries who could have spent ten years making disciples spend the same ten years simply doing 'mission work' because they lack the courage to cut the barren fig tree down and change their program."

(Wagner, 1974: 578)

Arthur's novel also warns of the dangers of holding onto the old ways:

"An easy, routine way of life which many associate with stability and security only gives man stagnation. Entrenched routine only spoils man and makes him simple and weak.

On the other hand, progressive resistance in life always has the potential to give man progressive strength, and to make man progressively wiser ...

Resistance makes a man think new thoughts he never thought before. It makes a man ask questions he never asked before. It makes a man seek answers he never sought before. It makes a man beg God for help that he never before realized he needed. These quests, quests of the heart and soul, eventually make a man deeper, wider, taller."

(Arthur, 1991: 249-250)

Some will resist change to church practices, as they feel such change would be disobedient to God Himself and to what they perceive, and are led to believe, are *His* traditions. God does give guidelines for our behavior, and His standards may be timeless, but our expressions of respect and obedience to those guidelines may, instead, reflect our culture at a point in time. John Bevere, in *The Fear of the Lord*, explains the principle of needing to separate our traditions and practices from our relationship with God. As an illustration, he looks at the Jewish traditions in force at the time of Jesus:

"[John the Baptist] was not sent to those who did not know the name of the Lord. He was sent to those in covenant with Jehovah. Israel had become religious, yet believed everything was fine. In truth God saw the Israelites as lost sheep. The thousands who faithfully attended the synagogue remained unaware of their true heart condition. They were deceived and thought their worship and service to be acceptable to God."

(Bevere, 1997: 58-59)

We may criticize the Jews of Jesus' day for being resistant to changes they perceived as against God's directives. Yet aren't we in danger of wearing our own set of blinkers, thinking we are likewise protecting Godly practices, when we are merely refusing to consider changes to the traditions of men? Frost and Hirsch strive to protect core principles while also challenging local church practices:

> *"While we admit to being unashamedly radical 'in the true sense of that word' in our reexamination of everything in relation to standard church practice, we are nonetheless quite deeply committed to the historic, orthodox, Christian faith. Don't be fooled by our somewhat unorthodox approach to life, mission, and church. While we are unafraid to critique church traditions, we are devoted to the Scriptures and unmoving on the core Christian doctrines. So, while you are reading this book and perhaps finding yourself bristling with objections, please be assured that what we are espousing is not unbiblical. Unconventional for the church in the West? Yes. Unbiblical? No."*

(Frost & Hirsch, 2003: ix)

Rinehart clearly separates the sacredness of core values from the expendable traditions:

> *"... the New Testament gives us the freedom to question ... established [church] forms because it makes only the essentials – God and His Word – holy. Systems and structures are human inventions to further divine ends. They are not sacred in themselves; they are expendable."*

(Rinehart, 1998: 143)

Frost and Hirsch summarize the need for change with a view that church traditions have become an idol:

> *"We can no longer afford our historical sentimentality, even addiction, to the past. Christendom is not the biblical mode of the church. It was/is merely one way in which the church has conceived of itself. In enshrining it as the sole form of the church, we have made it into an idol that has captivated our imaginations and enslaved us to a historical-cultural expression of the church. We have not answered the challenges of our times precisely because we refuse to let go of the idol. This must change!"*

(Frost & Hirsch, 2003: 15)

They deride the pointless repetition of modes of proven failure:

> *"If you are digging a hole in one place and you realize you need to dig it elsewhere, you don't get there by digging in the same place, only deeper. And yet churches, when they realize that the old attractional mode isn't working, seem to believe that if they just do attractional church better, it will work. And, let's face it, so many of the church growth seminars and conferences are simply repackaging the traditional-attractional mode and promoting it to small, struggling, and dying churches as the only way to grow. There is a whole industry devoted to such conferences and the production of such materials that simply encourage struggling congregations to keep digging the same hole deeper."*

(Frost & Hirsch, 2003: 62-63)

Not surprisingly, these authors recommend radical, revolutionary change rather than tinkering with the failed model:

"... we are advocating a wholesale change in the way Christians are doing and being the church ..."

(Frost & Hirsch, 2003: ix)

"We [asked] ... the question 'Evolution or Revolution?' The answer is revolution. For the early church it was always revolution, but revolution is especially necessary now. ... we feel that we are living in an incredibly urgent time that can be described as the greatest spiritual awakening in the history of Western culture, and the message of the church is not even getting any airplay. We cannot expect to impact Western culture by simply renovating disused pubs. A completely alternate model is required. If we fail at this point, history will judge us very harshly. It is likely ... that it will spell the church's demise as a significant spiritual force in our land, and the church will be consigned to being a footnote to history. The statistics bear this out right across the West. This is not a time for evolution, as if another desperate reworking of the old model is going to fix our problems and start a revival. It is time for a revolution in the way we do and are church."

(Frost & Hirsch, 2003: 16)

However, Brown warns that, while revolution may be necessary, it is not likely to be a pleasant experience:

"For many, however, the thought of revolution in the Church is unsettling. What if some of our spiritual foundations need adjusting? What if sweeping, even extreme, change is required? What if our very concept of 'church' must be overhauled? What if it costs some of us our jobs, our livelihoods, our careers?

Revolution, rightly understood, is a disturbing word. Simply stated, there is no such thing as a nice revolution. Or, to express it another way: A revolution that costs nothing is worth nothing. How revolutionary do you really want to be?

For years now we have bemoaned the state of the Western Church, longing for change, praying for revival, looking for new methods and programs and ideas. And God has answered us in many wonderful ways; some real progress has been made. But I fear that most of us have not yet realized how serious the problem is and have failed, therefore, to realize just how serious – how sweeping and wide-ranging and dramatic and radical – the solution must be."

(Brown, 2002: 12-13)

CHAPTER 4:
WHAT "CHURCH" IS NOT!!!

Before we can effectively consider different models of "church", we need to take some time to work towards a common understanding of the term, "church". We start by identifying some wrong, and hence dangerous, misconceptions. Oliver and Thwaites argue strongly for clear, sound thinking on this issue:

> *"We need to restore the name 'church', investing it again with the meaning, the purpose and the power God intended it to have all along. The Reformation did not change the doctrine of the church. The great revivals of the eighteenth century did not challenge the doctrine of the church. The Pentecostals and their close cousins the Charismatics left the doctrine of the church well intact. This time, it's time for it to change. We have hit the wall and it's not the devil, it's not the world, and it's not a lack of leadership, teaching or holiness. The wall we have hit is the wall at the back, front and two sides of our local (and, yes, even cell) church.*
>
> *If we are to see change come; if we are to see fire breathed into our understanding and way of work; if we are to be salt, light and leaven to the world; we need to see a revolution come to our vision of church. If we don't, we will remain inside our buildings, looking out, ever wondering why the world doesn't come in and join us. And inside our meetings we will be taught, led and challenged into cultural oblivion."*
>
> (Oliver & Thwaites, 2001: 43)

Confusion over Old Testament and New Testament models

Sometimes we see battles fought between truth and lies, but sometimes the struggles are between truth and tradition. Jesus shone the spotlight on this issue in His interaction with the Pharisees. They opposed Him, not because they had honestly and openly evaluated His claims and found them to be false, but because He challenged their traditions. In

Luke 5: 36-39, following a clash with the Pharisees, Jesus tells the parable of new wine having to go into new wineskins else it will burst the old. The message? That new teaching may well destroy old traditions—we need new, flexible ways if we are to accommodate the revolutionary teachings of Jesus.

David Pawson, an English pastor and author, spoke boldly in a sermon titled *God is Calling the Church to Change* (1984). His modern variation of Jesus' parable of the wineskins suggests you imagine you've come across a beggar wearing a shabby coat with the elbows worn out. You give him your nice new coat. He gets out a dirty old knife, cuts the elbows out of your coat, then pins the pieces over the holes. If we try to put God's new covenant as introduced by Jesus into old religious structures that reflect the traditions of the Old Testament, it just won't work!

But we may protest that we are already part of the new covenant, so these stories do not apply to us. Pawson is cutting in his exposure of how very far the typical local church is from the new covenant. Instead, he claims, it is commonly based on the old covenant, and no wonder the new won't fit. While very carefully stressing he is not attacking any specific denomination, he shows areas where "churches" are typically living under the old covenant. Under headings that reflect the old covenant, he compares Old Testament cultures with modern local church life, and concludes on each point that our practices often reflect the old rather than the new covenant.

- **Building-centered**

The old covenant had the temple (or tabernacle), along with all its adornments of holy articles (incense, vestments, etc.), at the center of worship.

The new covenant is intended to be centered on Jesus. It is understood that the New Testament church typically had no church buildings for the first few hundred years, yet most local churches today could not conceive operating without their "church" building.

- **Priests and people clearly separated**

The old covenant had a special class of people appointed as priests.

In the new covenant, all of the people are "*a royal priesthood*" (1 Peter 2: 9, 10), and we have only Jesus as our one High Priest (Hebrews).

Pawson, himself a pastor, expresses the opinion that having a professional minister is the biggest barrier to renewal. We *all* need to be performing the ministry God assigns. Pawson goes so far as to challenge those who make statements such as, "I'm going to Bible College to train for the ministry." If he comes across such an attitude, he counters by asking, "What ministry? Teaching, evangelism, administration, or what?" If they answer, "All", or just "*the* ministry", he believes they have not heard from God, as there is no such thing as '*the* ministry', or '*the* minister'. In the new covenant, different people from within the Body of Christ have different ministries, on a moment-by-moment basis, as led by the Holy Spirit.

Pawson believes that there is still room for people to be trained for a particular task, and that we still have a place for professionals, but not as "the minister." He also believes that, on the other side of the coin, we should have no place for "the laity"—we should all be involved in ministry.

- **Central, hierarchical government**

The old covenant governance model was strictly hierarchical, with the high priest at the top.

Jesus called us not to exercise authority in the manner typified by secular society, yet our churches today reflect so much of secular governance and authority.

- **Tribally divided or "denominated"**

The old covenant recognized the existence of discrete tribes within the nation of Israel.

In the new covenant, while there may be many fellowships, they should not be isolated into artificial denominations. Christ's church, the Body of Christ, is singular.

- **Membership via physical birth**

The people to whom the old covenant applied were, typically, physically "born into" the privileges and responsibilities of the covenant.

In new covenant, God has no grand-children—each individual must personally experience what Jesus called the second birth, namely a coming into His covenant by a spiritual "birth".

Pawson suggests this truth has implications for practices such as infant baptism.

- **Nationally limited**

The old covenant was centered on the nation of Israel.

Pawson notes that the new covenant should be international, not national. We should refer to Christ's Church, not the "church of Australia", the "church of America", or the "church of England"(!)

In their book titled *Invading Secular Space: Strategies for Tomorrow's Church*, Martin Robinson and Dwight Smith succinctly express similar views:

> "[We must be cautious in the application of] the teaching we find on leadership in the Old Testament. There we can identify some very important and universal truths, relevant for all generations of leadership. But when the structure of the leadership in the Old Testament, and especially with regard to Israel, is brought into the church, it is wrongly applied. The church knows no kings, save for King Jesus. The church does not practise the priesthood of Aaron, but the priesthood of every believer. The temple is no longer found in a tent or a building, but the people of Christ themselves ... are the temple in which and through which God dwells. In reality many churches have an Old Testament model of leadership in mind."
>
> (Robinson & Smith, 2003: 138-139)

Many leaders recognize that we should be living under a new covenant, but so many assume that the so-called "New Testament church" is a pure model of the new covenant, and one which we should strive to copy. However as Brown notes, defining the New Testament model is not easy:

> *"The pages that follow reflect years of wrestling through the issue of what really constitutes the New Testament norm for 'the Church.'"*
>
> (Brown, 2002: 7)

Discovery of the essence of the New Testament church is complicated by the fact that it had many divergent facets. For example, the New Testament church had apparently contradictory dimensions such as geographically static fellowships, yet mobility of its workers. In their articles, Arthur Glasser (*Crucial Dimensions in World Evangelization*) and William Smalley (*Cultural Implications of an Indigenous Church*), writing from a missionary perspective, state:

> *"... we cannot but conclude that both the congregational parish structure and the mobile missionary band structure are equally valid in God's sight. Neither has more right to the name 'church' since both are expressions of the life of the people of God."*
>
> (Glasser, 1976: 107)

> *"Sometimes in our search for an understanding of the nature of the church we turn to the New Testament ... and seek for it there. [But] ... the church of Jerusalem was apparently different even in operational matters from the churches in Europe, and it was certainly different in the outlook on the basic cultural issues which were so important to the Jews. ... [Where one] society differs from another (as the Greek world is different from the Jewish world) the church resulting is different."*
>
> (Smalley, in Winter et. al. 1981: 498)

So if we wish to model *our* local church on the New Testament model, should it reflect Greek or Jewish thinking? Should it be based in one static building, or have everyone abandon the building and go on missionary journeys, or what? There simply is not one "new Testament" model we can or should copy.

Even if we could distill one concise specification of what the New Testament church was, some such as Arthur Glasser warn against holding it up as an ideal as it, like some of our modern churches, was still influenced by the old covenant model.

> *"[The activities experienced by the New Testament church reflected] ... the pattern they formerly had followed at their old synagogue services. It was natural for them to consider the probability that God wanted them to continue this pattern."*
>
> (Glasser, 1976:102).

As just one example of the New Testament church exhibiting aspects that aligned with the Old Testament model, Glasser also states,

> *"... like Israel in the wilderness, [the New Testament church] had both leaders and followers."*
>
> (Glasser, 1976: 107)

If we try to shape our local fellowship on some concept of the New Testament church, and it was unwittingly influenced by the old covenant, we too will have dimensions that reflect the "old".

In spite of these difficulties, some still call for us to reflect the New Testament model:

> *"The answer to the problem of mission in the West requires something far more radical than reworking a dated and untenable model. It will require that we adopt something that looks far more like the early church …"*
>
> (Frost & Hirsch, 2003: 15)

However, the same authors also warn that we must not unthinkingly copy the New Testament church:

> *"[The new missional church] will be radical in its attempts to embrace biblical mandates for the life of locally based faith communities without feeling as though it has to reconstruct the first-century church in every detail."*
>
> (Frost & Hirsch, 2003: 22)

So should the local churches of our day look like the New Testament church, or not?

Don't base your doctrine on Paul & the apostles instead of on Jesus

Now here's the crunch. The New Testament church wasn't perfect. Nor should we expect it to be. Like the local churches of today, the people involved (including the leaders) were imperfect people. We must avoid mindlessly copying what the New Testament church did. But if we look beyond what they *did* and seek what Paul and others *taught* they should be doing, will we get it right?

We seem to be left with some uncertainty as to the applicability of New Testament church patterns. At this point, many turn to the teachings of the apostles, and especially Paul, for guidance. This attitude in some church circles is noted by Dennis Bennett in his book, *Nine O'clock in the Morning*:

> *"The Episcopal Church teaches that we 'continue steadfastly in the Apostles' doctrine and fellowship' which means that the same things the Apostles experienced we should expect to happen in the church today."*
>
> (Bennett, 1984: 31)

Just one of many examples of the reverence shown for Paul's writings seems evident when Gilley comfortably puts the writings of Jesus and the writings of Paul apparently on equal footing when he criticizes Christians who obtain:

> "... their philosophy for living from popular talk-show hosts [rather] than from Jesus and Paul."
>
> (Gilley, 2005: 60)

Gilley's book *This Little Church Went to Market* attempts to correct perceived errors in church models and trends, and calls the readers back to a biblical model. Gilley quotes extensively from the Bible, with well over 200 scriptures referenced. However, the emphasis is on the teaching of Paul, not Jesus. Only about one sixth of the quotes are from Jesus' teaching!

He goes further to claim that:

> "... the book of Acts [is our] ... divinely inspired church growth manual ..."
>
> (Gilley, 2005: 17).

Clearly, he sees the teaching and practices recorded in Acts as being authoritative for determining the model for "church".

In a similar manner, John McArthur gives me the impression that he bases his book *The Power of Integrity* on the example of Paul rather than that of Christ:

> "... How we can practically model <u>Paul's</u> integrity is the purpose of the remainder of this book." [Emphasis mine]
>
> (MacArthur, 1997: 99)

To me, Frost and Hirsch join the chorus of those holding to Paul's teaching as the foundation for what we should do today:

> "[The proposed model is] a mode of leadership that recognizes the fivefold model detailed by Paul in Ephesians 6."
>
> (Frost & Hirsch, 2003: 12)

> "Ephesians and its teaching forms part of Paul's fundamental ecclesiology, and as such, ought to be read as a fundamental description, even a prescription, of the church in all ages."
>
> (Frost & Hirsch, 2003: 167)

> "What we are arguing for here is a rediscovery of the fullness of Pauline teaching about Christian ministry."
>
> (Frost & Hirsch, 2003: 168)

Frost and Hirsch go even further, not only calling us to accept that Paul sets the pattern for us to follow, but declaring his views are so complete that no one should ever tamper with them. In the chapter titled, *The Genius of APEPT* [Apostle, Prophet, Evangelist, Pastor, Teacher], they strongly claim the list's perfection and completeness by asking the rhetorical questions:

> "Is any style or leadership factor missing? Does any factor need to be added?"
>
> (Frost & Hirsch, 2003: 175)

… and then stating:

> "We believe that APEPT is part of the DNA of the church and ought not to be tampered with."
>
> (Frost & Hirsch, 2003: 175)

One interesting observation is that Frost and Hirsch encourage us to consider the merits of the New Testament church "… *without feeling as though it has to reconstruct the first-century church in every detail.*" (22). While stating we must be free to adapt the practices of the New Testament church, they seem to counter this with the claim that we absolutely must not adapt (or "tamper with") Paul's Apostle, Prophet, Evangelist, Pastor, Teacher (APEPT) model.

As discussed below, we need to consider at least two aspects of Frost and Hirsch's position. Firstly, even if Paul's model was perfect in his day, we must thoughtfully consider how we apply any Biblical verses in situations today. And secondly, and even more fundamentally, we need to challenge any perceptions of perfection regarding Paul and his model.

Were Paul and the other apostles perfect? Of course not—they were human, not divine. A few simple examples of human frailty follow:

- Peter was a Jew, and had traditions that distanced him from interaction with gentiles. When God gave him a vision of a sheet containing both "clean" and "unclean" animals and ordered Peter to eat, he disobeyed the heavenly command and refused three times (Acts 10)! The NIV Study Bible notes the ingrained nature of Peter's traditions that made him unwilling to obey immediately even a direct instruction from God.

- Paul rejected the recommendation of Barnabas to include Mark in their travels (Acts 15: 36-40), but did later realize the value of Mark (2 Timothy 4:11). Paul's error of judgment regarding Mark was only a plain human error, as any of us can and do make. It is merely noted to demonstrate Paul's ability to make mistakes.

- The apostles in Judea were affronted by the inclusion of gentiles in the church, and criticized Peter regarding his acceptance of hospitality from Cornelius. The now-changed Peter had to confront them on their wrong theology (Acts 11). I repeat for emphasis that the *apostles got it wrong* and they had to be confronted.

The call to follow the teaching of the apostles would not be a problem either if the apostles were perfect (which they were not), or if their teaching as recorded in the New Testament could be applied uncritically to our situations (which it cannot). On the latter, Josh McDowell issues a warning in his book, *The New Evidence That Demands a Verdict*:

> "Basically there are only two qualifications to inerrancy: first, only the original manuscripts are inerrant, not the copies; second, only what the Bible affirms is inerrant, not everything it contains.
>
> To be sure, many complicated issues are involved in determining precisely what the Bible affirms in any given passage, including meaning, context, and literary form.

> *This, however, is not a question of inspiration but of interpretation. All would agree, for example, that the Bible contains lies, including Satan's lies. But the Bible does not affirm that these lies are true. All inerrancy claims is that the record of these lies is true.*
>
> *Not everyone would agree, on the other hand, that everything contained in the book of Ecclesiastes is true. Many Christian interpreters of Ecclesiastes view the statements in the middle of the book as simply a true record of the false views of natural man 'under the sun'.*
>
> *There seems to be room for difference of opinion here and in other like situations (the speeches of Job's friends, for example). Christians may differ as to what the Bible actually affirms in a given passage and what it merely records, but there should be no disagreement among us that what the Bible does affirm is inerrant. God cannot err."*
>
> (McDowell, 1999: 348)

If we encounter church leaders who defend their positions and actions based on what Paul literally said, we can and should challenge their simplistic application of Paul's views. Further, and even more importantly, we need to check if some of these views are out of line with the teaching and practices of Jesus.

Based on what McDowell teaches, we can benefit from the writings of Paul (and Peter, and Solomon, etc.), but their teaching is not to be taken as necessarily inerrant. The central issue is that those who are called Christians (i.e. 'followers of Christ') must be just that—followers of Christ—not followers of Paul. Even Paul himself at one time rebukes those who claim to be followers of himself or in fact anyone other than Christ (1Cor: 1).

In spite of earlier quotations by Frost and Hirsch that revere the teachings of Paul, these authors do in fact also explicitly note that we must follow Christ, not Paul:

> *"... Jesus is our primary model of mission, and the Gospels are our primary texts. This might sound somewhat prosaic, but it is actually a massive paradigm shift from the way the church has generally viewed Christology in the Christendom mode. Jesus has generally been read through dogmatic ontological frames (as in the creeds) or through the structures of Paulinism (as in the Reformation), both we believe obscuring the primary historical portrait of Jesus as found in the Gospels [i.e. the words and actions of Jesus]. The Christendom-era church has tended to load so much into the historic debates about the nature of Christ in his being that it has obscured the fact that Christ was a historic person who represents the principal model for mission, ministry, and discipleship, and the focal point of an authentic New Testament faith.*
>
> *We evangelicals have for too long read Jesus through predominantly what have been called Pauline eyes. We doubt the Apostle Paul read Jesus this way himself. But by reading the gospel through the Epistles [i.e. the words and actions of the apostles, not Jesus], a disturbing distortion develops. Effectively, the Gospels are not taken seriously as prescriptive texts for life, mission, and discipleship. Now let it be said that we affirm the Pauline view of Jesus. But our perspectives of Jesus can be so weighted by and*

filtered through the Pauline interpretation of the Messiah that we are unable to see him without hearing the Pauline formulas in our heads. Actually the problem is not Paul at all, the problem lies in Paulin-ism. Like always, the ism is the problem. It is worth being reminded that Paul himself was very keen to ensure that we focus on Jesus and not on him (1 Cor 1:11-17) and he encouraged us to follow him only insofar as he followed Messiah (1 Cor 11:1). Paul always pointed us to Jesus, and we need to take his advice again now as we find ourselves in a missional setting remarkably similar to the one Paul was in. ... [And rather than seeing Paul as our only guide,] we should read all the writers in Scripture through the perspective of the Gospels, including Paul. Jesus is my Lord and Savior, not Paul."

(Frost & Hirsch, 2003: 112-113)

Frost and Hirsch go on to demand that we base the required rethink of church practices on no one less than Jesus Himself:

"It is essential to a revolutionary new approach to church that there be a fundamental shift in our collective thinking. Essentially we need to recover the missional genius of the early church, which was modeled on Jesus. The problem the church faces today is that it is seeking to recover that genius from a viewpoint of two thousand years of Christianity in the West, much of it deeply grounded and indelibly shaped in the Christendom paradigm. To recover a primal sense of who Jesus was and how he engaged people missionally will require a fresh look at the central person of the faith.

We believe that an alternative, missional approach to being and doing church is best supported by an alternative approach to Christian spirituality. Too much Christendom spirituality has been concerned with retreat and reflection. While we acknowledge the value of a rich interior life, as well as the value of solitude in interiority, we believe that retreat and reflection should be embraced as part of a broader spirituality that values engagement and action. We need to find a renewed framework and basis for understanding everyday life and our actions as a vital source of experience of God. We believe in the need for the recovery of a messianic spirituality, one rooted primarily in the life and teaching of Jesus himself."

(Frost & Hirsch, 2003: 115-116)

Frost and Hirsch also warn that some churches may appear to so highly value their traditions that these could be seen to be more sacred than the teaching of Christ Himself. They clearly appear to oppose such prioritization, and suggest the proper sequence should be:

"Christ's Commands[:] ... No adaptation possible, nonnegotiable.

Biblical Principles[:] ... The essence is unchanging. Adapt only to maintain dynamic equivalent.

Apostolic Patterns[:] ... Interpret or contextualize to fit the culture.

Church Practices[:] ... Fully adaptable and flexible for the culture."

(Frost & Hirsch, 2003: 80)

To restate the theme, we are to base what the Body of Christ looks like on the teachings and examples of Jesus, not on the presumed perfect model of the New Testament church.

Confusing the local church with the universal Church

There are problems enough setting up the so-called New Testament church as some ideal against which we must measure our local churches. But much worse is confusing the local churches with "*the* Church".

Sometimes we might use the word "church" to refer to a building. We might say, "My church is at the corner of Main and Station Streets." Philip Yancey is an author I enjoy. However in his book, *Prayer*, he states:

> "God is present in … cathedrals and buildings constructed to God's glory."
>
> (Yancey, 2006: 43)

Given the context surrounding this excerpt, I suspect Yancey intends to convey the message that God is present amongst His people, whether they assemble in house churches, fine buildings, or wherever. I have no issue with this view, though I suggest God is also equally right beside a solitary, grieving individual walking the sands of a beach with the salt of tears mixing with the salt of sea spray. A Christian does not need the setting of a "church" to know God's presence. Again, I suspect Yancey would agree.

So why do I highlight Yancey's quotation? Primarily because I think we sometimes use language that would allow us to see God as somehow especially present in a building. And would this be true even if no-one were present? I think not. (And we could never find out unless we visited the building to test such a theory, at which point the building is no longer empty!) So we are left with God being present amongst His people when they are assembled in a building. But would He leave them if the same group met, but outside on a park lawn? Of course not! In stark contrast to the Old Testament and the temple, the buildings that may be used by New Testament believers are not special, and the buildings themselves do not represent "church".

In another context, some might use the word "church" to represent a particular denomination. Quotations have already been encountered, for example, Pope Gregory VII referring to his denomination as "the Roman church" (singular). But this thinking of one's own denomination as "church" is encountered amongst many groups. Ortiz comments on this error:

> "We don't [but should] think in terms of the whole Body of Christ. We think [instead] in terms of the Baptist segment of the Body of Christ, or the Presbyterian segment, or the Assemblies of God segment. We like to pretend that the part is the whole thing."
>
> (Ortiz, 1975: 103)

Rinehart notes the subtle and erroneous shift over time from seeing the Body of Christ as *the* Church to using the word "church" to describe a local, denominational assembly of believers:

WHAT "CHURCH" IS NOT!!!

> *"Whoever comes to God by faith is a citizen of the kingdom, a member of His universal and invisible church. … In order to appreciate the significance of being part of the people of God … we need to remember what happened at Pentecost. In Old Testament times God's Spirit 'came upon' particular individuals at specific times. In that day a leader such as Moses or Joshua was the direct link between God and the people …*
>
> *The situation changed after Christ went to be with the Father. From that point on, the Holy Spirit made His home in the life of each and every believer. God's people, then, are actually made up of individuals who have the very life of God moving in and through them. Leaders no longer have a monopoly on being led by God; all believers have access to His leadership.*
>
> *The truth that the church is the people of God is so wondrous that it can't be contained in one or two New Testament descriptions. Indeed, a number of metaphors describe what it means to be God's people: the Bride of Christ, a royal priesthood, a purchased possession, the body of Christ, a spiritual building. But the most familiar term for defining the people of God is 'the church.'*
>
> *With every generation since the time of Constantine, however, the word church has become more and more synonymous with an institution, a building, or an address in a particular locality. Lost to us is that true biblical sense of being a part of the church – God's people unleashed to do His bidding."*
>
> (Rinehart, 1998: 94-96)

Rinehart has noted how each generation has slipped further and further into this flawed thinking that somehow the local church equates to the universal Church. Mark Pearse touched on this topic in his beautiful book titled, *Thoughts on Holiness*, printed in the 1800s:

> *"What, then, is the Church which [Christ] loves with the love of delight and possession? Surely there can be but one answer. Forms, creeds, methods, sacraments, cannot create the Church; they may minister to its life, and do. But the Church of Christ is the whole body of those who have heard the voice of love and yielded to it. Every one who has accepted Him as He comes to us in His unutterable grace. All who have given themselves to Him, to love, honour, and obey Him, – this is the Church. This constitutes Church membership, a personal relation to the Lord Jesus Christ as supreme Head and Lover. We have known and believed the love that God hath to us. The Church is just everybody who lets Christ love him, and the way into the Church is letting Christ love us, listening to Him, believing Him, yielding ourselves to Him."*
>
> (Pearse, 1800s: 169-170)

The form of English language used may be a bit old-fashioned, but the message is as important today as ever.

This distinction between "*the* Church" (i.e. the Body of Christ), and local churches, can be presented graphically. The world's population can be split many ways. One dimension may be wealth (rich and poor). Another dimension may be first spoken language (those that speak English, Spanish, French, etc.). We look at two dimensions of interest to us.

One dimension in the diagram below relates to those who belong to, or are associated with, a "local church" gathering, versus those who are not. The second dimension relates to those who are genuine Christians, versus those who are not. At this point we need to be careful. Jesus clearly taught that not even those who call Him "Lord" are necessarily part of His kingdom (Matthew 7:21-27). He also taught that some that the religious look down on and judge as being unworthy, will actually be welcomed by Him. The key point is that God knows our hearts and we can and should safely leave it to Him to graciously decide who qualifies for membership in the Body of Christ.

	People who "belong" to a local church	People not associated with a local church
People who are Christians	A. Christians in the local church	C. Christians not associated with a local church
People who are not Christians	B. Non-Christians in the local church	D. Non-Christians not part of a local church

Some may remember a film from the 1960s called *A Thief in the Night*, where Christ returns and takes His followers home, leaving behind those who are not Christians. Independent of your view of the end times, the film portrayed a certain irony—that there were enough local church members left behind to have a church service the following Sunday, led by the pastor! The diagram above portrays, in the oval with a dotted outline, this sobering fact that not all who consider themselves part of a local church are necessarily Christians. Conversely, if we are genuine Christians, we are automatically part of the one, universal Church. Membership of the Body of Christ is portrayed as an oval with a solid outline.

Some may argue that all Christians *should* be actively involved in a local church. We will investigate this later, but for now let us accept that Christians in certain circumstances may not be part of a local church but are still members in *the* Church. Some examples may include:

- Christians jailed and in solitary confinement for their faith.
- Christians (such as Paul after his conversion) who are on "retreat" as God prepares them for His service.
- Christians involved in ministry organizations/parachurches who receive much of their fellowship from within the group.

The key point is that the oval with a dotted outline represents local church membership, and the oval with a solid outline represents "the Church". They are not the same thing.

In his article titled *A History of Christianity*, Kenneth Latourette succinctly expresses the same message as the preceding diagram:

WHAT "CHURCH" IS NOT!!!

"Through Christ there has come into being the [true] Church. The Church is never fully identical with ecclesiastical organizations. It is to be found in them, but not all of their members belong to it and it is greater than the sum of them all. Yet, though never fully visible as an institution, the Church has been and is a reality, more potent than any one or all of the churches. 'The blessed company of all faithful people,' it constitutes a fellowship which has been both aided and hampered by the churches, and is both in them and transcends them."

(Latourette, 1953: 165)

Pearse reinforces Latourette's view that not all in the local churches are Christians, and that there are Christians who are not part of any local church.

"Are we amongst [those who are part of the true Church because of our relationship with Christ]? There may be a belief in Christ; there may be an assured conviction that He loved all the world and died for all men on the Cross; there may be an ordering of our lives in obedience to the New Testament teaching, a rigid, exact, fierce obedience; and yet we may not know Him as our own Love, heart love, – love that embraces and cleaves to Him, – love that leans upon Him for strength and looks to Him for guidance, and rests in Him for satisfaction, – this is the condition, the only condition, of membership of His Church. Membership in the visible Church there may be without belonging to Jesus, and we may belong to Him without belonging to any visible Church."

(Pearse, 1800s: 170)

Sheldon is typical of the many who blur the boundaries between the one universal Body of Christ known as '*the* Church', and local churches (expressed in the plural form as there are many). While Christians take comfort in the words of Jesus that the gates of Hell will not prevail against His Church, Sheldon goes further, suggesting the invincibility of local churches also:

"[Jesus] is constantly reminding the Christians and the churches of their invincible power."

(Sheldon, 1999: 260)

Brown explicitly claims that the universal Church is the sum of all local churches:

"... all those churches together make up the Church."

(Brown, 2002: 43)

As portrayed in the earlier diagram, there are two major flaws with this argument. The first is that not all members of local churches are necessarily even Christians (even though they may proclaim to be), and the second that there are a number of Christians who are not necessarily aligned with a local church.

Angela Hunt's novel, *The Debt*, portrays a pastor who equates serving a local church with serving God. It is this very type of thinking that can enable some authoritarian church leaders to demand a loyalty that only belongs to God. The pastor's wife, trained to believe this, states to her husband:

> "I know this church is important to you, as well it should be. When you accepted Christ, you accepted the responsibility to build your life around this church and its Savior."

(Hunt, 2004: 176)

In a quotation partially repeated from earlier, we note that the Salvation Army's Articles of Marriage, commitment to the church was linked with commitment to God by the requirement that marriages must not:

> "...lessen in any way [the couple's] devotion to God and the Army."

(Hattersley, 2000: 281)

In direct contrast to the pastor in Hunt's fictional novel, and Booth's demands for loyalty to his church quoted above, Robinson and Smith appear to condemn the serving of the local church instead of serving God:

> "We can summarise the existing paradigm as one which centres on the minister (usually one with the gifts of pastor/teacher) as having a territorial emphasis (the parish or the community), and which sees the church as an organisation or institution. Such a model encourages us to think in terms of serving the church, whether as professional clergy or as lay people. The church is the focus of our concern and activity. The growth or otherwise of the church is the key measurement of success. Evangelistic strategy is concerned with how we bring people to church. Commitment to Jesus Christ is necessary because it is part of the package that enables us to join the church. A good result is that those who are drawn to the church become committed to the doctrine we espouse, but even more importantly, they join the church as active participants."

(Robinson & Smith, 2003: 108)

In *The Shaking*, John Noble identifies a similar risk in calling people to church instead of introducing them to Jesus:

> "Our focus [had] subtly moved from Jesus to our relationships ... Our invitation also moved from, 'Come and be joined to Jesus,' to 'Come and be joined to us.' The gospel of Christ had become the gospel of the church."

(Noble, 2002: 60-61)

Likewise, Buckingham warns of using the local church as a substitute for God:

> "Not being able to find our place in God, we try to localize Him. We build buildings and call them 'houses of God.' Unable to have a personal relationship, we insist on formalized prayer, bowing our heads, closing our eyes, going into the chapel, dropping on our knees – trying to nail God down for a few minutes so we can have a temporary place."

(Buckingham, 1980: 49)

Throughout Girard's book, he seems to suggest that, in his earlier days as a pastor, he had been confused with the separation between serving God and serving the local church:

"I still saw the church as an organization to be built and run and Christianity as receiving Christ and then 'getting involved' in the organization. After all, I was sure every program I planned was synonymous with 'the work of the Lord.' So, to be involved in the program was to be involved in Christian service. And to be involved in the institution was to be involved in Christ."

(Girard, 1972: 31)

We are meant to be serving God, not some institution. His Body, the true Church, has many responsibilities, one of them being support for the saints as they serve God. Instead, some seem to be suggesting that local churches expect to be served and supported by the saints:

"We have been accustomed to a situation where the people of God serve the church – as meeting and organisation – so that 'it' can do the works of ministry and thereby see the Kingdom grow. Most of the resources have been drawn into the household gathering to try and get it to fill the creation through its meetings, its leaders and its programmes. … The resources … are meant to be dispersed out there to equip the saints … These saints are the church … The church as construct, the church as separate, the church as meeting [i.e. traditional 'church'], cannot and will never fill creation. God never called it to, and the fact is that it is impossible for it to ever accomplish such a feat."

(Oliver & Thwaites, 2001: 57-58)

Brown tells the story of a person who served his denomination for decades, despite seeing major flaws. Brown then goes on to challenge all who serve their local church even if God calls them to break away. He expresses the consequences of this choice very strongly. And maybe you might react strongly to his position. But let's look first at what he has to say:

"I once spoke to a friend who, together with his wife, had served his denomination for more than thirty years. They had been home missionaries as well as foreign missionaries, often living sacrificially for the good of the work. Yet they were very frustrated with the organization's policies, calling them controlling, hindering and stifling. In fact, neither this man nor his wife had a single good thing to say about the denomination they represented. Their attitude was even marked by disdain.

'Then why do you stay with them?' I asked him. 'Why not work with others?'

'All my contacts are within the denomination,' he replied. 'All my financial support comes from them. Where would I go?' Outside the camp!

Why remain handcuffed to a system and handicapped by a system that is not going to change? And why dishonor the system by staying loyal to it on paper while expressing disrespect and even scorn for its leaders and policies? How can that be right in the sight of God?

Sadly I remembered having a similar conversation with this devoted brother more than fifteen years before; and now, more than a decade and a half later; his frustrations with the denomination were greater and his disagreements deeper. Still, it was next to impossible for him to make the break. This does not have to be your story, too.

One day you and I will stand before the Judge of all the earth and give an account for our lives. What will we say when He asks us why we failed to do what we knew was right, why the affirmation of man was more important to us than the affirmation of heaven, why we willingly deceived ourselves with cheap answers rather than walk the costly path of submission to the Father's will? How will we respond?"

(Brown, 2002: 186-187)

Before we pass judgment on Brown's view, let's look at what he seems to be saying. Attempting to put Brown's view in my own words, I think he is suggesting that God may well challenge us, in any given situation, to make a choice between what we believe He is asking of us and what the local church leaders may expect, or even demand, of us. And I think Brown is suggesting that the consequences of our response are pretty serious. For now, can we run with that view?

A man I know expressed the unequivocal view that "the institutional church is part of the Body of Christ". There is a danger here. If the church *institution* is truly part of the Body of Christ, then to attack the institution can be effectively viewed as an attack on Christ. Some use this very argument to resist any scrutiny. However, the claim is fundamentally flawed.

People can be members of the Body of Christ (or not). And people can be members of the local institutional organization known as, say, the Black Stump Baptist church (or not). But here's the rub. Jesus warned that not all that say, "Lord, Lord …" are part of His kingdom. It follows that not all that are members of a local church institution are necessarily even Christians (and that may potentially even include some in leadership).

If you find this hard to comprehend, consider the holy, set-apart nation of the Old Testament (the Israelites), and their dedicated temple. At times, the nation of Israel had corrupt kings. At times, those ministering in the temple that bore God's name were also doing wrong (for example, Eli's sons). And it was the leadership of the Jewish institution that wanted Jesus crucified. God sought out *people* he could work with, but was willing to let the set-apart nation be ransacked and the temple destroyed. People count in God's sight, but institutions are dispensable.

We need to separate the institution from any alignment with the Church universal, i.e. the Body of Christ. There are alignments between individual members of the church "club" and God's kingdom, but the institution can never be "holy".

Wayne Jacobsen and Dave Coleman, in *So You Don't Want to go to Church Anymore*, succinctly demonstrate that the true Church is the Body of Christ, not somewhere I can go.

> "Asking me where I go to church is like asking me where I go to Jacobsen. How do I answer that? I am a Jacobsen, and where I go a Jacobsen is. 'Church' is that kind of

word. It doesn't identify a location or an institution. It describes a people and how they relate to one another. If we lose sight of that, our understanding of the church will be distorted and we'll miss out on much of its joy."

(Jacobsen & Coleman, 2006: 170)

It is so easy to get tripped up by confusing use of the word "church". If we look again at a quotation presented earlier by Simson, a number of local churches could be described (perhaps somewhat pointedly) as:

"... [a] holy people coming regularly to a holy place on a holy day at a holy hour to participate in a holy ritual led by a holy man dressed in holy clothes for a holy fee."

(Wolfgang Simson in Houses that Changed the World, quoted in Brown, 2002: 50)

While that description may fit some local churches, it doesn't fit all, and it is a bit of a mouthful. For the sake of consistency (if not accuracy) I want a simple phrase that generically describes people gathering as a local assembly of Christians.

I could call it an "institutional church". Some such as Kevin DeYoung and Ted Kluck might be happy to use such a phrase—their book titled *Why We Love the Church* is subtitled, *In Praise of Institutions and Organized Religion*. Others might claim their own local church is anything but institutionalized, and may be offended to be so classified.

I could use the term "denominational church", but again some would say they don't fit as they attend a "free" or independent church that is not aligned with any denomination.

Maybe I could classify the collective of local churches as "traditional churches". Again I suspect some, if not many, would not align with this phrase, preferring to see themselves as "different" or even "revolutionary".

Even the expression "local church" might cause some debate, as some see their loyalty and allegiance tied to a "catholic church" (using the word "catholic" in one of its formal dictionary meanings to describe a universal/all-encompassing church rather than necessarily the "Roman" Catholic denomination). For such people, their emphasis could be focused on their global membership rather than membership in a local church.

And now I've just used the term "universal church" (!), which, for many, refers to the Body of Christ across all time.

You may not agree with any of my suggested solutions, but please, I am trying to nominate something that can be sufficient for us to move forward. As identified in the Introduction to this book, I refer to people who consciously and purposefully assemble as a local gathering of Christians, as a "local church", sometimes abbreviated by me and other quoted authors as simply "church" with a lowercase "c". And I use the term the "Body of Christ" to define all Christians, across time. This latter definition is again sometimes abbreviated by me, and other quoted authors, as "Church" with a capital "C", or as "the Church" (singular).

I have attempted to use the abbreviations consistently. But there is a small warning; some of the authors I have quoted use the word "church" in reference to the local church, and sometimes to the Body of Christ. I have tried to be faithful in my replication of these authors even if their use of the word, quite understandably, does not necessarily align with my terminology. So some confusion in the use of the term "church" may still remain.

CHAPTER 5:
SO WHAT SHOULD "CHURCH" LOOK LIKE?

Some options that have been tried and found wanting

Stan Telchin was a Jew, raised with Jewish traditions, who later came to accept Jesus Christ as the Messiah. He struggled to see how he could be true to his new-found faith while also retaining the essential elements of his Jewish heritage. While many of us may not be able to directly identify with his particular personal struggle, the question faces us all. Each of us has a personality that reflects our roots, our circle of friends, our socio-economic level, where we fit in our country as the predominant group or as one of the minorities, our identity based on career, our age, our gender, and so on. So for you and me, and for others, how should each of us express our faith? In his autobiography, *Betrayed*, Telchin articulates this struggle, saying:

> "The pattern was almost universal and it led to the question, 'How are we to live now that we believe?'
>
> ... old questions rose again: How are we Jews to function in what is primarily a Gentile world? Do we remain separate from Gentile believers, or do we worship with them? If we are to worship with them, will we have to go to churches? Won't this lead to assimilation? Mustn't this be avoided at all costs? Should we strive to create a synagogue for our worship? If so which kind, Orthodox, Conservative or Reform? If we establish synagogues what will happen to our Gentile brothers and sisters who want to worship with us? Won't this make them feel like second class citizens? If that happens, won't we be violating the Bible which tells us that we are to be 'one in the Body?' Is our concentration on preserving things Jewish, fear of man or a type of idolatry? How are we to reconcile the Word of God with the cultural differences and fears that still exist?

How are we to preserve our identity as Jews?"

(Telchin, 1981: 114)

Telchin lists a number of options for local church structuring, and there are more. Below is just a selection of perhaps some of the more common forms of "local church". Some have comments both in their favor and against; some are merely statements about an alternative style. This is nothing more than a very brief overview, highlighting some of the many current models, but not searching deeply into their relative merits or otherwise— some more fundamental issues underlie all these forms of church government and are addressed later. It is merely intended to provide a backdrop for our search, and to highlight the significant controversy over identification of a suitable structure for local churches.

One worldwide church, led by one central leader

Possibly the denomination that springs to mind if we talk of a model based on worldwide central control is the Catholic Church, if for no other reason than its sheer size. Noble appears to criticize Catholicism for

"... investing absolute authority in one man ..."

(Noble, 2002: 84)

and to challenge the belief of

"... the infallibility of the Pope."

(Noble, 2002: 84)

He also seems to question whether we can be confident that all church appointments to positions of authority are necessarily reflective of *God's* preferences:

"... it is difficult ... to believe that an unconverted bishop [i.e. one who has not had a 'conversion' experience leading him to a personal relationship with Christ] could impart the Holy Spirit and commission apostles simply because his church has given him the authority."

(Noble, 2002: 73)

Put simply, Noble and others give me the impression that they seriously challenge the wisdom of vesting total authority in one person.

City-based multi-church unions, led by an Apostle

Whereas some church models have one worldwide leader at the top, Noble's writing gives me the impression that he proposes a model with one person at the top of a collection of churches in a locality. He seems to argue for this leader having an "apostolic" ministry, the one he claims to be the most important of the five described by Paul in one part of the New Testament i.e. the ministries of the apostle, prophet, evangelist, pastor and teacher:

"Of all the ministry gifts expressed in [Jesus], this [apostolic ministry] was of primary importance ..."

(Noble, 2002: 69)

SO WHAT SHOULD "CHURCH" LOOK LIKE?

To apparently reinforce this view, Noble notes the view of Tony Morton who

> "... is clear on the primacy and visionary nature of apostles ..."
>
> (Noble, 2002: 69)

Noble then goes on to paint a picture that again places apostles in the top position, closest to Christ, and as the conduit for blessing from Christ to His people:

> "This oil, symbol of the Holy Spirit, is poured on Christ the Head. From him it runs down to the shoulders, the burden bearers, his chosen apostles and then on to the whole body. ...
>
> The apostolic power and anointing of the gospel flows from Jesus to his delegated leaders ..."
>
> (Noble, 2002: 71)

These especially selected delegates are then expected in turn to delegate to those that follow them, as

> "... the purpose of leadership in the church is to [perform] delegation [which] will free [the followers] to move to other fields of service."
>
> (Noble, 2002: 71)

Just as, for example, the Pope is revered within the Catholic Church, Noble seems to uphold the apostles as the 'cream of the crop':

> "Churches like Antioch, with their rich mix of culture, ministry and experience, release the cream of its leadership as 'hands,' in apostolic service to care for other parts of the body."
>
> (Noble, 2002: 97)

But where are all these apostolic leaders Noble wants at the helm to be found? Noble notes the diminished role of all five 'ministries' (apostle, prophet, evangelist, pastor and teacher) within local churches over the ages since Christ, but also suggests that there has been a progressive return over the more recent centuries. He also suggests that this return is happening in something like a reverse order—Paul mentioned these ministries starting at apostle, then prophet, evangelist, pastor and teacher—but Noble is suggesting that their reappearance started with pastor:

> "... primarily through the Catholic and orthodox churches ...[where] the pastor or priest plays the key role."
>
> (Noble, 2002: 75)

Then came the Reformation with

> "... the first major shaking the church had experienced for centuries ... Its strengths were preaching, exposition and a quest for truth. The pulpit was the central feature and the teacher played the key role."
>
> (Noble, 2002: 75)

Then followed the

> "... great evangelical missionary movements of the 18th and 19th centuries."
>
> (Noble, 2002: 68)

which exhibited

> "...zeal and a willingness to sacrifice all to preach the gospel to every people. The field was the central feature, [and] the evangelist was the key player ..."
>
> (Noble, 2002: 76)

More recently, the

> "... Pentecostal outpourings at the beginning of the 20th century."
>
> (Noble, 2002: 76)

delivered a tradition where

> "... the prophet has played a key role ..."
>
> (Noble, 2002: 77)

Finally, Noble argues that

> "... there is work to be done to bring the church into the fullness of her ministry [so the Holy Spirit] ... will raise up apostles to work to this end."
>
> (Noble, 2002: 74)

And the role of apostles within local churches? He proposes that they have authority over a collection of churches in a locality, as observed in Argentina:

> "The Argentinian revival has produced an understanding of God's heart for city-wide churches, and it's spreading. Corporate leadership, which transcends denominational allegiances and personal ambition, works together with apostolic ministries. The primary concern is for the health and expansion of the whole church in the city."
>
> (Noble, 2002: 88-89)

Multi-church unions, led by a consortium of ministries

Some churches have power centered in one person internationally, while Noble proposes one person (an 'apostle') leading all churches in a city. Frost and Hirsch offer a variation, still with city-wide leadership, but spread amongst a group of people that collectively represent all five of the ministries noted by Noble, namely the ministries of the apostle, prophet, evangelist, pastor and teacher.

Frost and Hirsch's book, *The Shaping of things to Come*, seems to build their whole argument for this structure on the list identified by Paul in Ephesians 4:11. To call for a complete reorganization of local church structures based on one list of ministries seems a questionable tactic, especially when it is noted that the New Testament provides other lists with a different mix of 'ministries', some of these also provided by Paul. Examples of other lists include:

- Apostles, prophets, teachers, miracle workers, healers, helpers, administrators, and those who "speak in tongues" (1 Corinthians 12:27-31).
- Prophets, servants, teachers, encouragers, financial givers, leaders, mercy-givers (Romans 12:6-8).
- Speakers, servants (1 Peter 4:10-11).
- People with wisdom, knowledge, faith, and gifts (such as for healing, performing, prophesy, discernment, speaking in tongues and interpretation of such utterances) (1 Corinthians 12:4-11).

So having a leadership team at a city level may seem to be a possibility, but to rigidly structure its membership based on the five classifications appearing in one text of the Bible seems risky at best. At worst it appears to be contrary to Jesus' wishes. Firstly, we need to note that the example and teaching of Jesus did not apply this five-point prescription presented later by Paul. Secondly, and more confronting, there is a stark contrast between Paul classifying several special leadership gifts, one of which is "teacher", and Jesus' explicit teaching in Matthew 23 that *no-one should be called "teacher"*.

Multi-church unions, with no elected hierarchy of oversight

If there are problems with a pastors' fraternity where some are appointed to hierarchical positions, could an alliance of pastors with no clear headship perhaps solve all problems? Through his novels' character, Arthur suggests not, identifying a more subtle form of control than that exhibited by appointed leadership, namely the control of the peer group.

In some circles, if one person dares to question the direction of the group, they risk being rejected by the group. Not only do they end up out in the cold, but the group loses its voice of conscience. And those still in the group may not associate with the expelled member in case they also get rejected:

> *"Of course, pastoral peer pressure does exist, and in a mighty way. I am now convinced that pastoral peer pressure can be just as harmful and destructive as worldly peer pressure. It can be rightly argued that pastoral peer pressure can be a positive motivational factor, but it can also be argued with just as much evidence that pastoral peer pressure can be a motivational factor in the 'wrong direction,' especially if all your peers are going in the wrong direction.*
>
> *If each of the peers is fearful of changing directions because of the risk of being condemned and ostracized by the others, the whole group is locked into an unchecked path.*
>
> *If one dares break free to question the legitimacy of the group's direction, he is quickly classified as a liberal, and thus ceases to wield any inside influence. None of the other pastors – again because of peer pressure – will give the guy a sympathetic or attentive ear. None of them will listen to his reasons or arguments. They will refuse to be associated with him, lest they, too, lose their acceptance.*

As shameful as it is, I honestly believe that most pastors in the legalistic camp are influenced more by peer pressure than Spirit pressure. It's obvious they are not listening to God's Spirit as long as they continue to preach and believe their extreme and senseless traditions of legalism, and with a self-righteous and know-it-all attitude.

They have become the Pharisees of our day, and their inner-circle peer pressure keeps them blinded to that fact."

(Arthur, 1991: 135)

Traditional local churches with democratic election of leaders, or with no leaders

As a pastor, Jamie Buckingham shares how he struggled with the democratic model, one observed consequence being that the people can end up controlling the church leaders in unhealthy ways:

"For years I had wrestled with being a 'hireling' to a group of people. As a minister I had always been paid by the church. I was controlled by an official board. There was no spiritual privilege which did not have a string attached – a string securely fastened around my wallet. I was told how to live, ...what to wear and what not to wear. Even my wife's wardrobe had to meet the approval of official and unofficial groups within the church."

(Buckingham, 1980: 79)

While some seek a democratic model to remove dangers of an appointed hierarchy, Tillapaugh notes the potentially cumbersome nature of a full church democracy, where the whole congregation must be called together before a decision can be made. He takes parts of the Baptist denomination as typical of this approach, stating:

"[The New Testament church] began acting like some modern-day Baptists who must call an all-church meeting to make a decision."

(Tillapaugh, 1982: 129)

My reading of Noble's position is that he also objects to the democratic model where a local church's members democratically appoint one person, or a team of elders, to leadership, and that he attacks the democratic model within churches, criticizing Protestantism for

"... allowing every individual equal authority."

(Noble, 2002: 84)

and quotes a statement he recorded from a conversation with a Catholic priest, Tom Forrest, suggesting that

"... every evangelical is his own pope and makes infallible statements every week!"

(Noble, 2002: 84)

Noble instead argues for a "theocratic" model:

> *"[Paul] ... was establishing a divine order for church, not a democracy, where everyone's opinions are of equal importance, but rather a theocracy where God reigns through respected leaders with proven ministries ..."*
>
> (Noble, 2002: 89)

Buckingham expresses reserve regarding the democratic model, as he perceives dangers in the masses dictating to the clergy.

I have no doubt that unhealthy control can be exerted by politically astute and power-hungry laity, just as much as unhealthy control can be exercised by power-hungry leadership. Tillapaugh's objections are perhaps softer as he suggests he fears decision-making may become unwieldy if left to the masses. But Noble's confrontation of the democratic model follows quite a different line of argument. While perhaps he may have no difficulty in accepting equality for all within a country's political system, he seems to suggest it must not be so within churches. He appears to be claiming we must not permit all believers to have equal authority. In fact, he is arguing that God's ultimate authority can and must be represented by His chosen leaders.

One resultant danger would appear to be the limited ability of a mere member of the Body of Christ to challenge leadership's views.

Home churches

Some have despaired of having effective local churches where there are church buildings, formally recognized church leaders, and so on. An alternative form is to have 'home church'. Brown argues that this approach does not really address the underlying problems of local churches:

> *"The simple act of moving from a big meeting in a 'church' building into a small meeting in a home will not change us in the least. The physical structure in which we meet is not the primary issue. The shift in our mentality is the primary issue. Do we go to church or are we the Church? Do we go to a building to watch a religious performance – or, if we are more spiritual, to participate in a religious service – or are we salt and light in our communities, fishers of lost men and women, witnesses for Jesus on a divine mission to glorify God by life or by death?"*
>
> (Brown, 2002: 45)

Para churches

Still others feel a calling to active ministry in so-called parachurch organizations. Noble again is critical of these:

> *"Nowhere in 'The Book' [i.e. the Bible] do we find para-church, which means 'beside church' or in the minds of some, 'not really church.' If para-church describes anything, it is the work of the Holy Spirit who comes alongside the church! The phrase has been conjured up to keep at bay those who seem to threaten what possessive and sometimes hierarchical church leaders have come to regard as their domain."*
>
> (Noble, 2002: 170-171)

24-hour a day churches

Noble states:

> "One of the great problems in the church today is the limitations of our gatherings, especially for those who meet only once or twice a week."

(Noble, 2002: 139)

The solution, according to Noble?

> "24-hour church is the answer!"

(Noble, 2002: 140)

This is to be provided by a network of co-operative local churches. To support the perceived need for 24 x 7 church, Noble quotes from Thwaites, co-author of *Church that Works*, with the extract stating:

> "Marriage, family and work fill the creation; meetings, programmes and building cannot. When the local gathering attempts to encompass the impossible it cannot help but falter."

(Noble, 2002: 139)

He seems to be entirely missing Thwaites' point. I interpret Thwaites as saying that buildings and programs of the "gathered" church simply cannot reach where families and workers go, and instead we must trust God to lead individuals to perform God's works in the world as He sees fit rather than via institutional programs. But Noble seems to want the weaknesses of one local church to be overcome by coordinated collections of church programs, running twenty-four hours a day, seven days a week, rather than trusting God to direct His army of front-line workers.

The above extracts are merely intended to draw attention to the diversity of opinions on recommended local church structures, and to suggest that each of these models is flawed. Noble summarizes his view on some of them:

> "At least some of today's models of leadership – for example, a one-man pastor; five elders in a small local church; worse still, an elected 'diaconate' which produces a democratic deadlock; or a strong dominating personality – have little to do with God's order for his people.
>
> A democratic system of voting may work well with mature Christians who have open and honest relationships, but most churches which operate in this way have histories of infighting and division or paralysis through fear of disagreement. Equally, a benevolent dictatorship can work if the 'dictator' is Spirit-filled. However these models are not likely to produce a plurality of leadership which empowers the people. Things the Lord tolerated in the past when we were moving from ignorance to understanding, will no longer be acceptable."

(Noble, 2002: 92-93)

That may leave us wondering where we go from here. A bold rethink may be required, as Albert Einstein notes:

> "We can't solve problems by using the same kind of thinking we used when we created them."

The need for a new perspective on "church"

Through the eyes of the central character in his novel, Arthur seems to present the stereotypical local church as having failed:

> "For the church to function as a spiritual support group as God intended ... it has got to be more than just an information center where we gather together passively week after week and sing repetitious songs and hear repetitious sermons from only one person."

(Arthur, 1993: 149)

The writer of the foreword to *Unleashing the Church* summarizes the author's criticism of many local churches as being

> "... introverted, concerned about attracting larger and larger congregations to their pulpit-centred services, increasing their budgets, improving and expanding their facilities while their members remain afflicted with arthritic spectatoritis."

(Tillapaugh, 1982: 5)

Tillapaugh notes a difference between the optimism engendered in trainee church leaders during their time in a seminary, as compared with the stark reality of their subsequent work as actual church leaders:

> "While in seminary we future pastors had visions of serving the radiant bride of Christ. Yet when we were called to serve a local church we found something that resembled a shriveled octopus more than a bride with a beautiful body. Our bride didn't have her own arms. Others had stuck their arms all over her. Her ministry activity was so small she had shrunk to a few programs, scores of committees and maintenance of a building or two.
>
> We went to our pulpits, opened our Bibles and preached, 'The Lord's message rang out from you not only in Macedonia and Achaia—your faith in God has become known everywhere' (1 Thess. 1:8). But our preaching had a hollow ring. Words like 'everywhere' stuck in our throats as we looked over congregations that had very little involvement or even contact with large segments of our community. We knew that the distance between the church spoken of in the Bible and the one we were serving was immense."

(Tillapaugh 1982: 47)

Frost and Hirsch recognize this difference between the expectations of trainee clergy and the reality they subsequently encounter, and have questioned practicing church leaders:

> *"If you [church leaders] could start all over again, would you do it the same way? ... Alan has asked this question many times in groups and churches who are struggling to revitalize the ministry of the church. In every setting, he has yet to hear someone say they would do it the same way. Well the [question] here is 'Why are you doing it the same way now?'"*
>
> (Frost & Hirsch, 2003: 193)

Tillapaugh also notes the reality that some people, to be effective, had to work outside of church structures:

> *"[Dawson Trotman, the founder of the Navigators] had to bypass the church to have an effective ministry with sailors."*
>
> (Tillapaugh, 1982: 15)

The quotes above should ring warning bells that all is not well with local church practices. Yancey goes further, seemingly suggesting that these practices are contrary to those of Jesus.

> *"As I reflect on Jesus' temptations ... I realize they centered on his reason for coming to earth, his 'style' of working. Satan was, in effect, dangling before Jesus a speeded-up way of accomplishing his mission. He could win over the crowds by creating food on demand and then take control of the kingdoms of the world, all the while protecting himself from danger. 'Why move thy feet so slow to what is best?' Satan jeered in Milton's version.*
>
> *I first found this insight in the writings of Dostoevsky, who made the Temptation scene the centerpiece of his great novel The Brothers Karamazov. The agnostic brother Ivan Karamazov writes a poem called 'The Grand Inquisitor' set in sixteenth-century Seville at the height of the Inquisition. In the poem, a disguised Jesus visits the city at a time when heretics are daily being burned at the stake. The Grand Inquisitor, a cardinal, 'an old man, almost ninety, tall and erect, with a withered face and sunken eyes,' recognizes Jesus and has him thrown into prison. There, the two visit in a scene intentionally reminiscent of the Temptation in the desert.*
>
> *The Inquisitor has an accusation to make: by turning down the three temptations, Jesus forfeited the three greatest powers at his disposal, 'miracle, mystery, and authority.' He should have followed Satan's advice and performed the miracles on demand in order to increase his fame among the people. He should have welcomed the offer of authority and power. Did Jesus not realize that people want more than anything else to worship what is established beyond dispute? 'Instead of taking possession of men's freedom, you increased it, and burdened the spiritual kingdom of mankind with its sufferings forever. You desired man's free love, that he should follow you freely, enticed and taken captive by you.'*
>
> *By resisting Satan's temptations to override human freedom, the Inquisitor maintains, Jesus made himself far too easy to reject. He surrendered his greatest advantage: the power to compel belief. Fortunately, continues the sly Inquisitor, the church recognized*

the error and corrected it, and has been relying on miracle, mystery, and authority ever since. For this reason, the Inquisitor must execute Jesus one more time, lest he hinder the church's work."

(Yancey, 1995: 74)

"If I read church history correctly, many other followers of Jesus have yielded to the very temptations he resisted. Dostoevsky shrewdly replayed the Temptation scene in the torture cell of the Grand Inquisitor. How could a church founded by the One who withstood the Temptation carry out an Inquisition of forced belief that lasted half a millennium? Meanwhile, in a milder Protestant version in the city of Geneva, officials were making attendance at church compulsory and refusal to take the Eucharist a crime. Heretics there, too, were burned at the stake.

To its shame, Christian history reveals unrelieved attempts to improve on the way of Christ."

(Yancey, 1995: 81)

McManus seems to claim the local church as an institution is in such a poor shape that only a revolution will bring the required change:

"Jesus is being lost in a religion bearing His name. People are being lost because they cannot reconcile Jesus ... with Christianity. Christianity has become docile, domesticated, civilized. We have forgotten that there is a kingdom of darkness stealing the hopes and dreams and souls of a humanity without God. It is time to hear the barbarian call, to form a barbarian tribe, and to unleash the barbarian revolt. Let the invasion begin ..."

(McManus, 2005: 17)

Before we launch out as agents of change, let us first spend a brief moment to define what the word "church" should *really* mean.

Expressing similar views to those expressed earlier in this book by Rinehart, Howard Snyder differentiates between the universal Body of Christ as the Church, and a local church gathering:

"It is critically important—especially in a worldwide, multicultural situation such as the Church faces today—to be clear that the essence of the Church is people, not organization; that it is a community, not an institution. The great divide in contemporary thinking about the Church is located precisely here. Biblically, the Church is the community of God's people, and this is a spiritual reality which is valid in every culture. But all ecclesiastical institutions—whether seminaries, denominational structures, mission boards, publishing houses or what have you—are not the Church. Rather, they are supportive institutions created to serve the Church in its life and mission. They are culturally bound and can be sociologically understood and evaluated. But they are not themselves the Church. And when such institutions are confused with the Church, or seen as part of its essence, all kinds of unfortunate

misunderstandings result, and the Church is bound to a particular, present cultural expression."

(Snyder, 1977: 121)

But what is this thing we call a local church?

We can have a herd of cattle, a flock of birds, or a school of fish. There is a Greek word that refers to a group of people. It could have been translated into English as a "mob", but was typically translated as "church". The New Testament refers to the group of Christians in a town as the "church", but it could equally have been expressed as the "mob" of Christians at the town. Similarly, the group that wanted to kill Paul could have been called a "mob", or the "church" that wanted to kill Paul. There was nothing religious about the term "church", other than what we've made it. Oliver and Thwaites go on to claim:

"Today when we refer to the church, it is nearly always in terms of what happens in a special building at special times on special days ...

... In other words, we see ourselves as church when we are gathered, worshipping, praying, listening and responding, but do we see ourselves, as the people of God when scattered, being as important and significant as the church gathered? Deliberately or unintentionally, we empower leaders, meetings, and resources, most of which go to maintain this thing which we call 'church'."

(Oliver & Thwaites, 2001: 7-8)

Oliver speaks of a

"...flawed theology of the church believing, in reality, that the church is synonymous with gathering or the meeting; that when we are not gathered, we are not truly or effectively the church."

(Oliver & Thwaites, 2001: 63)

Thwaites seems to make a serious charge against the concept of the church as an assembly (both traditional and "cell"), claiming that a reason why God's people have failed to prevail against the gates of hell is because

"... our doctrine or understanding of 'his church' has been severely limited. In a word, it's been 'defective'. Our problem is that we have kept the powerful name church inside the meetings, programmes and buildings of the local (or cell) expression of church. We have kept the name church under the managerial control of pastors and ministers, and have not released it to name and empower the saints in all of their life and work."

(Oliver & Thwaites, 2001: 42-43)

While many debate the form any given local church should take, it is perhaps not surprising that some of the church leaders have a vested interest, and still insist that the laity should hold the local church in almost reverent awe. Listen to the words of Jack Hayford, in his book, *Pastors of Promise*. As a pastor, he claims that the local church is the

SO WHAT SHOULD "CHURCH" LOOK LIKE?

"… one central and continuing place of God's timeless workings …"

(Hayford, 1997: 61)

In contrast, the following quotations expose us to a refreshing willingness to consider that God's people (i.e. the one universal Church, the Body of Christ) may actually be able to effectively perform ministry, have fellowship, and grow the Kingdom outside the constraints of a local church. And to redefine what might be meant by the term, "church"!

Oliver and Thwaites present two opposing ways of seeing "church". The first is the popular but flawed view (both current and historic) that church is *assembly* based. We *become* church when we assemble. When we wander home, we're no longer church. While some see home or cell church as a radical alternative to denominational, building-based local "church", it still suffers from the same flaw of "being" church when its members assemble. The second view of "church" is that we *are* Church, independent of where we might be:

"We have held the gathered church, under the wing of its leaders in a building or a house, to be the church proper and the church central. I remember speaking to one fellow who had been taught that the church was only the church if it gathered, because that's what he had been told the word 'ekklesia' means. I checked with him to make sure by asking: 'So if you are not physically proximate to another member of your congregation, then you are not church?' He stuck to his guns and so I asked one more question: 'Where does the church go when it's not meeting, does it disappear? If so, it must be one of the weakest things on earth.' He had no answer. Your doctrine of church may not be that strict, but this demonstrates the kind of thinking that is out there. Hence the need to look again at what '[God's] church' is and is not.

We have, as mentioned, made much of the word ekklesia; taking it to mean that the church gathered in a meeting is the central expression of church. This to my mind is not supported by Scripture. There was a church that gathered in the house of Apphia and Archippus (Philem. 1:2). The other eight references to the church being 'in' somewhere all speak of cities, none speak of buildings. The word used for 'assembling together', from the oft quoted 'not forsaking our own assembling together, as is the habit of some' (Heb.10:25 NASV), is not ekklesia, it's a word that simply means coming together. When the word church is used in Scripture, in key books like those of Ephesians or Romans, it is not used to refer to the gathering, rather it speaks of the body of Christ in all of life. An exception to this, one might think, is 1 Timothy 3:15, where the gathering of the church (as what Paul calls the household of God) is declared to be the church of the living God. However, quite simply here, as was the case with the gathering in the house of Apphia and Archippus, the church was first the church and then it gathered. The gathering did not make it the church. Words like 'household' and 'coming together' (assembly) are used to describe his body, the church, when it gathers. Never is the word ekklesia used of the gathering itself. This is not an exhaustive study, but it serves, I would hope, to help us to not mistake the word 'church' in Scripture for the act of meeting. They are two distinct words with different meanings."

(Oliver & Thwaites, 2001: 169-170)

Thwaites contrasts the view of "church" as people assembled into a congregation with what he believes is the biblical view of church, namely that "church" *is* the Body of Christ in every sphere, including (and especially) so-called "secular" work, whether paid or unpaid:

"... the church is the people of God living and working in every sphere of creation ..."

(Oliver & Thwaites, 2001: 55)

"We, as saints, are the church: our work is the work of the church; our work is on the front line of engagement of the gates of hell. Our work is not secular and temporal – it is sacred and eternal."

(Oliver & Thwaites, 2001: 59)

"The Son of God stands as head of his body the church over all things in creation. The church perpetually exists in him, and does not materialise or become real only when it meets. As we live, work and occupy, we are progressively joining together as members of his body in him."

(Oliver & Thwaites, 2001: 170)

"The logic is simple: if we are the church, then when we work we are that church, when we meet we are that church, when we sleep, take a meal with our family or have a coffee with our friends we are ... wait for it ... still the church. I know we know this, but in practice, we tend, for the most part, to talk and act as if we don't."

(Oliver & Thwaites, 2001: 168)

Foster shares personally how he seeks to experience God in all aspects of life, not just during assembly in a local church:

"My whole life, in one sense, has been an experiment in how to be a portable sanctuary – learning to practise the presence of God in the midst of the stresses and strains of contemporary life. Some people who read my books are surprised to learn that I have never been drawn to a monastic life ... For me, the great challenge has always been to experience the reality of God in the midst of going to work and raising kids and cleaning house and paying the bills."

(Foster, 1985: x)

All of this stands in sharp contrast with the more conventional "church" views. The views expressed seem to conclude that if gifted people end up working in the business world, such a calling is somehow less valuable than full-time ministry in a local church institution:

"The evidence suggests that [people with gifts other than pastor/teacher] have not made it through denominational selection processes that are looking for pastor/teachers. Instead, there has been a tendency to move such people into missions, or into para-church agencies (often they have begun new ones) or, tragically, they have simply gone into the business world without seeing that activity as a valid ministry.

The situation of the post-Christendom church in the West demands that such people are recruited as a matter of urgency into ministry."

(Robinson & Smith, 2003: 86-87)

"*Tragic*" if gifted people have "*simply gone into the business world*"? Such seems to be the view of those who cannot conceive of effective ministry outside of the assembled "church".

A simple alternative exists, so why is it being ignored?

In his book *Thoughts on Holiness*, Pearse presents a very simple solution—don't look for a model church, or for a church model. Instead, model your life on Jesus.

> "*Christ Himself in the heart is the only deliverance from the traditional religion or from the dead forms of the Temple service. He reveals the Father to us, and we worship Him in spirit and in truth. We hold communion with Him, and within us is restored the Holy of Holies. We hear the voice of the Father. We have His love shed abroad in the heart. The light of His countenance gladdens us. We have the glorious presence of the King. We know Him and delight in Him as the fairest among ten thousand, and the altogether lovely. 'We will come unto Him and take up our abode with Him,' is a promise that the Master waits to fulfil.*"

(Pearse, 1800s: 200-201)

It may sound simple, but its implications are profound. There are some lessons to be learned. So why are they being missed by so many? In part, the answer may be that we are spending too much time protecting our traditions, or the establishment, or the leaders. Or maybe the answer is even more serious. Maybe we are trying to run the show according to our own perceived wisdom rather than trusting God to run His Church. We need to recognize that we cannot achieve anything of real value on our own:

> "*What about the Holy Spirit? Where does He fit into all this?*
>
> *Usually, in our approach to things, He is sanctimoniously invited to bless what we've already planned, and asked to help in the things we cannot do for ourselves.*
>
> *But what we are depending on is the Sunday school, the sanctuary, the pastor, the Saturday newspaper ad, the sermon, the choir, the board, the ushers, the visitation teams, the greeters, the teachers, the sidewalk sign, the liturgy, the social, the rally, the camping program, the heavy schedule of activities, the 'revival' meeting, the clever communications piece, the new idea or program or leader or organ or classroom building or ….*
>
> *It is tough (!) to let go of all those handfuls of earthly sand we are clawing for and clinging to for dear life and growth and edification, and to begin clinging to the Rock — the Source of the things that build the spiritual church.*

> *Caught in the swirling sand of human, fleshly church 'necessities,' it is difficult to realize that the Spirit is not doing it — we are!*
>
> *He will do what He can as an 'add-on' to our programs and plans. Romans 8:28 will operate in spite of our willful or stupid or blind occupation of the place that belongs to Him. But only as the Holy Spirit is allowed His place as the actual Head of the Church, Lord, All in all, will the [modern church] begin to have any similarity to the Church of The Acts. Only as we see Him, and not ourselves, as the church's source of Life, leadership and energy to do its task, will our churches ever rise above the miserable limitations of our own human abilities, talents and intelligence, to become something clearly identifiable as a work of God.*
>
> *Until we come to real dependence on the Spirit of God in us and among us, and to a cessation of our dependence on what the flesh can do, the work of the church will always seem frustrating, weak and riddled with the diseases that plague all human institutions. Until we start to walk and live and operate our churches by faith on Him alone, there will be all too much about our churches that declare them to be little more than the frail efforts of dedicated men, trying to do something all by themselves and then, in vain, trying to convince the world and themselves that 'God did it'!"*
>
> (Girard, 1972: 70-71):

So, as Brown notes (and as quoted earlier), it's time for radical change, but it may be costly:

> "For years now we have bemoaned the state of the Western Church, longing for change, praying for revival, looking for new methods and programs, and ideas. And God has answered us in many wonderful ways; some real progress has been made. But I fear that most of us have not yet realized how serious the problem is, and have failed, therefore, to realize just how serious – how sweeping and wide-ranging and dramatic and radical – the solution must be."
>
> (Brown, 2002: 13)

An alternative exists. But are you willing to seek God for answers that may not be comfortable? And perhaps get rid of some old wine-skins along the way? Adrian Plass' book, *View From A Bouncy Castle*, seems to hold the view that some people live

> "...like a puppet, with some other powerful outsider pulling the strings, writing the script, making [them] do things that [are] foolish or wrong ..."
>
> (Plass, 1991: 157)

But why would anyone live like that, he asks? He tells of children raised in institutional homes who really want to live with foster parents but often fail to make the transition. He explains the problem this way:

> "One of the boys tried to explain it to me once.
>
> 'It's not that you don't want it to happen,' he said, 'and it's not that you don't feel excited and grateful and all that – it's just that you suddenly get frightened, and you

think you're going to mess it up anyway, like everything else has always got messed up, so you just make it happen early.'

'But what is it that makes you so frightened?' I asked.

'Being in a family,' he said, 'not knowing what you do or say. Not knowing if they'll just pretend they like you or whether they really will. Besides,' he added, 'it's easier being in [an institution] with all the other kids and staff and that …'

Like many of those who yearn to be part of God's family, he was unable to take a gamble on the reality of love. Better the spiritual half-life of familiar day-to-day existence, than risky meetings with a God who might not turn out to be as loving or forgiving or understanding as his publicity suggests.

You only find out the truth by trying, and it's a terrible fate to be cast for ever in the devil's soap opera [i.e. playing a role set by some script-writer rather than being the real person God intended you to be]. I'm glad I got out when I did."

(Plass, 1991: 158-159)

SECTION 2:

NO MORE "HOLY MEN"

Under the old covenant, God gave Moses the Ten Commandments. Judaism then elaborated on these, and identified 613 specific, detailed "mitzvot", or further commandments. And all of this in spite of Moses' final words in Deuteronomy 4: 1-2 where he advises the people to listen carefully to the laws as provided, but importantly he then clearly instructs them to avoiding adding new laws.

Jesus powerfully challenged both Judaism's expansion of God's laws, and the reverence shown by Jews of His day for the multitude of man-made extensions to God's laws. For example, His disciples were noted to have been in breach of the tradition of the elders when they ate food without first performing a ceremonial washing of their hands (Mark 7: 1-5). Not only did Jesus choose to ignore some of these man-made traditions, He went further and accused the religious leaders of actually breaking God's laws so they could uphold their own traditions. He quoted Isaiah and noted that the leaders' teachings are nothing more than man-made rules (Matthew 15: 3-9). This condemnation by Jesus of the rules of men parading as laws of God is reflected in this book's title.

And finally, Jesus condensed even the Ten Commandments into two essential commandments (Matthew 22: 37-40). So while religious leaders expanded the rules, Jesus challenged the extra rules and focused on essentials.

But just as the Jewish leaders of Jesus' day burdened their people with added rules, many churches have generated long lists of added traditions. It has reached the stage where, unfortunately, some people are rejecting the good news of Jesus because they can't stomach the bad news of church rules. It is vital that, like Jesus' response to the traditions of the elders, we challenge the church rules and traditions and see what basics are the essence of Christian faith, and what traditions of men parade as principles of God but are dispensable.

Pearse speaks very strongly of the problem of religious traditions, looking at how there was a "confusion" that had crept in between forms of worship, versus relationships with God.

> *"Religion had become very much a thing of tradition, an inherited custom. God was not to them the living God, after Whom the soul thirsted, and in Whom it delighted. They kneeled with lowly tones and confessed their sins, but without any deep contrition. They came with a sacrifice, but without desire or thought of anything further. They heard the benediction spoken, but without any sense of blessing; only a sigh of relief that it was done. That was the source of the confusion. Every age illustrates it. Then is everything wrong when religion comes to be a round of pious phrases without any grip of faith; pious tones without any heart-cleaving to the Lord; prating about sin, but going on with a self-satisfied goodness; saying, 'Lord, Lord,' – but without hallowed communion with Him, without any earnest effort to know His will, without any denying ourselves to please Him.*
>
> *Religion without a living God – then all this mischief assuredly creeps in. The service may be very grand, very stirring, very emotional, very solemn, – all that will help*

men to cheat themselves more perfectly. Many a man likes to be made to feel that life is a sacred and lofty thing – for an hour; he can the better afford to balance such solemnities by frittering life away in a thousand vanities. A man likes to wipe his eyes at the touching story of somebody else's generosity, his emotion makes him a sharer in the good deed; but that will not stop him from taking his poor neighbour by the throat and demanding his own with usury. Many a worshipper likes to worship awed and entranced amidst solemn appeals or melting music; and yet he can go straight home to be selfish, snappish, mean, to feel that life is a dull, colourless, dispiriting thing, when the music is hushed."

(Pearse, 1800s: 193-195)

Traditionally, the practices of Christendom tend to be centered on the local church.

- "Leadership" is commonly seen as the domain of the professional church leaders, though occasionally these leaders might trust very special laity with some minor roles, but still under the leaders' watchful eye.

- "Fellowship" is seen as taking place amongst the local church members, typically as part of formal services, and typically in a "church" building. Phrases such as, "Where do you fellowship?" underline this thinking. A visiting cynic might wonder how much real fellowship occurs when the people struggle to arrive in time for the service to start, stare at the back of each other's heads for an hour (with maybe a brief interlude for organized hugs and hand-shakes), then maybe have coffee with some while sometimes studiously avoiding others.

- "Ministry" is again typically the special domain of the church leaders, reinforced by phrases such as, "Chris is going to Bible college to prepare for ministry", or after graduation, "Meet our minister, Pastor Chris". But worse than that, ministry is seen as necessarily the responsibility of the local church to "organize". To some, the idea of real ministry happening outside of the structures of a local church is too dangerous to be allowed, and too hard to control.

Up to this point, I hope this book has drawn you to feel comfortable in questioning and challenging beliefs that have been fed to you.

We need to remove the "dead wood" of the traditions so we can see more clearly where we might head. It may help to look at the flaws in so many traditions we are likely to encounter. Many of the following chapters do just this, and later in the book we will turn our attention to looking at the foundations for a fresh, new way to move forward, and finally close with a look at how *you* might be part of an exciting break for freedom.

But for the moment, let's start looking at the traditions of men that need to be demolished. As a foundation for living in freedom, we need to discard the unhelpful (or even downright dangerous) traditions of men that parade as laws of God. You can expect to encounter external resistance to this dismantling, certainly from those with vested interest, but also from those who have not yet seen that they too can be free.

You need to also be aware that each of us can encounter our own internal resistance to change. Dismantling what has been part of us for so long can be painful–I struggled for quite some time. But in some way it can be like the treatment for some burns victims—the old, damaged flesh must first be removed, even though the process of removal of what is dead can be extremely traumatic and painful, before the healthy, new flesh can start to grow.

Are you willing to challenge the traditions of men? Are you willing to trust that God can use you as He chooses, even if it is in a way that is different to your ideas of a "traditional" Christian? Are you willing to move with God even if others stay in the safety of their traditions? I hope and pray so.

According to the Old Testament, God initially had a direct relationship with Adam and Eve. Much later, God again sought to have a personal relationship with His people, but they were too afraid, and instead wanted Moses to come between God and them. Even later again, instead of accepting God as King, His people wanted an earthly king, like the other nations had. It seems that the Biblical history contains a repeating theme of God wanting to relate personally, but instead the people wanting to have leaders that take responsibility for hearing from God on behalf of the people.

Today, the leadership issue is still debated. Some question whether we even need leaders, while others cry out for more leaders to be trained–without such leaders they fear that the Church cannot grow and reach its full potential.

Who is right? Are the local church leaders, in their many forms, a reflection of God's plan? Or are they more a reflection of dispensable traditions of men? And even if they do carry aspects of "tradition", are they necessarily unhelpful? If even the Old Testament, let alone the New, suggests God wants a direct relationship with each of us, are the church leaders getting in the way? The instruction (1 Timothy 2:5) to have no mediator between God and man other than Jesus stands in stark contrast with what is too often observed.

If we apply the analogy of the "body", there is one head. In the natural body, all parts have a role, but the brain has direct connection with the hands, the eyes, the ears, and so on. In the "Body of Christ", the New Testament clearly states that Jesus is the Head, yet we may observe too many cases where leaders presume the role of communicating to the parts on behalf of the Head.

Have we got it fundamentally wrong?

CHAPTER 6:
THE ISSUE OF PROFESSIONALISM

Martin Luther was the catalyst for the Reformation. At the very heart of the blood-stained struggle for freedom from the abuses of the Catholic Church was the contentious concept of the "priesthood of all believers". Centuries later, the Catholic Church still has its hierarchy of power, with a pope at the top, and he is still claimed to be infallible. But even the Protestant churches, whose foundations are built on the hard-won freedom from the evils of man-made chains-of-command, are still typically centered around a hierarchy of professional church leaders.

One view - "The ministry" of the professional church leaders

Reza Safa, a convert from Islam to Christianity, was raised in an Islamic culture. Through his book, *Blood of the Sword - Blood of the Cross*, he has given us his insight into the attitude Muslims have towards their leaders – insights that may provide a new perspective on our own attitudes to church leaders.

> *"My father ... had an unshakeable love in his heart for the imams (pontiffs) of Islam. However, there is no such thing as close contact or fellowship with God. God is too great a being to be contacted by man. Therefore the prophet and imams are the closest beings that man can approach and they are accounted so holy that there is awesome respect for them. Because the Shi'ite Muslims believe that these imams are very close to God, to express one's love toward them is to express one's love toward God ..."*

(Safa, 1990: 7)

As Christians, it may be easy to criticize Islam's elevation of its holy men, but an honest evaluation of the attitude of many Christians to their leaders suggests that these Christians, too, often see the leaders as "holy men", better able to mediate between God and man, rather than allowing Jesus to fulfil the role of mediator.

Jack Hayford had written to pastors across the USA asking about their reason for being *"in the ministry"* (Hayford, 1997: 20). He then went on to proclaim that the call to the ministry

> *"... extends deeper, wider and higher than any other sense of vocation, however valid, transcending even the inner urges of people who have lofty goals – those of scientists, writers, athletes, explorers and teachers."*
>
> (Hayford, 1997: 21)

It is certainly understandable that people can be passionate about their careers. In fact, we want to be treated by doctors, and taught by teachers, who have a sense of the importance of their role. However, we may take exception with an individual who implies, directly or subtly, that their particular calling is seen by them to be central in the scheme of things. Few may be surprised to encounter the odd politician or two that see their role as being of extreme importance, especially if they lead a country. So perhaps we should not be surprised to encounter a pastor or church leader who suggests that he or she and others with the same role fulfil the most important vocation of all possible. A bias that Hayford seemingly holds, and which I feel is reinforced by his statement that

> *"The call to shepherding ... [puts pastors/leaders] ... at the pivotal point of relaying and multiplying the spread of heaven's message to mankind."*
>
> (Hayford, 1997: 24)

My interpretation of Hayford's view is that it is blatant and explicit—and remember, Hayford is a pastor! Charles Sheldon's novel *Jesus is Here* I find to be a bit more subtle, presenting an assumption that there are "professional" Christians and others (non-professionals).

> *"Mr. Grey had begun his career as a professional evangelist. ... He had been very successful as an evangelist ... and when the mission there, started by his converts, had developed into a church, the people had clamored for him as their pastor. ... He was absolutely consecrated to religious work."*
>
> (Sheldon, 1999: 36-37)

Sheldon's perception that there exists a class of "professional" Christians is less direct than that of Hayford, but perhaps he has a similar set of beliefs as those underpinning Hayford's bold claims.

At the start of a new appointment in my home town of Melbourne, Australia, a team of church leaders were, in my opinion, a *bit* more balanced, seeing their role to develop the potential in the laity. Yet even here, I got the impression that they set themselves apart and claimed superior training and a need to "supervise" the laity. This seems to imply that the laity didn't have the gifting they themselves had:

> *"The Clergy's task is to train, coach, inspire and supervise lay persons in their ministry of caring, while also using the rich resources of their training, professional role, and pastoral office in doing their own caring work."*
>
> (Extract from a church newsletter in Berwick, Victoria, Australia)

MacArthur reinforces the role of church leaders by taking a swipe at lay people who dare to move into leadership roles but don't have, in his view, sufficient maturity for the job:

> *"Just as families today are dominated by their children, so are many churches. How tragic when the church's immature believers are among its most influential teachers and leaders."*

(MacArthur, 1997: 30)

The following handful of quotations reinforce the stance already expressed above. Firstly, Hunt seems to portray Abel as a minister who instructs his young church members to support his ministry, arguing that full-time ministry is the supreme calling:

> *"... we're teaching these young people to be servants while they follow the highest calling any believer could receive."*

(Hunt, 2004: 7)

Abel's wife, Emma Rose, initially shared his view. As a Bible college student, she noted:

> *"I never, ever thought that God would use me in what my fellow students called 'full-time ministry.' Those who had received a calling were revered on campus; even the professors looked at them as front-line warriors in training."*

(Hunt, 2004: 23)

This reverence for full-time ministry is not peculiar to Western culture. Esther Ahn Kim, a Korean woman, shared in her autobiography, *If I Perish*, that:

> *"... my mother had encouraged me to be a pastor's wife. I had insisted I would not marry a pastor. ...*
>
> *I had my way by marrying an engineer, but ... [my husband] decided to abandon his chosen profession and become a pastor. ... by this time I was as eager as he that he serve the Lord full time."*

(Kim, 1977: 255)

Hudson Taylor, the founder of the China Inland Mission, also showed his belief that working for an income is less honorable than working full time for God. His aim was to be a full-time evangelist, but if necessity forced him to work for an income, he would work as little as possible so that he could focus on "missionary efforts":

> *"I was willing to give up all my time to the service of evangelisation among the heathen if, by any means, He would supply the smallest amount on which I could live; and if He were not pleased to do this, I was prepared to undertake whatever work might be necessary to support myself, giving all the time that could be spared from such a calling to more distinctly missionary efforts."*

(Taylor & Taylor, 1911: 431)

The above quotations made me question if the authors hold the view that "holy men", "clergy", or "leaders" are special, and their followers, also known as the "laity", are somehow lesser beings, or at least expected to fulfil lesser roles while supporting their leaders.

Leadership in local churches may be seen by some as important, but it is also widely recognized that the power and authority of such leadership can be abused. In his book *Money, Sex and Power*, Foster points out the evils in abuse of power. He uses William Booth, the founder of the Salvation Army, as a case in point, noting the distinct contrast between the leadership style of Jesus and that of Booth. Yet in spite of this position, Foster still upholds the power-leadership model, arguing that while abuse of hierarchical structures is wrong, the structure itself is essential:

> "Authoritative leadership is essential in the community of faith. It is easy to forget this when we see leadership abused."
>
> (Foster, 1985: 634)

In response to abusive leadership, some seek an organizational structure with no leader. But even in such an organization, Tillapaugh suggests that some form of leader is still likely to emerge.

> "The local church soon becomes like its pastor, and this is true even of those groups who do not believe in pastors. The true pastor of such a group is not hard to identify; he is usually the one who can present the strongest argument against any church having a pastor."
>
> Tillapaugh (1982: 103), quoting A. W. Tozer:

Based on the quotations provided so far, it would appear that the general consensus is that we must have leaders, even though there are risks of them abusing the laity. This leaves us with the very important but unresolved question as to what leadership model we could pursue—and that is even if we need a leadership model.

Starting to question this view

The view of some that church leaders, and others called to "full-time" ministry, are special is well established. But is this a wholesome view? Not all think so.

It is not only Christendom that has struggled with the issue of whether or not there should be a special class of people who are paid to be professional religious leaders. Centuries ago, this was a controversial topic amongst the Jewish community, as noted in Jonathan Sacks' highly recommended book, *The Dignity of Difference*:

> "The greatest of medieval rabbis, Moses Maimonides, fought against the practice of supporting a leisured class of rabbinic scholars through public charitable funds. 'One who makes his mind up to study Torah and not to work but to live on charity', he wrote, 'profanes the name of God, brings the Torah into contempt, extinguishes the light of religion, brings evil upon himself, and deprives himself of life hereafter.' This was a controversial campaign, never entirely successful, for in Judaism study

is the highest value, and there were always those who believed that there should be a scholarly elite relieved of the burden of having to work for a living. Maimonides, though, saw the dangers of such an arrangement. It compromised the independence of the scholar. 'Better', he told his disciple Joseph ibn Aknin, 'to earn a penny as a tailor, carpenter or weaver than to depend on the income of the Exilarch.' It removed the rabbi from the world in which his disciples had to live. And it turned a religious vocation into a paid profession."

(Sacks, 2003: 95-96, including quotations from Maimonides)

Eugene Nida, in *Communication and Social Structure*, seems to warn against one particular and what I perceive to be a disturbing aspect of having church leaders as a special class, namely establishment of the church leaders as the spokespeople for God:

"… in the ministry … it is usual for the religious professional to do most of the talking. Too often the minister … regards himself solely as intermediary of a superior message from God … [The religious professional] has gone forth to tell people the truth, not to listen to other people's ideas about the truth."

(Nida, 1972: 431)

Girard was a minister. My reading of his book gave me the impression that he had an awakening when he realized he had set himself up as the intermediary between God and the laity within his congregation:

"[God desired to be] the Living Head of the Church Himself [but this could not happen] … as long as I kept impressing the church with my indispensability to it, as the only one who knew how to do a myriad of things, the only one who ever preached, the all-knowing authority on every matter, the only 'trained professional' counselor, the chairman of everything, the teacher of everything, the one responsible for everything, the one without whose blessing and prompting nobody acts or innovates or leads or does anything! Me: the 'great white father,' the 'all-spiritual high priest,' the one-man 'whirling dervish' and spiritual tornado, the 'little tin god.' "

(Girard, 1972: 90-91)

The possibility of seeing the church leaders as something special is dangerous due to its subtlety. Unless challenged, thinking that elevates clergy can slip in. Yancey is an internationally respected author. He tackles many thorny issues with insight and honesty. Yet he, like any of us, can be blindsided by assumptions. His apparent dependence on the church leaders as a class can be demonstrated when he says:

"As an adult I rely on public utilities to bring me electricity and fuel, vehicle manufacturers to provide me transportation, farmers to feed me, pastors and mentors to nourish me spiritually."

(Yancey, 2006: 27)

This dependency by the laity on the church leaders can leave the laity vulnerable, as ironically highlighted by a quotation two pages earlier in the same book by Yancey. The story is told of street people who lost their "minister" in tragic circumstances, and were subsequently at risk due to the dependence they had on the minister:

> "I cannot tell you what a blow that was for the people he ministered to. They barely hang on to life themselves, and then to have their pastor commit suicide ..."

(Yancey, 2006: 25)

Oliver gets even more direct. He speaks out against the fundamental issue of having even the concept of "full-time ministry", labeling it a

> "... flawed approach to ministry ... [that] has produced what we could safely call the Christian caste system, where all Christians are equal, but full-time Christians are more equal than others! The most damaging and vulgar expression of this caste system is the persistent use of the phrase 'full-time' to describe the upper or ruling class.
>
> The phrase 'full-time' is used only once in the entire scriptures – Romans 13:6. In that Scripture it refers to a local government employee in the inland revenue, who is also referred to as God's servant. If we persist in using the phrase, we deliberately demean 95 per cent or more of the church who, by the same definition, are not full-time and never can be. Many of my closest friends are paid by the church, and they are among the most supportive in the drive to be rid of the phrase. Why? Because it produces a two-tier Christianity, where those not paid by the church can never feel fully affirmed or released to do what they have been led to do. They will always feel second best, second rate and less spiritual. God forbid!"

(Oliver & Thwaites, 2001: 63)

While Oliver tackles the use of the phrase, "full-time ministry", Pawson (repeated from an earlier quotation) tackles the underlying phrase, "ministry". He suggests that each of us may be called to many ministries, but challenges people who vaguely state they are called to *"the* ministry". If someone makes this claim, Pawson then challenges them by asking,

> "Which ministry? Teaching, evangelism, administration, or what? If you answer, 'all', you haven't heard from God."

(Pawson, 1984)

But don't we need "leaders"? Jacobsen and Coleman suggest not, or at least nothing like what we've grown to accept as normal.

> "[Marvin:] '... how do leaders fit in all of this? Don't we need elders and pastors and apostles?'
>
> [John:] 'For what?'
>
> [Marvin:] 'Doesn't someone need to be in charge and organize things so people will know what to do?' Marvin was almost beside himself. I cringed inside, knowing he wasn't going to hear what he wanted.
>
> [John:] 'Why, so people can follow someone else instead of following Jesus? Don't you

see we already have a leader? The church gives Jesus first place in everything and it will refuse to let anyone else crawl up in his seat.'

[Marvin:] 'So leaders aren't important either?'

[John:] 'Not the way you've been taught to think of them. One can hardly conceive of body life today without an organization and a leader shaping others with his vision. Some love to lead; others desperately want to be led. This system has made God's people so passive most can't even imagine living without a human leader to identify with. Then we wonder why our spirituality falls so painfully short ….' "

(Jacobsen & Coleman, 2006: 140)

While the above authors challenge the theological concept of having special "holy men" within Christendom, Adrian Plass brings a touch of humor into the debate by presenting a satire that questions the motives of some "in ministry":

"I want to have a ministry.
I want to be profound,
I want to see the folks I touch
Go spinning to the ground.
I want to use a funny voice,
Mysterious and low,
I want to spot uneven legs,
I want to watch them grow.

I want to have a little team,
No more than two or three,
A totally devoted group
Whose ministry is – me!
They'd keep an eye upon my soul
And tell me how it looks,
And even more importantly,
They'd sell my tapes and books.

I want to send my prayer list out,
The printed sort looks flash,
The ones that say, 'I'm greatly blessed!
And could you send some cash?'
I'd send them out by first-class post,
And please the folk who got 'em,
By putting little written bits
In biro on the bottom.

I want to be a humble star
At national church events,
And lead obscure seminars
In great big leaky tents.

I want to say how I deplore
the famous Christian hunters,
I want to sign their Bibles
And refer to them as 'punters'.

I really want a ministry
I want to alter lives,
I want to pray for something dead
And see if it revives.
I do! I want a ministry,
I'm sure it's all been planned.
I'll make a start as soon as God,
Removes the job in hand."

(Plass, 1991: 148-149)

Should we simply abandon the church's leader/follower divide?

Opinions have been expressed that challenge the belief that there are special classes of Christians, particularly those that fulfil the role of leadership within local churches, and/or those that are "full-time" for God. But where does that leave us? Should there be no such classes at all? Are we all equal? Or are there some that are more equal than others?

The foundation - All are equal in the Body

Famous nineteenth century preacher, Dwight L. Moody, opens the debate in his book *The Faith Which Overcomes* by arguing that all are—or should be—workers in the Kingdom of God:

> *"I read some time ago of a man who took passage in a stage coach. There were first, second, and third-class passengers. But when he looked into the coach, he saw all the passengers sitting together without distinction. He could not understand it till by-and-by they came to a hill, and the coach stopped, and the driver called out, 'First-class passengers keep their seats; second-class passengers get out and walk; third-class passengers get behind and push.' Now, in the Church, we have no room for first-class passengers – people who think that salvation means an easy ride all the way to heaven. We have no room for second-class passengers – people who are carried most of the time, and who, when they must work out their own salvation, go trudging on, giving never a thought to helping their fellows along. All Church members ought to be third-class passengers – ready to dismount and push all together, and push with a will. That was John Wesley's definition of a Church – 'All at it, and always at it.' Every Christian ought to be a worker."*

(Moody, circa 1890: 115-116)

Rinehart argues that leaders who exercise demands for loyalty often base their actions on the presumption that they are somehow a cut above their followers, but warns that the resultant structure is not Godly:

> *"If leaders subtly present themselves as 'the anointed' or as somehow superior in their understanding of God and His word, and they use that image to demand loyalty, they create an unholy structure for control."*
>
> (Rinehart, 1998: 65)

In the foreword to Rinehart's book, Terry Taylor goes further. Not only should those labeled by some as leaders be reclassified as workers willing to push the coach uphill (to use Moody's analogy), but those classified by some as "mere" laity should be reclassified as members of the Body of Christ that are worthy of performing ministry as directed by God:

> *"There should be no clergy/laity caste system like the one that has built up over the ages. Everyone is [capable of ministry] in some realm, and all should submit to one another.*
>
> *... The Word of God strikes at the roots of the hierarchical structures that have grown up like a choking undergrowth that stifles new life. ... As Moses sought the release of the ancient people of Israel from soul-numbing slavery, Stacy wants to see the people of God released from false assumptions about who is qualified to perform ministry. Further, he wants to see each individual developed according to his or her gifting."*
>
> (Rinehart, 1998: 10)

Rinehart leaves no doubt as to whether or not some are members of a superior class:

> *"[God] has absolute authority. All citizens of His Kingdom are equal under His reign."*
>
> (Rinehart, 1998: 94)

> *"... there is no justification in the New Testament for a special category that places 'leaders' in a separate position above all others. We have a great High Priest who mediates between us and the Father. He has made each of us members of His royal priesthood."*
>
> (Rinehart, 1998: 108)

> *"Like the Pharisees and scribes of Jesus' day, church leaders have established traditions and systems that have become virtually sacred down through the ages. Whether it's declaring that bishops are a special class of believers, that the clergy alone has the right to read the Scriptures, or that one's forgiveness comes from a priest and not from God, the pages of history are filled with examples of power abused in the name of Christ.*
>
> *Abuses of power in our day are often more subtle. The layout of church office space, the titles we assign, the requirements for membership or for being a teacher – all indicate underlying beliefs about power."*
>
> (Rinehart, 1998: 48)

Rinehart attacks the belief system behind the so-called clergy/laity divide. David Pawson (1984) goes on to warn of the *consequences* of following a flawed belief system, expressing the opinion that having a professional minister is the biggest barrier to renewal.

Girard similarly notes that the sickness in local churches can be traced back to having the ministry left to the professionals rather than shared among the people:

> "It began to soak in that every individual Christian is a minister and a priest, whose spiritual ministry is deeply needed in the church. That the church is as sick as it is to a large degree because every individual Christian does not see himself as a minister and priest, nor is there any real encouragement for him to see himself that way. The spiritual ministry of each individual member must be a spiritual ministry — not just more involvement in the machinery of an organization."

(Girard, 1972: 45)

Condemning the distinction between church leaders & laity

Brown (in a partial re-quote) explains how:

> "In Old Testament times God set apart a special class of Israelites for divine service [but] ... this changed with the death and resurrection of Jesus. He made all believers holy priests, a revolutionary concept in world religions."

(Brown, 2002: 51)

He also points out the inherent evil in a religious caste system:

> "This concept ... [that] only a select few had direct access to God, while the others were somehow second class, dependent on the elite leaders with their sacred titles and sacred garments ... undermined the foundations of the new community Jesus was building."

(Brown, 2002: 51)

Commenting on the models adopted early in church history, Noble states:

> "The resulting, unbiblical, division between priest and congregation meant the masses were cut off from a direct relationship with Jesus. This situation was worsened because the Bible was not readily available to combat the teachings which locked people into such unscriptural authority."

(Noble, 2002: 65)

Brown argues the case that the term "priest" relates to the old covenant, not the new, other than when it applies to *all* Christians:

> "... the gospels, Acts and Hebrews speak of 'priests' more than 160 times –as in the Jewish Temple priests, or Jesus the High Priest, or Melchizedek the priest—but never once speak of a special church officer called priest. On the other hand, the few references to priests in 1 Peter and Revelation refer to all believers as part of a holy priesthood, performing priestly functions. All believers!"

(Brown, 2002: 52)

Girard agrees with Brown's theoretical position, but points out that it is only theoretical—the practical reality is quite different:

> *"In the Spirit's design for the church, every believer is ordained a priest. St. Jerome called baptism 'the ordination of the laity.'*
>
> *Every Christian, having the Life of Christ in him, is equipped for a personal ministry to his fellow believers and to unbelievers.*
>
> *All evangelicals agree with the theory. Every college course on church history credits Martin Luther with having revived 'the priesthood of believers.' We all recognize the existence of this priesthood — except that we make no provision for it in the structure of our churches."*

(Girard, 1972: 86)

Brown argues that, in spite of centuries of clear teaching on the concept of the priesthood of all believers, we so easily follow the traditional church ways

> *"... setting up distinctions the Word does not recognize, using terms and concepts the Word is against, and putting people in special outfits and giving them special titles that only re-erect the wall that the New Testament tore down. To put it another way, if the minister is a 'reverend,' what then is the average believer? Is he or she just a believer? To say that is to negate the priesthood of every believer."*

(Brown, 2002: 53)

Patterns of hierarchies of elite rooted in the Old Testament

Rinehart puts the case that those who practice this priesthood of the elite often use Old Testament teaching to support their view, and he claims that the New Covenant has made such thinking obsolete:

> *"The real ministry, whether large or small, is often reserved for the trained professional, and 'ordinary' folks cower in the background ... A host of needs goes unmet and multitudes of believers mistakenly assume there is no place for them to serve.*
>
> *Much of this mindset originates from a faulty concept ... We're often directed to Old Testament examples as justification for the 'leader-as-superstar' model. Moses, the great deliverer ... Joshua ... the consummate military leader ...*
>
> *The significant players in the New Testament church were not superstars. Rather, they were average men and women ..."*

(Rinehart, 1998: 102-103)

> *"The advent of the Holy Spirit made the Old Testament model of leadership obsolete and a super-star mentality, at best, unnecessary."*

(Rinehart, 1998: 106)

One of the frequently applied Old Testament principles of leadership comes from the story of Moses and his father-in-law, Jethro. Moses was called by God to lead the Israelites out of Egypt and through the desert to the Promised land. Along the way,

Moses assumed the role of judge for all the people. Moses had taken the position of judging between parties, and had also taken the responsibility of communicating his understanding of God's laws to them (Exodus 18: 16), but he was getting worn out trying to be the mediator between God and a whole nation.

Jethro then comes to him with a bit of fatherly advice. Instead of rolling up his sleeves and helping Moses direct the people to God, he begins by reinforcing Moses' role as God's go-between, saying Moses must continue to represent the people before God (Exodus 18: 19). However, to lighten the load, he then goes on to advise Moses to delegate authority through a hierarchy of leaders, with Moses only actively taking responsibility for the difficult cases (Exodus 18: 22).

Hudson Taylor, like Moses before him, had taken on a role of direct interaction with every problem. As recounted in *Hudson Taylor and the China Inland Mission – The Growth of a Work of God* (the biography of Hudson Taylor as written by his son and daughter-in law), Hudson, like Moses, got his own "Jethro" advice:

> *"The burden ... of directing the work in China from a distance, as well as attending to all that had to be done at home, was very heavy. He was toiling far beyond his strength. ... two old friends ... in London ... urged the advice of Jethro–to divide among a number such responsibility as could be delegated ..."*
>
> (Taylor & Taylor, 1918: 224-225)

In spite of the common application of Old Testament practices to today's situations, Simson clearly proclaims that the New Testament model is fundamentally different:

> *"No expression of a New Testament church is ever led by just one professional 'holy man' doing the business of communicating with God and then feeding some relatively passive religious consumers Moses-style. Christianity has adopted this method from pagan religions, or at best from the Old Testament.*
>
> *The heavy professionalization of the church since Constantine has now been a pervasive influence long enough, dividing the people of God artificially into an infantilized laity and a professional clergy, and developing power-based mentalities and pyramid structures. According to the New Testament (1 Tim. 2:5), 'there is one God, and one mediator also between God and men, the man Christ Jesus.' God simply does not bless religious professionals to force themselves in between Himself and His people."*
>
> (Wolfgang Simson, in Brown, 2002: 60-61)

Christ as our only mediator?

Ezekiel 34 marks a turning point. The shepherds had abused their role, and God clearly communicated he was going to take over. In the New Testament, as previously noted, the author of Timothy takes up this theme. There is not only just one God, but there must be only one mediator between us and God, and that is Jesus Himself. But this principle is broken again and again by church leaders who try to take the place of Jesus by being mediators for the laity.

THE ISSUE OF PROFESSIONALISM

Howard Snyder's *Liberating the Church: The Ecology of Church and Kingdom* puts this principle of no mediator between God and man in his own words, stating:

> "The church is a theocracy, not a democracy. But it is not hierarchical theocracy tracing from God down a ladder to the lay peasant. Rather, it is a family in which God rules supremely, but kindly and lovingly in a way that builds and affirms each member and makes hierarchy superfluous."
>
> (Snyder, 1983, in Rinehart, 1998: 50)

Rinehart puts it even more bluntly, saying that while we talk of the ministry of all believers, some practice the ministry of the elite:

> "In power-based ministry structures ... decisions, new initiatives, and long-range direction flow down from a select few, with little input from others. An emphasis on role and position, in effect, resorts to ministry by the priesthood of the elite, not by all believers."
>
> (Rinehart, 1998: 65)

> "[God] did not raise leaders to do the holy living for the people or to do the ministry for them. [Leaders] ... tend to hold to the doctrine of the priesthood of all believers even as [they] practice the 'doctrine of the elite'."
>
> (Rinehart, 1998: 132)

Noble argues that those in the role of church leader may facilitate a subtle form of idolatry, namely worship of the local church:

> "The worst aspects of this [pastor/priest] tradition are ecclesiolatry, or worship of the church, and abuse of the sacrament as the church [leadership] comes between the people and a direct relationship to Jesus."
>
> (Noble, 2002: 75)

Plass conveys the message that church leaders can take the place of God the Father in our relationships. He begins by looking at the joyful encounter between the Prodigal son and his father, and asks:

> "Why do so few church-going people seem to have experienced that joyful collision with God?"
>
> (Plass, 1991: 54)

Plass answers his own question by *re-telling* the story of the Prodigal son, but changes it by having the son encounter a well-intentioned but "deluded one" on his way home, who falsely mimics the real father. By implication, he refers to the church leaders as "deluded ones" whose actions are a mere mimic of the real relationships we should have with God our Father. This "deluded one" gives the prodigal son an imaginary cloak, ring and calf (the same items that the real father would genuinely provide), but they are only illusions of the real thing.

> " 'Hi!' [the deluded one says to] the trudging penitent. 'Good news – you've been forgiven!'

'Great!' says the prodigal.

'Here you are', says the deluded one, and he wraps an imaginary cloak around the lad's shoulders. He mimes the action of putting a ring on his finger. Together they sit down to eat a non-existent fatted calf with invisible knives and forks.

'Isn't it wonderful!' he enthuses.

'Oh yes!' responds the prodigal, intensely relieved that he is to be forgiven so painlessly. 'Yes it is!'

They meet regularly for mime sessions. They become very proficient at mime. At last the young man manages to express a growing concern.

'The, er ... cloak and the ring and the calf – they're not actually, er ... real, are they?"

(Plass, 1991: 55-56)

When the son questions the authenticity of these items:

"His lack of faith is rebuked and disciplined. He feels guilty and unhappy. He knows the things are not really there, and he doesn't actually feel forgiven. Where is the father?"

(Plass, 1991: 56)

Plass then goes on to challenge the reader by looking at the options facing the Prodigal son whose relationship with the father has been replaced with a relationship with a well-meaning and "...*enthusiastic but deluded*" impostor:

"Eventually [the son] either settles for the troubled half-life of tediously repetitive mime sessions [i.e. church traditions], or he goes back to the pigs; or, if he's got any sense, he leaves his mime instructor [the pastor, priest, or whatever he's called] behind and moves on down the road to risk a genuine encounter with his father, who is anxiously awaiting him with a real cloak, and a real ring, and a real fatted calf.

And real forgiveness."

(Plass, 1991: 56)

Such genuine encounters have, at times in history, been actively resisted by the church leaders. Brown points out the persecution by church leaders of those who dared to translate the Bible into English so that ordinary Christians could read it for themselves, and then goes on to say:

"How could those professing to be teachers of the Bible end up in such an unbiblical state?

The answer is simple: The Church embraced the false teaching that there are two classes of believers, clergy and laity, and then took that teaching to its logical extreme. Since only the clergy were considered qualified and holy, they alone had access to the Word of God. The effects of that doctrine are still felt today, more than we would like to believe. In this critically important area, we still need a revolution ..."

(Brown, 2002: 51)

Oliver and Thwaites concede that there is a general perception of "full-time" ministers as being special, but argue that such views must be actively attacked:

> *"One friend of mine, a respected church leader, was mystified by the fact that working men and women in his church groups did not feel fully affirmed or released. I wasn't mystified at all. This same leader genuinely holds the view that so-called 'full-time leaders' have a higher call than others. They can fulfil God's purpose more, and extend his Kingdom more effectively. We have had open, frank and reasonably heated discussions on this point, but his view is sincerely held."*
>
> (Oliver & Thwaites, 2001: 209)

> *"… I want to say loud and clear: let's give the name 'full-time' to all God's people. It needs to be said again and again, until a stronghold is broken and the heel of the church at work crushes the Christian caste system. This stronghold is powerful and, like the creeping weed varieties in my garden, regularly needs uprooting."*
>
> (Oliver & Thwaites, 2001: 210)

Examples of confusion over church leaders & laity

Any attempt to reach clarity on the merits or otherwise of having a distinct class of people called the clergy is made more difficult when some spokespeople on the matter appear to have contradictory views.

As is a common practice in many books, the publishers of Henri Nouwen's book, *The Wounded Healer*, include recommendations for the book from others. These commentators carry different messages about the suggested audience (clergy or laity) who might benefit from this book. Some examples are listed below.

- '*America*' suggests the audience should incorporate both clergy *and* laity:
  "[The book] describes a style of ministry desperately needed by <u>all</u> … Since we all minister to each other, the book is well recommended to those beyond the ranks of professional clergy." [Emphasis mine]

  (Nouwen, 1972: i)

- Similarly, '*The Christian Century*' suggests
  "… this small volume should prove exciting and intelligible for <u>both clergy and laity</u>."
  [Emphasis mine]

  (Nouwen, 1972: i)

- Also '*Review for Religious*' recommends the book
  "… to all priests, sisters, and brothers as well as to all who recognize that in calling themselves Christian they are called to be ministers of healing."

  (Nouwen, 1972: ii)

- In contrast, some recommend the book specifically to the clergy. For example, '*The Record*' says:
"*I wish I could send this book to every <u>seminary, rectory and parsonage</u> in the country*" [Emphasis mine]

(Nouwen, 1972: ii)

- The '*Virginia Kirkus Service*' seems to mix its message:
"*[The author's argument is based on]... the humanity <u>common to minister and believer</u> [yet they recommend it is] ... for use by <u>clergymen, both Catholic and Protestant</u>.*" [Emphasis mine]

(Nouwen, 1972: ii)

The above extracts relate to the views of those who are quoted as recommending Nouwen's book. Now we look at extracts from Nouwen himself. On the one hand, Nouwen portrays a counseling situation and concludes that such ministry

"*... is not just a possibility to be actualized by a well-trained theologian, but the responsibility of every Christian.*"

Nouwen (1972: 70)

On the other hand, in the introduction, Nouwen (1972: xv) is clearly targeting the book at those who "minister" and later expands on the term "minister" by explicitly referring to ministers as those in

"*... the ministerial profession itself.*"

(Nouwen, 1972: 83)

He appears to be talking about recognized church leaders (pastors, priests ...), not ordinary people in "ministry".

His conclusion after the last chapter carries mixed messages, too. Nouwen recognizes that

"*... there are many ways and forms in which a [regular, ordinary member of the laity] can be a Christian.*"

Nouwen (1972: 99)

Yet, in spite of the above statement, Nouwen seems to portray the lay people as being in need of a professional minister to help them in their search for God. He asserts:

"*The minister is the one who can make [each man's] search for authenticity possible*"

Nouwen (1972: 99)

Does it follow that it is impossible for each man to search for authenticity without the guidance of a "minister"? It would appear that Nouwen thinks so.

Are we all equal, but some more equal than others? It would seem that some believe this oxymoron to be true.

THE ISSUE OF PROFESSIONALISM

Hudson Taylor, in his work in sharing the Gospel in China, both practiced and preached the merits of using laity in front-line ministry. He notes the important work initiated spontaneously by lay people:

> "It was a day of new departures in the development of lay agency, and a striking fulfilment might be seen in many directions of the prophecy of Joel: 'Also upon the servants and the handmaids in those days I will pour out my Spirit.'
>
> To mention a few only of the evangelical movements that had their beginnings in that formative time: Mrs. Ranyard was pioneering in a way for the work of Biblewomen, and Mrs. Bayley for that of Mothers' Meetings; Miss Macpherson had just commenced Gospel services in Bird Fair, and the rescue of little waifs from the lowest slums of London; Miss Robarts, Mr. (afterwards Sir George) Williams, and others, were laying the foundations of the Young Men's and Young Women's Christian Associations; Mrs. Daniels and her helpers were developing work for soldiers, with their special needs; and Mr. and Mrs. Pennefather, at Mildmay, were launching out in the training of Deaconesses for all manner of home missions. All these were making use of the consecrated energies of young converts in their first love, many of them comparatively 'unlearned and ignorant men,' but no opening had as yet been found for a similar employment of lay agency on the foreign field.
>
> 'When travelling in England, Scotland, and the north of Ireland in 1859 and '60,' wrote a Christian leader from the Continent, 'I repeatedly asked myself, 'where is the channel through which simple-hearted labourers brought to Christ through these remarkable Revivals, wishing to devote themselves to missionary work in foreign lands may reach their object?' But I found no such channel. All the colleges for missionary training require a preliminary education which one would seek in vain in youths of this sort. ...'
>
> ... Christian hearts were ... awakened to the fact that God by His Holy Spirit was using a class of workers hitherto largely excluded from spiritual ministries of the Church."
>
> (Taylor & Taylor, 1918: 48-49)

While the above related largely to the work of other groups, the same principles of joining with good-hearted people, independent of formal training or even recognized talent, applied also to Taylor's work:

> "Duncan was not specially gifted or cultured, but he possessed grit and perseverance and a great love for souls."
>
> (Taylor & Taylor, 1918: 120)

> "Because the pioneers were for the most part young, at the beginning only of their missionary life, it was argued that it could not be right to use them in work so difficult and important. Undoubtedly they were ignorant and inexperienced as compared with older missionaries, especially with the able men to be found in the foremost ranks of other societies. No one would have been more thankful than Mr. Taylor to have seen such workers take the field. But they were all needed, more than needed

> *in their actual posts. There was no suggestion that some or any of them should be set free, though China was accessible at last, from end to end, to preachers of the Gospel. Was, then, no one to go because they could not send the best? Mr. Taylor had good reason to believe that these young workers had been given in answer to prayer, and that the hand of God was in the coincidence of their being ready, on the spot, when the Gates of the West were thrown open. He was doing all he could to liberate experienced missionaries, and was thankful to have reliable Chinese Christians to send with the younger evangelists. Experience, he well knew, would be one of the great gains that would come to them as they pursued their task; and meanwhile, if they were not burdened with much knowledge, which often spells discouragement, they had the health and hopefulness of youth; the buoyancy of body, mind, and spirit which is in itself so great a gift. If only their critics, and they were many, could come nearer – could meet and know the men in question, and hear from their own lips of the wonderful opportunities God was giving – objections, he had no doubt, would give place to sympathy."*

(Taylor & Taylor, 1918: 292-293)

Taylor also noted the same set of beliefs in another famous missionary, William Burns, who saw

> "...evangelism as the great work of the Church, and the order of lay-evangelists as a lost order that Scripture required to be restored ..."

(Taylor & Taylor, 1911: 381)

Yet in spite of all these outspoken claims on seeing God's hand on the ordinary laity, and Taylor's willingness to accept any workers whether ordained or not, he appeared to exhibit a bias as

> "... ordained men were specially asked for."

(Taylor & Taylor, 1918: 496)

Why were ordained men "specially" asked for? If the answer is because they were "special", aren't we again slipping into the mistaken belief that we are all equal but some especially so?

I highly recommend Stacy Rinehart's book on "upside down" leadership. He exposes the flaws of a culture where Christian leaders are often self-serving rather than serving the people. There can be no confusion as to the view held by Rinehart; he clearly teaches that those in leadership are there to serve:

> *"In servant leadership, serving is the expression of leadership, regardless of how people follow. Serving is both the end as well as the means."*

(Rinehart, 1998: 41)

Rinehart warns of the subtle way some leaders try to cloak their desire to have the laity serving them by in fact claiming the opposite—that they, as leaders, are there to serve:

> "... servant leadership is a popular term today in both business and power-oriented ministry worlds. But often those who speak and write about it focus on the second word: servant **leadership**. Viewed with this emphasis, serving is simply a means to an end: 'I'll serve you, so you'll respect my leadership and follow me. I prime the pump, so you will deliver.' This is just another subtle form of power leadership."
>
> (Rinehart, 1998: 41)

I like Rinehart's book. However, I suspect there is a danger introduced by his phrase "servant leadership". I have concerns for two reasons.

Firstly, dictionary definitions and common usage for words like "lead", "leader", and "leadership" include terms such as the "chief", the "most important", a "director", the "boss", the "principal", and the person "in control" or "in charge". I believe that Rinehart most definitely does not want to convey any such meaning as the target for servant leadership.

Rather, it is my understanding that he wishes to convey the message that a servant leader is nothing more than one who shows initiative, and who demonstrates ministry by example, rather than leading by control. This is in fact another valid dictionary meaning for leadership, where, as one Oxford dictionary puts it, to lead is to "... *draw along or ... [serve] as a guide ...*", or to motivate by one's example. While Rinehart does not portray "servant leaders" as those who dictate or are seen to be the most important, I suggest that the variations in the meaning of the word "leadership" run the risk of carrying a message other than that he intended.

Secondly, I have encountered several church leaders who declare themselves to be servants, but are not. It's a bit like the oxymoron of those who boast of their humility. A church leader who proclaims to be a "servant leader" but who expects others to serve his or her vision is living in contradiction to the image he or she wishes to portray.

So while I applaud many of the themes in Rinehart's book, I recommend we avoid his phrase of "servant leadership" as I suggest it may be a source of confusion, especially to those who do not deeply research his writings. Perhaps we could describe those who serve as God leads, and who inspire others by their service, simply as "servants"? After all, as recorded in Luke 17:9-10, Jesus seems to suggest that if we serve God in everything He may ask of us, we still may not expect any title fancier than just "servant".

The core question – are *you* obeying God, or man?

Now the debate on the value or otherwise of a clergy / laity distinction gets personal. Apart from all the theories about the "priesthood of all believers", how do *you* relate to God, and how do *you* look at church leaders? Put very bluntly, do you relate to God directly, seeking His call on your life? Or do you go via a church leader (or any other person for that matter, such as spiritual mentors or spiritual guides) as your mediator?

Hunt's novel appears to portray Abel as a pastor who arrogantly led the laity. For example, as a pastor, he *seems* to listen to his members' views:

> "... Abel will nod ... and thank the gentlemen for their concern."
>
> (Hunt, 2004: 71)

However, behind this pretense at listening to the opinions of the members, he

> "... of course, will proceed exactly as he feels the Lord wants him to proceed. There's a fine art in leading a church – the pastor is the shepherd, Abel says, and while the sheep may love to bleat and baa and balk, the shepherd is responsible to the One who owns the sheep."
>
> (Hunt, 2004: 71-72)

He gets away with his arrogant leadership because

> "... though [the 'sheep' i.e. the local church laity] are not the brightest animals on earth ... they will do almost anything to follow the shepherd they have learned to trust."
>
> (Hunt, 2004: 72)

The pastor's assumed position of mediator between God and man is eventually challenged by his wife, who says,

> "... the purpose of parenting is to teach children how to think for themselves. And you can't shepherd your flock forever – sooner or later people have to follow Jesus and learn to listen for his voice."
>
> (Hunt, 2004: 262)

The pastor's wife realizes that the people often blindly obey their pastor. She also comes to realize that she has assumed her role also is to simply follow his directives. Now she challenges her husband's right to lead the people, as well as questioning his right to lead her:

> "[As the pastor's wife,] I thought I had honed the Christian walk to an art form. I was living a blameless life, working in the ministry, serving a church and a godly husband, doing my part ...
>
> But who had called me. Jesus or Abel [my husband, the pastor]? When Abel proposed [marriage], did I automatically transfer my allegiance to him? He is a godly man, a wonderful pastor ...
>
> But Abel is not my Lord ...
>
> I love my husband ... but I can no longer seek Abel's will when I should be seeking my Savior's and listening for his holy voice."
>
> (Hunt, 2004: 309-310)

While expressing her love for her husband, she stresses the need for all to follow Jesus, not the pastor:

> "I love you, Abel. I know you are a righteous man who loves God. I know you try to do your best to lead the flock. But you know what? You're a sheep, too. Though the

> lambs can learn a lot from you … they have to … learn to follow Jesus. He's the true Shepherd."
>
> (Hunt, 2004: 313)

Then she cuts to the core issue, namely that in the final analysis she must be obedient to God and follow His call, not the call as seen by her husband.

> " 'I disobeyed the Spirit, Abel. … I heard him, and I ignored him. And now I'm wondering how many other times I've ignored him …'
>
> 'You've always followed Christ.' Abel speaks in the raspy voice of frustration. 'We've spent twenty-four years praying together, being a team –'
>
> 'We've spent twenty-four years following your vision, Abel. My prayers have been echoes of yours; my goals have always been whatever you put on my to-do list. I think it's time I asked the Lord what he wants me to do.'
>
> 'He wants you to keep on being the way you are [i.e. a submissive pastor's wife].'
>
> 'No – he doesn't. He wants me to look back to where I've come from. I know that world, and I know how to help the people who are mired in it [i.e. she discovers a personal call, different to the vague role of being a 'pastor's wife']."
>
> (Hunt, 2004: 314)

This practice of having a mere person act as a go-between effectively means that the church leaders are taking the place of God in the lives of those who unquestioningly follow the leader's vision. And the laity who follow them are allowing and even encouraging the leaders to take this position!

Hunt's fiction portrays a people looking to their human leader for direction, saying,

> "Thunderous applause fills the room at each thump of Abel's lectern, and I know these people are thrilled to be getting a sneak peek at what God is planning to do through their church and their prophet."
>
> (Hunt, 2004: 69)

While Hunt (above) provides a cynical view of mindless followers, some authors blatantly and openly preach a philosophy of blind obedience. Brown quotes from Bevere's book, Under Cover, where Bevere takes the position that:

> "It doesn't matter what you believe you've heard in prayer: you are rebelling against God's authority if it goes against the directives of authorities in your life!"
>
> (Brown, 2002: 216)

From my reading of Brown's book, it seems that Bevere believes you can disobey authorities only if

> "… they tell us to do something that <u>directly contradicts what God has stated in His Word</u>." [Emphasis mine]
>
> (Brown, 2002: 216)

However, as Brown points out, Bevere's teaching fails to address

> "... *issues of conscience or the clear directives of the Holy Spirit ...*"
>
> (Brown, 2002: 216)

Brown then goes on to say,

> "*Such statements do not factor in verses such as Romans 14:23, which teaches that whatever is not done in faith is sin. If a leader tells a congregant, therefore, to do something that violates his or her conscience and cannot be done in faith, that leader is actually telling the congregant to sin. Also, doesn't the Word itself teach us that there are certain times when we must obey God rather than man? If a leader tells a believer to disregard what the Spirit has spoken to him and submit to the leader's directives, that leader is telling the believer to disobey the Word.*"
>
> (Brown, 2002: 216)

Rinehart exposes the dangers of power-based hierarchies that not only practice authoritative direction-giving, but also try to make people feel guilty for even questioning this style:

> "*In a power-based structure, the real voice of authority comes from some combination of the leaders and the ministry structures they represent. The focus is on the leaders, who alone are charged with hearing from God and discerning direction for the ministry. The leaders filter God's voice and in turn make demands on the people to fulfill their vision. The people end up serving the leadership and the structure. In a power-based ministry structure, questioning the leadership is a guilt-ridden exercise that comes uncomfortably close to questioning God.*"
>
> (Rinehart, 1998: 64-65)

Some authors teach as a principle the expectation of obedience by the laity to the church leaders, while others clearly warn against this approach. And others seem to muddy the waters. The authors of *Invading Secular Space* start well; the Body of Christ will be effective when *all* its members are empowered by the Holy Spirit:

> "*The power of the church is the Holy Spirit working in and through all of God's people ...*" [Emphasis mine]
>
> (Robinson & Smith, 2003: 144)

But the sentence above is followed by the claim that this empowering ministry is actually dependent on

> "...*the empowering ministry of people called leaders, whom Christ has given to his people.*" [Emphasis mine]
>
> (Robinson & Smith, 2003: 144)

Surely it is the Holy Spirit who provides the "*empowering ministry*", not leaders. And the Holy Spirit does not require that the church leaders "empower" the regular members before those He calls can act on His orders!

Jesus clearly taught that we should not call anyone "father" as a title of respect (Matthew 23:9). Yet many church leaders demand such respect. Some do it blatantly by their titles, others by implication in their assumed role of "spiritual father". Examples of this type of teaching follow.

Firstly, we look at Hudson Taylor. His claim is that each individual Christian is not only shaped by his or her "spiritual" parent, but can never rise beyond the spiritual level of this "parent":

> *"What the spiritual children will be depends on what the spiritual father is. …*
> *The stream will never rise higher than its source, but it will not fall far short of it,*
> *circumstances permitting."*
>
> (Taylor & Taylor, 1918: 404)

If we follow Taylor's argument through to its logical conclusion, the followers of Christ are, by each generation, becoming less and less mature. If no one can ever exceed the maturity of their leader/mentor, then whatever level of maturity in Christ was shown in (say) the apostle Peter, then none of the thousands who were converted through his ministry could surpass him, and their converts in turn must be even less effective. Two thousand years later, we must be pretty poor specimens. It is obviously blatant foolishness to hold to such thinking.

And the flaw in the argument perhaps turns on the implication behind the phrase, *"The stream will never rise higher than its source"*. If the source of our growth is always totally none other than the person who introduced us to Christ, maybe Taylor is right. But if the source is God Himself, of course we may achieve far greater things than the mere man or woman who may have introduced us to *the* source.

Noble goes further, saying it is the role of church leaders to actively seek those who are "*orphans*" and ensure they have "*fathers*":

> *"… many today do not even know their biological parents and sense no need of*
> *spiritual ones. They have no identity, no one to respect. So, [spiritual] fathers must seek*
> *out the orphans inside and outside the church …"*
>
> (Noble, 2002: 122)

Once a church leader has attained the role of "spiritual father", Noble appears to claim that they are then entitled to discipline their spiritual children:

> *"This tension of respect and affection should be welcomed in our relationships with our*
> *… spiritual fathers – it's healthy!*
>
> *… Leaders should conduct themselves in a way which expresses genuine friendship*
> *and affection, whilst <u>maintaining the right to bring correction</u> in love."* [Emphasis mine]
>
> (Noble, 2002: 119-120)

Thankfully, there are those who speak out on the dangers of such teaching, reminding us that, in a spiritual sense, we have but one Father, who is God:

> *"We must be careful not to fall into the trap of looking to any human ministry organization – whether a church or parachurch – as a father figure to give us security or significance. No one can provide us with a truly safe harbor except the Lord."*
>
> (Rinehart, 1998: 154)

If the objections are so strong, why do we still have professional church leaders?

There are many voices, and have been for centuries, that have spoken out against the concept of a separate class for church leaders. So why do we still have church leaders? One cynical and obvious answer might be that the church leaders have power and influence in and over the local churches, and why would they speak out against the very role that gives them that power, prestige and money? But other than that answer (or perhaps in addition to that answer), what other reasons might there be for the on-going existence of church leaders as a class?

Laity want a professional who will do "it" for them

Just as the people cried out for Moses to "do it for them", so it is today. One sad reality is that many laity *want* the professionals. At one extreme, there appear to be people who are happy to toss in a few coins on a Sunday, and think they've done their bit—the rest is up to the professionals whom they have paid to do the religious stuff. They feel that they are now absolved of any further personal responsibility, and can leave it to those "professionals". So the best they can do is to try and find the most worthy possible leader to support, based on secular selection standards. Cymbala states,

> *"[When] we select leaders ... we go by resumes, seniority, image, education, and a half-dozen other human criteria."*
>
> (Cymbala, 1997: 181)

But there are also people who genuinely want to see the Kingdom of God advanced, and would be willing to sacrifice through active involvement, but simply feel unworthy. After all, they haven't been to Bible College, and they are told that the "real" ministers are full-time. They feel they aren't up to the mark.

This attitude is so ingrained. We think that if we want to serve God, the "best" way is to become a "minister". In my home town, an episode of the American serial, *7th Heaven*, was aired in 2001, where Lucy announces she wants to become a "minister". Her father, Eric, is a minister of religion. On his birthday, he is honored by many of the people he has ministered to through the years. Earlier in the episode, Lucy lovingly reaches through a wall of pain to a lady who hasn't spoken since her husband's death many years ago. She "ministers" to this lady. The show had many moving aspects. However, for me, I wanted to cry out to Lucy, "Can't you see that you already *are* a minister? You don't have to be ordained to become what you already are!"

Church leaders' pride in their role

Laity may feel unworthy to minister. Conversely, too many ministers take pride in their presumed ability to minister better than mere laity. Moody exposes this flawed thinking, starting by looking at the humility of John the Baptist:

> "One of the meekest characters in history was John the Baptist. You remember when a deputation was sent to him and asked if he was Elias, or this prophet, or that prophet, he said, 'No.' Now he might have said some very flattering things of himself. He might have said:
>
>> 'I am the son of the old priest Zacharias. Have you not heard of my fame as a preacher? I have baptized more people probably, than any man living. The world has never seen a preacher like myself.'
>
> I honestly believe that in the present day most men standing in his position would do that. ... [But John's attitude was different.]
>
> 'John,' they asked, 'who are you?'
>
> 'I am nobody. I am to be heard, not to be seen. I am only a voice. ...
>
> There cometh one mightier than I after me, the latchet of whose shoes I am not worthy to stoop down and unloose.' Think of that; and bear in mind that Christ was looked upon as a deceiver, a village carpenter, and yet here is John, the son of the old priest, who had a much higher position in the sight of men than that of Jesus. Great crowds were coming to hear him, and even Herod attended his meetings. ...
>
> [John went even further, stating,] '[Christ] must increase, but I must decrease.'"

(Moody, circa 1890: 85-87)

Having introduced John's humility, Moody then contrasts this with the pride of many church leaders, especially church leaders who like to be addressed in a manner that reflects their title:

> "Let us now turn the light upon ourselves. Have we been decreasing of late? Do we think less of ourselves and of our position than we did a year ago? ... Are we wanting to hold on to some title, and are we offended because we are not treated with the courtesy that we think is due to us? Some time ago I heard a man in the pulpit say that he should take offence if he was not addressed by his title. My dear friend, are you going to take that position that you must have a title ...? John did not want any title, and when we are right with God, we shall not be caring about titles."

(Moody, circa 1890: 87-88)

Although Moody's criticisms were made in the 1800s, I suspect that his concerns could be equally applied to many church leaders today.

A modernized republication of Sheldon's 19th century classic, *Jesus is Here*, several times and in different ways, exalts the role of the church leaders:

"I never felt so <u>proud</u> of being a minister and a church member as I do at this minute." [Emphasis mine]

(Sheldon, 1999: 242)

"[Jesus] was up there smiling, glad, triumphant, revealing to that gathering of tired, discouraged, bewildered, and even self-satisfied pastors and people the <u>grandeur of their call</u> ..." [Emphasis mine]

(Sheldon, 1999: 113-114)

The above two quotations share the glory across the leaders and the members. But then he singles out the ministers for special recognition:

"Do you realize what courage and power ... Jesus put into the ministers?"

(Sheldon, 1999: 131)

Philips' novel, *Dawn of Liberty*, subtly challenges these views of the superiority of the church leaders. It is often in fiction that people draw caricatures that seem laughable and larger-than-life. Then we stop and realize that perhaps they are very close to the truth.

Philips sets the scene with East and West Germany reunited, and former Iron Curtain countries now open to the Gospel. And along comes Darrell Montgomery, an arrogant, know-it-all leader who headed an organization that had

"... undertaken grandiose new methods to proclaim the gospel to every creature."

(Phillips, 1995:123)

His goal obviously has a scriptural basis. It's just that his methods were based on an assumption that he, above all others, knew the best way to achieve that goal.

But it was not just that one leader who suffered from an over-sized ego. By and large, all the speakers were presented as having the same issue.

"Notwithstanding the seeming rightness of it all, Matthew could not help but detect a spirit of self-promotion in the whole thing. Most of the speakers he had heard thus far used every opportunity to plug their own vision and program and books and tapes and products. All in the name of the gospel, of course. But there was such a sense of 'My way is best so all the rest of you ought to jump in and support what I am doing.'"

(Phillips, 1995: 199)

All of this focus on the leaders contrasts starkly with the way things should be. Brown notes:

"... if you asked a Greek-speaking believer in the first century, 'Who is your pastor?' his most natural response would be 'Jesus!' He is called the Good Shepherd (Pastor!), the Great Shepherd (Pastor!) and the Chief Shepherd (Pastor!); see John 10:14; Hebrews 13:20; 1 Peter 5:4."

(Brown, 2002: 220)

But today's pastors want to be recognized as *the* "shepherd" of *their* sheep.

THE ISSUE OF PROFESSIONALISM

Church leaders' pride in their titles ("Pastor", "Father", etc.)

One way the church leaders' pride in their roles is apparent is in their use of titles. Again and again, I have encountered pastors who introduce themselves as "Pastor Smith", or "Pastor Jeff", etc. And of course, their faithful followers also use the same form.

But does the pastor introduce his plumber as "Plumber Anderson". If not, there's a distinction of rank within the Body, and that goes against the Bible's teaching in Matthew 23:8-10, where Jesus clearly directs us to avoid the use of terms such as "Father" or "Teacher". And His reasoning? We are all equal as brothers, so we should not assign titles of respect to others within the Body of Christ based on their role, leaving titles such as Father for God and Teacher for Jesus Himself.

A pastor once told me that the reason he wanted to be called "Pastor Peter" was so that any visitor would know who to come to for assistance. That attitude seems to carry an implied message, namely that the leaders alone are the ones to provide "assistance" to enquirers. Surely God should not need permission to use *any* person there.

To assume that only a leader could be used in such a way is prideful. Foster argues that many people equate titles and position with power, but that the Bible teaches that real power comes from God, and the New Testament story is one of people without titles or training who nonetheless exercised real power. This perplexed the religious and political leaders who had positions and titles, but didn't have the power to stop the unlearned disciples.

> *"[The disciples] had no degrees, no titles of distinction, no human authorisation. Since their ability (power) came from God, human authorisation was irrelevant. Hence their authority flew in the face of the vested interests of those in power. Since the disciples had no need to be authorised, they could not be controlled."*
>
> (Foster, 1985: 615)

Phillips' novel *Mercy and Eagleflight* portrays the main character as realizing the pride behind religious titles:

> *"Reverend and Evangelist and Brother and Sister – they were all just labels to make us look spiritual and pious ... I don't want to even think of being called [by a special title] now, as if I were a special and more spiritual person than someone else. I'm not. I never was, and the very thought of how long I pretended to be makes me sorry."*
>
> (Phillips, 1996: 150)

Ackoff states that not all who are given rank and title are worthy of this recognition, and further, their use of title reflects more on the way they see themselves than how others necessarily regard them!

> *"The characteristics of a position or title that induces people to respect its occupant or holder is its uniqueness and the difficulty involved in getting it. Unfortunately, people can rise to respected positions without having any of the personal properties that we respect. Nevertheless, we are then expected to respect them because we do not know*

how to distinguish between respect for an individual and respect for the position he/she holds.

Degrees and titles, like uniforms, are better reflections of how their bearers feel about themselves than of how others feel about them."

(Ackoff, 1991: 179)

Yet in spite of outspoken criticism of the use of titles, the church leaders by-and-large continue to bask in the perceived respect associated with the titles assigned to them (or even assigned by themselves).

It "pays" to be a pastor

There are perhaps at least two major interpretations of the word, "professional". One is that the person is good at what they do. One might say that a retired carpenter "is a real professional", even though they no longer earn money from their trade. Sometimes the recognition as a "professional" is associated with a person's formal training or career, but at other times it is simply recognition of a job well done.

Another meaning relates to the payment for work done. My understanding is that many years ago, the Olympic Games were reserved for non-professionals—for example, if an athlete was paid money to play tennis, they could not compete in the Olympic Games. This rule has been changed, perhaps due in part to the efforts they went to in order to earn money but not have it classified as professional income. Whatever the reasoning, the fact remains that one meaning for "professional" is that the person is paid money to do a job.

This latter interpretation is at the heart of this section. Should there be a "professional" church leadership class? Does the fact that many church leaders get paid to do their "job" compromise the whole ministry of the church leaders, and accentuate the distinction between church leaders and the laity?

Alcoholics Anonymous (in *Twelve Steps and Twelve Traditions*) also grappled with the question of payment for service. Their program has a twelve-step process for restoration to health. The early steps relate to such things as honesty to oneself, and sorting out one's relationships with others and with God. The last step involves outreach to fellow sufferers. One could, perhaps, classify that as "ministry". But it is not ministry by professional counselors, and by this I use both meanings of the word. You don't wait until you have completed a social worker degree, or a degree in psychology, before you reach out. And you don't do it to get paid for the "ministry".

In contrast to A.A., although members do not receive payment for outreach to other alcoholics as part of their "twelfth step" of recovery, that does not mean that they cannot get paid to take a job as a secretary, or cleaner, or whatever, doing work for the A.A. organization. It's just that they don't get paid to "minister" the message of hope to others.

"When we had agreed that the Twelfth Step couldn't be sold for money, we had been wise. But when we had declared that our Fellowship couldn't hire service workers nor

could any A.A. member carry our knowledge into other fields, we were taking the counsel of fear, fear which today has largely dispelled in the light of experience."

(AAWS, 1953: 167)

"If we hired an alcoholic [to answer phones, pack mail ...] he'd receive only what we'd have to pay a nonalcoholic for the same job. The job was not to do Twelfth Step work; it was to make Twelfth Step work possible. It was a service proposition, pure and simple."

(AAWS, 1953: 168)

Alcoholics Anonymous recognized that while employment to do cleaning (for example) could be a job taken by anyone, some paid jobs did require a level of knowledge of the problem of alcoholism:

"... we couldn't employ nonalcoholics as secretaries; we had to have people who knew the A.A. pitch."

(AAWS, 1953: 168)

So while Alcoholics Anonymous members *and* those outside of A.A. could be employed for jobs that did not require knowledge of alcoholism, only Alcoholics Anonymous members could be employed where some personal knowledge of alcoholism was required. But members were *never* to be employed to "minister":

"For our purpose, we have discovered that at the point of professionalism money and spirituality do not mix."

(AAWS, 1957: 115)

Further, Alcoholics Anonymous made the observation that those receiving ministry (i.e. other alcoholics) were much less likely to listen to the message of someone who gets paid for his or her message!

"Alcoholics simply will not listen to a paid twelfth-stepper. Almost from the beginning, we have been positive that face-to-face work with the alcoholic who suffers could be based only on the desire to help and be helped. When an A.A. talks for money, whether at a meeting or to a single newcomer, it can have a very bad effect on him, too. The money motive compromises him and everything he says and does for his prospect. This has always been so obvious that only a very few A.A.'s have ever worked the Twelfth Step for a fee."

(AAWS, 1953: 166)

If we applied these principles to many local churches, the volunteer laity working in the local church office would get paid, and the "minister" would not! But I suspect that the paid church leaders wouldn't be supportive of losing their income, or of giving it to someone else!

CHAPTER 7:
THE ISSUE OF CONTROL

We have looked at one reason why the church leaders might wish to retain the status quo reflected in a clear separation between church leadership and the laity—they may simply want to guard their "professional" status. But now we address perhaps the most telling issue of all church leader / laity issues, the dimension of "control". They see their leadership role as being quite distinct. One could hope they do their job and leave the laity alone to do theirs. Unfortunately, the clergy can and often do try to control the actions and even thoughts of the laity.

Lord Acton stated:

> *"Power tends to corrupt, and absolute power corrupts absolutely."*
>
> John Emerich Edward Dalberg Acton

The United States president, Abraham Lincoln, also warned of the dangers of power when he said,

> *"If you want to test a man's character, give him power."*
>
> Abraham Lincoln

The church leaders often exercise power, both openly, and covertly. Has it corrupted the relationship they have with laity?

The problem of "control" in local churches

Unfortunately, many church leaders would fail Lincoln's test, and the damage resulting from the abuse of their power is enormous, holding God's people back from what they could be:

> *"… one of the greatest hindrances to Church revolution in our day [is] … the abuse of spiritual authority. This power-mongering, controlling mentality stands against liberty*

in the Spirit, against forward progress in the things of God, against the prophetic word from heaven, against dynamic spiritual growth and vitality. It must be confronted and dismantled."

(Brown, 2002: 86)

Rinehart suggests that these abusive structures can exist only when we suppress the recognition that every believer must have a direct and personal relationship with God, uncontrolled by others:

"A power structure is the only alternative if we remove Christ as authority in the minds of individual believers ... Without the priesthood of believers, where each person must listen and respond to the Lord, a vacuum develops; it will fill up with the abuse of authority and control."

(Rinehart, 1998: 65)

An example of where church leaders overrule God's Spirit speaking to an individual is presented by Tillapaugh, who portrays a scenario where an individual has the gifting and a clear calling to minister to refugees, but the church leaders have other ideas:

"If the church doesn't enable that person to minister to refugees but elects them, instead, to a kitchen committee, that church is disobeying the command that supercedes all commands."

(Tillapaugh, 1982: 128)

Finally, Brown takes us back to the standards of Jesus Himself, exposing the cancer that hides behind hierarchical structures in churches. He quotes Viola as stating:

"What Jesus is condemning in these passages [Matthew 20:25-28, Luke 22:25-27] is not oppressive leaders as such, but the hierarchical form of leadership that dominates the Gentile world... What is the hierarchical form of leadership? It is the leadership style that is rooted in the benighted idea that power and authority flow from the top down in a chain-of-command social structure. The hierarchical leadership style is based on a worldly concept of power. This explains why it is endemic to all traditional bureaucracies, from the vicious forms of liege-lord and master-slave relationships to the highly stylized and regulated spheres of modern military and corporate America."

(Brown, 2002: 217)

So what does "control" look like when it exists?

Firstly we must recognize that, even though it is so much a part of the fabric of secular systems, it has fundamental dangers:

"Command-and-control management styles both derive from and reinforce bureaucracy, power tripping and an overall culture of paranoia."

(Levine, Locke, Searls and Weinberger, 2000: xv)

Maybe if it was only present outside of the Kingdom of God, then God's people would stand in stark contrast to the power politics of the world. Unfortunately, this disease of abusive control is widespread throughout Christendom. Just as one example, we look at the foundations of the Salvation Army (even its name reflects the military-like command and control structures just mentioned by Levine et al). At an annual conference of the Mission that William Booth led, he gained:

> "… formal acceptance of the General Superintendent's [i.e. his] supreme authority."
>
> (Hattersley, 2000: 222)

Hattersley notes that Booth's success in achieving a position of "supreme authority" is ironic in that it

> "… was in conflict with the democratic traditions of the Methodism which William Booth had adopted."
>
> (Hattersley, 2000: 222)

More and more, the people under Booth's influence looked to him and his appointed leadership team, rather than looking to God directly and personally. This shift in focus from God to the leaders was highlighted in a report where Catherine Booth speaks of sending their daughter for overseas service, referring to this daughter's role as that of a "savior". The focus had shifted from Jesus as savior, to one of Booth's daughters in the role of savior. Yet Catherine Booth says of her daughter's role:

> "But, oh, the joy and honour of giving her to be the <u>saviour</u> of those sin-stricken masses." [Emphasis mine]
>
> (Hattersley, 2000: 288)

The controlling actions and practices of the Booths contrast with the standard set by Oliver and Thwaites for leaders:

> "… leaders must become aware, apart from the latest book on leadership [they] have read, that [they] are not in charge of the church as fullness. It has no king except Jesus and needs no king except Jesus. It does need servants, but it does not need managers pretending to be servants."
>
> (Oliver & Thwaites, 2001: 94-95)

Booth's dictatorial style was blatant, but as Rinehart explains, the control mechanisms of others can be subtle:

> "Control takes many insidious forms. Pressuring people into conformity, shaming their lack of performance, rewarding only what meets our standards, withholding relationship – these are some of the common ways we manipulate with illegitimate control. … In so doing, we assume the role of the Holy Spirit in people's lives."
>
> (Rinehart, 1998: 54)

Girard opposes such control strategies, and tells a true and refreshing story that exhibits the willingness of some with perceived authority to stand aside and let God deal with individuals.

"One of our growing new Christians had been reading an evangelical magazine and ran across a little article about dancing. Within minutes the parsonage phone was ringing. Audrey [Girard's wife] answered. The lady on the line immediately asked, 'Is it really wrong for a Christian to dance?'

She was a little chagrined when Audrey refused a direct answer. 'Look,' Audrey told her, 'I know it would be easy for both of us if I just answered 'yes' or 'no.' But that wouldn't help you to learn how to walk in the Spirit. It would only impose my convictions on you. If all you want is a set of rules, you might as well [follow a religion that dictates what you must do]. If you are honestly willing to do what God wants you to do in this area of your life, you can pray about it, read your Bible (Audrey listed one or two appropriate passages for her to read) and the Holy Spirit will show you what His answer is.' She did and He did."

(Girard, 1972: 25)

Catalysts for controlling structures

In *The Spontaneous Multiplication of Churches*, George Patterson gives us an insight into the problem of abusive control through his classifications of three levels of authority. The first level of authority he identifies relates to direct commands from God Himself such as commands to repent, to love, and to pray. These commands

"... *carry all the authority of Heaven.*"

(Patterson, in Winter et. al. 1981: 611)

The next level of authority he identifies relates to apostolic practices. Examples include holding possessions in common, laying hands on new believers, and serving the Lord's Supper frequently in homes. While these practices may be instructive, they

"... *carry only the authority of their example.*"

(Patterson, in Winter et. al. 1981: 611)

His final classification relates to human customs which include what each of us choose to practice but should not expect of others. He notes that

"*Only Christ has the authority to ordain what [people in local] churches must do.*"

(Patterson, in Winter et. al. 1981: 611)

Not even Paul or Peter in the past, nor our church leaders today, have the authority to "ordain what [we] must do". Patterson then states:

"*Nearly all church divisions and quarrels come from someone requiring [adherence to] apostolic practices or human customs ... as though they were divine commands ..."*

(Patterson, in Winter et. al. 1981: 611)

This, surely, shines a spotlight on the root of much abuse of power. Some church leaders dictate that the practices of the apostles, or past church leaders, or even themselves, set the standard by which all laity must abide.

But one may well question how such authoritarian practices sneak into churches, especially if the dangers of controlling structures are so well recognized in some quarters, and if the teaching of Jesus so clearly condemns the world's system of power hierarchies. The blunt answer is that some laity and a lot of church leaders want it that way!

The people want a leader!

Rinehart points out that the desire of the masses to have someone to lead them is an ancient problem, and one that has always got in the way, and continues to get in the way, of our relationship with God:

> *"Part of the pressure to lead from a position of authority and control comes from the very people we are meant to serve. All of us, at one time or another, will run into the same human cry that Samuel heard in the day of the judges. 'Give us a king!' the people demanded (1 Samuel 8:5-6). God was the one who was their King, but the Israelites insisted they must have someone in the flesh.*
>
> *That cry still rings out today. People gravitate toward a human personality in whom they can put their trust. It's easier that way. They assume a pseudo parent-child relationship with the leader who will think and choose for them. This is the motivation behind that common tendency to 'put someone on a pedestal.' If we can convince ourselves that a leader is not like us – human, flawed, dependent on God and others – then we can follow his vision without stopping to wait on the Lord ourselves."*
>
> (Rinehart, 1998: 154-155)

Buckingham observes that the expectations of the laity shape the training provided for church leaders, attempting to equip them to be super-leaders, capable of anything. And pity help the leader who doesn't measure up to this unrealistic expectation!

> *"Seminaries often teach young ministers that the pastor of a church needs to be a 'well-rounded' person. The minister, we were taught, should not only preach; he should be an administrator, an evangelist, a teacher, a shepherd and give spiritual oversight to the entire Body. In short, the seminary concept is that one man called 'the pastor' should do the work that the Apostle Paul said should be handled by at least five men. Not once in my four years of training in a theological seminary was I told to find my place and fulfill my dream as either an apostle, prophet, evangelist, pastor or teacher. It was just assumed I would be all five – despite Paul's admonition to the Ephesians (Ephesians 4: 11-16). But just because one has a pastor's heart does not make him a public teacher or an evangelist. Just because one has a burden for lost souls does not mean he is also gifted as a shepherd – or has the insight of a prophet.*
>
> *Over the years, as I have watched men fail in the ministry, it is often because they have been forced into roles where they were not gifted. The prophet, who had a great gift of preaching and deep spiritual insight, was forced to be a pastor– or an administrator. When he failed in that, and since his preaching was often irritating and pointed, he was forced out of the church. Or perhaps it was a man with a tender, shepherd's heart, who loved his sheep as deeply as he loved his own children. Yet because he was not a*

prophetic preacher or was a poor evangelist, those in the congregation who wanted to build a bigger, more efficient organization would finally see to it that he was replaced – usually by some kind of human dynamo who shot golf in the high 70s, remembered jokes like Bob Hope and was the darling of the social circle – but knew God only as a distant cousin.

When the church recognizes that God never intended for the spiritual leader to be all things to all people and when the spiritual leaders become secure enough in their gift that they are not threatened by others who can supplement their ministry and succeed in areas where they are weak, then the church will once again grow strong and healthy."

(Buckingham, 1980: 137-138)

Rather than the laity becoming part of the solution, the laity often expect the minister to provide all the answers on their behalf:

"The congregation, the program, the evangelism, the life of the church all seemed too overwhelmingly dependent on the pastors."

(Girard, 1972: 18-19)

But the church leaders are human, not divine. They can't know everything and have clear answers to all questions. In *Front Porch Tales*, Philip Gulley shared how his personality did not meet the demands of others, and the problems that caused him as a minister:

"Truth be told, I sometimes envy folks like my grandpa, folks who have this sixth sense concerning the life-path they need to take. As for me, I spend a lot of time roaming the back roads, never certain what I think about things most folks are clear on.

My grandpa eyeballs his compass, and down the road he goes. No situational ethics for him, by golly. Right is right, wrong is wrong, and let the chips fall where they may. I'm more of a on-the-one-hand-this-but-on-the-other-hand-that kind of guy.

This can cause problems when you're a minister. Folks expect me to know right where I stand, especially in church meetings. <u>*I don't know what this presumes about ministers, but I'm not encouraged.*</u>

I'll tell you where I stand. I stand for integrity and for erring on the side of grace and for reading to your children." [Emphasis mine]

(Gulley, 1997: 142-143)

… and the leaders want and need followers!

The unrealistic demands of the laity are compounded by those church leaders who actually *want* the power and prestige of being in charge of the flock, sometimes to try and compensate for a poor self-image.

Control mechanisms may emerge from the insecurity of pastors. Buckingham openly shares some of his own experiences of attempting to exert control, where God had the audacity to try to change his order of service. Buckingham won; God lost! And so did some hurting people whose needs didn't fit into the controlled order of service. Buckingham states:

> *"Most church leaders have a very low concept of God. To relinquish control of their lives, their finances or their churches to God's Spirit would be the equivalent of mayhem and devastation. Most church leaders, unfortunately, operate off a broad basis of insecurity. ... Let me recall an incident ... [At the start of the morning service] I was waylaid as [a] ... wretch of a man [brought by a friend of the alcoholic] reached out and tugged at my coat sleeves.*
>
> *My mind was a torrent of emotions. I wanted to stop and talk, but what would happen if I was not standing at the pulpit ... The entire service would come to an embarrassing, silent halt. ... Everything depended on my being up there to make things work.*
>
> *Yet here was this man, tugging at my coat sleeve. ... I am sure [the drunk's friend] expected me to take his drunk buddy right up on the platform with me and ask the people to pray for him.*
>
> *But I could not.*
>
> *... when I opened my eyes after the prayer and glanced in the direction of the front side pew, Stan was gone. He never returned. ...*
>
> *It was unthinkable ... to believe God could be so brash as to interrupt anything as sacred as a worship service ..."*
>
> (Buckingham, 1980: 95-98)

In *As Bill Sees It*, Bill gives a bit of personal insight to the impacts of insecurity, and concludes that the driven need of some to be at the top can be self-destructive:

> *"In my teens, I had to be an athlete because I was not an athlete. I had to be a musician because I could not carry a tune. I had to be the president of my class in boarding school. I had to be the first in everything because in my perverse heart I felt myself the least of God's creatures. I could not accept my deep sense of inferiority, and so I strove to become captain of the baseball team, and I did learn to play the fiddle. Lead I must – or else. This was the 'all or nothing' kind of demand that later did me in."*
>
> (Bill, 1967: 214)

He also warns of how our need to be top dog can impact others, and of the futility of such attempts:

> *"Most people try to live by self-propulsion. Each person is like an actor who wants to run the whole show and is forever trying to arrange the lights, the scenery, and the rest of the players in his own way. If his arrangements would only stay put, if only people would do as he wished, the show would be great.*

> *What usually happens? The show doesn't come off very well. Admitting he may be somewhat at fault, he is sure that other people are more to blame. He becomes angry, indignant, self-pitying.*
>
> *Is he not really a self-seeker even when trying to be useful? Is he not a victim of the delusion that he can wrest satisfaction and happiness out of this world if he only manages well?"*
>
> (Bill, 1967: 320)

Finally, in *If You Love the Lord*, Keith Green warns of how our striving to lead can impact our relationships with God:

> *"…we'd better realize we're all capable of pushing our own agenda ahead of God's agenda … protecting the Lord's reputation with ungodly methods, and hurting innocent people in the process. We forget God doesn't need or ask for our protection."*
>
> (Green, 2000: 93-94)

Secular leadership styles

Control structures are common within secular organizations, whether they be military, commercial or governmental structures. Rinehart talks of how he saw leaders in an earlier phase of his life:

> *"I saw the leader as being the most influential person. He was the one who got things done as he climbed the ladder of power.*
>
> *… You're a leader when you're in charge, when people work for you and you call the shots. …*
>
> *Whether military or civilian, being a leader was, in some way, a matter of climbing one's way up an invisible ladder to the top. There, at the top, the reward was power – power to make things happen, power to control the options, power to influence others."*
>
> (Rinehart, 1998: 17, 19)

In contrast, while Jesus noted that rulers in the secular world practice dominance over their subjects (Matthew 20:25), He clearly stated that this is *not* what He expects amongst His followers. Yet a simple look at what is happening within local churches shows the secular techniques are influencing the churches rather than the other way around:

> *"All too often … in churches and religious organizations … leadership practices … differ only slightly from those in the boardroom of any corporation. …*
>
> *What would happen if we lifted the lid on the average church or ministry organization today? Would we not, in many cases, find a detailed study in the use of ego, power, and control perfected to an art form? In a strange way, the misuse of power seems to flourish in religious institutions. Here human ambition can be coated with the veneer of spirituality."*
>
> (Rinehart, 1998: 23)

> *"[I attended] a conference entitled 'Leadership in the Church.' …*
>
> *Alas! For a whole week we received nothing but basic management principles derived from the business and military arenas. I'd heard it all before. This time, however, the same ideas were coated with enough spiritual veneer to camouflage their source."*
>
> (Rinehart, 1998: 27)

Yancey likewise laments the same trend of secular influence on church leaders:

> *"… I have watched a disturbing pattern in what we do to religious leaders today. We reward them with applause, fame, enticing new contracts and a flurry of requests for speaking engagements and media appearances. We push our pastors to function as psychotherapists, orators, priests and chief executive officers. When a leader shows unusual acumen, we dangle the temptation of a radio show or TV programme, complete with a fund-raising machine to float the organisation."*
>
> (Yancey, 2001: 160-161)

Some may reluctantly concede that the control structures within Christendom do look very much like the same structures in secular organizations, but perhaps feel this is not *too* bad, really. If it "works" for secular organizations, why not use it to make it work for us, too? Rinehart warns that the apparent success of following these secular control methods comes at a price:

> *"… tactics typified by dominance, rank, positional authority, and turf protection do seem to be effective in the short run.*
>
> *… In the long run, both leaders and followers burn out under these approaches."*
>
> (Rinehart, 1998: 22)

I clearly remember an inspiring old man of God who often said he'd rather burn out than rust out. He was a vigorous agent for good. Even as he approached his 100th birthday he spent much of his time visiting "the poor old shut-ins" who were often decades younger than he. But I believe Rinehart is warning against a different type of burnout. This gentleman had a call, and achieved great things in God's strength, and at His direction. However, if we burn out trying to achieve some fame and fortune for our own ego's sake, or for the sake of our leader's ego, that is totally different. The pain and disillusionment of those who give all at the expense of their own well-being, and end up needing support rather than giving it, is a type of burnout to be avoided.

But it's not just an issue of burnout. If this were the only problem, we might see local churches that march forward at a great speed, chewing up and spitting out their supporters as they go. And we do see that. But Rinehart goes even deeper in his exposition of the usage of control mechanisms. He starts by turning the spotlight on the emotional sickness of many who choose to exercise powerful control, using a quotation from Henri Nouwen's *In the Name of Jesus: Reflections on Christian Leadership*:

> *"Much Christian leadership … is exercised by people who do not know how to develop healthy, intimate relationships and have opted for power and control instead."*
>
> (Nouwen, 1989, in Rinehart, 1998: 49)

Unfortunately, there are those who are driven by their own inadequacies and are spurred on by theories that encourage "control" styles of leadership:

> "We seem convinced that control is essential to good leadership; therefore, leaders should be in control of their people. ... 'Control freaks' abound in ministry settings."
>
> (Rinehart, 1998: 54)

Some might argue that "everyone is doing it", and hence it must be right. Rinehart would agree that many are following this leadership style, but he sees it as an unhealthy epidemic rather than a vindication of its rightness:

> "Like the Sanhedrin of Jesus' day, much of what ministry leaders today believe and do in the realm of power, authority, and control has been borrowed not from Scriptures, but from the surrounding power institutions. ...
>
> Here's the reality: There is an epidemic of power leadership loose in churches and ministry organizations today. Power leaders are so common that we've lost our immunity to this style of leadership."
>
> (Rinehart, 1998: 44)

In contrast to the observed popularity of power leadership, Rinehart calls God's people to exercise a totally different style of "leadership", one that is small and hard to see:

> "... we've adopted a secular view regarding what it takes to be an effective entity in the world – namely, a power that can be touched, tabulated, and made tangible. Yet it is a power at odds with the mystery of the mustard seed and the grain of salt – a resurrection power so vital and alive that it can operate out of sight in small, quiet, but truly unassailable ways."
>
> (Rinehart, 1998: 48)

As noted earlier, Rinehart not only calls us to a life of service, but also warns against those who describe their role as one of "servant leadership" yet see their service as a means to an end:

> "I'll serve you, so you'll respect my leadership and follow me. I prime the pump, so you will deliver."
>
> (Rinehart, 1998: 41).

That's not servant leadership. It's what Rinehart calls "power leadership".

What has been observed in many local churches is a training or "discipleship" system aimed at preparing people for leadership. But it commonly has some fundamental flaws. For one thing, those trained are never expected (and are usually not *allowed*) to go above and beyond the current leader at the top of the hierarchy.

But there is a more subtle flaw that needs to be exposed, and it relates to training the would-be-leaders to obey. If they ask lots of questions, or hesitate to obey, they are seen to have failed the test and are rejected as unsuitable material for potential leadership. On the other hand, if they meekly submit and become "yes men", they can continue to be groomed for leadership, but always as leaders under the control of the more senior leaders who came before, and who will continue to expect unquestioning obedience forever.

Even if this perpetual subservience were not a factor, training people in ways of obedience, so that having done their time they can graduate and then call the shots, is in itself problematic. Rinehart states that any preparation we may make to better equip should be preparation for service. Training should not be

> *"... a type of internship we fulfill (in which we serve our time and then graduate into a place where we become the central figure – 'the leader')."*
>
> (Rinehart, 1998: 41)

Robinson and Smith go back to the foundations of Christianity, and note that the power hierarchies we observe today were also alive and well in Jesus' time. But they also note that Jesus boldly rejected the very concept of hierarchies as a model for His kingdom:

> *"The Jewish religious system of the day and the Roman political system were oppressive top-down systems. They were an exact incarnation of the man-at-the-top thinking that comes so naturally to unredeemed men [and I would suggest, to all men]. It seems that Jesus was saying, 'I know that this is the culture that surrounds you, and the flesh that possesses you.'*
>
> *All around us today there persists this same cultural reality, top-down, over-under. It is as natural as breathing for humanity. The same basic principle finds many cultural manifestations. It also dominates the religious landscape of the world we live in. By the second century after Jesus died, the most comfortable model of leadership found in man, the man at the top, was invading the church of Jesus.*
>
> *It is highly instructive that Jesus does not begin his monologue with the disciples explaining how they might redeem such a model, because this model is unredeemable!"*
>
> (Robinson & Smith, 2003: 140)

Church history: The growing dependence on hierarchies

We see the damage done today within Christendom by the application of secular control hierarchies. But as noted, it's not a new problem. Robinson and Smith not only soundly condemn the hierarchical approach as heretical, they point out that it has been present from early times within the churches, and that even when put aside by some, it keeps re-appearing. It seems to be a bit like a cancer that may go into remission only to come back strongly again to threaten life itself:

> *"For a number of reasons, the church has tended to focus solely on the gifts of pastor and teacher and we have often located these gifts in the office called minister, priest or pastor. To make matters worse, that 'office' has often been structured as the dominant leader in hierarchical terms. ...*

> *This distortion has been around so long as to feel natural. But it is as unnatural as any of the worst heresies fought during the first few centuries. It is not necessary to document the precise history of this development but it is clear that the process was underway at a fairly early point in the life of the church. A number of creative missionary periods in the history of the church have interrupted this pattern, only for the dominance of a single clergy person to reassert itself later."*
>
> (Robinson & Smith, 2003: 129)

I read and enjoyed *Upside Down* by Rinehart. My review of his work led me to conclude he really had a perspective that was worthy of consideration.

Rinehart explains how the rot started to set in early:

> *"As the body grew, after the death of the first-generation believers and apostles, the human propensity to walk by sight reared its ugly head. People are more comfortable seeing a representative of God than being directly in communication with the Living One. ... Thus they began to set up structures and leadership not unlike the well-known Jewish and pagan infrastructures. They soon forgot that Jesus was the head of the body as they began to transfer His leadership to human leaders and supporting administrative structures."*
>
> (Rinehart, 1998: 76-77)

Was this really the point where institutionalization of church structures commenced? His following observations appear to support this view.

Rinehart also notes that the early churches reacted poorly to pressures:

> *"... instead of entrusting themselves to the Holy Spirit ... they resorted to more pragmatic approaches.*
>
> *Their solution? Create a tighter organization. First, to refute certain false teachers who claimed lineage back to a specific apostle, the leaders produced a similar line of succession all the way back to their own apostle. Second, they determined that basic rules of order needed to be written down for general distribution to the fellowships. Thus, The Didache or Teaching of the Apostles was compiled. This was essentially a manual of discipline, giving guidelines for life and worship.*
>
> *Third, and most significantly, the foundational model of leadership changed. Ignatius articulated a doctrine significantly different from the servant model of Jesus ..."*
>
> (Rinehart, 1998: 77)

These power-centered leaders then went further to consolidate their power, proclaiming:

> *"... the bishop is representative of God the Father and the presbyters are the sanhedrin of God ... Nothing was done without the bishop. ... [Ignatius stated] that he who honors the bishop shall be honored by God."*
>
> (Rinehart, 1998: 77-78, quoting Kenneth Latourette's
History of Christianity, Volume 1: Beginnings to 1500, p. 117)

The power of church leaders was strengthened by their rejection of those who would question their right to such authority. Those who claimed to be special could now rebuke or even totally reject the members who would not submit:

> *"The leaders ... excluded those who would not submit ... A special class of priests held power over the spiritual well-being of those under their charge. The worship became increasingly formulaic, with decreasing participation by believers. Leaders adopted a distinctive style of dress and claimed special rights – the ability to grant forgiveness, to withhold the Lord's Supper, and to teach the Scriptures."*
>
> (Rinehart, 1998: 78)

The above recounting of church history seems to reflect an early appearance of some of the ills of today's church institutions. For example, Rinehart notes that Ignatius ushered in hierarchical power structures within churches; the Roman Emperor then moved in to use the emergent church structure for his own purposes, leading to the papal structures we still see today:

> *"Constantine proclaimed himself Pontifex Maximus – where the state and church joined. Pagans became 'converts' for political purposes, and sound theology took a secondary place to keeping control of the masses. The distinction between the called-out ones of God and the world became blurred.*
>
> *Augustine supported this trend, calling for an even closer alliance between the state and the church. ...*
>
> *Spiritual power progressively moved into the hands of a few men. The bishop of Rome assumed a greater role among the churches, ultimately assuming the title of Pope. Gradually, the hierarchy of the monarchical bishoprics centralized in Rome. The common people found themselves at the mercy of either the spirituality or the corruption of the clerics.*
>
> *The final transfer of power into the hand of a single individual came during the papacy of Gregory VII. He declared that the pope could use any available means to substantiate his authority, even if it contravened Scripture. As the earthly guardian of Scripture, this was within his right.*
>
> *Rampant abuse of power and all its trappings by the Roman church, combined with the hopeless passivity of the people, led to a church millennium with little evidence of the gospel's reality. ...*
>
> *What began as a shift in assumptions by Ignatius in the second century evolved into a full-fledged spiritual system. One man was designated as the physical head of the body on earth. Jesus became more and more a mere figurehead for His Bride."*
>
> (Rinehart, 1998: 79-80)

The new structure was not unopposed, but those in power were not about to give up their prestige and power without a fight:

> *"The Holy Spirit broke through repeatedly, though, raising up individuals with burning convictions. These faithful disciples proclaimed that the Imperial Church asserted power the gospel had never granted. ...*
>
> *Just as the Pharisees and Sadducees feared losing power and control over people, the institutional church sought vigorously to protect its political position and its perceived status as intermediary between God and people. If either of these eroded, those in power would lose their position, livelihood, and security."*
>
> (Rinehart, 1998: 80)

I asked myself if Rinehart's views reflected primarily on the Catholic Church? Some Protestants may happily point the finger at the Catholic Church, denouncing its authority structures. While we will very shortly look at the hypocrisy of such an attitude from sections of the Protestant community, I felt that the flaws in the world-wide hierarchical nature of the Catholic Church must be seriously challenged.

One of the most controlling attitudes that carry enormous potential for abuse is the papal claim of infallibility. As quoted earlier, Pope Gregory VII stated:

> *"The pope can be judged by no one; the Roman church has never erred and never will err till the end of time; the Roman church was founded by Christ alone; the pope alone can depose and restore bishops; he alone can make new laws, set up new bishoprics, and divide old ones; he alone can [transfer] bishops; he alone can call general councils and authorize canon law; he alone can revise his judgments; his legates, even though in inferior orders, have precedence over all bishops; an appeal to the papal courts inhibits judgment by all inferior courts; a duly ordained pope is undoubtedly made a saint by the merits of St. Peter."*
>
> Pope Gregory VII, eleventh century.
Cited in Benson Bobrick, Wide as the Waters: The Story of the English Bible
and the Revolution It Inspired. (Brown, 2002: 101)

Even as we start out in the 21st century, the official policy of papal infallibility has not been renounced!

Martin Luther is perhaps the most famous of all people raised within the Catholic Church who went on to denounce some of its flaws. On the topic of control of the masses by those appointed to the church hierarchy, Lindsay describes how Luther exposed the Pope's techniques. He commences by demonstrating that the pope claimed to be above the law of the land, stating that

> *"... the Temporal Power [i.e. secular government authorities] has no jurisdiction over the Spiritual ..."*
>
> (Lindsay, 1996: 86)

to which Luther countered:

> *"The Romanists assert that the Pope, bishops, priests and monks are the spiritual estate, while princes, lords, artificers and peasants are the temporal estate; but this is*

> simply an hypocritical device. All Christians are of the spiritual estate, and there is no difference between them save that of office and of work given to do. Every man has work given him to do for the commonwealth, and he may be restrained and punished if he does not do it properly, whether he be Pope, bishop, priest, monk, tailor, mason or cobbler."
>
> (Lindsay, 1996: 86)

Luther then stated that the second of the Pope's defenses for his abuse of authority was in claiming that the church leaders

> "... cannot be admonished from Scripture, since no one may interpret Scripture but the Pope ..."
>
> (Lindsay, 1996: 86)

Luther countered the above sarcastically:

> "As for the statement that the Pope alone can interpret Scripture – if that were true, what is the need for the Holy Scriptures? 'Let us burn them, and content ourselves with the unlearned gentlemen at Rome, in whom the Holy Ghost dwells, who, however, can dwell in pious souls only. If I had not read it, I could never have believed that the devil should have put forth such follies at Rome and find a following.'"
>
> (Lindsay, 1996: 86)

And the third argument from the "church" to keep the peasants in line was that the church

> "... cannot be called in question by a Council, because no man can call a Council but the Pope."
>
> (Lindsay, 1996: 86)

Luther replied,

> "... we are plainly taught in Scripture that if our brother offends we are to tell it to the Church, and if the Pope offends, as he often does, we can only obey the Word of God by calling a Council ..."
>
> (Lindsay, 1996: 86-87)

The Catholic Church may be seen as an obvious example of an international hierarchy. Less obvious to some are the subtle but still controlling hierarchies where control is wielded by a single leader but at the local church level. Two examples are given below.

The Methodist church was born from the Protestant reformation that opposed the central control of the Pope. In spite of these roots, a form of central control subsequently arose within Methodism. In response, a group of church leaders within the early Methodist church wanted to be free of this central authority. And the response from the power brokers at headquarters? The central authority accused them of

> "... obstinate and wilful resistance to authority."
>
> (Hattersley, 2000: 33)

The local leaders held their ground, and the cutting criticisms from the central office only strengthened their resolve for independence from central authority. However, in their new-found freedom from central control, these same leaders argued that

> "... each local society should have absolute power of discipline over its members ..."
>
> (Hattersley, 2000: 33)

This moved the domination of controlling leaders down the hierarchy, but still controlled the laity, albeit at a local level.

The control from the command center was even more obvious within the Salvation Army. In *They Found The Secret*, Edman tells of Samuel Brengle's move to join the Salvation Army, and highlights William Booth's condemnation of Brengle for his perceived independence from the head-office thinking:

> "Brengle, you belong to the dangerous classes. You have been your own boss for so long that I don't think you will want to submit to Salvation Army discipline. We are an Army, and we demand obedience."
>
> (Edman, 1960: 12)

The topic of a leader's fear of what is sometimes called "loose-cannon laity" is specifically addressed later in this book. For now, we must recognize that some leaders demand a style of allegiance that rejects an individual's freedom of thought, independent of whether the model is one of world-wide central control, or control centered on the local church.

The above extracts note how hierarchies embedded themselves into the fabric of local churches *after* the times of the first apostles. Some argue that it appears to be a natural tendency for man to establish power structures, with appointed heads and hierarchies. If this is true, did warning signs of this tendency appear even during the time of the first apostles?

Unfortunately, the answer is "Yes". Even while Jesus was alive, two of his disciples sought appointment over the others, asking to be seated beside Jesus in His new kingdom. After Jesus' death, the appointments continued. Just for example, there was the appointment of a replacement for Judas to fill a leadership gap. Later, there were appointments to roles such as "elders" and "deacons". Even the apostles did not want to wait on tables as they considered *their* work too important and chose others to do that work—the early signs of a class hierarchy had already appeared.

One can argue whether these appointments were just reflections of the human desire for order, structure and control. The desire of the two disciples to have official positions is beyond question an act of human desire—Jesus quickly exposed their wrong thinking. Some argue the appointment of elders was a bit like the Israelis of the Old Testament who wanted a king, even when God clearly wanted to relate to his people without this form of government. They hold the view that the establishment of "elders" was driven by a similar desire to have mediators between God and man, other than Jesus.

You may disagree with those who argue this way. All I ask at this stage is that you remain open to the possibility of the New Testament records being a factual representation of the events, but not necessarily a reflection of God's best, or a blueprint for us to follow.

Leadership by a team is still a hierarchical model

Most people will recognize the hierarchical model when the organization is dominated by one world leader. Some will still see it when there is a local, dominant leader. But less will see the presence of a hierarchical model if there is a leadership *team*.

One definition of the word "Hierarchy" (from Wikipedia) is as follows:

> *"A Hierarchy is a system of ranking and organizing things or people, where each element of the system (except for the top element) is subordinate to a single other element."*

(Wikipedia, October 28, 2006)

We can conclude that it doesn't matter whether the top "element" of a church hierarchy is one person (Pope, senior pastor, or whatever) or a group (such as a team of leaders, or an eldership group). Nor does it matter if the hierarchy has several levels (e.g. Pope, cardinals, bishops, through to lesser authorities) or just one level ("my pastor"). All are forms of a hierarchy if the people at the "bottom" are in any way subordinate and are considered to have less ability to discern God's direction than those at the "top", or if there is someone at the top, regardless of how benevolent he or she may be.

Frost and Hirsch appear to challenge hierarchical church structures in all forms:

> *"... the traditional church (Christendom) is hierarchical ... [and has an] overly religious, bureaucratic, top-down model of leadership, as opposed to one that is more structured around grassroots agendas. While some denominations are ideologically committed to a very top-down hierarchical model that includes archbishops, bishops, priests, and parish councils, others 'who call themselves low church' are equally indebted to top-down approaches via regional superintendents, senior pastors, associate pastors, youth pastors, and deacons. From Pentecostals to the Orthodox church, from Baptists to Episcopalians and Presbyterians, the hierarchical model seems to be universal."*

(Frost & Hirsch, 2003: 21)

They also appear to be supporting the philosophy of what many call the "priesthood of all believers", stating that all must exercise ministry gifts:

> *"... let us emphasize that for maximum, missional impact, [Apostle, Prophet, Evangelist, Pastor, and Teacher] functions must not merely be limited to the leadership community within the church, but must be exercized by the whole church."*

(Frost & Hirsch, 2003: 170)

However, an apparent inconsistency in their argument for lack of hierarchies and titles starts to appear. We have a community of believers that are equal in the exercising of ministry, but we also appear to have a hierarchy in that a special group titled the "leadership community" is identified. Let's look a bit closer.

We now look at a quotation from Frost and Hirsch that at face value seems to propose that the community of faith (i.e. all believers) should be egalitarian (i.e. the community should not be divided into classes). They again appear to criticize the use of titles that would set one class apart (as in the section above):

> *"... the yearning for an egalitarian, gracious community of faith requires that leadership be egalitarian and cooperative as well. We cannot find the term senior pastor in the New Testament ... And this is not just a criticism to be leveled at the Episcopal churches. The Evangelical and Pentecostal churches, with their hierarchies of pastors, are functioning with a priesthood in all but name."*
>
> (Frost & Hirsch, 2003: 68)

These authors appear to be proposing a community with no classes; where all are equal—that's what egalitarian means. To me, there appears to be a problem, though, in that in the above quotation they refer *also* to an egalitarian *leadership* class. So it turns out that they seem not to support an overall *"egalitarian, gracious community of faith"* at all, but rather propose we have two communities, one for those doing the leading, and one for those being led. Isn't it oxymoronic—self-contradictory—to suggest we have a community without classes, and then in the same breath to talk about a leadership community—a class of people with the title of "leader"—that is distinct from the rest?

My impression is that all they are doing is swapping a hierarchical model they oppose—with one supreme leader that dictates to the laity—with a *team* of "special" leaders that still is distinguishable from the Body at large.

Their argument for this position commences by proposing an egalitarian leadership community:

> *"[The proposed model] abandons the triangular hierarchies of the traditional church and embraces a biblical, flat-leadership community ..."*
>
> (Frost & Hirsch, 2003: 12)

I came away feeling that they sought a *leadership* community that has no classes (within this class of people called "leaders"), and that they are not seeking a total community of *all* believers without classes.

They reinforce that this leadership community is a part of the larger Christian community, but nonetheless distinct:

> *"... the New Testament [i.e. Paul, not Jesus] teaches a fivefold leadership matrix that implies a community of leadership made up of apostles, prophets, evangelists, pastors, and teachers ... [The local church should be] shepherded by godly leaders ('elders' to be precise), but we see Christian leadership operating best as a community within a community."*
>
> (Frost & Hirsch, 2003: 68)

I have encountered the phrase "first among equals". It is an oxymoron, but one that is popular amongst leaders who wish to retain their elevated class while appearing to be acting in a manner that refuses to have separate classes. Frost and Hirsch appear to go close to this level of self-contradiction when they, in effect, say that all are called, but some more so than others—a "calling within a calling":

"... we want to suggest a two-dimensional reading of [Apostle, Prophet, Evangelist, Pastor, and Teacher roles] – one dimension that describes the leadership system (the leadership matrix) and the other that describes the whole church's ministry (the ministry matrix). Some will be called as apostles, but the whole community is to be apostolic ... "

(Frost & Hirsch, 2003: 170)

"We see the leadership matrix as the community within the community, made up of certain people who are called to exemplify and embody these ministries in such a way as to be an [Apostle, Prophet, Evangelist, Pastor, or Teacher] leader to the rest of the ... body. ... This can be seen as a 'calling within the calling.' "

(Frost & Hirsch, 2003: 172)

Frost and Hirsch continue to give me the impression of contradiction in the following extracts. Firstly, they repeat their rejection of the hierarchical model with one person at the top:

"There is no room for the loner or the one-man band in the New Testament model. We repudiate the classic hierarchical, triangular model with so-called senior pastors at the top. Biblically, it must be [a team of apostles, prophets, evangelists, pastors, and teachers]."

(Frost & Hirsch, 2003: 173)

This is immediately followed by upholding as exemplary the story of the local church run by the wife of one of the authors, which is

"... under the <u>leadership and direction</u> of [the <u>one</u>] team leader Debra Hirsch." [Emphasis mine]

(Frost & Hirsch, 2003: 173)

So this church that they hold up as an ideal of a local church that is *not* under a hierarchical one-person band (they actually use the phrase "*one-man band*"), yet is actually led by one person. In their own defense, they do claim that

"No longer is the church run by pastors alone but by a developing APEPT leadership team whose aim is to help all the other ministers (everyone) to find their parts in the whole and to pursue them."

(Frost & Hirsch, 2003: 173)

They seem to be trying to say it's a team thing, yet in their own words, admit that the local church is under the "*leadership and direction*" of Debra Hirsch.

The authors hold up this illustration as a shining example of non-hierarchical church leadership as it should be; yet they appear to still have one supreme leader, plus a team of special people in leadership positions …and then the rest…

The authors then follow the story of Debra's local church with another that is less like a *"one-man band"*—it has *two* supreme leaders instead of one! It seems that many church leaders are getting defensive about hierarchical models, so will go to enormous lengths to try to show that *their* hierarchy is *not* hierarchical. I would argue that a hierarchy is any structure where one element is subservient to another element that is in charge of or has the responsibility for those that follow. It matters not whether the element in control is represented by one individual, or two, or a larger group. It is still a hierarchy.

And it is still a hierarchy no matter how it is drawn. It can be drawn pictorially as a triangle with the leader(s) at the top. It can be drawn as concentric circles, with the "most important people" in the middle. It doesn't matter how it's diagrammed—the principle doesn't change! Yet Robinson and Smith portray concentric circles as a revolutionary alternative to triangles! Instead of those at the top of the pile being special, it's those in the middle that are special. You've still got the "special" ones, and the "not-so-special" ones. They state:

> *"… the man-at-the-top pyramid, found in the pastoral model [that is] crippling us today, is the opposite of [Jesus'] model. …*
>
> *… leadership in the New Testament model is probably best seen as a series of concentric circles rather than a pyramid. The circles acknowledge the importance of leadership as foundational to the community of Jesus' people …"*
>
> (Robinson & Smith, 2003: 141)

As shown already, others try to demonstrate that if the local leadership, especially a team, is somehow "under" the authority of others, and if there is some level of mutual submission amongst those higher in the chain of command, then the "sheep" are no longer exposed to the dangers of the hierarchical model:

> *"Apostolic teams will network within nations and around the world. They will respect and submit to one another and to the local leaders they serve, working together within the limits of their calling and commissioning. Local eldership teams will be supported by these mobile apostles and will become true shepherds to the sheep because of mutual trust and interdependence."*
>
> (Noble, 2002: 84-85)

Finally, we return to Frost and Hirsch. Yet again they seem to decry the classification of church leadership as separate from laity:

> *"The idea of a separated clergy, we maintain, is as alien to a New Testament church as it is to a missional one."*
>
> (Frost & Hirsch, 2003: 227)

In spite of this, I interpret their whole book to be addressed to "leaders". It matters little whether we call the two classes of Christians—clergy and laity, or Apostles / Prophets / Evangelists / Pastors / Teachers and the rest, or leaders and the led. It *is* a hierarchical model if there are two or more classes of members. This two-class reality within their idealized structures is exemplified when they state:

"... leaders consider ... themselves and the people they lead."

(Frost & Hirsch, 2003: 217)

So, for all that Frost and Hirsch say to the contrary, it does boil down to the leaders and the led!

Techniques used to maintain control

As seen, many writers strongly condemn hierarchical power structures within Christendom. These structures are typically seen by them as, at best, unhelpful in encouraging each Christian to discover their own role and contribution, and possibly much worse. The hierarchies may need to be exposed and resisted, but there is a much more damning evil lurking behind many hierarchies of the past and present—the techniques employed by those in power to protect their position.

One technique I have observed and mentioned is a variety of personal attacks on individuals who question, challenge, express dissent or, worse still, dare to leave a local church. Mind you, there are those who do not get to make a choice about leaving. They are ushered out because they are seen as too divisive or confrontational or a bad influence, and therefore cannot remain. I have also seen them labeled as "having a Jezebel spirit"—apparently the ultimate insult.

On the less malicious end of the scale is the inference that those who left (or are helped to exit) are misguided, and those who remain loyal to the "true church" should pray for their enlightenment and return. If the level of dissent was higher, the remnant are sometimes warned of the dangers of association with these "deluded people" lest they come under their influence and themselves also end up misguided. Further down the scale is blatant attack on their personalities, with labels suggesting they are agents of Satan, and giving these ex-members titles such as Simon the Sorcerer, or Jezebel. Sound very cult-like? It does, but these reactions by leaders can be found in many denominations, including those that may well be classified as "mainstream".

As the author of Ecclesiastes suggests, there is little that is new under the sun. Attacks on those who question or challenge leaders still occur today, as they have in the past. Hattersley recounts the story of a Salvation Army officer, Colonel Lampard, who had been engaged to one of William Booth's daughters, but broke off the engagement. This was

"... regarded by General Booth as a betrayal of the Army as well as his daughter."

(Hattersley, 2000: 391)

In response,

> "... the Army issued what amounted to a medical bulletin:
>
> Since the inquiry [into the circumstances surrounding the broken engagement] took place, an opinion on the subject has been formed by the physician who enjoys a leading reputation in the treatment of mental disease. He states very explicitly that in this particular direction, Colonel Lampard was (in his opinion) so far mentally deranged as not to be responsible for his action. ...
>
> Few people, even at the time, believed the diagnosis to be medically reputable. It is more difficult to decide if William Booth cynically regarded Colonel Lampard's 'madness' as the best way of defending his daughter and the Army or if his admiration for both the woman and the organisation made him honestly believe that only a lunatic would miss the opportunity to become a Booth."
>
> (Hattersley, 2000: 392)

On another occasion one of Booth's senior officers, George Railton, had publicly expressed opposition to a fundraising scheme. Again, the Army's response was to cast doubt on the mental health of the independent officer:

> "It was just two years since The War Cry had published the 'eminent physician's diagnosis' of Colonel Lampard's state of mental health. The Army's senior officers were quick to act on the precedent. If refusing to marry William Booth's daughter was a sign of madness, insulting the General in public must be conclusive evidence of an even more serious condition."
>
> (Hattersley, 2000: 410)

Another control technique observed throughout history is where paranoid leaders have established reporting mechanisms for identification of those that might oppose them. It happened in blatant forms in communist Russia and Nazi Germany, and it happens today in the more extreme, cult-like denominations. But, even in less extreme local churches, it can appear subtly. For example, so-called "discipleship" systems at times encourage the reporting of those who are not seen to be suitably committed and dedicated, who don't turn up for prayer meetings, and the like.

Reporting of dissidents to the leadership, even on matters shared in confidence, is not new to our times. Again we take the old Salvation Army as an example of the historic presence of such controls. George Railton had been attacked for his open opposition. In response, he

> "... wrote to Arthur Booth-Clibborn, whom he thought to be his friend, and in what he believed to be confidence. Some of Railton's letters complained mildly against his treatment. Booth-Clibborn sent them on to the Chief of Staff."
>
> (Hattersley, 2000: 411)

Yet another control technique observed at a secular consultancy with world-wide presence allegedly had a deliberate policy of frequently relocating staff. The motivation, if the report was correct, was to psychologically tie staff to the company. The theory was that, if any person has frequent and unsettling change, they never get the opportunity to establish relationships with those outside of work—the only stability in their life is the employer, so loyalty to employer is reinforced. If this tactic is true, I suggest it is a very unhealthy and immoral approach.

Hattersley suggests that Bramwell Booth (William Booth's appointed heir to control of the Salvation Army) had a similar style, though driven by a different but equally unhealthy motivation. For Bramwell, it was a chance to flex his muscles and impress others with his power:

"... Bramwell decided that the time had come to impress his authority on the whole international organisation. ... [His actions] led to a reorganisation of commands which his brothers and sisters described as 'musical chairs'. Herbert, briefly back in London for a conference, was informed that he had been transferred (without consultation) to the Australian Command. Eva was to abandon her duties in the London training homes and succeed Herbert in Canada ... The Booth-Clibborns were moved from France and Switzerland to Holland and Belgium and the Booth-Hellborgs from India to France. Ballington Booth was relieved of the United States Command and recalled to London. The Booth-Tuckers, who had returned to London with the intention of becoming the joint Foreign Secretaries of the Army, were warned of the possibility that they would succeed him."

(Hattersley, 2000: 411-412)

This heavy-handed movement of people was not without a cost. Ballington openly rebelled, and organized a public rally to oppose the orders, and shortly after broke away completely from the Salvation Army. It is my understanding that this Salvation Army policy of frequently relocating staff (known as giving "farewell orders") is still practiced today, independent of the motivation.

Another technique to maintain control of others has been classified by some as "shunning". It is not uncommon for members of one denomination to be encouraged to see themselves as being part of the "true" church. In some cases, not only are the perceived shortcomings of other churches highlighted, but any fraternization with them is soundly condemned. Again, we take the Salvation Army's early history as an example. One critic of the Salvation Army noted that the Army's own 'Orders and Regulations

"... warned against fraternisation with other churches ..."

(Hattersley, 2000: 266)

As stated earlier, such approaches to control are symptomatic of cult-like behavior and must be condemned.

Time for a change

The previous chapter looked at how members of the church leadership class often see themselves as being superior. This chapter explains how some church leaders misuse power to retain control of the laity.

Power structures existed before Christ, in both secular and religious organizations. Jesus openly condemned them, but they reappeared within Christendom anyway, and have become so entrenched as to appear normal.

An extreme form of abusive control manifests itself in the teaching that we must obey the commands of our leaders, no matter what. Yet, I deduce from my reading, this is exactly what Bevere appears to teach, and which Brown appears to oppose:

> *"... [Bevere] specifically cites 1 Peter 2:13, 18 to call believers to submit to harsh and cruel authorities of every kind, just as slaves must submit to harsh and cruel masters. Quite explicitly in the context of Under Cover, therefore, this means that believers should submit in just the same way to harsh and cruel pastors and spiritual leaders. As we have emphasized, this is not the teaching of Scripture."*
>
> (Brown, 2002: 217)

Such misleading teaching must be corrected. We start by exposing some false ideas behind the perceptions of "strong" leadership.

Hattersley paints a picture of William Booth that fits the stereotype image of dictatorial arrogance giving the impression of self-confident certainty:

> *"General Booth's whole life was a triumph for certainty.*
>
> *He was not an easy man to serve, but he inspired unquestioning loyalty ... William Booth was both arrogant and autocratic in his relations with everyone except his wife. And he was at his most dictatorial and inhuman when he feared that personal failings and foibles imperiled his Army's good name. In all his relations – with the single exception of his marriage – he lacked warmth, sympathy and understanding."*
>
> (Hattersley, 2000: 437)

Oliver and Thwaites present a totally different view of "leadership", where leaders ebb and flow in their roles, at times stepping back to let others move up.

> *"Most of the current leadership approach tells us that ministry gifts need to get out ahead of the saints and keep ahead, so that there will be someone strong and visionary for them to follow. This makes its mark initially, in that people will generally respond more readily to something strong and clear. However, over time, the record shows that passivity, uniformity and dependence are usually the result of such leadership. Strong leaders who are incessant in their leadership do not create strong people, they create weak people.*
>
> *Is the answer, then, to have weak leaders? No. To my mind, we need leaders that know how to ebb and flow. Leaders need to weave in and serve the saints as their need and*

hunger require. They need to be good stewards, who give the saints food at the proper time (Matt. 24:45) and not overfeed them. At times, they will be strong and then they need to go weak. At times, they are present and then they will need to absent themselves, giving space for choice and time for truth to mix with desire to make the good work. They need to learn to dance, knowing when to lead and when to follow, but all along resisting the urge to become the DJ or manager of the club."

(Oliver & Thwaites, 2001: 149)

There is still the problem of a hierarchy, and one danger in adopting this approach is that it leaves the power to decide when to "ebb" or "flow" in the leaders' hands. History suggests many leaders simply would not ease off on the reins of control.

What should be the final nail in the coffin of any teaching that espouses "power" structures is Robinson and Smith's observation that such approaches are not the way of Jesus:

"The fact that the Bible does not address the purpose of the church as an integral part of the mission of Jesus has led some to ask whether Jesus ever intended to found the church. Hans Küng, among many others, is convinced that Jesus and his immediate followers preached about the kingdom of God and spent no time at all preparing the structure of a new organisation."

(Robinson & Smith, 2003: 40)

What is taught and how we live should consistently express our rejection of any vestige of control structures. For some, this might mean being tempted to go back to the roots of the Protestant Reformation.

Rinehart reminds us of the progress towards freedom made by the likes of Martin Luther:

"Martin Luther ..., John Calvin, and others sought to refocus on faith in Christ as the sole means of salvation, to restore purity and integrity in leadership, and to reinstate the priesthood of all believers in practice. They made great strides in these areas, particularly in publishing the Bible in common languages."

(Rinehart, 1998: 81)

It is interesting to note that the quotation above refers on the one hand to those in "leadership", and also includes the phrase "the priesthood of all believers". Luther and others involved in the Reformation are claimed to have recognized the need for integrity amongst those "special" people who are called apart to be leaders, and to have recognized the principle of the priesthood of all believers where we are all equal before God (i.e. there are no special people). There are problems with the internal lack of consistency in these attitudes.

So, in spite of the progress towards freedom that was realized by the Reformation, some saw that it had not gone far enough:

"The second wave of reformation ... brought along a group known as the Anabaptists. To them, the Reformation efforts had not gone far enough. The Anabaptists pushed

the starting point of right thinking about God's design for the church back to its New Testament roots."

(Rinehart, 1998: 81)

And some would argue that even going back to the so-called New Testament model (and there is great debate on what that term really means) is still not returning to our roots. Instead, we must go back to the teaching and example of Jesus:

"There is an old saying that 'Jesus will be central.' It doesn't matter what else we lift up in His place, it will always fail us or fall short, and we will be led, time and again, back to acknowledging His supremacy in our lives. Nothing can fill His place."

(Rinehart, 1998: 156)

We need to not only reject the idea of classes within Christendom, particularly classes relating to the leaders and the led, but we also need to stand against the control techniques of church leaders who don't want to lose their privileged positions.

CHAPTER 8:
CONTROL OF THE INDIVIDUAL EXEMPLIFIED

The preceding sections address the views of certain church leaders that (i) they belong to a special class, and (ii) they are ordained by God to be in control of the sheep. This chapter has a focused analysis of just one published work for the purpose of articulating a detailed commentary and critique of its views. It is my opinion that a thorough drill down into one book that I consider to be an example of some church leadership thinking (albeit taking one position on a continuum) is helpful in highlighting the dangers of such views. The book is Juan Ortiz' *Disciple*.

Ortiz was a church leader who had international influence during the charismatic renewal period surrounding the 1970s. Many would agree he spoke with conviction and clarity on topics such as the lordship of Christ. He certainly challenged me on this topic, and for this I am grateful.

Yet at the heart of his teaching is this same central theme of the church leaders being a distinct class, and the need for them to be in control. If I reached this conclusion merely from distant interpretation of his motives, I may be wrong. I have not met the man. However, I believe his own words portray him as one who, through his status as a church leader, saw himself as fulfilling a special role, and who set the expectation of obedience from those in his church.

In conveying a critical analysis of his position, I wish to be absolutely clear that I am not even hinting that Ortiz is an evil man, or anything approaching such a position. Of course he is imperfect, just like you and me. However, when I read a source whose message expounds a view that, on analytical reflection I feel to be dangerous, and when I perceive that individual is held by many to be an influential authority within Christian thinking, I felt motivated to challenge his view.

My analysis of certain aspects of his premise is based on his published beliefs. You, of course, are entitled to likewise critique his views, as well as my views for that matter. In fact, I encourage you to acquire the referenced book and conduct your own analysis. We should always strive to honestly and openly consider the opinions of others, but be absolutely free to disagree. We can also compare the views of others and ourselves with our understanding of the standards set by Jesus, always remembering that our interpretation of His words and actions may be flawed.

If we define a Christian as one who follows Christ, and if we look at the teachings of Jesus, the theme of obedience appears to be unavoidable. Jesus directly taught that our love and even our friendship towards Him cannot be considered real if we do not obey Him (John 14:15 and John 15:14). It would seem fundamental that Christians should not have any issues with the rights of Jesus to "run the show", so to speak. But, as noted in the previous chapter, it is a totally separate issue when a church leader claims the right to demand obedience, acting in the role of mediator between God and man, the role declared by Jesus to be His own exclusive right; this is the position of authority that my critique of Ortiz' writing leads me to believe he holds.

According to my interpretation of Ortiz' book, he paints a picture of the New Testament church having three distinct levels in a hierarchy. At the top is God. He is in charge. In the middle are the church leaders, who are supposedly appointed by God. And at the bottom is the laity, whose job it is (according to Ortiz) to simply obey the church leaders:

> *"[The New Testament church] was a church commanded by the head, not the feet. The power flowed from the top <u>through the middle</u> to the bottom." [Emphasis mine]*
>
> (Ortiz, 1975: 125)

> *"God commanded the apostles, <u>who told the people what he wanted</u>. They also put elders in the churches. Everyone was obedient." [Emphasis mine]*
>
> (Ortiz, 1975: 125)

Ortiz not only has a particular interpretation of the New Testament model and God's intentions as they relate to church leadership hierarchies but, I believe, he goes much further and applies the concept of "discipleship" (the theme of his book) to today's local churches. Ortiz seems to be teaching that today's disciples should be taking orders from church leaders, not directly from God.

In contrast, we look at Sheldon's book *In His Steps*. There, Sheldon repeatedly challenges those who would be disciples of Christ to ask themselves, "What would Jesus do?" in a given situation. These followers of Christ are encouraged to look to Jesus and make their own determination as to what is the right thing to do. But Ortiz appears to define a disciple as one who follows his or her human teacher. In other words, rather than Christians being disciples of Jesus, those in Ortiz' church seem to be directed to be disciples of those that Ortiz appoints as their mentors:

> *"A disciple is a person who learns to live the life his teacher lives. And gradually he teaches others to live the life he lives."*
>
> (Ortiz, 1975: 105)

CONTROL OF THE INDIVIDUAL EXEMPLIFIED

As I read Ortiz' words, he seemed to present two distinct types of authority structures. The first is a simple hierarchy *within* a local church. The pastor is at the top. He (or she) appoints trusted leaders who will take orders from the pastor. And then come the laity, who are to be obedient to the not only the pastor, but also to the leaders the pastor assigns.

Jesus has already declared the structure He intends, namely that there is to be no mediator between man and God other than Himself, yet it seems to me that Ortiz first inserts the senior pastor as an additional layer, and then puts in even more layers between God and man.

My interpretation of his writing led me to the conclusion that he sees the second authority structure as one that relates to the church leaders themselves. Ortiz proclaims that they too must be in submission. So he proclaims a system whereby he, as a pastor in one local church, is under the authority of others. He introduces the phrase "intersubmission", whereby he appears to suggest he willingly comes under the peer authority of others as a prerequisite for being able to have authority over those within his church—creating yet more layers between the laity and God.

Ortiz explains these multiple layers as follows:

> *"Only when I am in line can authority pass through me to others."*
>
> (Ortiz, 1975: 113)
>
> *"Formation [of disciples] requires not only submission but intersubmission.*
>
> *How did we implement these things in Buenos Aires? Well, the first thing was for me to come under the authority of the ministers of my city."*
>
> (Ortiz, 1975: 114)
>
> *"What if God has installed two or three levels above me? Fine."*
>
> (Ortiz, 1975: 113)

It sounds like the pastor is in submission, with the laity having protection because their human authority is in submission to higher authorities within the city. Let's look deeper into Ortiz' model.

Firstly, Ortiz defines all of the local churches in a city as in reality being just one church, perhaps a little like there was *one* church at Rome, *one* church at Corinth, and so on.

> *"In the New Testament they never had to think up a name for the church, because there was only one. When I was in Charlotte, North Carolina, I was told that there were 400 churches in that city. That's not really true. There is one church in Charlotte, broken into 400 pieces. There can only be one church in each locality. …*
>
> *[God] sees the different pastors of the city as all co-pastors of His one church. If they are co-pastors, they should meet together, have fellowship, love one another. They should almost live together as the twelve pastors of the Jerusalem church did. They are the presbytery of the city, the elders in charge of God's flock."*
>
> (Ortiz, 1975: 129)

Ortiz then paints an idealistic picture of all church leaders in the city working together, in mutual submission to each other, and discerning God's will for the city.

> *"If we pastors are not submissive to each other, how can we expect the people to submit to us?*
>
> *The other pastors of God's one church form an extremely important guarantee for the disciples that they will not be abused by a dictator. They know that their pastor is also a disciple, subject to the leadership of the city's presbytery."*
>
> (Ortiz, 1975: 132)
>
> *"As [the group of church leaders in one city] wait before the Lord and pray together and love one another, God reveals His purpose for their city. God is finally able to speak to His shepherds as a group."*
>
> (Ortiz, 1975: 132)
>
> *"Jesus gives each leader of the Church a piece of the puzzle. If each one of us came with a piece of the puzzle, we could see the whole picture. But the person who receives an experience and makes a denomination out of that is going the wrong way."*
>
> (Ortiz, 1975: 157)

So it seems, according to Ortiz, there are two types of hierarchies. The laity must submit to their assigned leaders who in turn submit to their one pastor, in a strictly hierarchical manner. And the pastors have this so-called intersubmission between themselves as equals.

Ortiz' arguments for hierarchical control

According to my analysis, there appears to be a number of flaws in Ortiz' argument. For one thing, as noted above, he seems to demand a strict hierarchy of submission for the laity, but has a different expectation for the church leaders. While he talks of layers of submission for church leaders (claiming he is comfortable with having several layers above himself), his model for leaders appears to not be a hierarchy at all, but rather a confederation of church leaders as equals. He does not appear to suggest that there be a senior leader for the city—just a mutual sharing.

Further, my understanding of his position is that he believes that God can speak to the *leaders*, with each one getting *"a piece of the puzzle"*. But if God can talk to the church leaders, is He impotent and unable to talk to the regular *members* of His Body? Or can he only talk to special people, namely the leaders? Do we really need a mediator, or a number of mediators, between God and man other than Christ? I think not.

In spite of what I see as serious flaws in his logic, Ortiz presents an argument for hierarchical control (of the laity, that is). He starts on solid foundations, namely the authority the Godhead has, or should have, over His people:

> *"We are like the medieval people who thought the earth was the center of the universe.*

> *They were wrong, and so are we. We think we are the center of the universe, and God and Jesus Christ and the angels all revolve around us. Heaven is for us; everything is for our benefit.*
>
> *We are wrong. God is the center. We must change our center of gravity. He is the sun, and we revolve around Him."*
>
> (Ortiz, 1975: 14-15)

Having made the point that the laity need to get used to taking orders (from God), he moves on to lay the foundations for us taking orders from the church leaders. To start with, he looks at the (perceived) important role of having the authority to baptize others (in spite of the fact that Jesus instructed *all* of His followers to make disciples and baptize them). He notes that Paul

> *"… baptized almost nobody …"*
>
> (Ortiz, 1975: 87)

He then also uses scripture to point out that many were being baptized. But he seems to jump to the conclusion that these baptisms must have involved the leaders and not the laity, without any proof, stating:

> *"Somebody was baptizing the new believers, and it wasn't Paul. It must have been Crispus, Gaius, and other <u>spiritual fathers</u> who right away began caring for their spiritual children." [Emphasis mine]*
>
> (Ortiz, 1975: 87)

My reading of Ortiz leads me towards the view that not only does he establish what he sees as an argument that important people do "important" things (the old "leaders are special" argument), but that he then moves on to the other major topic, namely "control". He appears to claim it as an eternal law of God that, as long as you are perceived to be under control of others (remember the line about being in submission to a confederation of pastors), then you have the right to *demand* control over those you lead.

> *"If you want the right to control others, you must be under the control of others yourself. It is an eternal law of God."*
>
> (Ortiz, 1975: 114)

From my interpretation, it seems that he then follows a "right" to control with an incredible (and unsubstantiated) claim that it is *only* through church leaders that the will of God is to be revealed!

> *"The will of God for today comes <u>only</u> in the group of ministers." [Emphasis mine]*
>
> (Ortiz, 1975: 132)

Perhaps you are already feeling uncomfortable with how I interpreted the direction of Ortiz' teaching. In my opinion, his teaching continues deeper into dangerous territory by him apparently suggesting that these leaders may be infallible! It seems that Ortiz argues that church leaders have the *potential* to be infallible, as long as they are filled with the Holy Spirit. He claims that the initial apostles achieved this status:

> *"The apostles ... had the right to define doctrine. The New Testament speaks often not of 'Jesus' doctrine' but of 'the apostles' doctrine.' They were infallible."*

(Ortiz, 1975: 126)

I believe that his claim is not only critically defective, but also very dangerous. We will look shortly at where Ortiz himself demonstrates elsewhere the imperfect nature of the apostles. Yet here he appears to build on this shaky foundation of the perceived perfection of the apostles to suggest that all church leaders *could* be perfect if only they were Spirit-filled:

> *"The problems arose when the theocratic church lost its charisma, its spiritual power. The leaders became more conscious of material, earthly power than what came from above. They kept the same form of government, but the spirit was gone."*

(Ortiz, 1975: 126)

The Catholic Church still maintains the doctrine of the Pope's infallibility. Ortiz, thankfully, doesn't see the Pope as infallible, but still claims he could have been if he had retained the "charisma":

> *"The pope continued to think of himself as infallible, and I can understand why. After all, the letters Peter had written, the letters of John and the others, were all the truth. Why shouldn't that continue? It could have; but without the charisma, the divine revelation from heaven, the Church became a dangerous thing in the world."*

(Ortiz, 1975: 126)

Ortiz then notes that some tried to bring back into the Catholic Church what the Popes were missing, but were rejected:

> *"Some of the sons of the [Catholic] Church—Savonarola, Huss, Luther, and others—tried to renew it, but the Church would not accept their ministries. They could have brought new life to the Catholic Church, but instead they were driven out. That is the problem of power without [Spirit-inspired] revelation."*

(Ortiz, 1975: 126)

By implication, it appears that Ortiz is suggesting that these leaders could have brought infallibility back, had they been Spirit-filled and Spirit-led, and had the Pope been willing to follow their leading!

So where does that leave us today? As quoted earlier, while Ortiz does not go so far as to say that today's leaders are infallible, he does claim that they are the only source of God's word to His people:

> *"The will of God for today comes <u>only</u> in the group of ministers."* [Emphasis mine]

(Ortiz, 1975: 132)

Ortiz has built this whole argument for the potential infallibility of today's church leaders on the belief that the apostles were infallible. Yet elsewhere Ortiz points out a number of examples of their fallibility. He starts by noting the difficulty often experienced by people in breaking with their traditions. And he notes this weakness amongst even those that followed Jesus, like Peter:

> "Traditions and structures are so strong! Sometimes I almost wonder if they don't have an evil spirit behind them. It's amazing to see the power of tradition even in an apostle like Peter when he was sent to Cornelius.
>
> Peter had been standing right there the day Jesus had said, 'Go therefore and make disciples of all nations' … He had also heard Jesus specifically command them to 'be My witnesses both in Jerusalem, and in all Judea and Samaria, and even to the remotest part of the earth' …
>
> But when it came right down to being a witness to Cornelius, a Gentile centurion, Peter's tradition wouldn't stretch. The Lord kept hitting him with the vision of the animals in the sheet and saying, 'What God has cleansed, no longer consider unholy' – and Peter kept insisting, 'By no means, Lord …'"

(Ortiz, 1975: 120-121)

> "An apostle of Jesus Christ – and he doesn't know what to do?! Even a small child would know. … But [Peter] is not willing to give the message. Why? Tradition."

(Ortiz, 1975: 122)

He also colorfully demonstrates this same fallibility amongst the leaders back in the Jerusalem church:

> "When [Peter and his colleagues] get back to Jerusalem, the news has already beaten them. Peter walks in. 'Hello, brother – how are you?' he says to someone.
>
> 'There's a board meeting at six o'clock.'
>
> 'What?'
>
> 'You heard me – a board meeting at six o'clock.'
>
> 'What for?'
>
> 'You'll find out when you get there.'
>
> The meeting opens. 'All right, Peter,' someone says, 'we've heard that you went into a Gentile home and ate with them! Don't touch us, don't touch us! Now, is that true?'
>
> Peter begins to tell the story. '… And as I began to speak, the Holy Spirit fell upon them –'
>
> 'No! No!'
>
> '– Just as He did upon us at the beginning –'
>
> 'No!'

> *'... If God therefore gave to them the same gift as He gave to us also after believing in the Lord Jesus Christ, who was I that I could stand in God's way?'*
>
> *Listen to what the Bible says: 'And when they heard this, they quieted down, and glorified God ...'* "
>
> (Ortiz, 1975: 123)

It appears that Ortiz would like the laity to obediently follow directives of the church leaders, especially with the implied potential for clerical infallibility if they are Spirit-filled. He bases his argument on the perceived infallibility of the apostles, yet also clearly demonstrates their ability to be wrong. There is a subtle irony in his argument. Ortiz himself claims to be Spirit-filled, and therefore presumably has the potential of infallibility, yet the holes in his arguments demonstrate his fallibility. Hopefully we can be very comfortable in abandoning any ideas relating to the possibility of infallibility within the church leaders we know!

The local church starts to take the place of God

One may question as to how a pastor such as Ortiz can get himself into a position where *he* is seen as an intermediary between God and man, to be obeyed by his followers as if he spoke for God Himself. One technique used, whether consciously or not, is to blur the boundaries between the role and authority of God, and the propounded role and authority of local churches and the leadership hierarchies within them. If we are to love and obey God wholeheartedly, and *if* the church leader is God's appointed representative, some argue we should therefore love and obey our pastor wholeheartedly. If we are to give of our time and money to God, then they also argue we should likewise give our time and money to the local church.

Excerpts of Ortiz' teaching along these lines follow. The emphases in the quotes are mine, intended to expose how his teaching moves so quickly and easily from our relationship to God to our relationship to the pastor and the local church.

Ortiz starts by stating that:

> "The only things Jesus talked about as being <u>given to Him</u> were gifts to the poor."
>
> (Ortiz, 1975: 39)

This line of reasoning is perhaps based on Jesus' words that if we give to the poor we are investing in treasures in heaven?

But even if we accept Ortiz' statement at face value, he seems to subtly shift the emphasis from giving to the poor to giving to the local church, claiming that we serve Jesus by giving offerings to the local church:

> "Servants don't say, 'Lord, do this and do that.' Servants say, 'Lord, what do You want me to do?' The satisfaction of the servant is to see the Lord satisfied. No wonder our churches don't work right. We have not begun to think about how to serve Jesus. Our

> *praises are His dinner. The hymns are the water on His table. The offering [to the local church] is yet another part of His meal."*
>
> (Ortiz, 1975: 38)

In Ortiz' defense, he does note that if we give to the local church so "… *we can air-condition the church* …" we have missed the point. To give to the local church for the benefit of others, not ourselves, would be an improvement. But a fundamental difference between Jesus' teaching and that of Ortiz needs to be highlighted. If Jesus had said we were to give our money to Him so He could give it to the poor, there might have been some closer parallels. But He said we are to give to the poor (directly), not letting our left hand know what our right hand is doing, and it will be counted to our credit.

Applying that teaching to you and me today, we can conclude that we can and should give directly, *as* God individually directs, *to whom* He directs and *when* He directs. Jesus' example does not translate to us giving to the local pastor so the pastor can presumably then seek God as to how to spend it. Nor can Jesus' teaching be extrapolated to suggest that if we give to the local church we are investing treasure for ourselves in heaven!

To hand over money to the church leaders so *they* can seek God is, at best, lazy on our part and, at worst, may result in our gifts going somewhere other than where God intended. We have looked at the issue of how we may need to differentiate between giving to God and giving to the local church. Now we look at how we give of our time.

Having gone through a list of the involvements expected of every disciple in Ortiz' church for seven nights of the week, Ortiz then goes on to elaborate how committed his disciples must be to the Kingdom to be able to keep up the pace of commitments to the church, stating:

> *"Now you can see why our people must be totally committed to the Kingdom! All day while they are working, they are thinking about what they are going to do after work for the Kingdom. They are disciples twenty-four hours a day. (I don't think I have to worry about people copying us without being submitted to Jesus. They wouldn't last very long.)"*
>
> (Ortiz, 1975: 135)

Again, I believe Ortiz blurs the lines. It seems inconceivable to Ortiz that some disciples of Christ might be called to commitments not organized and blessed by the church leaders!

Common sense and the Old Testament suggest if we have wronged someone, we must set the wrong right. For example, if we have stolen from someone we must pay them back (and if we use Exodus 22 as a reference, the payment may be quite a bit more than the value of what was stolen).

Ortiz seems to have a different view for the righting of wrongs. If we have committed what he is portraying as sins (such as smoking, going to a theatre or consuming alcohol), we can easily demonstrate a reversal of our ways by going to Sunday School, joining the choir, or giving money to the local church.

> "We can shut the window that lets in tobacco and open the window to Sunday school. We can shut the window to burlesque theatres and open the window to choir rehearsal. We can shut the window to liquor and open the window to giving money to the church."
>
> (Ortiz, 1975: 52-53)

The examples Ortiz provides of "wrongs" are themselves controversial. For example, he appears to be suggesting that liquor, in and of itself, is wrong. I doubt that many would question the problems of *abuse* of alcohol, but one must remember that even Jesus drank wine. But debating the rightness or otherwise of these external actions is not the point I wish to make. Rather, I wish to challenge the argument by Ortiz that becoming active in our local church is somehow opposite to these actions which he portrays as being wrongful. And is he implying that performing good deeds as faithful church members somehow cancels out the "wrongs"? If so, to me that sounds a bit like the concept of penance that harks back centuries within the Catholic church, and that stands in stark contrast to the message of "saved by grace", not by works.

Ortiz holds up for our viewing an example of the sort of commitment he considers commendable:

> "I have friends who have told me, 'Juan, I have given my life to God for your sake. If something happens to you, it happens to me. So my life is in your hands. If you need my blood, it's yours. So is my car, my home, everything.'"
>
> (Ortiz, 1975: 55)

If God is our "Lord", then *He* has rights to our time and possessions. For Juan Ortiz to allow or encourage that same level of commitment from "his" laity to himself seems to me to be a dangerous blurring of boundaries between God Himself and the church leaders—mere humans who claim to stand in His place. Our allegiance to God must be given to no other.

Submission to Christ becomes submission to church leaders

This misunderstanding of loyalty to God versus loyalty to a local pastor may be at its most dangerous and immoral when submission to the lordship of Christ becomes confused and turns into submission to the pastor as "lord".

In addressing social justice issues, Ortiz seems to suggest that any social justice action must start in the local church because that is, or should be, according to him

> "... where our [church leader's] own word is heard and <u>obeyed</u>." [Emphasis mine]
>
> (Ortiz, 1975: 135)

This position appears to be reinforced by teaching that

> "The congregation must be renewed in its understanding of the lordship of Christ and the role of the slave ..."
>
> (Ortiz, 1975: 131)

As seen in the following quotation, Ortiz seems to imply that the laity must learn to submit not just to the lordship of Christ, but also to the lordship of the pastor:

> "If we were under the lordship of Christ, He could just say the word, and we wouldn't need any soft organ music or soothing words from the pulpit – we would do as we were told. ... [Jesus] commanded, and [Jesus' disciples] did it. That is how disciples are formed.
>
> In order to form lives, [church leaders] must stop being speakers and start being fathers. Speakers have only hearers. Fathers have children. Learning doesn't come by hearing but by obeying [the pastor]."
>
> (Ortiz, 1975: 111)

It appears to me that, according to Ortiz, if the pastor is the representative of Christ, he has the authority to rebuke those who don't obey:

> "When Peter objected to the idea of the crucifixion, Jesus said, 'Get behind Me, Satan! You are a stumbling-block to Me' (Matthew 16:23). Can you imagine a modern pastor saying that to one of his flock?! Like it or not, rebuking is part of the formation process in discipleship."
>
> (Ortiz, 1975: 111)

Is Ortiz really laying the foundation for dictating the behavior of disciples in his church? It seems so, with him stating,

> "The further we went [in cell formation and discipleship], the more essential the lordship of Christ became – as you will see."
>
> (Ortiz, 1975: 133)

He then immediately goes on to describe what all his followers must do on each evening, even though

> "... nearly everyone is working all day long."
>
> (Ortiz, 1975: 133)

And his regime is not optional. For example:

> "A fifth night is given to the family. This is a _commandment_." [Emphasis mine]
>
> (Ortiz, 1975: 134)

> "A sixth night is given to rest. This too is a _commandment_. ..." [Emphasis mine]
>
> (Ortiz, 1975: 134)

And these rules apply to all, as clarified when Ortiz states:

> "Everyone stays home and sleeps until ten or eleven o'clock on Sunday morning."
>
> (Ortiz, 1975: 134)

At this point, it is arguable that Ortiz has become the leader of a centrally controlled system, telling people when to attend church meetings, and even when to sleep in!

The potential for this as a despotic system is arguably reinforced by use of language about what things people are permitted or forbidden to do:

> "After about six months ... I <u>allowed</u> my disciples to steal a few more members and begin making disciples of them themselves.
>
> ... we had to set up a number of cells. During the changeover [from more conventional church styles to cell-based styles], new people were being saved in the cells, but we <u>forbade</u> them to come to the club-type church ..." [Emphasis mine]

(Ortiz, 1975: 115)

Such an authoritarian structure would be unacceptable even if it were limited to church-related matters. But, according to his own words, apparently Ortiz' control reaches into the personal lives of those who follow him, with him arguing that God's rights, as Lord over all aspects of the lives of Christians, flows through to Ortiz' rights over the lives of the laity within his local church. For example, while the homes of the laity may be legally retained in the names of the individuals, Ortiz seems to claim the right to order how they are to be used:

> "When we first began to preach this message of discipleship ... our congregations were very willing to obey. Many of our members were bringing their homes and apartments to give to the church. ...
>
> We didn't know what to do with all these properties ...
>
> [After 6 months, the leaders said] 'We are going to return everyone's real estate. ... [God] wants a house with you inside taking care of it ... ready – for Him. He also wants your car, with you as the driver.
>
> 'Just remember, though, that it all still belongs to Him.'
>
> ... When visitors come to our congregation ... we say to someone, 'You, brother, you're going to take these people to your house.' <u>We don't ask; we command</u> ..." [Emphasis mine]

(Ortiz, 1975: 35-36)

Ortiz states that the homes and cars "... *still belong to Him*" i.e. they belong to God. But it appears that Ortiz is acting in the role of owner, seemingly commanding how they are used, without having to maintain these assets—the people do—but they are apparently required to be available at Ortiz' beck and call.

Similarly, my interpretation of Ortiz' writing is that God's rights over how we use our time have become Ortiz' rights over the laity's time:

> "Sometimes a Christian says to himself, 'Well, now that I'm finished working for the day, I'll go home and take a shower. Then I'll watch television for a while, and then I'll go to bed. Yes, I know there's a meeting tonight, but after all, pastor, I'm entitled to a little rest ...'

> *Entitled to what, Mr. Slave? You are entitled to nothing.* You are bought by Jesus Christ, and He owns all the hours of your day." [Emphasis mine]
>
> (Ortiz, 1975: 38)

And Ortiz' apparent total control over the lives of his followers seems to me to be held up as a shining example of the potential of his whole church to move as one—under Ortiz' control, of course!

> "You see, with this [hierarchical discipleship] structure, you [as church leaders] can do anything you want. You can pull the whole body together within a matter of hours if needed."
>
> (Ortiz, 1975: 116)

But can some laity chose to lay their lives on the altar (Ortiz' altar, not Christ's), while other laity within his church retain whatever level of individual control they desire? It would appear that they are no longer just "members", but Ortiz' slave-like "disciples".

> "We decided to stop using the word member, because it sounded too much like a club with no submission. We said we would use the word disciple instead. Everyone understood what a disciple was and knew that he was not there yet.
>
> … If you had asked [someone], 'Are you a disciple?' he would have said, 'Oh, no. Not yet. … [The pastor] hasn't placed me under someone to be formed into a disciple."
>
> (Ortiz, 1975: 114)

My interpretation of the material presented so far was that Ortiz had established a totalitarian hierarchy, and that in fact he was proud of what had been achieved in his church as highlighted by Ortiz in a story he tells. Ortiz decided to stage a *"mock persecution"* in which the local church was closed for a month, with people meeting in homes and visiting other congregations. As I read Ortiz' own account, it appeared that this visitation was not left to individuals or families to decide; instead, the leaders decided where the groups would go, and all cell members obeyed:

> "Cacho, for example – he's an auto body repairman who has 300 disciples in cells under him. … Cacho and his 300 went to a Baptist church …"
>
> (Ortiz, 1975: 115)

Ortiz does not seem to shy away from control, rather appearing to brazenly espouse it, and say it is the way it's meant to be (with him in charge, of course):

> "Club-type members don't submit. In fact, it's the other way around – they want the pastor to submit to them, because they hold the vote in the club. Again we are upside down. … In the … Kingdom, the arm [i.e. those higher up in the leadership hierarchy] controls the fingers, not the other way around."
>
> (Ortiz, 1975: 111)

A common trend in cults is the practice of suppression of questioning. The first section of this book addresses this topic at length. Ortiz' structure seems to follow the same direction, explicitly teaching the evils of "*speaking out against each other*".

> "*If you see a man cutting his foot with a knife, you will say, 'What in the world are you doing?'*
>
> '*I'm cutting my foot!*'
>
> '*Why?*'
>
> '*Because this foot stepped on the other one, and it said, 'Cut him!*' '
>
> *The man is out of his mind. He doesn't have the discernment to realize that both feet belong to the same body.*
>
> *… We must understand what the Body of Christ is. We must stop doing crazy things to ourselves, speaking against each other – no wonder we hurt. No wonder the church is weak and bleeding.*"
>
> (Ortiz, 1975: 104)

So it appears that Ortiz' "disciples" must not call to account, or criticize, him (or others). It is my opinion that such an attitude is reflective of controlling leadership, as noted early in this book, and that church leaders such as Ortiz who demonstrate a level of authority over the laity that must be rejected.

CHAPTER 9:
THE SUBTLE DANGERS OF "HIERARCHIES"

Mixed messages from a champion of freedom

Hudson Taylor gave his life in faithful service, sharing the good news with Chinese people, many of whom would otherwise not have been reached with the message. Not only did Taylor have a significant impact on a vast population of Chinese, he fearlessly broke with many traditions. For example, in spite of cutting criticism from other English people, he wore the clothes of those he wished to reach, rather than retaining English culture that would have been a barrier for many. He went into the Chinese interior when others preferred the safety of staying in or close to "treaty ports". And the list of radical changes goes on.

But perhaps one of the early and most striking examples of his freedom was his attitude to hierarchical structures. He was raised in a society steeped in class separation and the associated hierarchical structures of government, business, churches, and mission societies. When formal mission societies would not endorse him, he went to China anyway. When cautioned against going to the interior, he still proceeded. He was consistently polite to those in authority, yet exhibited an admirable freedom to act independently of their advice or approval. He followed what he believed was God's call, and could not be turned aside by those with rank and title.

To his credit, not only did Taylor display a personal freedom from subservience to those in authority, he initially expected others to relate to him, the founder of the China Inland Mission (CIM), with the same freedom. There are many who preach freedom from authority, but demand allegiance from *their* followers. Not so with Taylor at this early stage. One clear example relates to a missionary engaged by the CIM who had strongly divergent views than those of Taylor:

> "Mr. Cooper possessed strong individuality and was fearless as to his convictions. Mr. Taylor's relationship ... with this beloved friend ... may be judged from an incident that took place in the early days of the China Council.
>
> 'I do not like so often to oppose you,' said Mr. Cooper on one occasion; 'I think I had better resign.'
>
> 'No, indeed!' was the reply, 'I value such opposition; it saves me from many a mistake.'"
>
> (Taylor & Taylor, 1918: 554)

A similar attitude of freedom for others was shown when a Chinese local church, founded under the care of the CIM, appointed missionaries without the involvement of the CIM authorities. Rather than condemning them for their lack of consultation, their actions were merely reported in a manner that implies simple approval:

> "The Hang-Chow Church has sent out its first missionary, chosen by themselves and supported by their own gifts."
>
> (Taylor & Taylor, 1918: 255)

It is difficult to break totally free from the influences of our formative years and culture. Many who bring reform show evidence in their lives of ways they have sought to reject. For example, some suggest that while Martin Luther was the channel for radical "Reformation" within church practices in Germany, notably his championing of the concept of the "priesthood of all believers", he was also a victim of the traditions from which he was trying to break free. He taught on the priesthood of all believers, yet practiced the continuance of a clear role for church leaders.

Similarly, Taylor had some vestiges of his culture showing through in contrast to a life largely lived in freedom from the opinion of others. His own view on obedience to parents, expressed when he was in his mid-twenties and already in China following God's call on his life, was one of subservience.

> "If there was one thing of which Hudson Taylor had no doubt it was that the blessing of God rested upon obedience to parents or those in parental authority. Nothing would have induced him to act contrary to a command from his own parents, nor could he encourage the one he loved [i.e. his future wife, an orphan] to disregard her guardian's wishes. Years after, when experience had confirmed these convictions, he wrote upon this important subject:
>
>> I have never known the disobedience to the definite command of a parent, even if that parent were mistaken, that was not followed by retribution."
>
> (Taylor & Taylor, 1911: 437-438)

Such an attitude of absolute obedience to parents seems out of line with Jesus' confronting statement that, when compared to our love for Him, our relationship to even our parents should appear weak in comparison (Luke 14:26).

Also, within the context of what came to be the chain-of-command within the China Inland Mission, some mixed messages also appeared.

On the one hand, Taylor showed patience and grace in allowing those lower down in the hierarchy plenty of time to adapt to his appointment of leaders over them.

On the other hand, a hierarchy of command *was* established by Taylor. The supervision was to be motivated by love and by an attitude of service to those lower in rank. But still, rank was established, and it was presumed that Taylor believed that God Himself would eventually overcome dissent by showing the workers the "rightness" of the appointments. Taylor advised the leaders as follows:

> *"… above all, do not let [the rank-and-file missionaries] dream you [as Taylor's appointed leaders] are taking a higher place than their own: leave God to show that in due time. You are really their head as you become their servant and helper."*

(Taylor & Taylor, 1918: 393)

Further comments on the role of hierarchies

Often the laity place unfair expectations on their leaders. Rinehart exposes this pressure when he states:

> *"… the church groans under the weight of a flawed assumption that its spiritual leaders must be well educated, professional, and high-powered … The church as a whole pays a steep price for this false distinction [between professional leaders and 'ordinary' followers]."*

(Rinehart, 1998: 103)

Another source of expectations is peer pressure, where church leaders are spurred on to greater measurable achievements, such as higher attendance and offering statistics, in the context of comparison with other churches. This pressure may come via books (typically written by "successful" church leaders), by seminaries, or via conferences with the same "successful" leaders as guest speakers. I reviewed the quotation below. Was it possible that colleges and seminaries are actually success oriented? Girard's articulation certainly seems to suggest it is not just possible, but likely:

> *"Every book for pastors contains more clever ideas for doing it ourselves.*
>
> *Every Christian college and seminary aims at sending out ministers steeped in the glorious institutional idea that through enough hard work, clever manipulation of church members, effective organization and the profuse use of new ideas to 'get 'em involved' — 'you too can be a success.' (Incidentally, God will help you.)*
>
> *Every ministerial convention is more of the same. The pastors of the big, successful churches are there to tell you how it's done, how to organize, promote, advertise, preach and handle people so that 'you too can be a success.' At such meetings, the air is literally electrified with great ideas and challenge, challenge, challenge.*

> *A friend of mine came back from a ministerial convention recently with the comment, 'I'm so challenged, I'm limp!'*
>
> *To put into operation the wonderful ideas gleaned from just one ministerial convention would take the next five years! And each idea would probably work. Attendance would increase. Membership would grow. Offerings would swell. Involvement would reach a fever-pitch. Success would be assured.*
>
> *But the explosive, spontaneous life experienced by the New Testament Church would be no nearer than it was before the convention convened!*
>
> *But 'everybody's doing it.' It's the way to build a big church and to be a 'successful minister.' The accepted, approved, humanly desirable way. Guaranteed to bring much glory to the pastor, his local church, and the denomination whose 'glorious distinctives' he is seeking to spotlight."*
>
> (Girard, 1972: 64-65):

But sometimes the pressures for "success" come from the church leaders themselves, personally driven by their own mixed motives. Paul Hiebert, in *Culture and Cross-Cultural Differences, and Social Structure and Church Growth*, warns of empire builders who

> *"… gain personal followers and build large churches, schools, hospitals and other institutions that prove [their] worth."*
>
> (Hiebert in Winter et. al., 1981: 383)

Brown also identifies leaders' misguided motives:

> *"Their burning passion is not primarily to build the Messiah's Kingdom, to make His name known and to fulfill His goals as much as it is to fulfill their own vision, rallying people around themselves more than the Lord, guarding their reputations more carefully than they guard the reputation of the Lord. How unscriptural and offensive this is!"*
>
> (Brown, 2002: 59)

Girard cuts to the core issue, that too often those who establish hierarchical organizations, with themselves at the top, are doing just that—seeing themselves up at the top rather than establishing that God is in that place:

> *"It began to dawn on me that I had never allowed Christ to be Head of His own Body! I had been its head. In every church I'd ever seen in operation, even though we often spoke of Him as Head, in reality, it was a pastor or a board or a congregational meeting that ran the church. Not on the basis of a powerful sensed unity in the Spirit, but on the basis of majority rule. All the decisions were made by men. All the strategies, programs and organizations were arranged by human ingenuity; and then 'sanctified' by a quick glib prayer asking the Lord to 'bless these plans, this program, this organization.'"*
>
> (Girard, 1972: 51)

Hunt's novel, *The Debt*, highlights the same problem, with a cutting conclusion. She describes a pastor's wife who is questioning the role of the local church versus each individual following God's calling. She states,

> *"If our members attended every program we offered, they'd be at the church ten or twelve hours a day, seven days a week."*
>
> (Hunt, 2004: 263-264)

The husband's response shows his assumption that being totally centered on the Lord equates to a life centered on the local church, saying,

> *"And what's wrong with that? ... We are to center our lives around the Lord, we are commanded to fellowship together, we are to build up the body of Christ."*
>
> (Hunt, 2004: 264)

And the wife's response,

> *"Going to church does not equal living for Jesus."*
>
> (Hunt, 2004: 264)

This is a fundamental problem—having the church leaders assume the place of God. And we can see it played out across the three facets of the Godhead, with church leaders wanting to be a "father" for their followers, supplanting Jesus as the mediator between God and man, and acting as the conduit of revelation, taking the place of the Holy Spirit.

CHAPTER 10:
STOP SUPPORTING THE HIERARCHY

Hopefully you are beginning to see the need for a change from the tradition that divides Christianity into two groups—the professional clergy, leaders who strive to control the direction of God's people, and those who are controlled. Further, you may realize that while making a change is desirable, it comes at a price. You may be misunderstood and maligned, and you may need to consider the cost of finding freedom from control.

But where do you start in your journey to freedom? In the opening chapters we established the right, and the responsibility, to question. It is when we actually start to break free from the hierarchies of control that we may meet with the strongest opposition by those entrenched in the systems of "religion". They have invested much, and they will not want to lose their control over you. You must retain your right to question and challenge, and not cave to their pressures.

Your responsibility is to obey God, not man

We stated earlier how cults expect unthinking, unchallenged obedience. Brown cautions that our response to authority figures who demand our obedience should be a polite refusal:

> *"…when we say no to the system, it is not because we are simply fed up frustrated or disillusioned or disturbed, but because we are saying yes to God. When we say to an authority figure, 'I'm sorry, but I can't submit to your demands,' it is not because we are unsubmissive to leaders but because we are totally submitted to the Father."*
>
> (Brown, 2002: 91)

Quoting Watchman Nee's book, *Spiritual Authority*, Brown then goes on to clarify that

> *"Submission is a matter of attitude, while obedience is a matter of conduct."*
>
> (Brown, 2002: 91)

What does this mean? We can, and should, maintain an *attitude* of submission and respect for rightful authority. However, it is absolutely vital that we remind ourselves that any person who plays the role of an intermediary between God and man is not playing a "rightful" role. Putting that aside, there are still times when our *conduct*, or actions, must lead us to "disobey" even so-called "rightful" authority. Peter and John did not obey the religious leaders of their day when ordered not to preach again, and Jesus Himself broke many of the rules of these same leaders. There are times when we must make a stand.

> *"The midwives and Moses' mother both disobeyed the decrees of Pharaoh by preserving Moses … yet they were considered to be women of faith."*
>
> (Brown, 2002: 93)

An example a lot closer to home is the attitudes of children to their parents. Children may have an attitude of respect, yet should act in "disobedience" to parental directives if the parents order the children to break the law, be it God's law or man's.

> *"It is our submission to authority that empowers us to disobey authority in obedience to God."*
>
> (Brown, 2002: 93)

Brown then quotes Gandhi's statement that

> *"A non-violent revolution is not a program of seizure of power. It is a program of transformation of relationships, ending in a peaceful transfer of power."*
>
> (Brown, 2002: 95)

Brown comments that Gandhi

> *"… taught that by nonviolent refusal to cooperate with injustice, the power of injustice is broken."*
>
> (Brown, 2002: 95)

Brown calls for a revolution of Christians, but warns that it

> *"… is not simply a call to go against what is wrong with the current system, but to go with the Spirit and the Word. We emphasize doing things God's way, not merely bringing about change."*
>
> (Brown, 2002: 94)

It is to be noted that, while Brown quotes Nee, he also warns on the abuse that has arisen from those who quote Nee in an attempt to support their abusive leadership styles. In a footnote, and quoting Viola, Brown's book states that Nee's book, *Spiritual Authority*, is

> *"… one of the most abused pieces of literature ever to be written in this [20th] century. Virtually every recent authoritarian movement has gotten mileage out of this book to support the power of heavy-handed leadership."*
>
> (Brown, 2002: 214, quoting Viola)

Exposing the covering!

In reviewing Brown's book, I encountered the following statements. A detailed analysis led me to ask if Brown's views challenges ideas sometimes encountered on "covering", and obedience to leaders who might direct you regarding all sorts of aspects of personal and family life. He says:

> "If you say, 'We're called to obey our leaders no matter what,' that means you have to marry whom they tell you to marry, have as many kids as they tell you to have (or not have any kids if they say so), give as much money to the church as they tell you to give, live where they tell you to live and do whatever else they tell you to do – if they choose to make such demands.
>
> You reply, 'But God will protect me if they're wrong.'
>
> Says who? Why should God protect you or me if we fail to seek His face, fail to consult Him for His will, fail to use wisdom (or common sense!), fail to search the Scriptures for ourselves, fail to be responsible. Where is it written that if we simply submit to wrong counsel—no questions asked, no concerns raised—the Lord will bless us because we submitted?
>
> According to the Word of God every believer is a priest of the Most High God with direct access to His throne, and Jesus said that His sheep hear His voice (John 10: 1-5, 27), Paul taught that all of God's children are led by His Spirit (Romans 8:14-16) and John wrote that the anointing resides in each of us (1 John 2:20). On what scriptural basis can we shirk our responsibility to hear the Lord for our own lives and simply obey whatever the authority demands, regardless of how extreme or absurd those demands may be?
>
> Think back … Did the Hebrew midwives say, 'Our authority, Pharaoh, has commanded us to kill all male children born to our people, so we will obey him and God will bless us for that?' No. They disobeyed the demands of the authority and God blessed them for disobeying—because Pharaoh, their authority, stepped outside of his rightful bounds and ordered them to sin.
>
> 'But now you're missing the point,' you argue. 'When our authorities tell us to disobey the written Word, we don't obey. For everything else we obey.'
>
> I agree with the first half of this statement. But if that is the only time we can rightfully disobey, then, based on that logic, if your pastor tells you whom to marry, you do have to marry that person—and the Bible does not guarantee that God will bless you if you make the wrong choice. Also … the Scriptures teach that when the voice of God is in conflict with the voice of man, even if that voice is the voice of an authority, we must obey God rather than man (always with a submitted attitude, always with proper respect shown toward the authority and always accepting the consequences of our choices).

You ask, 'But what about 1 Peter 2:18? It is written there, 'Slaves, submit yourselves to your masters with all respect, not only to those who are good and considerate, but also to those who are harsh.' '

My friend, you are misusing the Word of God here. The pastor is not the master and the congregant is not the slave! In a master-slave relationship, the master owned the slave and had every legal right to work that slave to the bone. He was the absolute boss, and the slave lived to do his master's will. Obviously no Christian leader has any such rights over his congregants, and it is unacceptable that any pastor would try to use this verse to support his authoritarian rule over the flock. (To any believer enslaved in such an unscriptural church relationship, I recommend the counsel Paul had for slaves: 'If you can gain your freedom, do so!' In other words, get out as quickly as you can. Run for your life!)...

No minister or church owns you, and no one has the right to tell you that your convictions are not from the Lord unless those convictions are contrary to the Scriptures. In light of this, I find it interesting that many church leaders turn this upside down. They tell their congregants, 'You must submit to everything I say unless it runs contrary to the Scriptures,' rather than, 'You must hold fast to your convictions before the Lord unless those convictions run contrary to the Word.' There is quite a difference! ...

How this flies in the face of the typical, heavy-handed leadership!"

(Brown, 2002: 109-110, 114-115)

"*...every believer is ultimately accountable to Jesus, the Head of the Body and Lord of the Church. Therefore, when a leader demands that a believer go against his or her conscience he is asking that believer to act in a non-moral way. This is a serious issue. ... in the New Testament believers are never told they are 'accountable' to their leaders. Our primary accountability is to God.*"

(Brown, 2002: 115)

Frank Peretti's book, *The Visitation*, is a novel, but nonetheless contains some perspectives we would do well to consider. One of his characters states:

"I never believe anything just because a big-named Christian leader says it. I never do anything I don't want to do just because a pastor, presuming to be the voice of God, tries to coerce me with guilt or threats. I no longer respond to visions God gives to others about what I should or should not do, think, or be."

(Peretti, 1999: 323)

Follow God, not man

Girard declares the need for people to live under God's grace rather than the law of church leaders, and for all believers to live

"... personal lives of faith where they, <u>alone</u> with God, may experience His personal leadership, hear the voice of the Spirit speaking personally to them, and be led into and equipped for the kind of personal ministries that will make them really useful citizens in the Kingdom of God." [Emphasis mine]

(Girard, 1972: 119)

Hunt's novel shares on the same theme:

"... Chris's behavior had baffled me; now his actions make perfect sense. Like a dandelion seed blown by the breath of God, he has drifted throughout life, sharing God's love where and when he could.

But how can people who are tied to responsibilities live that way?

'The key is being obedient,' Chris murmurs. 'It's not so difficult. When you see a need and hear the Spirit's voice, you obey.'

Is it that easy? For him, maybe. For me ... it's never that simple. I have too many obligations, too many demands on my time.

... I realize it's been a long time since I consciously stopped in my busy routine to listen for the voice of God. ...

I have spent my entire adult life doing what I thought Christianity required me to do while Chris has been walking with an ear cocked to hear the voice of God."

(Hunt, 2004: 257-258)

Non-Christians, and Christians who have rejected institutional "church", are freed from Sunday morning rituals, from paying for the building fund or the clergy's salary, and from the need to get approval from the church leaders before they can do anything. But in our freedom, we need to make sure we are not abusing this freedom. The right to make choices should not translate into making wrong choices.

"Looking back, we see that our freedom to choose badly was not, after all, a very real freedom.

When we chose because we 'must,' this was not a free choice, either. But it got us started in the right direction.

When we chose because we 'ought to,' we were really doing better. This time we were earning some freedom, making ourselves ready for more.

But when, now and then, we could gladly make right choices without rebellion, holdout, or conflict, then we had our first view of what perfect freedom under God's will could be like."

(Bill, 1967: 124)

"At first glance legalism seems hard, but actually freedom in Christ is the harder way. It is relatively easy not to murder, hard to reach out in love; easy to avoid a neighbor's

bed, hard to keep a marriage alive; easy to pay taxes, hard to serve the poor. When living in freedom, I must remain open to the Spirit for guidance. I am more aware of what I have neglected than what I have achieved. I cannot hide behind a mask of behavior, like the hypocrites, nor can I hide behind facile comparisons with other Christians."

(Yancey, 1997: 209)

Our reading has set us on the path of identifying those traditions that have become so commonplace and "normal" that we may have difficulty in seeing any problem with them. We have looked at the dangers of installing church leaders as a distinct leadership class. The formation of a discrete class of Christians goes directly against the grain of the concept of the "body", where no part is more (or less) important.

Another practice in Christendom that also flies in the face of the "body" analogy is the suppression of individuality. In its extreme, conformity is a cult-like expectation, sometimes even down to the clothes to wear. In more subtle forms, it is the denigration of those who dare to be different.

One step towards freedom is the recognition and rejection of hierarchies. Another is the freedom to be the unique person God designed you to be. We'll go on to explore this.

SECTION 3:

NO MORE CONFORMITY

Having led you to think seriously about the legitimacy of 'holy men' in our community of believers, the next thing to consider relates to the topic of conformity.

Debates on the issue can get unnecessarily heated through misunderstanding of the words used in arguments. For example, unity and uniformity are easily confused. In some religious groups, members can be identified just by their dress. And I'm not just talking about Buddhist monks all dressing in orange. There are a number of what I will refer to as "fringe" Christian groups who expect all their members to dress alike, have similar hair styles, "enjoy" the same forms of entertainment, and so on.

That's uniformity. They all look alike. But there might be in-fighting amongst the members, indicating a lack of unity. In contrast, you can have a group of people who dress differently and have different life-styles but who demonstrate unity as they cooperate to achieve shared goals.

Some of the more mainstream Christian denominations influence members to look alike and, more concerning, to think alike. For example, there can be pressure to uphold the church leaders' vision rather than seek your own. Those who have the audacity to think for themselves and express views differing from those of the leaders, or to act differently from ways they are told to act, may well be labeled as having a "spirit of rebellion", or at least be seen as failing as a team player.

There is another pair of words that can cloud the discussion on conformity—individualism and individuality.

The term "individualism" has many definitions, and even those who espouse the values of individualism have divergent views as to its meaning. At the heart of the concept, though, are issues relating to who makes decisions, and who benefits from those decisions. In its extreme form, some will classify actions as demonstrating individualism if a person makes decisions for themselves, only for their own benefit, while a person who demonstrates what some call "collectivism" may instead believe that decisions should be made by the community, for the benefit of the community. An extract from Wikipedia (2008) defines individualism as:

- "the pursuit of personal happiness and independence rather than collective goals or interests".
- "the belief that society exists for the benefit of the individual, who must not be constrained by government interactions or made subordinate to collective interests".

Some church leaders actively warn against individualism. Many would perceive such attitudes as being selfish and self-centered. If a person held such views, it may be very difficult to see how they would fit in to the collective "Body of Christ".

Christ Himself prayed that we would be one. He sought unity. Paul taught that each member of the Body is unique, one being an eye, one being a hand, and so on. They are demonstrating individuality. Is there any conflict here? Thankfully, no—each and every member of the Body performs an important function as assigned by God, and each is as important as the other. We can be different, yet "one" in unity.

This New Testament teaching is not a compromise between extremes. Rather, it fully embraces some aspects of the richness and goodness that are reflected in both collectivism and individualism. On the one hand, all Christians are part of the Body of Christ. It is not a choice we make, and there are consequences and responsibilities attached to this reality. But on the other hand, we are all different, and that is exactly how our Maker designed us and intended us to be. We can celebrate and rejoice in our individuality while having a sensitivity and respect for the others that together, while different, also make the whole. It stands to reason that, because of our very differences, He also has different, and often unique, callings for each of us.

Christ's example encourages us all to be the God-designed individuals we are intended to be, for the benefit of the whole.

Some church leaders, in their attempts to suppress individuality of laity, misquote passages from the Old Testament relating to phrases such as Judges 17:6, where their interpretation of everyone doing what they thought to be right (because they didn't have a king) was that the people were living in a state of anarchy. The teaching goes along the lines that chaos abounded because the people were living according to their own selfish or misguided ethics, and if only they had a central authority in the shape of a king to set the direction for the nation, all would have been well.

Within local church contexts I have encountered this skewed teaching; the message is simple—the pastor is there to direct God's people, and any who do what is "right in their own eyes" are in sinful rebellion. Such a message suits those who seek to retain control of the laity. But it is an opportunistic misinterpretation.

Reading Samuel, it is abundantly clear that God doesn't want a king for His people. He is their king, and He wants the people to follow Him directly. It was the people who wanted a king. In 1 Samuel 8 the elders demanded that Samuel nominate a king to rule over them, because that's what the people were demanding. Perhaps Samuel might have felt a bit hurt, but God made it abundantly clear that the core issue was that they had rejected God Himself, not Samuel (1 Samuel 10:18-19).

At Samuel's farewell speech to the Israelites, he reminds them that it was they that demanded a king (1 Samuel 12:12. After a display of God's power, the people realized that their demand for a king added to their many other sins (1 Samuel 12:19) and yet subsequently went on and got their king anyway!

The sin was not that people did as they saw fit in the period before they had a king. The sin was in seeking to have a king to take the place of God. The New International Version (NIV) Study Bible commentary on Judges states:

> *"Throughout Judges the fundamental issue is the lordship of God in Israel – i.e., Israel's acknowledgement of and loyalty to his rule. His kingship over Israel had been uniquely established by the covenant at Sinai … In the very center of the cycle of the judges …*

Gideon had to remind Israel that the Lord was her King ... The recurring lament, and indictment, ... is: 'In those days Israel had no king; everyone did as he saw fit' ... The ... implicit charge is that Israel did not truly acknowledge or obey her heavenly King ..."

(The NIV Study Bible)

Do not let the church leaders use the phrase, "everyone did as he saw fit" to condemn you for being an individual and seeking God for yourself. And most certainly do not allow them to set themselves up as replacement "kings".

CHAPTER 11:
BLATANT EXPECTATIONS ON CONFORMITY

Some cultures value the expression of individuality, while others place a higher value on the group. For those of us raised in Western democracies, the workings of a group-based culture may seem strange. This contrast is powerfully exposed by Donald McGavran in *The Bridges of God*, where he looks at an entire community considering the claims of Christ:

> *"To understand the psychology of the innumerable sub-societies which make up non-Christian nations, it is essential that the leaders of the Churches and missions strive to see life from the point of view of a people, to whom individual action is treachery. Among those who think corporately only a rebel would strike out alone, without consultation and without companions. The individual does not think of himself as a self-sufficient unit, but as part of the group. His business affairs, his children's marriages, his personal problems, or the difficulties he has with his wife are properly settled by group thinking. Peoples become Christian as this group-mind is brought into a life-giving relationship to Jesus as Lord.*
>
> *It is important to note that the group decision is not the sum of separate individual decisions. The leader makes sure that his followers will follow. The followers make sure that they are not ahead of each other. Husbands sound out wives. Sons pledge their fathers. 'Will we as a group move if so-and-so does not come?' is a frequent question. As the group considers becoming Christian, tension mounts and excitement rises. Indeed, a prolonged informal vote-taking is underway. A change of religion involves a community change. Only as its members move together, does change become healthy and constructive."*
>
> (McGavran, 1981: 275)

McGavran articulates the reality of group-thinking in some cultures. But there are important questions that must be answered for us. What role does such group-thinking play within Christendom, or more significantly, what role *should* it play? Is it healthy or unhealthy? How much of conformity (and individuality) reflects traditional Western church tradition, and how much is God-ordained?

Cookie-cutter Christians?

Some people seem to oppose "difference". In an upcoming section, I analyze in some detail the teaching by Ortiz on "mashed potatoes", where he expresses the goal of people losing their individuality. Similarly, Watchman Nee, in *Changed into His Likeness*, seems to make sweeping generalizations, proposing that individualism is contrary to God's plan for the Body of Christ, even when expressed as individual (but not necessarily selfish) thinking.

> *"God must deliver us from the whole principle of individualism. He must save us from wanting to be outstanding individual Christians, and somehow make us one in His house. For it is the house of God that is His witness in the earth. Everyone knows how difficult it is for Christians to live together! When by the grace of God it happens, and continues to happen, even hell takes notice."*

(Nee, 1967: 40)

In direct contrast to the views above, other authors note the need for individual Christians to fearlessly go against the tide of common Christian thinking. They challenge individual Christians to be willing to be pioneers. For example, not only do Oliver and Thwaites challenge us to be different, but they warn us not to expect support and understanding from established local churches and their leaders.

> *"Apostolic individuals ... are often not understood and are called 'maverick' and somewhat reckless. They often experience difficulty fitting into the present church culture."*

(Oliver & Thwaites, 2001: 166)

> *"One thing that is sure about pioneering people is that, to this day, they are largely unaffirmed and unrecognised by pastors. ... These unlikely people hold an important key for this time. They have a God-given ability to penetrate the spheres of creation and make a way for the body to enter in to answer the cry."*

(Oliver & Thwaites, 2001: 167)

Brown seems to echo this theme, looking at history. He names many Christians from the past who he suggests are well regarded now but were opposed in their time. My interpretation of his historic analysis was that what made them stand out was that they were individualistic, *"each* [acting] *in his own distinctive way"*:

> *"William Booth. John Bunyan. Martin Luther. John Owen. William Seymour. John Wesley. George Whitefield. Roger Williams. What do these men have in common?*

All of them were famous Christian leaders, each in his own distinctive way. Booth founded the Salvation Army, spreading its radical and compassionate message to more than eighty nations. Bunyan wrote The Pilgrim's Progress, one of the most translated, widely read books in history. Luther provided the spark that ignited the Protestant Reformation. Owen was the most learned of the Puritan theologians. Seymour was the principal leader in the Azusa Street outpouring. Wesley was the father of the Methodist movement. Whitefield was the greatest preacher of the Great Awakening. Williams paved the way for the concept of the (proper) separation of church and state. These men not only touched their own generation but left behind a legacy that continues to touch lives today.

But these men have something else in common: Each one of them went against the religious grain of his day. Each one of them was a pioneer often scorned and rejected by the Church establishment. Each one of them had a conflict with the contemporary spiritual authorities, ultimately having to obey God rather than man. Yet we hail them today as heroes.

… The tune may be different but the words of the song are always the same: 'By what authority do you do these things? Who gave you the right?' That is how the established spiritual leadership opposes the new voice or move or church or message.

Jesus Himself experienced this kind of resistance."

(Brown, 2002: 141-143)

What are we to make of such divergent views? Noble seems to suggest that both extremes are dangerous. We should neither follow the crowd (even if the crowd be "God's people") nor, as individuals, be independent in our actions:

"Jesus is not coming back for a toe or finger, but for a body, a mature and holy bride. Israel understood the truth of corporate salvation, often neglecting their personal walk with God and bringing judgement on themselves. Western Christians, at the other extreme, are individualistic. This, too, is sin."

(Noble, 2002: 48)

There are obviously divergent views from many sources. But what does *God* want?

God loves diversity

God is a God of diversity. We are told each snowflake is unique, and that every zebra and giraffe has markings that are totally unique. We were designed in the image of God, yet God Himself has ensured diversity. Each of us can be uniquely distinguished by our fingerprints, our voice, and so many other characteristics. God *loves* diversity.

God also loves unity. It is clear that Jesus, too, desired a unity amongst His followers. Even if we dress differently we *can* have unity, are called to different ministries, and even have different theological interpretations. We are not the same, and do not need to be the same to have love one for another. Yet unfortunately, some assume that we can only have unity if we belong to the same denomination and even, within it, agree to the same set of beliefs. Brown thinks otherwise!

> *"How then does staying within ... denominations guarantee doctrinal accuracy? It does not. It guarantees doctrinal harmony only for those within their particular group. Yet this pressure toward uniformity and harmony is what holds many of us back. We must wholeheartedly reject this pressure. ...*
>
> *To state it again: 'The system' thrives on uniformity, which is then called orthodoxy; and thus, by circular reasoning, those within the system are considered orthodox and thought to be protected from heresy. How absurd! There is no biblical support for this position, nor is it even logical."*
>
> (Brown, 2002: 192-193)

Both McManus and Rinehart claim that it is the very act of pressuring believers into uniformity that robs us of our potential to be the unique and special person God intended:

> *"History again and again reveals to us that we are less likely to do good when we perceive ourselves [to be] a part of a larger crowd than if we make the choice standing alone. When we are in a crowd, we are more prone toward acts of evil or at least compliance to evil. For some reason the civilized can rationalize apathy and feel themselves absolved from personal responsibility. Good needs to be done, but someone else will take care of it."*
>
> (McManus, 2005: 123-124)

> *"Standardization ... can dictate the path of growth that every believer, ministry, or church needs to ... [follow, and] ... ignores the variety of creative ways God might choose to do things."*
>
> (Rinehart, 1998: 34)

> *"Conformity ... negates a sense of God's dealing in each person's inner life in unique ways."*
>
> (Rinehart, 1998: 35)

Rinehart uses a cutting analogy to suggest that uniformity's outworking might be mass-produced Christians:

> *"The industrial Revolution brought us its mass production quotas and standardization mentality ... As this kind of philosophy invaded the church, it produced something akin to a 'McChristian.' ... The idea is that by repeating the same steps, in the same order, with steady attention, one can produce maturing believers in a manner similar to mass produced burgers and fries."*
>
> (Rinehart, 1998: 117)

God help us if Christianity becomes "industrialized"—and yet in some ways, it is already suffering from this very malady.

In the 1500s, a law was passed in England called the Act of Uniformity, aimed at ensuring all people followed the prescribed religious ways of the official Anglican denomination. In the 1600s, not only were those who did not follow the established norms labeled as "Nonconformists", but the old Act of Uniformity was updated:

> *"In 1660 old acts against Nonconformists were revived. Meeting houses were closed; all persons were required under severe penalties to attend their parish church; it became illegal to conduct worship services except in accordance with Anglican ritual."*
>
> (Brown, 2002: 155)

John Bunyan, famed author of Pilgrim's Progress, was one of the Nonconformists imprisoned for non-compliance with the uniform practices of the denominational church. Perhaps today's church leaders would like to think they would not have reacted negatively to someone sent by God but different from their stereotype image. McManus challenges that maybe they might not have readily accepted even John the Baptist:

> *"How many of us would actually expect the person who came to prepare the way for Christ to present himself wearing animal skins, eating locusts, and wandering around in the desert? If he lived today, he would be medicated and diagnosed bipolar. He would be one more certified lunatic. And that's just what would happen if the church were in charge of his diagnosis. …*
>
> *Confronted by John, we have to stop and ask ourselves: 'If this is what the person looked like who prepared the way for Jesus, then what should a disciple of Jesus Christ look like who comes after Jesus? How is it possible that, for many of us, being a good Christian is really nothing more than being a good person?' The entire focus of our faith has been the elimination of sin, which is important but inadequate, rather than the unleashing of a unique, original, extraordinary, wonderfully untamed faith."*
>
> (McManus, 2005: 64-65)

And perhaps we too need to be free to have a radical expression of faith that is unlike that of the institutionalized practices that church leaders have put forward as the basis for unity?

CHAPTER 12:
SUPPRESSION THROUGH "ACCOUNTABILITY"

Attempts by many church leaders to turn all their followers into clones of themselves are obvious and can be seen (at least by outsiders) for what they really are. Those leaders think their way is the only way, and expect all their disciples to be faithful little copies of their masters. And their masters are the human leaders, not God.

Such behavior can be identified as being cult-like, and must be opposed, even if in more subtle forms such as proclamations of acceptable dress code for attendance at services. Some argue that a conservative dress code shows respect for God, but who defines what is appropriate? The human leader, of course. And in contrast, God Himself has said he judges our hearts, not our outward appearance.

Another somewhat different form of suppression of individuality relates to concepts such as accountability, discipleship, mentoring, fathering, and the like. In local churches where such concepts are upheld, some who attend may feel that they are still free to pursue God as He calls them. But you only have to scratch the surface to find that the freedom of individual expression is limited to the boundaries of what the assigned oversight deems to be acceptable.

Contradictions in teaching?

In the preceding paragraphs, we touched on some aspects of individual members of local churches being held "accountable". My reading of Richard Foster leads me to conclude that he looks at another aspect of so-called accountability, namely the accountability of those in leadership within church circles. He seems to take the position that church *leaders* who are not accountable to others are dangerous that they should be reined in using the model seen in the Benedictine structures of the Catholic Church.

> *"Those who are accountable to no one are especially susceptible to the corrupting influence of power. It was precisely this problem that caused Saint Benedict to establish the rule of stability. In the sixth century there were many wandering prophets and monks with no one to hold them accountable for what they said or did. But with the rule of stability they were drawn into communities in which mutual encouragement and discipline were possible. Today, most media preachers and itinerant evangelists suffer from exactly the same lack of accountability ... What is needed today is a modern Benedictine rule that would draw these powerful leaders into a disciplined and accountable fellowship."*

(Foster, 1985: 578-579)

It would appear that Foster expects *leaders* to participate in structures that would keep them "accountable". So, does Foster also expect *individuals* (laity) to also be placed in positions whereby they can be called to account? It would appear not. He cites as a desirable example his own recollections of a person who didn't restrict Foster's personal freedom by any "rules", Benedictine or otherwise, but rather shared truth and trusted God to guide him. He quotes his advisor as saying,

> *"... Let's be clear about one thing. My business, my only business, is to bring the truth of God as I see it, and then simply to love you regardless of what you do or don't do. It is not my business to straighten you out or to get you to do the right thing."*

(Foster, 1985: 607)

Apparently Foster sets one standard for leaders and another for regular laity.

Brown also seems to exhibit a level of confusion, but in a different manner. My analysis of his position seems to one the one hand condemn Christians who exhibit individual freedom, and on the other hand, applaud such freedom.

First, he unequivocally proclaims that it is unbiblical to have Christians act in a manner that is independent of others in the Body of Christ:

> *"There is no biblical justification for independent, unattached Christians."*

(Brown, 2002: 220)

Let us take one example where Christians might live a life that is effectively "independent and unattached" from other Christians, let alone from formal links to a local church. I know someone who chose to take God's love into a country torn by strife, and desperately in need of humanitarian aid. The government of that country often would not issue residential permits to any with a Christian faith. For this person's own safety, and for the safety of those whose lives were touched, the individual needed to be "independent" and "unattached". Would Brown condemn such lack of attachment as exhibiting unbiblical independence? I doubt it.

In fact, as quoted earlier, Brown upholds the need for each individual to be free of accountability to church leaders:

> "...every believer is ultimately accountable to Jesus, the Head of the Body and Lord of the Church. Therefore, when a leader demands that a believer go against his or her conscience he is asking that believer to act in a non-moral way. This is a serious issue. ... in the New Testament believers are never told they are 'accountable' to their leaders. Our primary accountability is to God."
>
> (Brown, 2002: 115)

I hesitate to judge Foster and Brown as being inconsistent in their beliefs. What I am trying to highlight is the ease with which a mixed message can be received by a reader, independent of whether the source has contradictions or not.

So does God expect us to live a life of freedom, independent from the constraints others may wish to place on us, or should we have some measure of "accountability"?

Let's look a bit deeper into this vexed topic.

Perceived dangers of "loose-cannon" individuals

Some authors appear to warn of dangers as they relate to individuality.

The first warning is of dangers an independent person might be to themselves. Green shared from his own observations of one such person:

> "I'll never forget one guy in particular, a new believer, who [dominated Bible studies and wouldn't listen]. ...
>
> As I listened to his experiences, I thought, Here's a brand-new believer who never got off the ground! He couldn't discern false teaching and wouldn't listen to anyone who might help him. He was completely derailed. All kinds of seeds of darkness had been sown in him, and he had no way to fend them off."
>
> (Green, 2000: 17)

In his book, *Confronting Power and Sex in the Catholic Church*, Geoffrey Robinson, a person with a refreshing personal level of independence despite being a bishop in the Catholic Church, also expounds on the merits of individuals having a community against which they can check their views:

> "It is not possible for individuals to form their consciences on all matters entirely on their own. People can form their consciences only by humbly joining with many others in the search for truth. If I have no respect for the collective wisdom of the community I belong to, I can hardly call myself a member of that community. One of the very first requirements of a true conscience is humility."
>
> (Robinson, 2007: 165)

A second danger of independence proposed by some authors arises from the possibility of the dangers to the larger community of which the individual is a part.

> *"A community must protect its members against the decisions of individuals that harm other people, even when these decisions are made in conscience. The state will imprison people who murder or steal, and a church community must, for example, dismiss from a teaching post a person who repeatedly displays racial bias against some students. Because harm is being caused to people, neither the state nor the church will accept conscience as a defense. There are serious difficulties and dangers in this field, but it cannot be ignored."*
>
> (Robinson, 2007: 169-170)

While Robinson takes some relatively strong examples to highlight the need for the community to protect itself against certain individuals, Cymbala uses a more moderate example, but one that nonetheless exhibits the need for a group to set boundaries. He tells of a member who

> *"... took it upon herself to lead out with a praise chorus now and then, jumping into the middle of whatever the pastor was trying to lead."*
>
> (Cymbala, 1997: 14)

In this context, it would appear that one individual's desire to express their rights to freedom was in conflict with the rights and freedoms of others.

Noble holds up his interpretation of the New Testament model as a solution to balancing individual freedom with protection of the larger community:

> *"New Testament leadership functioned in plurality and mutual submission, the final authority in the gathered church. ... No longer can independent, 'lone-ranger' itinerants roam the world foisting themselves on unwary churches and causing all kinds of damage and hurt."*
>
> (Noble, 2002: 110)

Weinberger also tackles a similar topic, this time based in the business world. He starts by warning of the danger of self-reliant individuals, stating:

> *"There's a dark side to self-reliance. It can encourage a type of arrogant cynicism that reacts to anything that [the establishment] tries to do for you with: 'I can do it better than that.' In this view of the world, there's what I can do with my own two hands and then there's red tape."*
>
> (Levine, Locke, Searls and Weinberger, 2000: 132)

Having warned of the dangers of unbalanced self-reliance, Weinberger then does go back to pointing out that self-reliance still has benefits over

> *"... resting comfortably in the assumed paternalism [of the establishment]"*
>
> (Levine, Locke, Searls and Weinberger, 2000: 132)

At first glance there seems to be danger in individuals acting outside the confines and controls of church, and danger in institutions defining boundaries within which individuals must remain.

SUPPRESSION THROUGH "ACCOUNTABILITY"

It is recognized widely that there are dangers in unchecked independence. But how great is the danger really?

An argument often raised against lay people developing ministries without "proper" leadership oversight is the danger of heretical teaching, rebellion, immorality, and such like. Tillapaugh recognized these as possible problem areas, but in his experience found little in the way of risk, and yet great benefit in trusting the Body to produce what it needed:

> *"A basic assumption in this approach to ministry is that lay people are capable of planning and carrying on a ministry.*
>
> *... What I have been describing will be difficult for many vocational and lay leaders in the church to accept. This style of ministry lessens their control. Unfortunately church leaders, vocational and lay, are often not accustomed to trusting people with ministry.*
>
> *... We have never had any of the feared heresy, rebellion or immorality usually predicted for such loosely controlled groups. We realized from the beginning that we would be taking risks if we didn't keep a tight rein on our people. But we chose to trust the Body to produce what it needed. As it turned out, the risk was small, the dividends huge."*
>
> Tillapaugh (1982: 76-79)

Girard likewise suggests that the feared dangers of freedom for individuals are rarely realized, as God Himself has a personal interest in bringing about healthy change in otherwise disruptive personalities. Girard suggests that, if we trust God, we may find that the act of getting out of God's way has unpredicted but positive results. He provides a list of experiences that are worthy of review and reflection:

> *"Our experience ... has shown us how the Holy Spirit can handle any situation in the church, if He is trusted with it.*
>
> *We have seen Him at work, working all things together for good, using problems, pressures and even failures ... We have trusted Him even in situations which we might formerly have viewed as cause for alarm or motivation for a campaign to solve things in the flesh. We've seen Him using such situations for our good.*
>
> *We have watched, or participated, as the Spirit has dealt with problems between people.*
>
> *He has beautifully shown Himself to be adequate to solve problems with false teachers who tried to enter our fellowship and disrupt it.*
>
> *We have sought to depend on the Spirit in matters of outward holiness ... The Spirit in the believer and speaking through the Word and the Body is dependable. He doesn't always deal with these matters in the order we would choose. Sometimes we wonder if He is dealing with them at all. But the Spirit can be trusted to make whatever changes in Christians He knows are needed, according to His own timetable. And when He does it, it's beautiful. The man is genuinely changed, not just conformed to some humanly-devised box we have designed to stuff him into.*

We have watched the Holy Spirit silence or remove divisive people and situations that had us worried and fretting. In His way and on His schedule (seldom according to our plans) He has handled, changed, solved or removed the forces of division, seeking to make us 'one in the Spirit.' "

(Girard, 1972: 74-75)

I do not believe Girard is saying there are no risks of individuals acting wrongly (be they church leaders or laity). Rather, I think he is suggesting we must consider that there will be times God may ask us to let Him sort things out without our involvement. As a pastor in search of a new model, Girard states:

"Since beginning to learn how to wait, we have seen Him work — singlehandedly — to get glory from predicaments involving false teachers, disruptive influences in the church, inter-personal problems, doctrinal differences, church finances, etc. We have seen Him alive, active and adequate for whatever it is — quite able to work His miracles without me always being in the middle of it, manipulating, protecting, guiding all affairs with my strong (?), finite hand."

(Girard, 1972: 121)

Cymbala tells that he had been warned that all evidence pointed to one of the ushers stealing from the collection plate. In God's own time, the Holy Spirit led the entire local church to a spontaneous time of intercession:

"Suddenly a young usher came running down the center aisle and threw himself on the altar ... ... I realized that he was apologizing for taking money from the offering plate. I stood speechless for a moment, bewildered by his unexpected confession ... ... I had not had to play detective, confront the culprit with his misdeed, or pressure him to confess."

(Cymbala, 1997: 19)

That's a good ending. But to take another example, if there is reason to believe someone is sexually abusing children in their trusted care, this is a matter for immediate protection of victims, *not* simply sitting back and hoping the problem sorts itself out.

Expect to encounter individuals who will act with a level of independence from local church hierarchies. Cautiously check the wisdom of their words and actions. But likewise—check the words, motives and actions of church leaders!

Proclaimed need for "submission"

There is a dangerous school of thought on submission that goes something like this: "Submission to the lordship of Christ is at the very heart of Christianity, and the practical outworking of this is to be applied in submission to those in responsible leadership positions within the church." While some of Michael Phillips' earlier books upheld the merits of individuals who exhibited a freedom from the views of men, in his book *The Garden at the Edge of Beyond*, he seems to have fallen for the trap of confusing submission to God with submission to men.

He rightly *starts* by clarifying our need for submission to God. He portrays a meeting on the borders of heaven between a man and other characters from history. In the man's encounter with Moses, Moses states:

> *"I drove Yahweh to anger ... I did not see that in obedience lay my safety."*
>
> (Phillips, 1998: 88)

Few Christians would question or challenge the need for obedience to God's directives if we are to consider ourselves followers of Christ—how can we be "followers" if we are not willing to follow! However, here Phillips seems to take obedience to the level of a fundamental absolute, namely that the entire purpose of our life is to learn dependence:

> *"I saw that through life we learn and accumulate, working for gain and prestige and recognition, doing all in our power to become self-sufficient. Dependency on others is considered the great evil, and escaping such dependency is the quest of so-called mature adult-hood.*
>
> *But I saw ... that this direction is erroneous ... [and] that the entire purpose of life on earth is to become not independent, but dependent."*
>
> (Phillips, 1998: 110-111)

It would appear that Phillips' teaching is in conflict with that of Jesus who said that the greatest command is to love the Lord our God with all our being. Yet my interpretation of this particular work by Phillips is that he is suggesting that the greatest thing (our "entire purpose of life") is to become dependent. Surely we can't have love as the greatest, and have dependence as the greatest? I would suggest that if we focus on loving God, we won't have to work at recognizing our dependence on His grace.

Phillips continues, appearing to move into even more dangerous territory where he holds in highest regard our submissive obedience not just to God, but also to others:

> *"With burning clarity I understood that when one who has plans and desires, goals and ambitions of his own, takes in the words of one over him that run counter to those wishes and replies, With pleasure shall I do what you say! – then does he reach to exalted heights of character. Such a one subserves his own wishes because the spirit of obedience dwells within him."*
>
> (Phillips, 1998: 91)

If we follow Phillips' new line of reasoning as it appears in this book, it seems that not only must we seek to please those "over" us in a hierarchical authority position, but that we must suppress our individuality. Does this mean that we would no longer have a right to retain the option of not "bowing down" to our church leader, for example?

> *"I saw that the very quality that would transform the stench of selfishness into the perfume of holiness was ... submission ...*
>
> *Lay down your own right to rule ... Put aside the cunning but soothing words of the ruling Self that feed the lower aspects of your nature. Listen not to its arguments that*

you are strong and capable, that you have <u>the right to think</u> and act and behave as an island, that you need bow before no other – neither parent nor spouse, teacher nor pastor, counselor nor elder, president nor king." [Emphasis mine]

(Phillips, 1998: 116-118)

But it seems that Phillips position gets worse. Much worse! Phillips appears to go on to teach that we must obey those in authority even when they are in error. I am not in any way suggesting Phillips has a mindset similar to that of the infamous Jim Jones, but doesn't this thinking reflect in part the mindless loyalty that is common in cults? If Jim Jones says to kill your kids, you obey him—he's the one in authority, after all. Phillips portrays a conversation between himself and Mary, the mother of Jesus:

" 'I was taught that we owe submission only to your Son and his Father,' I said after a pause.

'That is true enough, as far as it goes,' she replied. 'But my Son works through earthly relationships to deepen spiritual character.'

'I was also taught that if the one in authority – in human authority, I mean – is flawed and insensitive –'

'Then full submission is not required?' she said, finishing my thought.

I nodded, embarrassed. My eyes were sufficiently opened by now to see what an erroneous conclusion it was."

(Phillips, 1998: 122-123)

And if we don't obey these imperfect, human leaders, is Phillips concluding we are demonstrably in sin?

"[A well known man, respected as a 'man of God', said,] '... pride [is] the opposite of submission. But few recognize its other name, the name of the mask that shields it from public view. This is one of the great deceptions of the time in which you lived, my brother. Going by its other name, in fact, it was exalted as one of the great virtues. To need others, or to have others over you, was seen by our culture as weakness. What else was the enemy's lie in the Garden so long ago – 'You don't need God ... you can live without Him.' It was the deception of pride, cleverly disguised.'

'Disguised as what?' I asked. 'What is pride's other name?'

'Independence,' he answered. 'If submission was reviled by our world, Independence was exalted by it, praised and encouraged by peers and society. Ah, what a soothing balm to Self is the crafty and lying demon that goes by the name Independence.' "

(Phillips, 1998: 131)

"... thus, by what many would call a trivial sin – an independent spirit – did I prevent his perfecting that will within me."

(Phillips, 1998: 132)

You might find it incredible, but I heard of a woman who came back from a women's weekend and proclaimed that she now realized she must be *absolutely* obedient to her Christian husband, no matter what he asked of her. Apparently when pushed, she agreed that she would have to obey him even if he ordered her to kill her children as she trusted he would have a good reason for such an extreme demand, and he would have to take responsibility for his demands. Her role was merely to obey!

I have heard that she has since thankfully changed what I see as an extreme and unhealthy view, but this was the standard she lived by for quite some time, in obedience to those "over" her.

The above quotations from Phillips are sourced from the one book. Yet my reading of some of his earlier books, he took a different view. If so, one has to ask why he appears in his writing to have changed so dramatically from freedom to being subservient? In radical contrast to the quotations in the section above, my interpretation of his earlier views is that they tended to argue that some types of independence are healthy, noting the freedom to follow God's call even if in doing so we are totally alone. In fact, he articulates the virtues of a man that valued truth and was not afraid to find it for *himself* and follow it, independent of the opinions of others:

> *"He would think. He would look into those regions that most men avoided. He would not be afraid to examine his thoughts and feelings.*
>
> *He would do whatever it took to live by right and truth! He would walk a different road <u>even if he met no one else while traveling it</u>." [Emphasis mine]*

(Phillips, 1996: 209)

Phillips also seemed in this earlier book to suggest that some forms of independence are actually desirable:

> *"… some kinds of independence are good and necessary as one grows. But there is also a spirit of self-rule that can lead one away from what God wants if he or she seeks his or her own will instead."*

(Phillips, 1996: 87)

Exposing the concept of "covering"

In Phillips' book, *The Garden at the Edge of Beyond*, he espouses the value of having a covering, of having someone "over" you. Several other authors strongly argue against the whole idea of any such "covering".

Viola unequivocally claims that the Bible calls us to be accountable to God, but *never* to man:

> *"If the Bible is silent with respect to the idea of 'covering,' what do people mean when they ask, 'Who is your covering?' Most people (if pressed) would rephrase the question as: 'To what person are you accountable?' But this raises another sticky point: the Bible*

never consigns accountability to human beings. It consigns it exclusively to God (Matt. 12:36; 18:23; Luke 16:2; Rom. 3:19; 14:12; 1 Cor. 4:5; Heb. 4:13; 13:17; 1 Pet. 4:5)."

(Viola, in Brown, 2002: 217)

Don Clasen succinctly summarizes the thinking behind those who propose the need for a "covering":

"The idea is that standing in submission to one's authority protects a person from spiritual attack from Satan. Submission guarantees protection, thus the need for a covering. The term also implies that God will not allow the enemy to get to you as long as you are standing under that authority. If you get out from under, you become vulnerable to anything from deception to sinful activity."

(Clasen, quoted by Brown, 2002: 228)

With Clasen's definition of a "covering", Brown's book exposes the folly of the "safety" theme, and criticizes the flawed logic and unbiblical nature of the concept of a hierarchical pyramid of accountability. His careful and thoughtful development of the dangerous workings of hierarchical structures is worthy of review:

"... whether that fold is a denomination, an independent congregation, a small house church, ...[it] promises safety, and many believe that staying within the camp guarantees protection from deception, error and spiritual attack. Thus it is fear that often holds us back, and nothing paralyzes like fear.

Many leaders exploit this fear, sometimes out of pure motives and with real sincerity, seeking to protect the flock from perceived danger, and at other times out of selfishness and pride, not wanting to see their influence diminished. This, too, needs to be challenged. As Frank Viola explains,

> *The concept goes something like this: everyone must answer to someone else who is in a higher ecclesiastical position. In the garden-variety, post-war evangelical church, this translates into the 'laypeople' answering to the pastor. In turn, the pastor must answer to a person who has more authority.*
>
> *So the pastor will typically trace his accountability to a denominational headquarters, to another church (often called the 'mother church'), or to an influential Christian worker (who is perceived to have a higher rank in the ecclesiastical pyramid). As a result, the 'laypeople' are said to be 'covered' by the pastor, and the pastor is said to be 'covered' by the denomination, the mother church, or the Christian worker. The fact that people can trace their accountability to a higher ecclesiastical authority is the equivalent of being protected by that authority (so the thinking goes).*
>
> *But this line of thinking generates the following telling questions: Who covers the mother church? Who covers the denominational headquarters? And who covers the Christian worker? Some have offered the pat answer that God covers these 'higher' authorities. But such an answer begs the question; for why can't God be the covering*

for the 'laypeople,' or even the pastor? Of course, the real problem with the 'God-denominational-clergy-laity' model goes far beyond the incoherent, pretzel logic to which it leads. The chief problem is that it violates the spirit of the NT; for behind the pious rhetoric of 'providing accountability' and 'having a covering,' there looms a system of government that is bereft of Biblical support and driven by a spirit of control."

(Viola, in Brown, 2002: 190-192)

Owen seems to claim that the wielding of church authority over individuals and their relationship with Jesus results in

"... Jesus Christ [being] deposed from the sole power of lawmaking in his church. – that the true husband might be thrust aside, and adulterers of his spouse embraced. – that taskmasters might be appointed in and over his house, which he never gave to his church ..."

(Brown, 2002: 158)

By including Owen's statement in his book, is Brown suggesting that church leaders are effectively adulterers if they try to wield the authority that truly belongs to no-one but Jesus? Pretty strong words! But do many church leaders *really* take such an authoritarian role? Unfortunately, yes. And even those who are not so blatant about it can exhibit milder or more subtle forms of domination and direction. But to help us see the problem more clearly, let us now look in the following chapter at one pastor's seeming abuse of his authority—not in the words of others who may misunderstand him, but who, in his own words, appears to preach a doctrine of suppression of individuals.

CHAPTER 13:
BRAZEN OPPOSITION TO INDIVIDUALITY?

As quoted above, Brown records Viola as saying that some leaders act "*out of pure motives*" while others act "*out of selfishness and pride* [and a motivation that wants to prevent]… *their influence* [being] *diminished*".

Motives are not easily seen. But in this chapter, we look carefully at what one pastor, Juan Ortiz, has said in his own words. Even with diligent analysis, we cannot confidently judge motives, but we can think carefully about and draw our own conclusions as to his message.

Setting the scene for opposition to individuality

Ortiz makes the case that the New Testament recognizes the concept of discipleship, but not the concept of church membership:

> "… *we couldn't find the word member anywhere [in the Bible]. In all the accounts of the primitive church, we couldn't find where they took members into the church or made a special ceremony or anything.*
>
> *But in reading Acts, we found another word that really revolutionized our lives and our church – the word disciple.*"
>
> (Ortiz, 1975: 105)

In spite of the above, Ortiz does move back to recognition of membership within his local church. But he appears to redefine the concept.

> "*Eventually we came back to use the word member, but with a whole new definition. A body-type member is:*

(1) One who is dependent. You never see a nose walking along the street by itself. The body must be joined together as a body. If a member is independent, he is not part of the body."

(Ortiz, 1975: 116)

It is my understanding that within the field of counseling there is a recognition that the desired outcome is for the person being counseled to reach a stage of health such that they no longer 'need' the counselor. Or in other words, they become independent of the counselor. This healthy state appears to be explicitly opposed by Ortiz, where a part of the body simply cannot exist without being joined to another part within *his* local church. His list of definitions of a "member" continues, stating that a member must be

" *(2) A part of the body that unites two other parts. The forearm unites the hand with the upper arm."*

(Ortiz, 1975: 116)

This analogy is very hierarchical. Maybe it is not intended to be, but even so it is dangerous. Could Ortiz be quite deliberate in choosing an analogy where one member depends on another "upper" part that is closer to the "head"? Any doubt about Ortiz' intentions to establish a philosophy based on hierarchical authority structures disappears very quickly. In the following extract he is now talking about members that are "under" another, and that the nourishment comes from those above—I would suggest *clearly* hierarchical. According to Ortiz, a member is

" *(3) One who passes along nourishment. He receives nourishment for himself and for the other members <u>under</u> him." [Emphasis mine]*

(Ortiz, 1975: 116)

To me, it seems that the implication is that the nourishment does not reach an individual directly from God, and that God arranges the ordering of the hierarchy, stating that a member is

" *(4) One who sustains, who stays put. A member of the body can't be jerked out of the body. Does your wife ever say when you come home, 'Where did you lose your right leg?' Impossible. You don't lose your members."*

(Ortiz, 1975: 116-117)

This seems to me to be a very controlling statement. Is Ortiz really claiming that if any member dares to consider leaving the church led by Ortiz, such an action is analogous to tearing away part of the Body?

Finally, the "command-and-control" aspects of hierarchies are explicitly declared, as a member is

" *(5) One who passes along orders. The head gives an order to the hand, but it <u>must</u> be passed through other members in between. The hand never gets disgusted with the forearm and says, 'I think I'll detach myself from you and put in a cable from me directly to the head.' No. We are a body." [Emphasis mine]*

(Ortiz, 1975: 117)

In contrast to the analogy put forward by Ortiz, the body's muscles are actually each individually connected to the brain by a nervous system. The reason that body movements are coordinated is that the one brain tells each muscle what to do. We have one mediator between God and (every) man, which is Jesus.

My interpretation is that Ortiz preaches the value of flexibility within the Body of Christ, but his definition of flexibility seems to be conditional: you can be flexible as long as you are (1) dependent, (2) you only join to those parts the leaders dictate, (3) you only get nourishment from the person above you rather than from other sources, let alone God, (4) you don't leave your position, and (5) you obey orders and ensure those under you do likewise! He continues his definition of a member by stating that a member is

> " *(6) One who is elastic. Bodies are flexible. Organizations walk like robots. In the past, someone with a new idea or a new talent usually had to get out of the church in order to minister. People with vision had to go to Campus Crusade, to Youth for Christ, to the Navigators, or somewhere else to give expression to their vision.*
>
> *But when the church is a body of disciples, it is flexible."*

(Ortiz, 1975: 117)

The "benefits" of such flexibility would appear to allow Ortiz himself to command the troops to obey him in any aspect he chooses, rather than being flexibility for the individual.

Where hierarchical church frameworks exist, it is no surprise that the only people seen as having the power to bring change are the church leaders. Can members at the bottom of the hierarchy be respected as having the ability to think and act without leadership and oversight? We start by looking at a quotation that seems to have some subtle but concerning messages:

> "Paul and Barnabas, being master builders, were equipped to plant growing, living orchards."

(Ortiz, 1975: 98)

So if Paul and Barnabas are "master" builders, does that mean that others are less qualified? Or to really push the point, can ordinary laity "plant" new ministries, or is such noble work the exclusive domain of church leaders? History suggests that many ministries were started by lay people, in some cases with no help from established churches, and sometimes despite active opposition from the church leaders.

Ortiz appears to teach that it is the church leaders, and only the church leaders, that can bring about change. For example:

> "We <u>cannot</u> get our congregations to love if we [pastors] do not [love each other]. After all, we are the shepherds." [Emphasis mine]

(Ortiz, 1975: 55)

> *"Once [love] starts with us pastors, it will spread quickly to the other parts of the Body of Christ in our cities. But it <u>must</u> begin with us." [Emphasis mine]*
>
> (Ortiz, 1975: 59)

If my interpretation is correct, it is almost unbelievable: is Ortiz claiming that if my pastor is out of relation with another church leader, it is impossible for me to love others? And if I am in disagreement, I cannot resolve the dispute until the pastors resolve their differences? How come? Because, according to my understanding of Ortiz' claims, "… *it must begin with us*".

Not only am I, a lay-person, supposedly unable to love properly until shown how by the church leaders, it would appear from Ortiz's writing that I supposedly cannot mature beyond their level of maturity.

> *"Pastors must begin by reaching for maturity themselves first; then they will be ready to bring about the same growth in their sheep."*
>
> (Ortiz, 1975: 94)

> *"The church will be able to grow up in Christ as it sees its leadership really take hold."*
>
> (Ortiz, 1975: 96)

> *"… do you know what happens in the modern church? We pastors stop somewhere along the way … we stop moving. We become corks. The sheep grow and grow and start jamming up behind us, <u>unable to grow further until we grow some more ourselves</u>." [Emphasis mine]*
>
> (Ortiz, 1975: 97)

So we are "*unable to grow further*" until the church leaders grow? Let's analyze this for a moment. What Ortiz is effectively saying is that an individual can never grow to a greater level of maturity than the person in the local church who is acting as their immediate oversight and mentor. At best, the disciple may reach the level of their leader, but no further.

Let's take this to its "logical" conclusion. Assume Paul mentored Barnabas, but poor old Barnabas only got to 99% of Paul's stature. Then maybe the best of Barnabas' disciples only got to 99% of his maturity. So now we are down to about 98% of Paul's original maturity. Over time, some stunning disciples get to 100% of their master's level, and others struggle to get to 50%. By the time we get to the person who mentored Ortiz, we would be lucky if they had even 5% of Paul's original maturity.

If I am mentored by Ortiz, and reach only 80% of his maturity, I've only got 4% to pass on. Let's say that I am not pastored by Ortiz, and my assigned pastor is running a bit behind the pack. He's already down to 2%, so that's my ceiling. But I can't by-pass my oversight and go directly to Ortiz to get a top-up. It is only the church hierarchy who selects and appoints the discipleship hierarchy. I don't get a say.

> *"The father keeps turning over responsibility to his sons as they grow."*
>
> (Ortiz, 1975: 97)

Taking the line of thinking given by Ortiz, it seems as if we are in a pretty sad state. And we can't change a thing unless we are part of the chosen, the church leadership class, as

> "… through the leadership of the apostles and elders, the Kingdom of God must be brought to each place."
>
> (Ortiz, 1975: 130)

> "… discipleship has to start with pastors. … Discipleship <u>cannot</u> spread from bottom to top; it <u>must</u> go from top to bottom." [Emphasis mine]
>
> (Ortiz, 1975: 132)

It would seem that one product of this teaching is to keep the pastors important, relevant and needed, in at least their own eyes.

The "loose bricks" analogy

It would seem that we had better either plug in directly to Jesus, or else He needs to come back really soon, as according to the formula provided by Ortiz, there can't be much maturity left to share around! Yet just in case any underling thinks that they may be better off jumping the maturity level queue and getting close to Jesus individually, Ortiz seems to have foreseen such breaks for independence, and tried to cut them off at the pass with explicit teaching on staying put. He uses an analogy of each of us being a brick in a building.

But which building—the Body of Christ, or the local church institution? It would appear that Ortiz is talking of the need for each of us to be "put in place" (an interesting turn of phrase) by our local church leaders. And the reason is so that we don't get "stolen" by someone else.

> "Each member of the congregation is a brick, and we all work very hard to accumulate more and more bricks. …
>
> But there is a problem with loose bricks: They can be stolen [by another local church]."
>
> (Ortiz, 1975: 100)

Am I being too harsh, assuming Ortiz is worried about loose bricks ending up in someone else's church? At first glance, it may appear so. After all, he talks about us being God's bricks, in God's building:

> "We are God's bricks. But we have not been put into place in His building where we can support some weight and give strength."
>
> (Ortiz, 1975: 101)

But the reality appears to be otherwise. Ortiz is worried about losing "his" bricks:

> "The pastor and his people must be always on guard that someone from another church doesn't come along and steal bricks for their lot."
>
> (Ortiz, 1975: 100)

The solution to a pastor losing some of his bricks is to firmly cement them in place. He wants each of us to know our place:

> "[He wants each one of us to] know which bricks are under us, which are above us, and how we relate to each other."

(Ortiz, 1975: 101)

And if the bricks don't like being dictated to by the church leaders, then Ortiz may be seen to be teaching against such rebellion:

> "If the pastor tries to pick us up and put us in place in the building, we resist. The church must be run democratically, we say. We don't submit to any one person."

(Ortiz, 1975: 101)

Individuality vs. conformity

We have previously spoken about definitions of the term, "individualism", and its contrast with Christians who seek the collective good of the Body of Christ. Ortiz is very clear in his condemnation of individualism:

> "Darkness is individualism, selfishness. Light is love, communion, fellowship."

(Ortiz, 1975: 42)

One definition of individualism relates to each individual making decisions for him or herself, and for his or her own benefit. Some perceive the opposite of individualism being embodied in a local church where the elders make the decisions, for the perceived benefit of the church community. These polarized views are dangerous. For example, the option for an individual to follow God's distinct call on his or her life, in obedience to Christ Himself, is seen by Ortiz as being in rebellion against Christ!

> "I've heard Christians say very proudly, 'I don't follow any man—I follow Christ.' That sounds pious, but it's really a great mistake. It means the person wants to do his own will; he doesn't even realize what it means to follow Christ."

(Ortiz, 1975: 101)

The bible teaches that, while we are all made in God's image, we are all different (for example, refer to 1 Corinthians 12). In contrast, Ortiz teaches a "*mashed potato*" approach where it is impossible to discern individuals within the body:

> "God is doing even more than regrouping His people. He is uniting them. I can illustrate this with potatoes. Each potato plant in the garden has three, four, or five potatoes under it. Each individual potato belongs to one plant or another.
>
> When the harvest comes, all the potatoes are dug up and put into one sack. So they are regrouped. But they are not yet united. They may say, 'Oh, praise the Lord! Now we are all in the same sack.' But they are not yet one.
>
> They must be washed and peeled. They think they are closer yet. 'How nice is this love

among us!' they say.

But that's not all. They must be cut in pieces and mixed. They have now lost a lot of their individuality. They really think they are ready for the Master now.

But what God wants is mashed potatoes. Not many potatoes – one mashed potato. No potato can stand up and say, 'Here I am! I'm a potato.' The word must be we."

(Ortiz, 1975: 62)

It must be highlighted that in his writing Ortiz appears to confuse conformity with unity. He wants us all to have so lost our individuality that we cannot be discerned apart. But he takes the "mashed potato" analogy of loss of identity to teach what he proclaims is God's move to not just regroup people but to bring unity to them. What I conclude is that Ortiz seems incapable of perceiving unity amongst people who celebrate diversity. There can be no diversity in mashed potato. But in the Body of Christ, Jesus expects that there will be distinguishable parts, such as arms, legs, eyes and ears. A lump of mashed potato cannot do useful things like a hand or an eye can.

One irony is that Ortiz appears to not want *all* people to become unidentifiable "mashed potatoes". His book seems to suggest that, while the laity is to lose *their* identity, *he* still wants *his* leadership to be distinguishable from the masses!

The teaching of Ortiz on loss of identity reaches a further, disturbing climax. And if you find his analogy unpleasant, I apologize, but I feel the language he uses to condemn those who retain their individuality needs to be exposed:

"What things do we vomit? Things that won't digest. If something is digested, it doesn't come back up.

Vomited people are those people who refuse to be digested by the Lord Jesus Christ.

And digestion means getting lost. You're finished. Your life ends. You are transformed into Jesus. You are unmistakably associated with Him."

(Ortiz, 1975: 37)

Taking the statements above collectively, it appears that Ortiz is effectively teaching that unless your unique identity is totally lost within the local church, you should be, and will be, rejected by the Body.

Having roundly condemned any vestige of the individual being even vaguely discernable from the body-as-a-whole, Ortiz points out the significance of each individual member within his cell groups:

"Each member of the cell is important. The leader realizes that each person has his own aspirations and hopes. The cell ministers to the need of each person."

(Ortiz, 1975: 137)

This seems a strange conflict, until one realizes the reason for nurturing the individual is so that they can be useful to the group. In fact, if they are not out there recruiting more people to join their group, Ortiz states that they do not even have a valid reason for existence:

> "The cell also has a task; the Great Commission of the Lord Jesus Christ. They must be making disciples, or else there is no reason to exist."
>
> (Ortiz, 1975: 137-138)

Enslavement of the individual

I feel that the discipleship structure taught by Ortiz is designed to be beyond challenge or change, and what follows is that for those in Ortiz' church institution, there would appear to be no honorable escape, and if you disagree with the teaching and practices of Ortiz and would prefer to consider a change of leadership, there simply appears to be no option.

> "If a pastor is truly a father to his congregation, he cannot be changed ... every two or three years. What family changes fathers every two years? Maybe our churches are more like clubs that elect presidents for a certain term and then elect someone else. But if we are a family, we stay together."
>
> (Ortiz, 1975: 97)

It seems to me that the option of the individual leaving may be seen to be something like a "dishonorable discharge" from the armed services, and that anyone who leaves is likened to someone disowning their family and running away. These practices appear in many ways reflective of overly controlling behavior.

> "The only way I can form the lives of my four children is if they submit to me. Suppose each time I go to correct them, I run the risk of them running off to another father and saying, 'I don't want to be the child of Juan Carlos Ortiz anymore – I want to be your child.' And suppose that man would say, 'Oh, welcome – come on in.' I would have to stop correcting my children, because I don't want to lose them. I love them. But I do correct them, because I'm sure they are going to stay in my home no matter what. They are submitted.
>
> In the church, the pastors cannot form lives because if he gets too hard with one of his children, the child will run off to another orphanage."
>
> (Ortiz, 1975: 112)

No, it would seem Ortiz demands we must stay in the orphanage we have been placed in!

I don't know about you, but I don't want to be mashed or live in an orphanage—I want to live in relationship with my Heavenly Father.

CHAPTER 14:
WHY WE NEED INDIVIDUALS

There may be times we do actually have to rebel against the "party line" of church leadership. A glaring example comes from Nazi Germany, where some church leaders insisted on allegiance to Hitler. Those who held different views were not only ostracized, but sometimes killed. Yet Godly Christians did follow God's standard and rebel, not just against Hitler, but against church leaders who supported Hitler, in spite of the enormous cost.

We can be different from each other, and yet work in unity. We can hold different views without being rebellious. If we are obedient to *God* there is the possibility that some church leaders may still be offended because they perceive we are being "disobedient" to *them*. Brown clearly states where our loyalty must reside. He goes so far as to say that if we follow the commands of others rather than God, even if they be angels, we are in rebellion against God!

> *"... Owen allows for one ultimate allegiance for every believer: 'They will admit nothing, practice nothing, in the worship of God, private or public, but what they have his warrant for. Unless it comes in [Jesus'] name ... they will not hear an angel from heaven.' Jesus has the final word, and it is to that authoritative word we must bow. Dare we rebel against the Lord?"*

(Brown, 2002: 158-159)

Oliver and Thwaites note that what the church leaders mean by the phrase "church unity", really means *local* church unity, which in fact works against unity across the whole Body-of-Christ!

> *"... by defining the church primarily as congregation they have, in effect, worked to divide themselves from the body of Christ in the city."*

(Oliver & Thwaites, 2001: 173)

These authors also note that a focus on the local church robs the individual Christian of his or her potential to be salt and light in the world at large:

> "... a preoccupation with this expression of the church (one that sees it as central rather than servant) ends up limiting the overall impact of individual saints in regard to their works in creation. This is because the congregation focus eclipses that work, and uses up most of the energy, resource and affirmation in keeping the congregation and its activities going."

(Oliver & Thwaites, 2001: 156)

They conclude that we need a new perspective on the concept of unity. It must *not* be seen as members of a local congregation complying with the numbing uniformity of their local church norms. Rather, it should be a measure of how individuals, in their freedom, work in their own distinct ways but with a shared goal of sharing Christ's love to the world outside of their local church.

> "We need to redefine unity, no longer measuring it by meetings, but by the works of the saints [in their individual expression of ministry]."

(Oliver & Thwaites, 2001: 157)

Unless we grasp this truth, we will continue to see the members of the Body still chained to local church structures, under the control of the leaders.

Oliver and Thwaites recognize the need to set free those people who are *willing* to break away from the masses and move powerfully into new areas of outreach to others in need:

> "Pioneers are groundbreakers. The truth is that every saint has the capacity to break ground ...
>
> What I am referring to here is people who, in their profession, are able to take significant ground, via discoveries, establishing new businesses, bringing significant cultural change to organisations and ways of doing work and so on. What marks these people as being apostolic is that they are able to break new ground in the sphere of creation they engage through their work."

(Oliver & Thwaites, 2001: 166)

Unfortunately, local churches that attempt to control their members and turn them into clones of the church leaders are, by their very nature, unlikely to ever see pioneers arise from their ranks. And, even *if* it occurs, it is probable that such an outbreak of independent thinking and action will occur against the will of those who seek to retain "control". This will often mean that true pioneers have to be willing to act without the support of cheering crowds. Quite the reverse—they will often have to be able to cope with misunderstanding, if not outright opposition.

> "Those who exercise spiritual power must be prepared for aloneness. ... Aloneness means having to decide and act alone, for no others can share the burden or even understand the issues involved. Wise counselors, friends, the community of faith –all

are helpful, but only to a certain point. Most people have good intentions, but they simply do not understand spiritual power, and it is neither kind nor wise to ask them to help with decisions they can neither understand nor appreciate. We walk alone – well, not quite alone, for we have One who walks with us, but alone as far as human wisdom is concerned."

(Foster, 1985: 620)

Such lonely walks are not new to God's people. The Old Testament has many stories of pioneers who walked alone. In the New Testament, we may similarly start by looking at the life of John the Baptist, and even at Jesus Himself.

"One of the most touching themes in the Gospels is Jesus' aloneness."

(Foster, 1985: 620)

And if it's the path that Jesus took, we must be willing to walk a similar journey.

"We too must wrestle alone. We cannot even depend upon our husband or wife to understand what is occurring in the inner sanctuary of our soul."

(Foster, 1985: 620-621)

This does not mean that we cannot, or should not, consult others. The book of Proverbs encourages us with the wisdom of seeking advice. But when all is said and done, we must follow *God's* call on our life, even if it is a lonely calling.

Such concepts are totally foreign to those who would insist we must align with the vision of a pastor, and support only the ministry of his or her local church. Following God's leading in your own heart may take us on a very different path.

In the 1960s, Malvina Reynolds sang a song titled *Little Boxes*. In a humorous but challenging way, it showed the sameness of much of our lives. She portrayed a view that the homes where we live are just little boxes that "*... all look just the same*", and that some of educational institutions put students in little boxes (classrooms) that, like our homes, all look just the same. Worse than the sameness of appearance is the mass production of clones who think much alike. I suspect that while she did not specifically target seminaries and Bible colleges, the mass production of like-minded students applies equally. A Bible college graduate I know well expressed different views in one subject from those held by his supervisor, and was bluntly told he had a choice: conform to the party line, or fail.

Contrast this with God's creation. We are told that every snowflake is different, and that each of us has a unique fingerprint pattern. Being mashed together as demanded by Ortiz destroys that uniqueness.

Within the Body of Christ, God designed you to play a unique role, prepared just for you and only you. Despite discipleship programs, mentoring programs, "fathering" initiatives by pastors, and so on, our goal is not to turn out "just the same" as the pastor.

Levine shares the personal impact of being raised as the son of a potter who expressed personal creativity in his work. For Levine, his desire for creativity is expressed as

> "... a standard requiring constant exploration and reinvention, but also a certain studied ignorance of what's considered right and proper."
>
> (Levine, Locke, Searls and Weinberger, 2000: 48)

He suggests that artists

> "... at some level don't pay attention to what other people think ... [and have] ... a stubborn faith [that] ... shapes their work, [and] enables them to establish themselves as individuals ..."
>
> (Levine, Locke, Searls and Weinberger, 2000: 48-49)

McManus encourages us to be different, and to discover the unique path on which God wants to lead us.

> "[The apostle Peter] went on to describe us as aliens and strangers in the world; all of us different, but a part of the same tribe; all of us walking in the same direction, <u>but on a unique path</u>; all of us becoming what we could not be without the One who created us." [Emphasis mine]
>
> (McManus, 2005: 71)

Such freedom of thought will not go unnoticed. The very freedom that God wants for us may be opposed by those who do not want us to be free. Roger Williams came out from England to America in the 1600s. Because of his "religious non-conformity" that opposed the views of the official church and its representatives in the courts, the officials at Massachusetts

> "... banished him to England, but before he could be deported, he fled ... to ... uninhabited regions [further south in the United States]..."
>
> (Brown, 2002: 150)

Brown quotes Linder's *Dictionary of Christianity* in America as stating:

> "For the remainder of his life Williams would be a religious loner ... [who] ... clung tenaciously to ... his belief in religious liberty ... [, who] ... died an independent evangelical Christian without a denomination."
>
> (Brown, 2002: 151)

In the words of Williams,

> "God requireth not an uniformity of Religion."
>
> (Brown, 2002: 150)

Rather, Williams

> "... saw to it that all individuals and religious bodies enjoyed what he called 'soul liberty,' that is, religious freedom."
>
> (Brown, 2002: 150)

Based on his passion for such 'soul liberty', he set up Rhode Island with a

"... stress on freedom, individualism and being a place 'where no man should be molested for his conscience' "

(Brown, 2002: 151)

Many have fought for freedom. Let us not sacrifice it to local church programs and the dictates of the local church leadership.

Brown has written a delightful poem on this theme about the tension between church expectations and freedom for the individual. In analyzing it, I felt it hit the nail on the head as expressed in the following excerpt:

"'Submit! Conform! Become like us! Soon you'll fit our mold.

We'll cramp out your identity in our stranglehold.

'You're much too independent; you think you hear God well.

But if He has a word to speak, it's the group He'll tell!

…

So here is my conclusion. This is what I've found:

Maybe you are 'bonding'—but I don't want to be bound!"

(Brown, 2002: 219)

SECTION 4:

NO MORE INSTITUTIONALIZED MINISTRY

Since you're still hanging in with this book, hopefully you are starting to question the role of leaders as intermediaries, coming between you and God, telling you what God's plan is for your life, and making sure that your vision fits with theirs (if they will even allow you to have a vision). This practice typically weakens the power of church leaders enormously. Jesus has opened the way for us to commune with God as individuals. Many claim that every individual should have a personal relationship with God, but in practice they actually resist being cut out of the equation.

Holy men in holy robes (or leaders in any other guise) are not necessary. But the abolition of a special class of professional Christian raises questions. What happens to the "ministry" that has typically been tied to "full time" Christian workers such as missionaries and the clergy?

In his book *What's So Amazing about Grace?*, Yancey answers the question some may ask as to whether or not all ministry must be church-based by listing a number of notable ministries where the energy and vision came from individuals rather than church leaders, and the resultant ongoing work may have had little or nothing to do with local churches (Yancey, 1997: 266-268). He articulates a long list of ministries, demonstrating many of the forms that love-in-action may take. For example, he notes the Christian roots of the hospice movement, but comments that about half of modern hospices have a Christian base, and by implication, half do not. Similarly, while Alcoholics Anonymous had a Christian foundation, it is not run by any church organization. Again and again, individuals responded to a need that they felt well suited to address. And what God wants you to do is almost sure to be different again.

Yancey's list convinced me that individuals *can* deliver compassionate "ministry" independent of management by local churches. But is there a role for church-based ministry? Is it preferable?

CHAPTER 15:
EXPOSING MINISTRY INSTITUTIONALIZATION

The flaws of seeking "oversight"

The whole idea of having a governing body to manage the operations of a particular enterprise is a tactic commonly observed in secular institutions, but we need to question the effectiveness of such an approach applied to Christian work. We start by looking at the governance side effects as they have been discovered in a traditional "missions" environment. Smalley opens up the topic, noting that many Western organizations want the fruit of their labor to remain under their control and influence. Spontaneous, local forms of ministry are opposed, as they are seen as

> "... weeds, a nuisance, a hindrance in their carefully cultivated foreign mission garden, and all the time the carefully cultivated hothouse plants of the mission 'founded' church are unable to spread roots and to derive their nurture either from the soil of their own life or from the Word of God in the root-confining pots of the mission organization and culture."
>
> (Smalley, in Winter et. al. 1981: 501)

I have carefully read the extensive biography of Hudson Taylor, and sought to consider his historical experiences in the context of my current search for answers. I share my research with you, the reader, but in summary I came away with the impression that Hudson Taylor's experiences suggests an even more fundamental issue than ministry organizations based on "home" culture versus ministry organizations with a local expression. His experiences suggest that we do better looking to God than looking to *any* organization to support the ministry to which we feel called.

Taylor, perhaps like many, started looking for an established organization that might support him in the pursuit of his call. Initially he looked at church-based (denominational) groups, but all but one would only accept ordained church leaders, which Taylor wasn't:

> *"Missionary agencies were comparatively few and far between, and [Taylor] knew of only this one with which he as an unordained man could be connected."*
>
> (Taylor & Taylor, 1911: 176)

Still he remained confident that, as God had called him, God would open up a way to minister in spite of not finding a satisfactory church-based organization:

> *"But who is to send me? The Wesleyans have no station in China ... The Established Church have one or two, but I am not a churchman [i.e. not an ordained church leader] ... and would not do for them. The Baptists and Independents have stations there, but I do not hold their views ... The Chinese Association is very low in funds. So God and God alone is my hope, and I need no other."*
>
> (Taylor & Taylor, 1911: 99)

After the initial disappointment of not finding a suitable ministry organization, Taylor began to understand that he might be better off, and more free to follow God's call, if he was not indebted to a ministry organization:

> *"Previously ... [Taylor] had rather taken it for granted that the difficulty connected with his future would all vanish if some Society could be found to send him out. It was a youthful way of looking at things, and now with more experience he began to see that the very opposite might be the case. In London he had come to understand something of the working of a Society with its necessary rules and regulations, and he could not but see that to be under the direction of a Committee, while it would secure him a salary and other advantages, might greatly curtail his freedom of action, and in this way increase rather than lessen his trials."*
>
> (Taylor & Taylor, 1911: 172)

Taylor had received an offer to be educated as a surgeon, at the expense of a mission society. He refused their offer, believing:

> *"It is necessary for the well-being of the Society that its missionary should be subject to the Board of Management. ... Their rules are no doubt reasonable and essential for such an organisation. But to me, to be educated at their expense and of course subject to these regulations would be like removing myself from the direct and personal leading of God, because I should become the servant of the Society. Having no money I could not release myself honourably, and in any case, for nine months at least (the period required as notice) I should be unable to act. Now, it is possible to pay too dearly even for great advantages, and this is more than my conscience allows me to do."*
>
> (Taylor & Taylor, 1911: 177)

Taylor came to a revelation that to be under the authority of a ministry organization was in conflict with being under the Authority of God!

> *"This was the work to which the Lord had called him; deep down in his own soul he knew it beyond a doubt. But whether the Chinese Evangelisation Society would approve was quite another question.*
>
> *To judge from their Rules and Regulations they would expect, at any rate, to maintain absolute control over the movements of their representatives. These were spoken of as Agents, and were expected to subscribe to by-laws that perplexed him with their detailed requirements; and over against all this was his growing conviction about the work to which he personally was called. The hand of God was upon him. So far as he was concerned, this was the great fact, the chief consideration. And if the rightful authority of the Committee in London had to be considered as well, how would the two fit in?"*

(Taylor & Taylor, 1911: 175)

One of the lessons Taylor learned before heading off for China was that he must be free from the constraints of a ministry organization so he would be at liberty to obey God. Independence from any organization was central. But when he reached China, he learned another lesson. Being independent from organizational ties did not mean that he was independent from other members of the Body of Christ.

> *"He longed to be free and independent, and the Lord saw fit to keep him in the very opposite position, letting him learn from experience what it is to be poor and weak and indebted to others even for the necessaries of life. For His own, His well-beloved Son there was no better way; and there are lessons still that only can be learned in this school.*
>
> *But for such circumstances early in his missionary career, Hudson Taylor would never have been able to feel for others as it was necessary he should. By nature he was resourceful and independent to a fault. He had sacrificed, as we have seen, the hope and ambition of years, breaking off his medical curriculum before he could obtain a degree, simply that he might be free to follow the guidance of the Lord as it came to him personally, untrammelled by obligations even to the Society with which he was connected. And now at the very opening of his new life in China, he found himself cast upon the generosity of strangers, shut up to a position as little welcome, possibly, to them as to himself, and from which there seemed for a long time to come no hope of escape."*

(Taylor & Taylor, 1911: 219)

The lesson was not an easy one, but Taylor seemed to come to understand that his dependence on other members of the Body of Christ was good, and at times helpful, but he had to have an underlying, more fundamental, dependence on God Himself.

> *"… but for a growing rest of heart in God, Hudson Taylor would have been almost in despair. As it was, he was learning precious lessons of his own helplessness – and of Almighty strength."*

(Taylor & Taylor, 1911: 225)

Even though we may recognize that our support and affirmation does not come from ministry organizations, we cannot afford to feel so strong in ourselves that we don't need other people, unless that is a specific call.

> *"The devil often makes men strong, strong in themselves to do evil – great conquerors, great acquirers of wealth and power. The Lord on the contrary makes His servant weak, puts him in circumstances that will shew him his own nothingness, that he may lean upon the strength that is unfailing. It is a long lesson for most of us; but it cannot be passed over until deeply learned. And God Himself thinks no trouble too great, no care too costly to teach us this."*
>
> (Taylor & Taylor, 1911: 226)

The balance is in depending on God rather than on a ministry organization, while having the humility to realize it is God's plan that free individuals work together as and when He directs.

In a secular setting, Ackoff beautifully highlights the difference between the laudable goal of helping an individual acquire the skills to accomplish things ("power to"), and the undesirable position where one person or authority has "power over" another.

> *"Because development involves an increase in ability, it empowers, but only in a particular way: It increases power-to, not power-over. Power-over is authority, and authority is the ability to make someone do something he does not want to do, usually by threat of punishment. Therefore, to exercise power over others is to reduce their ability to satisfy their needs and desires. Power-to is the ability to implement decisions. This type of power increases with competence, hence development. In the ideal state, everyone would be able to get whatever he or she legitimately needed or wanted without the exercise of power-over. In states short of the ideal, politics has to do with the distribution of power-over. The political ideal, then, is a state in which no one has power over another but all have unlimited power-to. The ideal state is one in which there is no need for politics."*
>
> (Ackoff, 1991: 51)

Ackoff articulates his principle within the world of secular politics. However, within the Body of Christ, our goal is similar. Instead of people using their skills to achieve power *over* others, all may work to equip others so they, too, have the power to achieve their own individual full potential, as *God* leads.

This perhaps can be seen most clearly in the life of Jesus. If He wished, He could have exercised power over the Roman authorities, the religious leaders, and His disciples. Instead, He equipped those who wished to learn from Him so that they themselves could become agents of change and blessing to others. This equipping was intended to enable them to carry the good news and to make disciples. Sadly, some of their efforts also went into establishing institutions and leadership structures.

Man's natural desire to establish churches like organized clubs

God delights in people alive to Him, and obedient to Him. In contrast, many local churches are happy if their members are compliant and do little more than live lives that don't embarrass the leadership or church.

Girard suggested that many people were considered to be "spiritual" if they don't commit social sins such as drinking or smoking. Further, no great expectations were made on how the individual may respond to the needs of others:

> *"His life didn't really have to produce anything of witness in the outside world or love within the Body of believers."*

(Girard, 1972: 21)

Visible personal ministry was not only seen as unnecessary but as intrusive, and this is reinforced by the attitude that the local church is responsible for ministry. All its members have to do is support church activities and the leader's vision.

> *" 'The flesh' is represented by all the human, earthly things we expect to produce growth, maturity, spirituality and life in the church — instead of looking to the Holy Spirit for these things.*
>
> *For instance, in my ministry before our commitment to renewal, I depended on 'involvement' in the organization to produce spiritual maturity. The most mature Christian, I was sure, would be the one most 'involved' in the committees and activities of the church.*
>
> *Evangelism depended on my 'Sunday sales pitches' and invitations at the end of my sermons. Personal evangelism depended on training, careful organization and consistently applied pastoral pressure.*
>
> *A great church was dependent on great human leadership, a great program that 'involved' everyone in sight, great speaking, great music and a great number of people available to fill all the teaching positions, committees and work assignments that grew out of my great ideas. And surrounding all this and enhancing it must be the finest facilities the congregation can possibly afford (or perhaps even a little finer than that!)."*

(Girard, 1972: 68-69)

Phillips (1995: 154-157) tells of a conference aimed at reaching the once-closed Eastern Bloc countries. Or more precisely, setting up the strategy to reach them—the actual conference had no outreach. At a pair of sessions, opposing strategies were presented. At one, the speaker talked with passion of the need to be the hands of the gospel, to feed the hungry, to shelter the homeless, and so on. His vision was to raise huge funds via Western churches, to enlist the involvement of large numbers of volunteers who would work in his organization, to establish supply points, and so on. At the other session, a traditional "get the people saved" approach was presented. Print heaps of tracts, and hand them out, and the work will be done. Phillips' critique of the conference follows:

> *"Most of the key players at the conference sang the same tune. Money, money, money ... testaments ... literature ... tracts. Who was talking about prayer, about God's doing his work among men? Those on the other side of the continuum, those speaking about people's needs, weren't talking about God's role in their programs either.*
>
> *Where was the balance? Get involved in people's needs but never mention God – that was the evangelism advocated by the one extreme. Arm's length evangelism was the cry of the other. Come on, everyone, send us your money. It's clean and tidy. You won't have to actually do any down-and-dirty evangelism yourself in and around where you live. Let your money evangelize the world for you. Send cash and let the professional evangelists and preachers and missionaries do it for you."*
>
> (Phillips, 1995: 200)

In comparing notes, two attendees contrasted these two attitudes with that of a now deceased relative who, in their opinion, would have simply invited the hungry and cold people into his home, and let his Christian love do most of the talking–enacting a personal calling created by God.

Girard puts the choice in clear perspective. We can either have predictable organization, without any real life, or we can have life. He concludes that we really should not have a choice—we must not constrain or set expectations on the Holy Spirit.

> *"Man, depending on himself, feels safer with a static organization he can learn to control. New spiritual life, however, is based on a living relationship with the Divine Person. The moment it becomes static or routine, it has become a thing man is doing, and it is not His new life anymore."*
>
> (Girard, 1972: 211)

The creeping disease – turning "ministry" into tradition

In many walks of life, change can creep up almost unnoticed. On a personal level, it may be weight gain. On the national political scene, it may be almost imperceptible changes in attitudes that go unchallenged. Church institutions can also change without being noticed or challenged.

Just as one example, we look briefly at the changing role of Sunday Schools. They were originally intended only for the children of non-Christians.

> *"John Whitworth ... started an excellent innovation known as 'Sunday School.' Following the example of Mr. Raikes of Gloucester, he set about gathering in the untaught children of the streets."*
>
> (Taylor & Taylor, 1911: 23)

While Whitworth was providing Sunday School for children from non-Christian homes, Hudson Taylor's parents were, as Christians, ensuring that they did *not* send their children to Sunday School. They believed it was their own responsibility to school their children.

> *"The spiritual life of his children was equally the father's [as well as the mother's] care. Family worship he conducted regularly, after both breakfast and tea. … On Sundays he gave even more time to this home-ministry … While thoroughly approving of Sunday Schools for those who needed them, he did not consider his own children to be among the number, and would relinquish to no one the privilege of teaching them in the things of God."*
>
> (Taylor & Taylor, 1911: 48-49)

Today, many Christian parents may be criticized if they fail to send their children to Sunday School. The change from Sunday School being for children of non-Christians to being the common place for children of many Christian families is a major shift, and the radical change slipped in quietly over a long period of time.

But another aspect of change is to be noted. The Sunday School ministry was started by motivated individuals, but is now largely institutionalized within local church programs.

A pattern begins to emerge. Weinberger notes that moves by secular institutions to centralize control should start to ring warning bells:

> *"We all know enough about the inequities of history to smell something suspicious about the insistence on centralized control. Control and management are the mantras of the people who are in power, who judge personal success by power, and who use power to keep themselves at the top."*
>
> (Levine, Locke, Searls and Weinberger, 2000: 130)

The centralized control model is also prevalent within Christendom. Refreshingly, Yancey paints a picture that is in stark contrast to centralized control. Instead, he suggests that the example Jesus held up for achieving change is one of many individuals each doing their bit, yet this apparently uncoordinated rabble being powerful enough to change empires:

> *"Jesus' images portray the kingdom as a kind of secret force. Sheep among wolves, treasure hidden in a field, the tiniest seed in the garden, wheat growing among weeds, a pinch of yeast worked into bread dough, a sprinkling of salt on meat – all these hint at a movement that works within society, changing it from the inside out. You do not need a shovel full of salt to preserve a slab of ham; a dusting will suffice.*
>
> *Jesus did not leave an organized host of followers, for he knew that a handful of salt would gradually work its way through the mightiest empire in the world."*
>
> (Yancey, 1997: 260-261)

Lindsay notes that many great achievements have been made by individuals, just as Jesus said they would. He talks of the

> *"… genuine outcome of an honest human soul striving to humble itself before God …"*
>
> (Lindsay, 1996: 33-34)

He immediately goes on to warn of the consequences of institutionalization of these acts of individuals:

> "The evil came when spontaneous acts of repentance and honest endeavour after new obedience became stereotyped customs, then prescribed regulations ..."
>
> (Lindsay, 1996: 34)

Attempts to retain a move of God by institutionalizing what was originated by God's Spirit may have results that that look somewhat like the original, but in external appearance only. Just as dinosaur models may look like the original, they have no life.

> "Denominationalism is in many cases a result of the development of more or less indigenous churches in various subgroups or social levels of Western society. Usually they start in the lower brackets, fossilizing in their cultural forms as they move up in society and on through time. ... It is not until we are willing to let churches grow also [in their own, self-determined way] that we have learned to trust the Holy Spirit with society. We are treating him as a small child with a new toy too complicated and dangerous for him to handle. Our paternalism is not only a paternalism toward other peoples; it is also a paternalism towards God."
>
> (Smalley, in Winter et. al. 1981: 501-502)

Time and again, attempts by institutions to enshrine some ministry within their controlled programs only ends up in killing and fossilizing what was once a living thing.

CHAPTER 16:
CHURCH-GROWTH "MINISTRY"

The biography of Walter Betts clearly portrays him as an "evangelist", but I do find extremely distasteful the way Clarnette sees as comical a story of bullying tactics used to get a convert to Christianity:

> *"The family altar was always an important part of the daily programme. It was here that the youngsters early learned of sin and salvation and were introduced to the message that God used to reclaim so many around them. One day one of the boys collared a street urchin and urged him to 'get down on the footpath and give yourself to Christ or I'll hit you!'"*

(Clarnette, 1967: 69)

This story is apparently shared as a humorous example of evangelistic zeal. However, my critical review of the author's writing led me to conclude that such an approach is vulgar and offensive. Further, my reading of the book did not give me the impression that the author moved beyond his attempt at humor to condemnation of the offensive approach, presumably choosing to focus on what he sees as commendable enthusiasm.

I relate my own experience where I had developed a wonderful friendship with a neighbor, Keith. At times he asked questions about my faith. Sadly, his enquiries came to an abrupt and acrimonious end. Another person from the area, Kelvin, was a self-styled evangelist in his local church. Arriving at my home one day when Keith was visiting me, Kelvin started "bible bashing" Keith. This resulted in Keith not only turning away from asking really searching questions about God but he also thereafter avoided contact with me because he falsely believed that I was part of the abuse that had been handed out to him by Kelvin, when nothing could have been further from the truth.

This chapter is intended to challenge the actions that some place under the heading of "sharing the good news".

Crass evangelism parading as ministry

Many local churches carry the implicit message that sharing the good news is the job of the professional church leaders, with the laity doing their bit after being trained in the techniques of evangelism. Sadly, for many churches, the concept of sharing the good news has been polluted and diluted, and has become little more than well-directed marketing and sales to increase church membership numbers.

Unfortunately, some authors follow this line. It is my belief that we should be a friend to everyone we can, regardless of whether or not they are Christians. Surely that was the example set by Jesus. But to "intentionally" befriend people so we can get them to become church members strikes me as acting under false pretense. Let's have a look at the variety of views on this topic, and the subtlety of the message to befriend others so we can grow local churches.

Initially it may look like Frost and Hirsch also wish to suggest we simply reach out to those in need. They state that we shouldn't expect people to come to a local church. Instead we should get out to their world.

> *"... the traditional church plants itself within a particular community, neighborhood, or locale and expects that people will come to it to meet God and find fellowship with others. ... The Come-To-Us stance taken by the attractional church is unbiblical. It's not found in the Gospels or the Epistles. Jesus, Paul, the disciples, the early church leaders all had a Go-To-Them mentality."*
>
> (Frost & Hirsch, 2003: 18-19)

But are we getting out of the pews so we can be salt and light to others, or do we go out so that we might bring them back with us to the pews we temporarily left while on our recruitment drive? Are we recruiting them for our own church growth?

William Booth clearly opposed the idea of bringing people into a local church, but rather suggested we should go and reach out to those outside church. But the purpose? To *make* them come in!

> *"... the moral duty of God's ministers [is] to go out into the highways and byways and make them come in."*
>
> (Hattersley, 2000: 2-3)

George Railton, a close friend of the Booths and one of the Army's leading figures, stated that the purpose of the Army was to

> *"... save the people outside the church and then send them to the churches to be trained and cared for."*
>
> (Hattersley, 2000: 139)

This emphasis on church growth is not new.

> *"... the Roman church ... used monks ... to establish the church in large parts of Europe. Their mission often focused on a mission to the new rulers of Europe and*

at the very least the patronage of the nobility was sought in order to establish their mission work. In this, they could rely on the undoubted prestige that the Roman church began to enjoy. They were able to convey a sense that to be civilised, to be a true new European, it was necessary to become a Christian.

Their mission goal was to establish the church and to welcome people into the church. And it was the church that they brought. They did not just bring missionaries but full formed church structures which often included a bishop. ... Roman bishops were clearly in charge of the missionary enterprise. Their desire was to establish a diocese. The formation of a fully formed church structure was inseparable from the missionary enterprise."

(Robinson & Smith, 2003: 52)

"Taking the church to other lands was seen as the purpose of mission.

... mission was seen as a means of growing the church overseas and evangelism as a means of strengthening the church at home. But no matter whether at home or overseas the expansion of the church tended to become the chief end of both evangelism and mission. Mission was something that the church did to prosper its own life and witness. Evangelicals did have a vision of a changed society but that tended to be an outcome of a strengthened church and not part of mission as such. For evangelicals evangelism and mission were essentially programmes of the church, something that faithful churches did."

(Robinson & Smith, 2003: 55-56)

The Bible encourages us to share the good news of Jesus, but to put it bluntly, God's generous desire to reach out to needy people has often been corrupted by those who turn it into little more than a crass recruitment drive for their local church membership. As noted by Tillapaugh, those with such an attitude will only "minister" to those who are willing to become part of the organization.

"In the church we have developed a fortress mentality which says, 'We'll minister to anyone who will come and fit in with us.'"

(Tillapaugh, 1982: 52-53)

Oliver and Thwaites explain that some churches do actually reach out, but only after they've invested decades in getting their fortress safe. It may be argued that this is marginally better.

"Too often we establish a safe church subculture, grow it for twenty years and when it's strong enough, try to reach out from it. We then discover that what we have, in fact, created is a very strong sub-culture – one that is too much of a lump to salt, leaven and light the world."

(Oliver & Thwaites, 2001: 111-112)

Missionaries may be seen as the complete opposite of fortress-mentality local churches. Often at great personal cost, missionaries leave their familiar and comfortable homes to take the good news to foreign cultures. However, as noted earlier in great detail, many "missionary" ventures are little more than church-planting exercises. McGavran warns that the results can be the creation of an isolated, self-centered community where members cannot relate to their own people, nor sometimes even to the own families.

> *"... these mission station churches are ..., in truth, gathered churches, made up of [individuals that] have usually been disowned by their non-Christian relatives. The ... lives of these Christians have been so changed, and they find such satisfaction in the fellowship of their own sort (i.e. other mission station Christians) that they feel immeasurably superior to their own unconverted relatives. This is particularly true when they come from the oppressed classes. The second generation of Christians is even farther removed from their non-Christian relatives than the first, while in the third generation, in the very land where they live, the gathered church members know as a rule no non-Christian relatives at all. .... A new people has been established which intermarries only within itself and thinks of itself as a separate community."*
>
> (McGavran, 1981: 281)

The key message to be noted is that just as pastors struggle to conceive of a Godly and healthy Body of Christ without clergy at the helm, missionaries are unlikely to expect their sharing of the good news to be fruitful unless they can see evidence of their labor in the formation of local churches.

By way of contrast, Phillips openly condemns crass evangelism when people really need to be introduced to the power and love of God for real change:

> *"Ours is no calling merely to stand on the street corners of our cities preaching outmoded sermons to unconcerned passersby, satisfying our own need to feel important but doing little to impact those who hear us.*
>
> *Our calling is rather to take with transforming power the life of Christ to those in desperate need of it. To be astute and intellectually honed to stand on the cutting edge of today's world, to be compassionate and full of hearts that love, and to be battle-ready to face the cunning and evil resourcefulness of the enemy."*
>
> Phillips (1995: 234)

As Phillips notes, some may perform acts of "evangelism" without really caring for those they meet. And one may question whether such evangelism is little more than a recruitment drive. In contrast, in *Europe's Moravians: A Pioneer Missionary Church*, Colin Grant notes that the Moravians (a European denomination with history reaching back to the mid-1400s) had a focus on simple sharing of the good news rather than local church planting. Sadly, Grant sees this unpretentious attitude of the Moravians as a weakness:

> *"... Moravians had their weaknesses. They concentrated more on evangelism than on the actual planting of local churches and they were consequently very weak on developing Christian leadership. ... Since most of the early missionaries went out*

straight from 'the carpenter's bench' because of the spontaneous nature of their obedience, they were short on adequate preparation."

(Grant, 1976: 209)

It is ironic that Grant also suggests that the Moravians were successful *in spite* of these "weaknesses":

"[The Moravians] have left a record without parallel in the post-New Testament era of world evangelization, and we do well to look again at the main characteristics of this movement and learn the lessons God has for us."

(Grant, 1976: 206).

A case study in friendship with strings attached

Frost and Hirsch, having said earlier that we need to get out to where the people are rather than expect them to come in to local churches, start to show their hand. It appears to me that their driving force for friendships outside of the local church is intended to lead towards planting local churches. Agreed, they do not intend to bring them back to the original church, but the goal seems to be to get them into churches nonetheless.

"A church, a community of faith, centered in Christ, would then effectively be planted in that hangar [where a group of sky-diving enthusiasts have been 'reached for Christ' by church implants]. The goal would not be to bring a few newly converted skydivers into the church (whereupon they gradually replace all their skydiving friends with churchgoing ones and thus lose their places in their original 'tribe'), but to develop an incarnational Christian community within the skydiving fraternity."

(Frost & Hirsch, 2003: 51)

They refer to trying to "minister to" others, yet my analysis suggests that the stated goal may be one of church planting rather than any other form of ministry to the needs of others. It is assumed that getting others to join us must be good for them. It seems the missionary leaders will listen humbly, but only until they have got the pulse of the community, then they can show the unsaved how to behave like members of a local church:

"We would think like missionaries and spend more time listening to, eating with, and playing with the subculture or neighborhood we were trying to minister to. We would not assume to develop a model of church/community life <u>until</u> we had recognized and discerned the 'natural' ways in which a given group gathers and assembles." [Emphasis mine]

(Frost & Hirsch, 2003: 63)

Having strongly criticized what they call the "attractional" mode where the focus is on gathering, the authors quote Jonathan Campbell who says:

"The church is to share the good news of Jesus Christ in the power of the Holy Spirit

among all the social groupings and <u>gather</u> those who respond into disciple-making communities." [Emphasis mine]

(Frost & Hirsch, 2003: 66)

They then go on to elaborate Campbell's master plan, step-by-step. Firstly

"... an existing church commissions [a] church-planting team."

(Frost & Hirsch, 2003: 66)

Note that a "church" starts the ball rolling. It may be done with their "blessing", but the goal is to plant another local church.

Then an outgoing team

"... evangelizes strategic peoples."

(Frost & Hirsch, 2003: 66)

Their actions can be viewed as forming relationships under the pretense of friendship, but such friendship is really is aimed at gaining more members.

Finally, the team

"... with [the] new disciples, ... establishes an indigenous church."

(Frost & Hirsch, 2003: 66)

Yes, it may be on the home turf of the new 'disciples', but they are the disciples of those sent out rather than the disciples of Christ, and the church-planting team provides the expertise and direction of the base church.

... and then the theme repeats itself from the top, with the newly formed local church as the starting point for the next cycle.

Am I unkindly misunderstanding the true motives of Frost & Hirsch by suggesting they teach that we should deceptively join a group as if we want true friendship when what we are really seeking is to turn them into clones of ourselves and plant more of our own brand of churches? Let's look at the words of Frost and Hirsh themselves on this topic, and see if you agree with my concerns.

Frost and Hirsch start very well, actually condemning those who form less-than-genuine friendships just for the purposes of evangelism:

"There's very little genuine friendship happening. When churches do befriend unbelievers it's often so that they might become Christians. And it's assumed that the way to become Christian is for them to see how truly bad they are. Surely, not-yet-Christians see how disingenuous this is. True friendship is God's calling in and of itself. If people find friendship with Jesus through our friendship with them, that is the work of the Holy Spirit. Instead of having such a combative, manipulative spirituality of engagement with others, we believe [Christians need] to recover a spirituality of engagement that whispers into the souls of not-yet-Christians."

(Frost & Hirsch, 2003: 99)

They also take an example of a Christian opening a shoe store, but where the love of Christ shows through, rather than planting yet another church. Still sounds pretty good? Maybe, but the catch is that the shoe store is suggested as a better approach because church planting would not be *perceived* as beneficial for the community. So it would seem to boil down to taking actions to create a better perception. Hang the reality!

> "... no one in San Francisco wants another church, but they do want a cool shoe room. If we come to plant a church in a particular area, we're not <u>perceived</u> as doing anyone any favors. But if we're starting a café, an Internet launderette, or a day-care center, we're <u>seen</u> as bringing some intrinsic value to a community." [Emphasis mine]
>
> (Frost & Hirsch, 2003: 26)

Again, Frost and Hirsch encourage active participation in groups that try to improve the values in the community. But it seems to me that the motivation is to create opportunities for evangelism, rather than trying to bring justice, encourage the arts, be friends, or whatever.

> "... an interesting spin-off of seeing action as sacrament is that it allows others to join in around a common activity. ... Whether it is a socio-political cause (e.g., the campaign to free Nelson Mandela) or a social activity (e.g., a mural art project), the action itself can unite a wide variety of people around that activity. And these activities can become wonderful places for evangelism ..."
>
> (Frost & Hirsch, 2003: 144)

In summary, my interpretation is that Frost and Hirsch admit their motives. To me, they appear to be stating that our social interaction must be "intentional" i.e. directed at evangelization, no matter what it may *appear* to be.

> "Our point is that socializing <u>must</u> be <u>intentional</u>, <u>missional</u>, grace-filled, and generous. It must be seen as part of a broader pattern of infiltrating a community." [Emphasis mine]
>
> (Frost & Hirsch, 2003: 57)

But what about Jesus' example? He was known as a "friend of sinners". He just loved people, and had compassion for them, no matter what their political alignment, race, socio-economic position, or whatever. He just offered love to them all, even though some rejected the offer. He was not pretentious or devious—what you saw was what you got—He lived what He taught. By example, He demonstrated what James called "true religion"—the care of widows and orphans.

So a big question mark hangs over the "church planting" model. Jesus is the only model we need, and He demonstrated beautiful care for people, with no expectations of gaining a following. Those He ministered to did not have to follow Him, did not have to "catch His vision", pay tithes to Him, or change the way they dressed; they could just believe in Him if they chose to. Some responded by following Him, some didn't. He healed ten lepers, but only one bothered to even come back to thank Him. He cared nonetheless, and continued to reach out with compassion.

We need to be aware, however, that some might pretend to be followers of Jesus' example, befriending the vulnerable, but with a motivation of recruiting susceptible people into their own group. Cults do it—and so do churches.

CHAPTER 17:
MINISTRY WITHOUT INSTITUTIONS

It may be hard to imagine "ministry" without the oversight and support of local churches, but a number of authors challenge the assumptions behind church-based ministry.

Setting ministry free from "church"

In contrast to those who see "mission" as essentially an initiative of the local church, Frost and Hirsch teach:

> "Don't think church, think mission!"
>
> (Frost & Hirsch, 2003: 81)

Unfortunately, they address this teaching to "church planters". The overlap is that these church planters are ones who are

> "... interested in developing missional churches."
>
> (Frost & Hirsch, 2003: 81)

So on the one hand these authors appear to see mission and church planting to be inextricably linked. Yet on the other hand they encourage "mission" such as a businessman raising the standard of ethics in his sphere of influence. There seems to be a muddying of the waters from these authors.

However, they make an interesting observation as to one reason why we still see so much church-based ministry. They suggest it is often because initiatives outside of the local churches are not recognized as *real* mission. And they make the point that so many local churches will not support the individual ministry of their people unless such ministry is clearly focused on inviting those contacted to join the local church:

> "... we don't [but should] see businessmen, students, youth workers, lecturers, plumbers, electricians, and homemakers as having missional roles in their worlds. If a

businessman starts a prayer breakfast in a local restaurant, the church will notify its members and support the program. But if a businessman attempts to use his influence to develop ethical schemes through his business to serve the needy or create jobs for the unemployed we traditionally don't [but should] see this as mission. We ... [have not traditionally seen, but should see] the strong creation of friendships that parents make through the local school as being anything to do with mission (<u>unless they're inviting them to church</u>)." [Emphasis mine]

(Frost & Hirsch, 2003: 45)

Frost and Hirsch appear to condemn the lack of recognition by local churches of ministry *outside* of their influence and control. In contrast, it seems to me that Oliver and Thwaites condemn ministry *inside* local churches for the limitations imposed by this church-centric approach:

"We have, for too long, placed these creation-encompassing truths concerning the saints, the ministry gifts and the divine purpose, within the setting of the congregation. This placement has severely hindered the body in its calling to salt, light and leaven the earth. We can no longer afford such a strategic blunder."

(Oliver & Thwaites, 2001: 153)

In Hunt's novel, Chris is debating with Emma on the topic of reaching the world by getting involved where the people are at. Chris starts by quoting Jesus' prayer for His disciples not to be taken out of the world but to be kept safe from the evil one. He goes on to say,

"Jesus' prayer ... was meant for us, Emma. We were never meant to hide in our churches or in our sheltered social circles. Jesus wants us to advance into the world, not retreat from it. ...

... I've seen too many Christians cocooning as if the outside world doesn't exist. They build huge churches, Christian schools, recreation programs, even medical centers for their members – anything and everything possible to ensure they never have to venture into the world Christ wants us to embrace."

(Hunt, 2004: 223)

Emma counters with a quote from Scripture:

"Come out from them and separate yourselves from them, says the Lord. Don't touch their filthy things, and I will welcome you."

(Hunt, 2004: 223)

To which Chris replies,

"There's a difference ...between walking in the world and wallowing in it. We are the light of the world, but we have hidden our light inside our buildings and Christian programs. When the world looks at us, too often they see petty, self-absorbed people who wag their fingers and scold everyone else for misbehaviors, then retreat into ivory towers ..."

(Hunt, 2004: 223-224)

Foster encourages God's people to move beyond the safe and comfortable ministry performed in God's name in the security of local church confines, and challenges them to be agents of God's love where it is most needed—on the front line of life outside:

> *"It is all well and good to speak of service within the warm confines of the home or the believing fellowship, but what about the rough and tumble of the world of business and politics? To be a servant in a culture predicated upon competition may not be easy, but Jesus never suggested that discipleship would be effortless."*
>
> (Foster, 1985: 642)

Rinehart goes so far as to say that real impact is observed when the laity gets involved personally with those in need, rather than leaving it to the professional church leadership. But the reason for calling God's people to arms is not just that it is proven to be effective, but that ministry *by* the people is what God expects *of* His people!

> *"Looking at the scene worldwide, we see that the believing community is growing fastest where there is ministry of and by the people of God. The 'unqualified' and 'untrained' are being mightily used by the Holy Spirit because of their simple obedience to His call for holiness, faith, and commitment.*
>
> *In contrast, many churches and ministries in the United States are built in part on a relatively small core group of 'ministry professionals' who are committed to a particular vision. These individuals are much like the pillars of a North Carolina beach house – remove even one of them and the entire structure is severely weakened. Remove enough of them and the ministry itself falls.*
>
> *The fact that so many ministries depend upon the continuous output of so few individuals is alarming. Kingdom ministry is meant to be shared by each and every one of God's people."*
>
> (Rinehart, 1998: 128)

There are many consequences of ministry based within the programs of local churches. Not only does it lessen the effectiveness of sharing the good news with those "outside", it also has negative impacts on those "inside". And this is true of both the church leaders and the laity. Tillapaugh notes the widespread use of "motivation" by church leaders to try to get the people into action:

> *"It is sad to see pastors trying to motivate their people with fear, ought-to, or you'll-be-blessed motivations. God uses want-to motivation because that is the only kind of driving force which works for any length of time."*
>
> (Tillapaugh, 1982: 131)

Rinehart perhaps identifies one reason why these attempts at motivation are so common—the "professionals" are exhausted, and are often assigned to roles for which they are not gifted. He shares from his own early experiences before he adopted a new strategy:

> *"Every day as I got dressed to head off to my new job, I kept telling myself that if I tried hard and trusted God enough, I could rise to the occasion; God would honor my faith. And every day the tasks ... left me depleted. The function I served was important to the kingdom, but I was not drawn to it nor was I gifted for it."*
>
> (Rinehart, 1998: 115-116)

But it's not only the professionals who lose out with this approach. The laity misses out on the joy and fulfillment of achieving God's purposes for their lives. Donald McGavran warns:

> *"... the essential recognition [of the importance of God-directed work among people groups] is not often made by Christian leaders. Gifts of God come and go unrecognized; while <u>man</u>-directed ... work is carried faithfully, doggedly forward."* [Emphasis mine]
>
> (McGavran, 1981: 289)

A number of authors recognize the opportunities lost through attempting to run church-based ministry, and gently suggest a better way. But other authors are more damning in their outspoken condemnation. Vernon Grounds, the writer of the foreword to Tillapaugh's *Unleashing the Church*, criticizes the use of structures, and implies a level of slavery in the way people are bound to their local church. He calls for a reversal:

> *"Forget about binding members to an organization with ties of loyalty, cords of convivial programming, and busy intramural involvement."*
>
> (Tillapaugh, 1982: 5)

Tillapaugh notes the lack of creativity amongst church ministries. This is damning when the Holy Spirit is renowned for the unique and creative ways He calls people to respond to varying needs:

> *"One of the saddest commentaries on the ... church is its deadening sameness. One can look in the yellow pages and find Sunday School, worship, Sunday evening and midweek services listed with numbing regularity. If the church is one of the 37,000 Southern Baptist churches you can also expect to find Women's Missionary Union, Brotherhood, Girl's Auxiliary, Royal Ambassadors and Training Union. If it is not Southern Baptist, look for basically the same groups with different names. When Detroit mass-produces, all the models come off the assembly line looking the same. When the Holy Spirit creates, each one is unique."*
>
> (Tillapaugh, 1982: 73)

And Glasser speaks out in perhaps the boldest manner, suggesting that Satan himself uses organization structures within local churches to further his purposes:

> *"The spirit world is always present and the demons are never friendly. ... [We are called to] active resistance to all that hinders the ongoing purpose of God – the powers in religious structures ..."*
>
> (Glasser, 1976: 112)

Again we contrast the leadership style of Jesus with that so often encountered amongst church leaders. Not only does Yancey highlight this difference, he notes that he was actually schooled by church leaders in techniques of control and manipulation.

> "This quality of restraint in Jesus – one could almost call it a divine shyness – took me by surprise. I realized, as I absorbed the story of Jesus in the Gospels, that I had expected from him the same qualities I had met in the … church of my childhood. There, I often felt the victim of emotional pressures. Doctrine was dished out in a 'Believe and don't ask questions!' style. Wielding the power of miracle, mystery, and authority, the church left no place for doubt. I also learned manipulative techniques for 'soul-winning,' some of which involved misrepresenting myself to the person I was talking to. Yet now I am unable to find any of these qualities in the life of Jesus."

(Yancey, 1995: 80)

The need for freedom to perform ministry as God directs rather than as committees direct is highlighted in Edman's book *They Found the Secret*, where he tells the story of Amy Carmichael, a missionary to orphaned children in India in the early 1900's. He notes her willingness to act in freedom relating to the ministry she performed, even when explicitly ordered to submit to those who perceived they had authority over her.

> "[Her publication of her views] caused tremendous stir in India, and also in Britain; so much so that a committee on the field was appointed to ask her to return to England. [But rather than being cowed by opposition she stood firm and found that] … the Lord of the Harvest overruled in her behalf when others misunderstood her obedience to marching orders and her understanding of the battle."

(Edman, 1960: 28)

A more radical way: No leaders, no laity, just servants of Christ

The following stories are gathered from experiences in settings ranging from local churches, through overseas mission-based churches, to groups of Christians who meet in work places rather than in church settings. However, a theme is common in all, namely that individuals must seek God's call on their lives rather than getting the direction and blessing via a hierarchical organizational structure.

Oliver and Thwaites tell of a work-based gathering where there is a lack of formal organization. Instead, the group is free and dynamic. There are no formal leadership appointments, and ministry initiatives are dynamic.

> "The gatherings would be open for family, friends and clients. There would be no leader, but different people would come, from time to time, to input and teach. There would be no one worship leader, but different people would come and minister and then others would replace them."

(Oliver & Thwaites, 2001: 186)

Hiebert contrasts the church control mechanisms with which we are familiar with the Biblical role of brotherhood and servanthood he values. Note that the leader is dispensable!

> "There [may be] leadership in the Church ... but ... the leader ... [must be] dispensable ... for [it is the leader's task to] ... move on when his presence begins to hinder its growth."
>
> (Hiebert in Winter et. al., 1981: 383)

Rather than the pastor deciding to start (say) a street outreach and

> "... then go recruit laypeople to staff it."
>
> (Cymbala, 1997: 74)

Cymbala suggests we

> "... let God birth something in people who are spiritually sensitive, who begin to pray and feel a calling."
>
> (Cymbala, 1997: 74)

He points out that people motivated by God's calling are far less likely to toss in the towel when discouragement or complications set in than those appointed to fill the pastor's, or anyone else's, vision.

Likewise, Charles Sheldon portrays one of his characters seeking God's will for her life. She asks a friend, "What do you think?" Her friend replies:

> "You mustn't ask me to decide for you ... we must each one of us decide according to the judgment we feel for ourselves to be Christlike."
>
> (Sheldon, 1984: 55)

As Cymbala grappled with how to exercise leadership, he observed that his father-in-law

> "... didn't offer a lot of advice or perspective; I guess he thought I would learn more in the school of hard knocks. He often told me, 'Jim, you're just going to have to find your own way, under God, of ministering ...' "
>
> (Cymbala, 1997: 18)

These stories and examples reflect an opposition to the directive control mechanisms typically encountered in most local churches.

Buckingham shared what he believed was a personal message from God to him:

> "Jamie, don't let the world – or the church – mold you into its image."
>
> (Buckingham, 1980: 183)

Buckingham went on to say,

> "... I am determined to hear and do the will of God for me – despite what others think I should do. This does not mean I do not fail and need the correction and

adjustment of others. But it does mean that I shall not be ashamed – or afraid – of my imperfections."

(Buckingham, 1980: 183)

These statements demonstrate a real freedom from the words of others directing our lives. Instead, we can be directed by God, based on a mature relationship with Him—one of freedom. Rather than being frightened to take another step until God has spoken, Buckingham portrays a vibrant relationship where we are so close to the heartbeat of God that we can move with the sure knowledge that if we miss the mark occasionally (as we are sure to do), we will hear His gentle words of redirection.

"The higher way of guidance is not to follow the Lord but to go before Him as He directs. He longs to bring His children into such maturity that they can walk alone. He does not desire to hold us with a tight rein as a horse or mule but with freedom, guided only by His eye upon us. If at any moment we misstep, if our ear is tuned to His voice, He will speak softly and say, 'No, not that way, this is the way – walk ye in it."

(Buckingham, 1980: 113)

This observed freedom from the opinion or permission of others is nothing new. Many of the heroes of the Bible knew a similar freedom. Philip was called by God to minister to the Ethiopian eunuch. Philip did not seek approval from church leaders—he simply obeyed God.

But the best example is in the life of Jesus Himself. As a young man still in the care of His parents, He chose to stay at the temple, discussing matters of faith with the elders, and did not ask permission of His parents or even notify them of His choice! Such freedom may cause reaction, but we can nevertheless make the choice to live in freedom. This must not be fueled by rebelliousness and carelessness for the feelings of others. Instead, we can maintain a desire to avoid offense where possible; yet retain a God-led freedom, even if it results in being misunderstood.

We take a look at some stories of pastors who, in contrast to demanding the laity follow their lead, allow a level of liberty.

Arthur (1991: 197-200) tells the moving story of a local church where a "leader" allows the Holy Spirit to speak through others. In one scene, a member introduced a refugee family he had met and who were staying with him. The pastor put aside his planned sermon, and those attending prayed for this family. Then the treasurer (not the pastor) took the initiative to recommend that the local church give one third of the contents of their bank account to this family, and the people unanimously agreed. The suggestion did not come from the pastor, and it was the people who decided.

Arthur then tells how, at the next service, the pastor encouraged open discussion on what the ideal Christian should look like on the outside, and on the inside. Throughout the initial discussion, the pastor was silent. When he eventually spoke, it was merely to ask a question on the possibility of a country's culture becoming intertwined with positions of faith, and to point to the Bible's comments on how the Pharisees had mixed traditions with the teaching of Moses.

In analyzing Arthur's book, he appeared to condemn culturally based expectations of Christians such as dress codes, a simple example that I suspect many can relate to. His story, I suggest, is insightful and worthy of thoughtful consideration:

> " 'And now,' he said in his gentle, disarming old voice, 'everybody here has an image floating in their head of the ideal Christian. Describe that image in words. What does that ideal Christian look like on the outside? And what does he look like on the inside?'
>
> For the ten minutes allotted them, the people wrote. When they finished, the pastor asked them to each take twenty or thirty seconds and read aloud what they had written. Starting at one end of the outer circle and continuing around to the last person in the inner circle, they all read from their sheets of paper.
>
> When the reading was over, one man stood and said, 'I need to ask the Americans something. As most of you know, I became a convert to Christianity at home in France only five months ago. Now my greatest desire in life is to please my God. Several of you from America said the ideal Christian on the outside should be clean and well-groomed, neatly dressed, and things to that effect. This concept of the Christian testimony is foreign to me. But if it is really what God expects, then I want to know so I can make the necessary changes in my life. I need to be taught. So – what Scriptures must I read to learn of this idea that I should always look clean and neat?' His question was posed with obvious sincerity.
>
> The pastor sat in silence, listening and waiting.
>
> A woman with a Southern accent responded first. 'Well, I can't pinpoint the exact Scripture for you, but it must be there. Every church in America teaches it.'
>
> Several others spoke up, and the discussion continued in a lively exchange of ideas, feelings, questions, opinions, and Bible verses.
>
> The spontaneous interaction appeared to be something this group was used to, but Jason had never seen anything like it in a church service. It was as foreign to him as the concept of the 'well-groomed Christian' was to the Frenchman. Jason found it, though, to be thought-provoking, invigorating. As a matter of fact, he downright liked it.
>
> One of the Americans, a middle-aged man, conceded that the 'clean-cut' idea was perhaps culturally influenced. He then nodded to a few of the Europeans, Africans, and Asians, and asked them to read again what they had written. 'Hands that are willing to work hard,' said one. 'A tongue that speaks kind words,' said another. And another said, 'Ears that listen to things of worthwhile substance.'
>
> Soon the old pastor spoke again, <u>his first words since the discussion started</u>. 'I want all of us to ask ourselves a question: If Christianity is present in a country for a long time, and becomes tightly intertwined with the culture, is it possible that Christianity in that country could become more defined by the culture's qualities than by the actual teachings of the Bible?' ...

The pastor opened his Bible and read a passage from the book of Mark. Then he showed from the passage how the Pharisees sincerely but destructively passed off manmade traditions as the word of God.

That was all. He did not attempt to draw any conclusions, but simply ended the service with prayer." [Emphasis mine]

(Arthur, 1991: 200-202)

Arthur's stories are fictional, but he has crafted an image of a pastor that is very different to what many of us have seen.

Tillapaugh likewise establishes a distinction between common practice and the people in his story, but this time it is real-life. Note how an individual, a member of the laity, took the initiative to establish a new ministry. It was not "visioned" or approved by the pastor, orchestrated by the pastor, or resourced by those the pastor "appointed" to the ministry:

"One of the newest ministries in our church is a health-care ministry. The woman who heads it ... [initially advertised it] ... and held an open meeting for anyone interested. Several people showed up. Some were health-care professionals; others were interested in holistic health and nutrition. (Such initial brainstorming sessions are usually attended and conducted by <u>lay people only</u>. ...)

A second health-care meeting held shortly afterward produced a smaller group. These became the core people and they began to map out the structure of the ministry. ... Where this health-care ministry will go in the future remains to be seen. It will depend on the people God sends into the ministry, what He puts on their hearts, and the needs they see. The shape of this ministry ... is simple: the Holy Spirit leads people and people shape the Body." [Emphasis mine]

(Tillapaugh, 1982: 74-75)

As stated a little earlier, we are not seeking a "better church". These stories, while being found in the setting of local church structures, are only recounted to portray an important principle, irrespective of where it is played out.

The message is simple. Clergy dominating and dictating the ministry of the laity is unacceptable. Clergy who allow freedom amongst the laity is better. For individuals who are no longer part of the clergy/laity system and who live in freedom, it is far, far better. For them, it is not a matter of whether they are granted freedom by their pastor. They embrace a freedom granted by God. They live in a way that exhibits freedom, no matter what some people who claim "authority" may wish. For them, the role of the clergy, and being granted permission by such clergy, are simply irrelevant.

Jesus could have set up a kingdom of force, majesty and dominant authority, Yancey notes His style was, in fact, the reverse:

"The most influential person who has ever lived, Jesus held no office, had an attitude approaching contempt towards political power, and left no material possessions other than the robe on his back."

(Yancey, 2001: 165)

Having seen that Jesus did not fit the shape of influential people with fancy titles, Yancey also notes that Jesus chose as disciples those we would not classify as 'born leaders':

> *"I would have puzzled over the strange mixture represented by the Twelve. Simon the Zealot belongs to the party violently opposing Rome, while Matthew the tax collector has recently been employed by Rome's puppet ruler. No scholars like Nicodemus or wealthy patrons like Joseph of Arimethea have made it into the Twelve. One must look hard to detect any strong leadership abilities.*
>
> *...Jesus does not seem to choose his followers on the basis of native talent or perfectibility or potential for greatness. When he lived on earth he surrounded himself with ordinary people who misunderstood him, failed to exercise much spiritual power, and sometimes behaved like churlish school-children."*
>
> (Yancey, 1995: 99-100)

In Matthew 20: 25-28, Jesus taught that even if in other areas of life we might observe those who use their high position to dominate others, in the Kingdom of God, we are all to serve as He leads. He went further, and even forbade the use of titles that would set one person up as having a higher rank than others (Matthew 23:10)

If we encourage structures that allow freedom for the individual, we should not be surprised if we are opposed by those who desire to retain control and who don't want a message of freedom preached to those they direct. Lindsay tells of one of Luther's opponents who feared that if Luther's beliefs were accepted, they would destroy the control the church leaders had over the laity:

> *"[John Eck] saw that the theses [from Luther] were based on principles which would justify the opinions of John Huss, or, as they were commonly called, 'the Bohemian Heresy', and that if carried out they would destroy the whole medieval conception of the supernatural powers of the clergy, and the dominion over the laity which the gifts supposed to be bestowed in ordination gave them."*
>
> (Lindsay, 1996: 65)

In stark contrast, Tillapaugh describes a church structure based on relationships and trust rather than control structures. As quoted previously, he states that such an approach:

> *"... will be difficult for many vocational and lay leaders in the church to accept. This style of ministry lessens their control. Unfortunately church leaders, vocational and lay, are often not accustomed to trusting people with ministry."*
>
> (Tillapaugh, 1982: 77)

Tillapaugh then goes on to paint a picture of

> *"... fearful pastors [who] direct their vitality and strength into a strictly controlled and 'safe' series of programs."*
>
> (Tillapaugh, 1982: 80)

The power brokers of the local church institutions of Luther's day opposed any move that would lessen their influence. Tillapaugh clearly states that the same opposition continues to exist today. And Rinehart has a warning for these control-mongers:

> "Leaders … who strive to control lay ministry and want to keep the laity locked up under their 'leadership' … may get run over."
>
> (Rinehart, 1998: 13)

The alternative to being led by leaders – be led by the Holy Spirit!

Oliver and Thwaites suggest that clues to a new approach to ministry already exist—we just need to be able to "see" them. The trouble for some might be that the traditions of local churches are obstructing our vision:

> "The first thing we need to realise is that the [the Body of Christ as it brings salt and light outside of the local church environment] already exists in the landscape: it is already functioning. The problem has been that our doctrine or understanding of church has made it, for the most part, invisible to us. Hence the need for a theology of creation and of the church that enables us to see it."
>
> (Oliver & Thwaites, 2001: 94)

We don't have to wait until some remarkable event occurs (an angelic visitation, a word from a burning bush, or whatever) to get us started. Such thinking may be nothing more than seeking an excuse to do nothing. Oliver and Thwaites see your current "work" place (paid or unpaid) as a culture of which you are already part and where you can and should minister effectively. For example, they state:

> "How strong the imperative to recognise the many unnamed ministry gifts now residing in business, in healthcare, in home settings, in education and so on. How great the opportunity there is to … stand with and equip the saints in their works as the church as fullness. Like Jesus and John the Baptist, we need these ministry gifts in the market place; we need them in the byways of business and in the hallways of education; in the clinics and wards – not … as chaplains …, but as mentors, as friends, as Kingdom consultants, as human resource people, as teachers and communicators, networkers, servants, resource gatherers – extending the power of agreement, the knowledge of the Son of God, triggering the created gifts and traits in the saints to stir and equip them for good work."
>
> (Oliver & Thwaites, 2001: 160)

It may sound so obvious to say we should follow the leading of the Holy Spirit that one may ask why wouldn't anyone who claims to be a follower of Christ adopt this philosophy? Sometimes the answer is that church leaders teach us to follow *them*. Of course, they may not explicitly finish the sentence by saying we should follow them *instead* of following the Holy Spirit. In fact, many church leaders would argue that they are so good at hearing from God that following *them* is the same as following God.

> *"Centralization assumes that a leader speaks for God and that people are there to support the leader's vision of what needs to be accomplished. Following along with the leader or organization becomes a basic tenet of godliness. Failing to submit is to rebel against God Himself!"*
>
> (Rinehart, 1998: 36)

Sometimes the leaders want us to follow them. Sometimes the people would rather follow the leader than have a direct relationship with God. After introducing a quotation from Exodus 20, Bevere notes that Moses, the leader, chose a close relationship with God, but the people did not.

> *"Look at the difference in the responses to God's manifested glory: Israel drew back but Moses drew near. This illustrates the different responses of believers today."*
>
> (Bevere, 1997: 137)

Similarly, after quoting from Deuteronomy 5 (where the people asked Moses to interpret God's directives on their behalf), the author states:

> *"They cried out, 'We cannot approach His glorious presence nor stand in the midst of Him and live.' They wanted Moses to hear for them, and they promised to hear [Moses] and do whatever God said [via Moses] to do! They attempted to live by this pattern for thousands of years but could not obey His words. How different are we today? Do we get God's Word from our pastor and preachers …?"*
>
> (Bevere, 1997: 139-140)

Rinehart very clearly states that the message to seek God directly must be communicated by all who are in a position to share this challenge:

> *"The final goal [of those who find themselves in positions of influence] should be to direct people to the Trinity, not to the leader or the organization."*
>
> (Rinehart, 1998: 89)

When Hudson Taylor was seriously ill, his wife prayed for his recovery.

> *"Realising what it would mean to the Mission if he were taken suddenly, with no one in view to fill his place, she had been holding on to God in prayer and faith for his recovery."*
>
> (Taylor & Taylor, 1918: 579-580)

There is nothing surprising in Mrs. Taylor praying for her husband. Millions of Christians who believe in the effectiveness of prayer and see a loved one suffering would do the same. But she was not only praying for herself and for her husband. She perceived that the organization Hudson Taylor led was very dependent on him, and was worried at how the China Inland Mission would cope if he were taken. No person is irreplaceable, and to pray for the leader's recovery from ill health just *so that* "his" (or "her") ministry may continue indicates a misplaced dependency on the individual rather than God.

The story of Taylor is based in a "missions" setting. Ralph Winter and Steven Hawthorne, in the preface to the book they edited titled *Perspectives on the World Christian Movement*, teach some principles that are also based in a missions setting. They note that movements of God today bring blessing in the manner of God's interaction with Abraham—based on "obedience of faith." But that obedience must not be "organized":

> "... we do not contemplate any physical or human organizational centralization of that obedience."
>
> (Winter & Hawthorne, 1981: xiii)

Howard Snyder teaches that there should not be an organizational hierarchy within Christian institutions. He recognizes this dependency on leaders is evident within local churches and is accepted as the norm by many, but he nonetheless opposes the existence of such structures. But can Christian institutions actually exist without hierarchies? Is such a radical approach workable?

Perhaps some secular organizations such as the armed forces need hierarchies. It is not an area on which I wish to take a position, and certainly one in which I have almost no experience. But within Christendom, I believe a position is possible in which we can and should manage without a hierarchy, even if it may seem unworkable.

> "The church ... [should not be] ... a chain of command but a network of love. This is, of course, supremely impractical to people steeped in hierarchical concepts. But it is the way of the Kingdom."
>
> (Snyder, 1983, in Rinehart, 1998: 50)

Again we ask—can it really work this way? I personally believe it can *only* work if God is all He claims to be, and if He is *allowed* to be Who He is! He is more than capable of running the show, and we need to take Him at His word. Our actions should be based on a rock-solid belief that He will not fail without our interference.

If God's work in the Body of Christ cannot be achieved without man's interference because God is too weak and ineffective to move in the hearts of men, then I would argue He's a pretty impotent God. I don't want to be actively involved with any organization that depends on clever men or women. I would rather risk all on God's abilities. Either He "succeeds" (sometimes in ways we may not choose or even like—Jesus didn't enjoy the experience of dying on a Roman cross), or the whole faith thing seems flawed. Do we want a safety net or an insurance policy that depends on charming (or not so charming) leaders? Either God comes through, or the venture fails.

Some local church leaders brazenly and openly demand that the laity obey *their* interpretation of God's will for every individual, and commit loyally to *their* vision for the group. This style is, bluntly, cult-like.

Less confrontational, but just as dangerous, are those who come to you with a "word" from God. Unless it is confirmation of what *you* are hearing from God, it can probably be put aside.

Whether church leaders are overt or covert in their attempts to influence us, we must be aware of another danger, namely ourselves! We must guard our own attitudes in seeking a leader's interpretation of God's will for us. In her autobiography, *Salvation Creek*, Susan Duncan shares her own temptation to look to others for guidance. I suggest that her honest expression may reflect a danger common to many of us:

> *"I've always been tempted to hand over responsibility for my life to someone else, maybe because it's a lot easier than growing up."*
>
> (Duncan, 2006: 292)

I have encountered those who clamor for a "word" to direct them. There is wisdom in discussing a matter with others, but we must ultimately take the responsibility for our own walk with God.

I would really like to take a moment to clarify what I am seeking to communicate at this point. The issue is not whether a certain person with (or without) a leadership title is a "good" person or not, nor is it about whether they typically offer sound advice or not. It is about us, not them. Do we seek their advice either as the first port of call (rather than seeking God), or worse still, as the only source of direction?

Elkins suggests that this practice of seeking guidance from leadership can even open us up and make us more susceptible to cult leaders:

> *"Christians should put their faith in the Bible, not in men. But doesn't the Christian Church go against its own advice? Don't Christians elevate certain people to a celebrity status, and then place their trust in them? In fact, Christianity is loaded with so many experts and great teachers and Christian leaders that to some unsuspecting souls the Rev. Moon is just another star in the galaxy."*
>
> Elkins (1980: 141)

Novelist Francine Rivers succinctly clarifies that we are to follow Jesus, not the leading of men:

> *"The Debt is a wonderful story that reminds us not to follow in the footsteps of men, but in the footsteps of Jesus."*
>
> (Francine Rivers in Hunt, 2004: 'Advance Praise' section at start of book)

In a similar way, Robin Lee Hatcher states we are to follow Jesus, not church traditions:

> *"[Hunt's book] … will challenge you in many ways, and it just might shake you loose from your comfortable church pew and send you out to follow in the footsteps of Jesus."*
>
> (Robin Lee Hatcher in Hunt, 2004: 'Advance Praise' section at start of book)

It really is quite simple. *Nothing* should be a substitute for our personal relationship with Jesus, our responsibility to seek His guidance, and our willingness to follow in obedience.

For some American missions, the fieldwork was initially controlled from the sending country. Later, the work was controlled by the missionaries themselves, but as local representatives of the sending country. In contrast, as noted by R. Pierce Beaver in *The History of Mission Strategy*, some German missions depended on the work of the Holy Spirit in the lives of the local people:

> "... the missionaries were to regard themselves as assistants to the Holy Spirit. They were to be primarily messengers, evangelists, preachers, who were not to stress heavy theological doctrines but rather tell the simple gospel story of God's loving act of reconciliation of men to himself in Christ our Savior, who lived and died for all men. In God's providence the time would come when the Holy Spirit would bring converts ..."
>
> (Beaver, 1970: 198)

Trusting the Holy Spirit has been the key to much blessing. The challenge to you and me is to abandon the perceived safety net of church traditions, leadership and "oversight", and to wholly trust God to lead us. Of course, a lot of input comes to us from many sources, whether we read it (even in the Bible), or listening to strangers, or to the word of those we know. God may or may not be using these. They may be trying to control us—or they may not. The challenge is for us to measure that input against the inner witness of the Spirit who knows us and our needs, and is faithful to us in our particular journey.

> "Spontaneous expansion involves a full trust in the Holy Spirit and a recognition that the ecclesiastical traditions of the older Churches are not necessarily useful ..."
>
> (McGavran, 1981: 290)

We should not only trust the Holy Spirit to direct our own lives, but we should also trust that He is able to direct the lives of others. Girard developed a principle to trust the Holy Spirit to bring about change rather than having the church leaders enforce their own standards:

> "When we try to legislate and coerce people to accept certain outward standards of behavior which we think will make them 'more spiritual,' we are robbing them of some very precious experiences with the living Lord Himself. We are putting them into man-made 'boxes,' hemming them in spiritually, and stealing from them the beautiful experience of freedom to be personally led and taught by the Holy Spirit and the Word.
>
> When we get another believer to adjust his life to fit our moldy little molds, it's great for our own egos — but does nearly irreparable damage to that Christian's personal relationship to 'the law of the Spirit of life in Christ Jesus' (Romans 8:2). By imposing our own conscience on him, we kill in him some of the vitality and life of the Spirit (2 Corinthians 3:6). And the exciting person-to-Person aspect of his relationship with Christ is depersonalized. The abundant Christian life is reduced to the drudgery of a set of lifeless rules!"
>
> (Girard, 1972: 24-25)

We shouldn't need an organization to manage our assets

Little by little, we can see how wary we ought to be of the hierarchical structures embodied in local churches. We *must* break free from controlling church leaders. But many of us expect that, as a new ministry grows, surely we will need *some* management structure? We have argued previously that we don't need a hierarchy of authority to "control" the ministry, but it is often assumed that we will still need some organization to manage the assets which we may perhaps acquire as a part of ministry growth.

Firstly, we address the theory that local churches need buildings. John Taylor, in *Enough is Enough*, exposes some of the underlying, questionable aspects of the fancy buildings we create, supposedly "to the glory of God":

> "The cathedral symbol which has dominated our thinking and imagination for so long, and has dictated the forms and concepts of our building and decoration from actual cathedrals to country parish churches, is dead and had better be buried ... The cathedral typified wealth and power and esteem, if not downright human pride ... It was the fortress of faith, the stronghold of religion, the rhetorical assertion of the temporal triumph of Christendom."

(Bishop Dwyer of Reno, in Taylor, 1975: 75)

Frost and Hirsch provide an historical perspective, showing how the early church actually thrived without buildings, and also concluding that the focus on buildings has been detrimental to Christendom:

> "Christianity was at its most effective and most true to its nature as the people of God when it did not own any buildings. It was Christendom that gave us beautiful buildings and cathedrals and steeples and pews; all these have shaped us and imprisoned us and kept us from discovering real community for so long that it must be called a tragedy."

(Frost & Hirsch, 2003: 152)

Talking about one particular church building, they note:

> "The vast majority of the building was just row upon row of seating facing a large stage at the front featuring excellent lighting and sound equipment. So what indeed was the nonverbal message of that building? Our interpretation: the vast majority of the people were passive consumers. The few active people were the ones on the stage presented in a highly professional manner. They were the producers. The church looked like it was designed for the presentation of a show of some sort. The building exuded wealth, success, and professionalism. All the needs of the consumer were catered to. But what did that building (or even any traditional church building) say to the average not-yet-Christian about the gospel?"

(Frost & Hirsch, 2003: 152)

I don't know about you, but I have seen plenty of church buildings that fit that description!

Most religions of the world erect majestic buildings to impress—be it Islam with its mosques, Hinduism with temples, or Christianity with cathedrals and church buildings of every shape and size. Contrast this with Jesus, the one upon whom all the principles of Christianity are founded. He didn't have a place He could call His own, even to lay down and sleep. All He left behind in the way of tangible assets at His death was the clothes He had been wearing.

Although Jesus initially occasionally attended the synagogue, speaking to the assembled Jews there, he went on to speak and minister in the homes of friends (and sometimes strangers), or on convenient hills and boats on lakes. And it is to be noted that He did not acquire equipment for His ministry. No mobile tent ministries for him; He just used whatever was at hand.

Some may feel that a significant ministry must acquire assets to be able to perform its job. Alcoholics Anonymous (A.A.) likewise considered the potential of building research facilities and hospitals specializing in the needs of alcoholics. They chose against this course of action. Instead, individual members, as they felt called, supported others who were operating in this field. But the actual ministry of A.A. was run on a minimum of cash and assets—not completely without money, but a minimum. Extracts from other quotations emphasize their philosophy:

> *"The conservatives said, 'Why tempt ourselves with money? We don't need it. We can meet in homes and no group will have to have a treasury. Why do we need books and offices and world services? …' The radicals thought otherwise: 'Not only do we need essential services, we need plenty more. We need hospitals, paid therapists, traveling lecturers, rehabilitation centers, and heaven knows what else. It is going to take millions. …'*
>
> *After a while we awoke to the pleasant fact that A.A. as such was not going to require much money after all. … Not only would we have the least possible service organization; we would use the least possible money. For us this does not mean no money at all. But it does mean the least possible money to do the job well. It is in this sense that A.A. has declared for the principle of corporate poverty. It is a chief safeguard of our future."*

(AAWS, 1957: 110-111)

Foster's book, *Money, Sex & Power*, has at its heart the theme of balance between the extremes of abuse of wealth, sexuality and power versus the denial of any good in any of these facets of life. He has one chapter headed *The Dark Side of Money*, and the next is titled, *The Light Side of Money*. He states, for example,

> *"The issue of money would be much easier to deal with if it were all bad. Our task then would be to denounce it and withdraw from it. That, however, is the one thing we cannot do if we want to be faithful to the biblical witness."*

(Foster, 1985: 437)

In a similar manner A.A. learned to use assets, but to absolutely minimize ownership. We could well conclude that corporate assets are not needed to perform ministry.

We shouldn't need an organization to manage the plan

Some struggle to perceive a ministry without the backing of assets. Even more challenging to some is the concept of a ministry without a grand plan.

Within governments, businesses and military organizations, hierarchical structures are generally accepted as being essential, and for one very simple reason. If an organization has hundreds or thousands of staff, the person at the top simply cannot see the whole picture and relate personally to all the staff. It is just not humanly possible. Mechanisms such as hierarchies and delegation are sometimes needed.

And, where *needed*, these structures actually work, to a point. Yes, they often need checks and balances, which by their very nature are inefficient, but somehow the world seems to bump along. Occasionally, one organization seems to stand out from the pack. They grow fast, and are applauded for their success. Consultancy companies package their formula for success, and market it to others so they, too, can all be the best, even though it's impossible for all to be at the top. But the idea makes money.

Meanwhile, on the sidelines, church leaders watch with interest. Some seem to think that, maybe, if they applied the same marketing techniques, they, too, could be "successful"?

> *"Seminars offering the latest techniques for growing a church often feature 'CEO pastors' or business leaders who have succeeded in producing a large ministry. ... The assumption is: 'If it works, it must be good.' ... the Bible becomes a secondary authority, and what works becomes the primary value."*
>
> (Rinehart, 1998: 35)

Rather than Godly people setting an example for the world to follow, many church leaders are following the example of the world. Gilley's book *This Little Church Went to Market*, criticizes Christendom's application of "successful" marketing techniques to achieve church growth. Rinehart warns that judging the "rightness" of an approach by measuring its financial or numerical growth is flawed.

> *"As long as our ministry is growing rapidly, everything seems fine. ... When production is the overriding value, we often neglect to ask the hard questions [on integrity]. After all, who's going to argue with success?"*
>
> (Rinehart, 1998: 36)

There are even those who make a "ministry" of producing prolific amounts of literature on how to be a successful leader. Some even say that their way is the "irrefutable" way to do it!

So we can model a ministry on principles that are founded on secular organizations, or we can look to God for His way?

Secular models need mechanisms such as hierarchies to accommodate the limitations of human leadership. But if the "Boss" (and please, I do not mean to be irreverent) has all knowledge, is everywhere at once, never sleeps, knows the strengths and weakness of each member of the team, and has a strategy far superior to anything you or I could *ever* conceive, He doesn't need an army of underlings trying to manage the bits the workers think He can't get to. With God at the top, we do not need delegation—each can get his or her instructions direct from the "Boss". And as long as we all do our bit, the entire "organization", with millions of people, can still function, and function *really* well. (Even if some members falter at times, the all-seeing, all-knowing "Boss" knows best how to respond.)

Some might object to what may seem like individuals acting in chaotic freedom, but this is not what is being proposed. An analogy may help. Before an orchestra begins playing, there *is* chaos as individual instruments tune. Quite frankly, I think that this point in the proceedings is outright distasteful.

The individual has done their preparation; now it is time to come together as the conductor steps up. Each individual now turns their attention to, and takes their cue directly from, the conductor. And a beautiful harmony is the outcome. And that is nothing compared to what the Great Conductor can do with those who are looking to *Him* rather than to others.

So now we get to a critical point in our journey. If you believe in a "god" that is incapable of running the whole show, and that has short-comings that cannot be overcome without church leaders making up for his weaknesses, you believe in a different god to the One I choose to follow. Unless the God of the universe and all creation is all He claims to be, the new approach for freedom from local church constraints simply will not work, and we will have to continue to rely on church institutions that look, and are, frighteningly similar to secular organizational structures.

> *"Most Christians do not believe God really controls things. They look at their churches and see they are controlled by men. They see the infighting, the divisions, the jockeying for position, the political machinery, the worldly shepherds – and they conclude God cannot be trusted with important matters."*
>
> (Buckingham, 1980: 94)

As part of a proposed God-led approach, we will have people who, under God's direction, show initiative and inspire others. But their role is to serve, not to "lead" in the ways we have too often seen. Be warned, though. It will take courage and faith to believe that such a radically different approach can work.

> *"It's as though we believe, deep down, that Christ's teaching on [being a servant rather than a 'leader'] is an anachronism, better left to the dusty roads of Galilee with its ox-drawn carts. How could such [servitude] apply to our busy, pressure-filled age? Yet ... [it] is not an impossible ideal in our day. Rather, it should be the foundational cornerstone of our thinking about [serving]. Christ lived, taught, and modeled it for us, and it is our true distinctive as believers.*

We are meant to relate to each other in ways the world would like to emulate."

(Rinehart, 1998: 28)

If we allow God to *be* God, no longer can any of us call the shots. In very practical terms, this means that you and I cannot tell God how He should assign roles, nor for how long, nor instruct Him as to who we want to work with.

So to start with, we had better get used to the idea that each of us has responsibilities that God intends us to fulfil. We do our bit; others do theirs. But no one individual can do everything, and we need each other.

> "Though we are all brothers and sisters before Him, we have unique roles and contributions to make."
>
> (Rinehart, 1998: 89)

> "[There is an assumption] that believers are omnicompetent. The theory is that a committed follower ought to be able to do it all. ... The average person feels this heavy weight of excessive expectation."
>
> (Rinehart, 1998: 117)

> "[A sober judgment of our abilities] implies that each [of us] ... has clear limits set for him or her – limits of capacity and gifting."
>
> (Rinehart, 1998: 119)

> "[In the New Testament] individuals practiced the freedom to specialize in particular arenas of service. And they depended solely upon God to supply the complementary gifts and resultant ministries needed. There was no imperative then, nor is there one now, to be omnicompetent supermen and superwomen."
>
> (Rinehart, 1998: 122-123)

Not only does God have the right to assign us our roles, but may change them as He sees fit on a moment-by-moment basis. Today I might be expected to fulfil one task, and tomorrow I may see someone else called to take "my" place, and I may be called to do something totally different. We do not need to understand God's grand plan; we just act with the knowledge we already have, and to listen for new directions and obey, moment by moment. Individually, we each participate.

An example previously mentioned was Phillip in the New Testament, who left what he was doing and did what he was told to do: teach the Ethiopian. He didn't stop to make sure that there was someone to take over for him, nor did he make sure that he had permission from others to do what God was asking him to do. He simply obeyed the call *God* put on his life at that moment. Challenging, isn't it!

That leads to another realization. As we work in our corner, we may perceive unfilled needs close by. We may even feel indignant that others do not seem to be doing their bit. "Here I am working hard, but look at those 'so-called Christians' over there who aren't pitching in." We might fall into judgmental attitudes, or maybe try to "help" God by prodding others we *think* are well suited into action. But we must leave that to God.

"Even when vacancies scream to be filled, we must resist the tendency to fill them with any willing people who volunteer or by choosing who seem to be the most likely candidates. Getting the job done is not the key issue; that responsibility rests with the Lord. Our corporate faith will increase as we watch God raise up and place His man or woman in that position.

It will also force us to our knees to ask the Lord to provide just the right person, probably someone we never would have chosen on our own."

(Rinehart, 1998: 125)

SECTION 5:

NO MORE "HOLY HUDDLES"

We have looked at reasons why the role of the clergy may be up for question, and why ministry can occur outside of the formal institution of the local church. We now tackle another tradition—the perceived need to come together within the local church for "fellowship".

It is not uncommon to encounter subtle pressures for Christians to belong to a "fellowship" within a local church setting. "Fellowship" can be another name for the local church, as in "Where do you fellowship?", sometimes officially in its name. It can also refer to the act of having camaraderie with those in the local church.

More direct confrontation can also be encountered, sometimes in the form of condemnation against those who are perceived to be "backslidden" Christians. This may include those who are seen as being in active disobedience to Paul's command that we should not avoid meeting together (Hebrews 10:25). For example, I had a relative state that she would pray that I find a church to attend. I believe her intention was good, but I still found it was based on an assumption I needed to attend a church.

One question might be, "Is the local church the only place where Christians can enjoy fellowship?" Hopefully all would agree that the answer is, "No". A more telling question might be, "If we can find 'fellowship' in environments other than just the local church, is local church fellowship even necessary?" Some would argue that precious little real fellowship occurs within the local church anyway, and that many have greater and deeper fellowship at work and in other areas of their lives than as part of local church activities.

CHAPTER 18:
THE MYTHS OF "FELLOWSHIP"

Some believe the local church is synonymous with Christian "fellowship"

Even if local church fellowship leaves a lot to be desired, the foundational question remains: As Christians, are we expected to belong to the "fellowship" of a local church? Many arguments have been identified to suggest that this is so. Lawrence Richards, in the introduction to *Brethren, Hang Loose*, makes an assumption that

> *"... the Divine invitation to live together as the Body of Christ ..."*
>
> (Girard, 1972: 13)

is to be found within the local church. This view that fellowship and Body life are inseparable from the local "church" is commonly held.

It is a very natural human trait to desire fellowship and support. "Bill", a foundational person within Alcoholics Anonymous, notes that

> *"... most individuals [in this context, alcoholics] cannot recover unless there is a group. Realization dawns on each member that he is but a small part of a great whole; that no personal sacrifice is too great for preservation of the Fellowship. He learns that the clamor of desires and ambitions within him must be silenced whenever these could damage the group.*
>
> *It becomes plain that the group must survive or the individual will not."*
>
> (Bill, 1967: 9)

Bill's observation is a pragmatic one, noted within the framework of recovering alcoholics. Watchman Nee goes further within the context of Christendom, claiming that not only does experience teach us that we cannot flourish alone, but that God will sometimes humble us by forcing a realization of interdependency:

> *"It is a matter of experience that we cannot go on indefinitely, nor can we witness effectively, without fellowship. God often brings the most spiritually mature people up against a blank wall in order to teach them this. They reach an impasse, something they cannot deal with alone. Then they discover the absolute necessity of fellowship with others in Christ, and learn the practical values of the corporate life."*
>
> (Nee, 1967: 42)

J. Herbert Kane, in *The Work of Evangelism*, looks at the topic from the perspective of teaching on the Body of Christ, and concludes that we don't have a choice about being a member of Christ's "Body", i.e. the universal Church. But he goes further, and also seamlessly ties being a member of the universal Church with also being a member of a local church:

> *"Following conversion, the convert does not remain in isolation. He becomes a member of the universal church, the Body of Christ, by the baptism of the Holy Spirit. By an act of his own he joins a local congregation and becomes part of its fellowship, work, and witness."*
>
> (Kane, 1980: 566)

Alan Tippett, in a similar manner in his article *The Evangelization of Animists*, merges the necessity of a Christian's membership in the Body of Christ with an equal necessity to be part of a local church. He effectively claims that the Body of Christ is the "theological" dimension of the "church", and the local church is the practical outworking of the same reality:

> *"... the notion of the fellowship is crucial in biblical argument. True, we can speak of evangelism as bringing individual men face to face with Christ, but we cannot leave it there, because the New Testament did not leave it there. Christ is, of course, the Ultimate, and in that sense we need no more than to be with him. But for this present point of time in which he has been born, the convert has to be incorporated into some precise fellowship group, the Church, which is Christ's Body. In the records of the early Church (Acts) and the letters which tell us so much of its inner life, the configuration which holds it all together structurally is the church – be it theologically the Church Universal, or practically the local church. Remove that concept from the New Testament and look for a disembodied collection of isolated people who had met Christ, and you will soon be disillusioned."*
>
> (Tippett, 1975: 637-638)

Glasser brings the argument full circle. The quotations above suggest that new converts to the Christian faith must be incorporated into a local church; Glasser argues that there will not be any effective outreach to make new converts unless there is a local church from which to base the outreach:

> *"God's program for the evangelization of the world involves the local church. Unless local congregations are firmly established in each population center that has been evangelized, there is no satisfactory way of conserving the results of evangelistic efforts.*

> *Without local churches new converts cannot be readily trained, for that training involves working in a group and participating in group worship as well as walking alone with God. Without the varied, extensive outreach of a spiritually-minded church, it is difficult to train young converts to discharge their responsibility under God to participate in gospel outreach. In fact, it is almost impossible to evangelize souls and train converts adequately without the healthy functioning of a local church.*
>
> *Planting these churches, then, is ever the ultimate objective of all missionary work. Missionary labor, no matter how brilliant, will have little permanence unless this is accomplished. In the final analysis, it is the local congregations, rather than individual believers, that bring lasting changes to the spiritual life of a region."*
>
> (Glasser, 1976: 103)

Many recognize that "fellowship" may occur within parachurch situations such as a group of students joining together in a summer outreach program. Frost and Hirsch note this tendency:

> *"Many people find in a student body or in being part of a short-term mission team the very thing that ought to characterize being church: mission, passion, equipping, accountability, love and respect. Sadly, they often report that their home churches are so lacking in these characteristics they'd rather stay part of such temporary communities than settle for what the institutional church has to offer."*
>
> (Frost & Hirsch, 2003: 77)

However, Frost and Hirsch also argue that this should not be so, rejecting the idea of any form of parachurch being an alternative to local church-based-fellowship:

> *"Neither do we think that a group of Christians who gather for a specific missional purpose is necessarily a church. Although it could be said that student bodies in theological seminaries, kids at Christian youth summer camps, and people on short-term mission trips create temporary forms of church, we believe it is the very impermanence of those communities that precludes us from identifying them as churches."*
>
> (Frost & Hirsch, 2003: 76-77)

This particular line of argument focuses on the perceived short-term nature of parachurch initiatives. Their argument is flawed on many fronts. Firstly, some parachurch organizations have existed for decades or even centuries. Without entering into debates on their merits, or how closely they fit to anyone's definition of a "parachurch" organization, groups like the Navigators, Campus Crusades for Christ, and Wycliffe Bible Translators spring to mind as examples of parachurch organizations that have exhibited longevity. Secondly, there are many examples of local churches that do not exhibit much in the way of stability!

And finally, one could well say, "If God calls me into fellowship with some other Christians for a season, whether it is for a specific purpose or just for sharing our journey, why should any man condemn that?" Frost and Hirsch imply that some such interactions between Christians are nothing more than a "... *bunch of Christians* [who] ... *bumped into each other*". This seems to negate the possibility that God may have ordained the encounter:

> *"... the six of us sitting around that table that night were not a church. We had made no mutual commitments, shared no long-term calling, were completely unaccountable to one another, and our purpose for gathering was mainly social. Of course, as Christians, our conversation centered on Christian things, and by the end of the evening we were encouraged in our faith and individual callings. We were doing some of the things a church might do, but our involvement was not permanent.*
>
> *We don't think a church is just any old bunch of Christians who have bumped into each other."*
>
> (Frost & Hirsch, 2003: 76)

The interaction between Philip and the eunuch was certainly lacking permanence, yet I think it reasonable to assume that all would agree that God ordained it! But was it an example of essential "fellowship"?

Challenging the view

We have already looked at the dangers of confusing the local church with the Body of Christ. We have also previously noted that Body of Christ is not the sum of all local churches—some in local churches are not Christians, and some Christians are not linked to any local church. This must be recognized when considering what it means to have "fellowship".

Taking Glasser's position as an example, there are real dangers, such as confusing "bringing a person to Christ" with "bringing a person to church".

In the past, I was taught my role in sharing the good news was to bring people to the local church and then the professionals would do the rest. But that logic is flawed. We've visited the concept of paid professionals to do "ministry" and found it wanting. We want to introduce people to Christ Himself, not some organization that purports to represent Him. Even phrases such as the "unchurched", by which people typically really mean the "unsaved", are dangerous. The implication is that if I do not go to church (i.e. I am "unchurched") then I am not "saved".

We need to separate the concept of being part of the Body of Christ (i.e. the universal Church) from identification with a local church.

McDowell, like many others mentioned above, uses Hebrews 10:25 as the basis for teaching that we must join a local church. He implies that, if we are not part of a local church, we cannot be in fellowship with other Christians, going so far as to order us to join a local church, immediately:

> *"God's Word admonishes us not to forsake 'the assembling of ourselves together …' (Hebrews 10:25 NKJV). Several logs burn brightly together; but put one aside on the cold hearth and the fire goes out. So it is with your relationship to other Christians. If you do not belong to a church, do not wait to be invited. Take the initiative; call the pastor of a nearby church where Christ is honored and His Word is preached. Start this week, and make plans to attend regularly."*
>
> (McDowell, 1999: 760)

Brown also follows this common line of reasoning, stating,

> *"… every believer should be part of a regular gathering of believers (see, for example, Hebrews 10:25) …"*
>
> (Brown, 2002: 220)

and (as quoted earlier) that

> *"… there is no biblical justification for independent, unattached Christians."*
>
> (Brown, 2002: 220)

In contrast, (as also quoted earlier) the same author proclaims our indebtedness to Roger Williams, a

> *"… religious loner [who] …died an independent evangelical Christian without a denomination."*
>
> (Brown, 2002: 151)

There seem to be some differences of opinion, even within an author's statements. Given that so many who hold the position that we *must* join a local church "fellowship" base their view on their interpretation of this one verse (Hebrew 10:25), we need to take a look at this cornerstone of their argument.

Oliver and Thwaites express views that are in stark contrast to those of McDowell, Brown (and a few others). They suggest that Hebrews 10:25 is misused when applied to local church. They argue that we do not "go to church" at a local gathering, but rather we "are" the Church (universal), all the time, and anywhere. (This quotation is a partial replication of an earlier extract from Oliver and Thwaites):

> *"We have, as mentioned, made much of the word ekklesia; taking it to mean that the church gathered in a meeting is the central expression of church. This to my mind is not supported by Scripture. There was a church that gathered in the house of Apphia and Archippus (Philem. 1:2). The other eight references to the church being 'in' somewhere all speak of cities, none speak of buildings. The word used for 'assembling together', from the oft quoted 'not forsaking our own assembling together, as is the habit of some' (Heb.10:25 NASV), is not ekklesia, it's a word that simply means coming together. When the word church is used in Scripture, in key books like those of Ephesians or Romans, it is not used to refer to the gathering, rather it speaks of the body of Christ in all of life. An exception to this, one might think, is 1 Timothy 3:15,*

where the gathering of the church (as what Paul calls the household of God) is declared to be the church of the living God. However, quite simply here, as was the case with the gathering in the house of Apphia and Archippus, the church was first the church and then it gathered. The gathering did not make it the church. Words like 'household' and 'coming together' (assembly) are used to describe his body, the church, when it gathers. Never is the word ekklesia used of the gathering itself. This is not an exhaustive study, but it serves, I would hope, to help us to not mistake the word 'church' in Scripture for the act of meeting. They are two distinct words with different meanings."

(Oliver & Thwaites, 2001: 169-170)

Jacobsen and Coleman's novel tackles the critics of those who seek fellowship independent of church structures, explaining that Christians will still find ways to fellowship:

" 'But won't people who just 'follow Jesus' live independently from the body?' Marvin asked.

[John] 'Do you think that's possible?'

[Marvin] 'You don't?'

[John] 'That's the fear I hear all the time, but I don't see it. People who are growing in their relationship with Father will hunger for real connections with his family. …' "

(Jacobsen & Coleman, 2006: 112)

Some would argue that freedom from the confines of a local church opens the individual up to error. Again Jacobsen and Coleman dispel this myth:

"Shouldn't we be committed to a local fellowship?

That has been said so often today that most of us assume it is in the Bible somewhere. I haven't found it yet. Many of us have been led to believe that we can't possibly survive without the 'covering of the body' and will either fall into error or backslide into sin. But doesn't that happen inside our local congregations as well?

I know many people who live outside those structures and find not only an ever-deepening relationship with God, but also connections with other believers that run far deeper than they found in the institution. …

Scripture does encourage us to be devoted to one another, not committed to an institution."

(Jacobsen & Coleman, 2006: 171-172)

"But don't our institutions keep us from error?

I'm sorry to burst your bubble here, but every major heresy that has been inflicted on God's people for the last two thousand years has come from organized groups with 'leaders' who thought they knew God's mind better than anyone around them. Conversely, virtually every move of God among people hungering for him was rejected

> *by the 'church' of that day. The people were excluded, excommunicated, or executed for following God."*
>
> (Jacobsen & Coleman, 2006: 172)

The final inconsistency I wish to highlight relates to the double standard used by church leaders in their own practice of "fellowship". They preach that the laity must find their fellowship within the local church, through attendance, membership, and so on. But they themselves find "fellowship" outside of the local church, rather than relating to its members:

> *"The truth is that ... many ministers ... find it hard to locate their primary expression of church in their own congregation. The reason for this is that, as a leader, they have a different relationship to the congregation than everybody in it has. Hence, local church leaders seek out peers to play golf and pray with ... They attend conferences where other colleagues are often to be found and they fellowship there."*
>
> (Oliver & Thwaites, 2001: 181)

While not suggesting in any way that we should all become hermits, living in total isolation, I suggest we need to challenge the assumption some seem to make that all Christians need to be in regular contact with fellow Christians via "churchlike" activities if we are to be fruitful, or maybe even if our faith is to survive.

Some look to church fellowship (or marriage, etc.) as a solution to their loneliness. Nouwen suggests loneliness is not an evil to be avoided:

> *"... I would like to voice loudly and clearly what might seem unpopular and maybe even disturbing: The Christian way of life does not take away our loneliness; it protects and cherishes it as a precious gift. ...*
>
> *... when we want to give up our loneliness ... too soon, we easily relate to our human world with devastating expectations. We ignore what we already know ... that no love or friendship, no intimate embrace or tender kiss, no community, commune or collective, no man or woman, will ever be able to satisfy our desire to be released from our lonely condition."*
>
> (Nouwen, 1972: 84)

Nouwen encourages us to

> *"... face directly our own condition in all its beauty as well as misery."*
>
> (Nouwen, 1972: 91)

He states that this is

> *"... a very painful and lonely process ..."*
>
> (Nouwen, 1972: 91)

but encourages us that

> *"This experience tells us that we can only love because we are born out of love, that we can only give because our life is a gift, and that we can only make others free because*

we are set free by Him whose heart is greater than ours. When we have found the anchor places for our lives in our own center, we can be free to let others enter into the space created for them and allow them to dance their own dance, sing their own song and speak their own language without fear."

(Nouwen, 1972: 91-92)

It seems that, having clarified the need for each of us to face our own needs so that we minister to others because of *their* needs, not our own, Nouwen then concludes that the resultant sharing of honest, weak people brings fellowship, stating that

"... a shared pain is no longer paralyzing but mobilizing ...

[Through a shared search for life] ... this common search, [and the resultant] hospitality becomes community."

(Nouwen, 1972: 93)

Perhaps too often our security has been in the church system rather than in God himself. If this is so, then breaking free from this false security will be painful, but beneficial.

"God is setting you free from the things in which you used to find security in the past. They were in the way of God being the Father to you that he knew you wanted – and they were false hopes anyway. Losing them is always painful ..."

(Jacobsen & Coleman, 2006: 71)

Deep, meaningful "fellowship" with others can be a reality, whether they are Christians or not, and independent of where we meet. We can also learn to embrace times of loneliness, where we can perhaps learn more intensely of the fellowship we can have with God, our Father.

The parable of the "minister" who won't be programmed

Jacobsen and Coleman's novel has two main characters. There is John, whose life is a simple moment-by-moment walk as God leads—no plans, no schedules, just a delightful spontaneity as he responds to the emerging directions of the Spirit.

The other player is Jake who has been a faithful pastor, but is disillusioned. The following snippets provide insight into the underlying message.

What appears to Jake as a "chance" encounter has been of great value, and he wants to organize another meeting:

"[Jake asks John,] 'Do you live around here?'

'No. Actually this is the first time I have been to [your town].'

'Really? What brings you here?'

'Maybe your prayers,' he said, laughing. 'I'm not really sure.'

'Listen, I've got to go in a few minutes. Could we meet again sometime?'

'I don't know. I really don't have the freedom to commit to an appointment. If we need to get together again, I'm sure we will. This happened without a schedule.'"

(Jacobsen & Coleman, 2006: 16-17)

John's life is one of freedom and fruitfulness as he trusts God to orchestrate his life. He encourages Jake to discover the same freedom:

" 'Jake, you've learned to measure stability by your circumstances and by your ability to see how things will work out months in advance.'

'... Anything we do to try and guarantee stability on our own terms will actually rob us of the freedom to simply follow him today. We'll resort to our own wisdom instead of following his. The greatest freedom God can give you is to trust his ability to take care of you each day.'"

(Jacobsen & Coleman, 2006: 94)

Some of us have experienced institutionalized "fellowship", where the organization tries hard to develop an environment in which individuals can relate, under leadership control. This is contrasted with genuine friendships that arise organically.

In Jacobsen and Coleman's novel, a few people have discovered the pleasures of unstructured relationships, and one person comments about a distant friend who longs to enjoy a similar experience. He states:

"I have a friend in Georgia who just can't find anyone who wants this kind of life together ..."

(Jacobsen & Coleman, 2006: 113)

There is an irony. On the one hand, the caring friend has discovered the delights of friendships that grow *organically* without the need for organizational structures. Yet this same friend wonders if he can *structure* something so his friend can make the same discovery! John very quickly kills off such an idea:

"Father knows that [your friend desires deep friendships], too! Certainly there are others near him with a similar hunger, but if Father hasn't made those connections yet, your friend can rest in that. It's much easier for us to find it when we live contentedly in God's provision rather than being anxious for what we don't see. Encourage him to enjoy what Father is doing each day while keeping his eyes open for others. You never know how or when God will make connections."

(Jacobsen & Coleman, 2006: 113)

John shares a very simple foundation for discovery of true fellowship:

"What I hope you'll do is simply let God connect you with those brothers and sisters he wants you to walk with for now. Think less about 'starting' something than just learning to share your life in God with others on a similar journey."

(Jacobsen & Coleman, 2006: 85-86)

Out of our unstructured friendships, some "ministry" may arise. But if it does, it will not be formal with support provided by one with official titles and roles. Rather, it will be spontaneous, involving nothing more than friends helping others, as God leads. And it will be transitory. Today I help you, tomorrow someone helps me.

> "... there will be [those] God will give you [as fellow travelers and friends] as you simply follow him ... Some will help you for a time on your journey and others you will help on theirs, but mostly you will find yourself mutually sharing his life together."
>
> (Jacobsen & Coleman, 2006: 154)

One of the group, Bryce, is struggling with these informal dynamics, and looks for better answers from John.

> " 'Just ask [Jesus] whom he wants you to be walking with right now,' John offered. 'Don't try to sort out what you want or what you think is best. Follow the growing conviction he settles in your heart over time.' ....
>
> 'So it really is a day-to-day walk, letting Jesus sort out his way in us?' Bryce said.
>
> 'Yes, it is, Bryce, and when you learn to live that way you'll never want to go back. Jesus is really good at showing you how to do it, especially when your desire to please him is not competing with doing what you think is best or easiest.' "
>
> (Jacobsen & Coleman, 2006: 152)

Still there are some people who want to organize things. They want to know how such unstructured friendships and ministry will be structured(!), how it will work, what it will look like. John's patient answer follows:

> "It can look like a hundred different things because Father is so creative. Try to copy any of them and you'll find it turns lifeless and empty after the initial excitement of starting something new fades away. The church thrives where people are focused on Jesus, not where they are focused on church.
>
> This is a great time to learn to enjoy him together. Just keep living, loving, and listening, and he will lead you to whatever expression of church life best fits his plans. Don't be concerned if it's nothing you can point to and say, 'That is the church.' You are the church. Don't be afraid to live in that reality."
>
> (Jacobsen & Coleman, 2006: 140)

You might think the answer above would be sufficient for those steeped in local church life and its traditions to break free from traditional church structures. Do we need to hear the message again and again, maybe in different ways, before we embrace freedom? My analysis of the authors' story suggests this may be true.

> " 'You mean there isn't some way that we can gather as God's people that fulfills the hope of the New Testament church?'
>
> 'Oh, there's a gathering that does that,' John said with a certainty that took me by surprise.

'Really? I'd like to hear about it,' I said.

Just then another flock of squawking geese flew over the trees and drew all our eyes skyward and held our gaze as the ever-shifting V headed southward.

'They get it!' *John said with a smile as we all looked back down.*

'Get what?'

'There's a gathering going on. They are all headed south to warmer weather. It's not so important what group they're with at the moment, but that they're headed in the right direction.'

'So we should all fly south?' *Bryce asked, clueless as to what John was talking about.*

'You think of gatherings as meetings to go to and trying to craft the perfect format that will guarantee results that no meeting can guarantee. But you don't see yet that Jesus is always gathering his flock to himself. People from all over the world are finding their hunger for him eclipsing their hunger for anything else and that every substitute they try only adds to their restlessness. As they keep their eyes on him, not only do they grow closer to him with each passing day, but they find themselves alongside others who are headed that way, too. Geese fly together like that not because they are obligated to do so, but because it lightens their load and lifts them closer to their goal.'

John turned his head skyward again and we joined him, now seeing at least four different flocks all heading south. 'And all of those flocks will end up in the same place, together. That's all Jesus ever wanted – one flock drawn to him alone, and each helping lighten the load of others they find going the same direction as they are.

'That's the gathering. It's not when you meet, where you meet, or how you meet in meetings, but that you are gathering your heart to him. If that's happening, you usually won't find yourself going it alone very long. You'll find others heading the same direction, and by traveling together you'll be able to help one another along the way. That's why you only hurt yourself when you look for people who want to meet a certain way or think like you do about everything. Every person who crosses your path, believer or unbeliever, in an institution like this or outside of it, is a potential partner in this journey. By loving them to the degree that they allow, you'll participate in his great gathering.

'But the goal remains the same. It's him! It's always him – not a style of meeting or a preplanned program, not a safe salary, or a predictable future.' "

(Jacobsen & Coleman, 2006: 157-158)

That's just a fictional story, but does it suggest that even after the picture becomes clear, we may resist? My interpretation of this story seems to warn that long-standing traditions can be hard to break.

" 'I still don't know what to do,' *Bryce said, cracking a smile of feigned frustration.*

'Yes, you do,' *John said, smirking back.*

'I know.' Bryce shook his head. *'Follow him, every day! As scary as that sounds, there's a real freedom in it, isn't there?'* "

(Jacobsen & Coleman, 2006: 158)

The temptation might always be to go back to what we see as organized and predictable, but that's not the way to freedom. There may be a role for a bit of organization, and we will investigate the topic in more depth in a later chapter. It's enough at this point to say that, generally, less organization is better than more, and even the little you may have must be open to change.

SECTION 6:

EXPECT OPPOSITION

"During times of universal deceit, telling the truth becomes a revolutionary act."

George Orwell

Ackoff criticizes secular systems for their resistance to change, and more for their reluctance to even consider change:

"Most systems, like recalcitrant children, do not appreciate being beaten, even when the beating is good for them. This is especially true of bureaucracies. They find choice unsettling; they prefer a static equilibrium produced by complete conformity to rule in an unchanging environment: continuous repetition of the expected. Whatever else creativity implies, it implies production of the unexpected. It is the unexpected that produces the quantum leaps in development and quality of life."

(Ackoff, 1991: 42)

Ackoff takes the education system as an example with which he has familiarity:

"The educational system has demonstrated an unlimited ability to resist responding to any of its problems. When it does respond, it does so like a coiled spring, modifying itself as little as necessary to accommodate the pressure being applied to it, and returning to its original state as soon as the pressure is removed."

(Ackoff, 1991: 59)

Not only are established systems resistant to change; he argues that unfortunately they are likely to win in a tug-of-war against those who try to bring about change:

"... established social systems have the advantage; they are able to exert continuing energy in the service of their stable state, whereas those attacking can seldom sustain their attack."

(Quotation from Schon, in Ackoff, 1991: 59)

He then identifies what I believe to be a key dimension of the struggle for change—the established leaders are not about to weaken their position by considering that the rank and file might have a point!

"Suppliers of a service such as education who are not subject to control by those served (students and their parents or guardians) often assume they are infallible. This assumption deprives them of the ability to think creatively about their services or to learn from those who do so. Most educators believe that laymen cannot contribute to improvement of institutionalized education. This is nonsense."

(Ackoff, 1991: 63)

If you start to challenge the role of clergy, the necessity for ministry, and fellowship based in the local church, you can expect opposition. An understanding of how this has often worked in the past may help prepare you for what you may well face in the future.

CHAPTER 19 :
ANALYSIS OF PERSECUTION, RESISTANCE

Introduction

It seems to me that what Ackoff says about secular institutions can also be observed in many church institutions:

> *"... ours is not necessarily a popular message. We've become disturbingly aware through personal experience and observation that those who advocate such a thoroughgoing recalibration of the church will not always be met with open arms by the prevailing church leadership. And yet we feel compelled to lovingly challenge the church to dismantle many of the arcane institutional structures it is now beholden to and to bravely face the future with imagination and courage."*
>
> (Frost & Hirsch, 2003: ix)

In the quotation above, Frost and Hirsch appear to suggest that we should consider dismantling "*the arcane institutional structures*" so prevalent in local churches. One disturbing question might be, "How much might be left by the time we get rid of every trace of the '*arcane structures*' in local churches?" I think that the answer is probably, "Not much"—which is one reason why those who have their sense of self-worth so heavily tied to local church structures will resist change.

> *"It is worth noting here that part of the revolution of missional church, like all revolutions, will have to bring down the dominant ideological system that imposes the old system. We simply have to break the power of clericalism if we are going to see new movements start and flourish. Why? Because clericalism (the dominance of the ordained clergy class) serves to enshrine the old system and has too much to lose in the new – it will resist the change that disturbs the system that legitimizes it. Again we*

refer the reader to a study of movements in general. The dominant official leadership has always persecuted new movements. Witness the New Testament examples in Jesus and Paul. Witness the great missional movements and leaders in the church, the early monastics, Francis, Luther, Wesley, Booth, Martin Luther King Jr., the Pentecostals, etc. But as Jesus revolutionaries we do well to heed Jesus' old warning to his original disciples in not too different a situation than ours: 'Be wise as serpents and innocent as doves.'"

(Frost & Hirsch, 2003: 172)

This is the way it has been throughout history. The prophets of the Old Testament were often opposed, and sometimes even killed, by the people of their days. Jesus also encountered opposition by the church leaders of His day.

"Jesus Himself experienced ... resistance.

... the chief priests and the elders of the people came to him. 'By what authority are you doing these things?' they asked. ...

Isn't this remarkable? The blind and lame had been healed the day before, apparently right before these leaders' eyes ... Yet the leaders had only one question: By what authority are You doing these things? Who gave You the right?

'We are the religious leaders here, and You are challenging our system and upsetting our apple cart. You drive out the moneychangers, attack our whole method of operation, work all kinds of miracles and now set up shop in our Temple, teaching Your own doctrines. What right do You have to do this? Who gave You permission? Which group is sanctioning Your activities? What makes You think You have divine authority backing You?'"

(Brown, 2002: 143-144)

Just as Jesus was opposed by religious leaders, so were His disciples. For example, Peter had been used in God's healing of a lame man:

"[The leaders] could not deny the miracle, but because it did not originate under their auspices, did not have their approval and, worst of all, conflicted with their authority, they tried to shut it down. This is the religious way. It stands against spiritual progress and, when it resists the Word of God, must itself be resisted."

(Brown, 2002: 145)

We run the clock forward from Jesus' experiences to the 1500's AD. Martin Luther was troubled by the evils he saw within the church, and took action to right the wrongs:

"Luther began his work of reformation in an attack on what was called an Indulgence ..."

(Lindsay, 1996: 49)

In spite of clearly demonstrating opposition to certain practices within the institutional church, Luther also saw himself as

"... a devout and obedient son of that Church."

(Lindsay, 1996: 56-57).

He possibly took this position because he had no problem with its routines, hierarchy and structures. He felt such allegiance to church traditions that he

"... had a profound contempt for men who believe that they are born to set the world right."

(Lindsay, 1996: 57)

Yet in spite of his loyalty to church traditions, he also publicly criticized the institutional church (but it did not come easily):

"At length, after much hesitation and deep distress of mind, he felt compelled to interfere, and, as was usual when his mind was made up, he went unflinchingly to the root of the matter in the most direct and dauntless fashion."

(Lindsay, 1996: 57).

Lindsay lists a number of courageous criticisms Luther made of the institutional church (some of which have been quoted earlier):

"He exposes the gross exactions connected with the bestowal of the pallium on German prelates; the trafficking in beneficies, in all manner of exemptions and permissions to evade ecclesiastical laws and restrictions, the most shameless instances being those connected with marriage; and describes the Curial Court as a place 'where vows are annulled; where a monk gets leave to quit his Order; where priests can enter married life for money; where bastards can become legitimate; and dishonor and shame may arrive at high honours; all evil repute and disgrace is knighted and ennobled; where a marriage is suffered that is in a forbidden degree, or has some other defect ...there is a buying and a selling, a changing, blustering and bargaining, cheating and lying, robbing and stealing, debauchery and villainy, and all kinds of contempt of God that Antichrist could not reign worse.'"

(Lindsay, 1996: 88)

Yet after this scathing attack, Luther

"... proceeds to give some suggestions for amending matters – twenty-seven in number."

(Lindsay, 1996: 88)

It appears that Luther wanted to bring reformation to the Catholic Church, not to replace it. While openly attacking the Pope's position as supreme ruler, he also spoke kindly of the struggles of the local parish priests:

"In one of his suggestions ... he deals with the terribly sad condition of the German country parish priests, and he does this in a tender and sympathetic way."

(Lindsay, 1996: 89)

Lindsay says that Luther's goal was to have a church

> *"... altered in externals as little as possible, enough only to permit free scope to evangelical preaching and teaching."*
>
> Lindsay (1996: 129)

To adapt an analogy from Jesus, Luther wanted to put a new patch on the old cloth, or to put new wine in an old wineskin. And even though he was trying to turn the Catholic Church into a "better" church rather than totally rip it up, he was still violently opposed by the church leaders.

The liberators turn into captors

It is a sad observation that the hard-won freedom of the Reformation created church structures that, like the very structures they replaced, became resistant to change.

> *"... once power was wrested from the Roman Church, new structures and new hierarchies began to grow in their place. Within a relatively short period of time, reformation groups became state churches in their own right. Then they were as quick to defend their power and structures as was the Roman Church before them. Lutherans and Calvinists dealt with the Anabaptist movement by arresting its leaders and sometimes murdering them.*
>
> *For all the good that came out of the Reformation, it still serves to illustrate our stubborn tendency to use human means of power to build a manageable, controlled system. To have repudiated the papal system was remarkable. But the Reformation did, indeed, fall short. It failed, in many instances, to return to the Scriptures and to the Spirit that empowered its movement toward Christian liberty. How tragic!"*
>
> (Rinehart, 1998: 81-82)

As quoted earlier, not only were the new church institutions resistant to change, but like the Catholic Church of old, they were more than willing to punish those who did not "conform" to their model.

> *"In 1660 old acts against Nonconformists were revived. Meeting houses were closed; all persons were required under severe penalties to attend their parish church; it became illegal to conduct worship services except in accordance with [state-sanctioned] ritual."*
>
> (Brown, 2002: 155)

It is one thing to try to discredit opponents by labeling them as "heretics", and this was certainly done.

> *"God always reserved a seed for himself; a few that worshipped in spirit and in truth. I have often doubted, whether these were not the very persons whom the rich and honourable Christians, who will always have number as well as power on their side, did not stigmatize, from time to time, with the title of heretics."*
>
> (Brown, 2002: 182)

Yet it is incredible, but a sad fact of history, that those who defended their own particular way of doing things were willing to murder their fellow-Christians who saw things differently.

> "John Wycliffe was hunted like a criminal, and William Tyndale was killed for the crime of translating the Bible into English. And it was 'Christian' leaders who persecuted them."
>
> (Brown, 2002: 50-51)

The Old Testament prophets were opposed in their day. Jesus was opposed by the religious hierarchy of His day, as subsequently were His disciples. The Reformists were opposed by the Catholic Church. Then the Reformists opposed the new breed. If you or I are willing to challenge the current church power brokers, we must not be surprised if we, too, meet with opposition. In fact, we should be surprised if we are *not* strongly opposed!

It beggars belief that so-called Christian churches would oppose those who take the good news of Jesus to others. Yet this is an observed occurrence across history.

> "… <u>most</u> People Movements have actually been resisted by the leaders of the Church and mission where they started." [Emphasis mine]
>
> (McGavran, 1981: 288)

My reading of McGavran's material led me to question if some opposition comes from Christians who somehow see themselves as belonging to a superior class, and not wanting God's good news or freedom to reach people they consider beneath them. Extracts from previous quotations are repeated below to possibly assist in evaluation as to whether or not some might hold such a position:

> "Judson … was concerned with <u>more important</u> matters than a Christian movement among a backward tribe." [Emphasis mine]
>
> (McGavran, 1981: 285)

> "[The Churas of Pakistan] had been largely overlooked by the missionaries preaching Christ to the respectable members … The missionaries were at first dubious about admitting to the Christian fellowship these lowest of the low."
>
> (McGavran, 1981: 285-286)

In his article, *The New Macedonia: A Revolutionary New Era in Mission Begins*, Winter noted that John Wesley's outreach to miners resulted in the formation of local churches for the miners. Even though this strategy was extremely fruitful,

> "The results rocked … the existing churches … Not very many people favored Wesley's contact with the miners. Fewer still agreed that miners should have separate churches!"
>
> (Winter, 1974: 303)

If we tinker around the edges of institutionalized Christendom, we will get some resistance. But if we have a head-on frontal attack on the precious traditions of churches, we can expect a major battle. Frost and Hirsch warn:

> "... innovation, and therefore real progress, can so easily be marginalized and locked down in the Christendom paradigm of church. It is rare that an established institution can tolerate a serious questioning of its legitimacy implicit in a new, alternative model. It was Machiavelli who noted that innovators are always persecuted and their innovations resisted. In fact, the more compelling the innovation, the more powerful the resistance to it."
>
> (Frost & Hirsch, 2003: 191)

A cycle of opposition, acceptance, opposition, acceptance, and so on can be noted within Christian churches. The established "church" sees a threat, and opposes it. Nonetheless, the so-called "heretics" continue, and later become more acceptable across the general community. They settle in, once again become institutionalized, and then some in their ranks seek the freedom of following God instead of their rules. These new rebels are opposed, break free, get a following, become acceptable, and then settle down as a new institution. And so it goes.

Girard openly shares his initial reaction to a move of God with the Holy Spirit leading the people instead of the pastor leading the laity. He opposed it! Girard shares that his initial concern about God leading the show rather than him was that:

> "... evangelism would suffer, the professional ministry would suffer, my denomination would suffer, much that we count as progress would suffer, finances would suffer, and there would be too much freedom from needed pastoral control. Things would get out of hand!"
>
> (Girard, 1972: 79)

Then there was a change in his attitude, and he moved not just to acceptance, but he embraced this change enthusiastically, seeing its potential:

> "Those were my first thoughts. My second thought was, 'Wow! I'd love to see that — the church getting out of hand!'"
>
> (Girard, 1972: 79)

Not all embrace opportunities as readily as Girard did. Centuries earlier, a Church of England bishop from one diocese challenged John Wesley for preaching, asking him,

> "... by what authority he preached in his diocese."
>
> (Brown, 2002: 147)

The bishop then went on and

> "... forbade him to continue."
>
> (Brown, 2002: 147)

Sadly, the bishop was far from alone in his opposition.

> "The religious leadership of the Church of England opposed Wesley; many common people ... opposed him; even his own family opposed him. Yet none of this stopped

> *him. Wesley was convinced by the Word, by the Spirit, and by his own experience that the Gospel he preached was true. … By his teachings and his new 'Methodist' movement, he excommunicated the Church of England …"*

(Brown, 2002: 148)

The Church of England opposed Wesley. He pursued his call, undaunted. A new movement of freedom started. But the noted cycle of opposition/acceptance/opposition was lived out. The new "Methodist" movement gained acceptance, but then became institutionalized and in turn opposed others. This is in spite of the Methodist movement being founded by a person who exercised personal freedom in pursuing God's calling for his life:

> *"Sadly, one century later, when William Booth started the Salvation Army, ministering to the poorest of the poor in East London, many Methodists persecuted and opposed him."*

(Brown, 2002: 148)

Martin Luther broke free from some aspects of Catholic traditions, but retained others. For example, while he preached the principle of "the priesthood of all believers", he practiced the opposite, in the appointment of church leaders. We should be careful to not judge too harshly, however. We can boldly move along the paths that lead towards freedom, but we may never be fully aware of some of the prejudices we hold, let alone have the ability to break free from them all.

An honest recognition that we will never have a perfect understanding could discourage us from even trying to gain greater understanding, or it could be the humble motivator for us to choose a life-time of openness and learning. With that as a background, let us try to confront honestly the views of others we see to be dangerously flawed, but with the grace to accept honest criticism of our own views. Let us strive to never be so locked into our new "revelation" as to discount those who suggest room for improvement.

CHAPTER 20:
HONORABLE BUT MISGUIDED REASONS FOR RESISTANCE

Some church leaders believe that "churches" are essential

There are many good men and women in church leadership positions. In spite of my opposition to the *institution* of the local church, some of these church leaders remain my friends. Several of them admit problems with local churches, but still support the institution as they can see no alternative.

I remember attending the wedding of a long-term friend. My recollection of the wedding was that the pastor officiating at the wedding gave a very clear directive to the couple, warning them that they must be careful to always attend a local church on a Sunday morning. Taken in context, the message that I came away with was clear—attend church, or risk your marriage.

Noble notes that, in Jesus' conversation with the woman at the well,

> *"Jesus cut through it all and said, in effect, what many say who have nothing to do with Christianity, 'You don't have to go to church to be a Christian. It's what you believe and how you behave that counts.'"*

(Noble, 2002: 142)

Noble proclaims that this is the essence of *Jesus'* statement, but almost unbelievably appears to go on to say, in a sweeping statement that encompasses all who do not attend a local church,

> *"Of course, people who say that neither go to church nor behave properly: it's an excuse."*

(Noble, 2002: 142)

My analysis of the above two statements left me with an uncomfortable implication. If Noble believes that Jesus is one of the people who has made the claim that one doesn't need to go to church, and then Noble claims that people who make such statements do not behave properly, is he accusing Jesus of improper behavior, or flawed theology in believing church attendance is not essential? I doubt it. But in my mind it does throw into question the validity of his argument.

To be fair, Noble's words seem to suggest that he is trying to argue that it is *how* we worship that counts, not where. Yet in the development of his argument, he appears to effectively be saying that it's OK for Jesus to say we don't have to go to church to be a follower of God, but if we use the same message as used by the Son of God, we are to be labeled by Noble as those who do not come up to the mark.

The observation to be noted is that so many of the church leaders are willing to make generalizations about those that fail to attend church—and you, too, are likely to be criticized by them if you break free from church, even if their arguments don't hold water.

John Wesley broke many traditions, but was very conservative as to the role of the local church. At one stage, he actively opposed any preaching if it was to be outside the confines of the church building, saying:

> "[Preaching outdoors] is a mad notion."
>
> (Brown, 2002: 223)

He then went further, saying,

> "I should have thought the saving of souls almost a sin if it had not been in a church."
>
> (Brown, 2002: 223)

This prejudice is almost inconceivable if we take his claim that it is a "mad notion" to preach in the open air and compare it to the common actions of Jesus Himself. Yet such can be the blinding nature of prejudice against ministry outside of the "House of God". And it is still with us today.

The Church (i.e. the Body of Christ), by definition, includes all Christians, whether or not they are affiliated with local churches. It follows that all Christians participating in a "parachurch" organization are still part of the Body of Christ. However, my analysis of Robinson and Smith's writings seems to suggest that they lament the existence of parachurch organizations where they exist apart from local church organizations:

> *"Encapsulated in the body of para-church organisations are many of the evangelistic, discipleship, caring and church planting gifts and strategies necessary to impact the circle of accountability. In and of themselves, the para-church organisations can make a significant impact for the gospel with their particular Spirit-given gifts. But, significant as these impacts may appear to be, they pale in comparison with what can happen when the whole body of Christ is released into the telling of their particular grace stories, using their particular grace gifts.*

God did not design a small cadre of people, no matter how gifted or motivated, to do what he has designed the whole to do. Not only do we lose the full impact of numbers of people when we fail to mobilise the whole; more importantly we lose the full impact and colour of the diversity contained in the whole of the body. A union of like gifts can make a significant impact, but it will never be as great as what the world will see when a significant portion of the whole paints the world with the full diversity of God's creation in Christ's people.

It is for these reasons that movement demands that para-church organisations and their gifts do not perform for or in the place of the church. Rather, they need to become active instruments in the hands of the Spirit of God to motivate, train and release the church into full effectiveness."

(Robinson & Smith, 2003: 213-214)

My analysis leads me to question if Robinson and Smith see the only way to bring unity in the Body is for these outsiders to return to local churches, or at least to have the parachurch organization intrinsically tied to local churches? Surely Christians in parachurch organizations are just as much part of the true Church (Body of Christ) as are Christians within local churches, and that's where unity comes from? I get the impression that Robinson and Smith want to "release the church" by bringing gifted people in parachurches back into unity with local churches. My opinion? For God's sake (and I use that term literally and respectfully), don't force them back. Instead of trying to get motivated people back into "church", let's get the people in local churches motivated, and then get them out onto the front line as God leads each one!

In contrast to the calls of so many to get outreach workers back into local churches, Ralph Winter, in his article *The Two Structures of God's Redemptive Mission*, observes that local churches rarely reach out, but mission-based groups outside the churches do. However, he bemoans the fact that these outreach ministries seem to plant churches rather than planting more missions.

It's a good point, and perhaps the reason that many mission-based groups plant churches is that so many people simply cannot conceive of Christianity without local churches.

"… missions … have tended to assume that … churches … need to be established [i.e. they have typically not seen the need for establishment of independent organisations such as themselves that are outside of the church system]. Even in the case where mission work is being pursued by what are essentially semi-autonomous mission [groups], it is [churches], not [independent groups], that are the only goal. That is to say, the mission agencies (even those that [are the most independent from] denominations back home) have tended in their mission work very simply to set up churches and not to plant … [independent mission groups] in the so-called mission lands.

… In this blindness they have merely planted churches and have not effectively concerned themselves to make sure that the kind of mission structure within which they operate also be set up on the field."

(Winter, 1973: 188-189)

Until people start to realize that vibrant works of God can and actually do occur outside local churches, we may run in circles trying to get called people back into the confines of institutionalization.

Some church leaders believe that only they can understand God's word and ways

Jesus started His ministry with almost exclusively unschooled "lay" people. He did *not* seek to retrain and redirect the priests of His day. In contrast, it is all too common today to assume that only the trained church leaders can achieve anything of importance for God.

Below is just one simple quotation where it is assumed that "leaders", not the laity, have to find the way for the Body of Christ to move forward:

> "Whether by church planting or by expanding existing structures, <u>leaders</u> need to come to the place where they are determined to find a way to multiply and grow the church of Jesus Christ." [Emphasis mine]

(Robinson & Smith, 2003: 166)

This quotation may seem trivial. But entire books are written *by* church leaders, *for* church leaders, calling them to renew the local churches, mobilize the laity (while keeping them under careful supervision), catch the vision, develop new programs of outreach (to bring more people into the local church), and so on. Implicit in all such literature is the belief that it is the church *leaders* that hold the keys.

Within the history of Christendom, it was typically the church leaders who had an education, and were able to read and write.

> "The priesthood in ancient Israel was confined to Aaron and his sons. However in most premodern societies the priesthood had one notable characteristic. Priests could read and write. The word 'hieroglyphic' means 'priestly script'. To this day, the word 'clerical' in English has a double meaning, 'related to the clergy' and 'pertaining to a clerk or scribe' – a relic of the Middle Ages when ministers of religion held a near-monopoly of education."

(Sacks, 2003: 135)

Further, during the period when the Bible as we know it was only available in Latin, the chances of the laity being able to argue against errors held by the church leaders were slim, particularly if any dissent probably meant being executed as a heretic. It is no wonder that the inherited view is that it is the church leaders who are best positioned to understand the ways of God, and to interpret them for the laity.

Erwin McManus tells a story of an interaction with his 12-year-old daughter. His story challenged me, and may challenge you, too. McManus is a person with a high profile within Christian circles. Is it possible for a 12-year-old to hear more clearly from God than a respected senior? My interpretation of McManus' story is that it most certainly appears more than vaguely possible! It is easy to assume that "father knows best" (in some denominations, the church leaders actually assume the title of "father"), as they typically have more training or experience than the laity, but a critique of the following story led me to conclude that God can, and does, speak directly to all of His children who listen to Him:

" *'Daddy, one day I want to make a billion dollars, and I want to give it all away. I want to help the poor; I want to help the needy. I want to make a billion dollars, and I don't care if I have nothing, but I want to give it all to help people.'*

As I was listening to her dream, I thought, I can fix this. Because the dream was almost right.

But she kept saying, 'I want to make a billion dollars and give it away and help the poor, and I don't care if I'm homeless or have nothing. I just want to give it away to help people.'

I said, 'Mariah, I want you to make a billion dollars and give to the poor and the needy, but it's not a good idea that you have nothing. Then you would be needy and somebody would have to take care of you and you wouldn't be responsible.'

'I don't care if I don't have anything, Daddy,' Mariah responded. 'I just want to make a billion dollars and give it away. I don't care if I'm homeless. I don't care if I have nothing.'

'But if you're homeless, our taxes would have to pay for you.'

Looking at me as if to say, Daddy, you just don't understand, she continued, 'I don't care if I have nothing. I just want to make a billion dollars and give it all away. I don't care if I have nothing.'

I thought, Okay, I'm not really helping here. I was trying to help her understand that she needed to keep something, restructure it, and reinvest it so that she could make another billion and help another group of people. I just wasn't able to help her with her dream. And I thought, A metaphor – that will help.

'Honey, let's say you're a large tree bearing fruit for people to eat because they are hungry, and you want to give all your fruit away because you want to feed everyone, care for everyone. But because of that, you didn't care about your roots, and so you said, 'I'm going to uproot myself. Who cares about the soil and the water? I just want to bear all the fruit I can.' And then you will die. Then the next year you won't be able to bear fruit. It's better to take care of your roots, too, so that you can keep bearing fruit year after year after year.'

She said, 'Daddy, what in the world do roots have to do with this?'

I knew I wasn't making progress. We left the place and went to the car. I unlocked it, and she got into the car quickly. By the time I slid into the driver's seat, she was sobbing, and I didn't know what was going on. I asked, 'Mariah, are you okay?'

Just drenched in tears, she looked at me and said, 'Daddy, I want to change the world, but you can't appreciate my dream. I want to change the world.' She continued, 'I didn't say I would be homeless; I said I didn't care if I became homeless. I want to change the world. Can't you just hear my dream?'

I realized that instead of nurturing and unleashing the dream being born out of her heart for God, I was domesticating her dream and trying to civilize her raw and untamed faith, which was ironic since I was so excited that this was her heart.

'Well, honey, I am excited about your dream,' I said. 'Don't you think that we were a small part of trying to nurture your heart to have that dream?'

She said, 'Yeah, but I don't think you're getting it.'

I said, 'Well, I get it now. I get it now.'

It took me a little while, but suddenly I saw it clearly. I was experiencing a barbarian invasion. Mariah's heart was beating to the rhythm of the heart of God. And her dreams were way too raw for me. I didn't see it initially, but I was trying to civilize her instead of unleashing the untamed faith within her. After all, I am her dad. It's okay if I live a life of irrational faith and breathtaking adventure. I want something different for her. I want her to have security and safety – you know, a predictable, boring, mundane life where I never have to worry about her again. In that moment I realized Mariah would have none of that. For her there is only one path. Even at twelve she has already committed to it. Be still my heart, but my daughter has chosen the barbarian way out of civilization."

(McManus, 2005: 8-11)

It appears to be so easy for the "elders", be it McManus in the story above, or church "elders" or leaders, to simply miss the mark. For example, Winter suggests that local churches often don't even understand the possibility of separate congregations for different groups:

> "[Local churches] mistakenly think that being joined to Christ ought to include joining existing churches."

(Winter, 1974: 304)

Winter goes on to say that these converts:

> "... who would merely be considered somewhat odd additions to existing congregations, could be infusions of new life into whole new pockets of society where the church does not now exist at all!"

(Winter, 1974: 304)

Frost and Hirsch note that leaders of the establishment have invested so much of themselves they can't see anything differently from their traditions:

> "[A new way of thinking] begins to emerge, most often with opposition by those who still hold strongly to the established paradigm. Copernicus saved his neck only by recanting from the 'heresy' implied in his theory but was imprisoned for life. It is interesting that people are willing to persecute dissenters based on their assumptions about the world. This is probably because they have invested much of their sense of selfhood in the current paradigm and so receive their legitimacy from it. This is also why denominations seldom permit a questioning of their core organizations [sic] beliefs – commonly called sacred cows."
>
> (Frost & Hirsch, 2003: 191)

It is sobering to think that church leaders scorned the works of Copernicus that dared to suggest that the earth moved around the sun rather than the other way around. Church leaders today may still try to discredit you if they can.

George MacDonald provides a refreshing view that goes against the tide of church-leader-centric thinking. He takes the view that people are better off if they seek God for themselves – a truly radical view in some circles!

Speaking of a lady who, as a young girl with a heart for God, had been surrounded by teachers of tradition, MacDonald states:

> "Unhappily, she had not gone direct to the heavenly well – the very word of the Master himself. How could she? From very childhood her mind had been filled with traditional utterances concerning the divine character and divine plans – the merest inventions of men ...
>
> ... She had had a governess ... whose teaching [and] ... doctrines were so many smoked glasses held up between the mind of her pupil and the glory of the living God ..."
>
> (MacDonald, 1983(b): 44)

A Godly friend of this lady later counsels her to look to God rather than the teaching of others, warning that by listening to others we sometimes inherit their mistakes. If we seek God for ourselves, we, too, will at times make mistakes, but at least we don't compound them by the unchallenged and erroneous teaching of others:

> "Some go to other men to draw [an image of Jesus Christ] for them; and some go to others to tell them what they are to draw for themselves – thus getting all their blunders in addition to those they must make for themselves. But the nearest likeness you can see of him is the one drawn by yourself from thinking about him while you do what he tells you."
>
> (MacDonald, 1983(b): 98)

Some have noted that the seminaries where most church leaders are trained are apt to reinforce the errors of previous generations. Not only can the teaching be wrong yet repeated, but for some the status given to a theological training can be a barrier. MacDonald portrays a minister's daughter, who was well versed in theology, but,

> "... when she was near, you could not get within sight of God for her theology and herself together."
>
> (MacDonald, 1983(b): 48)

MacDonald succinctly summarizes the need to walk with God rather than try to learn about him through the teaching by theologians:

> "... the greater part of the teachers ... have always set themselves more to explain God than to obey him. The gospel is given not to redeem our understandings, but our hearts; that done, and only then, our understandings will be free. ... Nothing but Christ himself for your very own teacher and friend and brother, not all the doctrines about him, even if every one of them were true, can save you. ...
>
> If a man desires God, he cannot help knowing enough of him to be capable of learning more. His idea of him cannot be all wrong. But that does not make him fit to teach others all about him – only to go on to learn for himself."
>
> (MacDonald, 1983(b): 79)

Some church leaders want to maintain their "proper" roles

Robinson and Smith argue that it is the leaders that determine the success of a ministry, and that a lack of leaders will limit growth:

> "The success or otherwise of leaders in mobilising the giftedness of the whole church is the single biggest factor in determining the effectiveness of the church in mission."
>
> (Robinson & Smith, 2003: 103)

> "The recruitment and training of more leaders than you yourself can ever use is the key to the growth of movements. The lack of leadership development operates as the glass ceiling on the growth of every organisation. Developing innovative leadership training systems must be a high priority."
>
> (Robinson & Smith, 2003: 202)

Robinson and Smith support their argument by example, telling that

> "Some remarkable stories lie behind ... explosive [local church] growth."
>
> (Robinson & Smith, 2003: 188)

It is to be noted that it is these same authors who elsewhere seem to condemn a hierarchical model, yet in the following quotation appear to applaud the success of a particular local church, even though it appears to have a control-centred hierarchy. My interpretation leads me to conclude that this local church mandates that the vision of the leaders must be supported by all, that accountability is managed, that all are expected to report regularly on numerical growth, and that those at the top are somehow superior. To me, this view is reinforced by explicit thresholds for assignment to differing levels in the leadership hierarchy.

> *"Valerie Reshetinskiy leads Christian Hope Church in Kiev, a city of some 5,000,000 people. Valerie began his church with just six people in his living room in 1991. Today their congregation numbers more than 2,000. During this period they have planted more than 150 churches across the Ukraine, approximately half in Kiev itself. ...*
>
> *How did this growth take place?*
>
> *... Valerie ... has worked hard to build a leadership team in his own church which is deeply committed to the same vision and values. Valerie and the key leaders of Hope Church meet monthly. They revisit the vision, identify dates on the advance of the kingdom through them, resolve issues, and pray for God's strength and power. More than anything, these opportunities serve two important functions: to remind them why they exist and to ensure that they stay on track! Further, these meetings ensure accountability. Nobody is left out. Everyone is expected to be able to demonstrate what they have done to advance the kingdom of God in their particular circle. All are expected to report regularly on new church plants!*
>
> *The same vision and values have been communicated to every member. This is critical, because the members translate the vision into action. The leaders 'enable' the vision, but the members accomplish it together with the leaders. The leaders seek to create a ministry for every people group, geographical area and social need.*
>
> *... Because this model requires more leaders to make it function, the threshold for entry to leadership is lowered. The cell level of leadership demands less complex skills than those required to lead the whole church. The facilitator/leader of the small group is required to identify and train an assistant leader, ensuring future leaders for the expanding church."*
>
> (Robinson & Smith, 2003: 188-189, 191)

Of course such tightly managed expansion can be "successful" in God's Kingdom if measured simply by numbers. But on this basis, so is the McDonalds food chain!

Oliver and Thwaites go against the flow of those who, explicitly or implicitly, take the position that if the laity don't have lots of gifted leaders, they will simply be ineffective! They do note, however, that the above attitude is not uncommon.

> "Many leaders have become convinced that nothing much can happen unless <u>they</u> make it happen." [Emphasis mine]
>
> (Oliver & Thwaites, 2001: 94)

One sad reality is that there is truth in this opinion, not because the laity are incapable of achieving great things for God without the close scrutiny of "leaders", but because too often independent action is crushed if for no other reason than the leaders don't *want* anything to happen without them. Further, the laity have been trained to follow the vision of the leaders and not to trust or follow their own God-given visions. But Oliver and Thwaites appear to encourage us that it doesn't have to be so. They suggest that we may struggle to get alternative, laity-led ministry going while we're all busy propping up the old structures; but the scene is changing.

> *"... as more parables emerge on the landscape, an environment is set in place that encourages more of these pioneering people and works to emerge. It's as if a critical mass is formed, which propels the pioneers forward into the next level of breakthrough."*
>
> (Oliver & Thwaites, 2001: 167)

MacArthur typifies those who oppose laity who try to move into freedom, in what I feel to be the dubious belief that God actually intends the laity to submit to local church leaders. We have exposed this line of argument earlier, but it is presented below as an example of church leaders who may be well-intentioned but who hold to the party line of us submitting to them instead of to God:

> *"In addition to the work of His Spirit, God rules through the Spirit-controlled men who lead the church. ...*
>
> *God has designed His church in such a way that qualified, divinely appointed men preside over it and, with God's help, determine its direction, teach the Word, and give guidance and correction to the people. ...*
>
> *Since leaders are commanded to rule ... then those under them are also to submit ..."*
>
> (MacArthur, 1997: 119-120)

John, the disciple of Jesus, teaches in 1 John 4:20 that if we say we love God yet hate our brother, we are liars. He then goes on to say that any who love God must also love their brethren.

Over many years, I have encountered leaders who, in my view, twisted scripture to achieve domination by taking the words of John referenced above and then wrongfully extrapolating John's words. They seem to claim that we can only demonstrate an attitude of submission to God if we practice submission to the leader, who in turn claims to be God's representative. And on that basis, in my opinion they wield an ungodly authority, and take advantage of those who submit to them and their teaching.

MacArthur seems to follow a similar line of reasoning. Just because Jesus instructed us to "accept" others in an attitude that reflected accepting Christ Himself, surely this does not mean that we are to submit to church leaders as if they spoke for God? If this is the practice MacArthur is in fact wanting us to follow, I hold the view that it is a potential recipe for spiritual abuse:

> *"Jesus made the necessity of our submitting to spiritual authority even more imperative when He told the disciples, 'He who receives whomever I send receives Me; and he who receives Me receives Him who sent Me' (John 13:20). Our submission and obedience to the elders in our local church is equivalent to our submission and obedience to Christ."*
>
> (MacArthur, 1997: 120)

In summary, if those who oppose your moves to freedom try to use the big stick of claiming you must submit to them, I caution you not to be cowed by what I feel to be bullying behavior. They may (sometimes) mean well, but their actions could be those of a bully nonetheless.

Some church leaders want everything to be done "decently and in order"

I'm inspired by much of what Cymbala teaches. However, like many, he sees a "better church" as the solution to the woes of Christendom, and as such, advocates that evangelism should be done by the local church, not by parachurch groups. Jesus' command to share the good news was given to His disciples, not to the established religious hierarchy of His day. Yet Cymbala claims the role of evangelism as belonging to the local church:

> *"God's plan for the local church has always centered in evangelism. Those brought to Christ are thus born into the very place where they can be nurtured and discipled. This avoids the slippage we often see when parachurch ministries try to do the work mainly assigned to the local church."*
>
> (Cymbala, 1997: 179)

The great commission is to make disciples, not to plant local churches. Yet Cymbala would seem to be implying that Jesus' command to go into all the world and make disciples for Him should be applied via the local church institution. This practice is in stark contrast with the example of Jesus Himself, Who made disciples without the need for founding an institution, or appointing leaders, elders, buildings or an offering plate!

It is also sad when movements that claim to be initiated by God, and are often chaotic as they challenge the status quo of their day, feel the need to "get organized". The Pentecostal revival of the early 1900s saw significant growth that in turn generated challenges.

> *"By 1914, many ministers and laymen alike had begun to realize the rapid spread of the revival, and the many evangelistic outreaches it spawned had created a number of practical problems."*
>
> (Brown, 2002: 153)

And their assumed solution? Institutionalization!

> *"The need arose for formal recognition of ministers as well as approval and support of missionaries, with full accounting of funds. In addition, there was a growing demand for doctrinal unity, gospel literature, and a permanent Bible training school."*
>
> (Brown, 2002: 153)

Robinson and Smith proclaim that the current institutionalized local churches that have "ossified and declined" can be turned around. I challenge the value of even trying. But that is not the point I wish to highlight. Rather, I perceive that they insinuate that those who strike out in freedom to find life outside of their local church don't have the energy or gifting to bring about change. In my words, they seem to be saying that the faint-of-heart leave, and the real champions stay.

> *"… there are those who are sufficiently disenchanted with existing structures that they simply do not have the heart or the vision or the will to renew that which already*

exists. That can be a matter of call and gift. Some are not called or able to renew existing structures, and have no alternative but to strike out afresh. But it is not inevitable for movements to ossify or to decline ..."

(Robinson & Smith, 2003: 198)

Again, if we look at Jesus' life, He could have put His energy into bringing change in the synagogues. He didn't. He came to do a new thing!

Martin Luther taught the principle of the priesthood of all believers. His foundation for abandonment of the church leadership class is clearly stated by Professor Hendrik Kraemer, quoted in Brown:

"The fundamental ideas of the Reformation promised to inaugurate a radical change in the whole conception and place of the laity. Luther, at a decisive moment, rejected obedience to the Church as embodied in the hierarchical authority of the Pope, in the name of obedience to the Word of God. Luther's conception of the Church, especially in his earlier, militant writings, was a frontal attack on the hierarchical conception of the Church. The idea of the clergy as such was rejected. In principle the distinction of 'clergy' and 'laity' fell away..."

(Brown, 2002: 211)

Having just stated how Luther condemned the whole idea of a special class called to govern, Kraemer goes on to describe Luther's perceived need for professional oversight of a group:

"... For the sake of order alone certain people are set apart by the congregation, 'ministers' who were not priests in the cultural sense, mediators between God and the congregation of God and man, but 'ministers of the Word' (verbi divini ministry). But in principle all that was contained in the newly conceived ministry (to teach and preach, to baptize, to administer Holy Communion, to bind and loose sins, to make intercession, to judge about doctrine and discern the spirits) belonged of right to every baptized Christian ..."

(Brown, 2002: 211)

The intent was "for order alone". However, history proved that, over time, it turned out to be the thin edge of the wedge to reintroducing a church leader/laity distinction. God doesn't intend for church leaders to stand between us and God, and they are not needed to provide "order".

Oliver and Thwaites suggest one source of resistance to ministry moving beyond the local church is a perceived threat to congregational unity; but they point out that unity at the congregational level may by its very nature be a major threat to true unity in the Body at large!

"The fear that is often expressed regarding release, is that such will scatter the church and thus, undermine the unity of the body. ...

> *[There are so-called unity initiatives between congregations/denominations. For example,] ministers meet in larger numbers monthly, but it seems that after several unity events the congregations just seemed to return to the status quo. …*
>
> *So, what's the problem? The leader's belief that the church is primarily the congregation, is the very thing that works to ensure that the unity they are setting out to achieve will not happen. The reason? These leaders set out from the beginning of their church's history to establish unity in their congregation. The reason for this unity is that it produces a stronger congregation. I say this in passing, but it is of note, that the real or primary goal of pastors is not so much unity, rather, it is congregation. The building blocks for congregational unity are things like the leader's ministry emphasis, his doctrinal distinctives, his personality and, at the back of these, the history and traditions of the leader's own movement. All of these things work to create an intense and distinct culture within the congregation – one that makes it harder, if not impossible, for other distinct, but similarly intense, congregation-based churches to relate or join with them. Each congregation, in line with its doctrine of church, has created such a concentrated, narrow and uniform culture within, that it can no longer strongly link to other congregations in the city. In this way, our version of church unity becomes the very thing that works to divide the one church …"*
>
> (Oliver & Thwaites, 2001: 171-173)

Robinson and Smith argue that any movement needs structure, and that it is these very structures that provide direction for a movement:

> "There are many who see structure as the antithesis of movement. But in reality the creation of organisation actually adds power to the otherwise undirected energy of the initial movement."
>
> (Robinson & Smith, 2003: 197-198)

Since when did a static structure provide direction? And aren't we meant to be looking to the Holy Spirit for direction, not the local church constitution or institution? Finally, structures are by their very nature static, but those who are led the Holy Spirit are likened to the wind which blows where it will, unconstrained by any expectations of man (John 3:8).

Plass succinctly summarizes the objections to needing everything to be ordered:

> "Groups will develop a rigid structure of do's and don'ts, to protect themselves from the uncertainties and risks involved in grappling with the real world. Anyone who breaks one of the rules is threatening the security of the group, and must therefore be corrected or rejected.
>
> This is understandable, but has very little to do with the ideal outlook as Jesus taught it. He himself was a totally released and free person …"
>
> (Plass, 1991: 99)

Some church leaders perceive a need to protect "the church" institution

Some other authors, when talking about the business world, criticize what they see as a "fort mentality":

"It's in an imposing ... building that towers over the landscape.

Inside is everything we need.

And that's good because the outside is dangerous. We are under siege ... Thank God for the thick, high walls!

The king rules. If we have a wise king, we prosper.

The king has a court. The dukes, viscounts, and other sub-luminaries each receive their authority from the king. (The king even countenances an official fool. Within limits.)

We each have our role, our place. If we each do the job assigned to us by the king's minions, our fort will beat all those other stinking forts.

And then we will have succeeded – or, thinking it's the same thing, we will say we have 'won.' We get to dance a stupid jig while chanting 'Number one! Number one!'"

(Levine, Locke, Searls and Weinberger, 2000: 119)

Perhaps some would see such fort mentality also occurring in some local church scenes where the leadership strives to isolate "their" church from the threat of others. A number of Christian authors express this concern. For example, Rinehart provides a brief view of early church history, looking at how the church institution sacrificed liberty and vitality in the Holy Spirit by attempting to curtail a handful of individuals and beliefs that they saw as heretical:

"During the second century, in an effort to ensure doctrinal purity within a growing and far-flung church, a manual on church discipline was published in Syria. It was called the Didache. This document curtailed the use of the spiritual gifts and removed responsibility for spiritual leadership from the laity to a new class – the clergy, the ministry professionals. The individual believer was shackled and restrained from realizing his or her unique contributions to the body through the gifts of the Spirit. The Didache may have been effective in thwarting a few pockets of heresy, but it served to clamp the church in chains. We still drag those chains today."

(Rinehart, 1998: 116)

As Rinehart says above, the problems of this protectionist thinking are still with us today. And Brown warns of the consequences:

"... when you buck the system, even if God Himself has raised you up for this very purpose, you can expect to hear the same refrain: 'By what authority are you doing this?' This is the voice of traditional religion at its worst. God's words and deeds are not important. Tradition is!"

(Brown, 2002: 144)

If you walk in freedom, there will be opposition. But be encouraged, you won't be the first person to be misunderstood, and the path gets clearer as you keep on it.

In his book, *Disappointment with God*, Philip Yancey provides a quotation from William Thompson which paints a hypothetical scene set in the time period before God created our world and us. God discusses the risk of giving us freedom, yet decides to risk our rejection on the chance of winning our love:

> *"Imagine God in Heaven surrounded by the choirs of adoring angels singing hosannahs unendingly … 'If I create a perfect world, I know how it will turn out. In its absolute perfection, it will revolve like a perfect machine, never deviating from My absolute will.' Since God's imagination is perfect, there is no need for Him to create such a universe: it is enough for Him to imagine it to see it in all its details. Such a universe would not be very interesting to man or God, so we can assume that the Divinity continued His meditations. 'But what if I create a universe that is free, free even of me? What if I veil My Divinity so that the creatures are free to pursue their individual lives without being overwhelmed by My overpowering Presence? Will the creatures love Me? Can I be loved by creatures whom I have not programmed to adore me forever? Can love arise out of freedom? My angels love me unceasingly, but they can see Me at all times. What if I create beings in My own image as a Creator, beings who are free? But if I introduce freedom into this universe, I take the risk of introducing Evil into it as well, for if they are free, then they are free to deviate from My will. Hmmm. But what if I continue to interact with this dynamic universe, what if I and the creatures become the creators together of a great cosmic play? What if out of every occasion of evil, I respond with an unimaginable good, a good that overwhelms evil by springing out of the very attempts of evil to deny the Good? Will these new creatures of freedom then love Me, will they join with Me in creating Good out of Evil, novelty out of freedom? What if I join with them in the world of limitation and form, the world of suffering and evil? Ahh, in a truly free universe, even I do not know how it will turn out. Do I even dare to take that risk for love?'"*
>
> (William Thompson, in Yancey, 1988: 60-61)

Since God is willing to take such enormous risks in giving us freedom, never, ever, let any man chain you, especially on the pretext of protecting God and His kingdom, but in reality protecting the man-made church!

CHAPTER 21:
DISHONORABLE REASONS FOR RESISTANCE TO YOUR FREEDOM

As described above, some church leaders fiercely defend local churches as if they are "defending the faith". Their efforts may well be counter-productive to the expansion of God's kingdom, and sometimes, whether consciously or not, their motives may not be honorable.

Below is a skim over some of the darker motives that can exist behind the defense of local churches. It focuses on one case in point from another era, and you may well not relate directly and personally to many of the examples. It paints a fairly extreme picture of a leader who blatantly controlled his followers, but it is presented in the hope that the extreme nature of this leader's control may be helpful in detecting controlling attitudes in milder cases.

Some chinks in the armor

Some church leaders simply cannot conceive that they could possibly be wrong in their views. Any alternatives must, from their perspective, be automatically wrong, if not outright heresy. William and Catherine Booth, the founders of the Salvation Army, are described by Hattersley as

> *"... intolerant of disagreement (except between themselves) and incapable of considering the possibility that they were wrong."*
>
> (Hattersley, 2000: 81)

Booth effectively suppressed open discussion and debate at the annual conference of 1877. He condemned such practices in previous conferences by stating that

> *"... so large a proportion of the time [was] ... consumed in discussion of comparatively trivial matters."*
>
> (Hattersley, 2000: 225)

Hattersley goes on to explain how Booth argued that fundamental issues could not be trusted to the decisions of others, but needed to be made by him:

> *"William Booth set out to justify his proposals to avoid 'leaving essential principles and practices to be mangled about and decided by mere majorities'. He then described his plans for stifling democracy in a way of which any politician would have been proud. Answering his own question 'Why emasculate the Conference?', he avoided giving an answer by explaining that he proposed to replace the legislative assembly with a Council of War – which was represented as a superior form of democracy. In modern constitutional jargon, the Conference-turned-Council of War was purely advisory. The commander-in-chief [William Booth himself], by 'resolving upon a programme of action', removed all necessity for an executive committee to take decisions between Councils of War or at any other time. Clearly there was no need, in the circumstances, for a cumbersome executive to take decisions between conferences. That was the role of the commander-in-chief. Suddenly, the logic of the Presidential Address seemed impeccable: 'We thereby give up the Conference Committee. It seems almost useless to go into the reasons fully, but I may point out one or two. It seemed impossible to get a truly representative committee. …'*
>
> *In any event, reality about where power really lay made the change imperative: 'If you are in any trouble, you don't want to go to the Committee, you want to come to me …'*
>
> *[Booth] … established his control of the whole Mission – spiritual and administrative, local and national …"*

(Hattersley, 2000: 225-226)

Rinehart suggests that the root of much pride discovered in many church leaders is their belief that there really *is* a difference between them and the laity. In spite of verbal agreement with the philosophy of the "priesthood of all believers", there is limited practice of its principles.

> *"When leading seminars with ministry leaders, I ask them to list the elements of ministry. Usually at the top of their lists is the ministry of preaching and teaching the Word. Then I ask, 'Are you equipping the laity to do that ministry? Do you equip them to preach and teach?' The typical response is silence. If we are not equipping people for all of the ministry, including our own jobs, then do we really believe in the priesthood of believers?"*

(Rinehart, 1998: 133)

Rinehart also notes that the appearance of unity between leaders of separate local churches can be a veneer. The words may be about unity, but the reality is about competition:

> *"Most ministries today practice a congenial competition. While they mouth words of unity, there is little practical action to back up their pronouncements. Their real goal is to accumulate members in their ministry organisation or church while the lost still await the good news from a unified body of Christ."*

(Rinehart, 1998: 135)

If church leaders shy away from real unity for fear of losing followers, they are even less likely to release their laity to seek ministry options that might divert them from church projects considered more important by the leaders.

> "Releasing people for ministry requires trusting God and letting go of our tendency to hoard people for our own ministry agendas."
>
> (Rinehart, 1998: 129)

Even when church leaders do invest in other ministries, these are likely to be ministries that are seen as belonging to the "home church". Smalley claims that holders of the purse strings typically have financially supported

> "... churches which are their satellites, rather than into the grass roots growing development of an embarrassing indigenous church."
>
> (Smalley, in Winter et. al. 1981: 500)

In addition to desiring to have an outreach ministry reflect glory back to the source (i.e. the visionary church leader, not God), the founding leader prefers to retain control. He can't run the risk of "planting" a ministry and then seeing it taken over and heading in a direction differing to that of the "home" church.

> "... missionaries often do not like the product [i.e. the way an indigenous local church forms if they do not interfere]. Often a truly indigenous church is a source of concern and embarrassment to the mission bodies in the area."
>
> (Smalley, in Winter et. al. 1981: 498)

There are leaders who would rather oppose growth than see it take place outside their own paradigm. I see the following quotation as perhaps leaning in this direction:

> "A man who starts changing the system is dangerous. ... When a man starts shaking up the religious, political, and social system, the people in the system feel that they have to stop him."
>
> (Tom Skinner in Brown, 2002: 183)

Such attitudes on the part of the religious leaders of Jesus' day stirred them up to seeking to have Him killed. Thankfully, *physically* murdering someone is no longer considered appropriate in church circles, although still widely practiced until only a few centuries ago. Now character assassination—under the guise of opposing heresy—is far more common. The Inquisition lives on; it is just more subtle.

Oliver and Thwaites appear to address the same issue:

> "Many leaders are willing to permit a stronger release of the people of God into creation as long as their Sunday gathering and their oversight remains central to the process. They are releasing market-place ministries and kings to conquer the world of work, but are still reserving seats on Sunday and naming the people seated there as 'church central'. Such a controlled release – done in line with an old ecclesiology, and in response to a fear that if release is granted, then the people might not come back –

will not see the church as fullness rise. If the culture affirms the ecclesiastic mother ship as central, dominant and church primary, then, by definition, the rest of what happens will not be any of those things.

By the time that this kind of approach to things [reflecting] church [traditions] makes its way out into the world of work, the blaze of affirmation from the central campfire has now burned down to a smouldering stub in the hands of the saint. In the darkness all around them, this little light penetrates little darkness. It's hardly surprising that these saints are left pining for the bonfires of the church central to light up their life every Sunday. Hence the need, I believe, of taking away a centre that should not have been there in the first place. The church as fullness needs no king, no centre, and no lords to manage it. Jesus is its king and he alone is its centre.

Sounds scary? So it should, because it is. The main reason it is scary is because most leaders do not trust saints to be the church apart from their management of the process. Also, most leaders do not have a theology that can encompass this way of being church. Unless one has a vision and understanding of the church as fullness, the above description will sound like the end of the world."

(Oliver & Thwaites, 2001: 170-171)

It seems to me that these authors are suggesting that there are leaders who try to control different expressions of ministry to keep the local church traditions as the center of each believer's life.

A deep-dive analysis of one leader

Attempts to dominate are always a problem. To some, it may seem less of a problem when the leader has at least a veneer of outward respectability. In fact, I would argue that apparently "good" leaders may be all the more dangerous. But we'll put that aside for the moment, and look at what Hattersley says about William Booth.

My interpretation of Hattersley's book is that Booth argued that there were merits in taking action against individuals who expressed views at odds with those of himself. It seems that Booth labelled opposition as "apostasy" and "dissent", then went further and argued that such attitudes would lead to "moral deterioration".

Hattersley tells us that one of William Booth's followers had left the Salvation Army and sent a confrontational letter explaining his actions. Booth read the letter out at an annual conference, using it to support his own push for tighter control. He presented the letter

> "... as evidence of the moral deterioration which follows apostasy."

(Hattersley, 2000: 224)

Hattersley records that Booth went on to claim

> "The way to avoid the repetition of such deplorable conduct was ... to concentrate all power in the hands of William Booth himself ... [and that] ... the new discipline would stifle dissent."

(Hattersley, 2000: 224)

Perhaps Booth's motives were pure, driven by a desire to protect his followers from moral failure? Is Hattersley suggesting that Booth is correct in opposing individuals who think for themselves? Apparently not, as Hattersley also notes that

> "… there was no explanation of why that should be so [i.e. why the centralization of control would avoid 'deplorable conduct']."
>
> (Hattersley, 2000: 224)

My interpretation is that Hattersley calls into question Booth's rationale for centralization of control.

Hattersley presents another reason put forward by Booth for control of the individual. Booth apparently argued that military-style top-down command-&-control structures were central to military success, and extrapolated that reasoning to suggest the same formula for success in God's work. Under William Booth, the Mission adopted the name of the Salvation Army; it also adopted military attitudes:

> "Discipline was next to godliness: 'It was the discipline of the revolutionary armies, the stern unbending obedience which was enforced on all ranks from highest to lowest which created for Napoleon the admirable military instrument by which he shattered every throne in Europe.' … Decisions would be taken by those qualified to govern – 'not counting noses [i.e. democratic voting] but admitting no noses into the concern which are not willing to be guided by the directing brain'."
>
> (Hattersley, 2000: 373-374)

Hattersley appears to call into question the use of military style disciplines within this Christian organization. He comments on the inconsistency of William Booth's attitude to discipline, depending on whether he was giving or receiving the orders:

> "When he imposed [discipline], there could be no relaxation or exception. When it was imposed on him, he insisted that he accepted no other authority than God."
>
> (Hattersley, 2000: 5)

Hattersley also notes Booth's inconsistency towards restraints put on God's people:

> "… he who was so much against the restraints imposed by religious elders in societies to which he had once belonged, now imposed restraints on people under him."
>
> (Hattersley, 2000: 234)

While not explicitly damning a military style within the Salvation Army, my wider reading of Hattersley suggests he is not convinced by Booth's adoption of a command-&-control system.

Now my critique of Hattersley focused on an argument for opposing individual freedom based on the perceived efficiency of centralized decision-making. Hattersley states that Booth believed

> "… evangelism only prospered under strong leadership."
>
> (Hattersley, 2000: 224)

Perhaps having a dictatorial leader is more "efficient" than running a committee with diverse points of view that need some hard work to resolve, but surely that does not mean a single voice calling the shots is a better solution? It appears to me that Hattersley calls into question the accuracy of Booth's argument for efficiency, suggesting that Booth's recollections may not have been accurate:

> "By a remarkable rewriting of [Booth's] personal history, he went on to explain that ... conflicts ... had always been the result of the inevitably inefficient, and usually corrupt, committee system."
>
> (Hattersley, 2000: 224)

Is Hattersley challenging Booth's arguments behind the control Booth took over subordinates? I think so.

My reading of Hattersley suggests he is even more direct in his expression of concern around other aspects of Booth's control over those in the Salvation Army, and suppression of expressions of opposition or even questioning, highlighting Booth's egotistical nature as problematic. He writes:

> "William Booth was a man of unrestrained ambition. His principal aspirations were for the great cause which he had been called to serve but, like so many men of destiny, he did not believe that it could prosper without him."
>
> (Hattersley, 2000: 182)

Hattersley explicitly points out Booth's intolerance towards those who dared to express their own individual views of matters:

> "Certainty about his duty made him reckless, arrogant and impatient with even the friendliest disagreement ..."
>
> (Hattersley, 2000: 128)

It appears that Hattersley held the view that such intolerance was a negative trait. He highlights the negative side effects of Booth's unbending demands for loyalty, even if the challenges came from his own children, stating that even as death approached, William Booth

> "... would not have attempted to reunite his divided family. Kate, Ballington and Herbert had disobeyed their General and ignored the commandment to honour their father. For them, there could be no forgiveness. William Booth [was] ... an unsympathetic human being."
>
> (Hattersley, 2000: 436)

Hattersley leads me to believe that he is suggesting that Booth enshrined himself as the ultimate authority, as demonstrated in the following quotations:

> "It seemed that, with the Booths in charge, nothing could hold back the Mission's work. That was certainly William Booth's own view. And he grew increasingly impatient with the restraints which were occasionally imposed on his authority. He determined

to remove the impediments to his successful leadership by rewriting the Mission's constitution."

(Hattersley, 2000: 209)

At the 1876 Annual Conference, William Booth

"… used the occasion to impose his will on the increasingly unruly army as, in the previous year, he had taken complete control of the general staff."

(Hattersley, 2000: 213)

In one of his presentations at the conference, Booth taught

"… it is safest and best for society in all its grades and relations to feel that there is a real authority which must be respected and a real law and authority which must be obeyed."

(Hattersley, 2000: 213)

As a result of the proceedings of the conference there was a

"… shift of authority away from the individual mission towards the General Superintendent – the centralisation which many Methodists believed was the sin of the established Church …"

(Hattersley, 2000: 214)

Hattersley's book led me to believe that he disapproved of Booth's controlling nature, and its impact in the formative stages of the Salvation Army. Taking heed of Hattersley's reservations, and applying my own experiences, I believe that today's Salvation Army remains hierarchical in nature, and that, for example, its church leaders ("Officers") are still given "Marching Orders" to relocate their work to other regions at the whim of more senior ranks.

My conclusion after critiquing Hattersley's book is that while the Salvation Army (from Booth's day through to the present) provides commendable support to the vulnerable in society, nonetheless the foundations laid first by Booth's nature and then enshrined in the constitution are such that independent individuals who voice dissent are likely to be opposed. Perhaps those who oppose independent thinking genuinely believe that senior ranking leaders are better placed to understand God's ways and will? Perhaps, as seen in other settings, some feel that the organization must be protected from those who would undermine it?

We have considered some of Booth's many faults, not to perform character assassination on him, but rather to expose as an example just one leader who demanded subservience based on a pretext such as him overcoming character weaknesses in his followers.

Those that at one point in time followed Booth had a choice. They could have continued to trust Booth and to lean on him, or they could have trusted themselves to depend directly on Jesus. You and I must look to *no one* but Jesus, and *any* leader who tries to divert our allegiance must be shunned. Of course, such leaders are likely to oppose our freedom from their control, but we must break free, no matter how loudly they protest.

SECTION 7:

FIRST AID FOR THE DEAD?

Some people advocate improvement to the current local church structures little by little. They don't want to hurt people's feelings, or to be seen as harshly critical of what they perceive to be God's institution. They hope for neat little changes to what they already find not too uncomfortable.

Others can only see a radical surgery option. Rip out the cancerous bits, and if the patient doesn't survive, maybe they weren't meant to. They might argue that any attempt at remediation of local church structures will only delay the inevitable—death!

But what does *God* want His people to do? The dangers of making the wrong choice are enormous. If He wants us to heal and renew the local churches, dismantling what we've got will be destructive and in clear breach of His purposes. Conversely, if the answer is to throw away the old wineskin, simple application of a patch or two won't be enough.

CHAPTER 22:
CAN'T WE FIND SOME USE FOR LOCAL CHURCHES?

Trying to salvage something from the local church scrap heap

Some serious challenges to traditional church structures have been presented. Most would agree that there are problems with church institutions. Maybe some church leaders feel they are leading the perfect church, but we most definitely don't want anything to do with them anyway!

Some signposts to radical change have also been presented by a number of authors, but the messages aren't always clear. On the one hand, Robinson and Smith may appear to see life for the local church as long as it flows from mission. They argue that it will be a different shape to what many of us have experienced, but it will have life nonetheless:

> *"To return to mission as the core [reason for being] of the church will inevitably mean that the shape of the church will change. Our very failure may well assist us to return to that innovation stage of the life of the church when the church ceases to do church but to do mission. What flows from mission will still be the church but it will be a very different kind of church."*
>
> (Robinson & Smith, 2003: 56)

Conversely, Nee argues that there will be life in the one Church, the Body of Christ, as individuals perform their God-ordained ministry. Again, the shape may be quite unexpected, but the Church (universal, as distinct from local church institutions) will exist. In this context, he does not explicitly portray a role for local churches, but just for the one Church:

> *"But quietly, in many places and largely unseen, God is raising up a vessel which is truly His house. It consists not of single outstanding individuals, whether great in*

preaching or revival or anything else, but in humble men and women who have been welded into one by the Cross."

(Nee, 1967: 40)

It is easy to understand that many people do not want to totally abandon the concept of local churches. Perhaps they have been raised to believe they truly are representative of God's one universal Church, the Body of Christ. Or perhaps they cannot see another way, and genuinely want to make the very best of whatever they have to work with. Or perhaps they just are too complacent to even rock the boat.

Hunt portrays the image of a pastor's wife who has been radically challenged about the ineffectiveness of 'church' as her husband has been running it. In the past she has had a cocooned existence. She no longer wants to remain within the cocoon, yet neither does she want to grow beyond the cocoon and leave it forever. Rather, she now intends to enjoy the comfort of 'church' while planning to also reach out to those outside of church.

"Even as I stand on the brink of a new adventure with Christ, the dependability of this worship service comforts me as much as the hundreds of tip-tilted faces involved in worship. I have always been moved by the power of community, but through the music and sights of this service, I feel as though this body has slipped its arms around me. I see love in the faces that occasionally glance my way and smile; I feel the strength undergirding the aged saints who are lifting wizened hands to the Lord.

The body of Christ is a mighty force, and Abel is not wrong to serve it. He is a guardian of the sheep obeying the Lord's command. He is feeding them with what he has been given, he is teaching the young ones and helping them grow strong in wisdom and faith.

But I pray I will never again cocoon in this comfort. There are too many absent from this building, too many people waking to a Sunday morning filled with despair and loss."

(Hunt, 2004: 329)

But note what comforts her—the 'dependability' of her local church. Surely Christ's offer to us is the opposite —no guarantee other than a cross. And what does she offer those outside the local church? It seems she is suggesting that if they can be brought into the church building on a Sunday morning that will mean they can avoid waking in despair. But is it the local church or Christ to whom they are or should be looking for courage, strength and vision? Or are the local churches and Christ Himself somehow confused? We can't afford to give a mixed message. It is Christ and Christ alone who sustains and leads us.

Yet Lawrence Richards, in the introduction to *Brethren, Hang Loose*, expresses the view that

"... today's churches do not deserve abandonment".

(Girard, 1972: 13).

The book clearly spells out problems in the present church structures, and Girard expresses initial despair that change can ever come to traditional structures. However, it goes on to suggest new life can be brought to the old churches. But Girard also warns that his experience has shown that the simple addition of a few new ideas to a fundamentally unchanged church structure would produce only more of the same deadness:

> *"Our [local church] was rapidly developing some of the same old institutional diseases we had naively thought we could avoid, simply by starting a new church with a few new ideas."*

(Girard, 1972: 18)

Towards the end of the book, Girard suggests it is debatable that

> *"… the institutional church can be completely renewed without undergoing a revolution so radical as to destroy it as an institution …"*

(Girard, 1972: 204)

So where does this leave us? If we try to follow the views of Girard and some others quoted in his book, the local churches do not deserve to be abandoned, yet they need such radical renewal that they may be destroyed.

David Pawson (1984) spoke boldly on the topic of what we should do with local churches. He stressed the essential role of the Holy Spirit in bringing change, rather than man looking for new techniques or new programs. And he warned that it is the nature of the Holy Spirit to lead in unexpected ways. Pawson reasons that we should not be surprised if He moves outside of our comfortable traditions. Nor should we be surprised if the solution He leads one person towards is different to the solution for another.

Pawson taught that most people would currently find themselves in an "old covenant" church, i.e. one that was more aligned with the traditions and structures of the Old Testament rather than the New Testament teaching of Christ. Many would get defensive at such a suggestion, but whether you agree or not with his line of reasoning, the challenge that followed can be applied. What might God call *you* to do in response to recognition of imperfection in local church structures? Broadly speaking, Pawson presented three options, noting that whatever we do must be done in love:

- Stay in your current local church, but try to be an agent of change. However, Pawson noted that it is not good if one person has a vision for change and tries to force their vision on a group of people who don't want to change. He advises them not to stay out of some misguided loyalty, especially if they believe the Holy Spirit is telling them to go.

- Move to another local church that practices "new covenant" fellowship. Again, Pawson has a warning: don't move on if you're doing it because you're a "supermarket shopper", forever searching for something more pleasing to your wrong motives.

- Be a catalyst to start a new church. And the warning here is to be careful about initiating a new fellowship because all the existing ones are imperfect, especially if you think you can start the perfect church!

But Pawson's options are built around an assumption that we *need* local churches. Considering that Pawson is himself a pastor, perhaps he has not looked beyond options that still involve local churches, albeit in some improved form.

Lindsay noted that Luther encouraged people to look at the "machinery" of the church with balance and freedom. The balance allowed a person to evaluate what was useful for him or her. The freedom came from the ability to throw away anything that hindered a person getting close to God. In fact, Luther strongly recommended that anything that got in the way

"... ought to be changed or done away with ..."

Lindsay (1996: 82)

Hattersley notes the life of Francis Xavier, a Jesuit priest who *"converted half of Goa"*, but attributes part of his success to his act of

"... disowning the corrupt missionaries whom he found there ..."

(Hattersley, 2000: 294)

He, too, had the courage to abandon unhealthy practices.

In *The Problem of Wineskins*, Howard Snyder goes so far as to say that institutionalized traditions must be decisively removed:

"Protestantism is caught in a stifling web of institutionalism. The wineskins have grown rigid. It is not enough, therefore, merely to call for change or to proclaim the need. The whole problem of wineskins–the structure of the church–must be dealt with."

(Snyder, 1975: 50,51, in Tillapaugh, 1982: 80)

Some people defend church institutions based on the pragmatic evaluation that they do some good. Some could even argue that there was some good in the actions of Hitler, too. Having some good does not mean we should defend the source. Brown seems to suggest that the evidence of some local churches having produced some good does not mean we need them:

"It is one thing to affirm that God is working within all kinds of groups, structures and settings, and that He is active within 'the system.' But that does not mean that He wants us to let the system go unchallenged or that He will not call us to leave the system. He might very well lead us to march to the beat of a different drummer, and that means being out of step with many others."

Brown (2002: 185)

Girard appears to go even further, making a bold and confronting statement that:

"New Testament life can't happen within the organized church ... There is too much against it!" [Emphasis mine]

(Girard, 1972: 32)

He then goes on to succinctly summarize why we need change:

> "*Too many 'barnacles' from the past still cling to the old institutional church concept.*
>
> *Too much emphasis on buildings and budgets. Too much money needed just to keep the machine running. Too much pastoral and lay effort spent on oiling the gears of the organiza-tion. Too much energy expended keeping touchy members happy because you can't afford to lose them.*
>
> *Too much dependence on the pastor — and no way to change that.*
>
> *Too many comfortable pews all facing the front so no one has to relate to anyone else. Too easy for Christians to sit-listen-¬leave-and-forget without anything really happening in their lives.*
>
> *Too much holding one another at arm's length. Too little real fellowship — gut-level fellowship — inner circle fellowship.*
>
> *Nothing provided in the church to make it happen at that level.*
>
> *Too many rules. Too much government. Too many man-made standards. Too many reports to fill out.*
>
> *Too little time to enjoy life.*
>
> *Too little time with the family.*
>
> *Too little time to get to know God. Too little time to pray.*"

(Girard, 1972: 32-33)

What about a new start?

In spite of the many clear signposts pointing to freedom in Christ without the constraints of a church institution, some still won't give up the fight easily. The most common response to perceived flaws in one's current local church is to find another. Buckingham supports the freedom for change. Having stressed the preference for congregation members of a 'stuck-in-a-rut' pastor to be agents of change within the existing local church, Buckingham then goes on to state that

> "*… if [the pastor] refuses to move, the sheep must go on. For they, like him, are commanded to 'quench not the Holy Spirit.' Sad is the pastor who lies in the dust, trampled by sheep who wanted nothing more than for him to lead them.*"

(Buckingham, 1980: 101)

Tillapaugh expresses the opinion that the senior pastor's attitude to change is likely to carry major influence:

> "*If the senior pastor desires to see the church unleashed, it will likely happen. If not, it really doesn't matter much what others may try to do.*"

Tillapaugh (1982: 99)

So what should people do if they are in a local church where the leadership controls the laity? Tillapaugh doesn't hesitate to advise they move on, saying,

> *"Don't stay and fight; go elsewhere …"*
>
> Tillapaugh (1982: 103)

Being free to seek a "better church" is preferable to maintaining a cult-like loyalty to a current church, no matter what its errors. But what if you can't find a "better" church? Some authors suggest you start a new one! That was Girard's goal, but he encountered some fundamental issues in the flawed current church model. So starting yet another church was going to achieve little. (Further, it is to be noted that Girard assumed that the "New Testament" church model was an ideal that, if rediscovered, would solve the problems. This often-held view has been noted earlier as simplistic at best, and flawed and dangerous at worst.)

> *"I could see these things, but I did not know how else to operate. All my ministerial training in college had taught me how to function within this old mold. All my experience had been in making the old outdated machine run at top efficiency when in reality the old machine was almost ready for the junkpile. A new day demanded a new vehicle for moving the Great Commission forward.*
>
> *I became convinced that the organized church as I knew it – even my own new church – would never be that vehicle. There was too much against it.*
>
> *There was just no way.*
>
> *I deeply longed to lead my young congregation into the experience of the Church in Acts. But I'd tried every idea my cleverness could devise to lead it to such a life – but no program of mine could bring it off.*
>
> *I'd have been willing to listen to any advice that made any kind of sense and provided answers to any of the questions I was asking. But, who do you go to for advice when you are convinced that no other pastor you know is any freer from the institutional hang-ups than you are, and no church you know is any closer to the New Testament Ideal than the one you serve?"*
>
> (Girard, 1972: 33)

Girard describes the life-changing challenge he received at a minister's meeting. The tiredness of many ministers was identified, and contrasted with Christ's offer to give rest to all who were laboring and feeling under a heavy load (Matthew 11:28). For clergy to experience rest in Christ seemed impossible in local churches where, if the minister stopped pushing hard, pretty much everything stopped. The speaker's solution was simple—quit striving in your own strength.

> *"Begin to depend upon the Life of Jesus to live the Christian life in and through you. Quit trying to fulfill the Great Commission, obey the commandments, fulfill your ministerial calling. Instead, depend on the Life – His Life in you. If He doesn't do it, nobody should. Simply make your body available to Him. Quit! and let Jesus be in you*

> what the New Testament declares that He is. Don't try to be 'like Jesus.' Let Jesus live your life. Stop doing things for Him. Start letting Him do it.
>
> Rest! And watch what Jesus Christ alive in you can do."
>
> (Girard, 1972: 54-55)

Girard summarized his struggle, concluding that totally breaking away from institutionalized church might be the solution:

> "But how do we translate this [resting in Christ] into the practical aspects of church life? The institution in its present form will fight these concepts. Its very structure is against this new 'faith-rest' prin¬ciple. How can the people ever catch this for their lives? They're so bound by the organizational concept and its traditions.
>
> Perhaps leaving the institution is still the only answer."
>
> (Girard, 1972: 56)

For many, even to question or doubt the traditions of "church" can be daunting, I know it was for me at first. Michael Brown (quoting Dale Brown) challenges us to be brave and open enough to have:

> "… the security to question to the depths."
>
> Brown (2002: 181)

He refers to having the ability to honestly revisit our roots and see if we've lost our way. This openness can be applied to many topics. I want to suggest that we need to go back to our foundations for understanding church. And this means looking to the founder, Jesus. With this in mind, let's look at what Brown says:

> "Sometimes the most radical, revolutionary thing we can do is return to our roots. Sometimes the way to real progress involves going back and retrieving what was lost before moving forward into unexplored territory. Sometimes the most revolutionary thing we can do is to tear down and repair before trying to build something new. But this is costly, painful and quite unsettling."
>
> Brown (2002: 181)

We need to ask the hard question: "Is the institution of 'local church' going to work in any setting at all, or is it doomed?"

It's just not going to work

Plass addresses the problem of those who can see the faults in the traditions of others but replace them with their own flawed traditions. He provides a "dictionary" definition for "non-conformist" churches, declaring that they are:

> "… denominations that have broken away from spiritually atrophied mainline churches in order to be allowed to atrophy in a manner that is in accordance with their own understanding of Scripture."
>
> (Plass, 2007: 130)

For years Martin Luther cherished the hope that change could be brought about within the church as he knew it.

> *"He was as indifferent to forms of Church government as John Wesley, and, like Wesley, every step he took in providing for a separate organisation was forced upon him as a practical necessity. He cherished the hope that the new wine might be stored in the old bottles ..."*
>
> (Lindsay, 1996: 175).

Lindsay tells of Martin Luther's conviction that church tradition could be a useful means to an end, but should be removed if it is an obstacle. He then calls men to have the courage to change if necessary:

> *"[Luther] respected everything which had belonged to the past, and especially to that medieval Church into which he had been born. But these things were not required to make the Church. They were only modes ... and if they failed to conform to the precepts of the Word of God and had become full of human corruptions, thus degenerating into hindrances rather than remaining helps to the furtherance of the true religious life of the soul, they ought to be done away with, and something else should be put in their place. The fact that the human soul needs absolutely nothing in the last resort but the Word of God dwelling in it, ought to give men courage and calmness in demanding the change. The principle of the spiritual priesthood of all believers was able to deliver men from all fear in demanding such a reformation as the Church required ..."*
>
> Lindsay (1996: 177-178)

Martin Luther called men to have the courage to break free from stifling church traditions, including the tradition that the priesthood was a special class of Christians. In its place, he called for recognition of the principle of the priesthood of all believers. But in practice, he was dragged back to operate against his own principles, instead following the traditions he spoke so strongly against. The local churches he was instrumental in forming still had church leaders (of which he was one), and they still had laity.

Oliver and Thwaites argue that in a similar way local church institutions of *our* day are still imprisoning the laity by practicing anything but the priesthood of all believers:

> *"Even though the Reformers started well, the trouble was that the doctrine or understanding of the church was left basically unchanged from previous eras – dominated, in the main, by Roman Catholic teaching. The local church was still something separated from the real everyday lives of most of the saints out there. Inside, the ministers still taught from their pulpits and the church gathered was deemed to be primary. The rest of what the saints did was, by inference and definition, secondary. So, it followed that, over time, what started well with Luther and Calvin did not end well. Today we are still faced with the divide between church and life. A divide that conquers the saints and keeps them tied to the sanctuary – the birdcage. Speaking of birdcages, where are your wings? ...*

All over the Christian world there are chained eagles. Logs of false teaching, chains of false expectation and false doctrine are holding down some magnificent men and women who, deep down, are longing to fly. They are longing for permission, for understanding, for conviction; longing to feel the wind of the Spirit blow under outstretched wings, as they get lifted into the thermals high up in God's purpose. The [place] is here; the [time] is now. As you read, will you let the Word of God break those chains? Will you let his Spirit breathe into your faint hope, your faint faith, and let him stir you up, lift you up to something higher?"

(Oliver & Thwaites, 2001: 76-77)

We may try, like Luther, to bring change to the church system. But Jacobsen and Coleman suggest we will just go round yet another circle, and end up somewhat as we started:

"*People have been trying to reform [the local church institution] for two thousand years, and the result is almost always the same – a new system emerges to replace the old, but it eventually becomes a substitute of its own [for an individual's relationship with Jesus]. Have you ever noticed that those who share your hunger [for Jesus] don't share your passion to reform the machinery?*"

(Jacobsen & Coleman, 2006: 150)

Brown presents a challenge that might be uncomfortable for some to face. He questions what right any Christian has to remain as part of a local church institution that is limiting their obedience to God's spirit in what He may be calling them to do, and goes so far as to question the decency of their actions in deceitfully appearing to provide implicit support for a system they privately oppose:

"*If your traditions stifle the Word of God, why adhere to the traditions? Is it not clear by now that those traditions will not change or go away by themselves? If your structure stands in the way of the Spirit, why remain loyal to the structure? It has been here longer than you have, and if not challenged it will remain here long after you have gone. Why expect a metamorphosis in the establishment now? If your spiritual-political alliances keep you from fulfilling your calling, why maintain the carnal bond? Why perpetuate the sham?*

… Why remain handcuffed to a system and handicapped by a system that is not going to change? And why dishonor the system by staying loyal to it on paper while expressing disrespect and even scorn for its leaders and policies?"

Brown (2002: 186-187)

CHAPTER 23:
WHAT ABOUT "HOME CHURCHES" AS AN ALTERNATIVE?

A theme is emerging, that the more traditional building-based local churches are fundamentally (and fatally) flawed. Of course, they may live on as museums, in honor of the traditions of the men that sustained them, and to the glory of the men who built them (not to the glory of God as so many of their foundation stones proclaim). But before we finally lay "churches" to rest (in whatever form they may appear), some would argue that home churches are a viable alternative to the more conventional building-based local churches. Some see them as being fresh and new, while others see them as reflecting the very roots of Christendom.

Frost and Hirsch encourage the use of home churches, particularly as part of church-planting schemes:

> *"We suggest new-church planters ...[target their efforts at suitable individuals that] ... have good reputations, and have influence in the community ... [with the end goal being to] ... start new home-based churches."*

(Frost & Hirsch, 2003: 65)

They see it as essential that members of central local churches also belong to home churches:

> *"All those people who claim St Thomas's as their church <u>must</u> belong to a cell."* [Emphasis mine]

(Frost & Hirsch, 2003: 53)

They also see it as essential that all who are members of home churches attend central "*celebration*" meetings. There are clear aspects of the old hierarchical control appearing here. My interpretation is that the so-called "celebration" meetings are not just for celebration, but also for top-down, hierarchical direction setting, as,

"The celebration is a time for large-scale worship, <u>motivation, and vision casting</u>."
[Emphasis mine]

(Frost & Hirsch, 2003: 53)

In contrast to Frost and Hirsch, who see the two forms of church inextricably linked, Brown takes a few tentative steps to distance home churches from the central local church. Having been hurt (again) in a more traditional local church, Brown and some friends asked,

"Will the Church ever get things right, or will there have to be a whole new expression of the Body, an expression that would focus only on small house meetings without formal leadership or structure?"

(Brown, 2002: 184)

The Lausanne Committee for World Evangelization, in *Christian Witness to the Chinese People*, praised the merits of home churches as observed in China:

"Deprived of pastoral leadership since the mid-1950's, the house churches that emerged are largely a lay movement at the grass roots level, particularly in the villages. As a lay movement, house churches lay greater stress on Christian experience than theological formulation. When they come together, they share their experiences of God and of His Word in their lives. Prayer and fellowship, mutual encouragement and costly discipleship mark their living in koinonia."

(Lausanne Committee for World Evangelization, 1980: 675)

Robinson and Smith see home churches as having value, not just in mission settings for new converts, but as *the* best way to organize church. Whereas Frost and Hirsch saw home churches as an adjunct to the central church, Robinson & Smith see them as the universal, best, and *only* effective means of having 'church'. They could hardly be more glowing in their praise of the virtues of home churches, portraying them as being far superior to traditional institutionalized local churches.

"The term 'small groups' in this context is a generic description of a highly effective function that is universally required. Whatever we call them, people need to be organised into groups of ten to twelve ...

These forums are the natural place to gather new believers ... They are the safest and sanest place for interested people to continue asking questions about the gospel. They are the clearest place to see the gospel dressed in the lives of real people ...

These groups are the best place to keep all of Christ's people focused upon sharing the good news into all of their relationships ...

These groups are the best place to initiate leadership development.

... It is the <u>best</u> place to see how to mobilise people. It is the <u>best</u> place to measure the gifts and roles of every burgeoning leader. It is the <u>first</u> place that every new leader ought to start ..." [Emphasis mine]

(Robinson & Smith, 2003: 173-174)

Jacobsen and Coleman portray home church meetings where the *real* interaction happens before and after the formal bits of the evening, hence raising questions on the effectiveness of home churches.

> *"Let me guess … When you first get together there is a lot of energy and excitement. But about the time you start the meeting, things get awkward. Even your sharing seems a bit forced and artificial. When you finally end the meeting, the energy and excitement return as people pick up and leave. Is that close?"*
>
> (Jacobsen & Coleman, 2006: 105-106)

They then go on to challenge our motives as individuals. Are we going to a home church (or any church for that matter) to seek the support from others that we should be getting from God?

> *"Meeting together isn't the problem, but it's easy to get stuck in a way of meeting that is artificial and counterproductive.*
>
> *… [Meeting in a home can be more relational, but] it can also be a less-controlled replication of the same dynamic [that is otherwise encountered in building-based church settings]. We're trying to get from our brothers and sisters what we're not finding in Father himself. That's a recipe for disaster. Nothing we as believers can ever do together will make up for the lack of our own relationship with God. When we put the church in that place, we make it an idol and others will always end up disappointing us."*
>
> (Jacobsen & Coleman, 2006: 106)

But perhaps, if our motives are right, then home church is still OK? Or will any attempt to bring the organizational constructs of the building-based local church into the home church simply get in the way of the deep and meaningful relationships?

> *"… the more organization you bring to church life, the less life it will contain. … Instead of trying to build a house church, learn to love one another and share each other's journeys. Who is [Jesus] asking you to walk alongside right now and how can you encourage them? I love it when brothers and sisters choose to be intentional in sharing God's life together in a particular season. So, yes, experiment with community together. You'll learn a lot. Just avoid the desire to make it contrived, exclusive, or permanent. Relationships don't work that way."*
>
> (Jacobsen & Coleman, 2006: 110)

Oliver and Thwaites express the view that "*gathered*" church is fundamentally wrong, whether in a building or in a home. A repeat of an earlier quotation follows:

> *"We have held the gathered church, under the wing of its leaders <u>in a building or a house</u>, to be the church proper and the church central. I remember speaking to one fellow who had been taught that the church was only the church if it gathered, because that's what he had been told the word 'ekklesia' means. I checked with him to make sure by asking: 'So if you are not physically proximate to another member of your*

congregation, then you are not church?' He stuck to his guns and so I asked one more question: 'Where does the church go when it's not meeting, does it disappear? If so, it must be one of the weakest things on earth.' He had no answer. Your doctrine of church may not be that strict, but this demonstrates the kind of thinking that is out there. Hence the need to look again at what '[God's] church' is and is not." [Emphasis mine]

(Oliver & Thwaites, 2001: 169)

As quoted earlier, Brown goes further, explicitly stating that churches in a home are still just churches, and simply carry the old problems to a new setting:

"The simple act of moving from a big meeting in a 'church' building into a small meeting in a home will not change us in the least. The physical structure in which we meet is not the primary issue. The shift in our mentality is the primary issue. Do we go to church or are we the Church? Do we go to a building to watch a religious performance – or, if we are more spiritual, to participate in a religious service – or are we salt and light in our communities, fishers of lost men and women, witnesses for Jesus on a divine mission to glorify God by life or by death?"

(Brown, 2002: 45)

"... for many it is difficult to leave the security of the camp and the safety of the fold, whether that fold is a denomination, an independent congregation, a small house church or even a family tradition. Anything can become part of 'the establishment,' part of that which resists biblical change, part of 'the system.' "

(Brown, 2002: 190)

"... house meetings can be just as ineffective as liturgical services ... "

(Brown, 2002: 192)

In conclusion, to whatever level a home church reflects the traditional building-based church (its operations, methods, aims, leadership or functions), nothing significant has been gained. And by the time we cull away the last vestiges of the church institution, we might discover that we've got nothing left, other than relationships. And relationships don't need "home church", or "cell groups" as they are sometimes called. In fact, home church would only get in the way of relationships.

CHAPTER 24:
WE NEED MORE THAN A FACELIFT

Over the previous chapters, we have progressively challenged many of the core traditions that some follow as if they are mandates from God. We now pull together this thinking and reach some provocative conclusions.

Time to get real

Frost and Hirsch describe the experience of some Catholic nuns living and ministering in a housing estate. But even though the nuns do not see their home in the estate as "church", their links with a traditional denomination and the way they express their faith in this setting still ends up with the perception by the *people* that their apartment is an expression of the local church. You can't take the old ways, simply relocate them, and expect them to metamorphose.

> "While the [Catholic] sisters resist calling what they're doing 'church,' the rest of the community clearly identify the nuns' apartment as their chapel."
>
> (Frost & Hirsch, 2003: 24)

You can take a local church, and repackage it, but no matter how it is rewrapped, it is still a local church. If something waddles like a duck, quacks like a duck and swims like a duck, it probably is a duck even if it is disguised. And repackaging a church doesn't change it.

> "… Edward De Bono makes the seemingly self-evident observation that you cannot dig a hole in a different place by digging more in the same place. … This is similar to Einstein's remark about the impossibility of problem solving by using the same type of consciousness that created the problem in the first instance. It is also sometimes called organizational insanity – the belief that you can get significantly different results by doing the same thing 'better.' And yet this is precisely what we do all the time. Surely

Christendom has been worked and reworked and tweaked every which way possible, and yet we still persist in doing it the same way, only 'better.'"

(Frost & Hirsch, 2003: 196)

Words like "revolutionary", "radical", and "fundamentalist" tend to have negative connotations in the minds of many people. When we see news footage of radical fundamentalists who are willing to kill for their beliefs, the rejection of such attitudes is not only understandable, but appropriate. However, what the world needs, perhaps more than ever, are radical Christians who are willing to give their lives in sacrificial and loving service to others, as led by God.

Least needed are more unquestioning followers of a human leader. But we do need compassionate, brave followers of Christ who are willing to challenge the assumptions and belief systems of this sick world and sick churches who pretend to be a vibrant alternative to the world's systems.

It is blatantly insufficient to simply recoat the tomb of Christian church traditions with a nice clean coat of paint. It would be a bit like whitewashing a sepulcher.

"The old form has to die a death: it cannot dress up in suit and tie and move its business into the church as fullness."

(Oliver & Thwaites, 2001: 99)

But we don't want to run full steam ahead after any person's radical ideas. Each one of us needs to personally seek God's wisdom for our role in His strategy. And the place to start is humble prayer, recognizing that each of us individually needs His direction.

"We have lost the eternal youthfulness of Christianity and have aged into calculating manhood. We seldom pray in earnest for the extraordinary, the limitless, the glorious. We seldom pray with real confidence for any good to the realisation of which we cannot imagine a way. And yet we suppose ourselves to believe in an infinite Father."

(Taylor & Taylor, 1918: 348)

Rick Joyner has his fans and his critics. Independent of what view you may hold of him as an author, let us look at his book, *The Final Quest*, where he draws an analogy between the Civil War in America and the emerging struggles within the Church. He stresses the need for warfare. He identifies the cause as being a struggle for freedom from slavery. He clarifies that the real enemies are the church institutions and traditions, not the people that currently lead them. Given that he is himself a church leader, perhaps it is not surprising that he sees the problems more with traditions than the leaders who enshrine and perpetuate these traditions. Nonetheless, he warns that we must never accept any compromise with these institutions and traditions:

"... I sat pondering this dream. Alarmingly, certain events and conditions in the church had seemed to parallel just what I had seen ... I was then reminded of Abraham Lincoln. The only way that he could become 'the Emancipator,' and preserve the Union, was to be willing to fight a Civil War. He not only had to fight it, but fight with the

> *resolution not to compromise until the victory was complete. He also had to have the grace to fight the bloodiest war in [American] history without 'demonizing' the enemy with propaganda. If he had done that he might have been able to galvanize the resolve of the North much faster, and win a quicker military victory, but it would have made the reunion after the war much more difficult. Because he was truly fighting to preserve the Union, he never made the men and women of the South the enemy, but rather the evil that had them in bondage.*
>
> *A great spiritual civil war now looms before the church. Many will do everything that they can to avoid it. This is understandable, and even noble. However, compromise will never maintain a lasting peace. It will only make the ultimate conflict that much more difficult when it comes, and it will come.*
>
> *… The main issue will be slavery versus freedom. … Just as the American Civil War at times looked like it would destroy the entire nation, what is coming upon the church will at times appear as if it will be the end of the church. … The church will not be destroyed, but the institutions and doctrines that have kept men in spiritual slavery will be."*
>
> (Joyner, 1996: 36-37)

Many people believe we must not attack church institutions, as they hold the view that we might be guilty of attacking the very thing that *God* established. Let's take a look at careful look at this idea.

Firstly, it has been clarified that the heart of many practices in local churches is nothing more than the traditions of *men*. Jesus did not say "go and set up churches". But even *if* the local church structures were God-ordained, it wouldn't mean God cannot engage us in bringing about some change. McManus points out that this is exactly what God, through His Son, did to the institution of Judaism that He had founded because men demanded to have an intermediary:

> *"Two thousand years ago God started a revolt against the religion He started. So don't ever put it past God to cause a groundswell movement against churches and Christian institutions that bear His name. If He was willing to turn Judaism upside down, don't think for a moment our institutions are safe from a divine revolt. I am convinced that even now there are multitudes of followers of Jesus Christ who are sick and tired of the church playing games and playing down the call of God. My travels only confirm that the murmurings of revolution are everywhere. I am convinced that there is an uprising in the works and that no one less than God is behind it."*
>
> (McManus, 2005: 114)

We must be warned that if we are willing to challenge the system, we will face opposition. But the choice is obedience to God or submission to the human forces that pervade churches.

> *"… the enemy will essentially leave you alone if you are domesticated. He will not waste his energy destroying a civilized religion. If anything, he uses his energy to*

promote such activity. Religion can be one of the surest places to keep us from God. When our faith becomes refined, it is no longer dangerous to the dark kingdom.

Barbarians, on the other hand, are not to be trusted. They respect no borders that are established by powers or principalities. They have but one King, one Lord, and one mission. They are insolent enough to crash the gates of hell. For the sake of others, they are willing to risk their own lives and thrust themselves into the midst of peril."

(McManus, 2005: 128)

Some concrete steps to freedom

True freedom requires that we stake our claim and act on it.

Ask the hard questions

Very early in this book, we looked at cult-like behavior. One strong theme in cults and in more "regular" churches that exhibit some aspects of cult-like behavior is the suppression of questioning. If anyone tells you to stop asking questions, one immediate response should be to say, "Why?" In this one word, you are asking a question (the very thing you have been told not to do), as well as challenging their authority to gag you. But whether or not it is tolerated, asking questions is healthy and freeing. We don't need permission.

"Our need is for men and women who are free with the freedom of Christ, free to ask the awkward questions that have occurred to no one else, and free to come up with startling answers that no one else has dared to give."

(Taylor, 1975: 69)

Stop using old-church terminology.

There are two mythological concepts that are embedded in the language of church life. The first reflects a view that the church buildings are the location of the Church, and the second that the local church leaders are somehow especially "holy".

"... just as the New Testament does not recognize the concept of special holy buildings, instead calling all of us to be the temple of the Lord ... so also the New Testament does not recognize the concept of special holy people ... instead calling all of us to be holy."

(Brown, 2002: 52)

As quoted earlier, Brown quotes Professor Hendrik Kraemer as saying,

"The fundamental ideas of the Reformation promised to inaugurate a radical change in the whole conception and place of the laity. Luther, at a decisive moment, rejected obedience to the [Catholic] Church as embodied in the hierarchical authority of the Pope, in the name of obedience to the Word of God. ... The idea of the clergy as such was rejected. In principle the distinction of 'clergy' and 'laity' fell away ..."

(Brown, 2002: 211)

A friend wrote a challenging article titled, *Call No Man Father*, in which she confronts the practice of addressing church leaders with special titles. One step towards freedom is to follow her advice. If we are speaking to or about a member of the church leadership, we can simply use their given name. In some local church circles the people are familiar with introductions like, "This is pastor Jo, and here's elder Terry", but how about "I'd like you to meet plumber Alex and my close friend, accountant Sam"?

That is blatantly stupid. So let's cut the rubbish, and drop the titles for the church leaders, too. So if you had met with Joseph Ratzinger or Jorge Bergoglio, Popes from the Catholic Church, you should have greeted them as Joseph or Jorge, not as Holy Father, Your Holiness or any other such title— if they are Christians in the Body of Christ they are just members on the same level as you and me. And if you are meeting with a pastor from a local Pentecostal church, if his mum named him Fred, why not call him Fred instead of Pastor Fred?

If we stop using terms of endearment and authority we will be reinforcing our freedom to treat them as equals before God. My late mother was a nurse, and encountered some well-to-do patients who saw themselves as being somehow above the rest of humanity. At the risk of sounding crude, she apparently told one of them that when it came to cleaning their rear end after they've used the bed-pan, they all looked pretty much alike!

Another difficult challenge is what we do with the term "church". For some it means the local assembly of Christians in a particular denomination, or even just the building ("Can you please give me directions to the Baptist Church?"). For others it means the whole Body of Christ, including people from the past and people yet to be born.

As quoted earlier, Jacobsen and Coleman sheds some light on the topic when they state,

> *"Asking me where I go to church is like asking me where I go to Jacobsen. How do I answer that? I am a Jacobsen, and where I go a Jacobsen is. 'Church' is that kind of word. It doesn't identify a location or an institution. It describes a people and how they relate to one another. If we lose sight of that, our understanding of the church will be distorted and we'll miss out on much of its joy."*
>
> (Jacobsen & Coleman, 2006: 170)

Don't financially support the old ways

God doesn't need local church buildings for His work to be effective.

> *"[The outpouring of the Spirit on the day of Pentecost, as recorded in Acts] ... came with such strength that it captured the attention of multitudes in Jerusalem. There had been no radio, television, or newspaper announcements. No flyers were handed out. In fact, no meeting was even scheduled. Yet God so mightily manifested Himself that multitudes heard the anointed words of Peter and thousands were saved. This meeting was not held in a church, auditorium, or stadium, but rather outdoors in the streets."*
>
> (Bevere, 1997: 108)

When we look at the teaching of Christ, it is even more evident that He does not need buildings for ministry, and that in fact the living 'Body of Christ' is the "building" He chooses to occupy.

> *"Jesus, the Lamb of God, hung on the cross, shedding every drop of His innocent, royal blood for us. Once this was done, the veil of the temple was torn in two from top to bottom (Luke 23:45). God moved out! God's glory would never again be revealed in a building made with hands. Soon His glory would be revealed in the temple He had always longed to dwell in."*
>
> (Bevere, 1997: 61)

We contrast Jesus' instruction to go into all the world with what is typically practiced in Christendom today:

> *"Many Christians feel that church affairs are something quite beyond them. They have no intimate concern in them, because in the first place they have their 'minister' who is specially responsible for all such affairs, and then they have a great church building which seems so remote from their homes, and where matters are conducted so systematically and with such precision that one feels overpowered and bound in spirit."*
>
> (Brown, 2002: 46)

Frost and Hirsch cuttingly summarize the problem with local church buildings:

> *"In his classic 1975 book, The Problem of Wineskins, Howard Snyder writes that church buildings attest to five facts about the Western church: its immobility, inflexibility, lack of fellowship, pride, and class divisions. 'The gospel says 'Go,' but our church buildings say, 'Stay.' The gospel says, 'Seek the lost,' but our churches say, 'Let the lost seek the church.' "*
>
> (Frost & Hirsch, 2003: 69)

They go further to expose the error not only with "church" buildings, but with the special class of people who act as church leaders and who are often labeled "clergy".

> *"... the Christendom-mode of church has framed us and set us up for failure. Christendom is always associated with buildings, Sundays, and clergy! Always and everywhere. Yet the New Testament church had none of these."*
>
> (Frost & Hirsch, 2003: 193)

If Jesus truly is our Lord, then it follows that He has rights to our assets—our time, our skills, and our money. God can use our assets as He wishes. However, this doesn't mean we unthinkingly give our money to every "Christian" or non-Christian cause we encounter. It is our individual responsibility to discern when, if and how to give to a particular cause. And supporting a fund for building a local church "to the glory of God" or funding the salary of professional church leaders is not part of the scheme.

Take a break from "church" to gain a perspective

Adrian Plass' novel, *Stress Family Robinson*, tells the story of a family whose teenage son has ceased going to the local church, much to the disappointment of the parents. The son, Jack, explains why, and suggests that he needed a break from the institution to be able to see it more clearly:

> *"You know how in the old days the army used to dress up for battle in just about the most unsuitable gear you could possibly imagine? Most of it was much more decorative than practical, and those poor old foot soldiers in particular must have got so hot and uncomfortable ... They were trapped, really, in a load of traditional stuff that had no connection at all with what was going on, or the job that actually had to be done. But I don't suppose it occurred to many of them to complain about it, because that was just the way things were, and you'd have needed to be a real lateral thinker to picture it any differently. Well, I began to feel a bit like that in our church. It wasn't that I stopped believing in God or Jesus. ...*
>
> *I just needed some time to see what would happen if I took the old traditional uniform off and wore something more comfortable – more suitable, if you like. After all, the British army did that a long time ago – changed gear, I mean. I'd hate to think the church hasn't caught up with the army!"*
>
> (Plass, 1995: 216-217)

Oliver and Thwaites likewise suggest that time may be required to get one's bearings again after perhaps years or decades in a local church:

> *"... many, after twenty years of meetings had to take a break for a while to locate themselves again. Dangerous? Perhaps, but to my mind, not as dangerous as another twenty years of meetings attended by souls who have lost track of themselves along the way. True to human form, these people still talked to other saints, they still had coffee with a friend, and some even began to pray with their spouse. They met, but just didn't have a guitar in their midst when they did."*
>
> (Oliver & Thwaites, 2001: 177)

Some of these authors are implying that, following a break from "church", one may in fact return but with a new perspective, and settle back into the institution. My argument in this book is that, once free, you would do well to not return to the institutional way of Christian life. But if you are going to break free of the institution, there has to be a first time when you *don't* turn up! Seriously—why not next Sunday?

After encountering this challenge, a friend drew an analogy: Some smokers can give up smoking by going "cold turkey". Others struggle and may take a few attempts. Perhaps it may be similar for you with breaking free of the chains tying you to the local church. Some may be able to walk away and experience the fresh air of freedom immediately. For others, it may involve a series of small steps. I cannot tell you what to do. But I can suggest to you that, for some at least, an immediate and total break may be an option.

And what might the life of freedom look like? Read on.

SECTION 8:

SIGNPOSTS TO A BETTER WAY

Some of my friends have puzzled over what Christendom might look like if we no longer have local churches as the central expression of Christian life. Many agree with the condemnation of much of we see in "church". They also agree with many of the principles of freedom such as the individual's right (and responsibility) to follow God rather than being in slavery to the traditions of men. But they are uncomfortable with taking the big step away from the known. Unlike Abraham of old, they will not launch out into the unknown. They want a vision of what the replacement structure might look like before they abandon the "local church" ship. They state that we can't just burn the old ways without giving hope for a new and better way. One of the sticking points for them is that they are still looking for a structure. But God will not be put in a box. His call has always been a call to faith.

A number of authors provide snippets of an alternative to the traditional church practices. The catalyst for much of this thinking lies not in books on church reform written by pastors for pastors, in a Western society setting. Instead, some refreshingly different perspectives have come out of the thinking on "missions" that, if applied courageously to the situation "back home", would result in a revolution on how we live as the Body of Christ. Ministry becomes the domain and responsibility of *all* Christians, as led by the Holy Spirit, rather than deferring to church leaders as intermediaries, teachers, or "oversight". Fellowship occurs naturally as people with overlapping ministries interact. And the only "structure" needed is *God's* strategy, calling each of us to participate, even if we don't yet see God's "big picture".

Each of these facets of fellowship, leadership, and ministry are viewed in much more detail. It is new thinking on these fronts that will break the constraints and patterns that have enslaved and ensnared Christendom for far too long.

I do not mean to be irreverent, but I do make one assumption—that God is smarter than you or me. What I am saying is that many of the traditions of men reflect our own limitations. For example, we have hierarchies because *no* one man can directly lead the whole world-wide show, be conscious of what is happening everywhere at the moment (let alone have knowledge of what is yet to happen), and have the power to change history. So, we form a team to spread the responsibility, but all we end up with is a collection of fallible people with a jumble of ideas, and substituting our relationship with God for a relationship with them.

To put it very bluntly, if God is no more knowledgeable or powerful than I am, I don't want to follow Him. But given that He *does* have abilities far beyond our comprehension, we can and should be willing to trust Him to see the big picture and to direct His people as He sees fit, without having to get a leader's permission or each other's permission.

So here's the deal. If you believe that God is no better than you or a leader, I suggest you forget reading the rest of this book and just get on with managing your own life (or continue to let your pastor or leader run it for you!) and wear the consequences. But if you believe God *is* capable of and *wants* to provide direction, then let's look at what the

Body of Christ might look like if we *really* trusted Him rather than the church leaders or traditions of our comfortable, familiar denomination.

Sometimes God does give us a vision of what lies ahead. The spies who went into the Promised Land came back with a clear picture of the benefits of moving ahead. But they also brought back reports of some of the dangers of moving into new territory, and it was fear of these very challenges that held them back.

Sometimes God calls us to move even if we have no knowledge of the future. Much of Abraham's life reflects obedience without clear, detailed vision. Hudson Taylor perhaps drew some parallels with Abraham, moving in faith into the unknown.

Below we try to see if perhaps God may have given us some insight into what lies ahead, or to determine if we simply have to make a leap of faith.

CHAPTER 25:
NATURAL FELLOWSHIP

Setting the scene

Rinehart explains the necessity of fellowship:

> *"Christ said the world would recognize us as being His by the way we treat one another. Even as I write those words, I am convicted by their simple clarity and weightiness. Christ places such an emphasis on our relationships with one another that He makes them the litmus test of true spirituality. It is amazing and challenging. Clearly, He meant for our relationship to each other, and our willingness to serve each other, to be the greatest apologetic around.*
>
> *Building authentic community in the life of the body is not an addendum to the ministry; it is not something we hope will happen when there is time and energy available. Rather, it is the lifeblood of our ministry."*
>
> (Rinehart, 1998: 156)

Yet questions such as, "Where do you fellowship?" are at the heart of much misunderstanding. Such questions assume that fellowship occurs at a special place, with special people, namely the local church. In spite of the fact that local-church fellowship can often be shallow, this perception persists in the minds of many. Some go so far as to see it as an undesirable outcome to have any outreach or fellowship in other settings such as parachurch organizations. Frost and Hirsch reflect this thinking when they state,

> *"... the separation between the missioning and the worshiping communities within the church has been one of the tragedies of Christianity."*
>
> (Frost & Hirsch, 2003: 78)

Those who think in the way Frost and Hirsch seem to suggest we should think, want those with life and vision, who are operating outside the strangling confines of local church institutions, brought back into the fold. What they want is for this life to be transplanted into the dead institutions, not realizing that the very act of forcing these initiatives to align with local church governance will kill the vision rather than resuscitate the church institution.

Thankfully, there are alternatives to fellowship as the sole preserve of local churches. But before we look at ways to experience healthy fellowship outside of the local church, we must look briefly, but boldly, into some confronting, fundamental questions such as, "Why do you or I seek fellowship?" and, "Can we flourish and grow if God calls us apart from other Christians for a season?"

Philip Yancey's writings reveal from his own life and the lives of others, the reality of some being called away from the fellowship of others for a period. We should not be surprised at this. Looking back to our foundations, this same aspect has been revealed in the life of many including Abraham, Moses, Paul and, of course, Jesus Himself.

There is the reality that we are not designed to be hermits. Conversely, we must not become totally dependent on others for our survival and direction. In the words of a friend of mine, we all must be willing to "dig our own well", putting effort in to seeking God's day-by-day call on our own life. Bill speaks of a balance.

> "A.A. experience has taught us we cannot live alone with our pressing problems and the character defects which cause or aggravate them [but] ... We cannot wholly rely on friends to solve all our difficulties. A good adviser will never do all our thinking for us. He knows that each final choice must be ours. He will therefore help to eliminate fear, expediency, and self-deception, so enabling us to make choices which are loving, wise, and honest."

(Bill, 1967: 83)

Fellowship at the coal face of life

There is a radical alternative to institutional "fellowship". It is amazing in its simplicity. As we are obedient to God's daily leading in our life, we will find ourselves interacting with those in need, and perhaps with others who give their lives to being God's agent to meet those needs. We can experience real fellowship as we work and minister together for however long God calls us to walk together.

Nee stressed the need for fellowship to flow from vibrant life in Christ, not from a pre-ordained structure:

> "You cannot take a group of men and put God's principles of fellowship into it. Fellowship in Christ is a quite natural, effortless thing because it stems from the fact of the living Body of Christ, and there is therefore no need to plan or organize it. It flows spontaneously when our hearts are, as was Abraham's, 'unto the Lord'."

(Nee, 1967: 42)

He also warned of the folly of simply trying to follow a formula:

> *"But let us be careful. Is God's house a principle to be followed, or a life to be lived? Is it something to copy, or something to be? It would be easy, having seen the value of life together, to determine at all costs to apply the principles by which it should work. But this would not achieve the result. We must have the life of the Body, the shared life of Christ that comes from Him as Head, before we can abide by its principles. They cannot just be learned."*

(Nee, 1967: 40)

Even more fundamental than fellowship with fellow travelers is our fellowship with God. There may be times when we cannot have access to those who understand our journey; or in the extreme, we may be totally isolated from all other people, yet we can never be denied fellowship with God.

> *"The Lone member at sea, the A.A. at war in a far land – all these members know that they belong to A.A.'s world-wide community, that theirs is only a physical separation, that their fellows may be as near as the next port of call. Ever so importantly, they are certain that God's grace is just as much with them on the high seas or the lonely outpost as it is with them at home."*

(Bill, 1967: 9)

> *"Perhaps one of the greatest rewards of meditation and prayer is the sense of belonging that comes to us. We no longer live in a completely hostile world. We are no longer lost and frightened and purposeless.*
>
> *The moment we catch even a glimpse of God's will, the moment we begin to see truth, justice, and love as the real and eternal things in life, we are no longer deeply disturbed by all the seeming evidence to the contrary that surrounds us in purely human affairs. We know that God lovingly watches over us. We know that when we turn to Him, all will be well with us, here and hereafter."*

(Bill, 1967: 117)

We can find fellowship with those who travel beside us and, as God leads, we can share our lives, and invite others to share theirs (albeit with care and wisdom).

> *"When we reached A.A., and for the first time in our lives stood among people who seemed to understand, the sense of belonging was tremendously exciting. We thought the isolation problem had been solved.*
>
> *But we soon discovered that, while we weren't alone any more in a social sense, we still suffered many of the old pangs of anxious apartness. Until we had talked with complete candor of our conflicts, and had listened to someone else do the same thing, we still didn't belong."*

(Bill, 1967: 228)

Circumstances may deny us the common ties between people such as family bonds, but as long as we reach out and serve, we will find we are not alone.

> *"What can be said of many A.A. members who, for a variety of reasons, cannot have a family life? ... Surrounded by so many A.A. friends, the so-called loners tell us they no longer feel alone. In partnership with others – women and men – they can devote themselves to any number of ideas, people, and constructive projects. ... We daily see such members render prodigies of service, and receive great joys in return."*
>
> (Bill, 1967: 53)

Within the context of Alcoholics Anonymous groups, Bill advises that people support what is happening locally but also avoid becoming self-centered.

> *"While each A.A.'s interest should center principally in those about him and upon his own group, it is both necessary and desirable that we all get a larger vision of the whole."*
>
> (Bill, 1967: 297)

Far too many Christians have only experienced "fellowship" within the walls of the local church, or more realistically, with only a few selected ones from that church. Some seem to feel that that is enough, and go no further. Others share God's love with those they meet in the paths of their normal daily routine, and experience a richer and wider level of fellowship. Again, the danger can be a contentment that prevents us reaching even further. Bill challenges us to press on and discover all that God may have for us in the wider community. Of course, our motive is not just to feel good with an increased circle of friends, but that we may share hope with others. If God permits us to enjoy the wider circles of involvement, that's a bonus.

CHAPTER 26:
FREEDOM FROM STRUCTURES

Historical snippets of ministry without organization

When we look at history, we can see glimpses of what ministry might be like if it were freed from leaders, church institutions, and their constraints. Even though the Reformation of Luther's day resulted in many Protestant denominations structured around the local church, in its early days Luther's example in Germany demonstrated what could happen when men let God direct, without the constraints of structures.

> *"So the Reformation spread through Germany far and near in simple, natural fashion, without any attempt at preconcerted action, or any design to impose a new form of Church government, or a new and uniform order of public worship."*
>
> (Lindsay 1996: 129).

Luther's story may have been an unconscious outworking of the principles of freedom. In the beginning, Hudson Taylor's actions were likewise not based around structures. He consciously articulated the need for individuals to rise up and follow God's call, even if an organizational structure was not present to provide support. (James) Hudson Taylor's own words, recorded in his article *The Call to Service*, express a simple confidence in God rather than in structures:

> *"I saw that the apostolic plan was not to raise ways and means, but to go and do the work, trusting in His sure Word ...*
>
> *'And how do you propose to go [to China]?' [a minister of religion] inquired. I answered that I did not at all know; that it seemed to me probable that I should need to do as the Twelve and the Seventy had done in Judea – go without purse or scrip, relying on Him who had called me to supply all my need. Kindly placing his hand upon my shoulder, the minister replied, 'Ah, my boy, as you grow older you will get*

wiser than that. Such an idea would do very well in the days when Christ Himself was on earth, but not now.'

I have grown older since then, but not wiser. I am more than ever convinced that if we were to take the direction of our Master and the assurances He gave to His first disciples more fully as our guide, we should find them to be just as suited to our times as to those in which they were originally given."

(Taylor, J., circa 1865: 241, 238)

It's all about service

Alcoholics Anonymous label themselves as a fellowship, but its lack of structure and control as an organization may surprise many. *Individuals* perform "ministry", not the organization. A.A. groups do exist, but "service" is the *only* reason for these groups to exist, either at the local level or at state, national or international levels. This is not accidental; it is an intentional, clearly stated policy:

"A.A., as such, ought never to be organized; but we may create service boards or committees directly responsible to those they serve."

(AAWS, 1957: 78)

The theory may sound fine, but how does this work in practice? We take Alcoholics Anonymous as a real-life example of the outworking of the principle of groups existing only to serve, starting by observing their style at the local level. The importance of "getting it right" is strongly stated. This is not a matter of a self-interest group existing so the participants can have a bit of fun; for many of those in A.A. the issues are life-and-death. It is essential to get the principles right as to how we relate.

"The moment [outreach work results in formation of] a group, another discovery is made – that most individuals cannot recover unless there is a group. ... It becomes plain that the group must survive or the individual will not."

(AAWS, 1953: 130)

The local A.A. group may have a committee, but it is quite different to many local church committees. The A.A. group is there to serve only the members; many church committees exist to serve the church leaders. The A.A. group is appointed by the members; some church committees are appointed by the church hierarchy. (In fact, the A.A. has no command and control hierarchy.) And A.A. group is there to serve, and nothing more.

"[The committee members in the local group] are servants. Theirs is the sometimes thankless privilege of doing the group's chores. Headed by the chairman, they look after public relations and arrange meetings. Their treasurer, strictly accountable, takes money from the hat that is passed, banks it, pays the rent and other bills, and makes a regular report at business meetings. The secretary sees that literature is on the table, looks after the phone-answering service, answers the mail, and sends out notices of meetings. Such are the simple services that enable the group to function.

The committee gives no spiritual advice, judges no one's conduct, issues no orders. Every one of them may be promptly eliminated at the next election if they try this. And so they make the belated discovery that they are really servants, not senators. These are universal experiences. Thus throughout A.A. does the group conscience decree the terms upon which its leaders shall serve."

(AAWS, 1953: 134)

A.A. has local groups, but also has more centralized service groups. The central groups are a point of contact for anyone wishing to discover more, to buy literature, or to find a local group. Again, the principles are the same; it's just that the services provided are typically those that a local group may not be in a position to provide. Some simple examples include the production of publication material and the handling of correspondence from those who seek initial advice.

"When Dr. Bob and I realized on that fall day in 1937 that some two-score of us had recovered from alcoholism, we at once asked ourselves, 'How can this experience be shared? How can the word be spread?' … The number of alcoholics in the world who wanted to get well was reckoned in millions. … Word-of-mouth communication with the few alcoholics we could contact … would be not only slow but dangerous; dangerous because the recovery message in which we now had such high confidence might soon be garbled and twisted beyond recognition. Clearly our budding society and its message would have to be publicized."

(AAWS, 1957: 144)

"Pawing at random through the incoming mass of heartbreaking appeals, we found ourselves crying. What on earth could we do with them? We were really swamped.

We saw that we must have help. So we rounded up every A.A. woman and every A.A. wife who could use a typewriter. The upper floor of the Twenty-Fourth Street Club was converted into an emergency headquarters. For days Ruth and the volunteers tried to answer the ever increasing tide of mail. They were almost tempted into using form letters. But experience had shown that this would not do at all. A warm personal communication must be sent to every prospect and his family. The peak of the flood finally passed, but the regular correspondence traffic through Headquarters remained so great that we saw we would have to have permanent paid help. Volunteers could not handle the situation."

(AAWS, 1957: 191-192)

Some of the quotations shared above highlight the very real ability for people to be effective with no or minimal organization and structure. Whatever the differences between the examples cited, some themes were common—that each individual must respond to God rather than looking to an organization for support, and that where some organization might prove helpful, it was to be as little as possible, and only to serve those on the front line, not to direct them.

CHAPTER 27:
A CASE STUDY OF AN "ORGANIZATION" THAT ISN'T

We continue to look in more depth at the A.A. story. In the early stages of its formation, aspects began to appear that could have led it down the path of so many other "organizations". However, the lessons learned were distilled as guiding principles, and are very instructive if we have the humility to learn from them.

It looks like an organization

In its early days, A.A. was dependent on its founders for direction. Over time, the organization grew, but still retained this form of governance. Bill observed,

> "The main link between our world services and A.A. itself had been Dr. Bob, our secretarial staff, and me."

(AAWS, 1957: 210)

However, one of the founders was found to have a life-threatening illness.

> "... Dr. Bob had been stricken by an ailment that we all knew might prove fatal."

(AAWS, 1957: 209)

This forced a rethink. It was at this stage that elements of conventional institutions began to appear. Traditional boards with trustees were established.

> "Our first Board consisted of five Trustees."

(AAWS, 1957: 152)

Like many organizations, they began to capture in print the essence of their culture. Recommendations on methodologies, programs, steps, and the "traditions" were distilled and set in place for others to follow, and a magazine was initiated to carry the central message to all.

> "... we had enough background ... and at this point we would have to tell how our program for recovery from alcoholism really worked."
>
> (AAWS, 1957: 159)

> "... our literature would have to be as clear and comprehensive as possible. Our steps would have to be more explicit."
>
> (AAWS, 1957: 161)

> "Too many of us in our drinking days have suffered the terrible penalties of proud and angry pursuits to forget them now. These very pains have been the beginning of whatever wisdom we have since incorporated in A.A.'s Twelve Traditions."
>
> (AAWS, 1957: 234)

> "... A.A.'s Grapevine [magazine was] ...our biggest and best means of communicating current A.A. thought and experience ..."
>
> (AAWS, 1957: 31)

Based on observations by other authors in different settings, such acts run the risk of turning a dynamic organism into a set-in-stone organization, with the life gone forever. An extract from a more complete quotation appearing in a later section of this book summarizes the danger:

> "When man steps in with his reasons and fears to institutionalize and structure (or even record) that which is meant to flow free and unencumbered, life leaves."
>
> (Buckingham, 1980: 207)

This was not the A.A. experience, but the point is that such actions *could* have easily resulted in fossilization of what was intended to be a vibrant and dynamic ministry.

Not only was the culture of early A.A. practices captured in print, but the organization began to appoint paid staff, acquire real estate, and organize international conferences.

> "Our clubs were paying for caretakers ... Our New York office had just engaged ... a secretary."
>
> (AAWS, 1957: 194-195)

> "In 1940 we saw the establishment of the first clubhouse and the opening of the first rest farm."
>
> (AAWS, 1957: 180)

> "In the summer of 1950 we held our first international convention ... About 3,000 were in attendance."
>
> (AAWS, 1957: 212-213)

The role of A.A.'s principles

Actions as described above are typically hallmarks of a structured, institutionalized organization. And yet A.A. seemed to avoid these dangers. In part, it was the very principles that were captured and articulated that arguably contributed to the organization remaining adaptable and full of life, perhaps in spite of its early initiatives that could have taken it along the "institutionalization" path.

A.A. had recognized that, as a society, and as individuals, weaknesses existed. They assembled and distilled a number of guidelines that had proven helpful, to individuals and to groups.

> *"Our Traditions are a guide to better ways of working and living, and they are also an antidote for our various maladies. The Twelve Traditions are to group survival and harmony what A.A.'s Twelve Steps are to each member's sobriety and peace of mind.*
>
> *But the Twelve Traditions also point straight at many of our individual defects. By implication they ask each of us to lay aside pride and resentment. They ask for personal as well as group sacrifice. They ask us never to use the A.A. name in any quest for personal power or distinction or money."*

(AAWS, 1957: 96)

> *"As we had once struggled and prayed for individual recovery, just so earnestly did we commence to quest for the principles through which A.A. itself might survive."*

(AAWS, 1953: 130-131)

It is absolutely vital to note that the resultant principles, while promoting health of individuals and the group, were never to be enforced as "law". Perhaps it was this very flexibility and respect for individuals and groups to express themselves in different ways that protected A.A. from becoming a rigid, legalistic organization.

> *"In late 1945 a good A.A. friend suggested that all this mass of experience might be codified into a set of principles which could offer tested solutions to all our problems of living and working together and of relating our society to the world outside. If we had become sure enough of where we really stood on such matters as membership, group autonomy, singleness of purpose, nonendorsement of other enterprises, professionalism, public controversy, and anonymity in its several aspects, then such a set of principles could be written. A code of traditions could not, of course, ever become rule or law. But it might act as a guide for our Trustees, Headquarters people, and especially for A.A. groups with growing pains."*

(AAWS, 1957: 203)

Some of the core A.A. principles can be assembled into two groups, namely principles on simplicity in many aspects of life, and principles that protected the emerging organization from many of the pitfalls observed elsewhere when leaders abuse their authority.

The principles of simplicity

One of the two key founders of A.A., Bob, saw "simplicity" as a core virtue, and saw any practice that deviated from simplicity as a threat to the health of A.A. Maybe other organizations and ministries would do well to heed his advice.

> *"... I took my leave of Dr. Bob, knowing that the following week he was to undergo a very serious operation. ... We both knew this might well be the last [time we had together] ... [I recall the] wonderful, old, broad smile was on his face as he said almost jokingly, 'Remember, Bill, let's not louse this thing up. Let's keep it simple!' I turned away, unable to say a word. That was the last time I ever saw him."*
>
> (AAWS, 1957: 214)

Simplicity with money

On the topic of money, it is instructive to look at the teaching and practices of Jesus. It was a topic He confronted in a manner that was surprising to many. He warned of the difficulty of wealthy people truly entering the kingdom of God. He sent disciples out with a bare minimum of provisions. He taught that we should not worry about money, as surely the Father who cares for a sparrow can and will care for us.

It may have been possible for A.A. to follow the path of many churches and make sure that a large and continuing supply of funds was ensured. Some early A.A. initiates certainly were headed in that direction. At one fund raising function, the representative of a very wealthy businessman met with some A.A. members. He was very impressed by what A.A. was doing, and had heard of the expressed need for funds to build hospitals, print literature, and so on. Yet rather than giving funds, he confronted the A.A. people with the challenge:

> *"Won't money spoil this thing?"*
>
> (AAWS, 1957: 149)

Perhaps this response was providential; A.A. certainly saw it as pivotal in steering them away from focusing on money instead of focusing on ministry.

The apostle Paul teaches that the love of money is the source of evil. It is not *money* that is the problem, but the *love* of it. Paul also teaches that we should strive to be contented with what we have. Enough is enough.

A.A. also saw the need for a balance. It was impractical to have no money, and it was dangerous to have more than absolutely needed. As quoted earlier,

> *"The conservatives said, 'Why tempt ourselves with money? We don't need it. We can meet in homes and no group will have to have a treasury. Why do we need books and offices and world services? ...' The radicals thought otherwise: 'Not only do we need essential services, we need plenty more. We need hospitals, paid therapists, traveling lecturers, rehabilitation centers, and heaven knows what else. It is going to take millions. ...'*

> *After a while we awoke to the pleasant fact that A.A. as such was not going to require much money after all. ... Not only would we have the least possible service organization; we would use the least possible money. For us this does not mean no money at all. But it does mean the least possible money to do the job well. It is in this sense that A.A. has declared for the principle of corporate poverty. It is a chief safeguard of our future."*
>
> (AAWS, 1957: 110-111)

> *"... our Trustees wrote a bright page of A.A. history. They declared for the principle that A.A. must always stay poor. Reasonable running expenses plus a prudent reserve would henceforth be the ... financial policy. Regardless of current needs, the Trustees ... adopted a formal, airtight resolution that [outside donations, e.g. bequests of wills] would be ... declined. At that moment, the principle of corporate poverty was firmly and finally embedded in A.A. tradition."*
>
> (AAWS, 1957: 114)

In case you missed it, I want to highlight the above statement. If someone died and left millions of dollars in their will to Alcoholics Anonymous, the bequest would be refused. I am yet to find a local church that acts on such principles. Yet it seems to me to be much more closely aligned to the financial practices of Jesus and His disciples—carry a bit of money, but just enough and no more.

> *"In another meeting the whole subject of money in A.A. got a most healthy kicking around. A.A.'s principle of 'no compulsory fees or dues' can be construed and rationalized into 'no voluntary group or individual responsibility at all,' and this fallacy was exploded with a bang. There was complete unanimity that through voluntary contributions the legitimate bills of groups, areas, and A.A. as a whole must be paid or we could not properly carry our message. It was agreed that no A.A. treasury ought to get overstuffed or rich. Nevertheless, it was emphasized that the notion of keeping A.A. 'simple' and 'spiritual' by eliminating vital services that happened to cost a little time, trouble, and money was risky and absurd. It was the opinion of the meeting that oversimplification, which might lead us to muff our Twelfth Step work, area-wide and world-wide, could not be called either really simple or really spiritual."*
>
> (AAWS, 1957: 30)

When so many others saw a need for the wider community to fund the support of recovering alcoholics, A.A. saw it differently. They took the position that, for the well-being of the alcoholic, the individual must strive to take responsibility for their own recovery, and that an A.A. group must not be seen as a place to receive handouts.

> *"Self-supporting alcoholics? Whoever heard of such a thing? Yet we find that's what we have to be. This principle is telling evidence of the profound change that A.A. has wrought in all of us. Everybody knows that active alcoholics scream that they have no troubles money can't cure. Always, we've had our hands out. Time out of mind*

we've been dependent upon somebody, usually money-wise. When a society composed entirely of alcoholics says it's going to pay its bills, that's really news."

(AAWS, 1953: 160)

Within A.A., just as the individual was challenged with the responsibility of managing their own finances, the A.A. group also was charged with the responsibility of supporting itself rather than looking to the wider A.A. community.

"Every A.A. group ought to be fully self-supporting, declining outside contributions."

(AAWS, 1957: 78)

Finally, the same principle was applied to the central organization. It was not to look to others for funding.

"Whoever pays the piper is apt to call the tune, and if the A.A. Foundation obtained money from outside sources, its trustees might be tempted to run things without reference to the wishes of A.A. as a whole. ... [But with the alcoholics taking responsibility for expenses] the irresponsible had become responsible ..."

(AAWS, 1953: 164-165)

Simplicity with publicity

As with money, balance was sought in the arena of publicity. It was seen that there was merit in having a simple but well-presented portrayal of A.A. rather than leaving it entirely up to individuals. But again, the goal was simplicity; the central organization was not to become a self-seeking public relations venture promoting its own agenda, but rather a service for the benefit of the individual A.A. members.

"... we found that accurate and effective publicity about A.A. simply does not manufacture itself. Our over-all public relations couldn't be left entirely to chance encounters between reporters and A.A. members, who might or might not be well informed about our fellowship as a whole. This kind of unorganized 'simplicity' often garbled the true story of A.A. ..."

(AAWS, 1957: 35)

Simplicity of purpose

I have seen first-hand examples of local churches that not only try to be everything to their members, but actually teach that there are no needs that cannot be met by their own local expression of church. When someone encountered some "good" teaching elsewhere, in one case, instead of encouraging their members to look to these other sources to enrich their lives, this church acquired the teaching material, then modified it to "improve" it according to their own local prejudices. If someone dared to seek support elsewhere, this was seen as an act of disloyalty. Such attitudes reflect cult-like control of members.

The case above related to members *receiving* support from elsewhere. Another observed unhealthy behavior related to resisting members *providing* support elsewhere. The party line was to teach that all should put their money and time into the home church. So, in such a self-centered church:

- The leaders presented themselves and their chosen teams as all-sufficient.
- The members were expected to *seek* help from no other.
- The members were expected to *give* help to no other (unless authorized by the leaders).

My analysis of the following quotations leads me to conclude that the contrast between the above centralized control and the freedom within A.A. is stark. I am left with the understanding that A.A. does not even try to do anything other than help alcoholics recover, that they recognize the role of others in supporting recovery from alcoholism, and that they encourage their members to contribute in other ministries as each individual feels led:

> "Each group has but one primary purpose – to carry its message to the alcoholic who still suffers."
>
> (AAWS, 1957: 78)

> "… better do one thing supremely well than many badly. That is the central theme of this Tradition [Five]."
>
> (AAWS, 1953: 150)

> "Alcoholics Anonymous has no opinion on outside issues; hence the A.A. name ought never to be drawn into public controversy."
>
> (AAWS, 1957: 78)

> "An A.A. group ought never endorse, finance, or lend the A.A. name to any related facility or outside enterprise, lest problems of money, property, and prestige divert us from our primary purpose."
>
> (AAWS, 1957: 78)

> "In the old days our Foundation … was originally chartered to do everything but lobby for Prohibition. We were chartered for education; we were chartered for research; we could do almost anything. And we used to think we wanted a lot of money to do a lot of things. … If alcoholism could be licked, so could any problem! … Our principles might transform the world! …
>
> Long afterward we saw something else. We saw that the more A.A. minded its own business the greater its general influence would become … [A lot of other groups] began to spring up. They dealt with gambling, divorce, delinquency, dope addiction, mental illness, and the like. They, too, borrowed from A.A., but they made their own adaptations. They worked their own fields, and we did not have to endorse them or tell them how to live."
>
> (AAWS, 1957: 107, 109)

Simplicity in membership

In the very early days, A.A. had started to head down the route trodden by many organizations, especially churches, in having clearly articulated rules on what was required for an individual to be accepted as a member. The following extracts speak for themselves on how radical a change took place:

> "At one time ... every A.A. group had many membership rules. Everybody was scared witless that something or somebody would capsize the boat and dump us all back into the drink. [The central office] asked each group to send in its list of 'protective' regulations. The total list was a mile long. If all those rules had been in effect everywhere, nobody could have possibly have joined A.A. at all, so great was the sum of our anxiety and fear."
>
> (AAWS, 1953: 139-140)

> "Why did A.A. finally drop all its membership regulations? ... Why did we dare to say, contrary to the experience of society and government everywhere, that we would neither punish nor deprive any A.A. of membership, that we must never compel anyone to pay anything, believe anything, or conform to anything?
>
> The answer ... was simplicity itself. At last experience taught us that to take away any alcoholic's full chance was sometimes to pronounce his death sentence ... Who dared to be judge, jury, and executioner of his own sick brother?"
>
> (AAWS, 1953: 141)

An alcoholic with

> "... another addiction even worse ..."
>
> (AAWS, 1953: 142)

approached an A.A. group for help. Some felt the newcomer might bring trouble to the group. Another answered,

> "What we are really afraid of ... is our reputation. We are much more afraid of what people might say than the trouble this strange alcoholic might bring. As we've been talking, five short words have been running through my mind. Something keeps repeating to me, 'What would the Master do?'"
>
> (AAWS, 1953: 142)

> "[The newcomer was accepted and reached scores of others, and] ... never did he trouble anyone with his other difficulty."
>
> (AAWS, 1953: 142)

An atheist A.A. member, "Ed", was outspoken against others who believed in God. He made statements such as,

> "I can't stand this God stuff! It's a lot of malarkey for weak folks."
>
> (AAWS, 1953: 143)

A number of A.A. members took offence, and wanted him forced out of the group, but Ed held them to A.A.'s proclaimed standard of accepting all. Later Ed had a crisis and the "believers" amongst the group failed to help, but,

> "As he tossed on his bed, his hand brushed the bureau near by, touching a book. Opening the book, he read. It was a Gideon Bible. Ed never confided any more of what he saw and felt in that hotel room."
>
> (AAWS, 1953: 145)

But other A.A. members said,

> "What if we had actually succeed in throwing Ed out for blasphemy? What would have happened to him and all the others he later helped?"
>
> (AAWS, 1953: 145)

and then proclaimed that

> "… the hand of Providence early gave us a sign that any alcoholic is a member of our Society when he says so."
>
> (AAWS, 1953: 145)

It is again to be noted that A.A.'s final position on an open and accepting membership can be seen as so different to what is observed in some, if not most local churches.

Simplicity in service

Some may feel concerned that such freedom would result in anarchy. Again, a healthy balance between freedom and respect for the individual and simplicity of core values for the group seems to have been achieved.

> "Yearning for simplicity, we often wonder if we could not do away with many of A.A.'s present services. Wouldn't it be wonderful to have no bother, no politics, no expense, and no responsibility! But this is only a dream about simplicity; it would not be simplicity in fact. Without its essential services, A.A. would soon become a formless, confused, and irresponsible anarchy.
>
> Regarding any particular service, we need to ask only one question: 'Is this or that service really needed?' If it is not, then let it be eliminated. But if it is needed, then maintain it we must or fail in our mission to those who want and seek A.A."
>
> (AAWS, 1957: 140)

A centralized facility to provide printed material is one clear example of the potential of a service to be offered for those who might wish to avail themselves of such assistance.

> "[A.A. members from isolated regions] knew, as few did, how greatly A.A.'s literature and world services could help, for their sobriety had depended heavily upon the Big Book and those upon constant letters that came to them from Headquarters and fellow loners."
>
> (AAWS, 1957: 30)

The principles of delegating authority

A common series of events is observed as A.A. in a locality is formed and starts to grow. One visionary commences the work, and as others gather around this individual, he or she is naturally seen as the "leader".

> "Being the founder, he is at first the boss."
>
> (AAWS, 1953: 133)

The group grows, and responsibilities start to be shared beyond the central control of the original founder. But instead of one founder, there is now one core group! However, sometimes this core group may take the attitude that it has authority over others.

> "Perhaps it would be a good idea if we continue to keep a firm hand on A.A. in this town. After all, we are experienced. Besides, look at all the good we've done these drunks. They should be grateful!"
>
> (AAWS, 1953: 133)

If this attitude continues, the growing group may see itself as the replacement authority and push aside others, including even the founder, especially if the founder is seen as resisting the new directions of the group.

> "If the founder and his friends ... have heavily resisted ... they may be summarily beached."
>
> (AAWS, 1953: 134)

Independent of the rightness or otherwise of the actions of a particular group of people, the founder is responsible for his or her reactions. A warning exists for those founders who find themselves put to one side. They can graciously offer to share their experience, but as an equal, or they can become bitter and continue to fight the inevitable.

> "Let's turn again to the deposed founder and his friends. What becomes of them? ... Ultimately, they divide into two classes known in A.A. slang as 'elder statesmen' and 'bleeding deacons.' The elder statesman is the one who sees the wisdom of the group's decision, who holds no resentment over his reduced status, whose judgment, fortified by considerable experience, is sound, and who is willing to sit quietly on the sidelines patiently awaiting developments. The bleeding deacon is one who is just as surely convinced that the group cannot get along without him, who constantly connives for reelection to office, and who continues to be consumed with self-pity."
>
> (AAWS, 1953: 135)

It is recognized that there may well be a role for a person with vision, compassion and energy to initiate a work.

> "You must remember that every A.A. group starts, as it should, through the efforts of a single man and his friends – a founder and his hierarchy. There is no other way."
>
> (Bill, 1967: 269)

Yet in spite of this observed role of an individual starting a work, it is a sign of immaturity for the founder to hold onto his (or her) role.

> *"But when infancy is over, the original leaders always have to make way for that democracy which springs up through the grass roots and will eventually sweep aside the self-chosen leadership of the past."*
>
> (Bill, 1967: 269)

A.A. recognized that the principle of a local founder handing over to those who follow also applied to the central organization. Just as the local founder must trust the new members, the central organization had to trust its future to the groups.

> *"Everywhere the A.A. groups have taken their service affairs into their own hands. Local founders and their friends are now on the side lines. Why so many people forget that, when thinking of the future of our world services, I shall never understand. … The groups will eventually take over, and maybe they will squander their inheritance when they get it. It is probable, however, that they won't. Anyhow, they really have grown up; A.A. is theirs; let's give it to them."*
>
> (Bill, 1967: 269)

These principles of trusting the newer members were not mere rhetoric. The founders of the whole A.A. movement took concrete action to put this principle in practice.

> *"Standing before the Convention for the last time, I felt as all parents do when sons and daughters must begin to make their own decisions and to live their own lives. No more would I act for, decide for, or protect Alcoholics Anonymous. I saw that well-meaning parents who cling to their authority and overstay their time can do much damage. We old-timers must never do this to the A.A. family. When in the future they might ask us, we would gladly help them in the pinches. But that would be all. This new relationship was indeed the central meaning of what had just taken place.*
>
> *Like most parents at such an anxious time … I dreaded the coming change … but this mood quickly passed, and I knew that all worrying concern as a parent was now at an end. The conscience of Alcoholics Anonymous as moved by the guidance of God could be depended upon to insure A.A.'s future. Clearly my job henceforth was to let go and let God. Alcoholics Anonymous was at last safe – even from me."*
>
> (AAWS, 1957: 48)

The message is clear. God may use you or me to initiate a work, but that does not give us any rights to the work. God is the only authority that counts. A.A.'s Tradition Two explains that

> *"[There are principles for the individual, but] for our group purpose there is but one ultimate authority – a loving God as He may express Himself in our group conscience. Our leaders are but trusted servants; they do not govern."*
>
> (AAWS, 1957: 78)

A.A. organizational units may have a treasurer, board members, and so on, but these are appointed to positions of service, and do not carry any authority to direct. God is the only one with authority. That might sound an idealistic theory to many. So does it really work in practice?

> *"Where does A.A. get its direction? Who runs it? This ... is a puzzler for every friend and newcomer. When told that our Society has no president having authority to govern it, no treasurer who can compel the payment of any dues, no board of directors who can cast an erring member into outer darkness, when indeed no A.A. can give another a directive and enforce obedience, our friends gasp and exclaim, 'This simply can't be. There must be an angle somewhere.' These practical folk then read Tradition Two, and learn that the sole authority in A.A. is a loving God as He may express Himself in the group conscience. They dubiously ask an experienced A.A. member if this really works. The member, sane to all appearances, immediately answers, 'Yes! It definitely does.'"*

(AAWS, 1953: 132)

So the A.A. authors claim their principles work. The following section explains *how* it has worked in practice for them. Perhaps some of these lessons of experience may apply to you and me, in relation to any ministry God may set before us and call us to.

The outworking of the "authority" principles

Oliver and Thwaites were quoted earlier on the dangers of a culture that sees speakers from outside the group as somehow being superior to someone local. Such thinking obviously ignores the fact that a person, who for us is an external authority, has a home; for other people, he or she is merely a local speaker! And going beyond this, no matter where they come from, why is a person in the role of a speaker anything special?

A.A. could potentially have followed a similar path in seeking out "professional" workers to guide them. They resisted this, and instead took the position that the only people who would be paid for doing what they did were those such as accountants, receptionists or cleaners who served the organization rather than as people who led it.

> *"Alcoholics Anonymous should remain forever nonprofessional, but our service centers may employ special workers."*

(AAWS, 1957: 78)

A.A. went further. Not only would they resist the temptation to hire "professionals" in the work of recovery from alcoholism, they would oppose any self-appointed experts from within their own ranks rising to a perceived position of superiority or control.

> *"When we first put our world services into effect, Dr. Bob and I and our old-time friends were self-appointed guardians and custodians of this society. We took it upon ourselves to provide services. I do not mean it in any irreverent or exaggerated sense when I say that our setup of those days was a sort of double-headed papacy and a*

> college of cardinals. Structurally we had created a hierarchy of service.
>
> But we have learned that such a hierarchy cannot forever float alone; it must somehow be connected with the great sea of democracy all about it. The General Service Conference of Alcoholics Anonymous is now about to provide that permanent connection so much needed between our society and its Trustees. But our Conference will be more than a connection; it will represent the conscience of A.A. world-wide, to which our Trustees will in this very hour become directly accountable."

(AAWS, 1957: 225)

One of the mechanisms put in place to counter emergence of hierarchical leadership structures was the concept of "rotating" committee membership. This limits the potential for a local group's current committee to dominate the group.

> "… the group now has a so-called rotating committee, very sharply limited in its authority. In no sense whatever can its members govern or direct the group."

(AAWS, 1953: 134)

At another level, there could be potential for the central A.A. head office to attempt to establish some form of hierarchical control over local A.A. group committees. Again, a safety mechanism is in place to ensure that each local group is autonomous.

> "Tradition Four declares: 'Any two or three gathered together for sobriety may call themselves an A.A. group, provided that as a group they have no other affiliation.' … This means that these two or three alcoholics could try for sobriety in any way they liked. They could disagree with any or all of A.A.'s principles and still call themselves an A.A. group.
>
> But this ultra-liberty is not so risky as it looks. In the end the innovators would have to adopt A.A. principles – at least some of them – in order to remain sober at all. If, on the other hand, they found something better than A.A., or if they were able to improve on our methods, then in all probability we would adopt what they discovered for general use everywhere. This sort of liberty also prevents A.A. from becoming a frozen set of dogmatic principles that could not be changed even when obviously wrong. Healthy trial and error always have their day and place in A.A."

(AAWS, 1957: 105)

The freedom exercised by each group, and each member, may seem dangerous. A.A. has a simple and relaxed attitude, arguing that, on the one hand, God is capable of setting boundaries, and on the other hand, the natural consequences of ignoring wisdom also establishes boundaries.

> "Many people wonder how A.A. can function under such a seeming anarchy. Other societies have to have law and force and sanction and punishment, administered by authorized people. Happily for us, we found we need no human authority whatever. We have two authorities which are far more effective. One is benign, the other malign. There is God, our Father, who very simply says, 'I am waiting for you to do my

will.' The other authority is named John Barleycorn [i.e. alcohol], and he says, 'You had better do God's will or I will kill you.' And sometimes he does kill.... So there is authority enough, love enough, and punishment enough, all without any human being clutching the handles of power."

(AAWS, 1957: 105, 106)

"The A.A. Traditions are neither rules, regulations, nor laws. We obey them willingly because we ought to and because we want to. Perhaps the secret of their power lies in the fact that these life-giving communications spring out of living experience and are rooted in love."

(Bill, 1967: 319)

In looking back at the formation of A.A., it was recognized that it was shaped through the contributions of many individuals, as led by God.

"... A.A. Traditions were beaten out on the anvils of group experience. ... nobody had 'invented' Alcoholics Anonymous ... [Rather,] many streams of influence and many people, some of them nonalcoholics, had helped, by the Grace of God, to achieve A.A.'s purposes."

(AAWS, 1957: 2)

This was the final realization, but it developed over time. It was not always so. For example, there was a point in time where the Trustees of A.A. had the power, and the members of the organization were not in control of their own destiny.

"It was evident that here was a world-wide movement that had no direct access to its own principal service affairs. The Trustees had authority over our services; A.A. itself had no authority."

(AAWS, 1957: 210)

Even the *consideration* of a change to hand control to the ordinary members was not a decision made by the original founders, but a choice put to the members!

"[It was proposed that the] movement's delegates could come down to New York and see what A.A.'s world affairs were really like. They could then decide whether they would take responsibility or whether they would not. That would make it a movement decision, rather than one taken in silence by [the founders]."

(AAWS, 1957: 214)

It was one thing to reason that handing control to the members was the right thing to do ethically, but it raised a number of concerns on its possible outworking.

"But how, in electing delegates, could we cut down destructive politics with all the usual struggles for prestige and vainglory? How many delegates would be needed and from where should they come? When they arrived in New York, how could they be related to the Board of Trustees? What would be their actual powers and duties?"

(AAWS, 1957: 215)

A CASE STUDY OF AN "ORGANIZATION" THAT ISN'T

The election of delegates is taken as a working example of how these matters were resolved. A.A. established some principles for delegating responsibility from the members, through their assembly representatives, to conference delegates, and finally, to directors. The actual mechanics are not necessarily essential for copying into another context, but the underlying attitudes are instructive. The quotations below expose the underlying thought process of the author, which I consider to be vital. The actual mechanisms suggested may be challenged, varied, or tuned, but my analysis was not focused on the mechanics. Rather, I was trying to understand the way the author grappled with a problem and sought a process that respected the freedom of everyone involved.

> *"Each state and province might have one delegate each with the provision that those containing heavy A.A. population could have additional representation. To give the Conference continuity the delegates would be divided into two panels: Panel One to be elected in 1951 and Panel Two the following year. Hence only half the delegates would drop out at one time and the conference membership would rotate. Elections could take place at the largest centers of population in each state or province. Yet how could these assemblies of group representatives choose their committeemen and delegates without terrific political friction?*
>
> *As veterans of many a group hassle and Intergroup brawl, we worried seriously about this. Then came a happy thought. We knew that many of our election troubles were caused by personal nominations, whether from the floor of a meeting or by a self-appointed committee from a back room. Another prime cause of grief was the hotly contested close election, which nearly always left behind a large and discontented minority.*
>
> *We therefore devised a scheme of choosing committeemen out of Group Assemblies by written ballot with no personal nominations at all. But the chief friction would most certainly center around the election of the delegate. How could that pressure be kept down? It was stipulated that each delegate must receive a two-thirds vote of his Assembly for election. With a majority of this size the minority could not kick very much. But suppose the contest was a neck-and-neck affair, with nobody able to get the two-thirds vote? Here we would have to invent something. Maybe the lead man and one or two of his runners-up might place their names in a hat and take their chances on a drawing. The winner of such a painless lottery would become the delegate. Since the high men in the running would almost always be good ones, we could not miss getting a fine panel of delegates by such a method. Of course these ideas were quite speculative. We dearly hoped they were going to work. But would they?*
>
> *It was felt that the elected delegates, meeting in New York in conference, should have very real authority. Therefore the tentative Charter ... drawn for the Conference provided that the delegates, on a two-thirds vote, could issue flat directives to the Trustees. Even a simple majority could issue a strong suggestion to the Trustees. Nevertheless this type of suggestion would be a powerful one, because if it were not carried out the discontented majority could return home and see that contributions*

to Headquarters were cut. Under the proposed plan, it would also become traditional for the Trustees to submit the names of all proposed Board members to the Conference for confirmation. This would give the Conference an effective voice in the selection of Trustees."

(AAWS, 1957: 215-216)

These, then, were the principles, effectively giving representatives authority, but based on bottom-up delegation, not top-down appointment. How did they work in practice?

"I remember particularly the first tryout of the new plan in Boston. Before the meeting some of the elder politicos made a microscopic examination of the whole scheme and came up with the verdict that it was going to work. This was comforting, since those folks in Boston knew politics as few of the rest of us did. Their interest was everywhere intense, and members turned out in force for the mass meeting where I highlighted the Third Legacy plan. When the area's group representatives finally met to elect their committeemen and the delegate, the proceedings were as unruffled as a mill pond. The committeemen were duly elected and seated in front of the Assembly meeting. Then the Assemblymen voted and voted, but nobody could get a two-thirds majority. At last it was decided that the names of the whole committee be dumped into the hat. And out of that traditional receptacle there was drawn a fine delegate. Everybody was elated; we knew the heat was off. Right there we had our first glimmer that A.A. had begun to move from partisan politics into true statesmanship."

(AAWS, 1957: 217)

In the very early days of A.A. there were Trustees who were good men but who were not accountable to the regular members. As described above, a major shift occurred when the appointed delegates of the rank-and-file members were in a position to direct the Trustees. Another major change of responsibility occurred when an agreement was reached that the Trustees must consist of a two-thirds majority of alcoholic members!

"[In 1966, there was a] change in ratio of Trustees of the General Service Board to provide for a two-thirds majority of alcoholic members, the historic occasion on which the A.A. Fellowship accepts top responsibility for the future conduct of all its affairs."

(AAWS, 1957: page 'x')

The first real trial of Trustees having their direction set by members was a landmark occasion. While some of the delegated members may not have had as much experience in management of such responsibilities, as a group of individuals with wide and varying experiences, and with respect for the views of others, a richness in decision-making was noted:

"The Trustees submitted several of their own serious problems for the opinion of the Conference. With real dispatch the delegates handled several tough puzzlers about which we at Headquarters were in doubt. Though their advice was sometimes contrary to our own views, we saw they were frequently right. They were proving as never before that A.A.'s Tradition Two ['For our group purpose there is but one ultimate authority –

a loving God as He may express Himself in our group conscience. Our leaders are but trusted servants; they do not govern'] was correct. Our group conscience could safely act as the sole authority and sure guide for Alcoholics Anonymous. As the delegates returned home, they carried this deep conviction with them."

(AAWS, 1957: 218)

It may be hard to overstate the enormity of the change. A.A. had once been directed by its founders and Trustees, but was now in the hands of members, and God who spoke to them and through them.

"Speaking for co-founder Dr. Bob and for A.A.'s old-timers everywhere, I made the delivery of the [A.A. 'legacies'] to our whole society and its representative Conference. From that time A.A. went on its own, to serve God's purpose for so long as it was destined, under His providence, to endure.

... And when ... [the ordinary members] saw A.A.'s affairs delivered <u>entirely</u> into their own hands, they experienced a new realization of each individual's responsibility for the whole." [Emphasis mine]

(AAWS, 1957: 1-2)

Mechanisms were now established to facilitate the regular A.A. members in directing the affairs of their local group, and the organization as a whole. This bottom-up voice of the members was matched by mechanisms in the reverse direction—the articulation of the principle that those in positions of responsibility could never direct those "below" them.

Firstly, it was clearly stated that the central A.A. group could never direct a local group; each local group was autonomous and in charge of its own local affairs.

"Each group should be autonomous, except in matters affecting other groups or A.A. as a whole."

(AAWS, 1957: 78)

Maybe even more importantly, the appointed committee members in any local group could not direct the affairs of individual members. For example, one particular member had a personality that caused strong reservation in the quieter members, but was nonetheless trusted to reach out to others, albeit in his own rather robust way.

"... another famous early itinerant was Irwin M., a Cleveland A.A. who had become a champion salesman of Venetian blinds ... The prospect of Irwin [as a 'missionary' of A.A. principles to those outside of the early A.A. geographical reach] scared us rather badly. ... we had on file a long list of [alcoholics who had sent correspondence] ... who had not been personally visited. Irwin had long since broken all the rules of caution and discreet approach to newcomers, so it was with reluctance that we gave him the list. Then we waited – but not for long. Irwin ran them down, every single one, with his home-crashing tornado technique. ... Stunned but happy Southerners began to send their thanks to Headquarters."

(AAWS, 1957: 25)

One other rather telling area of potential abuse of control relates to the topic of excluding those who don't "fit" some perceived standard. However, within A.A.,

> "The only requirement for A.A. membership is a desire to stop drinking."
>
> (AAWS, 1957: 78)

Not only can any alcoholic with a wish to dry out join, he (or she) cannot be disciplined let alone expelled.

> "Does not nearly every society on earth give authority to some of its members to impose obedience upon the rest and to punish or expel offenders? ... To this rule Alcoholics Anonymous is a complete exception."
>
> (AAWS, 1957: 118)

It should be clear that A.A. does not direct its members. However, they realistically accept that there may be times when an individual's interpretation of God's will may be distorted by personal issues. In such cases, they wisely recognize that the larger group may, at times, provide another interpretation for the individual to consider. It is never a situation of the group deciding for the individual what he or she must do. At most, they can share their views, encourage the individual to seek God's will for his or her life, and to then stand back and trust God in the life of the individual.

Just because people gather together, they don't need to be "organized"

Alcoholics Anonymous *is* an "organization" from the external perspective of the law of the land—it is an incorporated body. Yet it is not "organized". Let us allow A.A. to explain this apparent contradiction in its own words, and as we analyze the quotations, ask ourselves if the underlying principles and humility could be applied in any ministry to which God may call you or me?

> "Tradition Nine states: 'A.A., as such, ought never to be organized, but we may create service boards or committees directly responsible to those they serve.' This one still puzzles a lot of people. How can you have a society that is unorganized, and at the same time organize services?"
>
> (AAWS, 1957: 118)

> "When Tradition Nine was first written, it said that 'Alcoholics Anonymous needs the least possible organization.' In years since then, we have changed our mind about that. Today, we are able to say with assurance that Alcoholics Anonymous – A.A. as a whole – should never be organized at all. Then, in seeming contradiction, we proceed to create special service boards and committees which in themselves are organized. How, then, can we have an unorganized movement which can and does create a service organization for itself? Scanning this puzzler, people say, 'What do they mean, no organization?'
>
> Well, let's see. Did anyone ever hear of a nation, a church, a political party, even a benevolent association that had no membership rules? Did anyone ever hear of

a society which couldn't somehow discipline its members and enforce obedience to necessary rules and regulations? Doesn't nearly every society on earth give authority to some of its members to impose obedience upon the rest and to punish or expel offenders? Therefore, every nation, in fact every form of society, has to be a government administered by human beings. Power to direct or govern is the essence of organization everywhere.

Yet Alcoholics Anonymous is an exception. It does not conform to this pattern. Neither its General Service Conference, its Foundation Board ... nor the humblest group committee can issue a single directive to an A.A. member and make it stick, let alone mete out any punishment. We've tried it lots of times, but utter failure is always the result. Groups have tried to expel members, but the banished have come back to sit in the meeting place, saying, 'This is life for us; you can't keep us out.' Committees have instructed many an A.A. to stop working on a chronic backslider, only to be told: 'How I do my Twelfth Step [outreach] work is my business. Who are you to judge?' This doesn't mean an A.A. won't take advice or suggestions from more experienced members, but he surely won't take orders. Who is more unpopular than the oldtime A.A., full of wisdom, who moves to another area and tries to tell the group there how to run its business? He and all like him who 'view with alarm for the good of A.A.' meet the most stubborn resistance or, worse still, laughter.

You might think A.A.'s headquarters in New York would be an exception. Surely, the people there would have to have some authority. But long ago, trustees and staff members alike found they could do no more than make suggestions, and very mild ones at that. They even had to coin a couple of sentences which still go into half the letters they write: 'Of course, you are at perfect liberty to handle this matter anyway you please. But the majority experience in A.A. does seem to suggest ...' Now, that attitude is far removed from central government, isn't it?"

(AAWS, 1953: 172-174)

"... it is now clear that we ought never to name boards to govern us. It is equally clear, however, that we shall always need to authorize workers to serve us. Here we discriminate between the spirit of vested authority and the spirit of service, concepts which are sometimes poles apart. It is in this spirit of service that we elect the A.A. groups' informal rotating committees, the Intergroup Associations of the area, and the General Service Conference for A.A. as a whole. Even our Trustees, once an independent body, are today directly accountable to our fellowship. They are the caretakers and expediters of our world services."

(AAWS, 1957: 120)

"While A.A. has to function, it must at the same time avoid wealth, prestige, and power, three great dangers which necessarily tempt nearly all human societies. Though Tradition Nine ['A.A., as such, ought never to be organized; but we may create service boards or committees directly responsible to those they serve'] at first sight seems to deal with purely practical matters, it embodies a deep spirituality in its actual *operation. A.A. is a society without organization, animated only by the spirit of service – a true fellowship."*

(AAWS, 1957: 120)

"Continuously since its beginning, and today, A.A. has been a fellowship and not an organization. Incorporation necessarily makes it an organization. ... We believe that 'spiritual faith' and a 'way of life' cannot be incorporated. ... A.A. can and will survive so long as it remains a spiritual faith and a way of life open to all men and women who suffer ..."

(AAWS, 1957: 127)

Could such principles of freedom actually work in a "Christian ministry" context? After reading the Alcoholics Anonymous books, I almost immediately had the opportunity to observe, and participate in, a form of ministry that was delightfully free of structure. There was a small group of people with a shared background and desire for healing that met somewhat regularly in an informal setting. One individual had been the visionary and facilitated us meeting each other, but he didn't "run the show". While he and a number of others were active Christians, several of the group were from outside the Christian context. It didn't matter, and all individuals were respected. It proved to be a healthy, healing and delightful "non-organization"!

My conclusion was that not only did it work for Alcoholics Anonymous, but it can and does work well in so-called "ministry". If we go back to Jesus himself, he had followers, but they could "un-follow" at any point if they chose. One did.

Arguably it is highly instructive that Jesus did not write constitutions or have schedules for regular meetings. My analysis of Alcoholics Anonymous is that they seem to reflect the anti-institution attitudes of the founder of Christianity!

CHAPTER 28:
YOU SAY, "BUT WHAT IF WE FIND A 'GOOD' LEADER?"

This is only one chapter, but it may be one of the most important for you. When you discover the style of your current leader is less than perfect, it is very tempting to look for a better leader. There can be comfort in being able to look up to someone who claims to have all the answers, or at least displays the confidence to be able to hear God better than you, and hence be a conduit for answers.

I am trying to show you the flaws in the "local church" scene. If I succeed in giving you the courage and conviction to move away from your current situation, only to have you gravitate to another scenario with a leader who is in a position of authority or influence over you, you have still not discovered the freedom God intends for you. I know–I have been there.

One huge danger for those who experience the discomfort of breaking with the traditions that have held them for so long, is to encounter a "leader" who proclaims that he or she shares the same values as you. Maybe he or she has read this very same book, and says nice things like, "There's a lot of merit in that book, but it takes a bit to put it into practice—perhaps I can help guide you?" The warning bells should be clanging loudly for you. Run a mile—fast. Especially if this "leader" classifies himself or herself as a "revolutionary", but under their facade of offering guidance, demonstrates they represent the same old hierarchical mold.

Examples of compromise across church history

The Jews of Jesus' day had a solid set of traditions, touted by their priestly class. It is instructive to note, though, that while Jesus exhibited a level of freedom from these traditions that startled and discomforted His own countrymen, His *own* disciples struggled to live in the freedom he exhibited. And the apostles and those who waited for the Holy Spirit to come also had to grapple with issues of tradition, especially as the group included people who were not from a Jewish culture. Yet so much of the early church culture reflected a Jewish model, including the setting up of a meeting place, with recognized leaders.

As Christendom became "respectable", especially under the influence of the fourth century Roman emperor Constantine, the traditions of the Christian church became increasingly formalized. In an extract from Beckham, *Second Reformation*, 42-43, Brown points out that Constantine's corrupting influence on Christianity is evident today:

> *"Using a combination of the Roman governmental and feudal systems, Emperor Constantine developed a church structure that has lasted ...*
>
> *People go to a building (cathedral)*
>
> *on a special day of the week (Sunday)*
>
> *and someone (a priest, or today, a pastor)*
>
> *does something to them (teaching, preaching, absolution or healing)*
>
> *or for them (a ritual or entertainment)*
>
> *for a price (offerings)."*

(Brown, 2002: 43-44)

It is not surprising that the Roman Empire centered the power of the institutionalized church in Rome. What *is* surprising is that, centuries later, the Roman Catholic Church *still* sees itself as the true center of Christendom, and continues to wield the power originally given to it by the Roman government.

Added to this exercising of a power granted by man rather than God, has been the corruption that spread within the institution. Many good people within its ranks have tried to bring about change, often at great cost to themselves. Recently an Australian bishop published a book crying out for change, and was shunned as a result. He was fortunate that this treatment was the only penalty. When Luther tried to do similar, the Catholic Church tried to kill him!

Yet for all the change that Luther brought about through the Reformation, his reforms only unwound in part the institutionalization that had crept into Christendom. He was deeply influenced by the very institution he opposed.

> *"If you have never read the 95 Theses [of Martin Luther], you would be surprised at how deeply they reflect the existing system, as Luther constantly refers to the proper role of the Pope (without in the least rejecting that office); does not dispute the specific class of priests (as opposed to arguing clearly for the priesthood of every believer; rather he refers to 'clergy' and 'laity'); speaks of purgatory; makes reference to the mother of God (the classic Catholic description of Mary) as well as to venial sins and the Mass; and does not at all repudiate indulgences, per se, but rather their abuses ..."*

(Brown, 2002: 221)

Brown observes how Luther initially tried to bring about change, but within the structure of the church institution. Later Luther distanced himself from the institutional church of his upbringing, but Lindsay tells of how he also found it impossible to completely break free of the traditions.

> *"[Luther had] ... a mode of thinking from which he never completely divested himself. With all his reverence for the Word of God he could never avoid giving the traditions of the Church a certain place beside the Scripture. We find this thought coming continually forward, sometimes quite unconsciously, in much of his reasonings about institutions and in doctrines."*
>
> (Lindsay, 1996: 202)

Luther was not able to break totally free, but neither was the Reformation movement he founded. It stood against the Roman Catholic Church, but retained so much of that institution's foundations.

> *"The Reformation was a revolt against papal authority but not against the Roman concept of the church as an institution."*
>
> Brown (2002: 36) (Quoting William R. Estep, The Anabaptist Story)

Much more recently, there have been attempts to bring life back into Christendom and to break free from so many of the stifling traditions. For example, in the latter half of the last century, there was a surge of attempts to rediscover expressions of Christian life through the practice of "Christian community". Similarly, there have been many attempts to bring life to "church" through the practice of home churches. But again and again, these efforts bring only partial freedom, as they are typically riddled with vestiges of the practices found in the very same institutions from which they are trying to break free.

A lesson emerges. We cannot hang onto the unhelpful traditions of Christendom and take them forward into the life-style of freedom in Christ. Like the patch from the new sewn onto the old, or the storing of new wine in old wineskins, it just won't work.

If we are to see real change, we must do more than shuffle the deck chairs on the Titanic. We must identify and uncompromisingly root out the traditions that have corrupted Christendom.

> *"That is what we are saying about the Church. There must be revolutionary change. ... Minor modifications and improvements will not produce the desired results—and the desired results are beyond our expectations and dreams."*
>
> Brown (2002: 200)

Examples of compromise in individuals

Stories are told of how, in the early stages of his ministry, Hudson Taylor, the much-revered founder of the China Inland Mission, shared his views in such a way as to convince rather than coerce others. Even in the case where Taylor felt a particular set of actions were "wrong" rather than ill-advised, he gave other individuals the time and space to consider his view, and to change course of their own will.

> *"What is spiritual ministry? It is that if you see me to be wrong you are able by prayer, by spiritual power, by tact, by love, forbearance and patience to enlighten my conscience, and thus cause me gladly to turn from my mistaken course to the right one."*
>
> (Taylor & Taylor, 1918: 582)

> *"Never can I forget how helpfully Mr. Taylor led us on to see the needs, so that we suggested the rules to be made and the line to be taken by the Council, wholly unaware at the moment of how he was guiding our thought."*
>
> (Taylor & Taylor, 1918: 492)

Taylor had moments in his life that exemplified freedom from tradition. He also had moments that showed how traditions from the past led him to compromise on his own stated positions. On the one hand, he articulated the view that the leader was to avoid "lording it over" those under his or her care, even if such an approach was costly to the leader:

> *"The principle of godly rule is a most important one, for it equally affects us all. It is this – the seeking to help, not to lord; to keep from wrong paths and lead into right paths, for the glory of God and the good of those guided, not for the gratification of the ruler. Such rule always leads the ruler to the Cross, and saves the ruled at the cost of the ruler. … Let us all drink into this spirit, then lording on the one hand and bondage on the other will be alike impossible."*
>
> (Taylor & Taylor, 1918: 421)

He refers to *"godly rule"*. The concept of having any leader in a position of rule, be it in a Godly way or not, is fundamentally flawed and extremely dangerous. We have one Lord. No one else must ever take God's place and be allowed to rule over our lives, our thoughts, our inclinations, our calling or our actions. Even when the "ruler" proclaims an intention to govern on behalf of God in a saintly or "godly" manner, there is the danger of dictatorial attitudes creeping in. Taylor was certainly not exempt from these dangers as shown in the quotation below.

> *"I was to be the leader in China, and my direction implicitly followed. There was no question as to who was to determine points at issue."*
>
> (Taylor & Taylor, 1918: 54)

Brown's choice of title for his book, *Revolution in the Church*, sets an image of Brown as a person who is more than willing to break with tradition, for the good of God's people. And in so many respects, I do see Brown's views as revolutionary. His opposition to the use of titles for people is but one example.

He quotes a letter from John Wesley who is appalled at one of the Methodists who has assumed the title of "bishop", and scathingly attacks this action:

> "How can you, how dare you, suffer yourselves to be called BISHOP. I shudder, I start at the very thought! Men may call me a knave or a fool; a rascal, a scoundrel, and I am content. But they shall never, by my consent, call me Bishop."
>
> (John Wesley, in Brown, 2002: 62)

(As a side note, in spite of Wesley's confronting attack on the use of titles that would set one apart as being "special" within the Body of Christ, it is to be noted that this very person whom Wesley challenges over the title of "Bishop" is a person that Wesley had himself "ordained", and by that very act made out to be someone special! It is frighteningly easy to be inconsistent when steeped in traditions.)

But let us return to Brown, and his opposition to titles. He tells this story to point out his own opposition to the use of special titles. He stresses that

> "... the Lord so strongly opposed special titles ... [and said that we are all] ...equal in status as children of God."
>
> (Brown, 2002: 57)

Not in an attempt to discredit Brown, but merely as an example of how easy it is to fall into traps of tradition, it is interesting to note that having condemned the use of titles, in his very next sentence he refers to **Saint** Paul. How is it that church leaders and teachers refer to Saint Peter and Saint Paul but I have never heard them refer to Saint Lazarus or Saint Martha! And it appears that Brown has perhaps unconsciously fallen for this trap, too, in spite of his conscious opposition to titles within Christendom.

For an author to so strongly condemn the use of titles, and then immediately refer to Peter and Paul as saints should be seen as a warning to each of us. It is so easy for us to unconsciously support traditions that we may consciously oppose. I will be disappointed if readers of this book are able to point to any inconsistencies that I may have, and examples where I hold up one standard but fail to live by it. I will be disappointed, but I will not be totally surprised. Our upbringing often has a hold on us that we find hard to see, let alone break free from. Perhaps the best we can do is to be aware of this danger, and to be humble in listening to others who expose us as being captives of tradition.

How "radical" are they, really?

The remainder of this chapter seeks to give us insight into another pair of authors who consider themselves revolutionaries, yet I am concerned that they often reflect "old" thinking.

At the outset, let's clearly establish beyond any doubt that Frost and Hirsch believe they are radical revolutionaries. The very first sentence in their book, *The Shaping of Things to Come*, proclaims,

> "In this book expect to encounter revolutionary ideas that will sometimes unnerve you."
>
> (Frost & Hirsch, 2003: ix)

The bio on the back cover of the book states that Alan Hirsch is "... *known for his radical approach ...*"

The page immediately before the table of contents quotes Hans Küng as saying,

> *"[We must] play down our longing for certainty, accept what is risky, live by improvisation and experiment."*
>
> (Hans Küng in Frost & Hirsch, 2003: vi)

In early parts of this book, I quoted Frost and Hirsch where they warn radicals to not be surprised if they receive opposition from church establishments, and I also quoted them as making points such as

- Western churches are bankrupt, and unfortunately, radicals who claim otherwise will be told to stay silent.

- Dependence on a church building is a tragedy.

- Simple variations on old church themes will not be sufficient to bring new life. We must challenge what *appears* to be working somewhat adequately, as these church traditions have actually become enslaving idols. In fact, we need wholesale change, a revolution rather than an evolution.

- There must *not* be a separation of Christ's Body into the two classes of church leaders and laity.

They certainly *sound* like radicals. But are they really?

It's an oxymoron to call someone a "conservative radical". Yet Frost and Hirsch claim for themselves the title of "radical" while seemingly expressing many beliefs that appear to me to be amazingly conservative. They have already been extensively quoted within this book to highlight their willingness to break with traditional patterns, yet, in contradiction, they have also been quoted to expose their apparent inability to even conceive of Christian life without the "safety net" they perceive to be offered by the local church institution. My reading of their book leads me to question if these two authors cannot conceive of Christian life without the active involvement of local churches.

So what's the problem? It seems to me that we have a couple of people who declare themselves to be radical, yet appear to be quite conservative in several areas. You may wonder why I am making such an issue of these well-intentioned authors who appear to struggle to achieve the level of change they are claiming is so much needed.

Moving on from Frost and Hirsch and looking more generally, I perceive that there is a danger that there are many who wear the badge of "radical" who may attract a following among those who see the need for sweeping changes within Christendom. One of the problems is that some self-proclaimed "radical" church leaders may have only a veneer of change but be really quite conservative under the covers. People who want deep change may align to such leaders, believing that their personal responsibilities to seek God directly can be put aside as they can now simply follow those who wear the right badge or say the right words.

All of this to say that one of the greatest dangers to *you* discovering freedom is to find people who declare themselves to be radical and able to show you the way, but who in fact may carry many quite conservative attitudes as baggage when it comes to retaining local churches. We must avoid those who say that they want a revolution, but they want it carefully managed by the local church leaders.

Claims that successful ministry needs "church" to succeed

Again, we take the church-centric nature of Frost and Hirsch as an example, and perform a closer analysis.

We must be very careful lest we dilute *our* calling to sweeping, drastic renewal. Frost and Hirsch note that there are encouraging signs of life within Christendom, observing that they have

> "... encountered a new breed of Christian leadership, young and feisty, willing to experiment with audacious new versions of Christian communities within unchurched subcultures."

(Frost & Hirsch, 2003: x)

It may sound pretty radical, but before we read any further, warning bells should start to ring.

Firstly, we could do well to ask if they are basing their views on an assumed retention of the old, traditional two-class hierarchy of the leaders and the led, no matter what they label the roles. These "young and feisty" people are part of a new breed of what? Christian leadership!

Secondly, are they equating non-Christians with "unchurched" by effectively stating that you can't be a Christian unless you belong to an institutionalized local church? To me, it doesn't take long to conclude that they are steeped in tradition when, in the same paragraph, they go on to warn,

> "... it seems to us [that these radical ministry forms] are more likely to succeed when legitimized, affirmed, and supported by the <u>more conventional</u>, established churches and denominational structures in their midst." [Emphasis mine]

(Frost & Hirsch, 2003: x)

They are proposing "...*audacious new versions of Christian communities*" that are to be "...*legitimized* ... *by conventional churches*". Isn't that like Jesus' ministry needing to be legitimized by the Scribes and Pharisees of His day?

Claims that change can only come via the church leaders

I conclude from the following statements of Frost and Hirsch below that they apparently cannot conceive of radical change occurring unless the change comes via church leadership.

> "... changed relations can <u>only</u> follow the inner change and preparation of the people

who lead, work, and sacrifice for the community. In other words, it <u>must</u> begin with leadership." [Emphasis mine]

(Frost & Hirsch, 2003: 156)

"It is within our power [as leaders] to make a difference in this area [i.e. restructuring the local church] if we will exercise strategic focus and discipline in recruiting, training, and mobilizing a full-fledged leadership and ministry matrix for our times."

(Frost & Hirsch, 2003: 180)

"... it is time for some 'reimagineering' to happen in our churches. And <u>it will be up to an emerging apostolic leadership to bring it about</u>." [Emphasis mine]

(Frost & Hirsch, 2003: 200)

"... <u>imaginative, godly, biblical leadership is absolutely vital</u>. It is the strategic area of leverage for change. We would focus on this first and keep focusing on it." [Emphasis mine]

(Frost & Hirsch, 2003: 67)

My critique of the work of Frost and Hirsch concluded that they are not only *perpetuating* the two-class structure, but seem to be *declaring* that there is no validity to another's ministry unless the "strategic" leadership have first done their "imagineering" and dictated the local church's direction. If we compare this proposed strategy to Jesus' approach to ministry, we might conclude that He should have become a leader in a synagogue and brought change through the 'system' rather than trusting His revolution to fishermen, tax collectors, and the like.

Claims that individual ministries must be church-centric

Jesus was known as a friend to those who were *outside* the established religious institutions, but His motive wasn't to get them to become "nice" little members of the local religious order. He simply loved them, and found their company more acceptable than that of those he chastised as being religious hypocrites.

Do the attitudes of Frost and Hirsch align with Jesus' attitudes? At first glance it may appear so—they encourage local churches to actually immerse themselves in "secular" groups. When I looked deeper, their motives appeared to me to be less pure, joining "secular" groups as part of infiltration exercises, with the local church apparently (1) "commissioning" them to do so, to (2) funding their clandestine activities, and (3) excusing them from Sunday morning services so as to allow them to engage with unchurched people. To me, the following excerpts demonstrate a lack of full transparency. Their strategy appears to actively encourage actions with an ulterior motive:

"[Adam and Amy met some people with an interest in skydiving.] In an incarnational church Adam and Amy and maybe some other Christians would be commissioned to join the skydiving club, to eat breakfast with them every Saturday, to develop a web of friendships, to share their faith ..."

(Frost & Hirsch, 2003: 51)

> *"[The fact that non-churched people are not attracted to the local church] emphasizes the importance of a group of Christians <u>infiltrating</u> a community ... It would be a decidedly incarnational choice if a few members of a local church, so moved by compassion for [as an example] the car enthusiasts right across the road, chose to buy a model car and join the club! This would be the kind of thinking and acting we're talking about. If the spirit of our missionary God were to sweep through such a church, we don't doubt that the church itself might buy a few model cars and <u>commission some of its members to miss the morning service</u> so they can fully enter into the community of the car club." [Emphasis mine]*
>
> (Frost & Hirsch, 2003: 42-43)

This apparent deception could be excused by some in the name of "converting" a few "heathen", calling on the abused phrase that "the end justifies the means". I'm led to think that the motivation for Frost and Hirsch is to get these poor lost souls into "church" rather than to simply offer them the "good news" of Jesus Christ.

> *"While it is a noble and, indeed, a godly activity for a Christian businessman to run a shoe shop and to try to be Christ to his customers, something is missing if a Christian faith community [i.e. a local 'church'] isn't part of the equation."*
>
> (Frost & Hirsch, 2003: 26-27)

Claims that we still need paid, professional leaders

Of more concern is Frost and Hirsch positioning their book as "missional", i.e. reaching out to the needy people in our communities. But to me it is quickly evident that the whole thing revolves around the local church. Are they of the opinion that the church leaders are too busy in committees and such-like to have the time to touch the lives of those outside the church institution? It appears so, as they recommend what seems to them to be an obvious solution—get the non-leader church members out doing the front-line "missional" work.

As well as this ministry work being really focused on getting "un-churched" people into new churches, albeit it new local churches that reflect their culture, there is another problem which I find surprising and unsettling, namely their openness to the idea of employing a professional evangelist. And yes, they mean "professional" in its full sense—an evangelist who gets paid to mix with the "not-yet-saved" members of the community who have been caught by the laity in a "net" of what I consider to be contrived friendships.

> *"... as these nets of friendship and service are strengthening, the ministry of the gifted evangelist comes into play. He or she shouldn't have to be a visiting preacher at a church service, but one of the links in the net. As I am building ever closer bonds between my Christian and not-yet-Christian friends, I should assume that God has gifted our church with an evangelist, one who can naturally and effectively proclaim Jesus in a contextualized and attractive manner. As the net is being repaired and tightened, my not-yet-Christians are bound to come into contact with my evangelist friend. We believe that if our not-yet-Christian friends were swept into a series of*

friendships with a number of incarnational Christians, at least one of whom is an evangelist, God will do his work of bringing people into a relationship with him."

(Frost & Hirsch, 2003: 58)

" 'Don't you know that those who work in the temple get their food from the temple, and those who serve at the altar share in what is offered on the altar? In the same way, the Lord has commanded that those who preach the gospel should receive their living from the gospel' (1 Cor 9:13-14). So wrote Paul, though he was quick to point out that he was not feathering his own nest. He told the Corinthians that he personally was not after any remuneration, only that the church should financially support the work of evangelists generally. It can be debated that this passage refers specifically to the early office of apostle and is therefore no longer applicable. If it is applied these days, is seems to take a stand for ministerial stipends for professional clergy. But the missional-incarnational church will recognize that the gifted evangelist will be in hot demand for dinner parties, lunches, late-night discussions, and gatherings of parents at the school gate after school. If the evangelist can surf, she should be at the beach regularly. If he skydives 'to use an earlier illustration', he should be at the airstrip every Saturday. If the evangelist is an artist, a classic-car enthusiast, a great cook, or an expert gardener, he or she must be free to interact with other members of the like-minded community. If this means working part time to be free to work the nets created by the church's friendships, then that church should consider supporting the evangelist financially.

Supporting those who proclaim the gospel, when applied to Western culture today, could be a healthy corrective for many people for whom the cycle of work, family, and church is so consuming that they never have time for building friendships with not-yet-Christians. Ironically, full-time clergy in the traditional-attractional churches often find themselves so run off their feet with the busyness of serving on various committees, attending myriad meetings, and running worship services, that they have very few social contacts with unbelievers. We think this is one of the great blights of the institutional church; it covertly withdraws its clergy from casual, social contact with the neighborhood community. The propensity for clergy to move regularly to different parishes means many don't have long-term friendships in any one area. And when a minister joins the local jogging club or the book-reading society at a local bookshop, he or she is often accused, by the congregation, of not doing the Lord's work."

(Frost & Hirsch, 2003: 58-59)

The above quotation seems to suggest that the expectations of clergy should be lightened to allow them more time to interact with a wider group in the general community. Are Frost and Hirsch seeking to weaken, or perhaps even remove, the clergy-laity divide? Perhaps, but my analysis of the following quote suggests that the class of "leader" remains, and is in fact seen as being essential by Frost and Hirsch. Are they suggesting that the work performed by the laity that might have been of value will, at best, fall into disrepair over time if not managed by "leadership"? It seems that is their view.

> *"... we want to explore perhaps one of the most significant aspects needed for the transition from Christendom mode to a missional mode of church; a shift to apostolic leadership. In fact, without this the missional church is unlikely to rise at all, and if it does manage to survive birth, it will not last long because it will lack the leadership structure to sustain it over the long distance. ... A renewed focus on leadership is absolutely essential to the renewal and growth of the church. ... This issue of the development of a new kind of leadership is possibly the single most important question of strategy in this decade, and whether the church responds correctly or not will determine to some extent its survival as a viable expression of the gospel in the years to come."*
>
> (Frost & Hirsch, 2003: 165)

It's bad enough that they seem to suggest the work of the laity may not survive unless there is oversight by leadership. Surely there is potential for *God* to use anyone, whether or not they are managed by "leadership"? We look deeper into these views of Frost and Hirsch in the following section.

Laity are to be bold and free (yet they must be under local church leadership?)

Frost and Hirsch talk of the "*shape of the missional church*". They appear to be critical of traditional local church structures. They also appear to have a passion for church-based "mission", and realize the need for laity to be mobilized. I questioned if there might be an inconsistency between their desire to "free" laity for mission, and yet to ensure that such laity are managed by "leadership", presumably based in local churches.

As we start to look at the apparent tensions between setting individuals free yet keeping them bound to the local church, we begin by Frost and Hirsch calling on people to be bold and free in Christ. A deliberately selective quote follows (with words reflecting the film, 'Chicken Run'):

> *"Toughen up! Get out of the chicken coop, trust God ... and let it happen. If you don't know what you're doing, follow Jesus; he's the best model of mission we know. It's time to fly the coop!"*
>
> (Frost & Hirsch, 2003: 162)

If that were the whole quote, one may reasonably conclude that Frost and Hirsch really want to set everyone free. But that's only part of the quote. My reading of Frost and Hirsch leads me to the view that they see the local church must carefully manage this breaking free from the chicken coop. On the one hand, the preceding quote suggests the authors are calling us to boldly trust God and to follow Jesus, but it appears to me that they want these "free" laity to be somewhat constrained. The full quote is,

> *"Toughen up! Get out of the chicken coop, trust God, <u>get accountable, go out in twos</u>, and let it happen. If you don't know what you're doing, follow Jesus; he's the best model of mission we know. It's time to fly the coop!"* [Emphasis mine]
>
> (Frost & Hirsch, 2003: 162)

Who are they accountable to? God? Or maybe to church "leadership, in which case I question the alleged freedom. And why are they expected to work in pairs? Perhaps it's an innocent copying of a precedent recorded in the New Testament. Perhaps it's for the safety of individuals. But perhaps there is an unconscious element of control, driven by a fear that one person could wander away from the "party line" into unorthodox thinking? I am certainly not accusing Frost and Hirsch of such motives. Nonetheless I do question if I, as a member of their church, could I go out on my own if I chose, and without having to report back to the authority to which I was "accountable"? You may feel this last hypothetical could never happen, but I've seen the "holy" spy network in action in unhealthy settings. Again, I am certainly not accusing these authors of such motives, but I feel a warning needs to be broadcast about the danger of such an approach being misused.

One of many baffling contradictions is that this call to go out in twos is on the page following a story of a person they hold up as a shining example of one who, on his own, boldly followed God. Let's embrace freedom, and refuse to be paired up at a leader's behest, and refuse to be "accountable" to hierarchical leadership.

As I read their book, there seemed to be another inconsistency. I got the impression that the authors expect courageous *leadership* within the management of the local church. Fine (as far as having any hierarchical leadership goes), but does this imply they don't actually expect the *laity* to be too bold?

> "A missional church is as imaginative as it is bold. And missional leadership is courageous and willing to try new things and risk all if necessary to see the kingdom come. Every church should have a Research and Development department ... And every authentic missional church will experiment like mad in order to find new and accessible ways of doing and being the people of God."
>
> (Frost & Hirsch, 2003: 189)

Moses and the Israelites established what might be labeled a "Research and Development" department by sending in the spies to check out what lay ahead. There was nothing wrong with this action. In fact God ordered it in that scenario. But there are two warnings relating to this story.

Firstly, the people followed the fear-based findings of the majority of the spies rather than seeking or understanding God's heart for themselves or considering the faith-based reports delivered by Joshua and Caleb. And secondly, even if it was right for Moses to do this bit of research, it was a one-off action under God's leading. Yet Frost and Hirsch seem to want the permanent establishment of such departments in their institutions.

If you think I am being a bit harsh in claiming Frost and Hirsch want us to play 'follow-the-leader', read on.

Vision is to come from the people, yet they must all align with the leader's vision

When you first read the following, you could easily conclude I must be wrong in criticizing Frost and Hirsch. Based on the following quotation, surely they do not expect the laity to follow the leader's vision.

> *"It is a disturbing trait of the more gung-ho Christian leader today to believe that he (usually male) is the sole visionary and the people are mere receivers of the vision and must adhere to it because of the position of the leader in the organization. While many of us reject this approach to leadership, a watered-down version of this kind of thinking exists in many so-called leadership development programs. They teach that all is well when graduates of these programs simply (super)impose their vision on a community without first listening very deeply to the longings and dreams of the local people in that community."*
>
> (Frost & Hirsch, 2003: 188)

Aren't Frost and Hirsch saying that good leaders will listen closely to the "longing and dreams" of the people rather than autocratically imposing their own vision? Isn't that good?

A perhaps more cynical interpretation of their approach follows. I conclude that they are suggesting that a leader will be able to articulate his or her own ideas, plant them like seeds in the minds of the followers, have the people go away to think about it, and come back thinking that God has stimulated like thinking in their heads, thinking it is God that has led them.

> *"… all that a great visionary leader does is awaken and harness the dreams and visions of the members of a given community and <u>give them deeper coherence by means of a grand vision</u> that ties together all the 'little visions' of the members of the group. The fact remains that no one will be prepared to die for my sense of purpose in life. She or he will die only for her or his own sense of purpose. <u>My task as a leader is to so articulate the vision that others are willing to embed their sense of purpose within the common vision</u> of the community. <u>Only if they think that the common vision legitimizes their vision will they be motivated by the leader's vision</u>. In this sense, <u>willingness to partake in corporate vision is the greatest compliment that a person can pay to leadership</u>. <u>It is holy ground and should be treated with reverence</u>."* [Emphasis mine]
>
> (Frost & Hirsch, 2003: 188)

It is my view that such thinking is extremely dangerous. It is couched as the leaders adding value to the visions of individuals. But look a little deeper. The visions of the individuals are labeled "little visions", whereas that of the leader is the "grand vision". Such an attitude devalues the vision of the individual. Also of concern is Frost and Hirsch's apparent assumption that God cannot give one individual a vision unless it aligns with that of the church leadership. It seems to be less about adding value to the vision of the individual, and more about the leadership retaining control. And just to really expose what I see as their class-based thinking, the leader's "*grand vision*" is declared to be "*holy ground and must be treated with reverence*"! It can be assumed from this that if a member of the laity has a different vision, he or she is wrong and must be managed.

Ministry depends on the people, yet ministry depends on the leaders

Frost and Hirsch identify the need for Christendom to rethink the way it works:

> *"The mission of the church needs constantly to be renewed and reconceived."*
>
> (Frost & Hirsch, 2003: 187)

Given their view that the local church needs to get a new vision (pulled together by the leadership), they at one point look to the laity to bring about change.

> *"... the people of God are to relentlessly reimagine their fundamental tasks in the world."*
>
> (Frost & Hirsch, 2003: 187)

However, all this "reimagination" amongst the laity is, based on my interpretation of the following quotation by Frost and Hirsch, to be carefully managed by the leaders:

> *"... it's one of the core tasks of leadership to help the community to dream again."*
>
> (Frost & Hirsch, 2003: 188)

Local leaders reflecting local culture or head office beliefs?

Over the next few quotations, we look at how Frost and Hirsch start by seeming to give groups some level of local ('indigenous") autonomy from the central church:

> *"First is the paramount importance placed on having indigenous leadership development. Whenever the church is led by 'outsiders' ... there will remain a suspicion that although Jesus has come into the host community, he is not really part of that community."*
>
> (Frost & Hirsch, 2003: 74)

Cracks in any appearance of local autonomy start to appear when it becomes obvious that the local leaders are not on their own. The imported leaders not only exist, but make the call as to when the locals can be trusted (or not trusted) to run the show without them!

> *"And so, second, and equally important, is the need for imported or itinerant leaders to know when to move on or to hand over complete leadership to local leaders."*
>
> (Frost & Hirsch, 2003: 74)

And even more fundamentally flawed is the revelation that the local leaders are hand-picked by the "outsiders". They are deemed suitable if, and only if, the local leaders align with the philosophies and visions that are deemed to be important to those central leaders making the selection.

> *"It will be important in planting incarnational churches that the leaders select a team only on the basis of a clear, demonstrated commitment to stated philosophy and vision."*
>
> (Frost & Hirsch, 2003: 67)

Based on my analysis, I suggest that Frost and Hirsch should be seen as also having a leadership style to avoid. I cannot see how they can be radical as long as they retain their roots still firmly planted in local church institutions, especially with a special leadership class.

CHAPTER 29:
A LINE IN THE SAND - STOP PLAYING 'FOLLOW THE LEADER'

Don't look for leaders

As far back as Moses' day, the people cried out for a leader. God challenged them, asking why they wanted one when He was their leader. He warned them of the consequences of demanding a king like other nations had, yet they still wanted a figurehead. And according to Rinehart, not much has changed over the centuries!

> *"A group of believers who demand a shiny elite and productive leader to do their ministry and to run their organization as they want him to are headed for trouble. Leaders who try to correct this error sometimes find themselves out of a job. God intended ministry to be shared. Where this is not happening, it may be due to the hardheartedness of the people as much as to the ambition of a leader."*
>
> (Rinehart, 1998: 132)

Having a leader might be fine if *God* didn't want to be our direct head (but He does), *and* if the leadership model wasn't so fundamentally flawed (which it is). The models used are not only corrupt, but seem to also be self-perpetuating, and built into the very fabric of our religious institutions.

> *"In the great majority of cases, these men and women of God are doing the best they know how to do, and even if their mindsets need adjusting and their methods need changing, this is probably the way they learned to do ministry in their home churches, or from their former pastors, or in Bible school or seminary, or through books and conferences, and it is probably the only way they understand."*
>
> (Brown, 2002: 126)

Often church leaders talk about the accountability and balance that can be achieved as they "submit" to each other in some sort of "pastoral fraternity". Brown draws an analogy between these groups and labor trade unions, where

> *"...the primary purpose of a union is to ensure the well-being and prosperity of the union members. It is to protect their rights. And doing this preserves solidarity within the union ranks."*
>
> (Brown, 2002: 130)

However, Brown suggests that these pastoral fraternities can be an excuse for pastors to gossip and complain about the problem laity that they "have to put up with". These meetings can turn into either mutual admiration societies or sources of bragging about growth by pastors who are insecure. Brown criticizes the pastoral fraternity model, where church leaders create a self-interest group, warning of

> *"... the wrongness of political alliances and siding with those in position rather than siding with truth. It has to do with the territorial mindset, which is antithetical to the Kingdom of God mentality."*
>
> (Brown, 2002: 133-134)

He describes some of the results of this, such as turning a blind eye to the problems with other pastors, or the double standards on how a pastor reacts when people join him from another local church compared with how they react when they leave him! He invites the readers to join him

> *"... in dismantling what can rightly be described as the ministerial labor union [that is] a system of spiritual territorialism, religious politics, and protection of position, often based on a leadership attitude of 'You scratch my back, I'll scratch yours.' It is not the Jesus way."*
>
> (Brown, 2002: 126-127)

Even if our pastor is not fraternizing with other church leaders, Brown suggests we still have a fundamental problem—the pastor!

> *"What makes this all the more striking is that the Greek noun poimen, 'pastor/shepherd,' is used with reference to a church leader only once in the entire New Testament—namely in Ephesians 4:11. Otherwise it always refers to Jesus. In contrast with this, outside of Ephesians 4:11, apostle is found five times (with reference to someone other than the twelve apostles or Paul), prophet is found eleven times, evangelist is found twice, and teacher occurs eleven times. Yet in many Pentecostal circles, if you are 'in the ministry' you are a pastor, unless you travel and speak, in which case you are an evangelist. But these are the ministry callings mentioned least in the New Testament! Where have all the others gone?"*
>
> (Brown, 2002: 136)

The roles of church leaders and laity can be viewed as somewhere on a continuum. At one extreme we can have the laity sitting back and doing nothing, leaving it all to the church leaders. Another extreme can be where the laity does what God directs them to do, totally independently of what the church leaders may think or say. Before we look at the latter radical position, we must first squarely face the consequences of a compromise. What if we retain church leaders, but just work alongside them? Can they keep their status and salary, while the laity shoulders more of the burden? And wouldn't that be a good thing?

It's interesting and instructive to look at how Jesus ushered in change. He could have tried to convince just the church leaders of His day to see the new kingdom He was delivering. There were plenty of gifted, well-educated people amongst the religious leaders. They had vast influence over the masses. Wouldn't it have been easier to bring change through the existing structure? Then, as a side-benefit, Jesus would have been part of the "in" crowd instead of being executed by them.

Sounds a good theory, perhaps. But Jesus realized it was harder to change religious traditions than it was to change the hearts of the ordinary people. And Oliver and Thwaites express a view that suggests that not much has changed:

> *"...with just one or two exceptions, the church, by and large, and church leadership in particular, has seemed more or less disinterested [in the message that it's time for releasing the laity]."*

(Oliver & Thwaites, 2001: 11)

So instead of trying to hope that the leaders would be open to embracing change, Jesus simply reached out to the people and started a new and different way, with *them*.

Was Jesus "anti-establishment"? He did see the leaders for who they were, but did He harbor a hatred for them? I do not believe so. In contrast, He showed a love for all people, no matter what their rank. He *welcomed* a religious leader, Nicodemus. He showed compassion to people in secular/military leadership—healing a centurion's servant, even though this man represented a forced rule by an external nation which was far from welcome in the eyes of most, if not all, Jews.

It is clear that Jesus loved all, but opposed the wrongful use of power by the religious elite. In fact, He called these religious leaders to account for the way they bound the people. The bottom line is that He chose to bring about radical change by employing the services of ordinary people, not by seeking "revival" within the organized circles of traditional, institutionalized religion. Nor should we wait for the church leaders of our day to change.

While I consider much of Girard's *Brethren, Hang Loose* to be commendable, it is still one pastor writing to others. Lawrence Richards, in the introduction to Girard's book, notes the existence of many publications that articulate the woes of local churches, and suggests principles and patterns for renewal (Girard, 1972: 13). That was true decades ago and little seems to have changed.

We don't need more books for the church leaders. We need the laity to stop looking to church leaders for answers, and to learn to let the laity look directly to God.

McGavran tells of church leaders who were pursuing ministry to the better-educated, wealthier, more acceptable people. Meanwhile, God was doing a work amongst the social outcasts, led by uneducated individuals. For example,

> "Adoniram Judson went to Burma as a missionary to the cultured Buddhist Burmese. ... [One of his helpers was] a rough character, by name Ko Tha Byu, a Karen by race. The Karens were among the backward tribes of Burma ... and were supposed by the Burmese to be stupid inferior people. 'You can teach a buffalo, but not a Karen,' was the common verdict. Judson ... was inclined to take the common verdict as true. However, he persisted, and a few months later Ko Tha Byu became a convinced, if not a highly illuminated, Christian."

(McGavran, 1981: 284)

Judson was

> "... speaking to the [influential] Burmese of that land, Ko Tha Byu ... spoke to the humble Karen ..."

(McGavran, 1981: 284)

Meanwhile, a large evangelistic movement began through the work of this undirected Karen, even though (as quoted earlier)

> "Judson ... was concerned with more important matters than a Christian movement among a backward tribe."

(McGavran, 1981: 285)

More important matters? More important than God touching the lives of an outcast people? In spite of the leader's prejudices, Ko Tha Byu pressed on, and the outcome was that

> "[The Christian movement] among the Karens may well be the source of a Church numbering millions, ...
>
> By contrast, the Mission Station Approach [exemplified and pursued by Judson] has yielded its ordinary quota of small, static mission station churches with a membership of perhaps 20,000 souls for all Burma."

(McGavran, 1981: 285)

A similar story, partially quoted earlier, is based on experiences in Pakistan:

> "Up in the north of Pakistan there was a lowly people called Churas. ... They had been largely overlooked by the missionaries preaching Christ to the respectable members of the Hindu and Muslim communities, and organizing their few hard-won converts into mission station churches. Then a man named Ditt from among the Churas turned to Christ, continued to live among his people, despite their attempts at ostracism, and gradually brought his relatives into the Christian faith."

(McGavran, 1981: 285-286)

And the initial reaction from the missionaries to this move of God?

> "The missionaries were at first dubious about admitting to the Christian fellowship these lowest of the low, lest the upper castes and the Muslims take offence."
>
> (McGavran, 1981: 286)

Thank God that He is more than capable of calling His people into action without the intervention of church leaders who purport to be acting and speaking on His behalf.

Don't seek permission for your own vision

I do hope that, as a member of the Body of Christ, you have been caused to question the seeking of another's interpretation of what God wants you to do, and have been encouraged to do the work that *God* has called you to do. There is no need to go to a church leader to ask for permission to act. Yet Frost and Hirsch seem to think we should:

> "The <u>leadership</u> of a given community <u>will need to give organizational permission</u> for rethinking and allow for lots of experimentation, recognizing that this process is dangerous, tricky, and inevitably chaotic." [Emphasis mine]
>
> (Frost & Hirsch, 2003: 196)

Yet even though these authors suggest that permission may be hard to acquire, they still expect it must be granted.

> "Giving space for those disturbers of the status quo will require massive permission-giving from all levels of the established denominations, who currently give little indication that they are really willing to let that happen."
>
> (Frost & Hirsch, 2003: 180)

Frost and Hirsch have warned that release may not be freely given, and they also seem to be saying we'd better not hold our breath waiting for release:

> "… there seems to be painfully little permission, either from denominational, local, or personal leadership, to 'go for it' and try new things."
>
> (Frost & Hirsch, 2003: 183)

My reading of Oliver and Thwaites suggests that they, like Frost and Hirsch, also point out that church leaders may be reluctant to change. Is it because some leaders raise (possibly misguided) theological arguments for retaining the central, hierarchical local church as the hub of activity and control? Or worse, may some leaders fear that some of their own personal benefits might walk out the door if change involves releasing the laity? Or maybe they may resist because

> "… the present status quo … makes it hard to re-envision the emerging shape [of the replacement of local church]."
>
> (Oliver & Thwaites, 2001: 109)

Nonetheless, Oliver and Thwaites throw out the challenge to leaders by saying that the leaders

> "... cannot hold on to the saints inside our church construct, calling them by that strange and unbiblical name 'my people', and pretend [they] are giving them the power of agreement they need to penetrate the darkness and shine the light into their world."
>
> (Oliver & Thwaites, 2001: 110)

Many books have squarely tackled the topic, demanding leadership set the laity free. For example, Rinehart's book, *Upside Down* (Rinehart, 1998) has a chapter titled, *Let My People Go! – Releasing God's People for Service* (Rinehart, 1998: 127-139), and entire books have been written on the topic, including Tillapaugh's *Unleashing the Church* (Tillapaugh, 1982). But by and large, the problems still persist.

Perhaps the church leaders just don't get it, or possibly they know what's right, but don't want to lose their position, prestige or income. Or possibly there are other reasons. But whatever the root cause, the church leaders are typically holding tight to the reins, even while some *talk* of empowering the laity. Talking in a different context, Sidney Poitier's autobiography, *The Measure of a Man*, nonetheless articulates the problem:

> "Wherever there's a configuration in which there are the powerful and the powerless, the powerful, by and large, aren't going to feel much of anything about this imbalance. After a while the powerful become accustomed to experiencing the power to their benefit in ways that are painless. It's the air they breathe, the water they swim in.
>
> The powerless, who aren't swimming in that comfort and that ease, look at the inequity quite differently than the guy ... who's in the comfort seat. ... However much prodding they get from the powerless or the disenfranchised or the slaves, those in power just aren't inclined toward introspection or remorse."
>
> (Poitier, 2001: 126)

Quoting a pastor in Brazil, Noble states,

> "... if someone committed to the church has a vision or wants to fulfil their calling, I simply ask two questions – what do you want to do? and, what do you need to do it? Then it's all systems go and people are allowed to make mistakes."
>
> (Noble, 2002: 126)

At first glance, this looks like the pastor in question is just what we are looking for—a pastor willing to freely support initiatives of the laity. But look a bit more closely. The pastor puts a condition on the freedom. There's an "if", and it is all about the pastor's local church. *If* the request for freedom comes from someone "... *committed to the local church* ..." then permission will be granted.

Oliver and Thwaites express a caution about such pastors who seem to grant freedom, but on *their* terms. Even if we are totally surprised by the church leaders truly setting us free (and not just saying the "right" words), they may retract their "permission" when the reality hits that we're following God's call instead of theirs!

> *"... when the release becomes too real, in that individuals start to bond more strongly with their work than they do their church, some leaders, feeling their support base under threat, begin to pull on the ecclesiastic band to draw the saints back into the congregational fold. Much of this release of saints by pastors did not come from a theological conviction on their part. Rather, it has come from the saints taking initiative and pastors, seeing the trend and deciding to catch up."*
>
> (Oliver & Thwaites, 2001: 33-34)

We have looked so far at the likelihood (or otherwise) of church leaders granting release. Yet so often it seems the laity seeks release even if the chances of being truly set free are slim. We don't need to, so why do we even *seek* the approval of the church leaders?

Girard paints a picture of how life might be if the laity is truly free:

> *"People learn to walk one-to-one with the Spirit of Jesus. They no longer wait for the pastor or the organized church to give them something to do. They find their own ministry of life under the leadership of the Holy Spirit. Sometimes this involves them in the organizational framework of the church. Often it does not.*
>
> *As long as I kept them tied to me or to the institution, they could only grow within that narrow framework. Once set free to the ministry of the Spirit and the Body — the extent of their spiritual growth is limited only by their own responsiveness to the will of God. They can grow past me. They can grow past the institution. 'Growing up into Christ in all things.'"*
>
> (Girard, 1972: 161):

Girard also notes that such freedom may never be discovered. Why? Because some people simply cannot envision life outside of a local church.

> *"There seems to be no way for people to get free from the notion that Christianity is activity in an organisation that owns a building someplace. There is no thought of finding one's own ministry under the personal leadership of the Holy Spirit. Christians never get that free from 'the Church.'"*
>
> (Girard, 1972: 33)

Oliver and Thwaites note that many people who work hard and succeed in business are

> *"... driven by a desire to prove to their fathers that they could succeed."*
>
> (Oliver & Thwaites, 2001: 105-106)

They also note that, in the absence of positive affirmation and growth, people

> *"... remain weak, become destructive or simply die."*
>
> (Oliver & Thwaites, 2001: 106)

The need for affirmation seems to be built in.

Oliver and Thwaites seem to recognize approval from the church leaders is unlikely, so they suggest we might get a bit of encouragement from other sources. One possible source is from our circle of friends, e.g. in the workplace. They may not even be Christians. Yet Oliver and Thwaites suggest this might be more meaningful:

> *"In many ways ... this [agreement from peers] is more important than the agreement you might gain from your minister."*
>
> (Oliver & Thwaites, 2001: 110)

Now reality starts to bite. We are going to be hard-pressed to get "permission" from church leaders, but even our Christian friends may not understand. Oliver and Thwaites express a view that might be considered unwelcome in many circles— that those outside of Christendom might be more attuned to the light and salt we are trying to deliver than those inside. Too often Christians think they have a monopoly on good works and compassion. Such an attitude is blatantly absurd, as expressed in a previous quotation:

> *"It is ... best that those we enter into agreement with are Christians, but sadly, at times, we may find it very hard or impossible to locate them. We will, however, in most settings generally find people who may not be Christians, but who love truth and want to see the good arise. ... Scripture records many instances where holy prophets would not touch unholy heathen, only to find that God was working all along to see these people come to truth."*
>
> (Oliver & Thwaites, 2001: 111)

> *"The reason [that many 'parables of the church at work on the factory floor, the executive chair, the family home, the A.A. meeting, etc. are emerging on the landscape] is that more of these parables are taking the name church to themselves. They are taking permission to be at the forefront of the Kingdom move into creation. They are building from the good desire of heart and will no longer be stopped or tied anymore by authority structures that set limits on their reach into creation.*
>
> *They don't want to be in adversarial relationship with leaders of local church settings, but they have been waiting for too many years for real permission to come from them, and are now drawing that permission from each other and from society, to do the good works and be the church they are and always have been."*
>
> (Oliver & Thwaites, 2001: 136)

> *"... things are on the move and more and more Christians are taking permission to build with others the new culture of being church."*
>
> (Oliver & Thwaites, 2001: 112)

But what if this last port of call (those *outside* of Christendom) also fails to support us? If God has called us to a work, then the only approval we need is *His*!

> *"Remember, you are the church and you have the agreement of heaven to be and build that church in all of life and work."*
>
> (Oliver & Thwaites, 2001: 110)

With the emotional freedom to move ahead even without the backing of *any* others, people can be truly free. And many *are* exercising just such freedom.

The need for praise from others should never be a motive, even if it is received. It may feel more pleasant if the church leaders give their blessing, but the core issue is about being faithful to *God's* calling, not feeling good because others applaud us. In reality, we are unlikely to get permission from others to act with the freedom that Jesus demonstrated. We may simply have to live in the freedom Jesus offers, no matter what the consequences. The leaders *can't* prevent true freedom of the spirit. The worst they can do is to kill us. And they might, as far as our reputation goes, if not physically. Just ask Jesus.

Without being irreverent I suggest that one of many good reasons to follow God rather than man is that He is much smarter! We can look up to those who are older, and who have more experience than us, and it is wise for us to listen to and learn from others. But it is foolish to seek and follow their advice unquestioningly, and it should never be taken as having greater authority than God!

As an "elder statesman", Hudson Taylor had been approached by a younger person interested in working in China. Taylor recommended a plan for this individual's preparation:

> *"T. J. Barnardo, coming to Coburn Street as a candidate for the China Inland Mission, was advised by Mr. Taylor to study medicine, and introduced accordingly to the London Hospital."*
>
> (Taylor & Taylor, 1918: 56)

However, God had different plans to those of the applicant, and of Taylor:

> *"Tom Barnardo was ... a bright lad of twenty whose interest in China ... was to bring him to his own among the waifs and strays of East London."*
>
> (Taylor & Taylor, 1918: 56)

God used his desire to serve, but not in the manner *Taylor* advised. If young Tom had simply followed the advice of Taylor he would have missed out on God's best.

So how do we begin our journey into freedom? Yancey asks a similar question. His answer is set in the restrictive communist regime of the 1900s. While our curtailing of freedom may not be as extreme, Yancey seems to suggest that we can draw on the strategies of the dissidents under communist government; we, too, can move towards freedom, not by asking for permission, but by simply living in our own (and God's) permission to be free.

> *"For many years dissidents in Eastern Europe met in secret, used code words, avoided public telephones, and published psuedonymous essays in underground papers. In the mid-1970s, however, these dissidents began to realize that their double lives had cost them dearly. By working in secret, always with a nervous glance over the shoulder, they had succumbed to fear, the goal of their Communist opponents all along. They made a conscious decision to change tactics. 'We will act as if we are free, at all costs,' ...*
>
> *In effect, the dissidents started acting in the way they thought society should act. If you want freedom of speech, speak freely. If you love the truth, tell the truth. The authorities did not know how to respond. Sometimes they cracked down – nearly all the dissidents spent time in prison – and sometimes they watched with frustration*

bordering on rage. Meanwhile the dissidents' brazen tactics made it far easier for them to connect with one another ... and a kind of 'freedom archipelago' took shape ..."

(Yancey, 1997: 261)

Locke shares an encounter that provoked him to think about the topic of permission to question, research, and speak out. His story relates to his career, and was set in Japan, but is nonetheless instructive as we consider Christendom:

"One day, I met with a researcher in a coffee shop. ... I had just been to the bookstore and was lugging a stack of books on highly advanced computer-science topics. It was all Greek to me, but I figured something might rub off. Suddenly the guy asks me, 'Who gives you permission to read those books?'

I was stunned. Bowled over. Did his puzzlement reflect some sort of cultural difference? I didn't think so. It struck me that this fellow was just being more honest and direct than an American might be. He was articulating what many people in today's world seem to assume: that official authorization is required to learn new things. I thought about this deeply, and I'm thinking about it still.

Who gives us permission to explore our world? The question implies that the world in fact belongs to someone else. Who gives us permission to communicate what we've experienced, what we believe, what we've discovered of that world for ourselves? The question betokens a history of voice suppressed, of whole cultures that have come to believe only power is sanctioned to speak. Because the ability to speak does involve power. It entails ownership and the control conferred by ownership. ...

Right then and there, in that chance encounter in some random Tokyo coffee shop, I gave myself blanket permission: to be curious, to learn, to speak, to write. But it's a long road from permission to practice, and there's plenty of negative reinforcement in between. Freedom of expression may be called out loftily in the U.S. Constitution, but even after two centuries of democracy, it's still a far cry from second nature."

(Levine, Locke, Searls and Weinberger, 2000: 28)

In general, the church leaders just don't get it that in God's kingdom we have one King and **all** of the rest are servants. There is simply no place for a special distinction or privilege for those who want or seek to be "first amongst equals", let alone those who blatantly seek to be positioned above the rest.

Jesus didn't seek or receive permission from leaders. He didn't ask if He could heal on a Sabbath, befriend social outcasts, etc. He didn't need to be granted freedom from the church leaders. And He wouldn't have been given permission even if He had asked. He simply *lived* in freedom. It's well and truly time that we followed Jesus in this manner, and claimed the freedom He died to give us.

It's time for us to break free

I don't know if you can sense the growing excitement amongst the people of God. We can live life to the full, as Jesus meant it to be, and we don't need the church leaders to give us permission!

The following story from Bennett gives a glimpse of what life can be like for those who have discovered freedom. And in this case, it is the story of a nine-year-old who perhaps was too young to realize that what he was doing wasn't in keeping with the church leaders' expectations! He just did it. Perhaps, like Jesus said, we need to be more childlike in the way we follow Him.

> *"... a young boy, age nine, entirely on his own initiative started a prayer and praise session among his elementary schoolmates. Every morning before school, some twenty-five of them met at the school for this purpose. There was no adult leadership, and the teachers were especially impressed because the youngsters would come down to have their meeting even though it was a school holiday!"*
>
> (Bennett, 1984: 234)

Oliver and Thwaites introduce the challenge: ministry led by the paid professionals has often failed to achieve its potential, so now it's up to the rest of us to leave the binding cocoon, spread our wings and fly, taking responsibility for God's calling on each of us.

> *"Church leaders have, for the most part, taken oversight and management over both the Kingdom culture of the saints, and the works of ministry that they do in and from the local church base. This results in too much authority being held by church leaders over the lives of Christians. Such an arrangement profoundly limits the scope and diversity of the culture in which the works of ministry are intended to be done.*
>
> *In the church as fullness, the saints are responsible for their own works of ministry in creation."*
>
> (Oliver & Thwaites, 2001: 96)

Brown reinforces their view. We cannot simply attend a local church and think we've done our bit.

> *"By going to a service and singing along with the choir and saying Amen! to the preacher, we give ourselves the impression that we are actually doing something, when we are merely being an audience, thereby deceiving ourselves. Jesus did not save us and call us to be an audience!*
>
> *Audiences do not change the world. Audiences do not start revolutions. Audiences do not advance the Kingdom. Audiences do not fulfill the Great Commission. And audiences do not threaten the devil one bit. We must destroy this audience mentality, although our entertainment-oriented culture, replete with slick mega-churches and superstar-preachers, makes this an uphill battle for sure. But change we must, since the devil's troops understand well how the battle must be won – and it is not with the audience mentality."*
>
> (Brown, 2002: 63)

Oliver and Thwaites remind us that this change of responsibility, from ministry led by church leaders to ministry simply performed by members of the Body, is not just some theoretical notion for some time in the future. It's very real, and it's for today.

> *"Saints, in every sphere of paid and unpaid work, are you ready to follow Jesus to the workplace. Are you ready to take the plunge into the sea of God's adventure, not even sure you can swim well enough, long enough, or in the right direction, but following his voice because you've heard it?*
>
> *[Are we willing to be] the church that works. The time is now; the opportunity of a millennium lies before us. As the clocks of church gathering and church programmes tick away around us, it's time to climb the stairs to the open door that stands before us. Through that open door stands a new landscape waiting for your involvement, your participation, your heart. If not you and me reader, then who else? Answer that for me please."*
>
> (Oliver & Thwaites, 2001: 213)

In the past, the laity have too often left ministry to the church leaders because they saw them as somehow special. There is another danger. Some members of the laity may think that while other members might actively participate in God's plan, perhaps that's best left to "special" laity, but certainly not them personally. Oliver and Thwaites clearly instruct us that ministry is for *all*:

> *"... we all have a commission in line with our own gifting and character, to both minister to others and do the work God created us to do."*
>
> (Oliver & Thwaites, 2001: 153)

McManus pushes this theme even harder (in a quotation partially presented earlier):

> *"For some reason the civilized can rationalize apathy and feel themselves absolved from personal responsibility. Good needs to be done, but someone else will take care of it.*
>
> *The barbarian revolt tolerates no such abdication of responsibility. Every citizen of the kingdom of God is brought into the heat of the conflict between good and evil. Everyone who swears allegiance to Christ bears responsibility for humanity. The power and force of the barbarian way are that each one who chooses His path must find the courage to jump."*
>
> (McManus, 2005: 124)

To move into this new realm, every individual member of the Body should make a choice to join in, and back up this decision with personal action. To do less, to not act when we should, is itself an act. When we do nothing, we are making a *choice* to do nothing.

While my earlier analysis of the publication by Frost and Hirsch raised concerns at what I saw as inconsistency over the matter of hierarchical church structures, my critique of their call to action for all impressed me.

"Obedience takes place on two levels. First, it is an act of the soul—an act that involves developing the right intention, that is, inward obedience. Second, it is an act of the body. It involves putting right intentions into actions – outward obedience."

(Frost & Hirsch, 2003: 140)

"Mission is a task! … An inactive, purely reflective, personal faith is not typical of that modeled by Christ. This isn't to say that the reflective practices are not helpful. They surely are, but only when part of a broader actional, missional Christian life. In fact, we believe one worships more fully, prays more deeply, and studies more diligently when all are done in the context of a life of action and spiritual momentum."

(Frost & Hirsch, 2003: 142-143)

"So much of Scripture puts emphasis on action and nonaction. A classic example is Matthew 25, which is literally made up of a series of parables of judgment culminating in the profoundly unsettling parable of the sheep and the goats, which places the emphasis on action or nonaction as the gauge for judgment. Any Christian that is not unsettled by that parable, and many like it, must surely be in denial and is more than likely quoting Paul in favor of what Bonhoeffer called 'cheap grace.' This is precisely the way we must not use Paul."

(Frost & Hirsch, 2003: 142)

CHAPTER 30:
INDIVIDUALITY AS GOD INTENDED

In the prelude to chapter 11 we looked at the belief system called "individualism", and noted its opposite, namely "collectivism". In its more extreme form, those who follow the creed of individualism believe the individual should make the decisions, and the individual should benefit from those decisions. Conversely, those who pursue collectivism would see the group as making the decisions, for the benefit of the group.

There are many other forms of decision-making, with different models for distribution of benefit. For example, the catch-cry of democracy, "government of the people, by the people, for the people" may be seen as one approach that attempts to balance the rights and responsibilities of the individual and the group.

While democracy has many commendable aspects, not all are convinced it is the appropriate model for the "kingdom of God". If it's a "kingdom", it has a king. If it's God's kingdom, God is the king.

In a so-called "theocracy", we revisit the criteria of who makes the decisions and who benefits, and it's pretty simple. God makes the decisions, and He allocates the benefits as He chooses. For some, they may receive benefits in this life, and for others it comes in the next life. Hebrews 11 tells of many, who by faith in God, received benefits in this life, but it also tells of those who suffered and died horrible deaths but who will still be rewarded. There are some important principles to recognize if we choose to be citizens of God's kingdom:

- In God's kingdom, it must be God who calls the shots. Of course, we may choose to obey or not, but neither we as individuals, nor any group, set the direction.

- Your responsibility (and mine) in the decision-making process is for each of us as individuals to seek to discern God's call on our life, and to follow that call, with or without the blessing, approval or even understanding of others.

- Our motivation for obedience must not be rooted in an expectation of reward.

Stories of freedom in action

George MacDonald's novel, *The Poet and the Pauper: The Baronet's Song*, portrays Sir Gibbie as a person who delights in pleasing others, and will happily follow "orders" if they seem right, but who on the other hand will politely act with independence if he sees a better way. In Gibbie's relationship with the minister's wife, MacDonald notes:

> "[The wife] had yet to discover that Gibbie had his own ideas too, that it was the general noble teachableness and affection of his nature that had brought about so speedy an understanding between them in everything wherein he saw she could show him the better way, but that nowhere else would he feel bound or inclined to follow her injunctions. Much and strongly as he was drawn to her by her ladyhood and the sense she gave him of refinement, he had no feeling that she had authority over him. … he had not an idea of owing obedience to any but [Jesus]."
>
> (MacDonald, 1983(a): 125)

The minister, Mr. Sclater, had sensed the freedom of Gibbie's nature, but nonetheless wanted to dominate. MacDonald states,

> "Mr. Sclater also had hitherto exercised prudence in his demands upon Gibbie – not that he desired anything less than unlimited authority with him but, knowing it would be hard to enforce, he sought to establish it by a gradual tightening of the rein. Gibbie had never yet refused to do anything he required of him, yet somehow Mr. Sclater could never feel that the lad was exactly obeying him. He thought it over but could not understand it and did not like it, for he was fond of authority. Gibbie in fact did whatever was required of him from his own delight in meeting the wish expressed, not from any sense of duty or of obligation to obedience."
>
> (MacDonald, 1983(a): 126)

Mr. Sclater's sense of inability to dominate Gibbie was soon made obvious. Gibbie had left the home of Mr. Sclater where he was boarding so he could visit his close friend, Donal, who was in town. Mr. Sclater was furious that Gibbie had not sought permission to visit. After pursuing Gibbie to Donal's dwelling, he vented his anger on Gibbie in front of Donal, and ordered him to come home immediately. Gibbie's polite but unbending response was,

> "Dear sir, I am going to slepe this night with Donal. The bed is bigg enuf for 2. Good night sir."
>
> (MacDonald, 1983(a): 127)

The example of Gibbie's freedom, while insightful, is fictional, being an extract from a novel. However the author of *Heavenly Deception*, Chris Elkins, tells a true story of an individual's freedom from domination. His friend, Alan, was being pressured to attend a meeting by a church leader who stated,

> "If Satan can keep you from coming, you have miserably failed God."
>
> Elkins (1980: 41)

Alan's response hits the nail on the head:

> "My commitment to God is between God and myself. No one else interprets it for me. No one intimidates me about it."
>
> Elkins (1980: 41)

As another example of freedom in action, we look at the experiences of Henry Frost. We tend to see Hudson Taylor as a man of God with a courageous, clear vision of precisely God's plans and purposes. Yet the biographers also expose times when Taylor made decisions that, in hindsight, showed he had missed the mark. For example, there was a young American individual who personally felt a call of God, yet Taylor opposed the young man's call until he was effectively *forced* to concede it was from God.

Not only does this story reinforce *our* need to individually hear from God (as did the American young man – in the face of significant opposition), it also underlines the message that we must reject any authority in matters of God's call on *our* life from those who may believe they have some claim over us due to their perceived experience and maturity.

The details of this story are instructive. It starts with Henry Frost, a God-fearing American young man. He was so convinced that God wanted him to support the work in China that he traveled across the Atlantic to England, to meet Hudson Taylor, the self-appointed leader of the China Inland Mission. To put this in context, such a voyage in the 1880s was slow and expensive. To make such a trip without first communicating with Taylor to ensure a welcome was a great step of faith.

Frost's goal was to seek Taylor's support for establishment of an American branch of the China Inland Mission (C.I.M.). However, Taylor could not see how it would work:

> *"... Mr. Taylor could not see his way to the establishment of an American branch. It would be, he suggested, far better for Mr. Frost to start a fresh organisation, on the lines of the C.I.M. if he pleased, but something that would be native in its inception and development; for a transplanted mission, like a transplanted tree, would have difficulty in striking root in the new soil. Needless to say, this was a great disappointment [for Frost]."*
>
> (Taylor & Taylor, 1918: 438)

A great disappointment? That appears to be a gross understatement. Let Frost share his feelings, in his own words.

> *"On reaching my lodgings ... I had one of the most sorrowful experiences of my life. At the threshold of my room, Satan seemed to meet me and envelop me in darkness. ... I had come over three thousand miles only to receive to my request the answer, No. But this was not the worst of it. I had had positive assurance that the Lord had Himself guided me in my prayer, and had led me to take the long journey and make the request that had been made; but now I felt I could never again be sure whether my prayers were or were not of God, or whether I was or was not being guided of Him."*
>
> (Taylor & Taylor, 1918: 438)

Frost had travelled a huge distance, at great cost, only to have his vision politely but firmly rejected by the man he assumed would confirm God's call on his life. Taylor had a reputation and track record of following God's call on his *own* life. Surely Taylor would also discern God's stamp of approval on Frost's vision. Apparently not. And the effect was to cause Frost to have lost confidence in his ability to hear from God, because he was depending on *Taylor* to validate what God Himself had already put in his heart.

Frost returns home, disillusioned. We now follow the saga, from Taylor's perspective. Circumstances align such that he ends up travelling to China via America, but he still has no vision at all of the C.I.M. opening an American branch, as originally envisaged by Frost. In fact, Taylor can see no real purpose in the American visit that has been thrust upon him by circumstances.

> *"I had not the remotest idea in coming to America ... that anything specially bearing upon the work of the China Inland Mission would grow out of it."*
>
> (Taylor & Taylor, 1918: 442)

In spite of Taylor's thoughts and attitudes, God starts to get his attention. It's a slow awakening, but the realization of a greater purpose has its dim beginnings.

> *"... it was not until Mr. Taylor had been nearly a month in America that it began to dawn upon him that there was a larger purpose concerning this visit than any he had in view."*
>
> (Taylor & Taylor, 1918: 444-445)

Following a conference, the attendees were moved to offer financial support for missionaries. Frost was present at the conference, though without the knowledge or support of Taylor. And God orchestrated Frost's role to come back into view.

> *"... promises and money came flowing in, until ... [Frost] had scarcely a place to put them. There [Frost] stood in the midst of the assembly – without ever wishing it or thinking such a thing could be – suddenly transformed into an impromptu Treasurer of the China Inland Mission."*
>
> (Taylor & Taylor, 1918: 447)

Frost had believed he was called to a role in the formation of an American branch of the C.I.M., and God was not going to be stopped, not even by the very founder and self-appointed leader of the C.I.M. itself! Frost's personal vision was being vindicated by God, *in spite of Taylor*.

> *"Returning to his room that summer morning Mr. Frost could not but remember the sorrowful experience through which he had passed in London, when he had wondered whether he could ever know that prayer was really answered, or be assured of the guidance of God again. The faith that had sustained him then was being exchanged for sight, and as he poured out his heart in wondering thankfulness he realised how safe and good it is 'not only to wait upon God, but also to wait for Him.'"*
>
> (Taylor & Taylor, 1918: 447)

Frost graciously reports Taylor's growing awareness of the correctness of Frost's original vision, as shared with and initially rejected by Taylor:

> *"It was becoming clear to [Taylor], as to me, that my visit to London and appeal for a branch of the Mission to be established on this continent had been more providential than was at first recognised."*
>
> (Taylor & Taylor, 1918: 448)

The story continues. Frost gives the collected money to Taylor, and Taylor now sees the need for an American branch of the C.I.M. Taylor also recognizes the need for people to staff the branch, but still cannot see that *God* has called Frost to this role, even though God used Frost in management of the collection money and Frost was effectively standing there waiting to be "given permission" to take up the mantle. Frost's call was clear, and obviously supported by *God's* overriding actions, but *still* the "man of God", Taylor, could not see what God was directing, and *still* Frost was relying on Taylor.

> *"For the problem that faced [Taylor i.e. the need to set up the American branch of the C.I.M.], after little more than three weeks in America, was no simple one, and as yet the man at his side [i.e. Frost], young and retiring as he was, had not yet been recognised as the providential solution."*
>
> (Taylor & Taylor, 1918: 448)

It would be easy to understand if Frost had lost patience with Taylor. Frost felt vindicated in his calling, in spite of Taylor's original rejection. And here were Frost and Taylor again, and as before, the self-appointed leader of the C.I.M. was still too slow to catch up with where Frost and God were travelling! It is interesting to note Frost's two-fold response. Firstly, he prayed, and God gave him plenty of opportunity for prayer. And secondly, he acted. He had not been recognized, but nonetheless, was proactive in following the call that *God* had so clearly made, continuing in his role as (unofficial) treasurer, and also taking the initiative to send out correspondence in the role of secretary, even though this role, too, was unofficial.

> *"But all the while, out of sight, there was a quiet force of prayer at work that went far to account for the wonderful things that were happening. Mr. Taylor and his party were so carried forward on a tide of interest and enthusiasm that it was all they could do to keep up with their programme, and prolonged seasons of prayer – save for his early morning hour – were impossible. But in the retirement of that country home at Attica a man was on his knees, prevailing with God.*
>
> *For, strange to say, Mr. Henry W. Frost was not much in evidence at the meetings. A serious illness that threatened the life of his father kept him from travelling, and when not required in the sick room he had more leisure than usual for thought and prayer. He saw, with the clearness of a listening soul, the way in which things were tending. Money continued to come to him for the support of missionaries in China, and in the middle of August he sent out a circular letter to the contributors asking 'many and fervent prayers' that the right persons might be chosen, and that some might be ready*

> *to sail without delay, that the opportunity of Mr. Taylor's escort might not be lost."*
>
> (Taylor & Taylor, 1918: 449-450)

Frost's confidence in the rightness of his call was building. He was already, patiently and unobtrusively, acting out the part of the American representative of the C.I.M. It would be understandable if he were to challenge Taylor forcefully, yet Frost's approach was to simply act in obedience to God, and try to graciously encourage Taylor to reconsider his initial rejection. He writes to Taylor offering the use of his home, and the use of his services:

> *"This quiet home is most blessed in one respect ... I have much opportunity for prayer, and I do praise God for it. I am sure it is what He wants just now, and I do count it a great privilege to tell Him of all our hopes and fears at this critical time. It makes me realise the force of that definition of prayer that one has given, 'Prayer is the attitude of a needy and helpless soul whose only refuge is in God': for I feel our need and I feel our helplessness; yet I feel at the same time what a great and sure refuge we have in our God. Praise His holy Name, He has made us 'prisoners in Christ' ... and from this vantage-ground we may ask what we will!*
>
> *Please very specially remember the C.I.M's relation to America. I dare not seek to influence you, yet I ask most earnestly that you will consider the question, Will it not be well to establish a branch here? I have much to say to you upon this, if you are led to listen to it."*
>
> (Taylor & Taylor, 1918: 450)

It is almost unbelievable that Taylor had *still* not caught the vision, or maybe he was struggling to concede that he had been wrong in his earlier judgments. It was only the sheer necessity of receiving extra help when Taylor himself could no longer cope that forced Taylor to thankfully accept Frost's offer. Frost did not force Taylor, but God left Taylor with very little in the way of choices!

> *"By the middle of September Mr. Frost's prayers seemed more than answered. The number of applicants to join the Mission had risen to over forty, out-distancing even his faith and expectations. Hundreds of letters had poured in, and Mr. Taylor was wholly unable to cope with the correspondence necessary for completing the cases of candidates. It was with thankfulness, therefore, he fell back on Mr. Frost's suggestion of a reunion of the outgoing party at Attica, when he might be able to hand over much of the work that remained to his willing hands."*
>
> (Taylor & Taylor, 1918: 452)

> *"Surely not the least remarkable of the converging providences by which Mr. Taylor was led to go forward in these matters was the generous, devoted co-operation of Mr. Frost, and the way in which he was ready to assume whatever of responsibility Mr. Taylor <u>had</u> to devolve." [Emphasis mine]*
>
> (Taylor & Taylor, 1918: 453)

Even at this late stage, it was when Taylor *"had to devolve"* responsibility that it was handed to Frost. Presumably, if Taylor had the energy, time, and resources to continue to manage the American operation himself, he *still* would have done so. This story underlines two principles. Firstly, even so-called "great" men of God should not be assumed to be sympathetic or understanding of God's call on an individual. And secondly, it is up to the *individual* to seek and discover God's plan for his or her own life, and to follow God's plan even if not supported by others, no matter what status some may see them as holding.

Some principles of freedom

One aspect of freedom is a willingness to be different. When I was a youngster, one of my favorite pastimes was racing home-made billy-carts (known by some as soap boxes) down the steep hills of my home town. My friends and I also enjoyed trying to make them look like other vehicles. We painted them red and had make-believe water containers so they could become fire engines. We also tried to turn them into the covered wagons of America's Wild West – this was definitely a failure, because at speed the hoops holding the sheets collapsed, blocking all view of the street for the driver, with skinned knees and elbows the immediate result.

Then came the attempt to mimic drag-racing cars. Those who followed this fashion put big ball-bearing wheels on the back, and small ones on the front. This made the "chassis" (a piece of timber down the middle of the billy-cart) lower at the front. Unfortunately, our local council didn't worry about uneven footpaths. With the front of the billy-cart almost touching the ground, any raised concrete sections brought the billy-cart to a sudden and spectacular stop.

As a young lad, though, I had gone against the crowd. I had considered the uneven concrete footpaths, and had argued that the big wheels should be on the front. That way, when a bump was encountered, the back end of the billy-cart would simply scrape over the lump and keep going instead of coming to a bone-jarring stop. The motor mechanic that supplied the ball bearing wheels emphatically declared the design was wrong, but I didn't waver. I also encountered peer pressure from my friends, but stuck to my guns. Eventually my design was seen by others as saving many grazes.

This is a simple but true tale. I had been raised by parents that encouraged me to feel comfortable with being different, and I was willing to be mocked for what I believed. And God calls each one of us, as individuals, to also be fearless in going against the flow.

We live in God's kingdom and our King values diversity. We should not go against the principles of His kingdom by trying to make His children look the same, believe the same, or act the same—let alone being clones of some church leader. We are all unique, and He intended it that way. We are called to be different, as a people *and* as individuals. Our choice is either to rise to the challenge, or to disobey. Buckingham puts it this way:

> *"Salvation, in its purest sense, is becoming the person you really are – the person God*

created you to be. It is possible, I can report, to live above the humanism of this world and to achieve the individuality and personal identity with God that each man yearns for. But it can be done only when a man comes to grips with the fact he is different, that God has a unique place and purpose for him in life, and he does not need to defend his status – just live it out."

(Buckingham, 1980: 185)

Another aspect of freedom is exemplified by Hudson Taylor who, in his role as an English missionary to China, ventured into remote parts of the country. In an inland city in the 1850s he encountered an individual who sought truth for himself. Taylor shares his meeting with this elderly citizen:

"I found ... a private residence, the home of a fine old gentleman, eighty years of age, who had formerly been a Mandarin at Soo-chow. Taken to the guest-hall, I noticed over the entrance this inscription, 'Act morally and you will obtain Happiness.' I took the lowest chair of course, nearest the door, but in a little while the master of the house appeared and with much ceremony insisted on my moving to a higher seat.

When I offered him a selection of our books, he told me he also had books to give, and made me a present of three works of his own, in ten volumes, beautifully got up and treating of almost every imaginable subject. There was a little astronomy, a little meteorology, a little geography, some mathematics, and so on. But he said he had one superlative idea which he was delighted to have the opportunity of imparting to me.

Three great kingdoms existed in the world he said, England, Russia and China, but his discovery was as yet unknown in any of them. Confucius himself was ignorant of it, and likewise all the Sages. In short it was known to but one person – himself; and he was now eighty years of age. This long prelude and the importance of his manner made me wonder what could be coming, and it was hard to repress a smile when it proved to be that the sun stood still and the earth travelled round it."

(Taylor & Taylor, 1911: 297-298)

We, too, can smile at this story; but there is a strong message. It is those who are willing to seek for truth and knowledge beyond that of their "teachers" who are most likely to pioneer new ground, whether it be in areas of science or faith.

In the exercise of our freedom, we need to interact with others without being controlled by them. Weinberger contrasts hierarchical command-and-control structures with the freedom experienced on the World Wide Web, where we see

"... connections made by real individuals based on what they care about and what they know, [and] ... paths that emerge because that's where the feet are walking, as opposed to the highways bulldozed into existence according to a centralized plan."

(Levine, Locke, Searls and Weinberger, 2000: 121)

It is when individuals are free to walk in the paths of God's leading rather than down the highways of tradition that new paths will emerge. A key point to be noted, however, is that the individuals network with other freedom-loving people. They are neither hermits nor subservient clones of some religious leader.

To be free we need to be able to adapt. Under pressure, organizations may fail, but the otherwise apparently weak and insignificant individuals that God has chosen remain; they can survive and even be fruitful, while organizations, like dinosaurs, cannot adapt sufficiently quickly.

> *"... when disappointment came and unexpected failure the great majority ceased to help or care ... [and] more than one society in aid of the work actually ceased to exist. But here and there in His own training-schools were those the Lord could count upon: little and weak perhaps, unknown and unimportant, but willing to go all lengths in carrying out His purposes, ready through His grace to meet the conditions and pay the price."*
>
> (Taylor & Taylor, 1911: 122)

Rinehart notes that some church leaders try to direct their followers to become a herd of look-alikes. He boldly opposes such attitudes and proclaims the need and health of an approach where each individual can minister as God leads:

> *"Conformity treats all believers alike ...*
>
> *In contrast, [we should] equip and develop people in ways that empower and release them to live according to their gifting and God-given calling. Individuals experience great freedom in the Spirit, as their contribution to the body is expected to be unlike anyone else's."*
>
> (Rinehart, 1998: 39)

> *"[We should assume] that God has a different standard of evaluation for each person and ministry. It is God alone who produces fruit; we are fellow workers with Him in His harvest. His fruit is often hidden and always defies measurement. He uses different people in different ways through different processes. The value of authenticity allows people the freedom to do things in ministry that may seem to fail in the short run. But failure in our eyes may not be failure in God's eyes at all."*
>
> (Rinehart, 1998: 40)

Thankfully, there are bold individuals who break away from the crowd and discover liberty in sharing God's love in the way *He* designed for them.

> *"A growing number of believers are earnestly seeking their unique niche of service in the body of Christ. This is one of the healthiest trends for God's people in this century. So much latent power and potential exists in an energized laity whose members are freed to contribute their unique talents."*
>
> (Rinehart, 1998: 118)

If each individual is led personally by God, the results may appear chaotic to those traditional leaders who want everything to be nice, predictable, and under their control.

McManus encourages the opposite. He prefers freedom ahead of 'good order'.

> "When Christianity becomes just another religion ... to keep people in line, we build our own Christian civilization and then demand that everyone who believes in Jesus become a good citizen.
>
> It's hard to imagine that Jesus would endure the agony of the Cross just to keep us in line. Jesus began a revolution to secure our freedom. The new covenant that He established puts its trust not in the law, but in the transforming power of God's Spirit living within us."

(McManus, 2005: 6-7)

Interaction with others

Some leaders openly and brazenly teach that it is the job of the "followers" simply to follow— not to question, and not to think. Some even teach that if the leaders make mistakes, while they will be judged for their errors, their followers will not be held accountable for obeying, regardless of what their own conscience may say. One extreme of this thinking was observed in the Jonestown massacre, where parents murdered their children because Jim Jones told them to. According to such perverse teaching, Jim Jones may be held accountable for ordering the execution of innocent children, but not the parents who slaughtered their own children in obedience to their leader's demand.

In refreshing contrast, Alcoholic Anonymous not only places the responsibility for actions with the individual, but warns the group *against* taking responsibility for the individual.

> "An A.A. group, as such, cannot take on all the personal problems of its members, let alone those of nonalcoholics in the world around us. The A.A. group is not, for example, a mediator of domestic relations, nor does it furnish personal financial aid to anyone.
>
> Though a member may sometimes be helped in such matters by his friends in A.A., the primary responsibility for the solutions of all his problems of living and growing rests squarely upon the individual himself. Should an A.A. group attempt this sort of help, its effectiveness and energy would be hopelessly dissipated."

(Bill, 1967: 79)

A.A. goes further, stating that the individual is also responsible to give time and love freely to others, without any expectations of reward, other than the enrichment of having helped another:

> "Watch any A.A. of six months [working with a newcomer]. If the newcomer says, 'To the devil with you,' the twelfth-stepper only smiles and finds another alcoholic to help. He doesn't feel frustrated or rejected. If his next drunk responds, and in turn starts to give love and attention to other sufferers, yet gives none back to him, the

> *sponsor is happy about it anyway. He still doesn't feel rejected; instead he rejoices that his former prospect is sober and happy.*
>
> *And he well knows that his own life has been made richer, as an extra dividend of giving to another without any demand for a return."*

(Bill, 1967: 69)

There is an expectation that there will be a brotherhood amongst the members. But it is one where individuals see their own responsibility is to reach out to others, rather than having an expectation or demand that others must love them. I am responsible for giving where and to whom God directs; I cannot demand that others must feel a responsibility to give to me.

> *"As we made spiritual progress, it became clear that, if we ever were to feel emotionally secure, we would have to put our lives on a give-and-take basis; we would have to develop the sense of being in partnership or brotherhood with all those around us. We saw that we would need to give constantly of ourselves without demand for repayment. When we persistently did this, we gradually found that people were attracted to us as never before. And even if they failed us, we could be understanding and not too seriously affected."*

(Bill, 1967: 220)

Some people stress the need for "fellowship" with other people, even though God clearly, at times, may call an individual aside from others. And if He ordains it that way, we should not fight against His purposes. A.A. makes the observation that many so-called "loners" may actually have the privilege of serving others in a way denied to those with, for example, family responsibilities, stating that

> *"They can participate in enterprises which would be denied to family men and women."*

(Bill, 1967: 53)

If we are blessed with an enriching family circle, we are to be grateful; but no matter what our circumstances, we are always individuals with responsibilities for our own actions, and for loving others who need our support, whether or not that love is returned.

While it is the duty of each of us to personally seek God's direction for our life, we lack wisdom and humility if we believe we can learn nothing of God's ways from others.

> *"I am a firm believer in both guidance and prayer. But I am fully aware, and humble enough, I hope, to see there may be nothing infallible about my guidance.*
>
> *The minute I figure I have got a perfectly clear pipeline to God, I have become egotistical enough to get into real trouble. Nobody can cause more needless grief than a power-driver who thinks he has got it straight from God."*

(Bill, 1967: 38)

Bill shares a simple, true story of the danger of going solo:

> *"Going it alone in spiritual matters is dangerous. How many times have we heard well-intentioned people claim the guidance of God when it was plain that they were mistaken? Lacking both practice and humility, they had deluded themselves and so were able to justify the most arrant nonsense on the ground that this was what God had told them."*
>
> (Bill, 1967: 274)

> *"Because of drinking, my friend Henry had lost a high-salaried job. There remained a fine house – with a budget three times his reduced earnings.*
>
> *He could have rented the house for enough to carry it. But no! Henry said he knew that God wanted him to live there, and He would see that the costs were paid. So Henry went on running up bills and glowing with faith. Not surprisingly, his creditors finally took over the place."*
>
> (Bill, 1967: 84)

Within the safety net of respecting the views of others, Bill shares how he, as an individual, seeks to discern God's leading, starting out by checking on his own personal motives.

> *"Man is supposed to think, and act. He wasn't made in God's image to be an automaton.*
>
> *My own formula along this line runs as follows: First, think through every situation pro and con, praying meanwhile that I be not influenced by ego considerations. Affirm that I would like to do God's will.*
>
> *Then, having turned the problem over in this fashion and getting no conclusive or compelling answer, I wait for further guidance, which may come into the mind directly or through other people or through circumstances.*
>
> *If I feel I can't wait, and still get no definite indication, I repeat the first measure several times, try to pick out the best course, and then proceed to act. I know if I am wrong, the heavens won't fall. A lesson will be learned, in any case."*
>
> (Bill, 1967: 55)

It may seem to be a contradiction to say that we are well advised to seek the counsel of others in our search for discernment of God's will, and yet also to say that we must be shaped by God, not others. However, it is not to be a contest between the views of others and our understanding of what God is saying. There is wisdom in listening and considering the views of others; but we should not feel, having sought their opinions, that we would be offending them by acting otherwise, if that is our considered conclusion. It *must* be God who has the final say.

Buckingham looks at the way Jesus trained His disciples to function without having the need to run back to him for instructions on every matter. They had to be prepared to listen to God's voice in their own heart, as would be the case after He had left them to carry on His mission without His physical presence.

> *"Jesus, in a magnificent briefing with His disciples, told them He had a job for them. 'I send you out as sheep in the midst of wolves,' He said in Matthew 10:16. But as we read on, we find Jesus gave them absolutely no instructions on how to contact Him in case of an emergency. What [modern-day] discipler would send his disciples out without giving them the hot-line number back to the church? But Jesus had a purpose in this. He was training them for the time which was to come when He would be gone and they would have to depend entirely on an invisible Spirit to lead them. Now He was there in the flesh. But the time was soon to come when He would no longer be among them. No longer visible. He wanted each man to have an independent relationship with God Himself.*
>
> *That was the whole purpose of Jesus' ministry among men – to bring men to a place of independent relationship with God. He did not want them related to an earthly disciple-maker the rest of their lives. He knew His followers would have to function everywhere. Alone in courtrooms. In jails. In the quiet of their homes. In the jungles, when nobody else was within a hundred miles. They needed to learn to stand alone, if necessary, simply having fellowship with the invisible Spirit."*
>
> (Buckingham, 1980: 49-50)

We should not allow others to shape us, even though some may *demand* it as their right due to their position in the local church hierarchy. Neither should we *offer* to them a role where they can shape us, thus abdicating our responsibilities in our personal walk with God. It is *God's* sole prerogative to mold us as *He* sees fit.

Yet how many church leaders wish to shape individuals by so-called fathering / mentoring / discipling / teaching / leading them? If the answer was only one such pastor, that is one too many. We must get them out of the way and let God shape each of us.

> *"C.S. Lewis once said that when an individual was wholly God's he would be more himself than ever before. In that incredible statement he captured the essence of why any equipping process must respect the uniqueness of the individual. People don't come to us as blank slates upon which we write whatever we need them to be at the moment.*
>
> *… God has a purpose and a plan for each of His children that in some mysterious way fulfills a larger plan than any one of us can grasp."*
>
> (Rinehart, 1998: 133, 134)

Buckingham feels so strongly on this matter he has written a reminder to himself to remain true to God's call even if the resultant "shape" of what he turns out to be does not meet with the approval of others, as noted in the partially repeated quotation below:

> *"In the flyleaf of my Bible I have written a number of messages to myself – personal messages from God to me. One of them says: 'Jamie, don't let the world – or the church – mold you into its image.' Some of my friends do not understand my sometimes strange ways, but I am determined to hear and do the will of God for me – despite what others think I should do. This does not mean I do not fail and need the correction and adjustment of others. But it does mean that I shall not be ashamed – or afraid – of*

my imperfections. And I shall push on, despite my flaws, and present my body a living sacrifice, blemishes and all, and believe I am acceptable to His service. For it is far better to risk and fail than to count myself unworthy and not risk at all.

That means I must be willing to be myself – and live with others' anger and not grow angry in return."

(Buckingham, 1980: 183)

Jacobsen and Coleman's novel portrays a picture of a man called John being valued by others for his words of wisdom. As he is about to head off a little early from a barbeque, one of his friends appeals to him:

"... we have so many ... things we would love to ask!"

(Jacobsen & Coleman, 2006: 142)

Rather than perhaps enjoying the dependence of people on him, John points them to Jesus, answering,

"Then ask Jesus ... I could answer questions all day and it wouldn't make a difference. This life can't be neatly sewn up in the intellect. It must be uncovered in the journey. He'll make things clear to you as you need them."

(Jacobsen & Coleman, 2006: 142)

It is such a pity that many church leaders, instead of pointing us to Jesus, take the responsibility for answering on His behalf–in fact, it is shameful.

We must each be careful to avoid two things. We must avoid allowing others to become dependent on us; and we must never become dependent on anyone but Jesus.

We have both the right and the responsibility to act in freedom and to follow God, even if that takes us in a different direction to any group with which we may be associated. But how might such apparent tension between the freedom of the individual and the cohesion of the group works out in practice?

For Alcoholics Anonymous, the rights of the individual are paramount.

" 'Does this mean,' some will anxiously ask, 'that in A.A. the individual doesn't count for much? Is he to be dominated by his group and swallowed up in it?'

We may certainly answer this question with a loud 'No!' We believe there isn't a fellowship on earth which lavishes more devoted care upon its individual members; surely there is none which more jealously guards the individual's right to think, talk, and act as he wishes. No A.A. can compel another to do anything; nobody can be punished or expelled. Our Twelve Steps to recovery are suggestions; the Twelve Traditions which guarantee A.A.'s unity contain not a single 'Don't.' They repeatedly say 'We ought ...' but never 'You must!'

To many minds all this liberty for the individual spells sheer anarchy. Every newcomer, every friend who looks at A.A. for the first time is greatly puzzled. They see liberty

verging on license, yet they recognize at once that A.A. has an irresistible strength of purpose and action. 'How,' they ask, 'can such a crowd of anarchists function at all? How can they possibly place their common welfare first? What in Heaven's name holds them together?'

Those who look closely soon have the key to this strange paradox. The A.A. member has to conform to the principles of recovery. His life actually depends upon obedience to spiritual principles. If he deviates too far, the penalty is sure and swift; he sickens and dies. At first he goes along because he must, but later he discovers a way of life he really wants to live. Moreover, he finds he cannot keep this priceless gift unless he gives it away. Neither he nor anybody else can survive unless he carries the A.A. message."

(AAWS, 1953: 129-130)

Some members of A.A. could be tempted to look to the organization to direct them in their individual ministry. While certain members of the group, as individuals, may support various ministries, the group as an entity never does. The group has only one role—to minister to alcoholics. The individuals in the group may be led to other external ministries, but the group itself must never take on such responsibilities.

"Of course [as a group] we [potentially could] interest ourselves in [many] fields ... But, as a society [i.e. a single-purpose group], should we? Our experience says that we definitely should not. We can and we do help, as individuals, in those fields. That is good. But, as a fellowship, we know that we must not be diverted."

(AAWS, 1957: 106)

Not only do the groups *never* support a ministry other than the group's primary goal, they go so far as to avoid taking sides in public controversies. A.A.'s tenth tradition states:

"Alcoholics Anonymous has no opinion on outside issues; hence the A.A. name ought never be drawn into public controversy."

(AAWS, 1953: 176)

It explains that, as a whole,

"... we must never, no matter what the provocation, publicly take sides in any fight, even a worthy one."

(AAWS, 1953: 176)

However, the role of individuals is quite different to that of the group:

"Nor does [Tradition Ten as it applies to the entire group] ... mean that the members of Alcoholics Anonymous, now restored as citizens of the world, are going to back away from their individual responsibilities to act as they see the right upon issues of our time."

(AAWS, 1953: 177)

Brown also comments on the topic of potential tension between the roles of individuals and the role of the group. On the one hand, he notes that

"... team ministry can succeed only when personal agendas are crucified ..."

(Brown, 2002: 219)

However, he also notes that the group

"... must not quench individual gifting and calling ..."

(Brown, 2002: 219)

Brown recognizes the potential to hold such different views in tension, but in practice his observation was that groups tended to have

"... an unhealthy team emphasis ... [and a resultant] ... group smothering [of] the individual"

(Brown, 2002: 219)

Buckingham succinctly summarizes the topic of the group vs. the individual. If we have individuals led by God, and God alone, we will have unity within the Body under God's direction and according to His plan.

"As each man finds his place in the Body, ... determined not to be anyone else but to be the person God created him to be ... it is then that believers, as individuals and in true oneness, will be within the Spirit's control."

(Buckingham, 1980: 137)

Some steps towards freedom

We all need to allow and even encourage a check on our motives. Put bluntly, if we perform a "ministry" so as to gain commendation for our good works, our motives are seriously flawed. If we want to be "different" so that we can stand out from the crowd and be noticed, the catalyst for our work is absolutely wrong.

I have been fortunate enough to indirectly be made aware of some people whose lives are in complete contrast to those who seek recognition for their work. In all cases, you will never read of their work, simply because the life they live might be well described as living behind the enemy lines. They choose to give of themselves in service to the needy in countries and cultures where, if their work was to be broadcast, they would at least be forced out of their place of ministry, if not jailed or even executed.

They are what I call "hidden heroes". Their way of life is most certainly different to what it was in the culture of their birth. They exhibit amazing freedom in following God, not in seeking public recognition nor even the "blessing" of a sending church. It may be far too dangerous to allow even their home circle of friends to know the details of their calling.

In some ways, their lives are a little like police force members who go "undercover". Even their close friends and family cannot know of their work, and they may be despised by some for what appears to be a lifestyle far from that of an honorable citizen.

Are you and I willing to suffer misunderstanding so that we can faithfully pursue God's call should He design a pathway for us that is far from the "norm"? Do we feel we must have a "respectable" answer as to the way we practice our faith? Will we only be obedient to God's call if we can be rewarded with fame and glory for our sacrifices? Bill sums up the true rewards of faithful service:

> *"How wonderful is the feeling that we do not have to be specially distinguished among our fellows in order to be useful and profoundly happy. Not many of us can be leaders of prominence, nor do we wish to be.*
>
> *Service gladly rendered, obligations squarely met, troubles well accepted or solved with God's help, the knowledge that at home or in the world outside we are partners in a common effort, the fact that in God's sight all human beings are important, the proof that love freely given brings a full return, the certainty that we are no longer isolated and alone in self-constructed prisons, the surety that we can fit and belong in God's scheme of things – these are the satisfactions of right living for which no pomp and circumstance, no heap of material possessions, could possibly be substitutes."*
>
> (Bill, 1967: 254)

Frank Peretti's autobiography, *The Wounded Spirit*, is a touching, disturbing and challenging book as it reveals from the "inside" the pain of those who are bullied for being "different". In spite of the pain he experienced, Peretti encourages us all to grasp that

> *"God has created us in His image and put each of us here on earth for specific purposes."*
>
> (Peretti, 2000: 119)

Each of us has been created as an individual with unique, God-designed purposes. We do need to be careful we don't spend our lives seeking the *one* big thing we think God has designed us for—because perhaps today He wants us to help a neighbor. Possibly tomorrow He will call us to support a community initiative. Maybe the next day, something else. Yes, there could be a few "big" things He intends for us to do. Perhaps. Or maybe we are just to be faithful in the little things that might go unnoticed by others.

Peretti's statement is made in the context of Micah 6:8, where God tells us that he desires we exercise justice and mercy in a spirit of humility. That's enough. We don't need to have miraculous signs and wonders to get started. All we need to know is that God wants us to stand for justice and mercy, as He does, and to care for the "little" people of this world, be they the poor, the widowed, the orphaned, or whatever. To do nothing because we don't have a hand-written note appearing on our wall is an excuse that just won't cut it.

When Hudson Taylor first started out in the ministry God gave him, perhaps more than many of his era, he followed a calling that went against the flow of conventional Christian practice. He was fearless in pursuit of God's calling, even if it generated disapproval. Yet this fierce yet polite individuality proved to be his strength.

> *"… he was alone, and with growing experience was able to strike out on lines more characteristically his own."*
>
> (Taylor & Taylor, 1911: 293)

As noted earlier, it is sometimes the periods where one is away from "fellowship" that God shapes us as only He can.

> *"And the Lord was not only with him amid those lonely labours. He did more than protect His servant, and supply needed grace. It was, if one may say so reverently, His opportunity. And He drew very near revealing Himself and His purposes as He only can perhaps when one is much alone."*
>
> (Taylor & Taylor, 1911: 294)

Taylor's desire to reduce any unnecessary gap between himself and the people he wished to reach in love resulted in him adopting Chinese dress, hair style, and food. And the reaction from fellow Englishmen also working in China? Rejection!

> *"The covert sneer or undisguised contempt of the European community he found less difficult to bear than the disapproval of fellow-missionaries. But this also had to be faced, for he was practically alone in his convictions, and certainly the only one to carry them into effect."*
>
> (Taylor & Taylor, 1911: 320)

One could easily conclude that Taylor was so independent that he was not able to consider the merits of views held by others. Instead, in his freedom to follow his own distinct calling, he was also humble in learning from others. He encountered another missionary, William Burns, who, like Taylor, was an individual with his own approach—his own "line of work" or "calling". However, Burns' style impressed Taylor, and he was willing to alter his own individual style to those aspects of Burns' work that seemed appropriate to adopt.

> *"Practical and methodical in all his ways, Mr. Burns had a line of his own in such work that [Hudson Taylor] was glad to follow."*
>
> (Taylor & Taylor, 1911: 341)

These were two individuals who were fearless in pursuing their individual callings, but Taylor was willing to learn from Burns. And this was not a one-way domination of one character over another. Rather, Burns was also impressed by Taylor, and also made changes to his style from lessons learned from Taylor.

> *"... four weeks ago ... I put on Chinese dress, which I am now wearing. Mr. Taylor had made this change a few months before, and I found that he was in consequence so much less incommoded in preaching, etc., by the crowd, that I concluded it was my duty to follow his example."*
>
> (Taylor & Taylor, 1911: 344)

Surely this is true freedom: an individual, taking no care for criticisms of one's actions, other than a healthy openness to the challenge as to whether he has indeed heard God's voice. We do need to remain constantly open to learning from others and open to refining our own path when challenged. We need to be free to be different and free to adopt the styles of others—but only as far as God wants, because He may have a different path for us.

We want to be careful when we consider the views of others, as we need to check their motives and perspectives, and our own inclinations, against what *God* wants. But here is a problem. Can we confidently presume to have a complete and perfect understanding of God's plan? We will look at this sometimes perplexing problem in more depth in a later chapter, but for now I suggest that a lack of certainty on our part need not hold us back. While we need to always remain open to gaining a better understanding of our Father and His ways, we can humbly accept that we may get just enough light to take the next step, but we must seek that light then move boldly.

> *"Light will no doubt be given you. Do not forget, however, in seeking more, the importance of walking according to the light you have. If you feel called to the work, do not be anxious as to the time and way. He will make it plain. … I desire increasingly to leave all my affairs in the hands of God, who alone can, and who assuredly will, lead us aright if humbly and in faith we seek His aid. …*
>
> *I am sure you will forgive me if I urge on you … the importance of seeking guidance from God for yourself personally, apart from the movements of others. Each one of us has an individual duty and responsibility toward Him. The conduct of others cannot make duty, for me, of that which is not so; nor can the claims of duty be lessened because of the action, right or wrong, of others. We may and should thank God for all the help He gives us through others in the performance of duty. But let us seek to see our own way clearly in the light of His will, and then in trial and perplexity we shall be 'stedfast, unmovable,' not having trusted to an arm of flesh. The Lord guide and bless you, and give you ever to lean unshaken on His faithfulness."*
>
> (Taylor & Taylor, 1911: 372-373)

People are often attracted to places and charismatic characters that seem to be at the center of a "move of God". The focus seems to be on a central person, or a particular place and time, and some individuals want to be part of the excitement. Sometimes the desire for involvement may be more for the individual's own blessing than for what they may give out to others. It is also not good to copy what God is doing with others. Rather than being swept along with the crowd, we must individually stop and ask God where He wants us to be. Such was the case for one person who supported Taylor, and who saw a number of large, powerful revival meetings sweeping England. Yet God called him to a different path.

> *"I feel so cold and lifeless, and long to be in the heart of these mighty workings. But such is not my privilege. One has to learn to deal with the Lord alone, and not to limit His power to seasons or even places."*
>
> (Taylor & Taylor, 1911: 500)

We can look at the life of John the Baptist, and of Jesus. Their lifestyles were radically different (what they wore, what they ate, and what they drank, for example), as noted by the Pharisees. But more importantly within the context of this particular discussion, while both fulfilled the purposes of their ministry, their ministries were radically different. John's role can be summarized as preparing the way for the Messiah, and Jesus *was* the Messiah. We, too, must consider that our path may be set in a different direction to where the crowds are heading, even if they seem to be in the center of what may appear to be the spotlight of God's blessing.

Why would we consider joining a team? Aren't we being encouraged to be individuals, not look-alikes in a clone factory all doing what we are told by the leader? The reality is that the God's path for us will intersect with the paths of others. For a period of time we may be finding ourselves working for some common goals. But this is fundamentally different to formally "joining" a church or parachurch organization.

And if I find myself working alongside others for a season, it should not be for what I can get out of it. If God leads others to work in such a way that the ministry He has called me to is blessed, that's great. But my motive must be to obey God and be a blessing to others. Then we are not caught in a web of obligation.

There will be times when God calls others into our lives, but it is not because they are obliged to support us. We may need the support of others from time to time, but it is God we look to for ultimate support, and cannot demand it of others. The following quotes from Bill helped me cement my views on the balance between reaching out to others while not becoming totally dependent on them.

> *"When we insisted, like infants, that people protect and take care of us or that the world owed us a living, then the result was unfortunate. The people we most loved often pushed us aside or perhaps deserted us entirely. Our disillusionment was hard to bear.*
>
> *We failed to see that, though adult in years, we were still behaving childishly, trying to turn everybody – friends, wives, husbands, even the world itself – into protective parents. We refused to learn that overdependence upon people is unsuccessful because all people are fallible, and even the best of them will sometimes let us down, especially when our demands for attention become unreasonable.*
>
> *We are now on a different basis: the basis of trusting and relying upon God. We trust infinite God rather than our finite selves. Just to the extent that we do as we think He would have us do, and humbly rely on Him, does He enable us to match calamity with serenity."*
>
> (Bill, 1967: 265)

The preceding quotes highlight the dangers of overdependence on others. The next paragraph highlights how, within A.A., individual freedom is held in tension with the acknowledgement that we need each other.

> *"Few indeed are those who, assailed by the tyrant alcohol, have ever won through in singlehanded combat. It is a statistical fact that alcoholics almost never recover on their personal resources alone".*
>
> (Bill, 1967: 245)

Our strength comes from a willingness to stand alone, balanced with a willingness to stand with others in *their* hour of need (as God calls), and the humility to accept support in *our* hour of need. We are not bound together by some constitution developed by church leadership. We are bound together in love, under *God's* leadership, responding as He, the Master Tactician, calls our lives to cross paths.

McManus paints two distinctly different pictures, both of Christians moving together with others. The first follows:

> *"When [Christians freed from 'church' expectations] travel together, they do not march in single file. There is no forced conformity. They are not required or expected to keep in step. They walk together as free individuals joined not by standardization, but by spirit."*

(McManus, 2005: 71)

Here McManus condemns the idea of Christians walking in a line, but it's a particular type of line he opposes. He stands against a single file, with one in front leading and all other following in step.

In the next quotation, McManus presents a different picture. It's another line, but fundamentally different. This time, Christ's followers are soldiers lined up across the battle front. They are equals, side by side. They have no leader other than Christ, and they only follow *His* orders. The power of this unity comes from Christ the Master Strategist; each individual only has to obey His orders.

> *"Although the force of one person fully committed to God is tremendous, it pales in comparison to the force of God's people moving together. One barbarian wandering through civilization can be discarded as nothing more than an oddity. But when members of the barbarian tribe line up across the battlefield, side by side, something amazing begins to happen. Dark kingdoms tremble; the dungeons and prisons that hold men, women, and children captive crumble; prison doors open; chains unlock; and multitudes come to freedom. ...*
>
> *... We fight violence with peace, hatred with love, and oppression with servanthood. While never violating our uniqueness, we move together, united in heart and soul."*

(McManus, 2005: 134)

CHAPTER 31:
MINISTRY SET FREE

Make sure the "good news" is free

Many people enter into debates as to the relative merits of "evangelism" in contrast to what is commonly classified as the "social gospel", or "walking the walk rather than just talking the talk".

It would appear that Jesus ministered in both ways. He called those who assembled to hear Him to change their lives, and to seek God's kingdom. He also cared for the hungry, the sick and the downtrodden.

Further, He commanded His disciples to be bearers of the good news, while teaching that "true religion" includes acts such as caring for widows and orphans (sadly, the Apostles in the church in Acts failed in this and ordered deacons to do this work). Samuel Moffett, in *Evangelism: The Leading Partner*, and Frank Tillapaugh, in *Unleashing the Church*, continue this theme of ministering to the inner needs of people as well as their physical needs:

> "There is nothing quite so crippling to both evangelism and social action as to confuse them in definition or to separate them in practice. Our evangelists sometimes seem to be calling us to accept the King without his kingdom; while our prophets, just as narrow in their own way, seem to be trying to build the kingdom without the saving King."
>
> (Moffett, in Winter et. al. 1981: 730)

> "Evangelicals are coming out of an era that was shaped by the modernist-fundamentalist controversy in the early twentieth century. Many church historians believe that each side came away from the debate with only half the gospel.

The fundamentalist held onto the half that saves the soul; the modernists held onto the half that ministers to the body."

(Tillapaugh, 1982: 58)

Bill likewise encourages A.A. members to act on both fronts. On the one hand this involves sharing the good message (in this context, as it relates to alcoholics):

"We must carry the message, else we ourselves can wither and those who haven't been given the truth may die.

... May we ... continually seek the wisdom and the willingness by which we may well fulfill that immense trust which the Giver of all perfects gifts has placed in our hands."

(Bill, 1967: 13)

Bill also notes the need for acts of love to the suffering. A.A. members are encouraged to individually respond to the practical needs of fellow sufferers as they feel led. And if they are badly treated by those they try to help, they are encouraged to simply keep sharing. As previously quoted, Bill states:

"If the newcomer [to A.A.] says, 'To the devil with you,' the [one ministering] only smiles and finds another alcoholic to help. He doesn't feel frustrated or rejected. If his next drunk responds, and in turn starts to give love and attention to other sufferers, yet gives none back to him, the sponsor is happy about it anyway. He still doesn't feel rejected; instead he rejoices that his former prospect is sober and happy.

And he well knows that his own life has been made richer, as an extra dividend of giving to another without any demand for a return."

(Bill, 1967: 69)

Jesus came across many needy people, and simply reached out in love. He didn't organize a "ministry" to lepers or tax collectors or Samaritans. He didn't recruit them into some organization. He just loved them where they were.

Some followed Him; many didn't. For example, He healed ten lepers, and only one even returned to thank Him. If we wish to follow Jesus' example, we won't be showing love as a means to the end of building up "our ministry". We will just love people as God gives us opportunity in the day-to-day walk of life.

Love those who are different

Jesus' life clearly demonstrates He was comfortable with breaking the rules of His own culture. He comfortably interacted with soldiers from the army that had invaded His country. He broke with tradition by speaking to the Samaritan woman at the well. He lunched with tax collectors; and the list goes on.

It is clear that if we are to follow Jesus' example, we must be much more relaxed about the cultural practices of those we befriend. But can one go too far by accepting everything they do?

The Lausanne Committee, in *The Willowbank Report*, points out extremes of where this cannot be acceptable, and closes with the challenge of seeing how much of another group's practices can be retained, and perhaps modified (but only where necessary). The example is based on missionaries who encountered murderous practices amongst one culture, but it may be instructive to us in other circumstances:

> *"We have emphasized that the [need for Christians from other cultures] to 'celebrate, sing and dance' the gospel in its own cultural medium. At the same time, we wish to be alert to the dangers of this process. ...*
>
> *Applied to 19th century Fiji ... there would be 'direct encounter' with such inhuman practices as cannibalism, widow-strangling, infanticide, and patricide, and that converts would be expected to abandon these customs upon conversion. 'Indirect' encounter would take place, however, either when the moral issue was not so clear-cut (e.g., some marriage customs, initiation rites, festivals and musical celebrations involving song, dance and instruments) or when it becomes apparent only after the convert has begun to work out his or her new faith in the applied Christian life. Some of these practices will not need to be discarded, but rather to be purged of unclean elements and invested with Christian meaning. Old customs can be given new symbolism, old dances can celebrate new blessings, and old crafts can serve new purposes. To borrow an expression from the Old Testament, swords can be hammered into plows and spears into pruning-knives."*
>
> (Lausanne Committee for World Evangelization, 1978: 531, 536)

The authors above have clearly stated that the Christians from one culture should not be so egotistical as to impose their culture on any who would also express faith in Christ. Putting aside such extremes as cannibalism, some may still be concerned that the welcoming acceptance of people from another culture will result in a mix of inconsistent core Christian and "ungodly" cultural expressions. The Lausanne committee proposes a balance:

> *"We advocate neither the arrogance which imposes our culture on others, nor the syncretism which mixes the gospel with cultural elements incompatible with it ..."*
>
> (Lausanne Committee for World Evangelization, 1978: 519)

Winter makes it clear we do not have to have an "either/or" choice. Rather, we want to get rid of the unnecessary bits of *our* belief system so we can share the essential, core beliefs of our faith.

> *"[The purpose of cross-cultural evangelism] is not to let down the standards and make the Gospel easy – it is to disentangle the irrelevant elements and to make the Gospel clear."*
>
> (Winter, 1974: 306)

I have taken cannibalism as an example of an aspect of another's culture that we may wish to change, particularly if we suspect we might be on the menu! But where do we draw the line? The simple answer is that it is not simple! Just as an example, we look at

John Stott (in his article *The Bible in World Evangelization*), and others like him who teach on more classical evangelism; and their debate regarding how to "package" the gospel message:

> *"As we turn to the Bible for our message, ... we are immediately confronted with a dilemma. On the one hand, the message is given to us. We are not left to invent it ... On the other hand, it has not been given to us as a single, neat, mathematical formula...*
>
> *The gospel is thus seen to be one, yet diverse. It is 'given,' yet culturally adapted to its audience. Once we grasp this, we shall be saved from making two opposite mistakes. The first I will call 'total fluidity.' I recently heard an English church leader declare that there is no such thing as the gospel until we enter the situation in which we are to witness. We take nothing with us into the situation, he said; we discover the gospel only when we have arrived there. Now I am in full agreement with the need to be sensitive to each situation, but if this was the point which the leader in question was wanting to make, he grossly overstated it. There is such a thing as a revealed or given gospel, which we have no liberty to falsify.*
>
> *The opposite mistake I will call 'total rigidity.' In this case the evangelist behaves as if God has given a series of precise formulas that we have to repeat more or less word for word, and certain images that we must invariably employ. This leads to bondage to either words or images or both. Some evangelists lapse into the use of stale jargon, while others feel obliged on every occasion to mention 'the blood of Christ' or 'justification by faith' or 'the kingdom of God' or some other image."*
>
> (Stott, 1980: 5)

Moving beyond the mechanics of gospel presentation, Stott cuts deeper on the underlying attitudes we may have, including arrogant presumptions on the rightness of *our* culture:

> *"Some of us refuse to identify with the people we claim to be serving. We ... practice a double kind of cultural imperialism, imposing our own culture on others and despising theirs. But this was not the way of Christ, who emptied himself of his glory and humbled himself to serve."*
>
> (Stott, 1980: 7)

However, he also warns of an opposite attitude—that which so devalues our background that we have nothing left of God's message of hope:

> *"Other cross-cultural messengers of the gospel make the opposite mistake. So determined are they to identify with the people to whom they go that they surrender even their Christian standards and values. But again this was not Christ's way, since in becoming human he remained truly divine."*
>
> (Stott, 1980: 7)

So where is the balance? Jesus made friends with people from all backgrounds, including Roman invaders, despised Samaritans, prostitutes, and so on. Yet Jesus also challenged all peoples with a standard He held over and above the cultures.

> *"Of course Christ challenges every culture. ... Jesus Christ confronts them with his demand to dislodge whatever has thus far secured their allegiance and replace it with himself. He is Lord of every person and every culture. That threat, that confrontation, cannot be avoided. But does the gospel we proclaim present people with other threats that are unnecessary, because it calls for the abolition of harmless customs or appears destructive of national art, architecture, music, and festivals, or because we who share it are culture-proud and culture-blind?"*
>
> (Stott, 1980: 7)

So where does all of this leave us? Our first and primary goal is to love all. That is the great commandment. Jesus demonstrated love to those within His community who shared a common cultural foundation, as well those from diverse backgrounds.

And I suggest we may assume that any apparent clash between the practices of others and our past experiences with "traditional" Christianity may well reflect a mixture of our own prejudices with our faith rather than differences of a fundamental nature.

Jesus offended many of the religious leaders of His day by challenging the very Jewish traditions in the society of which He was a part. Jesus set a clear example of freedom from religious customs, yet the New Testament church also struggled to separate Jewish and Greek cultural aspects from core fundamentals of the Christian faith, and retained many aspects of the old religious systems. If we exhibit freedom and grace towards those who are different, we may well encounter opposition from "traditionalists". Jesus did, so the opposition doesn't necessarily prove our position to be wrong.

Some may give theoretic assent to "allowing" others to practice their Christian faith in a different way as long as they stay at a distance! They want to maintain the unity of their own group. However, Winter explains that there is a danger in assuming unity is the same as uniformity. He warns that

> *"... Christian unity cannot be healthy if it infringes upon Christian liberty."*
>
> (Winter, 1974: 307)

He concludes that we are to welcome people from varied backgrounds, and to not only allow them to retain their culture, but also allow them to interact closely with us:

> *"Let us glory in the fact that the world Christian family now already includes representatives of more different languages and cultures than any other organization or movement in human history. [Some] may be baffled and perplexed by world diversity. God is not. Let us glory in the fact that God has allowed different life-styles to exist in different forms, and that this flexibility has been exercised throughout history. Let us never be content with mere isolation, but let us everlastingly emphasize that the great richness of our Christian tradition can only be realized as these differing life ways maintain creative contact. But let us be cautious about hastening to uniformity. If the whole world church could be gathered into a single congregation, Sunday after Sunday, there would eventually and inevitably be a loss of a great deal of the rich diversity of the present Christian traditions. Does God want this? Do we want this?"*
>
> (Winter, 1974: 311)

Let us look at some examples of how diversity enabled outreach to a quite specific "culture"— that of sailors:

> "Back in the early forties, God gave Dawson Trotman a burning desire to reach sailors for Christ. Out of his ministry came the present-day worldwide ministry of the Navigators. ... It wasn't possible to minister to sailors in the majority of local churches in the 1940s nor is it possible today."
>
> (Tillapaugh, 1982: 15)

I suggest that we can draw at least two conclusions from this. Firstly, it is fully acceptable for them to maintain an expression of their Christian faith that is different from that of others. And secondly, those who do not belong to the fraternity of sailors should make sailors welcome to join their circle of friends, should the sailors choose to do so.

Jesus repeatedly crossed cultural boundaries. He demonstrated a delightful freedom from the expectations of what might be classified as normal for a Jew of His day. He didn't have to become a Samaritan or a Roman to be able to relate to such groups. In their article, *Bonding and the Missionary Task: Establishing a Sense of Belonging*, Thomas and Elizabeth Brewster suggest a healthy individual will comfortably recognize their roots, while discovering that the act of embracing a new culture *alongside* their birth culture, rather than *replacing* it, enriches them.

> "The concept of bonding implies a bi-cultural individual with a healthy self-image. Bonding and 'going native' are not the same thing. 'Going native' generally implies the rejection of one's first culture – a reaction which is seldom seen and which may not be possible for normal, emotionally stable individuals. Nor is being bi-cultural the same as being schizophrenic. The schizophrenic is a broken, fragmented self. But the bi-cultural person is developing a new self – a new personality."
>
> (Brewster & Brewster, in Winter et. al. 1981: 460)

Set God's love free

There is a saying that "a need doesn't constitute a call". Put another way, no one individual is capable of solving all the world's problems, nor every problem they encounter. However, the wisdom behind this saying also runs the risk of any one of us failing to respond to the needs that God *does* expect us to meet. We must be open to reaching out a helping hand to those in our immediate family and circle of friends, and be open to reaching out to those whose culture we might, quite frankly, not even understand well.

Many would be familiar with the story of David Wilkerson and Nicky Cruz in *The Cross and the Switchblade*. A similar story comes from my home town. A Christian decided to reach out a hand of love to bikies. He bought a bike, but initially lacked the skills to ride to such an extent he acquired the nickname of Autumn Leaf—he kept falling off. But he kept reaching out to the group of bikies, and love won out in the end.

What God lays on your heart may be a similar, clear and radical call. Or it may be a call to simple acts of love along life's journey. Or both!

The following is the expression of a pastor to other pastors, advising them to let God's people move in whatever way God (not the pastor) directs them:

> "Encourage people to find their own ministry of life. Let them use their own ideas and make their own mistakes. Don't always protect them from embarrassment and failure. Allow time for them to personally seek, find, and obey the Spirit's leadership. Don't be so busy getting them busy that they can't go their own way following the Spirit, because they're too tied up going your way."
>
> (Girard, 1972: 120)

It is refreshing to see such words from a pastor, even if he does want to still keep them in the church. However, as discussed already, you don't need permission to fly on the Spirit's wings!

In *The Church that Works*, the story is told of health workers who had a vision of ministry for God through their employment setting, totally independent from *any* local church. Having started in freedom, as God led each individual, Thwaites noted that they then risked compromising this very freedom by looking to outsider "specialists" to bolster their profile. The authors warn that even where a ministry is planted and growing without the direct influence of any local church and its leadership, the danger remains that what I will call "local church thinking" can still appear, especially in the form of an "expert" from outside overriding what God is doing dynamically within the group. They warn that,

> "If someone from elsewhere came with a powerful word, it might eclipse the words of others."
>
> (Oliver & Thwaites, 2001: 163)

Perhaps through lack of confidence in ourselves, or in God's ability to use us, we too often look outside of ourselves for support and direction. Our culture assumes that,

> "... unless we get in a known speaker, we don't think much will happen ..."
>
> (Oliver & Thwaites, 2001: 163)

Oliver and Thwaites express the view that, if the vision is grown organically by the people, and they share in their own natural way, it is more likely to be heard by their colleagues and to spread effectively.

Keith Green was a man with a passion for Christ and an internationally recognized ministry through his music. Two things are to be noted. Firstly, although he could easily have seen his "ministry" as singing, he also reached out in many other ways. For example he and his wife, Melody, provided accommodation for needy people. And secondly, much of his ministry involved a personal response to what he felt God had put on his heart, and was not directed by church leaders.

Melody Green, in her introduction to Keith's book, encourages us to also find our role, saying,

> "I ... pray that [Keith's] book will help you discover your own unique voice. And when you do, I encourage you to speak boldly as the Lord leads you ..."
>
> (Green, 2000: 9)

It's one thing to get out of the local church fortress and to seek to bring hope and healing to others. But if we do it in safe little teams assembled from like-minded folk from our home church, we have merely turned the fixed fortress into a semi-portable one.

God *may* call us to work with other Christians. Another scenario might be Him calling us to trust Him by going solo. Yet another alternative might be Him calling us to work with those who are not Christians. This last option may take many people by surprise, especially if they arrogantly think it is only Christians who have compassion and a message to tell.

Oliver and Thwaites reflect a bit of conservative thinking, stating that working with Christians is the "best" way. However, they do somewhat reluctantly open the door to working with others.

> "It is ... best that those we enter into agreement with are Christians, but sadly, at times, we may find it very hard or impossible to locate them. We will, however, in most settings generally find people who may not be Christians, but who love truth and want to see the good arise. ... Scripture records many instances where holy prophets would not touch unholy heathen, only to find that God was working all along to see these people come to truth."
>
> (Oliver & Thwaites, 2001: 111)

Frost and Hirsch go a little bit further, recognizing that it may not only be non-Christians who join *us* in pursuing our calling, but maybe we can join in and support *them* in the pursuit of their ministry.

> "... missional church thinking values the development of shared or joint projects between the Christian community and its host community. ... Shared projects allow the Christians to partner with [others] in useful, intrinsically valuable activities within the community. In the context of that partnership, significant connections can be established. [Christians] ... can initiate these shared projects ... or the Christian community can simply get behind existing projects."
>
> (Frost & Hirsch, 2003: 25)

A story from the experiences of Alcoholics Anonymous beautifully articulates that sometimes we may end up doing things differently, yet still achieve progress and retain respect for the views of others.

> "[Kaye] looked up Johnny Howe of the city's Probation Department. ... When he was shown the book Alcoholics Anonymous and was told what Kaye had seen ... he ... asked Kaye to join forces with him, but with certain reservations. Johnny had been running instruction classes for his alcoholic customers on a strictly psychological basis. ... The A.A. book was a revelation to him, but it was a revelation he did not much like

at first. He could not go for that 'surrender to the higher Power' business. The spiritual side of A.A. simply was not for Johnny.

Legend has it that he and Kaye compromised. Johnny would continue his lectures to inmates as before. But he and Kaye would try out certain A.A. ideas on some of the parolees. The prospects were told that they could try Kaye's ideas, or Johnny's, or both. Of course this sort of approach was not exactly orthodox A.A. Nevertheless it produced some results."

(AAWS, 1957: 91-92)

John Taylor, in his challenging book, *Enough is Enough*, really lays it on the line, and strongly challenges the prejudices that keep Christians comfortable only with their own circles.

"[An earlier reference] to Mao [Tsetung] need not alarm us. If Christians are going to defy the assumptions and the values of the affluent industrialized societies we have to be very sure about the road we have chosen to walk and about our reasons for walking it. And when we find, as we shall, that we are accompanied over a considerable stretch of the road by unexpected traveling-companions, this should neither deflect us nor turn us back. President Julius Nyerere, speaking as a fellow-Christian to the Maryknoll Missionary Order in New York in the autumn of 1970, warned that this would happen:

It is necessary to recognize, however, that others will also be working to promote social justice; we have no monopoly of virtue ... It is not necessary to agree with everything a man believes, or says, in order to work with him ... What right ... have we to reject those who serve mankind, simply because they refuse to accept the leadership of the Church, or refuse to acknowledge the divinity of Jesus or the existence of God? ... If God were to ask the wretched of the earth who are their friends, are we so sure that we know their answer?"

(Taylor, 1975: 82-83)

David Pawson (1984) tells the story of planning to construct a new church building that required some creativity in its design. Instead of using a Christian architect, Pawson felt called to use a secular architect. Not only did they end up with a great design but, through the interaction, the architect came to know Jesus.

Some may be comfortable with this story. They may conclude that the "normal" position is to work with Christians, but if God specifically directs to engage with non-Christians, and "conversion" results, then that may be OK. But such an attitude reeks of the old issue of pretending to get close and build friendships with others just so we can "convert" them. Thankfully, there are others who have a more wholesome and less deceptive view—who happily work with those who do not share our faith because they are people of worth and have much to contribute.

Melody Green shares some experiences of spontaneous response to perceived ministry opportunities. They were unplanned, and certainly not according to some pre-ordained "calling". For example, after meeting a needy but total stranger on the beach, she shares,

> *"Hoping that Keith might know what to do, I went and told him everything. Keith immediately got up and went to her side. His eyes were filled with compassion as he said a few comforting words of encouragement. She really responded to his kindness. And then I heard him say, 'Why don't you come home with us? Come and live with us. We'll help you.'*
>
> *I was probably as surprised as Cassie by Keith's invitation. I thought, Come and live with us? Is he serious? We don't even know her.*
>
> *But as I thought about it for a minute, I realized that Keith saw exactly what she needed – someone to love her enough to take her in and walk through this terrible time with her. And there was also a second little life at stake. It really seemed like God brought us together so we could help her, and I was glad Keith asked her to move in with us."*
>
> (Green & Hazard, 1989: 140)

Or another time they met a single mother:

> *"Keith and I ... told her she and Kelly could move in with us if they wanted. They did. ... Now she and Kelly shared one of our three bedrooms, leaving the one remaining bedroom for us, and a music room.*
>
> *But there was still more room at the inn.*
>
> *A short time later, I struck up a conversation with a young woman at the health club Keith and I belonged to. We were always trying to keep in shape, but I admit I spent most of my time in the jacuzzi. In fact, that's where I was when I met Maureen. She looked sad, and we got to talking. She was going through a personal crisis and was very open when I started to talk about Jesus. ... one thing led to another. Pretty soon, I was asking Keith if she could come and live with us, too.*
>
> *Some people thought we were crazy for having so many people move in with us. ... They'd say things like, 'You guys are nuts. You haven't even been married that long. You need time alone.' It was true we were young in our marriage, and even younger in the Lord – but it just didn't seem like the urgent needs of these people were going to wait. Where else were they going to go while we made sure we got our time alone? So we did what we felt the Lord wanted us to do – we kept our home and our hearts open to anyone who needed help. It gave us a deep sense of joy to know we could be used to make a difference in someone else's life."*
>
> (Green & Hazard, 1989: 141-142)

What the Greens taught by example, Tillapaugh summarizes succinctly:

> *"We don't need to wait until we have everything figured out before we begin a ministry. We don't need to kill a ministry by assigning a committee to study it. Let's start the ministry! Let's risk making mistakes and learn in the process of ministering."*
>
> (Tillapaugh, 1982: 55)

Maybe you have not heard an audible voice from heaven telling you what to do, nor seen writing appear on a wall. Most don't. However, not receiving some miraculous sign does not excuse you from acting. If you don't know where to start, you can try obeying the Bible's clear mandates for care and justice. Care for the widows and orphans, stand up for the underdog, fight for justice, and oppose domination by the powerful. And whatever your hand finds to do, do it with all your energy and strength. But make a start. Today. Now. Not just responding to every need, but as with Keith and Melody Green, remain open and listen to God.

Keith and Melody Green didn't wait until they were "mature in the Lord" before they reached out to others. As we have the opportunity, we should also encourage those we touch to likewise reach out. And they must act as God directs them, not look to us or others to direct their lives.

Alcoholics Anonymous also teaches those it helps to also reach out to others, perhaps initially with fellow alcoholics, but then to the wider community.

> *"Each of us ... spends a very large amount of time on [outreach to fellow alcoholics] in the early years. ... However, sooner or later most of us are presented with other obligations – to family, friends, and country. ...I just know that you are expected, at some point, to do more than carry the message of A.A. to other alcoholics. In A.A. we aim not only for sobriety – we try again to become citizens of the world that we rejected, and of the world that once rejected us."*
>
> (Bill, 1967: 21)

I think McManus might agree that if, God willing, you and I are agents of change in the lives of others, we can multiply the good news by teaching the recipients to also reach out and share.

> *"One of the tragedies of a civilized society is that no one wants to get involved. What becomes appropriate is to mind our own business. When we join a community that lacks a passionate heart for the world, we soon find ourselves acquiescing to apathy. It is a painful tragedy to see a brand-new follower of Christ alive with a barbarian spirit soon conformed to the status quo."*
>
> (McManus, 2005: 123)

Some may push back against the idea of "less mature" Christians performing meaningful ministry. McManus' book looks at the phrase, "born again". One the one hand he looks at the reality that a newly born baby, in the physical world, cannot be expected to make any contribution to society; the baby is totally dependent on others. On the other hand, I was challenged by a refreshing perspective that a newly born again Christian can contribute immediately.

> *"[We sometimes] perceive people who are new in the faith as nothing more than brand-new babes. They're innocent and helpless and incapable of caring for themselves, much less serving others. Yet the phrase that Jesus used can also be translated not as*

'born again,' but as 'born from above.' Jesus connected this birth not with a mother's womb, but with the Spirit of God descending from heaven and moving with power.

My point is this: the metaphor of new birth has led us to some wrong conclusions. When we are born of flesh and blood, we are helpless and dependent on others even for our own survival. That is not the case when we are born of Spirit. John spoke of the first birth as one of water and the second birth as one of Spirit. Strangely enough John the Baptist made a similar distinction in Luke 3:16 when he declared, 'I baptize you with water. But one more powerful than I will come, the thongs of whose sandals I am not worthy to untie. He will baptize you with the Holy Spirit and with fire.'

When we are born again, we are dropped not into a maternity ward, but into a war zone."

(McManus, 2005: 125-126)

I surmise that last sentence is a game-changer. Those new to Christ may exhibit a freshness and bravery that has not been spoiled by old-style leaders exhorting them to behave in a "proper" manner befitting of the standards of club membership. Are there risks? Of course! But that's where we must trust the Holy Spirit. And maybe we need to challenge ourselves to personally rediscover His freshness!

CHAPTER 32:
IDENTIFYING THE FREEDOM PRINCIPLES

We have looked at some individual parts of the jigsaw puzzle which depicts a radically different way of living out our Christian faith. We now assemble some of these pieces to create a sketch of how these principles might work in practice.

What you do: The dynamic ministry principle

We may be tempted to wait until some grand vision is fully understood, or maybe a new ministry has actually been formed (along with an elaborate constitution, a good bank balance, appointed staff, and a company car for each of us). If that's what we're waiting for, we have completely missed the message. God has given each of us enough to make a start with what we already have.

We need to be willing to do the little, unhidden, unspectacular, mundane things that come our way in life. We don't expect them—they just happen. And we are unlikely to plan for them. However, if we take seriously Jesus' command to be bearers of good news, not just to those in our inner circle but also to those outside of our circle of friends, there may be some things we might consider doing.

It must be noted that these so-called ministries are not mutually exclusive. You may be involved in one or several ministries at the same time, in different capacities. Your ministry may change over time, as you are led. This was my experience, too. At one point, we encountered a mother and her children who had escaped from domestic violence, and we gave support. At another we provided weekend respite to a single mother with two special-needs children. And more, just responding as needs arose and we felt called to respond.

Just being busy in some larger or more visible ministries does not excuse you from continuing to be alert to God's prompts to help in small ways. Remember the story of the "good Samaritan"? We could equally refer to it as the story of the "dysfunctional church leaders". The religious leaders of the "church" of Jesus' day were so busy in what *they* considered to be their prime ministry that they didn't have time to stop for their needy neighbor.

We have enough to make a start. It's always good to be open to learning new things, but we need not wait until we've learned it all before making a start. After all, making mistakes can be a part of the learning!

I interpret the foundational theme of Oliver and Thwaites' book as stating that your work (paid or unpaid) *is* ministry. We don't have to set sail to some foreign country as a missionary to begin to reach out to others. But the idea of "work" being part of God's plan for our lives is not something many would even consider. The following quotes provide a thread through their work as it relates to this matter seems to me to begin with a warning that passively listening is counter to action.

> *"We have become addicted to teaching in our present culture of church. We hear so much of such intensity and import so often, that much of the meaning in what we hear is lost before we drive out of the church car park. ... If we know too much more than our life experience can match, then that knowledge becomes counterproductive to our growth."*
>
> (Oliver & Thwaites, 2001: 119)

Oliver and Thwaites don't seem to be outright condemning teaching, but rather suggesting less teaching, with more open questions. Whatever small amount of teaching we listen to should be little more than opening up topics and letting God run with the outcome.

> *"The approach I am suggesting is one where we don't swamp the landscape with teaching tapes and videos and, in particular, that bane of Christian life – the method men. Dare I say it: we are obsessed with product, particularly product that has buttons and levers to push and pull, things to do and say and when to do and say them. ...*
>
> *So, we don't need too much teaching up front. ... The less that we give closure to people, the more they will have to learn to find the arrival places in life."*
>
> (Oliver & Thwaites, 2001: 122-123)

> *"How does this translate? So, you want a method do you?*
>
> *To speak plainly now (so you might perhaps think I am speaking from God!) I would suggest the following. Do sketch an outline and do teach some about the Hebrew vision of creation and the church as the fullness of him who came to fill all things, but don't offer closure and don't map it out in a method. In effect, speak it out and let the content sit there for a time. Give things time to stir up the good and the not so good things within people. Let responses arise and then discuss them, leaving more things open; again, not rushing to closure. Of course you can do whatever you want, in that this 'non-method' method I am suggesting needs to suit the situation, and situations are different and complex. What I am suggesting, however, is that truth be given time to leaven its way through, rather than being allowed to form its own sermon-series*

IDENTIFYING THE FREEDOM PRINCIPLES

lump with bells, whistles, guarantees, buttons, methods, pseudo-arrivals and vision statements attached."

(Oliver & Thwaites, 2001: 124-125)

Oliver and Thwaites lead me to a view that they not only warn about excessive teaching, but also warn about meetings in general. As we start launching out, they appear to caution against getting organized and trying to define when, how and where "we" will meet. They stress that it's not about meeting. It's about doing.

"So this new wineskin is not about defining how we <u>meet</u>, it's about <u>being</u> the [Body] in the place of work and in all of creation. It's about the way we think: think about God, think about what he calls church [His people, on the front line, not in a building] and think about his world of work" [Emphasis mine]

(Oliver & Thwaites, 2001: 37)

They present a though-provoking balance on the "work" front. We have jobs, whether paid or not, and it should be seen as important in what we do for God.

"... millions and millions of saints are going to work each day and most of them haven't got a clue as to the relationship between their work and the purposes of God on earth."

(Oliver & Thwaites, 2001: 117)

If the idea that "work is ministry" is strange to many laity, it is even less likely to be recognized by some church leaders.

"... no thought is given to establish what <u>church members</u> are already doing in their neighborhood and places of work. No attempt is made, for example, to identify the medical practitioner who has changed the approach to patients by providing counseling and practical support rather than just curative care. ... And no attempt is made to see one family's care for their disabled child as a ministry worthy of the church's support and prayers." [Emphasis mine]

(Charles Ringma, quoted in Frost & Hirsch, 2003: 45)

One reason given for church leaders not recognizing the ministry of the laity in their work-place relates to a false distinction made between the "spiritual" work of the local church and the "secular" work of the laity as they toil during the week.

"... the Christendom-mode church ... separates the sacred from the profane, the holy from the unholy, the in from the out. ... We talk routinely about the 'world out there.' What else can that mean other than that we, the church people, are 'in here'! This dualism has over 1,700 years created Christians that cannot relate their interior faith to their exterior practice, and this affects their ethics, their lifestyles, and their capacity to share their faith meaningfully with others."

(Frost & Hirsch, 2003: 19)

Even if the individual member of the laity recognizes their own God-ordained ministry, they may be disappointed if they look to the church leaders for support and encouragement.

> *"In the almost thirty years of my professional career, my church has never once suggested that there be any type of accounting of my on-the-job ministry to others. My church has never once offered to improve those skills which could make me a better minister, nor has it ever asked if I needed any kind of support in what I was doing. There has never been an inquiry into the types of ethical decisions I must face, or whether I seek to communicate the faith to my coworkers. I have never been in a congregation where there was any type of public affirmation of a ministry in my career. In short, I must conclude that my church really doesn't have the least interest whether or how I minister in my daily work."*
>
> (William Diehl, quoted from an extract in Robert Banks' *Christianity and Real Life,* in Frost & Hirsch, 2003: 20)

The authors quoted above as recognizing the validity of ministry in the workplace speak out against a false separation of sacred and secular. Yet I believe they also fall all too easily into the traps of traditional thinking. If we take an example of those "tentmakers" who live in a culture as paid foreigners so that they might have opportunities to share their faith, Frost and Hirsch see the income-earning job as just a means to an end. It supplies money so that the worker can then perform the "real" ministry.

> *"[In a] bi-vocational support or tentmaking [role, the one doing the ministry] ... works two places at once. He or she might work in non-church-based settings in order to support himself or herself for ministry in the direct missional setting."*
>
> (Frost & Hirsch, 2003: 217)

The authors don't follow through consistently by criticizing those that separate *"... the holy from the unholy ..."* (e.g. those that separate *"work in non-church based settings"* from *"direct missional"* work), and then make exactly this distinction themselves. In earlier quotations, they are clearly stating that the work *is* the ministry. Then in the quotation above, they are saying that those doing "tentmaking" have a job to earn money so that they can support themselves for the *real* ministry. The clear implication is that their money-earning job isn't *real* ministry.

I am only guessing, but maybe they do have a genuine desire for radically new forms of ministry, with the laity set free, but find a total, clean break from "church" traditions so very difficult. Old thinking is comfortable and familiar, and will creep in unless we carefully challenge ourselves and others.

It is good to start being a messenger of hope and love within your work environment. But even there, it is too easy to just love those that are easy to love. It is good that we demonstrate love to those with whom we naturally associate, but we must always challenge ourselves to reach further.

In the context of traditional "mission", Winter notes that, while *"near-neighbor evangelism"* (i.e. outreach to those in your own culture) is desirable and efficient, it is not enough. In the mid-1970s he estimated that,

> "... in the world today 2,700,000,000 men and women cannot hear the gospel by [such means]. They can hear only it by ... [those] who cross cultural, linguistic and geographical barriers ..."
>
> Winter (1974: 293)

To make this challenge a little more concrete, let's take a real example. In the 1970s, the attitude of many people towards homosexuals ranged from disassociation through to physical violence. I worked in a factory environment at the time, and one individual was assumed by many to be homosexual. Whether he was or not, he was certainly labeled as such. As a Christian, and totally putting aside the views you or others may hold on the "theology" of homosexuality, I had a choice. I could either stay comfortably in the circle of my core friendships, or I could expand it to include others whose lifestyles were different to my own–I chose the latter. Jesus certainly included and accepted many that brought Him into disrepute with more judgmental onlookers. We too must reach out to all, even if some of our friends do not understand why we are relating to those who are different.

In the areas of outreach, we have to move away from the local church model. A new understanding and a whole new practice is required.

> "... our definition of [ministries such as apostles or prophets] as mostly or only being 'full-time', local or para-church based ministries is far too narrow."
>
> (Oliver & Thwaites, 2001: 153)

The world we live in moves fast. Once, we had time to brew tea in a teapot, to develop a career over time by starting as an apprentice, to save for goods before thinking of buying them, to reign in our sexual drive and wait for its full expression with a life partner. Now the pressures of society and marketing push us towards instant gratification. It is tempting to assume that a new approach will appear immediately, already in its full, mature form. The reality is that it will more likely take time to materialize.

> "It is hard to imagine these gifts [i.e. apostles, prophets, evangelists, pastors, teachers] of the risen Lord functioning in a different way to that which we have seen, but I believe that we need to start doing so. The church as fullness is in great need of these resources of heaven. When we start to try and see these ministries differently, our definition of them will get fuzzy for a time, before the shape of the new begins to emerge."
>
> (Oliver & Thwaites, 2001: 150)

As noted above, the new way not only may take some time to emerge, but when it does, it should never be locked down or organized—it should always remain fluid. Weinberger looks at how the 'command and control' hierarchical approach to running commercial business has begun to be challenged as individuals start to network. But this totally different approach raises many questions. Weinberger suggests that we don't yet have the answers, but advises:

"Epochal changes are not [question and answer] sessions. ... It's a time to make things up, try them out, fail a thousand times, and laugh at how stupid you look.

[He also warns that] the urge to 'solve the problem' is nothing but the voice of the old command-and-control psychosis trying to reassert itself."

(Levine, Locke, Searls and Weinberger, 2000: 129)

Instead of running everything according to man-made rules, McManus encourages each of us to be free, to work with God directly to discover our own vision (*not* that of someone else), and see what happens!!!

"My goal is not to cast a vision that everyone buys into, but to create a visional community where everyone who enters in begins to have wild and God-sized dreams and visions. There is a price to pay, of course, when you choose this particular path; you end up with an unruly barbarian tribe. They keep getting called by God to do things you didn't expect or really didn't want them to do."

(McManus, 2005: 103)

Smalley, from a traditional "missions" perspective, gives guidelines for sharing the Good News with others. He suggests our teaching should include the following aspects:

- We should teach that the Bible has a cultural perspective, relevant to its original recipients, and that we need to take care that we don't apply in a literal manner what it says to people from another culture.

- In apparent contrast to the above, we need to teach that man's basic needs, nature, relationship to God, etc. are unchanging across time and culture.

- Finally, we need to instruct the people that their own outworking or expression of Christian faith is likely to be different, and that *they* must take the responsibility for praying and seeking God's message to them individually.

"It is our work first of all to see the Bible in its cultural perspective, to see God dealing with men through different cultural situations. It is our responsibility to see him change in his dealing with men as the cultural history of the Jews changes, to recognize that God has always, everywhere, dealt with men in terms of their culture. It is next our responsibility to take new Christians to the Bible and to help them see in the Bible God interacting with other people, people whose emotions and problems were very similar to their own so far as their fundamental nature is concerned, but also at times very different from their own in the specific objective or working of their forms of life. It is our responsibility to lead them in prayer to find what God would have them do as they study His Word and seek the interpretation and leadership of the Holy Spirit."

(Smalley, in Winter et. al. 1981: 499)

Thankfully, those who introduced McManus to Jesus did not try to shape him to fit their expectations of Christianity.

> *"Those who brought me to the faith did not take the time to civilize me. They brought me to the barbarian way and never tried to make me like them – only like Christ. They brought me into the presence of the living God and knew that His presence would both consume me and transform me."*
>
> (McManus, 2005: 77)

Likewise, we should not try to shape any Christian to fit our expectations, and we should not be dismayed if the way God leads turns out contrary to some of our precious beliefs.

> *"...mission is usually surprised at which seeds grow. Often they have the tendency to consider the seeds which do grow in any proliferation to be weeds ..."*
>
> (Smalley, in Winter et. al. 1981: 500-501)

Following the significant growth of the Pentecostal movement of the early 1900s, leaders met to take action to *manage* the movement. For a movement purportedly emphasizing the need for each individual to experience the Holy Spirit in their lives, it is interesting to observe the leaders' desire to control the movement:

> *"These concerned leaders realized that to protect and preserve the results of the revival the thousands of newly Spirit-baptized believers should be united in a cooperative fellowship. ... The five reasons they listed for calling the meeting were: doctrinal unity, conservation of the work, foreign missions interests, chartering churches under a common name for legal purposes, and the need for a Bible training school."*
>
> (Brown, 2002: 153)

It is clear that the desire to capture for all times the move of the Spirit can lead to church structures being enshrined. Perhaps we can see the dangers in such a setting; we need to take care that, in our freedom, we don't fall for the same trap.

Just to reinforce the dangers, we look one more time at the practice of structuring organizations as observed amongst denominational churches. Speaking of leaders who impose their will over individuals, and by this act come between those individuals and Jesus, Brown quotes Owen and adds his comments:

> *"And all this comes from 'the wills and fancies of men, under the name of order, decency, and authority of the church.' We cannot bow down to this!"*
>
> (Brown, 2002: 158)

We must never be constrained by the wishes of others to conform to their expectations, and we must never place these expectations on others.

Rinehart notes that Jesus did not specify a "model" for how His followers were to operate:

> *"In all His preparation of the twelve disciples, Jesus never emphasized any continuing organization. ... Jesus prayed that His disciples might be one ... While this certainly implied a close and continuing fellowship, it hardly specified any visible structure."*
>
> (Rinehart, 1998: 72)

Rather, Jesus simply taught His disciples to get into action, with the understanding that the Spirit would guide them with enough insight and direction to take the next step of faith, whatever that single step might turn out to be.

> "At the time of His ascension, Jesus instructed the disciples to wait before they went anywhere or did anything; God alone knew what should be done and how. Their part was to adopt an attitude of readiness and obedience."
>
> (Rinehart, 1998: 72)

We, too, need to heed Jesus' instructions, be obedient, and let God take responsibility for the "master" plan. The New Testament church is held in such high esteem, and many seek to go back to its historical roots, rather than its *real* spiritual roots, namely Jesus. However, the historical roots were corrupted. It is such a shame that the disciples, having received the Holy Spirit, and Jesus' instructions, then went on to fall into the old "church" mold by appointing formal leadership roles and telling others what they could or could not do. They took responsibility for appointing people to ministries, for directing lives, and for calling people to account for failures. These should be left as responsibilities for God, not any church hierarchy.

Who works with you: The dynamic involvement principle

Below I share some quotations from a book, *The Cluetrain Manifesto*. It's about the business world, but many business leaders might find the book confronting and irreverent. We have already looked at the dangers of church strategies and management styles that are based on the business world. So am I now going against this very principle by quoting from a business-related book? I say, "No", for two reasons.

Firstly, Levine et al's book is not pro-business (as we typically see it). It is perhaps better classified as "anti-establishment".

And secondly (and I hope this hits hard), I suggest that it's an indictment against Christendom that I have had to look to this anti-business-model book for quotations that oppose the very business models that churches copy from the business world!

Levine et al's observations suggest that liberated workers who network with other workers and the larger community are threatening the hierarchical power structures in business. In a similar manner, liberated Christians who form ministry-based communities of connected individuals may (hopefully!) threaten the hierarchical power structures of local churches.

In the section he labels *Decentralizing the Fort*, Weinberger challenges the 'centralized' model as it applies to the commercial world of "business".

> "Traditionally, business is an indoor sport.
>
> Businesses by their very nature are centralized (or so we think). Even if you are a global enterprise, your organization consists of a headquarters with regional offices.

> *A business is, after all, a bringing together of talented people who agree to work to achieve some common goals. We've assumed that 'together' means we have to centralize power, control, and resources. But there are lots of ways to be together."*
>
> (Levine, Locke, Searls and Weinberger, 2000: 129)

If we analyze his words, and consider if his comments on the business world could be applied to churches, possibly we can gain insight into foundational problems with centralized church models? You might agree that church practices are "an indoor sport", that they, "by their very nature", are centralized, and that church leaders presume we must be assembled "together" to be effective. Many Christians brought up in local churches have heard church leaders bemoan the lack of activity amongst the laity. Perhaps if they dismantled the central control, ordinary people would find God's ministry for themselves. In the business context, Weinberger notes:

> *"In a decentralized environment, people figure out that they have to do things themselves. Indeed, they want to do things themselves."*
>
> (Levine, Locke, Searls and Weinberger, 2000: 131)

Local churches often have a "fort" mentality, reinforced by the concept of membership. Weinberger firstly portrays the fort mentality by describing it as a

> *"... world of closed rooms and weekly meetings [where] you're a member or not. To join, you have to commit to sitting in a room at a particular time."*
>
> (Levine, Locke, Searls and Weinberger, 2000: 155)

He then goes on to contrast this fort membership model with *linked communities* where the individual can

> *"... check out what a particular group is doing [and] ... join [a] discussion group or visit ...",*
>
> (Levine, Locke, Searls and Weinberger, 2000: 155)

and states,

> *" ... membership isn't a yes-or-no decision."*
>
> (Levine, Locke, Searls and Weinberger, 2000: 155)

He concludes:

> *"When the hurdles to membership lower, the boundaries blur."*
>
> (Levine, Locke, Searls and Weinberger, 2000: 155)

People dynamically link to form living communities of connected individuals. Again as we read Weinberger's words as applied to the business world, we may find it challenging to consider if we can perhaps get an insight as to how the principles of freedom articulated for the business world may apply to church institutions?

> *"The business [set free of centralized control] now consists of a shifting set of hyperlinked groups, self-organizing, inviting in participants ... regardless of where–*

and whether–they are on the org chart. Management is simply an impediment to these groups. In fact, rather than employees feeling that they must constantly justify themselves to management, management now needs to give workers a single reason why it should be involved in the life of the business it used to believe it ran.

Hyperlinks [i.e. communities of connected individuals] subvert hierarchy. Hyperlinks subvert Fort Business."

(Levine, Locke, Searls and Weinberger, 2000: 158)

Searls argues that networked communities can, in practice, achieve a lot more than just conversations. He analyzes what has happened with the Internet. Firstly, he looks at what might have happened if big business had been tasked with the responsibility of coordinating Internet-related efforts. He says,

"What if the task of building the Internet had been jobbed out to the leaders of the communications business: to online services like AOL and Compuserve, to network companies like Novell and 3Com, to telecom companies like AT&T and Northern Telecom, to software companies like Microsoft and Lotus?"

(Levine, Locke, Searls and Weinberger, 2000: 85)

And he answers his own question by stating,

"It would never have happened ... Every one of those companies would have looked for a way to control it, to make it theirs."

(Levine, Locke, Searls and Weinberger, 2000: 85)

Searls then goes on to contrast the predicted inability of centralized businesses to build what we now call the Internet, with the way it actually developed. He suggests that the source of its development was

"...behind-the-scenes work by what amounts to a loosely organized, Internet-mediated software craft guild. ...

In fact, nearly a third of the world's Web servers are powered by Linux, the dark-horse challenger to Microsoft's previously unquestioned software hegemony. Linux was initiated by a young, unknown software developer, Linus Torvalds. He needed it, so he crafted it–and then he made it available to the rest of the world through the Internet. He published not just the finished product but, far more important, its source code. Anyone with software engineering tools and the technical chops could add to it, modify it, craft it into precisely the tool they needed. As a result, Linux has rapidly become one of the most sophisticated, powerful, and configurable software products in history–all without anyone managing or controlling it.

Eric Raymond ... describes the dynamics of this distributed and self-motivated community of independent programmers. How was it possible that a seemingly disorganized, seemingly undirected band of renegade hackers could rise to such prominence and threaten the world's largest, most powerful high-tech corporation ...?"

(Levine, Locke, Searls and Weinberger, 2000: 85-86)

The answer to this question is that

> "... the Internet and Linux ... show what can happen when people are able to communicate without either the constraints of command-and-control management, or the straightjacket of one-message-fits-all."
>
> (Levine, Locke, Searls and Weinberger, 2000: 86)

Locke predicts how things might be if individuals claim the freedom to which they are entitled:

> "... the future ... will be about subtle differences, not wholesale conformity; about diversity, not homogeneity; about breaking rules, not enforcing them; about pushing the envelope ...; about invitation, not protection; about doing it first [i.e. a pioneering spirit], not doing it 'right'; about making it better, not making it perfect; about telling the truth, not spinning bigger lies; about turning people on, not 'packaging' them; and perhaps above all, about building convivial communities ..."
>
> (Levine, Locke, Searls and Weinberger, 2000: 17)

And how will these communities of connected individuals be formed? Weinberger states,

> "These hyperlinked relationships are, like the Web of hyperlinked documents, a shifting context of links of varying importance and quality. They are self-asserting, not requiring anyone else's authority to be put in place."
>
> (Levine, Locke, Searls and Weinberger, 2000: 128)

It would appear that we don't need centralized control to achieve great things. It seems John Taylor would wholeheartedly agree:

> "... I do not put my faith in the big battalions. I distrust the pedlars of over-all strategy and I despair of the busy housemaids of the church endlessly tidying up its inconsistencies. The great ecclesiastical centralizers, like King Saul of old, put their trust in heavy accoutrements and expensive weapons. He could not bear to see the shepherd boy going unarmed into the contest with Goliath, and almost smothered him in excess of equipment. But David knew better."
>
> (Taylor, 1975: 87-88)

Oliver and Thwaites speak of the human need to enjoy relationships. If we abandon all "church" meetings, people will still meet, but in new and healthier ways that are relevant to their culture. They suggest that, for some, this may include spontaneous and informal times of sharing the Christian journey with mutual friends. It most certainly will *not* be in the form of regular Wednesday night cell group meetings.

> "These are simply places to come and worship, talk some and go. Little or no teaching is given. They are not held regularly, so as to break the weekly pattern that causes people to turn up because it's Wednesday."
>
> (Oliver & Thwaites, 2001: 187)

For others, the reason to meet is based on

> "... a common passion or a desire – third world debt, development, government, education ..."
>
> (Oliver & Thwaites, 2001: 187)

The key message is that *if* people meet it's because they *want* to, and in a way that is spontaneous and natural, not institutionalized, formal or regular.

> *"Each one of these gatherings is no longer in the shadows of the building. They are no longer an extension of the church of elsewhere; they are now populated by people who know they are his body, the church."*
>
> (Oliver & Thwaites, 2001: 188)

We may struggle to conceive of an organization that is not organized! Surely such a thing would be an oxymoron—a contradiction of terms. Yet my reading of Rinehart suggests he proposes something along these lines:

> *"... the basis of a structure that serves people and enables them to grow is a relational one. Its form should be that of a living organism ... The design resembles a matrix, an interweaving of individual lives into a rich tapestry of truth and love.*
>
> *... There are many parts but one body. These relationships of interdependence – with each other in the Lord – are the foundational dynamic of kingdom life. And as the word dynamic implies, their life-giving quality comes from a recognition that relationships flourish in an atmosphere of freedom.*
>
> (Rinehart, 1998: 144-145)

Can fluid relationships without an overriding management structure actually work for us? Rinehart seems to suggest so, highlighting how the Trinity has a foundation of loving relationships yet each member is a distinct individual.

> *"... if we look to the triune God, we see that He has modeled [relationships] for us. His [relationship] values and principles are everywhere in the Scriptures. While God has not given us a formula or rigid prescription, neither has He left us groping in the dark, waiting on the next new management seminar to give us direction."*
>
> (Rinehart, 1998: 86)

> *"What we see in the Godhead is an incredible picture of interdependence, and of unity and diversity ... Equality is the basis of their relationship, yet there is also a role differentiation among the Trinity. They share [responsibility], yet each has a different function. There is no jealousy or competition in their midst – only harmony and unity."*
>
> (Rinehart, 1998: 88)

So often, money, time, materials, effort and planning go into how to formalize a ministry, rather than simply performing the ministry. Instead, we should have as little as possible of defined structure, because by tomorrow it may be a different shape or a totally different ministry altogether. Rinehart describes this dynamic as follows:

> *"The true nature of life and ministry is an ebb and flow. The structure and forms change constantly as people develop and their needs evolve. This reality requires that … we stay flexible and adaptable, able to let go when needed. We must hold our ministry with an open hand, or we will squeeze out its very life. If our identity becomes confused with our position or responsibility …, we will then leave behind our calling to be a servant."*
>
> (Rinehart, 1998: 153)

Levine et al have painted a picture of how things could be, and actually might be, as workers break free and interconnect.

An example in action

Without fuss or fanfare, my late father achieved some of this freedom. He acted as he felt called to do, and he, like Levine et al, encouraged and experienced interconnection with other free souls.

My home country of Australia has vast areas of hot, arid desert. Today, most travelers to the more remote regions use 4WDs equipped with satellite phones or long-range radios. They can carry emergency position-indicating radio beacons (EPIRBs) to call for help in life-threatening situations. They often use global positioning system (GPS) devices to guide them along poorly marked dirt tracks. That's today.

In the middle of the last century, a single woman shared a vision of taking the Good News to families on huge properties in these far-flung areas.

This courageous woman needed a vehicle. A carpenter by trade, Dad built a caravan body on the chassis of a light truck. It was made of wood bent in steam to form a curved frame, with plywood overlaid to form a skin. Weatherproofing was nothing more than some canvas stretched across the ply and painted with an oil-based paint—pretty cheap, and pretty crude, but sufficient for this front-line soldier of the Cross. And her appreciation for dad's work was reflected in the naming of this truck – "Hephzibah" – which I am told is Hebrew for "my delight is in her".

She would drive for days, following a pair of wheel ruts in the desert, and sometimes find a family living at the end of the road, sometimes not. As with so many others, we often cannot measure the fruit from seeds planted by this lady, but if we are called to sow, we do not need to count the strike rate.

No local church leaders brought dad together with this courageous lady to fulfil some vision she had. God brought them together. We do not need much to be able to serve—at least, not much more than a willingness to serve. And we don't need to worry about how God will bring others across our paths. It is His strategy, not ours. Our job is to trust and obey, and to live in the freedom that will allow us to serve without having to be granted permission from church leaders.

Let us see how all these aspects of dynamic relationships could work. Perhaps yesterday's start-up ministry involving only you, may today gain momentum and involve others.

How are we to relate to those who come along to join in, especially when they come in different shapes and sizes and are not what we might have picked as colleagues? Rinehart emphasizes several principles:

- We are equals.
- Our equality is in worth, not role. We each have a unique contribution to make.
- Our roles can change over time.
- The role we play at one point in time may be filled by another later. We must be willing to step back and let others take "our" place, and God will move us on to His next role for us.
- The foundation for any joint ministry is relationships between the participants. Jesus said we would be known by how we loved each other.

"We are a team of co-equals, each with a different set of gifts and callings, each with a particular contribution to make. We make our contribution and then step back to allow another to do the same."

(Rinehart, 1998: 137)

"While each member of the family of Christ has his or her special roles to play in accomplishing kingdom purposes, the relationships among its members are critically important. Those relationships do not emphasize rank. Instead, we stand shoulder to shoulder, mutually supporting and deferring to one another. We step up to make our contribution and then step back into our place to encourage and applaud the contributions of others."

(Rinehart, 1998: 145)

In practical terms, this might mean that yesterday I saw a need and responded as God directed. Today, others who observed my actions might feel called to contribute. We now work together. It is no longer "my" ministry. (In fact, it was always God's, not mine.) Tomorrow the role I played as the founder has been superseded by others. I step back, and find that I am now free to contribute in a new way. And the day after, I am totally obsolete as others have replaced me. And perhaps at some future time, the whole ministry passes its shelf life. I simply move on to the next call that God places on my life, without regret. Stay fluid and don't hold on to "ministry".

Of course, the story can be told the other way around. Instead of looking at how a ministry I may have initiated plays out its life, I may join in and play changing roles in the work others began.

One interesting aspect of this whole changing scenario is that those that come and go *may* be Christians, and maybe they are not. Christians do not have a monopoly on "good works", and we should be humble enough to realize that.

IDENTIFYING THE FREEDOM PRINCIPLES

Who leads: The dynamic leadership principle

Rinehart condemns the leadership models so often found within Christendom. He also offers an alternative, which focuses on service (not just some church leader boasting about being a servant). Sometimes our examples may inspire and encourage others, but as previously stated, we do not become their leader. That is God's role.

> "Christ's disciples didn't see themselves as 'junior Nehemiahs' charged with the task of discerning God's mind for His people and then instructing everyone accordingly. Jesus instituted a different order based on ... mutuality and interdependence ...
>
> ... He said, 'You are not to be called 'Rabbi,' for you have only one Master and you are all brothers' (Matthew 23:8, NIV)."
>
> (Rinehart, 1998: 104)

> "[The Holy Spirit] enables every follower of Jesus to influence others spiritually ... [We] no longer have to be viewed as the ones who make it all happen. This eliminates an elite model of leadership, which can be so discouraging to the untrained follower of Jesus.
>
> ... each believer can be [an inspiration and example] in the arena of his or her particular gifting. Conversely, every believer ... [may be inspired by others] as well. This happens when believers defer to one another in the area of their gifts."
>
> (Rinehart, 1998: 106)

> "In the final analysis, we are all [servants who may inspire others] by serving the Lord and each other through the Spirit's work and unique gifting in our lives."
>
> (Rinehart, 1998: 108)

Rinehart suggests that the way we apply these principles in shared ministries can be shaped by what we observe of the relationship between the members of the Godhead:

> "[The concept of shared servanthood and responsibility] flows from the model of the Trinity."
>
> (Rinehart, 1998: 89)

Rinehart goes further, stating that even having shared responsibilities is not enough. All must be willing to share responsibilities in a *fluid* manner, with a willingness to change roles, as God directs:

> "We recognize and deeply respect each other's callings, strengths, spiritual gifts, and contributions. We have roles to play because of our gifts, and we each offer [inspiration] to the group in those special areas. Our focus is to recognize what God wants to accomplish ..."
>
> (Rinehart, 1998: 92)

At any one time, each person should be willing to show initiative in their area of calling, with others showing love and respect to the uniqueness and gifting of each individual.

Some examples of the principles in action

Sometimes it is helpful to see the application of principles. Theory is one thing, but what does it look like in real life? A small handful of stories follow, some of which are about people from within my own circle of contacts. Possibly you could add many more of your own. But hopefully these will be enough to fire your imagination as to what God's people can accomplish. I call them "hidden heroes", as they are faithful servants who typically labor without recognition, happy to simply wait for God's "well done" at the end of their journey.

The stories are varied, but there are common themes. Just as my father and the lady did with Hephzibah, these individuals responded to God's individual call. Sometimes they labored alone, or sometimes God brought fellow workers across their paths for a season. Sometimes the resultant ministry required service for much of their adult life, while other stories are examples of short-term ministries that came and went. But it didn't matter to these people—they served where God wanted, for as long as He wanted.

An unstoppable country lad

When I was much younger, I was blessed to know a man in his golden years who had many stories he could have told. But it was only as you spent the time with Des' wife and friends that you were able to draw out pieces of the rich tapestry of this man's life. Like many who were on the front line of the World Wars, this man rarely talked about his own experiences.

Des was raised as a farmer's son, in very hard times. Some could afford tractors, but Des still used horses for the farm work. He did not have the opportunities given to many to gain much of an education, but this very quiet man simply improvised. He mounted a bookstand on the handles of his horse-drawn plough, and read, day after day in the blazing sun. My own grandfather taught me that, with a good team of horses, the farmer directed them for the first trip around a paddock, but after that, the lead horse would follow the furrows from the previous lap. "All" the farmer had to do was to fight with heavy soils, unwanted roots and rocks, and miles and miles of walking. Yet this harsh environment was the schoolroom for Des.

And his favorite book? The Bible. Hour after hour, day after day, year after year, Des soaked himself in God's word. No seminary training was available for Des, but he knew God's word, and he knew God.

Then came the Second World War. Des ended up a prisoner of war in Asia, used as forced labor to build a railway line for the Japanese. There was a set amount of track work to complete each day, and punishment was extreme for any that fell short. With poor food, poor health, and demanding labor, many men died. In spite of sheer exhaustion, Des would spend many nights boiling and distilling water to nurse those with dysentery. He had no training as a nurse, but knew enough to realize that sick men with diarrhea needed clean water. And after a taxing night, he had to then turn up again for another full day of cruel labor.

Many fellow prisoners did not share Des' faith in God, but they were moved by his compassion for them and their fellow prisoners. Often, even though they themselves were sorely pressed, they would together take on some of Des' assigned length of track work to allow him a break, realizing that the next night he would most probably be up again, nursing the sick. Des deeply appreciated this sacrifice by his fellow prisoners, and would slip away into the bamboo forest for a bit of respite. Yet even in these moments, he would often use the time to cry out to God for his colleagues, preferring to seek God's blessing for them than to sleep.

Many years later, when I first met Des, he was still the same quiet man who served others where he could. He served them, but he always took his orders from God, not man. A number of Christians in a fairly remote part of the country had been used to attending a local church where they received their "teaching". But the pastor had left, and the denominational headquarters was unable to find a replacement.

Des saw the need, and saw a solution. He simply suggested that, if the people still wanted to meet, he would share with them what he knew of God and His ways. Problem solved? Well, yes, in some ways. But apparently the denomination was perplexed. Des had not asked their permission to teach, he just did it. And—horror of horrors—he had no recognized theological training; just years of reading God's word attached to the plow handles, combined with proving God at the war front—arguably a far better education than many ordained pastors.

And here he was, with no "authority", fulfilling the role of teaching God's word. In spite of the denomination's discomfort, he did not move aside (and there was still no one to replace him anyhow). It wasn't that he was trying to prove they couldn't boss him around. He simply ignored any concerns they had and pressed on with what he believed God wanted him to do. And the people were not about to let head office remove Des anyhow. Possibly quite frustrating for the hierarchy!

I cannot help but smile when I recollect what Des told me about the denomination's final solution. He told me that they had strict rules as to the requirements for ordination (formal training, evaluation by the central authority …)—all of which Des "failed" to meet. In spite of this, apparently they broke their own rules and gave him the necessary honorary titles to "allow" him to continue to lead. This presumably made *them* happy, and made not one iota of difference to Des. He simply continued doing what he understood God required, for a season, performing the same task he had done before receiving their "official blessing". That's freedom.

An exuberant city worker

Oliver and Thwaites recount a fairly long story, but one worth the telling. The setting for this story is a factory floor in England, in the latter half of the 1900s.

The first (long) extract sets the scene and I include it here as I was impressed by how a small group of Christians brought about massive change, notably without the oversight of a local church or its leaders. Please read it and enjoy it, but be prepared for an unexpected twist that caught me by surprise, presented in the subsequent quotation.

> *"I worked for an engineering company in Sheffield England, which made clutches, overdrives for cars, and certain garage equipment. The company had about 1,200 employees. My job at the company was a 'setter' and what I used to do was 'set' machines up or operations on machines for operators to command the machines and do a good job. At that particular time, the company was very union oriented (as were a lot of companies at that time). The union had an iron grip on the company and everybody that worked there had to pay subs to the union every week. The union did do some good things, don't get me wrong, but they did do some silly things, because they had too much power.*
>
> *Where I was based in the factory, there were two Christians. One was a very keen Christian and the other was a fairly keen Christian, but not quite as keen as the other one. This was because he kept on witnessing to his wife and tried to get her to go to church. She told him to cool it or she would go back to her mother's. And so, from then on, he had stopped going to church. He played a big part in my becoming a Christian even so. The other lad was a more regular churchgoer. Lunchtimes were great times. We used to play cards or dominoes. These two Christians used to sit and read the Bible and discuss it. I became very curious about what they were doing. I'd had a church background, in that I had always been in Sunday school, the Cubs, Boy's Brigades, the Scouts and the youth club, so I didn't feel embarrassed to talk to them. I spent some time talking to them about the Bible and I came up with some very good arguments, because I knew my Bible stories. There was one thing that they shared more than once that I couldn't get my head around and that was their own personal testimonies of how they had become Christians. I didn't have an argument for that because it was their own personal experience.*
>
> *God began to speak to me around the time my girlfriend's father died. We used to spend a lot of time together working on our cars and I used to get along with him well. I had not been touched by any death on my side of the family so it hit me in a big way. God started to speak to me more and more through that. At that time, God seemed to be in everything I did or said. I would look at the stars, and the wonder of creation made me think about God. I went to the coast for a day or so and seeing the sea made me think about God. I went to the country and God spoke to me, and I got to a point where there was nowhere to turn, everywhere God was prompting me to make a decision. I felt the Lord say, 'Jimmy, [it's] time to make a decision. You're at the point of no return: repent and ask me into your life.'*
>
> *One day when I got up early for work, I felt a bit weird. It felt as if it was going to be a 'different' day that day. It was while I was at work setting up a machine and operating it that God started to speak to me very strongly and I knew I had to make a decision – I couldn't hold out any longer. So I stopped the machine right there, and on the spot I prayed, repented and asked God into my life.*

I went around immediately telling everyone on the shop floor. I was so excited, and although some people didn't agree with what I was saying or didn't understand what I was saying, they could see my excitement. People were saying, 'look we don't know what's happened to Jim but something has happened to him'. Within a few days or so, a dozen of my friends and colleagues had become Christians and, from then on, there was someone saved every single day. It didn't just stay in the factory, but spilled out outside, because our girlfriends, wives, parents, brothers, sisters and cousins all started to become Christians. My wife became a Christian, and so did her sister. Since then, my wife has probably helped lead thousands of people who came from the factory to Christ.

All we had to share with people was our testimony, because we didn't really know the Bible. We didn't know anything about the Holy Spirit, the 'Second Blessing', renewal, revival. All we knew or had heard of was God. A friend of mine at the time said, 'Jim, I don't understand this – it's like a massive wave of God over which we have no control, no control at all'.

We felt that it was quite important to learn a bit more about the Bible, and found out about something that was called the 'Topical Memory System', from which you would get Bible verses through the post on little cards to memorise. So, each day we would get our memory verse and stick it on our machine, on the workbench or drawing-board, and we would learn the scripture. Then at lunch-time we would test each other and discuss what we had learnt that day, what we had learnt that week and what we had learnt over the past few weeks and months. So we learnt a lot of the Bible and it did help us in our witnessing.

Each person discipled another person. I had someone disciple me and I would disciple another, so that everybody was discipled by somebody else. There was much to do in the evenings because that's when we would do the discipling. We were happy to be so busy, because we were doing what God wanted us to do.

It was getting very exciting at work now. I can't explain the experience of work – it was absolutely incredible. There were a lot of us by now, so the company gave us the boardroom to meet in to have prayer in the mornings and Bible study in the evening. Actually, we had our Bible study as soon as work finished at 4.30 p.m., so we didn't go home until after it had finished.

We started to print our own magazine and put testimonies in that magazine. These were very relevant, because they were read by guys who were working next to the guys who had their testimonies in there. We used to put in tips on things like gardening, fishing and cooking, which people found really useful. The company bosses gave us permission to be at the gate five minutes before everybody else, so that we could go outside with big cardboard boxes full of newsletters to give out. Everybody used to take one, because the topics in there were the topics of discussion on the shop floor for the rest of the week. We never found any on the floor – that's incredible isn't it – everybody used to take them.

We prayed every morning. I used to get up at about quarter to five. All sorts of people were saved – from labourers to managers – no grade was excluded. All the 'girly' calendars came down and the company let us put Christian posters up. Also, the toilets were repainted to cover up all the rude jokes and pictures. Christians took over all the positions of shop stewards, because there were so many of us now. So, as all the shop stewards were Christians, there were no more strikes.

About half of the workers at the company became Christians. Productions levels went up by 60 per cent, because we were working harder, and scrap levels came right down. The ceiling was taken off the bonus earnings and our bosses doubled our wages overnight without us even asking, because we were doing so well.

The company began to supply free overalls and free safety wear. They built us a sports club, tennis courts, bowling green and children's area. This was the new environment God had created for us to work in. The company started a fishing club, cricket club, arts teams, cycling teams, bowling club, archery and football club and probably others that I can't remember as well. They even organised and paid for day trips to the coast for all the families. We began to get sent work from other factories within the group, because we were so efficient. The company built the finest training centre for apprentices in the country and, in fact, the finest in Europe (although I must be modest). The company took over our magazine: produced it, paid for it and it went out with our wages. You couldn't get your wages without getting one of our magazines."

(Oliver & Thwaites, 2001: 139-143)

I read the above, and was struck by the way something "unplanned" worked out so amazingly.

Could we ask ourselves if we could replicate the approach, and replicate the outcome, by copying what Jim had done? My guess is the advisable answer is, "No". What God did amongst Jim and his colleagues was probably unique. Moreover, if we ever try to bottle a move of the Spirit and control it for our own ministry, that's counter to how the Holy Spirit works. He's not going to be contained and ordered around by us to work in the same way just because it's what we want.

Could we also ask ourselves how such an outreach might interact with established, traditional churches? As I analyzed the following presentation by Oliver and Thwaites, I believe they alluded to a disturbing answer:

"We decided to send people out to churches because there were so many of us and thought we should get them to church. I suppose we were already a church in our own right, but because the church had no influence in what God was doing we started to get people into churches in the area, in the city where they lived. Unfortunately, the church didn't seem to appreciate what God had done and told us that they should have been saved at church and not at work. But we carried on trying to get people integrated into churches. This caused many problems, but that's another story."

(Oliver & Thwaites, 2001: 139-143)

My conclusion? Not only should we embrace the freedom to work with God outside of traditional church structures, but we should not later try to the incorporate the work back into churches. The message I gleaned from the story told by Oliver and Thwaites was that trying to formalize a work of God by placing it under the covering of a "church" can be the death of the work!

Feeding the body and the soul

Some friends of mine were aware of two related matters. One was the poverty of many in the suburb in which they lived, where even the basics of life were not easily attainable for many of the population. And the other reality was that a local bakery threw out food each Saturday that was still suitable for consumption but that would not be suitable for sale at the start of the new week.

These friends approached the shop, and received permission to collect and distribute the unsold food each weekend. The food was then freely distributed to the needy neighbors. Trust was built, and those receiving the food started to share deeper, personal issues. Both body and soul were nourished.

Over time, the needs grew, but so did the number of those willing to pitch in and help. It is my understanding that the initiative was not the result of some church leader's vision.

Friends at work

Sometimes people can see the fruit of their labors, sometimes not. John had a work colleague, Terry, who despised Christians and openly ridiculed them. Terry had been raised in an area that some regarded as "on the wrong side of the tracks". Many of the practices that "nice" Christians judge to be undesirable were very much part of Terry's life. But he was a survivor. He knew how to win street fights even if he didn't fight "clean". For example, if confronted by a larger, stronger opponent, he resorted to his own "left-hook special"—while the other person was watching the approaching right fist, Terry would down him with a left knee in the groin.

John was an IT professional, and Terry was a self-styled jack-of-all-trades in the general office. Unschooled but extremely bright, Terry was given the jobs from the "too-hard" basket. As it turned out, Terry and John were repeatedly thrown together on joint work assignments. When a crisis arose, management often teamed them up to solve the unsolvable.

Often they would work extremely long hours. At one time, for weeks on end, they only got home for a few hours of sleep and then headed back to another 16, 17 or 18-hour day. While having disparate views on matters of faith, they became close friends.

John had a real burden to pray for Terry's eternal welfare. Occasionally, Terry would ask questions about Christianity, but would only permit John to answer his immediate questions, but no more. After a few years of working together, they went separate ways as far as employment was concerned. Yet the friendship continued and, over the years, if there were challenges, they would get together to help each other. And all this time,

Terry kept a tight defense against matters of faith, with only the occasional lowering of his guard. And John kept praying.

A quarter of a century after first working together, Terry was dying. In a frank exchange on things that mattered, John quietly told of his disappointment in failing to be effective in the sharing of his personal faith in Jesus. Usually, Terry was blunt, cynical, cutting and foulmouthed in his conversations. However, in this case, his response had a note of softness. All he said was that John might be surprised at how much he had affected Terry's views.

They spoke for the last time only days before Terry died. Terry still gave nothing away. As John headed to Terry's funeral, he felt devastated that while this man whom he had prayed for over several decades had softened just the smallest bit, he not taken the step of receiving a saving faith. Imagine John's surprise to hear at the funeral a close friend of Terry share that in Terry's closing time, he actually made a decision for Christ.

If it were not for this revelation at the funeral, John may well have felt that his prayers for years had been unanswered. It is our job to sow love and care; we may not always see the fruit of our labor.

A hitchhiker

While it may be a real encouragement to see the fruit of our labor, our job is to be obedient, and to leave the outcome of our sharing to God. And it is this attitude that was important for Anne.

Driving along a country highway on her own late at night, she saw a male hitchhiker. She felt that God wanted her to give the hitchhiker a ride, but as a woman she would not normally consider giving a male a ride in a remote country setting. She drove on.

She had given up on the idea, but God had not, telling her to go back and pick up the hitchhiker. Quite some time later, she allowed God a small victory. She would go back, and if the hitchhiker was still there, she would pick him up. Just to increase her chances of avoiding such an outcome, she drove back, but via a less-than direct route! But he was still there.

Even the hitchhiker commented on the fact that a woman on her own had picked him up, and Anne shared the dialogue she had had with God. A valuable exchange followed. So much so, that Anne drove past the turn-off to her home and instead drove him all the way to his destination—something like an extra fifty kilometers (thirty miles) round trip.

Finally, Anne offered him the Bible she carried in her handbag. The hitchhiker politely refused, explaining that his mother had packed a Bible in his backpack. Up to now, he had not looked at it, but he said he now would.

The final outcome—who knows? Anne doesn't. But it doesn't matter. We play our part in God's strategy, and leave the outcome to Him.

My dad

Most of the stories I have shared relate to people I personally knew. Now I want to tell another story of the man who introduced me to Jesus—my own father. He was a layperson, not a member of the church leadership "class". He had no formal theological training. He was no more than a faithful servant, but that is more than enough for anyone.

Dad was a carpenter. But he saw his workplace as a place of ministry. His apprentice, Gordon, was a hard-drinking young man. It was not uncommon to see him turn up for work quite the worse for wear. Dad and he lived lives that were opposites in so many ways, yet Dad was able to reach out in love to this young man and subsequently led him to a personal, saving faith in Jesus. Gordon went on to later head up a state-wide outreach to drug and alcohol addicts, street kids, members of violent gangs, and prostitutes.

I only knew Dad for a bit over a decade before he died, but in that time I saw this quiet, shy, unschooled man of God touch so many lives. He simply grabbed every opportunity that arose to share his reason for hope.

I remember visiting him in hospital. Ron, the patient in the next bed, had a family. Even though dad had life-threatening troubles of his own, he reached out in kindness to Ron's children—country kids visiting a city hospital with a seriously ill dad. Dad didn't have much with which to entertain these youngsters, but he improvised. He took his handkerchief and tied a few knots in it, forming a "rabbit" with ears and a tail. He lightened the tensions in that hospital, told stories, created games, and befriended the family—and introduced them all to Jesus. To the best of my knowledge, decades later, and generations later, this farming family continues to carry God's torch in their country community.

Another story that may bring a smile to your face also relates to creativity in Dad's sharing of his faith. He was visiting the city with several fellow Christians, and encountered a rather abusive person who, while despising Christianity, needed a lift home that evening to Dad's country town. He agreed to accept a lift as long as Dad and his mates promised to never once talk about their faith. Dad agreed, and instead of *talking* about their faith, he and his friends simply *sang* hymns and choruses all the way! The Holy Spirit used the words of the songs, and the man begged Dad to tell him more about Jesus.

Dad reached out to all. There was trouble on the streets where we lived, with rival gangs forming. These types of kids would rarely even consider attending any activities related to Christianity. Dad's solution? At the end of the work week, he would empty his tradesman's truck of its tools, and load it up with seats. He would then drive around, and pick up these street kids, and run a regular program that attracted them. Not a typical "Sunday School", but one aimed at their interests. I believe that one of the young men that Dad befriended is now a leading Christian apologist. And who knows how the lives of so many others he touched may have turned out?

And there are many more stories of how he just followed God's leading every day, and the great impact he had on the lives of many others.

These stories hopefully convey the image of a person who quietly sought opportunities to share love and hope with others. These were not ministries established and approved by church leaders. Dad simply acted as God directed.

Ministering without being a "minister"

I have previously mentioned Hunt's fictional novel, *The Debt*, which tells the story of a clash of two cultures. A woman, Emma, was raised to respect and honor the local church as an institution; she was the wife of a pastor. She had conceived a son in earlier years but had adopted him out. This son, Chris, returned, and though Emma tried, she simply could not understand her long-lost but now returned son who served God in freedom *outside* of the constraints of the local church institution.

As I read this part of Hunt's novel, I wondered how challenged church leaders might feel if one of their own offspring initiated a ministry that was exercised outside of "church"?

The dialogue begins as the two try to convey totally different understandings of the term, "minister".

> "[Chris says,] 'I'm a minister.' …
>
> [Emma responds,] 'Why, that's wonderful! What church are you working with? …'
>
> [Chris] 'I'm doing parachurch work, non-denominational. I minister to people where I find them.' …
>
> [Emma] 'Well … it's wonderful that you've received the call. Tell me about it – did God call you in seminary? …'
>
> [Chris] 'We're all called, Emma. The moment we surrender our lives to Jesus we are called to follow him. And he leads us down paths that are as different as our personalities.' …
>
> [Emma] 'Yes, I know we're all supposed to serve God. But the call to pastoral ministry – surely that was different for you.'
>
> [Chris] … 'Afraid not.'
>
> [Emma] 'So … you were never called to be a pastor?'
>
> [Chris] … 'I was called to minister as a follower of Christ, Emma. I've been called to obey.' …
>
> [Emma] Somehow, somewhere, someone failed to teach this boy about ministry in the real world. … 'The call of a pastor is a unique thing,' I explained, folding my hands. 'Abel [her husband] was sixteen when he heard the call, and he knew his life would always be different. He stopped going to parties and school dances, he began to search for a good Christian college, he started listening to the great preachers. From that moment on, he knew what his life's work would be.'
>
> [Chris] … 'I know what my life's work will be, too.'

[Emma] 'What?'

[Chris] 'Following Christ.'

[Emma] I bite back a sigh of pure exasperation. 'God calls us to tasks. There's that verse about how God outfits the church by giving us pastors and teachers and evangelists and prophets–'

[Chris] 'You're absolutely right …But tell me – is every Sunday school teacher at your church on staff?'

[Emma] I shake my head. 'Of course not.'

[Chris] 'Yet their gift is as God-given as the pastor's. So why is one calling more sacred than another? No, Emma – we are all called to follow Christ. He has given us special gifts, and he expects us to use them as we move through the world. I used to think that being a Christian meant doing my religious duty – now I know that only God knows what my duty is from minute to minute. My job is to follow and obey.'

…

[Again, Chris states,] 'I told you, I'm a minister.'

[Emma] 'But you don't work for a church.'

[Chris] 'Call me self-employed and God-directed.' "

(Hunt, 2004: 152-154, 225)

Another dialogue centers on Emma's discomfort at meeting Chris in a pub, which is exactly where Chris often goes to meet needy people.

"[Chris] 'Coming here bothered you, didn't it?'.

[Emma] … 'Yes, it did. If anyone other than you had asked, I wouldn't have come. …'

[Chris] … 'There are people here, Emma. I go where the people are.'

[Emma] 'There are people everywhere … Even at church. If you want fellowship, you should visit a more appropriate place.'

[Chris] 'But if I want to minister … what better place than this?'

[Emma] It is a reasonable answer, but for some reason it stings.

[Chris] 'Tell me… if you didn't have your cell phone and your car broke down in front of this place, would you come inside to call for help?'

[Emma] 'Well … yes, if I had to. It'd be an emergency and it'd only take a minute.'

[Chris] 'So, you'd set your standards aside to rescue a car? Yet how much more valuable is a person than your wheels? It is perfectly right to do good [wherever we are] … God wants us to be merciful; he doesn't care about the little sacrifices we make to show others we're spiritual.' "

(Hunt, 2004: 159-160)

Of course this will mean we encounter people whom some might not classify as 'nice', but as Chris says,

> "... don't let guys like him rattle you. I've learned not to be surprised when sinners sin."
>
> (Hunt, 2004: 167)

As Chris interacts with people who are struggling, he finds many opportunities to selflessly reach out. Not without cost, but in obedience as God leads him to help people, one by one. Initially, Chris shares some photos with Emma of the real people that he is interacting with.

> " 'This is Melinda.' He slides the picture toward me. 'She's only fourteen, but she was kicked out of her home about six weeks ago. She's using drugs, drinking, suffering the abuse of practically every man who enters the crackhouse where she's staying. But the house is warmer than the street, and I've been taking her a couple of hot meals every day.' "
>
> (Hunt, 2004: 225)

Subsequently, Chris' adoptive parents also share some photos with Emma.

> "This is Shirley, from O'Shays. ... And this one ... is Judd, who was sleeping on the sidewalk before Chris took him home and gave him a bed."
>
> (Hunt, 2004: 299)

In Hunt's novel, Chris is presented as an example of reaching out in obedience to God. He had not called any others to support his "ministry". He has just been faithful, and led by example. As part of the story line, Chris dies in a road accident. After his death, Emma now states,

> "I may never understand how or when he took his pictures [of those he reached out to], but in a flash of insight I understand why: These people and their needs are now my responsibility."
>
> (Hunt, 2004: 300)

Even after Chris' death, God is faithful in enlisting the help of others to carry forward the work Chris had been doing, because it was never Chris' work, it was God's, and He can continue it even after an individual has moved on. We too need to respond as God leads, and leave the master strategy to God.

I found that a moving story. And challenging! I asked myself, and hopefully will continue to ask, "How does my life align with the spontaneity of Chris in freely following God's prompting? Perhaps that is a question we may all embrace?

CHAPTER 33:
APPLYING THE FREEDOM PRINCIPLES

We have just looked at some of the principles of operating in freedom. We also looked at a few examples of people who lived out aspects of these principles.

My granddad's axe?

You may have heard the story about a person who claimed to have his granddad's original axe? The handle had been replaced five times, and the head twice, but he still claimed it was the axe his granddad had owned and used. The moral of the story is that you can only change just so much before a thing is no longer what it used to be.

So here's the question. If we apply the principles of freedom to a local church, will it have changed so much we can no longer call it a church? It's only a hypothetical, but it may be insightful. Let's try it.

In this hypothetical "improved" church institution, the roles of individuals would look surprisingly different.

- The **founders** of the ministry would have stepped aside. They might subsequently offer advice based on lessons learned, but their views would be taken as just the views of *one* of the group. In this new setting, the founders would not take any offense if their advice was ignored by others. These others may be thankful for the founders' efforts in starting the ministry, but the founders would have *no* authority. Those who had been leaders would now be just some of the many individuals, and they would trust God to direct those who had subsequently joined, and not try to interfere.

- *Everyone* would be a "**minister**"— *every* individual would minister to the needs of others. In obedience to God, they would minister; so by definition they would be ministers. But unlike the ministers in your typical local church, they would not be paid, they would not be ordained, and there would be no titles for *any* role.

- There would be **no leaders**. From a casual observation, there might *appear* to be leaders. One person may seem to be more active in befriending newcomers. Another might seem to be leading by example in care for the elderly. But when you look a little closer, you might observe that what one person did at one point in time is not necessarily the same the next time, not because they have assigned roles and rosters saying when they should be performing, but because each follows God on a moment-by-moment basis. If I see a need, and if I am the first to respond, one could say I am leading. But as others respond to what they see me doing, some with greater ability may step in to help, and God may use them to move the ministry in a new way. Without any fuss or fancy appointments, these other individuals might be labeled by the casual observer as now "leading". And God might call me to new areas, or humbly to support the work as it moves in a new direction. Who cares who is seen to be leading? No one. Because no one is ever recognized as a leader, and it is only God who directs anyway.

- There would be **no "tithes"** or **"offerings"** because each individual would give the amount that God tells them to give to whom and to where He tells them. It may be to a neighbor who is struggling, it may be to a charity, it may be to someone they are passing on the street (because God knows the needs).

- **Time** would be spent as God sees fit. There would be no fixed prayer meetings (each person would be praying how, when and where God tells them to), no deacons or elders meetings (there would not be deacons or elders), no finance committee meetings (there would not be a finance committee), no evangelical society meetings (there would not be such a society because each person is doing what God tells them to do), no time spent in leadership meetings (there would be no leadership), and so on. Each person would be responsible to God and to Him alone for what He wants them to do with their time.

Think of all the benefits—time spent doing what God wants instead of feeling guilty, or being made to feel guilty, if you have to miss a meeting or service, money spent God's way instead of giving it to the church leaders to spend on salaries and buildings and other money-wasting things, to the detriment of those who actually *do* need your time and money.

In summary, I believe God is calling His people to get out of the pews and be on the front-line for Him, with Him as the Boss.

Final advice on how to define a model? "Don't do it"

Earlier in this book we spoke about how this might all come together. We recognized that some want a clear and fully articulated "model" to follow. We did not even try to elaborate a "model". What we did offer was a few pieces of the jig-saw puzzle, and a handful of underlying principles as a guide. But it is not a nicely packaged, complete (and static) out-of-the-box model.

But even the analogy of a jigsaw puzzle has dangers. The ones we are used to, when assembled, are fixed. There is only one way for each bit to fit together, and once they're in place, they should not be moved. In contrast, I believe that God has in mind for our lives to be a continuous adventure, with each of us willing to be where God may place us for a season, but also ready to move at a moment's notice. Like the people of Israel in the desert—when the cloud or pillar of fire stopped, they stopped, and when it moved, so did they, even in the middle of the night.

The "jigsaw puzzle" pieces are intended to give a glimpse of what this dynamic life might reflect at times. But the responsibility remains with you to see what pieces God wants you to apply. In other words, there are enough overall hints to remind us of what's so wrong with local church structures, but these hints also teach us obedience and faith. Isn't that the way it was always meant to be?!

Much of our human nature likes simple solutions to our problems. Whether it is three easy steps to losing weight, becoming wealthy, or finding a life partner—the idea that someone else has distilled the essence ready for us to consume seems to lure many people. In the world of sales and marketing, it can be a little dangerous, tempting us to part with our money on a remedy that may turn out to be a disappointment. But in the world of Christian faith, the promise of following people who proclaim they have the answers is still tempting to some—but with potentially much more serious consequences. So beware the desire for models.

On the other hand, I have some thoughtful friends who are not looking for the easy answers, but nonetheless quite reasonably want a picture of how Christian life *might* "work" if we no longer have churches and leaders. Some argue that even if there is no single, simple model, surely we can present some examples of those who have lived life in freedom from church constraints?

Oliver and Thwaites argue that many "saints" (i.e. Christians) have their vision so dominated by church-centric practices that we *need* to offer them a vision of an alternative:

> *"At the moment, because the church as construct, or as meetings, is the centre and focus for the saints, they have very little sight of each other as the church in their world of work. Hence, the importance of giving them a vision of each other as the body and also a greater awareness of Christ the head of that body standing in the sphere of creation in which they live and work."*
>
> (Oliver & Thwaites, 2001: 93)

I have sought in preceding pages to offer snippets from the stories of those who have gone before *and* demonstrated a life lived according to the Holy Spirit's calling, rather than being defined by the leadership. But there are dangers in holding up the lives and actions of others. Many authors in many books share how God led them, but warn the readers not to simplistically apply the same ways as a "formula". We must exercise the same caution when looking at the examples just listed. We can learn from them but we must not be tempted to copy them. God's direction for one person or group may not be His pattern for others. It may not even be His pattern for the same people next time around!

If others in the past had been constrained by the models they had already seen, Hudson Taylor would not have gone to China without the backing of a mission society, he would not have left the coastal "safe" areas, and he would not have reached the people by abandoning English customs in favor of those he sought to reach–and what a loss that would have been.

Similarly, Florence Nightingale broke the pattern. She lived in a period where the nursing profession was restricted to males. But she had a vision that was different, and single-handedly brought about a revolution in health care.

These examples of freedom are inspirational, but we must not copy them unthinkingly, or all Christians might end up as nurses in China!

It is not uncommon for a dedicated Christian to be keen to be "doing" something for God. In Jacobsen and Coleman's novel, Jake is struggling with waiting for God to show the way, and John provides some wise counsel:

> "[John] '... We only need to do what God puts on our heart to do, and doubting his ability to work beyond us is not the best way to hear him. ... Our worst moments result from grabbing for ourselves that which Father has not given us. ... Our biggest messes come when we try to do something for God that we're convinced he can't do for himself.'
>
> [Jake] 'Then what do I do, just sit around and wait for God?'
>
> [John] 'Who said anything about sitting around? Learning to live by trusting Father is the most difficult part of this journey. So much of what we do is driven by our anxiety that God is not working on our behalf, that we have no idea of the actions that trust produces. Trusting doesn't make you a couch potato. As you follow him, Jake, you'll find yourself doing more than you've ever done, but it won't be the frantic activity of a desperate person, it will be the simple obedience of a loved child. That's all Father desires.' "

(Jacobsen & Coleman, 2006: 95-96)

Adrian Plass nicely summarizes the simplicity of working with God:

> "I hate the thought that my pet formulae might obscure or postpone the work that the Holy Spirit wants to do. Perhaps, rather, we should aim ... to find out what God is doing, and then join in."

(Plass, 1991: 206)

Please be encouraged by the glimpses of an approach I have shared. Now please put them aside and wait on God for His leading in your life. Oliver and Thwaites suggest that we can relatively quickly establish a dance or music performance that can be showcased to demonstrate what we are doing, but many works in the new landscape

> *"… take a lot longer to mature and are not as easily paraded …"*
>
> (Oliver & Thwaites, 2001: 178)

If what you want is public applause in recognition of what a wonderful person you are, you may be able to engineer the praise you are seeking. But it will be praise focused on you, not on God. He may even move on to look for others He can work with who are humble and moldable.

Instead, maybe we would do better to simply seek God's strategy and you partner with Him.

SECTION 9:

CHECK OUT THE PLANK IN YOUR OWN EYE

It is a good start to question and challenge the traditions of men which too often have been considered as God's traditions. He is a God of creativity, and He is not constrained to do today what He did yesterday.

It is also good to get an understanding of a new and different way of relating to God and our fellow men. But if this head knowledge ends there and there is no action, it is questionable how much benefit has been gained. We need to apply the knowledge.

The remainder of this book guides us to realizing the potential for a new-found freedom. We start by considering personal change.

CHAPTER 34:
YOU MAY NEED TO CHANGE

We have looked at a number of serious flaws in the church traditions, and by implication, some of those individuals who hold leadership positions in those churches. Now I want to address another challenge—that of your own heart.

Jesus taught we can also be slaves to the wrong desires in our hearts (John 8:34-36).

Jesus also instructs us as to the futility of trying to help remove a splinter from the eye of another while not taking the time to remove the plank in our own eye. If we hope to clearly see the faults in the church and leadership systems, we should be willing to address our own faults.

It may be a comfort to realize that we are not the only ones who struggle with our inner selves. Many would recognize Hudson Taylor as a man of prayer, faith, vision and commitment to God's work, but may be surprised at the depth of his struggles.

> *"Were it not recorded in his own words it would be difficult to believe, certainly impossible to imagine, such conflict, suffering, almost despair in spiritual things in one who had long and truly known the Lord. Ah, was it not that very fact that made it possible? Nearness to Christ had been to him so real and blessed that any distance was unbearable. So deeply did he love that any clouding of the Master's face was felt, and felt at once with anguish of heart. It is the bride who mourns the absence of the bridegroom, not one who has been a stranger to His love."*
>
> (Taylor & Taylor, 1918: 170)

The authors of Taylor's biography note:

> *"To know that [closeness of one's walk with God] … in fuller measure was Mr. Taylor's deepest longing; but oh, how different were the actual experiences of his soul! … Sometimes he was buoyed up by hope, sometimes almost in despair."*
>
> (Taylor & Taylor, 1918: 165)

Taylor's own words show the enormity of his battle:

> *"My own position becomes more and more responsible, and my need greater of special grace to fill it; but I have continually to mourn that I follow at such a distance and learn so slowly to imitate my precious Master. I cannot tell you how I am buffeted sometimes by temptation. I never knew how bad a heart I had. Yet I do know that I love God and love His work, and desire to serve Him only and in all things. And I value above all things that precious Saviour in Whom alone I can be accepted. Often I am tempted to think that one so full of sin cannot be a child of God at all; but I try to throw it back, and rejoice all the more in the preciousness of Jesus, and in the riches of that grace that has made us 'accepted in the Beloved.' Beloved He is of God; beloved He ought to be of us. But oh, how short I fall here again! May God help me to love Him more and serve Him better. Do pray for me. Pray that the Lord will keep me from sin, will sanctify me wholly, will use me more largely in His service."*
>
> (Taylor & Taylor, 1918: 166-167)

George Müller was the founder of a faith-based work among orphans in England. He recognized the inefficiency of trying to accomplish things in one's own strength, and the necessity of making time for fellowship with God.

> *"If I had strength to work twenty-four hours every day I could not half accomplish what is ready for my hands and feet and head and heart. ... Yet with all this, I consider my first business to be, and my most important business every day, to get blessing in my own soul – for my own soul to be happy in the Lord, and then to work, and to work with all diligence."*
>
> (George Müller, quoted in Taylor & Taylor, 1918: 177-178)

Taylor likewise notes the need for walking closely with God, and shares how he strikingly missed the fellowship with God at any time he had allowed something to spoil the relationship:

> *"Fellowship with God was to [Taylor] a great reality, a great necessity. He had known much of it; much too of the terrible void of losing it. 'Like a diver under water without air, or a fireman on a burning building with an empty hose,' he found himself face to face with ... all the claims that pressed upon him, but alas! too often out of touch with Christ."*
>
> (Taylor & Taylor, 1918: 164)

It's not always an easy or pleasant task to seek change in your own life, but Taylor suggests that it is the internal, hidden victories that count more than the external, visible ones:

> *"[The] noblest work is that wrought in the secret of the soul. Not the conquest of kingdoms, but self-conquest; not the renunciation of anything external merely, but self-renunciation; not the consecration of substance, but self-consecration in the service of God and man – these are the hardest deeds to accomplish, and the most divine attainments. They shine with the peculiar light of Calvary."*
>
> (Taylor & Taylor, 1918: 262)

It is not enough to just "believe in God"; we must experience a personal walk with Him.

> *"Somehow Christianity has become a nonmystical religion. It's about a reasonable faith. If we believe the right things, then we are orthodox. Frankly whether we ever actually connect to God or experience His undeniable presence has become incidental, if not irrelevant. We have become believers rather than experiencers."*
>
> (McManus, 2005: 61)

If we desire to walk with Him, it must be on *His* terms.

> *"For just so long as we were convinced that we could live exclusively by our own individual strength and intelligence, for just that long was a working faith in a Higher Power impossible.*
>
> *This was true even when we believed that God existed. We could actually have earnest religious beliefs which remained barren because we were still trying to play God ourselves. As long as we placed self-reliance first, a genuine reliance upon a Higher Power was out of the question.*
>
> *That basic ingredient of all humility, a desire to seek and do God's will, was missing."*
>
> (Bill, 1967: 139)

Moody describes this humility coming from an honest appraisal of our weaknesses. His quotation may reflect English expressions of a past era, but there are still some lessons to be learned from his warnings:

> *"It is wrong for a man or woman to profess what they do not possess. If you are not overcoming temptations, the world is overcoming you. Just get on your knees and ask God to help you. Let us go to God and ask Him to search us. Let us ask Him to wake us up; and let us not think that just because we are Church members we are all right."*
>
> (Moody, circa 1890: 16)

Bill describes the need for honesty in admission of our weaknesses, but not an attitude that demeans us as a person:

> *"... we should be ... humble without being servile or scraping. As God's people, we stand on our feet; we don't crawl before anyone."*
>
> (Bill, 1967: 277)

All of us have a continuing need to change. As Bill points out above, we do not need to dwell on our failings (real as they may be), but rather look to God to change us for the better, and then move on to our next challenge. But where do we start? A number of authors suggest we can look at our relationship with God, our relationships with others, and how we even "relate" to our own self. Those three topics are addressed in some detail in the next three chapters.

CHAPTER 35:
CHECK OUT YOUR RELATIONSHIP WITH GOD

The "Lordship of Christ"

One of several confronting aspects of Jesus' teaching was His claim to be God, and the need for His followers to accept Him as "Lord". This phrase has lost much of its meaning in our culture. It is a title still given in some cultures such as in Great Britain, as a mark of respect. However, in its earlier setting, it referred to an absolute authority. Within the Roman Empire, to have Jesus claim to be "Lord" was seen by some as a threat to Caesar's rule as Caesar too claimed that title.

Today, if we seriously consider what it means to be a follower of Christ, we must squarely face Christ's claim to be the ultimate authority in our lives. In fact, if the meaning of the term "Christian" is defined as one who follows Christ, then if we do not follow Christ, it is reasonable to ask if we are even Christians. In his book, *A Daughter's Devotion*, George McDonald states:

> "A Christian is one that does what the Lord Jesus tells him. Neither more nor less than that makes a Christian. It is not even understanding the Lord Jesus that makes one a Christian. It is doing what he tells us that makes us Christians, and that is the only way to understand him. …
>
> I want you to look out for his will, and find it, and do it. I want you not only to do it, though that is the main thing, when you think of it, but to look for it, to actively seek it that you may do it. … The man who does what God tells him, sits at his Father's feet, and looks up in his Father's face. Such a man is a true Christian."
>
> (MacDonald, 1988: 80-81)

George MacDonald claims that obedience to God is a greater thing than the finest works of art. There can be great beauty in artistic creation, and it may well be God-inspired. I do not believe MacDonald is trying to belittle stirring works of art. Rather, I take it that he is suggesting that, in spite of their grandeur and worth, to achieve what God has intended for us is an even higher aspiration:

> *"... the highest creation of which man is capable ... is to will the will of the Father. ...*
>
> *To do what we ought to do, as children of God, is an altogether higher, more divine, more potent, more creative thing, than to write the grandest poem, paint the most beautiful picture, carve the mightiest statue, build the most magnificent temple, dream out the most enchanting symphony."*
>
> (MacDonald, 1988: 122-123)

Taylor teaches a radical and uncomfortable level of obedience. He points out that we would rather be "lords" of our own lives than follow Jesus absolutely:

> *"Shall we definitely drop the title Lord as applied to Him, and take the ground that we are quite willing to recognise Him as our Saviour, so far as the penalty of sin is concerned, but are not prepared to own ourselves 'bought with a price,' or Him as having any claim to our unquestioning obedience? Shall we say that we are our own masters, willing to yield something as His due, who bought us with His blood, provided He does not ask too much? Our lives, our loved ones, our possessions are our own not His: we will give Him what we think fit, and obey any of His requirements that do not demand too great a sacrifice? To be taken to heaven by Jesus Christ we are more than willing, but we will not have this Man to reign over us?*
>
> *The heart of every Christian will undoubtedly reject the proposition, so formulated; but have not countless lives in each generation been lived as though it were proper ground to take? How few of the Lord's people have practically recognised the truth that Christ is either Lord of all, or is not Lord at all! If we can judge God's Word, instead of being judged by that Word; if we can give to God as much or as little as we like, then we are lords and He is the indebted one, to be grateful for our dole and obliged by our compliance with His wishes. If, on the other hand, He is Lord, let us treat Him as such. 'Why call ye Me, Lord, Lord, and do not the things which I say?'"*
>
> (Taylor & Taylor, 1918: 477-478)

> *"You cannot be your own Saviour, either in whole or in part."*
>
> (Taylor & Taylor, quoting from an 1868 Keswick article titled 'The Way of Holiness', 1918: 165)

We may be tempted to write off Taylor as a leader from another century but irrelevant to today. I personally believe we can learn from his experiences on many fronts, including the role of prayer, the exercise of faith, and God's authority over us. While we should heed Taylor's advice to accept God's authority, we must also beware those who would apply such teaching in a way that positions them as God's representative in anyone else's life. God has a right to train and mentor us; others don't!

Brown suggests that a phrase such as "being discipled" by a mentor in our local church has at least two unfortunate consequences. Firstly, it dilutes the meaning of being a disciple. If we don't like what our mentor teaches, we can go find another. And secondly, it is very dangerous—putting our lives under the direction of another person is allowing someone to mediate between God and man—a role reserved exclusively for Jesus. Brown's teaching on Jesus' role is just as radical today as was Taylor's from another century.

> "But there is another side to the story. Jesus demands radical, absolute obedience from His followers, an obedience so extreme that to most of the world (and much of the Church) it appears fanatical, even cult-like. Jesus calls us to be His disciples. Do we really know what this means?
>
> For most of us, the answer is no. We have taken the punch out of the word so that the thought of being a disciple does not seem too threatening. After all, don't most serious believers want to be 'discipled'? Isn't one of the great needs in the Body today the need for more discipling? A disciple is a devoted learner and a devoted follower. Who doesn't want to be a disciple?
>
> Perhaps we are asking the wrong questions. Perhaps it would be better to ask, 'Who wants to be a disciple of Jesus?' That puts everything in a different light. Are you sure you want to be one of His disciples? ...
>
> ... The Word of God never calls people to 'become Christians,' especially as we commonly use the term. And the goal of the Great Commission is not to win people to a new religion, which is what 'becoming a Christian' means to most people today. Rather, it is a call to make disciples – true disciples, obedient to the Lord...
>
> ... You may ask, 'Are you saying, then, that we need to quit our jobs, drop out of school, leave our families, sell our possessions, put a few cans of food into a backpack and go hiking into the wilderness somewhere 'with Jesus'?
>
> Hardly. But I am saying you must reorient your whole life so that living for the Lord becomes your all-consuming passion, the preeminent force in your life, that which drives you and motivates you, the standard by which every other area of life is judged and the criterion by which everything is evaluated. That is what it means to be a disciple. It means being utterly absorbed with Jesus and His mission. It means a total revolution in your life and the total consecration of your life to the Jesus revolution."
>
> (Brown, 2002: 69-70, 78)

Will a lifestyle of such absolute obedience to God be costly to us as individuals? Of course it will. In so many small and large ways, it will mean death to our self-centered dreams for our lives. It is to be noted that the way of the cross is in stark contrast to the teaching that suggests the Christian life is one of unbounded blessing and prosperity (especially financial, of course!), with no cost.

One thing that will have to "die" will be the applause of many who do not understand the ways of Christ.

"One who is the servant of the Lord will often be found doing things the world cannot understand."

(MacDonald, 1988: 238)

But even more, Taylor suggests that the call of Christ will not only involve submission to directions we may not choose, but active seeking of His will, no matter what the cost:

"... none but fully consecrated men will accomplish much. Comfort-seeking, etc., won't do there. Cross-loving men are needed. Where are they to be found? Alas – where! Oh, may God make you and me of this spirit! and may our only prayer be, 'Lord, what wilt Thou have me to do?'"

(Taylor & Taylor, 1918: 296)

Miss Blatchley, one of Hudson Taylor's workers in the C.I.M., who personally knew much of the cost of following Christ, wrote:

"The shadow of a cross falls deep and broad;
With Thee I enter, trembling, the shade:–
Whence this new light which brightens round me, Lord?
'The fellowship of suffering,' He said."

(Taylor & Taylor, 1918: 187)

The 'Love of Christ'

All this talk on bearing one's cross and submission to Jesus as Lord can sound very unattractive. And if it was based just on domination by Jesus at our expense and for His selfish pleasure, it most certainly would be unattractive. Depending on your theology, one could argue that God, as the creator and master of the universe, could beat and bully us into quivering submission as fearful subjects if He wanted to.

Thankfully, this is not the image of the Father as presented to us through Jesus. His *love* for us is exemplified in the cross. Colin Grant writes of what can be experienced in our love for Him. This love shone through the lives of the Moravians, and touched the hearts of many.

"... this surging zeal had as its prime motivation a deep, ongoing passion and love for Christ ... William Wilberforce, the great evangelical English social reformer, wrote of the Moravians: 'They are a body who have perhaps excelled all mankind in solid and unequivocal proofs of the love of Christ and ardent, active zeal in his service. It is a zeal tempered with prudence, softened with meekness and supported by a courage which no danger can intimidate and a quiet certainty no hardship can exhaust.' Today, we need a full theological formulation of our motivation in mission and an adequate grasp of what we believe. But if there is no passionate love for Christ at the center of everything, we will only jingle and jangle our way across the world, merely making a noise as we go."

(Grant, 1976: 207-208)

Taylor, who is quoted as so strongly stressing the need for obedience to Jesus as Lord, shares in a letter to his sister how the relationship with Christ is one of richness and blessing. There is a paradox. If we abandon the self-centered search for our own happiness and instead seek God's Kingdom, we will discover a peace and contentment we may not have expected.

> *"If you want blessing … 'seek … first the Kingdom of God and His righteousness,' and you will be on the high road to all other good. Some people forget this and seek happiness in the world, but it eludes their grasp … They think, plan, contrive, and try this means and that, but get no nearer the mark. While there are others who, seeking nothing for themselves, have joy and peace poured into their hearts. For they put first 'the Kingdom of God and His righteousness,' and 'all these things' are 'added to them.' This I have proved by my own experience, and I can assure you that so it is.*
>
> *Pray earnestly, perseveringly, till your prayers are answered, to be truly made a child of God. Then remember you are His … but still a child. Your Father knows best where you should be and how. So ask to do His will as the true, the only way to happiness and content. Remember too, when saved you are His servant. All you possess is His. Use it as such. … If as His servant you are true to Christ, He as your Master will provide for you and that liberally. It is the Principal of any concern who has the burden of responsibility. So avoid seeking to be head. … Be the servant and child in all things. … Look for guidance, and commit your way unto the Lord. Thus you will prosper in temporal as in spiritual things, and avoid those grinding cares which wear one down more than actual labour, and sometimes make life itself a burden. And remember to pray for your absent brother who finds it much easier to tell you what to do than to act it out himself. But he does try to do so, and can tell you that he has never tried altogether in vain; for if he has not come up to the mark he is always blessed in his own soul for trying."*
>
> (Taylor & Taylor, 1911: 378)
>
> *"I am more happy in the Lord than I have ever been, and enjoy more leisure of soul, casting more fully every burden on Him Who alone is able to bear all. To be content with God's will and way is rest. Things may not be in many respects as I would wish them; but if God permits them to be so, or so orders them, I may well be content. Mine is to obey, His to direct. Hence I am not only able to bear up against the new trial … but to be fully satisfied about it , not to wish it otherwise, but to thank God for it. 'Even so, Father, for it seemed good in Thy sight.' "*
>
> (Taylor & Taylor, 1918: 180)

It can be so easy to assume that to please Christ we must work hard. As taught in James, there is a place for work, but underpinning whatever work we may perform must be a relationship with Christ. He wants our love *ahead* of our service. If our love is sound, there will be service, but not with the goal of winning His love. There will be times when He will ask us to make sacrifices, but that is totally different to us making sacrifices to win His approval. Hudson Taylor and his wife discovered the pleasure of simply resting in Christ. We start by looking at how Mrs. Taylor expressed her experience:

> " 'It was just resting in Jesus,' as she expressed it, 'and letting Him do the work' – a little sentence, but one that really lived out made her life the strength to the mission that Mr. Taylor had often realised it to be."

(Taylor & Taylor, 1918: 184)

Hudson Taylor reflects similar sentiments:

> *"It is a bright, sunny morning, but the sunshine without is as nothing to the sunshine within. He has taught me something of what is meant by 'Rejoice in the Lord'; and rejoice I must, and rejoice I do. I want you too to have fellowship, partnership in this joy. It is not that I have anything new to tell you, but I am feeling it all anew. …*
> *I now see it is not in what He is to me, not in what He is working, or has worked, or may work in, for or by me, but in Himself I am to rejoice; in what He is and has in Himself absolutely.*
>
> *And this, it appears to me, is the only possible or even legitimate ground for constant, unchanging, full joy. We cannot but rejoice, when our oneness with Him is realised, in His preciousness, grace, love, holiness, indeed in all His perfections. He is 'the same, yesterday, and to-day and for ever.' If our joy be in His keeping down sin in us, a fall or two destroys that; if it be in His working in or through us, we may not be conscious of the measure in which He is doing so, and may be puffed up or cast down without due reason; but if it be in Him as He is, this cannot change or fluctuate. … what ground for changeless joy we have in Jesus!"*

(Taylor & Taylor, 1918: 184-185)

Taylor then goes on to talk about the fruitfulness we experience if we rest and live in the company of Christ. At this stage, he talks of *not* striving in prayer and meditation, but instead simply *allowing* ourselves to focus our thoughts and affections on Christ:

> *"Apart from Him we have nothing, are nothing, cannot bring forth any fruit to God. He will not give some of His riches to you and some to me, to use and live on away from Himself. But in Him all is ours."*

(Taylor & Taylor, 1918: 317)

> *"How does the branch bear fruit? … Not by incessant effort for sunshine and air; not by vain struggles for those vivifying influences which give beauty to the blossom, and verdure to the leaf: it simply abides in the vine, in silent and undisturbed union, and blossoms and fruit appear as of spontaneous growth.*
>
> *How, then, shall a Christian bear fruit? By efforts and struggles to obtain that which is freely given; by meditations on watchfulness, on prayer, on action, on temptation, and on dangers? No: there must be a full concentration of the thoughts and affections on Christ; a complete surrender of the whole being to Him; a constant looking to Him for grace. Christians in whom these dispositions are once firmly fixed go on calmly as the*

infant borne in the arms of its mother. Christ reminds them of every duty in its time and place, reproves them for every error, councils them in every difficulty, excites them to every needful activity. In spiritual as in temporal matters they take no thought for the morrow; for they know that Christ will be as accessible to-morrow as to-day, and that time imposes no barrier on His love. Their hope and trust rest solely on what He is willing and able to do for them; on nothing that they suppose themselves able and willing to do for Him. Their talisman for every temptation and sorrow is their oft-repeated child-like surrender of their whole being to Him."

(Taylor & Taylor, 1918: 186)

Hopefully it is clear that we are not to strive to work and please Christ, but rather we should simply enjoy His presence. But Taylor discovered an even greater level of resting in Him. At one stage, realizing the value and necessity of abiding in Christ, Taylor worked hard to be conscious of Him. But this too is "work".

Instead, perhaps a bit like forms of dancing where one leads and another follows—Taylor simply trusted himself to Jesus to lead; all Taylor had to do was follow.

"Once I used to try to think very much and very often about Jesus, but I often forgot Him: now I trust Jesus to keep my heart remembering Him, and He does so. This is the best way. …

Oh! it is joy to feel Jesus living in you … to find your heart all taken up by Him; to be reminded of His love by His seeking communion with you at all times, not by your painful attempts to abide in Him. …

I have not to seek Him now; He never leaves me."

(Taylor & Taylor, 1918: 204, 206, 209)

The peace that Taylor talked of was not just something he claimed to have experienced, but something that was clearly evident to others.

"He was an object lesson in quietness. He drew from the Bank of Heaven every farthing of his daily income – 'My peace I give unto you.' Whatever did not agitate the Saviour, or ruffle His spirit was not to agitate him. The serenity of the Lord Jesus concerning any matter and at its most critical moment, this was his ideal and practical possession. He knew nothing of rush or hurry, of quivering nerves or vexation of spirit. He knew there was a peace passing all understanding, and that he could not do without it.

… Are you in a hurry, flurried, distressed? Look up! See the Man in the Glory! Let the face of Jesus shine upon you – the face of the Lord Jesus Christ. Is He worried, troubled, distressed? There is no wrinkle on His brow, no least shade of anxiety. Yet the affairs are His as much as yours.

… he was delightfully free and natural. I can find no words to describe it save the Scriptural expression 'in God.' He was 'in God' all the time, and God in him. It was that true 'abiding' of John xv. But oh, the lover-like attitude that underlay it!

He had in relation to Christ a most bountiful experience of the Song of Solomon. It was a wonderful combination – the strength and tenderness of one who, amid stern preoccupation, like that of a judge on the bench, carried in his heart the light and love of home.

(Taylor & Taylor, 1918: 493-495) (writings of Rev. Macartney, host for Taylor, in Australia)

Taylor beautifully summarized his rest in Christ. It is not something we need to strive for in the conscious; but only be sensitive to the times when we lose that peace and the sense of His presence.

"One asked [Taylor] the question: 'Are you always conscious of abiding in Christ?'

'While sleeping last night,' he replied, 'did I cease to abide in your house because I was unconscious of the fact? We should never be conscious of not abiding in Christ.'"

(Taylor & Taylor, 1918: 444)

Combining Lordship & love

There is to be a balance. We are to obediently follow Jesus as Lord, and we are to enjoy our love relationship with Him. As we abide in Christ, we will be fruitful in His service, for instead of us trying to achieve much for Him, we can let Him lead us as He knows best. Rinehart touches on this dichotomy:

"[Christ] tells us that no matter how gifted or talented we are or how much we know, if we do not abide in Him our efforts will be wasted (John 15:1-6)

… Our influence grows out of the fertile soil of personal spirituality. It stems not from what we know but from Who we know – and how well."

(Rinehart, 1998: 108, 109)

The Bible speaks of the fear of God, but it is not a fear based on dread of an all-powerful ogre. Rather, it is a fear of the consequences of moving outside of His love. If we seek to follow God's wise plan for our lives, we can then be free of all other fears.

"We are called to fear only God. There is an important reason for this. What we fear is what we're subject to; our fears define our master."

(McManus, 2005: 101)

Nicholas Herman (perhaps better known as Brother Lawrence, author of *The Practice of the Presence of God*), writing in the language of the 15th century, tells of God's great mercy rather than fear.

"I consider myself as the most wretched of men, full of sores and corruption, and who has committed all sorts of crimes against his King. Touched with a sensible regret, I confess to Him all my wickedness, I ask His forgiveness, I abandon myself in His hands, that He may do what He pleases with me. The King, full of mercy and goodness, very far from chastising me, embraces me with love, makes me eat at His table, serves

me with His own hands, gives me the key of His treasures; He converses and delights Himself with me incessantly, in a thousand and a thousand ways, and treats me in all respects as His favorite. It is thus I consider myself from time to time in His holy presence."

(Herman, circa 1666: 36-37)

CHAPTER 36:
CHECK OUT YOUR RELATIONSHIP WITH OTHERS

We have looked briefly at aspects of our relationship with God. Now we turn our attention to how we relate to other people, initially looking at those who represent the "old" way that we are trying to leave behind.

Relating to the old-school clergy who won't change

We may perceive wrongs within Christendom as it is practiced today. One response could be to take a page from the dark ages. Maybe we could raise up armies like the Crusaders of old, and overrun countries whose leaders and cultures can't see the "truth" as defined by us; or do as the Roman Catholic Church did through the inquisitors, and torture even our own citizens if they were found to be following heresy or failing to follow the party line.

God forbid!

Another path might be to simply ignore those who peddle what we perceive to be false doctrine, or who control and manipulate their followers. We could simply get on with living our own lives within truth as we know it. But there is a saying that *"Evil prospers when good men do nothing"*. To hide our heads in the sand and pretend problems don't exist is not a real solution, either.

Yet another saying is that *"the pen is mightier than the sword"*. The response of a number of individuals has been to publish their views. Again and again, writers have bravely exposed the inner workings of the group they have been part of. Typically, the price they pay is to be shunned by those who were once their friends, and sometimes even their own family. Hopefully they may have saved some others from unnecessary pain, but often at real cost to themselves.

So how are we to respond?

Taylor and others like him were often opposed in their work, but they did not seek revenge on those who attacked them. For example:

> *"Returning from a meeting on one occasion [Taylor] was accosted by a couple of men who appeared to be friendly. Engaged in conversation with one of them he did not notice the movements of the other, who suddenly rubbed into his eyes a mixture of pounded glass and mud calculated to blind him for life. Sightless and in desperate pain Taylor was wholly at their mercy, and there is no knowing what might have happened had not Joseph Beckett coming down Church Street at the time hastened to his assistance. Seeing the magistrate the ruffians made off, but not before Mr. Beckett had recognised one of them, a professed infidel and no friend to the Methodists in Barnsley. Poor Taylor was taken home in great suffering, and it was fully three months before he could return to work again. His employer urged him to take out a summons, having himself witnessed the occurrence. But [Taylor] would not hear of it.*
>
> *'No,' he said, 'the Lord is well able to deal with them. I would rather leave it in His hands.'*
>
> *This did not satisfy the magistrate, however, who decided to carry the prosecution through on his own account. In the witness-box the culprit denied the charge, calling upon God to strike him blind if he had had anything to do with the outrage. Shortly after, all Barnsley knew that he had lost his sight. For the rest of his life he had to be led by a dog through the familiar streets, and ultimately sunk into extreme poverty. His accomplice also was obliged to confess that nothing ever prospered with him from the time of their cruel attack on James Taylor."*

(Taylor & Taylor, 1911: 13-14)

What conclusions might we draw from this story? That Taylor did the right thing in refusing to press charges? Or that Taylor failed to call others to account for their actions, so another, Joseph Beckett (the magistrate), had to do what Taylor failed to do? I hesitate to make a judgment, but do wish to note the difference of response.

Taylor often left things "in God's hands", but not always. He saw it as one thing to refuse to speak up for his own personal rights, but as quite another thing to fail to speak up for others. He had been put in a position of providing for new missionaries (a married couple), but without the means. He and they had to depend on the kindness of missionaries from other societies. To make matters even worse, those who had sent out Taylor, and who should have provided for the couple but didn't, were in open criticism of the society that showed compassion and stepped in to provide support and accommodation. Taylor felt he had to make a stand:

> *"In addition to their own difficulties about which he had to write, Hudson Taylor was suffering from imprudent statements in [the society's magazine] calculated to give serious offense to the L.M.S. missionaries in Shanghai; 'men who,' as he put it,*

'however much you may differ from them in judgment, are more thoughtful for the shelter and support of your missionaries than the Society that sends them out ...'"

(Taylor & Taylor, 1911: 250)

Taylor then goes on to clarify why he must speak up, even at risk of causing offense:

"For though I feel these things and feel them keenly, were it not for the sake of others and the good of the Society I would pass over them in silence. To do this, however, would be unfaithfulness on my part. For ... [it is] morally wrong and thoughtless in the extreme to act as the Society has acted ..."

(Taylor & Taylor, 1911: 250)

Taylor does not pull punches, even with friends.

"Now you cannot but see, I am sure, what evidence this is of gross neglect. We do, at any rate. And while we both cherish the warmest and most affectionate regard for many of the Committee personally, and especially for its Secretaries, we cannot but feel that the Society had acted disgracefully."

(Taylor & Taylor, 1911: 251)

Foster suggests that we need to speak up, not only on behalf of others who may not be able to speak effectively for themselves, but also for ourselves where we need to take a stand against abuse:

"How do we serve others in the world? We serve them by a firm refusal to allow them to misuse and abuse us. To allow people to walk over us as one would a doormat is not service, but subservience. It is not healthy for us or for others. Service must not be identified with a false modesty or a Caspar Milquetoast personality. On the contrary, service resonates well with forthrightness and courageous action.

Therefore, if others try to walk over us and take advantage of our serving spirit, we stand up to the abuse. Our concern is not to defend 'our rights', for we have already given those to God. Firmly, we press others to respect all people – including us – as fully human. The issues can be many and varied – low salary, heavy workload, lack of advancement – the resolve is always the same: never to be 'thing-a-fied.'"

(Foster, 1985: 644)

Sometimes our opposition to abuse is demonstrated by speaking out. But as Yancey recounts from Martin Luther King, we sometimes may have to practice civil disobedience where the law is unjust:

"[Martin Luther King Jr] travelled with his wife to India in 1959 to observe first-hand the impact of a non-violent revolution. 'I left India,' he reported, 'more convinced than ever before that nonviolent resistance is the most potent weapon available to oppressed people in their struggle for freedom.' For other models, he looked back to Daniel and his three friends, who disobeyed the laws of Nebuchadnezzar, and to the early Christians who faced hungry lions rather than submit to unjust laws of the Roman

Empire. As he later articulated, 'One who breaks an unjust law must do so openly, lovingly and with a willingness to accept the penalty.' "

(Yancey, 2001: 24)

Jesus spoke boldly, and walked in freedom. He opposed wrongful traditions, but did not exhibit hatred for those that supported those practices. But just as Martin Luther King peacefully flouted unjust laws of the land, we may need to consider flouting "laws" enshrined as church traditions and, like King, be willing to suffer the consequences.

"[Martin Luther King Jr reminded] demonstrators that moral change is not accomplished through immoral means. He had learned that principle from the Sermon on the Mount, and almost all his speeches reiterated the message. 'Christianity,' he said, 'has always insisted that the cross we bear precedes the crown we wear. To be a Christian one must take up his cross, with all its difficulties and agonizing and tension-packed content, and carry it until that very cross leaves its mark upon us and redeems us to that more excellent way which comes only through suffering.'

King clung to non-violence because he profoundly believed that only a movement based on love could keep the oppressed from becoming a mirror image of their oppressors. He wanted to change the hearts of the white people, yes, but in a way that did not in the process harden the hearts of the blacks he was leading towards freedom. Non-violence, he believed, 'will save the Negro from seeking to substitute one tyranny for another.' "

(Yancey, 2001: 25)

Brown likewise stresses that God's way is not a way of violence:

"Jesus ... cannot be party to those who ... seek to improve the world by violence, a violence which begins with a hate-filled defamation and escalates to bloody terror, to torture and mass murder, where one party shifts all the blame on the opponent ... The errors of church history, crusades, inquisition, and religious wars, should put us on guard, today especially, against a romantic justification of revolutionary violence ... Jesus pointed a quite different way with agape: the way of nonviolent protest and willingness to suffer, a way which deserves more fully the designation 'revolutionary' than does the old, primitive way of violence."

(Martin Hengel in Brown, 2002: 84-85)

Yancey's book, *Soul Survivor*, highlighted for me that not only was Martin Luther King opposed to physical violence, but he went further, accepting hurtful mudslinging, name-calling and hostility. He encouraged young people to adopt a similar attitude that may be instructive for us as we seek to live a life that could well trigger opposition.

"Martin Luther King Jr ... sensed the students' temptation to become bitter, and then to turn on opponents in the same spirit of hostility they had been receiving – to become the enemy, in other words.

A big danger for us is the temptation to follow the people we are opposing. They call us names, so we call them names. Our names may not be 'redneck' or 'cracker'; they may be names that have a sociological or psychological veneer to them, a gloss; but they are names, nonetheless – 'ignorant', or 'brainwashed', or 'duped' or 'hysterical' or 'poor-white' or 'consumed by hate'. I know you will all give me plenty of evidence in support of those categories. But I urge you to think of them as that – as categories; and I remind you that in many people, in many people called segregationists, there are other things going on in their lives: this person or that person, standing here or there may also be other things – kind to neighbors and family, helpful and good-spirited at work.

You all know, I think, what I am trying to say – that we must try not to end up with stereotypes of those we oppose, even as they slip all of us into their stereotypes. And who are we? Let us not do to ourselves as others (as our opponents) do to us: try to put ourselves into one all-inclusive category – the virtuous ones as against the evil ones, or the decent ones as against the malicious, prejudiced ones, or the well-educated as against the ignorant. You can see that I can go on and on – and there is the danger: the 'us' or 'them' mentality takes hold, and we do, actually, begin to run the risk of joining ranks with the very people we are opposing. I worry about this a lot these days.

(From The Call of Service)"

(Yancey, 2001: 102-103)

I've observed that Tanya Levin clearly opposes the practices of one particular church and its leaders. She also graciously recognizes that those who stand for the very things we oppose may be victims of their denomination, or even victims of the structures of their own making! While standing against their practices we must give them the option and opportunity to break free if they have the courage to do so.

Levin shares her opinion as to what may be going on in the heads of church leaders. My interpretation of her perspective suggests that being held in high regard as a leader has a trap, namely that the esteemed leader can't afford to show human frailty.

> "Church growth is [seen as] a sign of God's blessing. If it's bigger, God is there more. Why else would all those people go? You have to keep working hard for church growth. Then you can put in a praise report at the next conference. Make sure you don't drop out of the loop. At the many conferences you are expected to attend, you still have to look cool and carefree. You have to look strong and successful, which costs money and more stress.
>
> The pressure can creep up. … Sometimes it's hard to sustain kindness towards a demanding flock. Strains on the family can start to show.
>
> [Church leaders] … will only ask for help as a desperate last resort. Needing help is a sign of not coping. Not coping is a sign of lack of faith. Or an abundance of sin. And not enough hard work. It's this type of person that can develop a negative attitude and become part of the problem, not part of the solution. We can't have leaders who aren't coping. Maybe leadership isn't the right place for you right now. Maybe you need a little time off.

> *[Brian Houston, the senior pastor at Hillsong, Australia] often says, emphatically, that he does not care to be around negative people. He won't spend time with people who are defeated, and who complain about the way things aren't. Brian likes to be around people who are excited about God, and have a vision and a purpose.*
>
> *A man says yes as a sign of faith. He doesn't say no because he's not afraid. He is never uncertain. He is in partnership with the Almighty. A real man is committed to the things of God no matter what it costs.*
>
> *If a man is not careful, he could lose his church. If he shows signs of one weakness, then what others will develop in him? Is he really fit to lead? If he's not, how soon can we get a replacement?*
>
> *I don't know of any insurance against this kind of thing happening. Like a crooked cop, an ex-pastor [may feel trapped because he/she] has no other training."*
>
> (Levin, 2007: 184-185)

I think there may be more than one response to Levin's insights. Perhaps we could show more grace to flawed leaders, and arguably that's a good thing to do. An alternative, arguably better, response would be to encourage dismantling of a hierarchical system that puts unrealistic demands on mere humans.

Locke highlights the fact that enterprises are really nothing more than their people. He states,

> *"... the first bit of news is that it isn't about us and them. It's about us [the people]. Them [the corporations, institutions, and I suggest, 'churches'] don't exist. Not really. Corporations are legal fictions, willing suspensions of disbelief. Pry the roof off any company and what do you find inside? The Cracker Jack prize is ourselves, just ordinary people. We come in all flavors: funny, cantankerous, neurotic, compassionate, avaricious, generous, scheming, lackadaisical, brilliant, and a million other things. It's true that the higher up the food chain you go, the more likely you are to encounter the arrogant and self-deluded, but even top management types are mostly harmless when you get to know them. Given lots of love, some even make good pets.*
>
> *Inside companies, outside companies, there are only people."*
>
> (Levine, Locke, Searls and Weinberger, 2000: 35-36)

Locke expresses some revolutionary attitudes, and by adapting his statements to apply to Christendom, one quotation now reads:

> *"Fact is, we don't care about ... [the established church] – per se, per diem, au gratin. Given half a chance, we'd burn the whole constellation of obsolete ... concepts to the waterline. ... [Tithes, membership, church mortgages] – if you're a ... [church], that's your problem. But if you [as an individual person] think of yourself as a ... [church], you've got much bigger worries. We strongly suggest you repeat the following mantra as often as possible until you feel better: 'I am not a [church]. I am a human being.' "*
>
> (Levine, Locke, Searls and Weinberger, 2000: 182)

Within the context of Christendom, Girard explains we have no choice but to move forward *beyond* the church structures. But he also warns that we must not abandon the people who are still trapped. We must oppose the institutions, but reach out to the people, even those who currently assume the titles belonging to the church leadership structures.

> *"In the first place, wherever there are true believers in Jesus, the Spirit of God is already working. These believers may be involved in the kind of church structure that stifles the sharing of life in Christ together, and inhibits spiritual growth. They may be all entangled in the red tape of the ecclesiastical bureaucracy that exists in many denominations. They may have prejudices, wrong ideas, and know nothing of dependence on the Spirit in any kind of practical, day-by-day way. They may seem to be almost mummified in the grave dressings of unbiblical church tradition. They may be opposed to anything that would disturb the status quo. But that doesn't alter the fact that if they have thrown themselves on Christ for salvation and He lives in them, they are a part of the Body of Christ.*
>
> *They cannot just be 'written off'!*
>
> *We must not fit their mold, or pamper them in their immaturity, or back down in the face of their carnal outbursts. We must not stop seeking to bring renewal and revival to the church just because they don't like it.*
>
> *But neither can we just write them off. They are brothers and sisters. Jesus said, if we do not have love for them, the world has a right to come to the conclusion that we are really not Christians at all.*
>
> *For these reasons, those who want to see church renewal cannot just 'forget' the institutional church. The people of God are there. The Spirit is there, in the people. I need those brothers and sisters very much. And they need me.*
>
> *I may be committed to tearing down the old man-made traditions and trying to replace institutionalism with something better, but I dare not be committed to forsaking my fellow members of the Body of Christ. Or to belittling in any way what the Spirit is doing in and through them. How can I? I share with them the same Body and the same Life."*

(Girard, 1972: 182-183)

Elissa Wall made several heart-wrenching claims about an appalling childhood in a (supposedly Christian) polygamous group. The leader at the time, Warren Jeffs, is now incarcerated in jail as a result of several convictions related to mistreatment of children. Without going into details here, Elissa's book makes confronting claims of horrific treatment, yet, after she had broken free, she retained a love for those group members she had left behind. Her appeal to the public was to show love to these people. Her argument was that by showing love, you may be the catalyst for their freedom.

> *"I wanted to say to the public, 'If you see them in the grocery store, give them a kind word instead of a cruel one, because you never know if that one kind word would*

make the difference for them.' All they know about people on the outside is what they have been taught; that they are evil, and the thing that had surprised me most in my transcendent journey from the FLDS to the life I live now is that good, honest, and respectful people lived out here and are nothing like what we'd been taught they are."

(Wall, 2008: 420-421)

The picture Elissa paints is of suffering and abuse beyond what I hope is the experience of most readers. Nonetheless, we all will have experienced wrong at the hands of others.

There is a time for bravely standing against such wrong, and Elisa joined with others in exposing evil. Heavy sentences were applied in subsequent court hearings.

There is also a time for love and grace. Elissa's compassion for those she left behind is, for me, a shining example. Perhaps as we, too, come to see local churches in a new light we may experience pain, and choose to distance ourselves from them to gain our freedom. The pain may come from a feeling of disillusionment as we wonder how church leaders can really believe they are the superior class in their tiered, hierarchical society. Or maybe the pain may come from us wondering how we bought the deception for so long and put so much of our lives into supporting such a system.

To add to the pain we may find that as we break free from the church institution and leadership control, many of our friends are also relating to us in new ways. Some may continue as good friends, even though we now have different viewpoints. But don't be surprised if true friends are few and far between. You may find some remain "friends" but only so they can stay close enough to convince you of the error of your ways. Others won't have time for you as they are too busy still doing "church" things, and if you are not part of this circle, you may find you don't even appear on their radar screen. Or perhaps the most cutting will be when the church leaders warn "the faithful" that you are now an apostate, and are to be shunned. They may teach that anyone who associates with you is in danger of losing their own salvation. In some of the more extreme cases, even family members are ordered to cut you off.

In our escape from the bondage of the institution, we should remain loving. As we move away from past unhealthy practices, it may be easy to be judgmental of others who remain tied to traditions, including traditions that we once embraced! Green and Hazard clearly saw what was perceived as issues worthy of confronting, and quote Green's late husband, Keith, noting that it may be tempting to act in unloving ways, by being

"... hurt, independent, talkative, stubborn, unteachable, and unyielding."

(Green & Hazard, 1989: 313)

So what's the antidote? While not compromising our beliefs, they encourage us to demonstrate

"... kindness, gentleness, self-control, and long-suffering ..."

(Green & Hazard, 1989: 313)

Stepping away from the institution and its control will bring its pain, and the choice to express that pain in negative ways will be ever before you. However, this is not the answer and would, no doubt, come back to bite you. We can strive for freedom in acknowledging our pain, yet always show grace in our responses to others.

Brown encourages us to be revolutionary, but warns us to avoid wrong attitudes and motives creeping in:

> *"If we are to take a stand for truth even when others call us extremists; if we are to refuse unrighteousness even when pressured to compromise; if we are to call for radical change and swim against the tide even at great personal cost – we must be sure our motivations are not fleshly. If they are, we are simply rebels with a cause, manifesting our own independence.*
>
> *Put another way, if you really want to be a Jesus revolutionary, you must crucify rebellion, independence, pride, self-will, ambition, anger, rage, retaliation and all related carnal behavior. You must cultivate humility, longsuffering and willingness to bear reproach; you must learn to turn the other cheek and overcome evil through good. The true Jesus revolutionary is a person whose flesh has been nailed to the cross. That is radical!*
>
> *The plain fact is that almost every earthly revolution contains a strong element of rebellion against authority, and God hates rebellion."*
>
> (Brown, 2002: 89-90)

He then goes on to note,

> *"I am aware that the slogan of the American Revolution was 'Rebellion Against Tyrants Is Obedience to God,' but I would still argue that the greater force driving the revolution was the cry for liberty rather than a call to rebellion in and of itself. Rather, the rebellion was a protest against oppression and injustice. In any event, the key is the last part of the phrase: 'Obedience to God' – that must always be the dominant factor."*
>
> (Brown, 2002: 214)

All of this is not to say that our pain is not real and must somehow be ignored or suppressed. Rather, in spite of our pain, we must never allow ourselves to lash out and hurt others.

It is important to note that the healthy response to the pain of loss is to not to attempt to recreate the familiar but unhealthy past. We may need to look at the topic of forgiveness toward those who have hurt us, but we must not try to return to the system, having now obtained our freedom. Although perhaps a poor analogy, we might look at those who have suffered abuse from a spouse or a parent. The victim may choose to work on forgiveness for past abuse, but should not confuse this with putting himself back in a vulnerable position under the control of the abuser. Likewise, we may choose to reach out in forgiveness to those who have hurt us in their roles within local churches, but we should not return to a position that will result in further abuse.

John Mott, in *The Responsibility of the Young People for the Evangelization of the World*, states:

> *"Let each one act for himself. Forget the others. If you feel the pressure … of the spirit of the living God, be serious and be obedient. It is a great thing to have dealings with the living God. Responsibility is individual, untransferable, urgent."*

(Mott, 1901: 271)

To respond to God's call on your life may mean that others, including those still at the local church you used to call "home", may not understand you, and may even throw barbs at you. To accept misunderstanding and still show the fruit of the spirit is not easy. But if I read my Bible correctly, this was the way that Jesus Himself walked, and He calls us to follow.

Relating to a new circle of friends

If you have accepted the challenge to be part of God's plan for your life, if you are willing to take on menial tasks rather than waiting for the grand ministry, and if you are opening up a dialogue with God as best you know how, that's great. But whereas in the closeted environment of a local church you may have related to others with much the same world view as your own, you are now living in the community at large. God might present you with opportunities to reach out in love to others who are "different". That can be anything from a different language group or faith, right down to differences in recreational interests and circles of friends.

Some of the following material comes from "missionary" teaching. If you struggle with stereotypes of missionaries in pith helmets, I ask that you please put aside such imagery and look at the message behind the quotations. In essence, it boils down to reaching out and loving those whose backgrounds are different to ours, and that is precisely what Jesus taught by example as he relaxed and befriended people from many walks of life, those often scorned by the religious leaders of His day.

One of the things that may potentially hinder us is our unconscious and hence unrecognized ways of doing things that set us apart. We need to work to understand our own culture and to get an understanding of how others see us.

We also need to understand ways we can better bridge the gap. It is not good enough to expect people to become like us. We must meet them on their own turf, just as Jesus did when He touched the lives of Samaritans, Romans, prostitutes, and tax collectors. We don't have to become one of them, but we must get close enough to be a friend.

We start by seeing what we can do to better understand our own culture. Lloyd Kwast, in *Understanding Culture*, suggests that

> *"… a thorough understanding of the meaning of culture is prerequisite to any effective communication of God's good news to a different people group.*

The most basic procedure in a study of culture is to become a master of one's own. ...

One helpful method is to view [our own culture as if] ... through the eyes of an alien space visitor."

(Kwast, in Winter et. al. 1981: 361)

It is easy to assume that there is not too large a difference between our own world view and that of others, but maybe the gap is larger than we perceive? Kwast challenged me by presenting a hypothetical that is both entertaining and instructive, where a Martian visits a classroom:

"The first thing that the newly arrived visitor would notice is the people's behavior. ... [For example, one] person enters dressed quite differently than the rest, and moves quickly to an obviously prearranged position facing the others, and begins to speak. ...

In observing the inhabitants, our alien begins to realize that many of the behaviors observed are apparently dictated by ... choices that people in the society have made. These choices inevitably reflect the issue of cultural values ... These issues always concern choices about what is 'good,' what is 'beneficial,' or what is 'best.' ...

Beyond the questions of behavior and values, we face a more fundamental question in the nature of culture. This takes us to a deeper level of understanding, that of cultural beliefs. These beliefs answer for that culture the question: 'What is true?' ...

Interestingly, our alien interrogator might discover that different people in [the classroom], while exhibiting similar behavior and values, might profess totally different beliefs about them. Further, he might find that the values and behaviors were opposed to the beliefs which supposedly produced them. This problem arises from the confusion within the culture between operating beliefs (beliefs that affect values and behavior) and theoretical beliefs (stated creeds which have little practical impact on values and behavior).

At the very heart of any culture is its world view, answering the most basic question: 'What is real?' This area of culture concerns itself with the great 'ultimate' questions of reality, questions which are seldom asked, but to which culture provides its most important answers."

(Kwast, in Winter et. al. 1981: 361-363)

Hudson Taylor of the China Inland Mission caused quite a stir when he chose to identify with the Chinese by adopting their clothes, diet, etc. His desire was to lay down his life for the people he loved, and to remove any obstacle. Hiebert warns that it is not just outward assimilation that is important:

"The real test of identification is not what we do in formal, structured situations. It is how we handle our informal time, and our most precious belongings. When the committee meeting is over, do we go aside with fellow Americans to discuss cameras, and thereby exclude our national colleagues ...? Do we frown on our children playing with the local children?

> *... The basic issue in identification is not formal equivalence – living in the same houses, eating the same food and wearing the same dress. We can do so and still communicate to people the mental distinction we make between them and us. ... [In contrast, if] we, indeed, see and feel ourselves to be one of them, this message will come through, even if we have different life styles."*
>
> (Hiebert, in Winter et. al. 1981: 384)

If our desire is to reach out and help others, we may impatiently try to convince them of a "better" way. Speaking from the context of "missionaries", David J. Hesselgrave, in *The Role of Culture in Communication, and World-view and Contextualization*, advises that first we must show humility and learn from *them*!

> *"Missionaries should prepare for this frustration [of effectively communicating to a different people]. They have been preoccupied with their message! By believing it, they were saved. By studying it they have been strengthened. Now they want to preach it to those who have not heard it, for that is a great part of what it means to be a missionary! But before they can do so effectively, they must study again – not just the language, but also the audience. They must learn before they can teach, and listen before they can speak. They need to know the message for the world, but also the world in which the message must be communicated."*
>
> (Hesselgrave, 1978: 392)

One task for your own personal growth is to try to recognize the cultural background of those who wrote the Bible, and then grapple with how your own culture may affect the way you understand what has been written. That's you trying to understand the words coming from another culture. Now we swap sides. In touching the lives of others, we must be willing to try and *present* the Gospel in terms that are relevant to the intended recipient's people group.

> *"... missionaries can temporarily adopt the world view of their non-Christian respondents. Then, by reexamining their message in the light of the respondent world view, they can adapt the message, encoding it in such a way that it will become meaningful to the respondents. This approach is not easy, but it is both possible and practical. Complete communication may not be attainable. Perfection seldom is. But effective communication is possible if missionaries take the initiative and pay the price. And true missionary motivation is to communicate a message, not simply dispense it.*
>
> *... With God's ends in view [the missionary] begins with [the starting point of the people he is reaching out to]. What they believe concerning the existence and nature of reality, the world around them, and man in relationship to the whole is of the essence. Adaptation to those beliefs is one of the first requirements of missionary communication. This process will affect the source, substance, and style of the missionary message."*
>
> (Hesselgrave, 1978: 402)

Here we go on humility again. In relating to others, we must respect the strengths in their culture rather than attacking any perceived weaknesses.

> *"Missionary communication is not enhanced by an arrogant show of superiority, or by ridiculing or downgrading other views, or by repeatedly pointing out their inconsistencies. ... This approach may serve the ego but it betrays the kingdom. The weaknesses, inconsistencies, and inadequacies of false systems of philosophy and religion are not to be overlooked. But missionaries must also deal with them at the points of their strength. ... We must learn to deal with the best case that non-Christians can make, not with their weakest case, lest we succeed only in pricking balloons and knocking down straw men."*
>
> (Hesselgrave, 1978: 403)

Phil Parshall, in *God's Communicator in the 80's*, goes so far as to recommend, within the "missions" perspective, dismantling of all mission compounds, as these reflect a desire for the "missionary" to retain their own superior culture. Perhaps you and I may not live in mission compounds in distant lands, but what fortresses might we unconsciously build to protect ourselves unnecessarily from becoming one with those we profess to love?

> *"These [western-styled mission compounds] are still found throughout the developing world. They are often misunderstood and, in some cases, despised by the nationals. A convert questioned their existence by asking, 'Am I wrong if I say that mission bungalows are often a partition wall between the hearts of the people and the missionaries?' ...*
>
> *It is my personal conviction that remaining mission compounds should be dismantled. This would free the missionary to move into the community and share his incarnational testimony among them, rather than being shut off in a large plot of land that has a very negative appraisal in the minds of the people."*
>
> (Parshall, 1979: 478)

We need to be willing to recognize and dismantle our own protective fortresses.

CHAPTER 37:
CHECK OUT YOURSELF

You can buy many books describing how to live a life pleasing to God, how to pray more or better, how to overcome those wrong thoughts, how to exhibit the fruit of the Spirit, how to …

Or to put it another way, how to live in guilt because you don't measure up to some implied standard such as how many times a day you should pray! God does set a standard for us, but He also shows more grace to us than we often show to ourselves.

At the end of the day, if we have an open, honest and loving relationship with God, things such as talking to Him, and issues of our weaknesses will fall into place. Nonetheless, I have included some quotations on these topics of "right living", but only where I have felt they offer unusual insight, present a healthy challenge, or movingly articulate a point in a way that may gently encourage us to a closer walk with our Heavenly Father.

Some may read this book as a call to arms against the traditions of men, a call to action for those stuck in local church pews under the control of others, or a call to discovery and fulfillment of God's specific call on your life. To an extent, you may feel there is some truth in all of these. But before we launch out in exploits "for God" (or at least in actions we believe are in line with His directives for us), we must first be willing to wait and listen, and to spend time in hidden preparation.

> "If we expect to engage in … ministry … we must understand the hidden preparation through which God puts his ministers. …
>
> *All of us must experience this hidden preparation. Time spent being instructed by God is well spent and never wasted. In hiddenness we learn to see life spiritually – to see what is important and what is of little consequence. Often God completely reverses our priorities. What we once saw as great and wonderful shrinks down to trivial and insignificant. Gaining recognition, success, wealth, and autonomy no longer attracts us. We learn to let go of all humanly initiated bids for power. Things we once*

considered unimportant and beneath us become matters of genuine consequence. We begin to value simple acts of kindness and neighbourliness. Small ordinary tasks become genuinely significant to us."

(Foster, 1985: 616-618)

In the language and culture of His day, Jesus expressed Himself in ways we might find uncomfortable. In Luke He taught that unless we hated our family members, we could not be a disciple of His. He used such hyperbole to show that, in comparison to our love for Him, our relations to others should seem quite poor. Taylor expresses this theme of loving Christ deeply in a slightly different way, but in a manner that I believe is not inconsistent with the teaching of Jesus:

"With the love with which you love your husband (in fact or in anticipation) you are to love the Lord Jesus, nay more. Are you lonely when he leaves you? So you should be while Jesus is absent. Do you long for the time when you can always be together? So you should for the return of Jesus to take you to Himself. Is service for your loved one freedom? 'No,' you will say, 'that is far too cold a word. Freedom! It is joy, delight, the desire of my heart.' So should you serve Jesus. Would you do what you could to remove the obstacles and hasten the day of your union? Then look for and hasten the day of His return. ... See Jesus in everything, then in everything you will find blessing. Keep looking to Jesus. Do nothing but for Him, but as in Him and by His strength and direction. Christ [is] all and in all! And may He abundantly and personally manifest Himself to you."

(Taylor & Taylor, 1911: 427)

Some leaders may be considered "successful" if measured by numbers of followers. Yet how many reports have you heard of "successful" leaders who have been brought down by the revelation of their own scandalous behavior? There are many.

"We may be able to compensate for lack of experience, skills, or education – in many areas of leadership. But deficiencies in character will contradict our message and undermine our credibility."

(Rinehart, 1998: 109)

Rinehart presents a familiar and challenging test for us:

"An insightful individual once noted that character is 'who you are when no one is looking.' If my character is authentic, then it will be consistent with what I profess, even when no one is around."

(Rinehart, 1998: 110)

If we are honest with ourselves, each one of us will admit to shortcomings. So can we ever sufficiently meet a standard where we qualify as being "good enough" to be useful to God?

"There is only one way for any of us to resolve the tension between the high ideals of the gospel and the grim reality of ourselves: to accept that we will never measure up,

but that we do not have to. We are judged by the righteousness of the Christ who lives within, not our own. Tolstoy got it halfway right: anything that makes me feel comfort with God's moral standard, anything that makes me feel, 'At last I have arrived,' is a cruel deception. But Dostoevsky got the other half right: anything that makes me feel discomfort with God's forgiving love is also a cruel deception. 'There is now no condemnation for those who are in Christ Jesus': that message, Leo Tolstoy never fully grasped.

Absolute ideals and absolute grace: after learning that dual message from Russian novelists, I returned to Jesus and found that it suffuses his teaching throughout the Gospels and especially in the Sermon on the Mount. In his response to the rich young ruler, in the parable of the Good Samaritan, in his comments about divorce, money, or any other moral issue, Jesus never lowered God's Ideal. 'Be perfect, therefore, as your heavenly Father is perfect,' he said. 'Love the Lord your God with all your heart and with all your soul and with all your mind.' Not Tolstoy, not Francis of Assisi, not Mother Teresa, not anyone has completely fulfilled those commands.

Yet the same Jesus tenderly offered absolute grace. Jesus forgave an adulteress, a thief on the cross, a disciple who had denied ever knowing him. He tapped that traitorous disciple, Peter, to found his church and for the next advance turned to a man called Saul, who had made his mark persecuting Christians. Grace is absolute, inflexible, all-encompassing. It extends even to the people who nailed Jesus to the cross: 'Father, forgive them, for they do not know what they are doing' were among the last words Jesus spoke on earth.

For years I had felt so unworthy before the absolute ideals of the Sermon on the Mount that I had missed in it any notion of grace. Once I understood the dual message, however, I went back and found that the message of grace gusts through the entire speech. It begins with the Beatitudes – Blessed are the poor in spirit, those who mourn, the meek; blessed are the desperate – and it moves toward the Lord's Prayer: 'Forgive us our debts ... deliver us from the evil one.' Jesus began this great sermon with gentle words for those in need and continued on with a prayer that has formed a model for all twelve-step groups. 'One day at a time,' say the alcoholics in AA; 'Give us this day our daily bread,' say the Christians. Grace is for the desperate, the needy, the broken, those who cannot make it on their own. Grace is for all of us.

For years I had thought of the Sermon on the Mount as a blueprint for human behavior that no one could possibly follow. Reading it again, I found that Jesus gave these words not to cumber us, but to tell us what God is like. The character of God is the urtext of the Sermon of the Mount. Why should we love our enemies? Because our clement Father causes his sun to rise on the evil and the good. Why be perfect? Because God is perfect. Why store up treasures in heaven? Because the Father lives there and will lavishly reward us. Why live without fear and worry? Because the same God who clothes the lilies and the grass of the field has promised to take care of us. Why pray? If an earthly father gives his son bread or fish, how much more will the Father in heaven give good gifts to those who ask him.

How could I have missed it? Jesus did not proclaim the Sermon on the Mount so that we would, Tolstoy-like, furrow our brows in despair over our failure to achieve perfection. He gave it to impart to us God's Ideal toward which we should never stop striving, but also to show that none of us will ever reach that Ideal. The Sermon on the Mount forces us to recognize the great distance between God and us, and any attempt to reduce that distance by somehow moderating its demands misses the point altogether.

The worst tragedy would be to turn the Sermon on the Mount into another form of legalism; it should rather put an end to all legalism. Legalism like the Pharisees' will always fail, not because it is too strict but because it is not strict enough. Thunderously, inarguably, the Sermon on the Mount proves that before God we all stand on level ground: murderers and temper-throwers, adulterers and lusters, thieves and coveters. We are all desperate, and that is in fact the only state appropriate to a human being who wants to know God. Having fallen from the absolute Ideal, we have nowhere to land but in the safety net of absolute grace."

(Yancey, 1995: 142-144)

As Christians, we are called to prayer. To clarify, I am not here talking about the practice of repeating formal prayers written by others. Instead, I am referring to the simple act of chatting with our Heavenly Father, sharing our thoughts, dreams, fears and even just day-to-day experiences. Hudson Taylor saw prayer as the foundational activity that allowed progress on other fronts.

"He encouraged his fellow-workers also in putting prayer, definite, believing prayer, before any other means ... and in seeking to live the life that makes such prayer possible."

(Taylor & Taylor, 1918: 73)

Cymbala also shares a refreshing experience where people had gathered for activity in a particular ministry (in this case, choir practice) but ended up just enjoying God's presence:

"... many nights there was more prayer and worship than there was [choir] practicing; sometimes the choir never got around to singing at all."

(Cymbala, 1997: 32)

The importance of prayer in Cymbala's life is touchingly portrayed by a personal story from his family life. In the chapter headed, *The Greatest Discovery of All Time*, he tells of God prompting people to pray for his wayward daughter, and God meeting her at exactly the same moment:

"One cold Tuesday night during the prayer meeting, I talked from Acts 4 about the church boldly calling on God in the face of persecution. ... An usher handed me a note. A young woman whom I felt to be spiritually sensitive had written: Pastor Cymbala, I feel impressed that we should stop the meeting and all pray for your daughter, ...

There arose a groaning, a sense of desperate determination, as if to say, 'Satan, you will not have this girl. Take your hands off her – she's coming back!' … The force of that vast throng calling on God almost literally knocked me over. …

Thirty-two hours later, on Thursday morning, as I was shaving, Carol suddenly burst through the door, her eyes wide. 'Go downstairs!' she blurted. 'Chrissy's here.'

'Chrissy's here?'

'Yes! Go down!'

'But Carol – I – '

'Just go down,' she urged. 'It's you she wants to see.'

I wiped off the shaving foam and headed down the stairs, my heart pounding. As I came around the corner, I saw my daughter on the kitchen floor, rocking on her hands and knees, sobbing. Cautiously I spoke her name:

'Chrissy?'

She grabbed my pant leg and began pouring out her anguish. 'Daddy – Daddy – I've sinned against God. I've sinned against myself. I've sinned against you and Mommy. Please forgive me – '

My vision was as clouded by tears as hers. I pulled her up from the floor and held her close as we cried together.

Suddenly she drew back. 'Daddy,' she said with a start, 'who was praying for me? Who was praying for me?' Her voice was like that of a cross-examining attorney.

'What do you mean, Chrissy?'

'On Tuesday night, Daddy – who was praying for me?' I didn't say anything, so she continued:

'In the middle of the night, God woke me and showed me I was heading toward this abyss. There was no bottom to it – it scared me to death. I was so frightened. I realized how hard I've been, how wrong, how rebellious.

'But at the same time, it was like God wrapped his arms around me and held me tight. He kept me from sliding any farther as he said, 'I still love you.'

'Daddy, tell me the truth – who was praying for me Tuesday night?'

I looked into her bloodshot eyes, and once again I recognized the daughter we had raised."

(Cymbala, 1997: 63-65)

God does not always answer our prayers as we may expect, nor necessarily in such a spectacular and touching manner as recounted above. But we can, and should, always share our dreams and our hurts with our Heavenly Father, and trust Him to answer as and when is best.

As Christians, many of us have been encouraged to spend time reading our Bibles. Others may have belonged to church institutions that discouraged or even forbade laity from reading the Bible for themselves, but that is nothing short of cultic behavior. But even for those of us encouraged to read for ourselves, or who have attended "Bible-based" local churches, there is the danger that the teaching we received may have led us from the truth rather than towards it. The Bible holds vital messages for us, but are there dangers in the way we read and interpret the Bible?

Through his novel's character, Randall Arthur summarizes the more extreme approaches to interpretation of the Bible:

> "... there are only three basic ways the Scriptures can be approached:
>
> (1) They can be accepted as they are, without being added to or subtracted from – the literalist approach.
>
> (2) They can be accepted in their entirety, then added to - the far-right or legalistic approach.
>
> (3) They can be critically dissected, and then deleted from - the far-left or liberal approach.
>
> *To the extremes are the legalists and the liberals. The legalists, of which in the past I was one of the most devout, add to the Bible their own set of denominational prejudices, their favorite teachings by idolized leaders, and the particular preferences of their native culture. All this 'tradition' becomes embedded into their definition of Christianity. The legalists will then elevate these manmade teachings to the very level of Scripture. They preach them dogmatically and universally in the name of God, and imprison people with them.*
>
> *This approach is destructive in the sense that it gives people a wrong concept of what Christianity is. (For example, Christianity is NOT physical cleanliness, nineteenth-century hymns, unfaltering patriotism, and one-hundred percent Sunday School attendance.) It also ladens people with an unnecessary load of false guilt, and turns its adherents into merciless and self-righteous judges who think that they and they alone have developed Christianity to its maximum potential.*
>
> *To the other extreme are the liberals, of whom I've also been a part. They conveniently delete passages and teachings from the Bible, not because the passages have in any way been scientifically proven false, but simply because they are the cause of personal offense, or are difficult for the logical mind to believe (for example – the teaching of the lake of fire, or the physical resurrection of Christ, or His exclusive saviorhood). This approach is also destructive in that it reduces Christianity to a personalized religion of subjective relativism, implying that finite and mortal man is his own god who can decide what is or is not divine revelation. In this setting, man will never believe any teaching that would uncomfortably regulate his lifestyle, thus rendering Christianity ineffective and creating a spiritual anarchy.*

Inevitably, a person who becomes his own god tends to fuel his own basic selfishness. At a great expense to others, he ultimately ends up respecting no one but himself.

Having personally experienced the destructiveness of both the legalistic and liberal extremes, I now take the third approach ... I am a literalist. I accept the Bible as it is. I don't purposely or consciously add to its teachings, even if I think it should speak out on an issue about which it is silent. Likewise, I don't purposely or consciously subtract from it, even if some of its pages cause me personal offense and are hard for me to understand. I trust that it is what it claims to be – the inspired and preserved Word of God, irrefutable, sufficient, and trustworthy in its entirety."

(Arthur, 1993: 215-216)

Arthur's character has argued above for what he calls a literalist approach. But is there danger in simply reading the Bible in a "literal" manner? Lindsay notes how wrong interpretation based on what had earlier been the teaching from his superiors misled Martin Luther for many years:

"[Luther] still prescribed penances, for he thought that commanded in the Bible. Where the Greek word we translate 'repent' occurred, the Vulgate or Latin Bible, which Luther had, read 'do penance'. Years afterwards Melanchthon showed him that the real scriptural word meant 'change your mind'. "

(Lindsay, 1996: 39)

There is much theology relating to interpretation of the Bible. As an example, the words used in one person's day can have significantly changed in meaning, and we need to be careful not to simplistically assume the same meaning when we read them today.

"The ... first responsibility is to study the Scriptures, in the original languages if possible, but always in terms of the 'Bible culture context.' Any sound system of hermeneutics must take into account the cultural context in which the message was originally communicated, the background and syntax and style, the characteristics of the audience, and the special circumstances in which the message was given. This process is essential to Bible exegesis. The important thing, after all, is not what the Bible reader or interpreter feels the meaning to be; the important thing is what the source intended that his respondents should understand by his message! The Bible interpreter is constantly tempted to project the meanings of his own cultural background into the exegetical process with the result that the original meaning is missed or perverted. This temptation is heightened by the fact that, for the most part, all of us learn our own culture quite unconsciously and uncritically."

(Hesselgrave, 1978: 394)

The Lausanne Committee similarly warns of the dangers in some approaches to Biblical interpretation, but goes on to challenge us to not just read the Bible, but to also allow it to be a catalyst for personal response.

"The commonest [or 'popular'] way [for interpretation and application of Scripture] *is to come straight to the words of the biblical text, and to study them without any awareness that the writer's cultural context differs from the reader's. The reader interprets the text as if it had been written in his own language, culture and time. ...*

A second approach takes with due seriousness the original historical and cultural context. It seeks also to discover what the text meant in its original language, and how it relates to the rest of Scripture. ...

The weakness of this 'historical' approach, however, is that it fails to consider what scripture may be saying to the contemporary reader. It stops short at the meaning of the Bible in its own time and culture. It is thus liable to analyse the text without applying it, and to acquire academic knowledge without obedience. ...

A third approach begins by combining the positive elements of both the 'popular' and the 'historical' approaches. From the 'historical' it takes the necessity of studying the original context and language, and from the 'popular' the necessity of listening to God's word and obeying it. But it goes further than this. It takes seriously the cultural context of the contemporary readers as well as of the biblical text, and recognizes that a dialogue must develop between the two.

It is the need for this dynamic interplay between text and interpreters which we wish to emphasize. Today's readers cannot come to the text in a personal vacuum, and should not try to. Instead, they should come with an awareness of concerns stemming from their cultural background, personal situation, and responsibility to others. These concerns will influence the questions which are put to the Scriptures. What is received back, however, will not be answers only, but more questions. As we address Scripture, Scripture addresses us. We find that our culturally conditioned presuppositions are being challenged and our questions corrected. In fact, we are compelled to reformulate our previous questions and to ask fresh ones. So the living interaction proceeds.

In this process of interaction our knowledge of God and our response to his will are continuously being deepened. The more we come to know him, the greater our responsibility becomes to obey him in our own situation, and the more we respond obediently, the more he makes himself known.

It is this continuous growth in knowledge, love and obedience which is the purpose and profit of the 'contextual' approach. Out of the context in which his word was originally given, we hear God speaking to us in our contemporary context, and we find it a transforming experience. This process is a kind of upward spiral in which Scripture remains always central and normative."

(Lausanne Committee for World Evangelization, 1978: 512-513)

Jesus repeatedly taught the need for us to act in faith. For some who feel their faith is not big enough to amount to much, Yancey offers encouragement:

"As a child, I strove for ever more faith. Adults urged me to develop faith, and I had few clues as to how to proceed. Reading all the healing stories together, I now detect

> *in the Gospels a kind of 'ladder of faith.' At the top of the ladder stand those people who impressed Jesus with bold, unshakeable faith: a centurion, an impertinent blind beggar, a persistent Canaanite woman. These stories of gristly faith threaten me, because seldom do I have such faith. I am easily discouraged by the silence of God. When my prayers are not answered, I am tempted to give up and not ask again. For this reason, I look down the ladder to find people of lesser faith, and it heartens me to learn that Jesus seemed willing to work with whatever tiny glimmer of faith came to light. I cling to the tender accounts of how Jesus treated the disciples who forsook and then doubted him. The same Jesus who praised the bold faith of those high up the ladder also gently quickened the flagging faith of his disciples. And I take special comfort in the confession of the father of the demon-possessed boy who said to Jesus, 'I do believe; help me overcome my unbelief!' Even that wavering man got his request granted."*

(Yancey, 1995: 181)

We can get excited about what we believe God could be calling us to do. He might give us a glimpse of what the future holds, but it cannot be guaranteed to be a complete vision. Some of it may relate to where we may eventually be heading, but not necessarily be marching orders for today. Girard cautions us to wait on, and for, the Holy Spirit:

> "*Depending on the Spirit inevitably and invariably involves learning to wait.*
> *To stop our own activity and wait for His.*"

(Girard, 1972: 75)

Girard looks at the lives of Jesus' disciples and notes that they were not naturally inclined to waiting:

> "*[Jesus] had trained and shared with these men for three years. He had just told them that they were commissioned to make disciples of people everywhere. After seeing Him alive from the dead, they were convinced that He was the Messiah, Savior and Son of God. They had a fantastic story to tell.*
>
> *Here was impetuous, impatient Peter. Hot-blooded Simon the Zealot was there. And those ambitious sons of thunder, James and John. Levi, the tax collector, a short-cut expert if there ever was one.*
>
> *Waiting was simply not their bag. They were men of action. Men with drive. Men with ideas and solutions. They all had active adrenalin glands.*
>
> *But Jesus' instructions read: 'Wait!'*
>
> *Wait for God's promise. Wait for the Spirit. Don't try anything — not one testimony or sermon or evangelistic crusade or missionary journey. Don't plan anything — not one scheme designed to carry out the Lord's command.*
>
> *Wait! Until you are filled with the Spirit.*
>
> *Wait! Until God takes control of you.*

Wait! Until He begins to do the work through you.

Waiting isn't easy. If we are going to trust Him to do it for us and in us and through us, we can't do it with an alternate plan in mind in case the Spirit's program doesn't come off on our pre-announced time schedule."

(Girard, 1972: 76)

Gulley talks of the need for perseverance, of not getting discouraged, and of organizing yourself to increase your chances of finding answers. While the Bible talks about knocking on the door and finding answers, he points out that while some knock and may quickly find their answers, that is not the experience of all:

"... for every one of those happy finders, I've met a weary knocker. Lifelong seekers whose knuckles are bloody-raw in their quest for the divine."

(Gulley, 1997: 155)

The race God calls us to run is more likely to be a marathon than a sprint!

It is my prayer that I, and you as readers of this book, would be catalysts of change—that we would be bold and visionary as we seek to undo the wrongs of the past and present, and seek to get closer to Jesus as the true foundation of our lives rather than allow man-made institutions, traditions and leaders, to come between us and God. While there may be times where we see some areas of service more clearly than others, we should also remain humble and willing to learn, even from those who disagree with us.

"I only urge caution to all who would challenge this system. It is costly and treacherous to go against the grain, since the moment we imagine ourselves to be God's elite, last-days remnant, we have fallen into spiritual pride, which itself is an insidious part of the system we desire to change. Let us proceed with humility, then, asking the Lord to search our hearts first, to strip us of all religious pretension and to deliver us from bondage to dead tradition. Let the revolution begin with us!"

(Brown, 2002: 8)

Finally on the topic of checking out ourselves, Taylor reminds us that it is not just what we do that needs to be constantly checked against God's standards, but also what we fail to do. Every little act we do today, or fail to do today, can have longer-term repercussions.

"... the reader is reminded that every act in this life and every omission too has a direct and important bearing on the future – his own and that of others."

(Taylor & Taylor, 1918: 38)

CHAPTER 38:
HIGH AIMS BALANCED WITH GRACE

Stay open to being personally challenged and changed

Bill from Alcoholics Anonymous writes of the necessity for each individual to honestly face his own issues and take responsibility for what he finds, rather than trying to shift the blame to others:

> "A business which takes no regular inventory usually goes broke. Taking a commercial inventory is a fact-finding and a fact-facing process. It is an effort to discover the truth about the stock in trade. One object is to disclose damaged or unsaleable goods, to get rid of them promptly and without regret. If the owner of the business is to be successful, he cannot fool himself about values.
>
> We had to do exactly the same thing with our lives. We had to take stock honestly."
>
> (Bill, 1967: 173)

> "Too much of my life has been spent in dwelling upon the faults of others. This is a most subtle and perverse form of self-satisfaction, which permits us to remain comfortably unaware of our own defects. Too often we are heard to say, 'If it weren't for him (or her), how happy I'd be!'"
>
> (Bill, 1967: 44)

It is one thing for us to take stock of our flaws. It is quite another thing when someone else points out what they see as areas for improvement in us! Again Bill shares from his experience that we need to listen to these criticisms, humbly learn from what is valid, and graciously put aside topics that we feel are not well-founded, without rejecting the one who expresses their concerns:

> "If this [group] was ruffled, if individuals were deeply disturbed – I say, 'This is fine.' What parliament, what republic, what democracy has not been disturbed? Friction of opposing viewpoints is the very modus operandi on which they proceed. Then what should we be afraid of?"
>
> (Bill, 1967: 82)

> "There are those in A.A. whom we call 'destructive' critics. They power-drive, they are 'politickers,' they make accusations to gain their ends – all for the good of A.A., of course! But we have learned that these folks need not be really destructive.
>
> We ought to listen carefully to what they say. Sometimes they are telling the whole truth; at other times, a little truth. If we are within their range, the whole truth, the half-truth, or no truth at all can prove equally unpleasant to us. If they have got the whole truth, or even a little truth, then we had better thank them and get on with our respective inventories, admitting we were wrong. If they are talking nonsense, we can ignore it, or else try to persuade them. Failing this, we can be sorry they are too thick to listen, and we can try to forget the whole business.
>
> There are few better means of self-survey and of developing patience than the workouts these usually well-meaning but erratic members so often afford us."
>
> (Bill, 1967: 215)

> "Few of us are any longer afraid of what any newcomer can do to [our] reputation or effectiveness. Those who slip, those who [beg in the streets], those who scandalize, those with mental twists, those who rebel ... – all such persons seldom harm [our] group for long.
>
> Some of these have become our most respected and best loved. Some have remained to try our patience, sober nevertheless. Others have drifted away. We have begun to regard the troublesome ones not as menaces, but rather as our teachers. They oblige us to cultivate patience, tolerance, and humility. We finally see that they are only people sicker than the rest of us, that we who condemn them are the Pharisees whose false righteousness does our group the deeper spiritual damage."
>
> (Bill, 1967: 28)

> "... Resentment is the Number One offender ... Given enough anger, both unity and purpose are lost. Given still more 'righteous' indignation, the group can disintegrate; it can actually die. This is why we prescribe no punishments for any misbehaviour, no matter how grievous. Indeed, no [individual] can be deprived of his [association with the group] for any reason whatever. ... Punishment never heals. Only love can heal."
>
> (Bill, 1967: 98)

Not only do we need to take responsibility for honest self-assessment and openly consider the comments of others (even if they convey their message in a rough manner); we also need to act courageously on what we discover.

> "The wise have always known that no one can make much of his life until self-searching becomes a regular habit, until he is able to admit and accept what he finds, and until he patiently and persistently tries to correct what is wrong."
>
> (Bill, 1967: 216)

> "Let us never fear needed change. Certainly we have to discriminate between changes for worse and changes for better. But once a need becomes clearly apparent in an

individual, in a group, or in A.A. as a whole, it has long since been found out that we cannot stand still and look the other way.

The essence of all growth is a willingness to change for the better and then an unremitting willingness to shoulder whatever responsibility this entails."

(Bill, 1967: 115)

High aims for yourself, gentleness towards others

As we become aware of our weaknesses, we can look to God's standards as the goal for our lives. Bill expresses the view that while setting our sights on such lofty goals can, on the one hand, result in despair at their lack of attainability, or on the other hand result in false pride from a misguided belief we have attained them, we still need to recognize God's standard:

"Many people will have no truck at all with absolute spiritual values. Perfectionists, they say, are either full of conceit because they fancy they have reached some impossible goal, or else they are swamped in self-condemnation because they have not done so.

Yet I think that we should not hold this view. It is not the fault of great ideals that they are sometimes misused and so become shallow excuses for guilt, rebellion, and pride. On the contrary, we cannot grow very much unless we constantly try to envision what the eternal spiritual values are …

Day by day, we try to move a little toward God's perfection. So we need not be consumed by maudlin guilt for failure to achieve His likeness and image by Thursday next. Progress is our aim, and His perfection is the beacon, light-years away, that draws us on."

(Bill, 1967: 15)

"I may attain 'humility for today' only to the extent that I am able to avoid the bog of guilt and rebellion on one hand and, on the other hand, that fair but deceiving land which is strewn with the fool's-gold coins of pride. This is how I can find and stay on the highroad to humility, which lies between these extremes. Therefore, a constant inventory which can reveal when I am off the road is always in order."

(Bill, 1967: 12)

Lack of ability to live up to God's standards is not the problem it might seem. In fact, Bill suggests that our struggles within ourselves and with each other are an essential part of growing towards maturity:

"Within A.A., I suppose, we shall always quarrel a good bit. Mostly, I think, about how to do the greatest good for the greatest number of drunks. We shall have our childish spats and snits over small questions of money management and who is going to run our groups for the next six months. Any bunch of growing children (and that is what we are) would hardly be in character if they did less.

These are the growing pains of infancy, and we actually thrive on them. Surmounting such problems, in A.A.'s rather rugged school of life, is a healthy exercise."

(Bill, 1967: 143)

It can be easy to be enthusiastic in sharing with others a newly discovered "truth", but we need to check the motives behind our enthusiasm. If you are now free and have moved outside the confines of the local church, that is wonderful. But is your desire to share this freedom based solely on a desire to see others set free, or is there an element of desire to have companionship on *your* journey so you are less lonely? Could it be said of you or me that:

"... you're still trying to make others do it, instead of living it yourself. It's natural for us to deal with our own emptiness by trying to get others around us to change. That's why so much body life today is built around accountability and human effort: if we could just get everyone else to do what's right, everything would be better for us."

(Jacobsen & Coleman, 2006: 51)

In contrast to urging others to agree with us to make *our* lives simpler, we need the genuine freedom to be willing to be misunderstood and even ostracized, while remaining generous and courteous to those who are travelling a different path.

"... you need to follow Jesus, even when it creates conflict. Always be gentle and gracious to everyone, but never compromise what is in your heart just to get along."

(Jacobsen & Coleman, 2006: 153)

This theme is reinforced in Jacobsen and Coleman's novel when John corrects Jake's misinterpretation of their relationship. Jake had thought John had pushed him in a certain direction that, while ending well, had been rocky on the way:

"[Jake] 'Well, it wasn't easy at the beginning. You really got me into trouble.'

[John] 'Oh, no I didn't. I never told you to do one thing. I simply made some observations, asked some questions, and gave you some options. The choices were all yours.'"

(Jacobsen & Coleman, 2006: 160)

John then goes on to suggest that Jake adopt a similar attitude in his interactions with others:

"... if you listen to nothing else I say, listen to this: don't use our conversations to try to change others. I'm only trying to help you learn to live in God's freedom. Until they are looking for the same things you are, people will not understand ..."

(Jacobsen & Coleman, 2006: 50)

Bill is realistic in that we may not always *feel* love for others. However, we can and should *act* in a gracious manner.

"Not many people can truthfully assert that they love everybody. Most of us must

> admit that we have loved but a few; that we have been quite indifferent to the many. As for the remainder – well, we have really disliked or hated them.
>
> We A.A.'s find we need something much better than this in order to keep our balance. The idea that we can be possessively loving of a few, can ignore the many, and can continue to fear or hate anybody at all, has to be abandoned, if only a little at a time.
>
> We can try to stop making unreasonable demands upon those we love. We can show kindness where we had formerly shown none. With those we dislike we can at least begin to practice justice and courtesy, perhaps going out of our way at times to understand and help them."

(Bill, 1967: 230)

There is a balance. We should not care so much about the opinion of others that we are controlled by trying to please them. But nor should we, in our freedom, show a disregard for the truths we may learn from others. Rather, we can gently share our journey, and provide further insight *if* they wish to gain greater understanding of our perspective.

> "[Jesus] can help you sense when people are ready and when you need to hold back. Make sure you really have their best interests in mind – that you are not using them to validate your own choice by pushing them to agree with you. That never works. Also, listen to the questions people are asking and it will help you know if they're hungry for more. Even with Jake, I've put nuggets out there and watched to see what he did with them. If he listened, struggled, and asked more, I took him further. If he didn't, I let it go! I was trying to serve him. I didn't need to validate myself."

(Jacobsen & Coleman, 2006: 153-154)

'The exchanged life'

In the notes above, Bill has encouraged us to show grace in our actions to others. Perhaps we also need to show ourselves grace as we fail to live perfectly! As noted, there are many books on the topics briefly introduced earlier on prayer, faith, Bible reading and so on. Hudson Taylor had spent years trying to apply the principles that seemed to be necessary for a "holy" life, but found the effort tiring and limited in value.

> "… I now think that this striving, effort, longing, hoping for better days to come [in the sense of closer fellowship with God], is not the true way to happiness, holiness or usefulness: better, no doubt far better, than being satisfied with our poor attainments, but not the best way after all."

(Taylor & Taylor, 1918: 168)

Instead, Taylor experienced a major personal breakthrough which he called the "Exchanged Life".

He had been painfully aware of problem areas in his own life. He had a deep desire to walk close to God, but again and again the reality seemed to be a distance from God and a series of failures in overcoming his areas of struggle. He accepted in theory that Christ was the source of his hope, and that he needed to tap into a living faith, but Taylor also felt deeply what he interpreted as a smallness of faith on his own part.

Then Taylor started to see things differently. Instead of striving for more faith, Taylor saw he could rest in the Faithful one. Instead of trying to "get" Christ, he saw he could accept that he is part of the vine and is already one with Him. Instead of working to see what he could do for God, he saw he could rest in the realization that it is God's responsibility to equip him for whatever He asks him to do.

This life of resting in God does not guarantee we will never sin again, but it does guarantee that we don't *have to* sin!

In a long but expressive letter to his sister, Taylor pours out his heart as he shares his newfound freedom:

> *"So many thanks for your long, dear letter … I do not think you have written me such a letter since we have been in China. I know it is with you as with me – you cannot, not you will not. Mind and body will not bear more than a certain amount of strain, or do more than a certain amount of work. As to work, mine was never so plentiful, so responsible, or so difficult; but the weight and strain are all gone. The last month or more has been perhaps, the happiest of my life; and I long to tell you a little of what the Lord has done for my soul. I do not know how far I may be able to make myself intelligible about it, for there is nothing new or strange or wonderful – and yet, all is new! In a word, 'Whereas once I was blind, now I see.'*
>
> *Perhaps I shall make myself more clear if I go back a little. Well, dearie, my mind has been greatly exercised for six or eight months past, feeling the need personally, and for our Mission, of more holiness, life, power in our souls. But personal need stood first and was the greatest. I felt the ingratitude, the danger, the sin of not living nearer to God. I prayed, agonised, fasted, strove, made resolutions, read the Word more diligently, sought more time for retirement and meditation – but all was without effect. Every day, almost every hour, a consciousness of sin oppressed me. I knew that if I could only abide in Christ all would be well, but I could not. I began the day with prayer, determined not to take my eye from Him for a moment; but pressure of duties, sometimes very trying, constant interruptions apt to be so wearing, often caused me to forget Him. Then one's nerves get so fretted in this climate that temptations to irritability, hard thoughts, and sometimes unkind words are all the more difficult to control. Each day brought its register of sin and failure, of lack of power. To will was indeed present with me, but how to perform I found not.*
>
> *Then came the question, 'Is there no rescue? Must it be thus to the end – constant conflict and, instead of victory, too often defeat?' How, too, could I preach with sincerity that to those who receive Jesus, 'to them gave He power to become the sons of God' (i.e. God-like) when it was not so in my own experience? Instead of growing stronger, I seemed to be getting weaker and to have less power against sin; and no wonder, for faith and even hope were getting very low. I hated myself; I hated my sin;*

and yet I gained no strength against it. I felt I was a child of God; His Spirit in my heart would cry, in spite of all, 'Abba, Father': but to rise to my privileges as a child, I was utterly powerless. I thought that holiness, practical holiness, was to be gradually attained by a diligent use of the means of grace. I felt that there was nothing I so much desired in this world, nothing I so much needed. But so far from in any measure attaining it, the more I pursued and strove after it, the more it eluded my grasp; till hope itself almost died out, and I began to think that, perhaps to make heaven the sweeter, God would not give it down here. I do not think I was striving to attain it in my own strength. I knew I was powerless. I told the Lord so, and asked Him to give me help and strength; and sometimes I almost believed He would keep and uphold me. But on looking back in the evening, alas! there was but sin and failure to confess and mourn before God.

I would not give you the impression that this was the daily experience of all those long, weary months. It was a too frequent state of soul; that toward which I was tending, and which almost ended in despair. And yet never did Christ seem more precious – a Saviour who could and would save such a sinner! … And sometimes there were seasons not only of peace but of joy in the Lord. But they were transitory, and at best there was a sad lack of power. Oh, how good the Lord was in bringing this conflict to an end!

All the time I felt assured that there was in Christ all I needed, but the practical question was how to get it out. He was rich, truly, but I was poor; He was strong, but I weak. I knew full well that there was in the root, the stem, abundant fatness; but how to get it into my puny little branch was the question. As gradually the light was dawning on me, I saw that faith was the only pre-requisite, was the hand to lay hold on His fulness and make it my own. But I had not this faith. I strove for it, but it would not come; tried to exercise it, but in vain. Seeing more and more the wondrous supply of grace laid up in Jesus, the fulness of our precious Saviour – my helplessness and guilt seemed to increase. Sins committed appeared but as trifles compared with the sin of unbelief which was their cause, which could not or would not take God at His word, but rather made Him a liar! Unbelief was, I felt, the damning sin of the world – yet I indulged in it. I prayed for faith, but it came not. What was I to do?

When my agony of soul was at its height, a sentence in a letter from dear McCarthy was used to remove the scales from my eyes, and the Spirit of God revealed the truth of our oneness with Jesus as I had never known it before. McCarthy, who had been much exercised by the same sense of failure, but saw the light before I did, wrote (I quote from memory):

> *'But how to get faith strengthened? Not by striving after faith, but by resting on the Faithful One.'*

As I read I saw it all! 'If we believe not, He abideth faithful.' I looked to Jesus and saw (and when I saw, oh, how joy flowed!) that He had said, 'I will never leave you.' 'Ah, there is rest!' I thought. 'I have striven in vain to rest in Him. I'll strive no more. For has He not promised to abide with me – never to leave me, never to fail me?' And, dearie, He never will!

But this was not all He showed me, nor one half. As I thought of the Vine and the branches, what light the blessed Spirit poured direct into my soul! How great seemed my mistake in having wished to get the sap, the fulness out of Him. I saw not only that Jesus would never leave me, but that I was a member of His body, of His flesh and of His bones. The vine now I see, is not the root merely, but all – root, stem, branches, twigs, leaves, flowers, fruit: and Jesus is not only that: He is soil and sunshine, air and showers, and ten thousand times more than we have ever dreamed, wished for, or needed. Oh, the joy of seeing this truth! I do pray that the eyes of your understanding may be enlightened, that you may know and enjoy the riches freely given us in Christ.

Oh, my dear sister, it is a wonderful thing to be really one with a risen and exalted Saviour; to be a member of Christ! Think what it involves. Can Christ be rich and I poor? Can your right hand be rich and the left poor? or your head be well fed while your body starves? Again, think of its bearing on prayer. Could a bank clerk say to a customer, 'It was only your hand wrote that cheque, not you,' or, 'I cannot pay this sum to your hand, but only to yourself'? No more can your prayers, or mine, be discredited if offered in the name of Jesus (i.e. not in our own name, or for the sake of Jesus merely, but on the ground that we are His, His members) so long as we keep within the extent of Christ's credit – a tolerably wide limit! If we ask anything unscriptural or not in accordance with the will of God, Christ Himself could not do that; but, 'If we ask anything according to His will, He heareth us, and … we know that we have the petitions that we desire of Him.'

The sweetest part, if one may speak of one part being sweeter than another, is the rest which full identification with Christ brings. I am no longer anxious about anything, as I realise this; for He, I know, is able to carry out His will, and His will is mine. It makes no matter where He places me, or how. That is rather for Him to consider than for me; for in the easiest positions He must give me His grace, and in the most difficult His grace is sufficient. It little matters to my servant whether I send him to buy a few cash worth of things, or the most expensive articles. In either case he looks to me for the money, and brings me his purchases. So, if God place me in great perplexity, must He not give me much guidance; in positions of great difficulty, much grace; in circumstances of great pressure and trial, much strength? No fear that His resources will be unequal to the emergency! And His resources are mine, for He is mine, and is with me and dwells in me. All this springs from the believer's oneness with Christ. And since Christ has thus dwelt in my heart by faith, how happy I have been! I wish I could tell you, instead of writing about it.

I am no better than before (may I not say, in a sense, I do not wish to be, nor am I striving to be); but I am dead and buried with Christ – aye, and risen too, and ascended; and now Christ lives in me, and 'the life that I now live in the flesh, I live by the faith of the Son of God, Who loved me, and gave Himself for me.' I now believe

I am dead to sin. God reckons me so, and tells me to reckon myself so. He knows best. All my past experience may have shown that it was not so; but I dare not say it is not now, when He says it is. I feel and know that old things have passed away. I am as capable of sinning as ever, but Christ is realised as present as never before. He cannot sin; and He can keep me from sinning. I cannot say (I am sorry to have to confess it) that since I have seen this light I have not sinned; but I do feel there was no need to have done so. And further – walking more in the light, my conscience has been more tender; sin has been instantly seen, confessed, pardoned; and peace and joy (with humility) instantly restored: with one exception, when for several hours peace and joy did not return – from want, as I had to learn, of full confession, and from some attempt to justify self.

Faith, I now see, is 'the substance of things hoped for,' and not mere shadow. It is not less than sight, but more. Sight only shows the outward forms of things; faith gives the substance. You can rest on substance, feed on substance. Christ dwelling in the heart by faith (i.e. His Word of Promise credited) is power indeed, is life indeed. And Christ and sin will not dwell together; nor can we have His presence with love of the world, or carefulness about 'many things.'

And now I must close. I have not said half I would, nor as I would had I more time. May God give you to lay hold on these blessed truths. Do not let us continue to say, in effect, 'Who shall ascend into heaven, that is to bring Christ down from above.' In other words, do not let us consider Him as afar off, when God has made us one with Him, members of His very body. Nor should we look upon this experience, these truths, as for the few. They are the birthright of every child of God, and no one can dispense with them without dishonour to our Lord. The only power for deliverance from sin or for true service is Christ."

(Taylor & Taylor, 1918: 173-177)

SECTION 10:

LAUNCH OUT IN FREEDOM

We have seen how others have found real freedom in their individual relationships with God. There is another dimension to freedom, and it requires freedom in how we exercise our responsibilities in reaching out as an agent of God's love.

Being an Australian, I am not well versed in the history of the fight for freedom of slaves in the USA, but from the little I do know, achieving the *right* to freedom was part of the story. But for a people who had been living in slavery for generations, they also had another challenge, namely to start *actually living* in freedom, in spite of any obstacles.

We, too, must first acknowledge the right and responsibility we have to follow God without having anyone try to assert their perceived authority to mediate and interpret God's will for us. But then we must take *actual* steps to put the right for freedom into practice.

CHAPTER 39:
BOLDNESS IN THE FACE OF MISUNDERSTANDING

Essential attitudes towards those who oppose our freedoms

To be free, we must simply accept that there will be those who not only oppose our position, but also turn that opposition into a personal attack. It's part of the price of freedom.

> *"Following your convictions will prove costly. Following the moving of the Spirit – remember, He is not standing still – will mean much agony in intercession and stretching of the soul. Following your Master closely will mean crucifixion, rejection, reproach and shame.*
>
> *Most of the opposition you experience will come from brothers and sisters in the Lord, from fellow workers and friends. It will come from 'the mainstream,' from those who are 'sound in the faith,' from those who are 'established in the truth,' even from those who are 'on fire for the Lord.' Often it will come from those whose acceptance you value.*
>
> *Yet that is the path of obedience, the price of being a pioneer. Who among us will make the break? Will you? What price must you pay to be fully faithful to the Lord? What will He require of you?"*
>
> (Brown, 2002: 185-186)

We are not responsible for how others react to our message and actions of freedom; however, we *are* responsible for how we react to *them*. We must be uncompromising in walking in freedom, even if our very freedom offends others. Living in freedom under Jesus' leadership will upset local church leaders who don't want us to be free but want us to follow them instead. But while we accept suffering as part of our call, we must not cause suffering through attitudes of superiority or revenge.

> *"That is how our Lord responds to that which is wrong: He seeks to make it right. And that means conflict and misunderstanding. Yet we seek to smooth things over and make everything nice. How contrary this is to the Jesus pattern! (Once again I add this caution: Following the Jesus pattern means acting in humility, coming as a servant rather than a boss, walking in grace and longsuffering, overcoming evil with good, honoring authority and living in peace as much as it lies with you, and losing your life rather than saving it. It does not give you or me the right to be nasty, contentious or obnoxious. But it does call us to be advocates of radical change regardless of the cost or consequences.) …*
>
> *On the one hand, that place outside the [local church] is a place of glory, of divine habitation, of spiritual vitality, of holy power, a place inhabited by multitudes of God's people. On the other hand, it is a place of challenge and confrontation, a place that is often lonely and painful, a place that will be small before it is large, rejected before it is honored and scorned before it is respected. Will we follow Jesus there?"*
>
> (Brown, 2002: 198-199, 201-202)

The journey will be painful, especially when those we have shared closeness with now treat us as outcasts. Yet we must not waste our pain. If we take up our cross as we are called to do, we may well look back and see the very pain we would prefer to avoid has been part of a path towards growth.

> *"An easy, routine way of life which many associate with stability and security only gives man stagnation. Entrenched routine only spoils man and makes him simple and weak. On the other hand, progressive resistance in life always has the potential to give many progressive strength, and to make man progressively wiser.*
>
> *The truth is this: Most if not all the true wisdom of God, the true insight of God, and the true knowledge of God that a man holds in his heart he has learned from resistance and affliction.*
>
> *Resistance makes a man think new thoughts he never considered before. It makes a man ask questions he never asked before. It makes a man seek answers he never sought before. It makes a man beg God for help that he never before realized he needed. These quests, quests of the heart and soul, eventually make a man deeper, wider, taller.*
>
> *Therefore man should fear the easy routine way of life that weakens, but he should welcome the resistance-filled life that strengthens and makes wise."*
>
> (Arthur, 1991: 217)

We must make a choice, and accept the consequences. We can live in slavery to the traditions of local institutions and to the leaders, or we can break free and be obedient to Jesus. It is not easy, but you cannot be totally dependent on Jesus as Lord until you have boldly and defiantly made your personal declaration of independence from the stifling traditions that men wrongly call "church".

There is a danger in being completely isolated from the advice of others, of being impervious to correction. We can discount all views that contradict our own, but then we run the risk of being no freer or wiser than those we oppose. We should listen to all criticism, and consider where improvement needs to occur, take it to God, seek His direction, and ask for the grace and courage to make changes where He indicates.

Conversely, we can believe everything we hear. And that too is dangerous. You may remember the story of the man and his son taking a donkey to market. At one stage they all walked, and one passer-by criticized him for not making use of the donkey to carry one of them, so he gave his son a ride. Another criticized the son for riding while his elderly father walked, so they swapped places. Another then criticized the father for making his young son walk, so they both got on. And as I recollect, they were about to be criticized for the cruelty of both riding the poor donkey when the bridge they were crossing broke under the combined weight, with great loss.

So, maintaining a sensitive balance between hearing others and standing firmly in our own conviction, we walk on with Jesus, regardless of opposition from those who do not understand.

> *"Not to advance [when opportunities were there for the taking] would be to retreat from the position of faith taken up at the beginning. It would be to look at difficulties rather than at the living God."*
>
> (Taylor & Taylor, 1918: 355)

At the end of the day, we focus on our responsibility. Friends and family may reject the call to freedom. But how will *you* respond? You (and I) must not wait until such a movement is popular, and has the backing of the masses. We must act individually now with the light we have.

Philip Yancey records such a challenge presented to him by Mahatma Ghandi:

> *"[Gandhi] shifts the spotlight away from movements and leaders of history and focuses it instead on himself. The crucial question for him was not how other Christians, Hindus or Muslims had acted in the past, but how he was acting in the present. Confronting Gandhi, I am forced to turn from an armchair review of Christian history to a much more painful look at myself as an individual follower of Jesus."*
>
> (Yancey, 2001: 157)

> *"In his own study of the New Testament, Gandhi found the counsel to seek truth with the whole heart, expecting nothing, regardless of results. He used to sing an Indian poem as he walked among the rice paddies at a time when his own people were persecuting him, 'If they answer not your call, walk alone, walk alone.' In countries like the US that message, frankly, does not sell."*
>
> (Yancey, 2001: 153)

The call to follow Jesus is not for those who want a soft ride. Jesus warned us that if He was persecuted for His actions and beliefs then we too must not be surprised if we are treated likewise. God's people are called to go against the flow, to be radical agents of change.

One tragic consequence of trying to be accepted by the "in" crowd is that we may end up compromising our values. Instead, we must be willing to stand apart. As quoted earlier, McManus states,

> *"One of the tragedies of a civilized society is that no one wants to get involved. What becomes appropriate is to mind our own business. When we join a community that lacks a passionate heart for the world, we soon find ourselves acquiescing to apathy. It is a painful tragedy to see a brand-new follower of Christ alive with a barbarian spirit soon conformed to the status quo."*
>
> (McManus, 2005: 123)

Cymbala points out that so often our preachers put a positive spin on everything, and won't face the reality that the local church is sick. We are in a serious battle, and

> *"... our stance must remain militant, aggressive, bold.*
>
> *That is what characterized General William Booth and the early Salvation Army as they invaded the slums of London. It characterized the early mission movements, such as the Moravians. It characterized Hudson Taylor in China as well as revivalists on the American frontier. These Christians were not bulls in a china shop, but they did speak the truth in love – fearlessly."*
>
> (Cymbala, 1997: 97-98)

It is to be noted that William Booth is held up by Cymbala as an example of courage in the face of opposition. We give credit where credit is due—Booth *was* courageous. We, too, are called to be courageous, but hopefully we will avoid the heavy-handed, hierarchical control mechanisms later employed by Booth.

One responsibility in taking a radical stance for Christ is to speak out against the very institution that would deny freedom to His followers.

> *"... a true biblical maverick acts in a prophetic manner by exposing the lies that the dominant group tells itself in order to sustain its shared illusions ..."*
>
> (Frost & Hirsch, 2003: 195)

Another responsibility is to not only speak out, but to act in whatever way God calls us. We *must* follow Him. Any lack of "proper preparation" as man judges is not an excuse. Many of those who have made their mark on the world were not trained according to prevailing standards, but God used them nonetheless. Or maybe He was able to use them *because* they had not been shaped by man's institutions!

> *"The heroes of church history whom we now revere were not known for their cleverness; they were warriors for God. Moody was never ordained to the ministry.*

> *Finney never went to seminary. Yet whole cities were visited by God as a result of their anointed work."*
>
> (Cymbala, 1997: 182)

So will you respond to the call?

> *"Will we be revolutionaries for Jesus if it means the loss of titles and prestige and power?*
>
> *Will we be revolutionaries for Jesus if it means the loss of friends and family?*
>
> *Will we be revolutionaries for Jesus if it means the loss of money?*
>
> *Will we be revolutionaries for Jesus if it means misunderstanding and even expulsion?*
>
> *Will we be revolutionaries for Jesus if it means we question the purpose of our multimillion-dollar church building used a precious few hours a week?*
>
> *Will we be revolutionaries for Jesus if it means massive personal upheaval?*
>
> *Will we? Will you?*
>
> *A growing army of holy radicals is saying Yes! to all the above. Their example should give you courage and faith to take a bold, even militant new stand. Their example should give you strength to get out of the boat and walk on the water toward Jesus. Their example should inspire you to fly.*
>
> *In reality, we have no other choice. It is revolution or bust, revolution or we die, revolution or …"*
>
> (Brown, 2002: 17)

For those with eyes to see it, the revolution has already begun, and in fact commenced when Jesus Himself walked on the Earth.

> *"A barbarian invasion is taking place even right now. [Christians with a revolutionary attitude] are coming from the four corners of the earth and they are numbered among the unlikely. From the moment Jesus walked among us the invasion began. And just as with those who crossed paths with Him here on earth, those who are most religious will be most offended and indignant. Barbarians are not welcome among the civilized and are feared among the domesticated. The way of Jesus is far too savage for their sensibilities. The sacrifice of God's Son, the way of the Cross, the call to die to ourselves, all lack the dignity of a refined faith. Why insist on such a barbaric way? Why a reckless call to awaken the barbarian faith within us at the risk of endangering … [what some see as a 'great civilization'] we have come to know as Christianity?*
>
> *Because Jesus did not suffer and die so that we could build for ourselves havens, but so that we might expand the kingdom of His love. Because invisible kingdoms are at war for the hearts and lives of every human being who walks on the face of this earth."*
>
> (McManus, 2005: 15-16)

McManus shares a vision of what unfettered followers of Jesus might become:

> *"[A group of] bees are called swarms, and ants are called colonies …*

But my favorite of all is the group designation for rhinos. You see, rhinos can run at thirty miles an hour, which is pretty fast when you consider how much weight they're pulling. They're actually faster than squirrels, which can run at up to twenty-six miles an hour. And even then, who's going to live in dread of a charging squirrel? ... Just one problem with this phenomenon. Rhinos can see only thirty feet in front of them. Can you imagine something that large moving in concert as a group, plowing ahead at thirty miles an hour with no idea what's at thirty-one feet? You would think that they would be far too timid to pick up full steam, that their inability to see far enough ahead would paralyze them to immobility. But with that horn pointing the way, rhinos run forward full steam ahead without apprehension, which leads us to their name.

Rhinos moving together at full speed are known as a crash. Even when they're just hanging around enjoying the watershed, they're called a crash because of their potential. You've got to love that. I think that's what we're supposed to be. That's what happens when we become barbarians and shake free of domestication and civility. ... We become an unstoppable force. We don't have to pretend we know the future. Who cares that we can see only thirty feet ahead? Whatever's at thirty-one feet needs to care that we're coming and better get out of the way."

(McManus, 2005: 136, 137-138)

The loneliness of the journey to freedom

Some argue that we need "fellowship", but what they actually mean is that we need to be strongly associated with a local church. Jacobsen and Coleman expose that error but also warn that, while it is healthy and normal to seek true friendship and fellowship without the conditions enforced by the local church, there may be times when the journey is lonely:

"But don't we need regular fellowship?

I wouldn't say we need it. If we were in a place where we couldn't find other believers, Jesus certainly would be able to take care of us. Thus, I'd phrase that a bit differently: will people who are growing to know the living God also desire real and meaningful connections with other believers? Absolutely!

... But sometimes that kind of fellowship is not easy to find. Periodically on this journey we may go through times when we can't seem to find any other believers who share our hunger. That's especially true for those who find that conforming to the expectations of the religious institutions around them diminishes their relationship with Jesus. They may find themselves excluded by believers with whom they've shared close friendship."

(Jacobsen & Coleman, 2006: 171)

Not only may the journey be lonely, but you may have to accept that some you called close friends may never understand. And in this state, we must learn to lean on God

Himself. Leigh Hatcher's autobiography, *I'm Not Crazy, I'm Just A Little Unwell*, reveals some of the pain he encountered as he journeyed along a path some others did not understand:

> *"It was only when I discovered how vulnerable I was that I really came to appreciate the size and scope of God – to know, in the depths of my being, his mercy and grace.*
>
> *Reading the living history of the Bible, I saw how unmistakable it is that God sometimes leads his great people of faith through the wilderness, often for a long time. Yet it is there that God reveals himself profoundly. What God had revealed to me especially was his utter trustworthiness. Even when events seemed to be spinning out of control, even when my best laid plans went up in smoke, even when others disappointed me and led me to despair – there was still One in whom I could trust. I now believed that the biggest lesson we can draw from the entire biblical narrative is how God can be trusted, always. And the biggest thing that God surely wants of us is simply to trust him.*
>
> *None of this ever dawned on me until, like Joseph, I went down into the pit. It completely revolutionised my whole understanding of life and faith.*
>
> *Unfortunately, it also set me apart from my old Christian community. I felt acutely how sad it was that many people had been unable to come alongside me in acceptance and understanding as I went through this experience. …*
>
> *… I felt the 'new me' had nowhere to go to have my new insights and understandings affirmed and understood, let alone embraced. I found it impossible simply to walk away from the experiences and insights won in the midst of suffering. They were too real and tough for me to just pack them away in a box and move on as if nothing had happened.*
>
> *At the end of the day, all this created a significant disconnection from my old stream of church life. For one reason and another, attempts to achieve a reconciliation and accommodation kept on hitting a wall. Sadly, I still found myself feeling alienated, alone and damaged, even in the midst of [significant personal well-being]."*
>
> (Hatcher, 2005: 97-98)

CHAPTER 40:
TIMID FEELINGS, BRAVE ACTIONS

If you or I saw a person limping because they had a stone in their shoe, we would wonder why they didn't stop and remove the stone. Yet sometimes some of us may be limping along in life, yet we do not stop to remove some unhealthy dimension that holds us back from freedom and wholesome living. There may be many reasons. Perhaps we are not fully aware of the symptom – after all, it's been part of our "normal" for so long. Or possibly we have a level of awareness, but cannot see another way, or fear that the cost of change may exceed the benefits.

The following story looks at this issue. The entire chapter could be summarized as a case study of two people living in an extremely abusive situation. Both were deeply unhappy by aspects of control as exercised by their church leaders, One person wanted to break free, and struggled to do so, but did eventually succeed. Her mother likewise spoke on the topic of escaping, but could not bring herself to do so.

McManus' words on the crash of rhinos and their possible implications for us are both stirring and encouraging. But while we are inspired to break free, there are two realities we must face. The first is that some we love and care for will feel unable to make such a massive change. And secondly, even for us, it won't be easy. McManus talks of a bold, brave charge towards the unseen. For some it will be a mixture of fear and uncertainty on the one hand, combined with a resolution to break free no matter what the price.

The following extracts are from the heart-rending story of Elissa Wall, who was raised in a polygamous sect, forced into marriage as a fourteen-year-old by the church head, and repeatedly raped by her husband.

You may read this chapter and see it being as such an extreme situation that you question its relevance to your life. I am genuinely hopeful that your experiences are nothing like the story that follows. However, I have provided extracts with commentary to demonstrate how Elissa struggled with timid feelings but nonetheless acted bravely, as stated in the chapter title.

The reason for the inclusion of my review of this story is simple. Often when we see an extreme scenario, we can more clearly see the more subtle parallels in our own lives, and help you gain an understanding of the real struggles that we may face in leaving "church". Elissa did eventually break free from her church, but her mother, though also emotionally torn apart by the actions of the sect's leaders, was unable to make a similar decision.

Understanding the background to one controlling group

The story starts with a tiny glimpse of some aspects of the behavior of the Fundamentalist Church of Latter Day Saints (FLDS). This is essential background to understanding the level of control exercised by the FLDS leaders described in Elissa's book, and the subsequent difficulties experienced by their followers in breaking free.

Unfortunately it is not unusual to encounter groups often labeled as "cults", where the leaders are exclusively male and where their position of authority is used to selfishly dominate women, sometimes for sexual purposes. In the FLDS, the most senior church leader (called the "prophet") had total authority. He taught that:

> "... a man must have a minimum of three wives to gain admittance to the highest of the three levels of heaven ... for himself and his family."
>
> (Wall, 2008: 9)

The "prophet" Rulon led by example. He had in excess of sixty wives! (Wall, 2008: 213).

Elissa and several of her many brothers and sisters were frequently disciplined because they dared to ask questions.

> *"Craig [one of Elissa's brothers] possessed a fiery intelligence and a quick mind. When he was still a high school student at Alta Academy, he had begun to examine aspects of our religion in his quest to gain a deeper understanding of our faith. Uncle Warren didn't seem to like Craig because he wasn't just another sheep willing to follow the flock. He was an enthusiastic student, and in priesthood history, he often asked pointed questions that would back Warren into a corner in front of the whole class. While he was eagerly trying to understand how the teachings and our culture all fit together, Warren was threatened by my brother's inquisitiveness and labeled him as trouble. ...*
>
> *Warren's attitude toward Craig and many of my siblings seemed to come not just from displeasure with their behavior but from a larger, more fundamental problem with the Wall family. It was almost as though he felt threatened by us. The fact that many in my family were smart, strong-willed, and unafraid to ask questions when things did not feel right made it hard to keep a tight hold on us. Warren didn't like having to deal with disobedience and questions concerning the priesthood. Our religion left no room*

for logical reasoning and honest questioning. Warren made no attempt to understand or tolerate any of this, deeming it as absolute rebellion."

(Wall, 2008: 44)

For *any* church leader to condemn questioning is evil—there can *never* be any excuse for such a mandate. Such control is even more evil if the leader forbids his or her followers to have interaction with people outside of their group, thus denying the possibility of their exposure to alternative views.

Warren Jeffs, a son of the "prophet" Rulon, and his eventual successor, had no intention of allowing his people to even *consider* other ways of thinking. He was responsible for the curriculum of the church's closed school, the Alta Academy, and for authoring much of the written material and the "teaching" that was broadcast over the loudspeakers. Elissa shares her observations as to how Warren isolated the pupils from exposure to differing views:

"As we advanced into higher grades, the religious aspects of our education, which had always been present, became all-consuming. Little by little, Uncle Warren had been removing traditional age-appropriate curriculum and replacing it with teachings from the church, as well as many of his own. …

In addition, he had rewritten our coursework to fit his designs. Books by authors outside the church were destroyed and replaced with church-approved ones. Subjects such as science and current events became less important, and instead the focus was on our religious teachings. Unapproved pictures were removed from textbooks, and anything that had to do with evolution or human anatomy was excised. In fact, anything that did not conform to our strict religious teachings and beliefs was removed from the lesson plans, and pages of books that dealt with conflicting subject matter were simply ripped out. …

Through these and other methods of indoctrination, Uncle Warren was slowly cultivating a generation of loyal followers. Most of us had attended Alta Academy since our youngest years. Almost everything that we knew about the priesthood had come from him. Warren had shaped our vision of the religion and the world; and we had learned only what Warren wanted us to."

(Wall, 2008: 71-72)

If someone from outside the sect was presented with some of Elissa's views, they may well have judged them to be neither reasonable nor logical. But as she explains, when a person is raised in a closed community from childhood, the church leaders can often train them to believe almost anything:

"Now that I no longer belong to the FLDS, I can understand how an outsider would find [our beliefs] ludicrous. But having spent my entire life listening only to this powerful rhetoric, to the constant repetition of these extreme beliefs, I was completely conditioned to believe whatever I was told by the people I believed to be God's

messengers. Though the FLDS are understandably offended by the word brainwashed, the truth is, I was, and I could not access, let alone act on, my inherent doubts."

(Wall, 2008: 226)

In spite of the system of indoctrination, some of the other FLDS members did ask questions and express doubts about the belief system. How were these questioning minds handled by the leadership? If they were males and deemed too old for reform they were often summarily ejected from the community with little more than the clothes they stood in, while females were married off to males that could be trusted to "keep them in line". When one of Elissa's sisters, Teressa, resisted marriage, she was sent to an environment deliberately intended to break her.

"Teressa's rebellion invited pressure to marry. Now I see that it was a common practice that a girl who had 'problems' with obedience should be married and made pregnant as soon as possible to help pull her from her wicked ways and push her to conform to the FLDS ideal of womanhood. Our mother and some of our older sisters began urging Teressa to 'turn herself in to the prophet for marriage,' but true to herself, Teressa refused. ... Warren later ordered her off church-owned land, allowing her only to go to the community in Bountiful, Canada, to work, repent, and learn about her proper role in our society. ...

[She, and two others,] went to work at a church-owned post and pole manufacturing mill in remote Alberta, almost seven hours north of Bountiful. Once there, they were all put to hard manual labor alongside other boys and occasionally a girl or two who had been sent there to reform. 'Work them so they can't find time to get into trouble' was the saying. Their primary task was to turn trees into poles. This was rigorous for all ... of them, but especially hard on Teressa in her long prairie-style dresses. Frequently they worked the night shift, even in sub-zero [Fahrenheit] temperatures; and there was little safety equipment. They received no pay, only room and board.

There was little attempt to hide the purpose of subjecting Teressa to this regimen. The point was to break her spirit by working her into submission. Marriage was dangled in front of her as the only reprieve from the work. It was a battle of wills and they were determined to undermine hers. After many months, Teressa finally gave in ...

It had taken the bitter cold of Canada, manual labor, and intense pressures, but finally Teressa had been broken. She was seventeen years old when she got married, and the most beautiful bride I'd ever seen. She had golden blond hair and fiery blue eyes. She was stunning on the surface, but beneath that veneer, I knew she hated that they'd defeated her."

(Wall, 2008: 80-82)

For those of us not living in such a controlling environment, we may ask why people didn't just leave. But not only were they psychologically tied to the sect, they were also held by family and financial ties.

"It was a common practice to expel men, and in extreme cases women, whom the priesthood considered a threat and could weaken the faith of other members. It doesn't

> take a religious ordinance or excommunication for a man to lose his priesthood. All that's required is for the prophet or someone acting at his direction to say: 'You have lost your priesthood.' The significance of this is enormous for believers, as it creates a culture of fear. If a husband loses his priesthood, his family is literally no longer his. In addition, he has to leave his land and home because his home is owned by the FLDS Church and controlled by the priesthood. Faithful wives and children will accept these decisions and wait to be reassigned to another man. In the meantime, the father is told that his only chance to win back his family is to leave and repent at a distance.
>
> If men want to remain faithful members of the church and not lose their home and family, they must obey the priesthood's rules and teachings in every facet of life."

(Wall, 2008: 18)

Perhaps the cruelest practice for those the church rejected was their total alienation from even contacting their old friends and family. One of Elissa's brothers had broken free, but at great personal cost.

> "Because [my brother, Travis, had] left the church in the middle of his 'reforming' in [a church community], he was now labeled an apostate. To be an apostate was even worse than being a gentile. Gentile was the term given to all non-FLDS people, no matter their religion, but an apostate was someone who had lost faith or had left the church, turning their back on the priesthood. Apostates were viewed as one of the worst kinds of evil. FLDS teachings demanded that all members abandon people who choose to apostatize – even members of your own family."

(Wall, 2008: 83-84)

The consequences of being ejected from the community were great. An atmosphere of fear was created by the threat of any perceived disobedience being punished by rejection. This was heightened by a practice of the faithful members actively reporting those they considered less than perfect.

> "What had once been a community of industrious people who lived by the motto 'Love thy neighbor as thyself' had slowly shifted to become a society of paranoid and fearful souls. Everyone was looking over his shoulder to see what his neighbor was doing, and Warren was encouraging people to report any wrongdoings. It seemed his goal was to rid the society of those he deemed unworthy and who would prevent the rest of us from being lifted up at the end of the world.
>
> Our new prophet's teachings became more severe and apocalyptic. 'Soon the Lord is going to cleanse the people,' he warned. 'And it will be revealed to the prophet those who are halfhearted, and they will be weeded out.' The mood in [the community] continued to grow more sullen and uneasy. Life had become all about 'perfection' and watching your neighbor and turning him in if deemed necessary to prove 'perfect obedience.' "

(Wall, 2008: 243-244)

Elissa's mother just can't break free

This was the background environment in which both Elissa and her mother grew up. Elissa was finally able to break free, but her mother failed to do so. Before we judge her mother, perhaps we need to look at the extracts below, and to concede that it is sometimes very difficult to make decisions that go against a lifetime of conditioning.

Something we may be able to identify with if *we* consider leaving a group is the investment we have already put into it. For some, there is the family name on a church pew donated by an ancestor, or maybe even by us! For others, it is the time and money already sacrificially given to the "cause". And of course there are typically investments in deep friendships—if we leave, historical evidence of others in similar circumstances indicates that friendships may be weakened if not totally lost.

Elissa's mother had similar tensions. There were times she may have wanted to take a path other than that demanded by her "priesthood" husband or the church's "prophet", but any sign of challenge on her part could mean all she had put into the local church could be irrevocably removed, let alone the fear and mistaken belief that she could also lose her salvation.

> *"There would be extreme consequences for her if she overstepped her role as a submissive wife, and her eternal salvation, for which she had already sacrificed so much, could be taken away in an instant."*
>
> (Wall, 2008: 133)

Even in the extreme circumstance of having an "unworthy" husband removed and another husband of the church's selection assigned, she still felt she could not risk her investment in this controlling church.

> *"I could sense mom was terrified at the prospect of never reaching Zion, and she quietly fretted over her uncertain future. Once again, she was losing a husband due to the prophet's decision. And as a believer, she didn't want to have sacrificed so much just to lose it all."*
>
> (Wall, 2008: 283)

When Elissa did at last break free from the clutches of the church, her mother was faced with a choice. Would she too leave? After almost an entire life-time in the FLDS, such decisions become increasingly difficult.

> *"Like so many things about the FLDS, her words were one big contradiction. While she was genuinely sorry about how my life had turned out, it seemed she couldn't see that there was any way other than that of the church. She'd lived her entire life in the FLDS, and she didn't have the mental capacity to question beyond its walls. This conversation was one of the rare times I'd ever heard her express doubts. Her willingness to actually raise questions made me cautiously optimistic that she would continue on this road, but only time would tell if she would actually be able to change her beliefs. At fifty-four, this would be a monumental feat, to reverse a lifetime of conditioning."*
>
> (Wall, 2008: 328-329)

Elissa's parents and others like them made decisions that affected much more than their own lives. Even relationships with those they loved were sacrificed for the church.

Warren Jeffs ordered Elissa's father to relocate, but also communicated that the sons who were still living in his home were not to go with him.

> "... parents were required to abandon 'unworthy' children ... At the prophet's request, FLDS fathers drove problem children to neighboring towns, dropped them off, and told them never to contact their family again. Though I'm sure Dad didn't want to abandon his sons, his devotion to the priesthood, like that of hundreds of other parents, was blind and absolute. He followed Warren's command and told all of his sons that they could not join him and Audrey [in the church community] in Short Creek."
>
> (Wall, 2008: 198-199)

Elissa's father was ordered to abandon his sons, and as an obedient church member, he followed orders. He had also ordered one of his wives, Elissa's mother, to abandon another of their sons, Craig.

Just as Elissa's father obeyed the church hierarchy, her mother obeyed her husband whom she had been trained to believe was her "priesthood head".

> "Years later, my mother would tell me that leaving Craig by the side of the road that day was one of the most painful things she ever had to do. At the time, though, she was as silent as any perfect FLDS wife should be. Casting out her son was her duty. She could not object, and even if she did, her opinion would not matter. She had to follow the orders of her husband; that was the command of the church, and she obeyed it no matter how much pain it caused her."
>
> (Wall, 2008: 47-48)

Another two sons had escaped the clutches of the controlling church. Now free, they rang their mother.

> "... they begged her to come back to Salt Lake and take care of them. When she said she couldn't, they accused her of choosing her religion over them. Her heart was torn in two, but the reality was apparent: her faith required that she choose the prophet and religion over everything else. It didn't matter how much she loved us, missed us, or wanted us by her side. She could not forsake her duty to the prophet and priesthood."
>
> (Wall, 2008: 117)

As a fourteen-year-old, Elissa was being pressured by the spokesperson of the "prophet" to marry her first cousin whom she detested. Elissa was resisting. Although her mother showed understanding and support at first, the leadership had then compelled the mother to align with them against Elissa.

> "'You have to do this,' Mom admitted. 'You have no other choice.'
>
> It was hard hearing those words from her. Her support from the previous week seemed to evaporate that night, and suddenly I felt hurt that she was giving in. I didn't

> *understand what had caused the shift, and I was crushed to have the most important person in my life surrendering to Uncles Warren and Fred. At that moment, I felt angry at the whole world. What I didn't know then was that Mom had been secretly pulled aside and told that it was her responsibility to make sure that the marriage took place, as the prophet had directed. She'd been instructed to make it happen 'or else.'*
>
> *So many people find it difficult to understand why I am no longer angry with my mother. It is hard for outsiders to comprehend the mind-set that came with our culture. We were taught that the priesthood and the prophet come before anything else, and Mom had already been forced to make this choice with six of her own children. It's hard to explain why she just didn't pack me up and take me away, but in her mind making that step would have damned us both. She was already a part [of] God's chosen people and she didn't want to give up the utopia she believed she was already in.*
>
> *To her, the outside world was like stepping into hell and nothing was worth trading that for. Because Fred and Warren were holding her accountable, if I failed to follow through with the marriage I would not only condemn myself, I would condemn her, too. Not only would she be risking eternal life, she would be also forced to choose the loss of home and community, and a relationship with the older and younger daughters she still had in the FLDS. As such, her feelings were rooted in a concern not just for my salvation, but for her own and for the safety of her two youngest daughters. Like so many FLDS members, Mom was a true follower. She'd been taught to strictly conform to the priesthood. Knowing the strength of my mother's belief, I guess it never crossed her mind to question whether this church, this life, was right if it forced her fourteen-year-old daughter into marriage. If she did question that, she would have to face many other decisions she had made in her painful past.*
>
> *Even then, I knew she had no 'real' choice. The church was her home. It was all she'd ever known, and she, like thousands of others, couldn't leave or risk giving up her and her children's place among the faithful."*
>
> (Wall, 2008: 150-151)

Elissa had shown grace when her mother chose her religion over her family. One of Elissa's sisters confronted their mother over her inability to protect her own children against the rule of the church leaders. Rather than conceding the truth, the mother turned on them for opposing the church leaders.

> *"'I'd rather see you die than fight the priesthood,' Mom said. Her words were a hard slap on the face. Everything Mom had ever done had been influenced by her loyalty to the church above all else, but to hear her phrase it in such indisputable terms was upsetting."*
>
> (Wall, 2008: 338)

The conclusion was clear. Their mother was simply not able to oppose abuse of her own offspring by those church leaders that she blindly obeyed.

Elissa was trapped, too

Elissa had the same church background as her mother. She, too, felt the pressures of the church leaders to conform, and had her own struggles to find freedom. The difference was that she *did* find freedom. It wasn't easy, and it carried a huge price tag, but one she was willing to pay.

Perhaps the one area that Elissa most strongly disagreed with the leadership on was their mandate that, as a fourteen year old, she marry her first cousin whom she despised. This issue was the catalyst for her questioning and challenging the hierarchy. Their abusive control of her rights was evil, yet they were stating that it was Elissa who would be acting in an evil manner if she disobeyed the "prophet", and that the consequences would be huge.

Without marriage to a "priesthood" man, Elissa was informed she could not attain heaven. And if she rejected the proposed marriage to her abusive cousin (subsequently charged for raping her), she may never again be given the opportunity by the FLDS leaders to marry. What's more, her act of disobedience would preclude her from living in the home with her mother. Her step-father stated,

> "Well, I just want you to know that if you turn down the prophet's offer [for marriage to your cousin], it's very likely you will never get married …
>
> And I could not have you welcome in this house anymore …"
>
> (Wall, 2008: 144)

Elissa considers her options:

> "Marriage to Allen wasn't just permanent, it was infinite – a punishment that would continue through this life and into the next.
>
> If I didn't marry him, I'd be left with no other options. For a fourteen-year-old girl with no family and no place to live, it might as well be a death sentence. I had always been an optimistic person, but as I stared the possibility of this bleak future in the face, I realized that even I was unwilling to push the limits of hope that far. I couldn't go to the local police [many of whom were faithful FLDS members]; I feared they would just bring me back to Fred and report me to Warren. I contemplated going outside the community, but my fear of that evil world was overpowering."
>
> (Wall, 2008: 144)

For people living outside of controlling churches such as the FLDS, one can usually turn to other family members. But for Elissa, whose father and brothers had fallen from grace within the eyes of the church leadership, they had been cut off from her and she could not contact them to seek support.

> "I stared … at the majestic red mountains and thought about jumping off one of the sheer faces of rock. It wouldn't be hard to climb up there, and I was sure it was high enough that the jump would kill me. As hard as it was for me to accept, at fourteen, I was actually contemplating suicide.

It was in that moment that I should have realized that the priesthood made it impossible for a woman to make decisions about her life – even if she knew what was right for her. Marriage wasn't about God, or the prophet, or any of that. It was about controlling women, trapping them into believing that they didn't have any other options and the only way out was a leap into the arms of the Lord from hundreds of feet in the air. Yet I still believed.

I hadn't spoken to my dad since I'd been removed from his home nearly two years before, but after church that day, my every moment was consumed by a vision of being rescued by Dad, Brad, and Caleb. They would come by in the middle of the night, and we would all escape under the cover of darkness. The only clues we'd leave behind would be our footsteps in the house and our tire tracks in the gravel. In the morning, people would wake up and gasp. I'd be condemned as a sinner and cursed by Warren and Fred. My mother and sisters would be devastated that I'd left them, but at least I would be alive. It made more sense to leave them alive than to die where I was. All I needed was for someone to save me, someone to give me a place to go.

But all this was just a fantasy. I had no way to contact Dad, Brad, and Caleb, and they didn't know about my impending marriage."

(Wall, 2008: 146-147)

Years later her husband faced trial in a court for raping her. She was questioned as to what options she had at the time to escape from the edict of marriage handed down by the representatives of the "prophet". As a young teenager Elissa simply did not have the choices we take for granted. She was forced into an arranged marriage and had no support system and no way of escape.

"'Did you consider other options?'

'I didn't have other options.'

'Was there a bus stop in Hildale?'

'No, there wasn't.'

'Did you have a friend with a car who could have –?'

'No, I did not.'

'Did you have any money of your own?'

'No.'

'Any credit cards?'

'No, I did not.'

These were simple questions – even obvious. But they were necessary to establish that all these everyday options that people on the outside take for granted simply are not part of life in [the FLDS church community]."

(Wall, 2008: 385)

While the whole process of forcing her into an unwelcome marriage had started to stir a desire for freedom, the horrors of the ensuing marriage only served to strengthen Elissa's yearning for a life beyond the church edicts.

> "The way [my husband] was treating me I felt like he viewed me not as a partner and equal, but as a possession. Something deep in my heart knew that no man, woman, or child should be anyone's chattel and be robbed of their God-given free will."
>
> (Wall, 2008: 206)

Elissa and her siblings had the fiery constitution required to question and challenge rules set by the church leaders. The hierarchy tried to break this independent spirit, but their abusive control only served to fortify it.

> "It felt to us like the people in Fred's home were trying to break our spirits in order to make us conform more strictly to the FLDS religion as they knew it. Even so, I held on to my belief that the spunk which had gotten us into trouble so many times in the past was also what would help us to stay strong and true to ourselves."
>
> (Wall, 2008: 98)

The church taught that they and they alone represented goodness and truth, and that those outside their particular denomination were not only in error, but evil. Such teaching, whether explicit or just implied, is not uncommon in even more moderate settings. However, interaction with the world "out there" started to unconsciously challenge the correctness of such teaching. The family had lost their home in a fire, and the regular community responded with compassion.

> "Our family was shocked by the outpouring of kindness from people outside our church. Their actions contradicted what we had long been taught about the 'evil' character of outsiders. Here were so many non-FLDS people offering help in our time of need, despite knowing about the secret and misunderstood life our family led."
>
> (Wall, 2008: 24)

Similarly, the family was on a holiday beside a lake, and observed the pure innocence of children at play. They had been taught that such people were evil, but a simple observation challenged such teaching.

> "At one point during the festivities, my attention was drawn to another group of children in swimsuits frolicking in the water. They were not from the FLDS, but they too were with their families on vacation. Like a scientist, I paused to study them. I was curious because I had been taught that outsiders were evil, but at first glance they didn't look that way to me.
>
> … I was young enough to still believe what I had been taught, simply because it was all I knew, but seeing that family gave me a shocking new point of view about the church's teachings. I didn't say anything to anyone. I kept it to myself.
>
> Later on in life, I would realize that standing there and watching those kids was the first time I ever questioned FLDS teachings, even if it was only subconsciously."
>
> (Wall, 2008: 68-69)

Another aspect of the sect's teaching was the prejudice against people with other than white skin. It is hard to imagine Elissa's shock to discover a brother who had broken away from the sect had a partner who was Afro-American. Again, an encounter with the real world outside of the closed community added to the growing doubts about the teachings of the church.

> *"The mother of his child was African-American. Hearing this came as a huge shock to me, although today I am embarrassed to admit it. All I could think of were Warren's words from Alta Academy that nonwhite people were the most evil of all outsiders. His racist remarks and hate-filled bigotry were a routine part of the classroom experience at Alta Academy, and from them, I had developed a prejudice about anyone whose skin looked different from my own. I had been told that my brother was damned to hell for even associating with Whitney.*
>
> *When I met Whitney that day, it was the first time I'd ever been introduced to an African-American. I didn't know what to expect or whether Warren's words would be true, but within minutes, my unease dissipated as I instantly liked Whitney and their baby. Whitney was so different from what I had pictured in my mind. She was clearly not the evil person that Uncle Warren had described. She was kind and welcoming to my siblings and me, despite our differences. ...*
>
> *As I sat there talking to Whitney, I found myself thinking that all it took was contact with the outside world and the barriers of fear that Warren constructed came tumbling down."*
>
> (Wall, 2008: 235)

The accidental encounters with the outside world chipped away at the authority of the sect's exclusive teaching. However, at one point several of Elissa's siblings who were now on the outside quite deliberately architected opportunities to challenge Elissa in a gentle and loving way.

> *"[My brother, Craig,] produced a jogging suit for me to wear, informing me that we would take a sunrise walk on the beach together. I had never seen the ocean and was excited by the prospect of getting my first look at the big waves. Changing out of my long dress into a pair of soft, comfortable pants was a thrill too. My brother and I walked way out onto the breakers in the fading gray mist of morning. Standing there as the waves crashed on the rocks beneath us was unlike anything I'd experienced.*
>
> *'You abandoned Mom,' I told him, my pent-up anger suddenly unleashed.*
>
> *Craig let my words hang in the air for a moment. Then he responded with a question, asking me why I continued to stay in the community. He was patient with me, and cautiously explained some of the journey that he had taken thus far.*
>
> *He told me he'd gone to Colorado to get some space from the confines of the religion so he could think with a clearer mind and begin to do some research. He was convinced that there was no divine revelation behind our teachings. It was Craig's firm belief that a group of old men had been dictating the lives of everyone else. It was earth-*

shattering to him at the time to such a point that he became deathly ill. Listening to him tell it now, I was upset as well. But Craig was sensitive to where I was in my life and knew that I wasn't ready to absorb what he'd come to believe. He treaded lightly and did not try to sway my beliefs. Instead, he prepared me with thought-provoking questions in an attempt to understand where I stood. It was clear that the priesthood still had a great hold over me and that I was not at all ready to dismiss all that I had been taught.

I returned to Kassandra and Ryan's apartment feeling refreshed and – even so many miles away – somehow at home. That morning was the beginning of what would prove to be an incredibly eye-opening trip during which I started to ask inner questions of my religion that I had never before dared to ask. Watching Kassandra's little family and seeing joy on the faces of three of my brothers was a necessary lesson for me. My siblings had fallen from grace in the eyes of the priesthood, and they had supposedly signed themselves up for hell. However, being in their company confirmed the suspicion that I'd had all those years ago at Bear Lake: people on the outside are not wicked at all. They might live in a world of Hallmark holidays, cropped pants, and haircuts, but they are nothing like the demons that [the FLDS "prophet"] spoke of.

This was my first solid look at life beyond the high walls of [my church's closed community], and it impacted my entire view of the world. In a bold move, I cut some of my hair in the front, making chic bangs. I also started wearing capris and some of the other modern styles Kassandra was into. One day, I joined Kassandra on a trip to the supermarket, donning my new pants, a pair of flip-flops, and a stylish short-sleeved top. As we walked from aisle to aisle, no one stared at me. It was the first time I'd been outside [the church community] without people noticing me. I felt unbelievably free. No one raised an eyebrow or tried to stifle laughter when I walked by. I looked just like everybody else. …

In retrospect I understand that my siblings – Kassandra and Craig especially – were laying the groundwork for what they knew I needed to do. They were not only exposing me to the simple joys of the real world but also zeroing in on me with thought-provoking questions and remarks about my life at home. I ate sushi for the first time and went out late-night bowling. Everything I did reminded me of my time with [a friend who also sought discovery of life beyond the FLDS community], and I did things that I never could have dreamed of back [in the church community]. I was hungry for life, and everywhere I looked things were glossy and new."

(Wall, 2008: 260-262)

Demonstrating to those locked inside church cultures that the world outside is not as evil as may be portrayed is part of helping our loved ones to find freedom. Another totally different tack is to prod them into a realization that, just as the outside world is not as evil as the church hierarchy would have us believe, that very same church hierarchy is not as pure as they try to make out!

One of Elissa's sisters, Kassandra, had been married off to the "prophet" Rulon. After Rulon's death, his son Warren not only orchestrated to be the replacement "prophet", but also secretly married seven of his late father's younger wives. When Kassandra found she was being prepared for this remarriage, she decided it was time to escape. She told Elissa of some of the hidden, dirty secrets of these male church leaders.

> *"I was shocked to hear about what had been going on inside the prophet's home. In the days after Warren married those first seven women, he'd begun to arrange for the marriages of some of [his late father's] other young wives. He declared it their new mission in life to be married, explaining that this was the 'next step' that Father wanted them to take. Kassandra told me of her panic as she watched her sister wives being given to the men that Warren deemed worthy, among them his brothers Isaac, Nephi, and Seth. Warren had even gone so far as to present her with a list of 'worthy' men that she could marry. Suddenly, her escape made a lot more sense, and I felt bad about carrying around my anger over her unexplained departure."*
>
> (Wall, 2008: 262-263)

Having exposed Elissa to the healthy lives of outsiders, and the corruption inside, Elissa's siblings then lovingly but directly challenged Elissa to decide if she would remain under the control of the church to which she belonged.

> *"One of my last nights was celebrated with a picnic on the beach. ... As we sat laughing and munching on the delicious food, the conversation shifted from light to deep. My siblings put me on the spot, questioning me about why I remained in the FLDS and trying to convince me to leave.*
>
> *'Do you honestly believe in Warren?'*
>
> *I had no answer.*
>
> *'Why are you still there?' they pushed.*
>
> *'I have to take care of Ally and Sherrie!' I retorted, the sting of abandonment still remembered in my heart. At the time I thought that neither Kassandra nor Craig had any idea what it had felt like to be deserted. It had happened to me six times, and the thought of inflicting that kind of a wound on Sherrie and Ally was deplorable.*
>
> *It was a hard conversation, but in the end it was helpful for all of us. I finally felt free to confront Kassandra about the pain she had put me through when she fled. 'I felt like you just left me.'*
>
> *She understood how I had felt and told me how sorry she was that she couldn't be there for me at that time. We hugged in reconciliation and I was relieved to be free of the weighty and difficult feelings of betrayal that I'd been carrying with me all this time. Then they told me something that was important for me to hear.*
>
> *'You would not be an evil person if you left,' Craig told me firmly. 'You are whatever you decide to be.'*

The sun had long since disappeared over the glittering ocean, leaving us with only the flickering light from our fire to see by. I felt so warm and comforted beside them even with the new unsettling thoughts that swam around in my mind. I had been in Oregon for what felt like a short time, but already something in me was changing. I wasn't ready to take the big leap, and I appreciated that my brothers and sister could see that. Nonetheless, my eyes were opening to a new and different world, one that would allow me to be anyone I wanted. …

My taste of freedom and real life had been a thrilling adventure, but I knew my time in Oregon was over. My belief system had begun to fray at the edges, but it was far from gone, and my obligation to Mom and the girls weighed heavily on my mind. Quietly I still wondered: If I left, would I really be okay? Or would doomsday arrive and leave my wasted body behind while the righteous were lifted up to heaven?

I boarded a plane in my long, drab FLDS skirt and top, a far cry from the comfortable and stylish clothes I'd been loving in Oregon. [My 'husband', Allen, from the arranged and enforced marriage] was waiting for me when I arrived in Vegas, wearing a look of frustrated disdain. I could see he was irritated with me and berated me during the trip home. 'I'm your priesthood head!' he exclaimed, exasperated. 'I am done sitting by and excusing your terrible behavior.'

After a while I just stopped listening. I was shocked and amused to discover that all I could think to my self was, 'I don't care.' "

(Wall, 2008: 263-265)

Elissa's unquestioning loyalty to the church was slipping! Thank God. But at that point she was still unable to make the final decision to break free. Sometimes it's just not that easy. The indoctrination that led to the binding belief that her church was the sole custodian of truth, and anyone leaving it was damned, was still a chain restricting her free choice.

" *'If I leave Allen, can I still go to heaven?' I asked, probably sounding somewhat like a scared young child.*

'All I know,' [a friend] said, 'is that you have to make a choice in your own heart, and I believe that your heart will tell you right whatever it is.' "

(Wall, 2008: 304-305)

In spite of encouragement that she would not be damned for leaving, and glimmers of hope for a life of love and freedom outside, this courageous girl was still not ready to leave.

"*Still, for all of [my] optimism, I was not ready to take the leap of faith and leave the FLDS.*"

(Wall, 2008: 307)

Part of her hesitancy was she had been deeply hurt when several of her siblings had broken away from the sect, leaving her behind. In some cases they had been forced out, and in other cases they had fled secretly, but in all cases she had felt the pain of their departure. She did not want to leave her two younger sisters behind, especially as she wanted to protect them from becoming child brides as she had been.

> *"I didn't know how to make this giant leap into the unknown. Each time I pictured my future on the outside, images of my mother and sisters flooded into my mind. I knew all too well the feelings of abandonment that Sherrie and Ally would experience, and I didn't want to subject them to that. If I wasn't there, who would protect them from being married off when they were still kids? I had already seen that Mom didn't have the ability to stand up for them. There was nothing I feared more than the girls experiencing my fate."*
>
> (Wall, 2008: 305)

Elissa found love with another man, Lamont, who also had been under the control of the same church. Over a lengthy period, they had grown closer. Aspects of the relationship had brought the issue of leaving to a head.

> *"It always would have been difficult, but now it would be necessary. It was time for me to stop talking about leaving and actually do it."*
>
> (Wall, 2008: 309)

In spite of the recognized need to *"stop talking about leaving and [to] actually do it"*, Elissa still hesitated. There are two ironies in the final outcome. Firstly, she was not given a choice about leaving—she was forced out. And secondly, her prime reason for staying was to protect her siblings, but the church authorities, in ejecting her from the church community, ruled that there must never be any further contact between her and the family that remained in the church.

> *"[The "prophet" declared,] '... I want you to know that you are no longer welcome to see your mother or be in Fred's home. You're to treat your mother and your sisters as though they are dead to you.'*
>
> *Now I broke into hysterics. What I had feared for months had finally come to pass. Warren had enough power to take from me everything that I held dear in that community. I would never be allowed to see my mother or my little sisters again. All these years of pain and suffering had been for absolutely nothing. The only reason I had endured for so long ... was to be close to my mother and sisters. Now I would have to live without them. It was the harshest verdict he could have delivered ...."*
>
> (Wall, 2008: 318)

Freedom at last

Elissa had been ejected from her community because of her relationship with Lamont. Her father was already a lesser member of the church, and had lost two of his wives, including Elissa's mother. Rather than breaking free from the church, the father was now trying to work towards being accepted again. Elissa initially stayed with her father, but found his focus on gaining acceptance by the church at odds with her new direction.

> *"As tempted as I was to stay there, Dad and Audrey were still fighting to remain in the church. They were too intricately connected to the world I needed to leave behind. In the letter, I told Dad that Mom, Ally, and Sherrie were the only reasons I had remained here all this time. If I couldn't be with them, then I didn't want to stay ..."*
>
> (Wall, 2008: 321)

That was the last link broken. She was now free.

> *"The thought of raising a child without my mother's beautiful singing voice and her loving gaze was almost too much, and again I broke down crying. I was making this choice to leave, not just for me and not just for Lamont, but for our child. I was making this choice so that our child, be it a girl or a boy, could grow up in a world without the walls and boundaries of the priesthood, a world where God and faith are instruments of hope, not tools of manipulation. I was making the choice that my mother had been unable to make for me and my siblings. I was choosing to give my child the power of choice."*
>
> (Wall, 2008: 321)

While she was now free, she had yet to adjust to life beyond the strict practices of her former religion. For those of us who make a break from more traditional mainstream churches, the impact of such a choice may not be as extreme. But for Elissa, almost everything about her new life was challenging.

> *"Leaving the FLDS had drained me of strength and left me emotional, washed up, and exhausted. It was as if all the pain, loss, and uncertainty that I'd tried to 'put on a shelf' over the past eight years suddenly fell on top of me.*
>
> *I finally mustered the strength to venture out of our house, but it was unsettling to feel so out of touch with my surroundings. ... Everything about our new life was strange and unfamiliar. ... The tiny house that Lamont rented for us in Hurricane was on a quiet street inhabited by 'normal' families, who shot us confused glances because of how we were dressed.*
>
> *I tried to conquer this awkwardness by dressing differently, but it wasn't that simple. ... I'd always wanted to wear normal clothes and had done so on occasion as part of my attempt to test my individuality, but with nothing familiar to cling to, I sought refuge in my old FLDS wardrobe.*
>
> *My hair, too, was a huge source of worry for me. Because FLDS women were all raised to keep their hair long, I'd never had a haircut aside from a few wispy bangs, and now my thick, blond locks fell down past my waist. ... Seeing strangers with their hair in shoulder-length blunt cuts or easy free curls made me long to look like them, but I just didn't know how.*
>
> *Part of what made our transition so difficult was that we barely had the financial resources to cover our bills, let alone acquire new clothes. In Colorado City there is no*

such thing as a mortgage or rent payment. A church-run trust called the United Effort Plan or UEP owns the land on which the people reside, and lots are awarded to worthy members of the priesthood to build on with the expectation of a monthly donation to the church of 10 percent of a man's income. Of course, members are encouraged to donate as much as they can, and many contribute significantly more. A portion of the monthly tithing is used to fund the communal storehouse where we purchased some of our food, paper goods, and other necessities at a very low cost. We had lived our lives in big families and the shopping was done for us and usually in bulk at stores like Costco.

As a result, we'd never had to think about everyday money issues. Lamont and I were now confronting the jaw-dropping prices at the local grocery stores. …

The financial pressures would have been hard for anyone, but we knew absolutely nothing about money management."

(Wall, 2008: 325-327)

The new freedom involved a whole new approach to life. It also meant, for Elissa and her new husband, a painful adjustment to life without many of their family and friends. This, too, can be the experience of those who leave mainstream churches. I know!

"Though Lamont and I remained in love and hopeful that we would adjust, those first weeks offered a frustrating overall picture of our new reality. Gone was our vision of escaping and simply starting anew. It would be an arduous road, but it was one that we needed to travel. …

Getting out wasn't just about starting a fresh routine, it was about establishing a totally new way of thinking. When you leave the FLDS, your whole foundation crumbles. You have to start from scratch and think about large, far-reaching questions, like What do I believe in? What about heaven? What are morals? What will I fight for? We had gained freedom and each other, but we had lost the ground beneath our feet. It made it even harder when our thoughts turned to the families we'd both lost. While I was now without my mom and sisters, Lamont too had lost his family."

(Wall, 2008: 329)

Some notes for you

While it is my earnest hope that you have not been part of such a strict church culture as experienced by Elissa Wall, I wish to warn you that change may not be as easy as you would hope. Little things, like what to do at 11:00 am on a Sunday morning, may disturb some and threaten you with feelings of guilt as it did for me. More significantly, there may be some family and friends who simply do not understand your departure from the local church, or who may go further and condemn you as a heretic, a back-slider or even now as a non-Christian! Still, the question remains. Will you choose freedom no matter what the price?

You must make your own choice for freedom. No-one else can. But if you do choose freedom, you must also choose how to relate to those still involved in institutional church. Based on Elissa's experiences, you will need to be gentle in offering them an alternative. We condemn the church leaders who are heavy-handed and intolerant of those who see things differently, yet if we are harsh towards those we have left behind in the local church, we may be equally guilty. As those who are now exiles from local churches and their controlling leadership, we must take care we treat with grace the vulnerable ones we have left behind. Most telling will be the way we treat others, as Jonathan Sacks notes,

> "... civilizations survive not by strength but by how they respond to the weak; not by wealth but by the care they show for the poor; not by power but by their concern for the powerless."

(Sacks, 2003: 195)

Let us be bold and consistent in choosing freedom for ourselves, and persistent but loving in offering the choice of freedom to others, recognizing that it may take some time for them to adjust to the huge change abandonment of the church system involves.

> "Maimonides points out that 'man, according to his nature, is not capable of abandoning suddenly all to which he was accustomed'. ... as the Jewish folk-saying puts it: It took one day to lead the Israelites out of Egypt, but forty years to take Egypt out of the Israelites ..."

(Sacks, 2003: 69, including quotation from Maimonides 'Guide for the Perplexed', III:32)

For those who make the brave decision to leave behind the familiar but enslaving patterns of the past, there still may be times of grieving for what has been. Some may have suffered abuse, yet also hold happy memories of good times with family and friends. While honestly admitting to the grief, we also must look forward to the future.

Jamie Buckingham encountered memories of the past that caused pain in the present. He had been visiting a nursing home, and one old lady expressed how much she missed her daddy, who had died many, many years earlier, in 1914.

> "Her eyes filled with tears and her chin began to quiver. 'At Thanksgiving daddy would walk around the big table and lay his hands on our heads, asking God to bless us.' She began to sob. 'I'm so homesick.'"

(Buckingham, 1978: 32)

Buckingham goes on to say,

> "Earthly daddies and mothers die. The old homesites, once so precious, fall into decay or are destroyed. Only the faded memories linger to haunt our loneliness. Homesickness is the backward call into a world to which we can never return. Faith is lifting up our feeble eyes and fixing them on another Father who stands in the future, beckoning us onward."

(Buckingham, 1978: 32)

We may wish to recapture some of the good times from our past, even if they also included unhealthy institutional control. Yet, painful as it might be, we must try to move forward to the great and wonderful freedom that God has planned for us.

CHAPTER 41:
DISCERN GOD'S CURRENT CALL ON YOUR LIFE

As we have noted previously, it is a poor approach to sit back and wait for leaders to radically change. We would probably be sitting in a pew a very long time! It is better to decide that *we* will make a change, and get involved in being salt and light in this troubled world in obedience to God's call on our lives.

But we will still miss the mark if we, as individual Christians living in freedom, go back to anyone else to find out what *they* think we should be doing. It's not enough to be Christians-in-action. We must be acting according to *God's* vision for us, not according to anyone else's vision.

Imagine how different history would be if Abraham had ignored God's call to step out into the unknown and followed His leading!

At a local church I once attended, one of the explicit pre-conditions of being admitted to the inner-circle of the leadership team was a willingness to "share the pastor's vision", i.e. accept it, absorb it, and follow it. Brown warns of the dangers of thinking that

> "… we will spend the rest of our lives merely supporting 'the pastor's vision' …"
>
> (Brown, 2002: 59)

He also presents a simple alternative—we should be

> "… finding our place …, rolling our sleeves up and getting into the game."
>
> (Brown, 2002: 59)

Rinehart explains what he sees as the benefits of each person finding their unique role in the Body:

> "As each individual member of the body is transformed more and more into the image of Christ, the whole body grows stronger."
>
> (Rinehart, 1998: 131)

But some of us are so used to waiting for God's calling through the channels of the church hierarchy we may be uneasy when we begin to listen to God for ourselves.

Does God speak through circumstances?

There can be many ways God may try to catch our attention. It will not necessarily be through an audible voice coming from a burning bush! He may quicken a passage of Scripture to us. He may prod our conscience about what we should or should not be doing. And sometimes He may expect us to use the brain He gave us!

Another way that God may tap us on the shoulder might be through circumstances. If we are genuinely trying to walk in His ways, we may be surprised at the number of little "miracles" that occur just in the timing of events. The events may be easy to explain in natural terms, but God's timing in their appearance on our radar screen may catch our attention and make us stop and question whether God is behind what we see happening.

There may be traps in any of these approaches. If all the indicators seem to line up, maybe that might be enough for us to proceed, always recognizing that our hearing and understanding are imperfect.

Hudson Taylor shares some of his own experiences. The first extract shows obstacles were not to stand in the way of his obedience to God. With patience and determination he pressed ahead against circumstances that seemed to form opposition.

> *"We believe ... that the time has come for doing more fully what the Master commanded us; and by His grace we intend to do it – not to try, for we see no scriptural authority for trying. 'Try' is a word constantly on the lips of unbelievers. 'We must do what we can,' they say; and too often the same attitude is taken up by the child of God. In our experience, to try has usually meant to fail. The Lord's word in reference to His various commands is not 'Do your best,' but 'Do it'; that is, do the thing commanded. We are therefore making arrangements for commencing work in each of these nine provinces – without haste, for 'he that believeth shall not make haste,' but also without unnecessary delay. ... 'If ye be willing and obedient, ye shall eat of the good of the land.' 'Whatsoever He saith unto you, do it.'"*

(Taylor & Taylor, 1918: 277)

In the next extracts, Taylor's reaction to obstacles was the very opposite. Instead of forging ahead in spite of the difficulties, he saw the difficulties and obstacles as God's intervention to prevent him making mistakes:

> *"Very easily, as one can see, might the whole Mission have become absorbed in that one coast-board province, small though it was among all the provinces of China. But, providentially, door after door was closed. Riots, disturbances, sickness, and other troubles hindered developments that would have tended in this direction, and gradually, almost insensibly, Mr. Taylor's own way seemed guided northward."*

(Taylor & Taylor, 1918: 133)

It was events surrounding his work that effectively forced him to take a different direction. In the next story, we see how God used seemingly unwelcome events to change the course of the larger work:

> *"Then came the gradual paralysis of the lower limbs, and the doctor's verdict that consigned him to absolute rest in bed. Stricken down in the prime of his days, he could only lie in that upstairs room conscious of all there was to be done, of all that was not being attended to – lie there and rejoice in God.*
>
> *Yes, rejoice in God! With desires and hopes as limitless as the needs that pressed upon his heart; with the prayer he had prayed, and the answers God had given; with opportunities opening in China, and a wave of spiritual blessing reviving the churches at home that he longed to see turned into missionary channels; with the 'sentence of death' in himself, and only the faintest hope that he would ever stand or walk again, the deepest thing of all was that unquestioning acceptance of the will of God, as wise, as kind, as best. Certain it is that from that quiet room, that room of suffering, sprang all the larger growth of the China Inland Mission."*
>
> (Taylor & Taylor, 1918: 263-264)

Taking another story from Taylor in the 1870s, China and England were on the point of declaration of war. People were advising Taylor not only that he should not return to China, but of the foolishness of sending additional missionaries when it was likely that those already in China may be expelled, or worse. Nonetheless, Taylor continued to send available missionaries out to China in expectation that God would overrule in some manner.

> *"More alive to the situation [of looming war] than his fellows, the Viceroy Li Hung-chang hurried to the coast, overtaking the British Ambassador just in time to reopen negotiations; and there, at Chefoo, was signed the memorable Convention which threw open the door of access at last to the remotest parts of China. This was the news that awaited Mr. Taylor on his arrival in Shanghai, the agreement having been signed within a week of his leaving England; and already three parties of the Eighteen had set out and were well on their way to the interior.*
>
> *'Just as our brethren were ready,' he wrote, 'not too soon and not too late the long-closed door opened to them of its own accord.'"*
>
> (Taylor & Taylor, 1918: 284)

> *"This journey and another taken in 1875 – a few months only after the murder of Margary – shows that the pioneers who were ready did not wait for the Chefoo Convention, or any other government assistance, thankful though they were for the new Treaty when it came."*
>
> (Taylor & Taylor, 1918: 286)

What conclusions can one draw? We must remember that Taylor's keenest desire was to be in close relationship with his God. If our desire is to walk with Him in such closeness, we are better placed to discern whether circumstances are a warning from God to change direction or to press ahead in faithful defiance of the circumstances. Hopefully the topics that follow may assist in gaining the discernment needed for such decisions.

Hearing through others vs. hearing for yourself

Are there any dangers in the individual seeking his or her own understanding of God's direction for their lives? Of course there are. In extreme cases, people have even committed murders because they believed that "God told them to". Alcoholics Anonymous shares their recognition of the dangers related to unchecked, individual "guidance" from God:

> "We have seen A.A.'s ask with much earnestness and faith for God's explicit guidance on matters ranging all the way from a shattering domestic or financial crisis to a minor personal fault, like tardiness. A man who tries to run his life rigidly by this kind of prayer, by this self-serving demand of God for replies, is a particularly disconcerting individual. To any questioning or criticism of his actions, he instantly proffers his reliance upon prayer for guidance in all matters great or small.
>
> He may have forgotten the possibility that his own wishful thinking and the human tendency to rationalize have distorted his so-called guidance. With the best of intentions, he tends to force his will into all sorts of situations and problems with the comfortable assurance that he is acting under God's specific direction."

(Bill, 1967: 170)

Bill shares his own experience where the voice of his friends contradicted what he believed he had heard from God. And his friends were right!

> "I had a flash of seeming divine guidance. It was only a single sentence, but it was most convincing. In fact, it came right out of the Bible. [But Bill's group of friends expressed a different view, and on further consideration, Bill came to the conclusion that] ... the group was right and I was wrong; the voice on the subway was not the voice of God. Here was the true voice welling up out of my friends. I listened and – thank God – I obeyed."

(AAWS, 1957: 100-101)

Of course there is an extreme in listening to others, where we abdicate our own responsibility and lean on the advice of our friends. We must remember that they, too, can have failings in "hearing", especially if it is on a topic that for them is the focus of much passion. Ask a person who is ministering to homeless youth if they think God might be calling you to the same vision, and their objectivity is likely to be affected by their own zeal.

Keith Green shared that hundreds (!!!) of people had perceived a call on his life. He listened to them, but because God did not confirm it personally, he left their advice on the shelf.

> " 'As far as I know,' Keith said, 'I'm not a prophet. And I don't want to be. In fact, since I've been a Christian I've had hundreds of people tell me I'm a prophet. Except I've never had God tell me I'm a prophet. And I figure that He's the one that ought to know. So I decided I want to be just a plain-old Christian. If I could just stand before the Lord and hear Him say, 'Well done. You were a good and faithful Christian,' I'd be really happy.' "
>
> (Green & Hazard, 1989: 287)

The voices of others may be well intentioned but wrong. Rinehart points out that we may need to actively 'tune out' these voices, as well as those of our own making, if we are to improve our chances of hearing correctly.

> "How do we become sensitive to the leading of the Spirit? It comes when we learn to tune out the cacophony of conflicting demands – of self and others – and simply listen for His still, small voice to speak. What freedom it brings!"
>
> (Rinehart, 1998: 147)

Taylor shares some hard-won wisdom. Instead of developing our own plans then asking God to bless them, he advises us to seek God's plans and prayerfully follow them as they are progressively revealed:

> "There are several different ways of working for God ...
>
> One is to make the best plans we can, and carry them out to the best of our ability. This may be better than working without plan, but it is by no means the best way of serving our Master. Or, having carefully laid our plans and determined to carry them through, we may ask God to help us, and to prosper us in connection with them. Yet another way of working is to begin with God; to ask His plans, and to offer ourselves to Him to carry out His purposes.
>
> ...Going about it in this way ... we leave the responsibility with the Great Designer, and find His service one of sweet restfulness. We have no responsibility save to follow as we are led; and we serve One Who is able both to design and to execute, and Whose work never fails."
>
> (Taylor & Taylor, 1918: 355-356)

When Jesus left His disciples, He clearly stated that they were not going to be left alone, but that He would send a comforter, the Holy Spirit. At this point, possibly a few readers are going to react. The Pentecostal/Charismatic types may wonder what took me so long to get to this point. And the rest of you may wonder if I am going to head off into Pentecostal extremes.

I hope to strike a balance, not a compromise. I am going to make a simple but strong statement. If Jesus thinks we need the Holy Spirit, then we do. And if one of the Spirit's jobs is to lead us, we'd better get to know this oft-overlooked member of the Trinity. And based on the Bible's description of the Holy Spirit we should not demand He acts in a prescribed way.

Taylor tells of the way one of the team approached the topic in a delightfully uncomplicated way:

> "One young worker from the interior ... was ... stirred with a sense of need and longing as never before. ... Praying in anguish ... for light and help, ... an entire stranger – a Christian seaman – came up to her and said earnestly:
>
> 'Are you filled with the Holy Ghost?'
>
> Filled with the Holy Ghost? She remembered no more of the conversation, but that question burned deeper and deeper into her heart. This, then, was the explanation of all the inward failure, the sorrow that seemed unavailing, the purposes that came to nothing. God had made a provision, given a Gift that she had never definitely accepted. She knew that the Holy Spirit must be her life in a certain sense, for 'if any man have not the Spirit of Christ, he is none of His.' And yet, just as certainly, she knew that she was not 'filled with the Spirit,' and was experiencing little of His power.
>
> But how afraid she was of being misled, of running into error and mistaking emotion for reality! The Word of God was full, now she came to study the subject, of the personality and power of the Holy Spirit. The Acts of the Apostles – what was it but the acts of the Holy Ghost, transforming and quickening lives just as she knew she needed to be quickened and transformed? Oh, yes, why had she never seen it! It was indeed the Holy Spirit she needed; the fulness of the Holy Spirit, to make unseen things real to her and impossible things possible. And there stood out in Gal. iii 13, 14 the words:
>
>> 'Christ hath redeemed us from the curse of the law, having been made a curse for us ... that we might receive the promise of the Spirit through faith.'
>
> What was she doing with the infinite Gift purchased at such a cost? She saw that just as Christ is ours by the gift of God, and yet we have each one personally to receive Him, so with the Holy Spirit. She saw that He too was a Person, just as real as the Lord Jesus, and to be just as truly welcomed by faith into the heart that cannot do without Him as a living link with the risen, glorious Lord. All the rest that can be told is that she took the step, though with fear and trembling – scarce knowing what it meant – and trusted the Holy Spirit to come in and possess her fully, just as she had trusted the Lord Jesus to be her Saviour. Feeling nothing, realising nothing, she just took God at His word, and then and there asked that the promise might be fulfilled."

(Taylor & Taylor, 1918: 509-510)

This colleague of Taylor's sought to be "filled" by the Holy Spirit. Such terminology can bring a whole lot of images to mind, some of which are, quite frankly, questionable. According to Taylor, our role in seeking filling with the Holy Spirit should be no more than to remove what shouldn't be there, and then simply ask and trust. In my opinion, we most certainly should not try to manufacture some visible "sign" just to pander to the expectations of others. If God wants us to have a relationship with this member of the trinity, let's ask Him and then trust Him to respond any way *He* chooses.

> *"If at any time you are conscious of failure or sin, or even if you stand in doubt about anything, confess it at once to Him, and accept His promise of immediate cleansing and restoration. ...*
>
> *Now the heart can no more be filled with two things at the same time than a tumbler can be filled with both air and water at the same time. If you want a tumbler full of water to be filled with air, it has first to be emptied of the water. This shows us why prayer to be filled with the Spirit is often gradually answered. We have to be shown our sins, our faults, our prepossessions, and to be delivered from them. Faith is the channel by which all grace and blessing are received; and that which is accepted by faith, God bestows in fact. Being filled does not always lead to exalted feeling or uniform manifestation, but God always keeps His word. We have to look to His promises or rest in them, expecting their literal fulfilment. Some put asking in the place of accepting; some wish it were so, instead of believing that it is so. We have never to wait for God's giving, for God has already 'blessed us with all spiritual blessings in heavenly things in Christ.' We may reverently say, He has nothing more to give; for He has given His all. Yet, just as the room is full of air, but none can get into the tumbler save as far as the water is emptied out, so we may be unable to receive all He has given, if the self-life is filling to some extent our hearts and lives."*
>
> (Taylor & Taylor, 1918: 574-575)

There was a time where I was actively involved in a group who passionately wanted to be on the "cutting edge", to be agents of change in our world. We were willing to make sacrifices to achieve our vision.

Bill comments on the role of having a vision for the future, suggesting it is not an abandonment of day-by-day "faith" to have a vision:

> *"Vision is, I think, the ability to make good estimates, both for the immediate and for the more distant future. Some might feel this sort of striving to be heresy against 'One day at a time.' But that valuable principle really refers to our mental and emotional lives and means chiefly that we are not foolishly to repine over the past nor wishfully to daydream about the future.*
>
> *As individuals and as a fellowship, we shall surely suffer if we cast the whole job of planning for tomorrow onto a fatuous idea of providence. God's real providence has endowed us human beings with a considerable capability for foresight, and He evidently expects us to use it. Of course, we shall often miscalculate the future in whole or in part, but that is better than to refuse to think at all."*
>
> (Bill, 1967: 317)

So how did the vision work out for the group of which I was part? A total disaster! Relationships, including my marriage, were torn apart, finances were ruined through misuse of funds, trust was broken, and young girls later reported that they had been sexually abused by the self-appointed leader. Sadly, in spite of my best attempts, including action through the courts, I was unable to protect my own children when their mother returned shortly after our entire family had left the group. The damage from that period remains as scars on the lives of many people.

How did things go so wrong for what had started out as a dynamic group of Christians? I will not even try to answer on behalf of others, especially those responsible for the abuse of the more vulnerable members. But through much soul-searching as to how I could have become part of a group that turned out to be so dysfunctional, I have come to a conclusion where I must take responsibility. My error is quite simple, really. I adopted the "vision" of the leader as my own instead of seeking God's vision for me, and progressively sought and accepted the leader's interpretation of God's will for my life rather than seeking God directly. Others must take accountability for their own actions, especially those who were party to evil abuse. I must take accountability for not having had a strong, independent relationship with God at that time.

In contrast to my own lack of direct reliance on God at that time, MacDonald's character, Janet, was the wife of a poor but honest and God-fearing shepherd, living in remote Scottish highlands. She had a simple but effective faith, learned from the heart of God Himself.

> *"Not for years and years had Janet been to church. She had long been unable to walk so far; and having no book but the [Bible], and no help to understand it but the highest, her faith was simple, strong, real, all-pervading. Day by day she pored over the great gospel until she had grown to be one of the noble ladies of the kingdom of heaven – one of those who inherit the earth and are ripening to see God. For the Master, and His mind in hers, was her teacher. She had little or no theology save what He taught her. To Janet, Jesus Christ was no object of so-called theological speculation, but a living Man who somehow or other heard her when she called to Him, and sent her the help she needed."*
>
> (MacDonald, 1983(a): 39)

If we seek to know God, we shall find He is more than capable of meeting our needs. But we must approach Him on His terms, and accept His guidance.

> *"The real Jesus was greater than the best show any man could put on. He was greater than any building you could put him in or any tradition you could wrap around him or any expectations you could impose on him. Throughout my life, in a variety of ways, I'd tried to do all four of those things, but now I was learning – again – that it's only when you're willing to know him on his terms, for who he is, that you really start to know him at all."*
>
> (Peretti, 1999: 475)

We may get some balance in the tension about hearing from God. We must walk in trust, but we will find God to be trustworthy. A conversation in Jacobsen and Coleman's novel presents the case:

> *"[John] 'If I've encouraged you to follow [Jesus] a bit more closely and to trust him with greater freedom, he'll sort out the rest. ...'*

[Roary] 'I'd like to believe it's that simple, but something tells me I'll mess it up. Do you really believe we're good enough to hear God's voice every day?'

[John] 'What a question! ... Of course not ... None of us are that good. But I think you're asking the wrong question. Let's phrase it like this: is Jesus big enough to get through to you every day? Do you think he is big enough to get past your blind spots, overcome your doubts, and show you his way? Doesn't that get a resounding yes?'"

(Jacobsen & Coleman, 2006: 114)

Prayer

Do we want to hear from God as to His call on our life? Phillips gets to the core of the matter that may so easily be missed. It is so basic one wonders why it even needs to be said. But I know I need to be reminded that if we are to get an answer, we'd better ask a question!

"I don't care much what you call it. ... But if he's the Boss and you're joining the team, you'd better start talking to him, or else you'll never know what he wants you to do. Call it praying. Call it whatever you want. But if you're going to be his follower, then you've got to talk to him so you'll know where he's heading and where you're supposed to follow."

(Phillips, 1996: 224)

John Mott sets the scene: if we are to achieve things for God, we had better lay the foundations in prayer. Time spent in prayer is an investment, rather than being an activity that robs us of time for what we might consider to be more important things.

"Among the different ways of helping in the present world crisis, there is none which will compare in vital importance with that of wielding the force of prayer. More important than the most earnest thinking upon a problem, more important than a personal interview to influence an individual, more important than addressing and swaying an audience – far more important than these and all other forms of activity is the act of coming into vital communion with God. Those who spend enough time in actual communion with God to become really conscious of their absolute dependence on Him, shall change the mere energy of the flesh for the power of God. ...

It is indeed true that he that saveth his time from prayer shall lose it. And that he that loseth his time, for communion with God, shall find it again in added blessing and power and fruitfulness."

(John R. Mott, in Taylor & Taylor, 1918: 436)

Time in prayer is not only important; Taylor argues that it actually achieves great things. It is not just a "spiritual" activity for our own improved perceptions; it brings change we might not otherwise achieve.

"Shall we not each one of us determine to labour more in prayer; to cultivate more intimate communion with God by His help; thinking less of our working and more of

His working, that He may in very deed be glorified in and through us? ... The people that do know their God shall be strong and do exploits."

(Taylor & Taylor, 1918: 275)

We are also reminded that effective prayer does not involve the simplistic and unthinking rite of repeating prayers from some prayer-book collection, nor does it involve repeated whining to have our demands met like some spoiled child.

"It is pointed out that we are to pray not as the heathen who use vain repetitions, nor as the worldly-minded who ask principally if not solely for their own benefit. 'After this manner therefore pray ye,' putting the kingdom of God first, and His righteousness."

(Taylor & Taylor, 1918: 38)

Spoiled children try to wear their parents down, to get their own way, even if the parent has decided it unwise to meet the demands. But this is totally different to a child making their needs known to a loving parent.

"Nothing is more striking in the records of the period than Mr. Taylor's dependence upon prayer, real dependence for every detail, every need. He leaned his whole weight on God, pleading the promises. Was it Lae-djün's affairs, the wife and child who needed him, or the difficulties of their long task; was it a question of health, their own or the children's, of house-moving, money for daily bread, or guidance as to their return to China? All, all was brought to their Heavenly Father with the directness of little children, and the conviction that He could and would undertake, direct and provide. It was all so real, so practical!"

(Taylor & Taylor, 1918: 22)

Taylor lived and taught the principle that God's work must not be funded by emotional appeals to others for money. A direct consequence of this stance is that we must make talk over such matters with God, to share our needs, and to be open to Him directing us in a different way.

"Let us never forget that, if we make no appeal to man, we need very, very definitely to continue our appeal to God."

(Taylor & Taylor, 1918: 432)

We are encouraged by Taylor to pray when things seem to be going poorly:

"Wishes, cares, anxieties prepare the heart for prayer, but are not prayer until they are converted into direct address, supplication, and cry unto God."

(Adolph Saphir, in Taylor & Taylor, 1918: 436)

We are also encouraged by Taylor to pray when things are going well. He argued that an abundance that is not used wisely can be even more disastrous than a lack. A bequest from a deceased benefactor had set aside a relatively huge source of funds for a period of ten years. While being extremely grateful for the opportunities this opened up, Taylor also had a cautionary note:

> "It meant not only great possible development, but great possible difficulty at the end of the period when, the last instalment having been paid, the new undertakings would have to be carried on. Mr. Taylor had no doubt whatever but that the whole thing – the form of the bequest as well as the gift itself – was of God, and had no hesitation in accepting it; but he saw that to go forward and enlarge the work without an increase of faith, prayer, and spiritual power, which alone could make it fruitful and sustain it, would be to court disaster.
>
> 'There probably never was a time when we needed divine guidance more than at present,' he had written to Mr. Stevenson before leaving England. 'We sorely need fresh life infusing into every part of our work, without which this large legacy which has been left us may prove the greatest misfortune we have had for a long time.' …
>
> Not that this was any argument for holding back. It simply meant that whatever was undertaken must be begun, as it could alone be continued, in God."
>
> (Taylor & Taylor, 1918: 569-570)

Faith

Having put our needs before God, faith is required—to trust Him to respond in His way and in His time. If we are going to seek God's call on our lives, we must count the cost. He may answer in a way that severely stretches our faith.

But do we have enough faith? Jesus says that faith as small as a mustard seed is enough to move mountains, and yet we sometimes feel condemned. If such a little faith can achieve so much, how come I don't have enough faith to believe for healing from a cold, let alone faith for recovery from cancer of a loved one? Some cruel people will go so far as to blame the death of another on the perceived lack of faith of the sick person, or the person praying for them.

Such issues are large topics in their own right which we are not addressing here. But we will explore the exercising of faith in matters of money. This is not because money is to be a central theme. Rather, it is put forward as a very practical and tangible topic in which Hudson Taylor exercised the faith to act for God even if certain practicalities were not evident.

Taylor immediately puts the issue in perspective, and removes the dimension of guilt. We are not to seek a great faith, but to rest in a faithful God with whatever little faith we may have.

> "It was just in his usual reading, as he often related, that he was struck with the words, 'Ekete pistin Theou.' How strangely new they seemed! <u>Have (or hold) the faithfulness of God</u>': surely it was a passage he had never seen before? Turning to the corresponding words in English he read (Mark xi. 22): 'Have faith in God.' Ah, that was familiar enough; and something within him whispered, 'the old difficulty!' How gladly would he have and increase in faith in God, if only he knew how! But this seemed entirely

> *different. It laid the emphasis on another side of the matter in a way he found surprisingly helpful. It was not 'have' in your own heart and mind, however you can get it, 'faith in God,' but simply 'hold fast, count upon His faithfulness'; and different indeed he saw the one to be from the other. Not my faith but God's faithfulness – what a rest that was!" [Emphasis mine]*
>
> (Taylor & Taylor, 1918: 278)

> *"The Lord is always faithful. ... People say, 'Lord, increase our faith.' Did not the Lord rebuke His disciples for that prayer? It is not great faith you need, He said in effect, but faith in a great God. Though your faith were as small as a grain of mustard-seed, it would suffice to remove mountains. We need a faith that rests on a great God, and expects Him to keep His own word and to do just as He has promised."*
>
> (Taylor & Taylor, 1918: 428-429)

So then, what is our part in the equation? Simply, as best we are able, to seek God's path for our lives. And God knows we will not be perfect. All He asks is that we wholeheartedly *seek* His Kingdom. That is enough.

> *"That Word had said, 'Seek first the Kingdom of God and His righteousness, and all these things (food and raiment) shall be added unto you.' If any one did not believe that God spoke the truth, it would be better for him not to go to China to propagate the faith. If he did believe it, surely the promise sufficed. Again, 'No good thing will He withhold from them that walk uprightly.' If any one did not mean to walk uprightly, he had better stay at home; if he did mean to walk uprightly, he had all he needed in the shape of a guarantee fund. God owns all the gold and silver in the world, and the cattle on a thousand hills."*
>
> (Taylor & Taylor, 1918: 42)

It can be easy to say that we depend on God. Words can be cheap. And it is not that we are being deliberately deceptive to impress others with our spirituality (though that may be a temptation). Sometimes we can believe we are placing our trust in God but it might be in our spouse or our retirement fund!

Taylor's wife had had a lifetime of opportunities to set her faith solidly on none other than God.

> *"It was not her husband's faith ... upon which she leaned, great as were her joy and confidence in him. From girlhood, orphaned of both parents, she had put to the test for herself the Heavenly Father's faithfulness."*
>
> (Taylor & Taylor, 1918: 37)

Yet even for a giant of the faith such as Mrs. Taylor, events occurred to remind her of where her trust must lay. She was ill; one of their children was fighting for her life, and her husband absent. In these circumstances, she was able to reflect:

> *"How much we lean upon each other for comfort or counsel we only find out when long separated, and perhaps He is trying to teach us to lean in the same way, and to a yet fuller extent upon Himself – our Heavenly Husband."*
>
> (Taylor & Taylor, 1918: 142)

DISCERN GOD'S CURRENT CALL ON YOUR LIFE

The Taylors personally lived a life of faith. Further, they felt that not only could they not enlist others unless they also had similar faith, but that to do so would be detrimental to the individual's relationship with God.

> "The Mission is supported by donations, not subscriptions. We have, therefore, no guaranteed income, and can only minister to our missionaries as we ourselves are ministered to by God. We do not send men to China as our agents. But men who believe that God has called them to the work, who go there to labour for God, and can therefore trust Him Whose they are and Whom they serve to supply their temporal needs, we gladly co-operate with – providing, if needful, outfit and passage money, and such a measure of support as circumstances call for and we are enabled to supply."
>
> (Taylor & Taylor, 1918: 268-269)

> "Each individual member must know that he or she was sent of God, and must be able to trust Him for supplies – strength, grace, protection, enablement for every emergency, as well as daily bread. No other basis would be possible [for joining the mission]. If the Mission were to be fruitful, were to continue at all amid the perils that must be faced, it could only be as each one connected with it continued his quota of faith in the living God."
>
> (Taylor & Taylor, 1918: 41)

Such guidelines may sound risky to some. Taylor felt that obedience to God's principles is wiser than taking actions of apparent safety.

> "Instance after instance is given from Mr. Taylor's experience of direct, unmistakable answers to prayer, and the deduction drawn is that with such a God it is safe and wise to go forward in the pathway of obedience – is indeed the only safe and wise thing to do."
>
> (Taylor & Taylor, 1918: 41)

Some today might suggest that "living by faith" might be well and good for those like Taylor a century or two ago, but that in today's modern world this cannot be done. It is interesting to note that Taylor encountered just such an argument in the 1850s! He had shared of his desire to serve God in China with a minister from a local church.

> " 'And how do you propose to go there?' [the local minister] inquired.
>
> I answered that I did not at all know; that it seemed to me probable that I should need to do as the Twelve and the Seventy had done in Judea, go without purse or scrip, relying on Him who sent me to supply all my need.
>
> Kindly placing his hand on my shoulder, the minister replied, 'Ah, my boy, as you grow older you will become wiser than that. Such an idea would do very well in the days when Christ Himself was on earth, but not now.'
>
> I have grown older since then, but not wiser. I am more and more convinced that if we were to take the directions of our Master and the assurance He gave to His first

disciples more fully as our guide, we should find them just as suited to our times as to those in which they were originally given."

(Taylor & Taylor, 1911: 85) [Note that this quotation is provided through Winter & Hawthorne earlier in this book]

By his reference to going *"… without purse …"* we can reasonably assume that Taylor was referring to the time Jesus sent out His disciples basically empty-handed, depending on the hospitality of those who might kindly invite them into their home (Luke 10). In Luke 22, Jesus also sent out disciples, but this time instructed them to take purses if possible. We do well to seek a thorough knowledge of the Bible, but taking this simple contrast as an example, we must also be careful to see what instructions applied to a particular audience at a particular time, and seek God's guidance as to how lessons from the past can be applied today.

Taylor set an example of living by faith. Yet Plass calls attention to the potential abuse of the concept of "living by faith", which he defines as

"… a good idea as long as my living by faith doesn't have to be financed by someone else working twice as hard to make sure that God provides for my needs as well as theirs."

(Plass, 2007: 112)

If we heed Plass' warning, it would seem that Taylor did in fact achieve the status of "living by faith" but at the expense of others. One benefactor makes it clear that his generosity has been costly:

"It does not represent any superabundance of wealth, as my business affairs will miss it. But if you, for Christ's sake, can [leave all behind in your home country], I cannot give less than this."

(Taylor & Taylor, 1918: 313)

For another, the cost of supporting those who lived by faith was not financial, but rather the taking on the care of additional children when she was already hard pressed. Mrs. Taylor wanted to return to China, but doing so meant having to leave her children behind for others to raise.

"At first, indeed, [Mrs. Taylor] could not see it to be called for [i.e. returning to China to care for families there while she left her family behind]. Her husband in poor health and overwhelmed with work surely needed her, to say nothing of the children. …

Meanwhile, Mrs. Broomhall … heard of the proposed step … [and, despite already having many children to look after, responded,] 'If Jenny is called to go to China … [then] I am called to care for her children.'"

(Taylor & Taylor, 1918: 310, 312)

Is there a balance? It would seem that Hudson Taylor was enabled to follow his calling at the expense of others. Perhaps there are a number of aspects to consider. Firstly, Taylor's calling was at great expense to himself also. He did not lead a life of *leisure* at the expense of others. Secondly, he did not *seek* the support he received. Others felt called by God to offer it, but it wasn't the result of Taylor applying pressure.

Was Taylor always right in his actions? Unless he was perfect, the answer is obvious. Was he right in these noted cases? Only God can really judge. But that is not the issue—the issue is rather, are you, am I, gaining benefit at the expense of others in a way that is not Godly?

Sometimes our perceived need for additional funds may stem from the standard we expect to be our right. I remember clearly a pastor who wanted his church to fund his home improvements. He established the benchmark of how he wanted to live by comparing his current life-style with the well-to-do in the community outside the church.

In contrast, Taylor's biography quotes a poem that expresses joy in God's presence, not joy in the physical location or comforts.

> *"O Thou, by long experience tried,*
> *Near whom no grief can long abide;*
> *My Lord, how full of sweet content,*
> *I pass my years of banishment.*
>
> *All scenes alike engaging prove*
> *To souls impress'd with sacred love!*
> *Where'er they dwell, they dwell in Thee;*
> *In heaven, on earth, or the sea.*
>
> *To me remains nor place nor time,*
> *My country is in every clime;*
> *I can be calm and free from care*
> *On any shore, since God is there.*
>
> *While place we seek or place we shun,*
> *The soul finds happiness in none;*
> *But with my God to guide my way*
> *'Tis equal joy to go or stay.*
>
> *Could I be cast where Thou art not,*
> *That were indeed, a dreadful thought;*
> *But regions none remote I call,*
> *Secure in finding God in all."*
>
> (Madame Guyon, in Taylor & Taylor, 1911: 200)

The author of Taylor's biography also comments on a fellow missionary, William Burns:

> "The presence of the Lord was the one thing real to him in China as it had been at home. 'He did not consider that he had a warrant to proceed in any sacred duty,' his biographer tells us, 'without a consciousness of that divine presence. Without it, he could not speak even to a handful of little children in a Sunday School; with it he could stand unabashed before the mightiest and wisest in the land.'

> *Ruled by such a master-principle, it was no wonder there was something about his life that impressed and attracted others even while it inspired a sense of awe. The brightest lamp will burn dim in an impure or rarified atmosphere, but William Burns was enabled so to keep himself 'in the love of God' that he was but little affected by his surroundings. Prayer was as natural to him as breathing, and the Word of God as necessary as daily food. He was always cheerful, always happy, witnessing to the truth of his own memorable words:*
>
>> *I think I can say, through grace, that God's presence or absence alone distinguishes places to me.*
>
> *Simplicity in living was his great delight. 'He enjoyed quietness and the luxury of having few things to take care of,' and thought the happiest state on earth for a Christian was 'that he should have few wants.'*
>
> *'If a man have Christ in his heart,' he used to say, 'heaven before his eyes, and only as much of temporal blessing as is just needful to carry him safely through life, then pain and sorrow have little to shoot at. ... To be in union with Him Who is the Shepherd of Israel, to walk very near Him Who is both sun and shield, comprehends all a poor sinner requires to make him happy between this and heaven.'*
>
> *Cultured, genial and overflowing with mother-wit, he was a delightful companion, and the contrast – for those who knew him in China – was very marked between 'the mind and thoughts so trained to higher things and the heart so content with that which was lowly.'"*
>
> (Taylor & Taylor, 1911: 346-347)

When circumstances forced a separation between Taylor and his close friend, William Burns, another poem demonstrates the attitude of contentedness, independent of surroundings.

> "Ill that God blesses is our good,
> And unblest good is ill:
> And all is right that seems most wrong
> If it be His sweet will."

(Taylor & Taylor, 1911: 358)

This relaxed attitude did not go without being tested. The mission had grown to the point where

> "Mr. Taylor's estimate of a hundred pounds a week as a working average could not be considered extravagant."

(Taylor & Taylor, 1918: 234)

Yet when they reached a point of being severely short funds, an administrator wrote to Taylor,

> "Twenty-five cents plus all the promises of God ... why, one felt ... rich ..."

(Taylor & Taylor, 1918: 256)

And what was Taylor's mind-set when confronted by tight financial conditions or even physical dangers for him and his workers?

> "How blessed it is to trust in Him. It is far happier to want, trusting Him, than to be richly supplied, leaning on supplies rather than on the Supplier."
>
> (Taylor & Taylor, 1918: 274)

> "Some around him could hardly understand this joy and rest, especially when fellow-workers were in danger. A budget of letters arriving on one occasion, as Mr. Nicoll relates, brought news of serious rioting in two different stations. Standing at his desk to read them, Mr. Taylor mentioned what was happening and that immediate help was necessary. Feeling that he might wish to be alone, the younger man was about to withdraw, when, to his surprise, some one began to whistle. It was the soft refrain of the same well-loved hymn:
>
> > Jesus, I am resting, resting, in the joy of what Thou art …
>
> Turning back, Mr. Nicoll could not help exclaiming, 'How can you whistle, when our friends are in such danger!'
>
> 'Would you have me anxious and troubled?' was the long-remembered answer. 'That would not help them, and would certainly incapacitate me for my work. I have just to roll the burden on the Lord.'
>
> Day and night that was his secret, 'just to roll the burden on the Lord.' Frequently those who were wakeful in the little house at Chin-kiang might hear, at two or three o'clock in the morning, the soft refrain of Mr. Taylor's favourite hymn. He had learned that, for him, only one life was possible – just that blessed life of resting and rejoicing in the Lord under all circumstances, while He dealt with the difficulties inward and outward, great and small."
>
> (Taylor & Taylor, 1918: 290-291)

Yet even this man who had learned so much of resting in God had physical and maybe emotional limits. China was embroiled in a vicious, bloody civil war, and the missionaries were not spared from the indiscriminate killing. The loss of close friends took a terrible toll on Hudson Taylor, yet his faith in God remained. Taylor wrote,

> "… telegram after telegram was received telling of riots, massacres, and the hunting down of refugees in station after station of the Mission – until the heart that so long, in joy and sorrow, had upheld these beloved fellow-workers before the Lord could endure no more, and almost ceased to beat. …
>
> 'I cannot read,' he said when things were at their worst; 'I cannot think; I cannot even pray; but I can trust.' "
>
> (Taylor & Taylor, 1918: 586-587)

Prayer, faith, ... *and* action

Hudson Taylor was undoubtedly a man of prayer, and a man of faith. The New Testament author James challenges us that we need more than passive faith. We must put the faith into action. And this Taylor certainly did. Yet the necessity of plenty of action did not lessen the need for prayer, but perhaps made it even more essential.

> "Was there a need just [when they were overwhelmingly busy] for a reminder that work cannot take the place of prayer? ... it certainly would not have been surprising if that little circle had been tempted to curtail quiet times of waiting upon God. ...
>
> [Yet] the last day of December was set apart ... as a day of fasting and prayer ... fitly closing the year that had witnessed the inauguration of a Mission so completely dependent upon God."
>
> (Taylor & Taylor, 1918: 46-47)

We must pray, yes, but we must also actively pursue what we believe is God's call. Taylor's parents heard his views on a calling and encouraged him to actively prepare.

> "My beloved parents neither disapproved nor encouraged my desire to engage in missionary work. They advised me, with such convictions, to use all the means in my power to develop the resources of body, mind and soul, and to wait prayerfully upon God, quite willing, should He show me that I was mistaken, to follow His guidance, or to go forward if in due time He should open the way ..."
>
> (Taylor & Taylor, 1911: 85)

Some see the use of practical means at our disposal as a lack of faith. Taylor grappled with such issues early in his active ministry, and came to the conclusion that to use what God has put at our disposal does not mean a lessening of faith. Further, to *not* use the practical things at hand can be negligent. The following extracts are set on a ship at sea in threatening conditions.

> "One thing was a great trouble to me that night. I was a very young believer, and had not sufficient faith in God to see Him in and through the use of means. I had felt it a duty to comply with the earnest wish of my beloved and honoured mother, and for her sake to procure a swimming-belt [for the sea journey]. But in my own soul I felt as if I could not simply trust in God while I had this swimming-belt, and my heart had no rest until on that night, after all hope of being saved was gone, I had given it away. Then I had perfect peace, and strange to say put several light things together, likely to float at the time we struck, without any thought of inconsistency or scruple.
>
> Ever since, I have seen clearly the mistake I made; a mistake that is very common in these days, when erroneous teaching on faith-healing does much harm, misleading some as to the purposes of God, shaking the faith of others and distressing the minds of many. The use of means ought not to lessen our faith in God, and our faith in God ought not to hinder our using whatever means He has given us for the accomplishment of His own purposes.

> *For years after this I always took a swimming-belt with me and never had any trouble about it; for after the storm was over, the question was settled for me through the prayerful study of the Scriptures. God gave me then to see my mistake, probably to deliver me from a great deal of trouble on similar questions now so constantly raised. When in medical or surgical charge of any case, I have never thought of neglecting to ask God's guidance and blessing in the use of appropriate means, nor yet of omitting to give thanks for answered prayer and restored health. But to me it would appear as presumptuous and wrong to neglect the use of those measures which He Himself has put within our reach as to neglect to take daily food, and suppose that life and health might be maintained by prayer alone."*
>
> (Taylor & Taylor, 1911: 191)

In summary, we are to pray, *and* to act.

> *"Mr. Taylor not only prayed [for unity at the upcoming conference]; he did all that in him lay to promote the unity he felt to be of such importance …"*
>
> (Taylor & Taylor, 1918: 292)

> *"You can work without praying, but it is a bad plan … but you cannot pray in earnest without working. … Do not be so busy with work for Christ that you have no strength left for praying. True prayer requires strength."*
>
> (Taylor & Taylor, 1918: 444)

An analogy of God's guidance likens us to a ship. A ship has a rudder for steering, but it is totally useless until the ship starts moving. Similarly, there are times God calls us to start moving with the little vision and faith we have, confident in His ability to direct as we move forward, not necessarily before we start.

> *"We felt we were going forward in this matter not knowing when, how, or where God would have the new work begun, but assured that, in the way, needed light and leading would be given; and we have not been disappointed."*
>
> (Taylor & Taylor, 1918: 570-571)

Be content doing the "little" things

If you or I are looking too hard to find what God wants us to do, there is a danger. You might be looking for large, spectacular "ministries", when maybe all God wants you to do at that time is to love your neighbor. He has already told us that to look after the poor and vulnerable of this world (James 1), to oppose injustice, to feed and clothe the poor (Isaiah 58), to act justly, to love mercy and to walk humbly with our God (Micah 6:8), to share the good news, and so much more. We don't need "special" revelation to obey the instructions we already have.

> *"… you find out what he's already told you to do and start right in doing that. …*
>
> *There are hundreds of things he's told his followers to do. … So that's where we start – doing those. …*

> *... If we don't do the first things he's said about how folks ... are to behave, he's not going to show us anything else. When we do those, he'll show us other things to do.*
>
> *[And the key to discovering these first things begins if we read] ... the four Gospels ... Matthew, Mark, Luke, and John ..."*

(Phillips, 1996: 224-225)

Sometimes God may give a person a view of His long-term plans. He did that for Hudson Taylor, letting him know that outreach in China was to be his life's work. But even then, God had many day-to-day tasks for Taylor to do. So whether or not we have any idea of where we might end up, let's keep talking to God about what we do in the next twenty-four hours. We need this daily communication, partly because that's where we are trained and tested for the future, and partly because the big-picture goals may be too grand for us to cope with. In a different setting, Bill from Alcoholics Anonymous shares his views on focusing on today.

> *"Most people feel more secure on the twenty-four-hour basis than they do in the resolution that they will never drink again. Most of them have broken too many resolutions. It's really a matter of personal choice; every A.A. has the privilege of interpreting the program as he likes.*
>
> *Personally, I take the attitude that I intend never to drink again. This is somewhat different from saying, 'I will never drink again.' The latter attitude sometimes gets people in trouble because it is undertaking on a personal basis to do what we alcoholics never could do. It is too much an act of will and leaves too little room for the idea that God will release us from the drink obsession provided we follow the A.A. program."*

(Bill, 1967: 16)

Yancey, too, encourages us to focus on the little things of today:

> *"In his recent volume The Longing for Home, Buechner draws a contrast between the news of the day reported on television each night – wars, elections, natural disasters – and the news of the day that transpires in our private worlds. Some of the things that happen there are so small that we hardly notice them, yet they help compose the day-by-day story of who we are. 'Their news is the news of what we are becoming or failing to become,' he says, which may be the most important news of all.*
>
> *In the same vein, Buechner believes that if God speaks at all in this world, it is into our everyday personal lives. In searching for God, many people tend to look for the miraculous and supernatural. Instead we should be attending to the ordinary: waking and sleeping and above all dreaming, what we remember and what we forget, what makes us smile and what makes us cry, what delights and what depresses us. In the most commonplace events of a day, God speaks, and Buechner demonstrates through his writing how to listen.*

> *Buechner recommends reviewing this more intimate news during the nightly interval when you first turn out the light and lie in the dark waiting for sleep to come. That is when the events of the day – an unanswered letter, a phone conversation, a tone of voice, a chance meeting at the post office, an unexpected lump in the throat – hint at other, subsurface meanings.*
>
> *If I was called upon to state in a few words the essence of everything I was trying to say … it would be something like this: Listen to your life. See it for the fathomless mystery it is. In the boredom and pain of it no less than in the excitement and gladness; touch, taste, smell your way to the holy and hidden heart of it because in the last analysis all moments are key moments, and life itself is grace.*
>
> *(From Now and Then)"*
>
> (Yancey, 2001: 247-248)

Angela Hunt's novel, *The Debt*, portrays Emma as a pastor's wife confronted by a scene of great need, with her son Chris apparently oblivious to the needs of all but one person. Emma proclaims,

> "What about the others? We need to do something about that situation; we can't just leave that child."
>
> (Hunt, 2004: 280)

Chris has compassion for the others, and the identified needs of the child are later addressed. But for today, Chris responds,

> "One person at a time, Emma. … I spoke to the Father this morning; this is Melinda's day."
>
> (Hunt, 2004: 281)

Today, neither you nor I can change the entire world. But we can make a difference, one person at a time.

CHAPTER 42:
BEWARE THE COMFORT OF THE FAMILIAR

For some people, freedom from the local church model and its leadership is not as simple as walking away. In extreme cases such as cults in walled compounds, such simple choices do not exist. As Bridges notes in his book, *Pursuit of Holiness*:

> *"You cannot say to a slave, 'Live as a free man,' but you can say that to someone delivered from slavery."*

(Bridges, 1985: 60)

Thankfully, most of us can walk away, even though it may be costly in terms of friendships, and many may misunderstand or criticize us. But we *can* walk away. However, Bridges notes that even those who can walk to freedom do not necessarily do so:

> *"… do you suppose that when slaves were freed by President Lincoln's Emancipation Proclamation, they immediately began to think as free men? Undoubtedly they still tended to act as slaves because they had developed habit patterns of slavery."*

(Bridges, 1985: 59)

We need to take care that "old thinking" does not continue to enslave us when it need no longer do so.

The lure of past traditions

Locke and Weinberger comment on the difficulty establishments have in changing direction even if the old way is known to be flawed:

> *"Command and control is widely perceived as dysfunctional, but it's a hard-to-break habit. Many … leaders are well aware that bureaucratic hierarchy works against*

needed knowledge and communication, yet inertia is a powerful force."

(Levine, Locke, Searls and Weinberger, 2000: 163-164)

Not only can old routines be hard to break. They can also tend to draw us back even after we've made a break. The familiar can draw us unconsciously.

"... radical thinking does not describe the paradigm shift that is necessary ... [because] ... the parish model still looms over such talk as the dominant model which will always strive to reassert itself. The default position of the church is always that of a church as an institution.

... [New ways of thinking are] not so hard to express, describe, grasp. The difficulty arises in actually living the paradigm because the old one constantly draws us back. All too often the best we can manage are initiatives that come out of the old paradigm and allow us to live in the new paradigm for a while. Constructing a new model, which we live within as a permanent reality, is much more difficult."

(Robinson & Smith, 2003: 109)

One reason the old systems draw people back even after they have broken free is that the old system has almost become part of us.

"Although a system may cease to exist in the legal sense or as a structure of power, its values (or anti-values), its philosophy, its teachings remain in us. They rule our thinking, our conduct, our attitude to others. The situation is a demonic paradox: we have toppled the system but we still carry its genes."

(Ryszard Kapuscinski in Levine, Locke, Searls and Weinberger, 2000: 177)

After the Israelites had eventually escaped from slavery, they did not immediately enter the Promised Land. Even though God supplied manna for food, at no cost—all they had to do was to gather it—they grumbled and thought back to the variety of food they ate in Egypt (Numbers 11). They longed for the leeks and garlic, and forgot the slavery that accompanied such food.

"The land of promise was not a land free from dangers. The milk and honey they were promised awaited them amid a land of giants.

It is no different for us. As it was for them, freedom is a return not to Paradise Lost, but to a promised land that we must win. Like Israel, who longed for Egypt because the journey was more difficult than the people expected, we must be aware of the temptation to return to the captivity from which we were freed. There is but one path to freedom."

(McManus, 2005: 139-140)

To discover freedom, we must leave the old behind and push forward, in spite of hardship or danger. But if we have been raised on sermons that focus almost exclusively on God's goodness, love and promises, and have not been exposed to the teaching on the cost of following God, we may be tempted to pull back as soon as things get a bit tough. We may wonder if God could really be leading us if our "Promised Land" appears to have dangers.

McManus challenges that God's ways often purposefully include apparent (and real) dangers that will strengthen our faith, if not kill us! He shares how he reacted to his child's sense of adventure and danger. The family lived in a house where, if one tried hard enough, they could get from the bathroom window and up to the roof. McManus and his wife, Kim, were in the front yard.

> "… all of a sudden, we heard a little voice calling for us from the roof. As soon as Kim saw [our son], her nurturing instinct kicked in, and she started commanding him to get back inside. I have to admit I was kind of proud of him right then, but what he did next totally surprised me.
>
> Looking past his mom, he … shouted, 'Dad, can I jump?' Kim answered on my behalf, 'No, you can't jump. Get back inside.'
>
> As if he hadn't heard anything at all, he asked me again, 'Dad, can I jump?'
>
> Now I know what I was supposed to do. A dad is never supposed to override the mom (I'm working on it). I'm just telling you what really happened. After all, he did ask me. I answered, 'Yeah, go ahead.'"
>
> (McManus, 2005: 117-118)

Their son did jump, and no damage was done. Sometimes a parent will allow a child to experience a little danger as part of the growing process. McManus also raised his kids to accept that sometimes following the call of God may put any or all of us in danger. Some parents would rather avoid danger for their children than follow God's call. And danger can be physical (e.g. living in a country with less medical facilities than at "home") or moral danger (as a couple working with street people in Amsterdam experienced). McManus' son wondered if his dad would also take risks in his obedience.

> "Not long ago Aaron asked me, 'Dad, would you purposefully put us in danger?'
>
> 'Yes,' I answered, 'of course.'
>
> Without blinking an eye his response was simply, 'That's what I thought. I was just making sure.'"
>
> (McManus, 2005: 107)

If a human parent would permit risks for themselves and others as the price of furthering God's Kingdom, would God do the same for His children?

> "I wonder how many of us have actually had this conversation with God: 'Abba, Father, Dad, would You purposefully put me in danger?' I think a lot of us haven't asked God that question because we went ahead and answered it for Him. Of course He wouldn't do that. We're His children. We're family. He wouldn't purposefully endanger us, not even to accomplish a higher or nobler purpose. Or would He?

Maybe you should stop and ask Him. His answer might surprise you. It certainly surprised John the Baptist."

(McManus, 2005: 108)

It can be hard to change, and even harder to trust, especially where trust in earthly leaders has been abused. The predictability of the status quo can make our current situation seem attractive, even if flawed.

"I was afraid to climb out of the nest ... After all, it's cozy there ... and I was happy being among friends-of-a-feather. But one day I clambered up on the edge, looked out at the world, and ... asked God to help me fly ..."

(Hunt, 2004: 254)

The path to freedom may seem frightening, but it is essential.

"I have been so wrapped up in good things – Christian forms, Christian functions – for so many years that the idea of breaking free is a little frightening. And yet I must do it."

(Hunt, 2004: 332)

Many Australians have their cultural roots in Europe, where Christmas celebrations include hot meals enjoyed during northern hemisphere winters. Yet Christmas Day in Australia can bring temperatures that soften the surface of the roads, and for those in rural regions, the heat can also bring life-threatening wildfires. The last thing many people want is a hot roast and hot pudding. Cooking on an outside barbeque, or better yet, having cold meat and salad followed by ice-cream, is more in order.

Yet in spite of the logic of such a choice, peer pressure for many demands slaving over a hot stove to prepare a traditional Christmas meal. Those who do otherwise can be criticized, and sometimes concede to the expectations of others rather than being willing to be different.

Whether Australians celebrate Christmas with a roast-and-pudding, or ice-cream, is not the issue. Rather, on matters of greater importance, are you and I bowing to the expectations of others?

"Unfortunately, other Christians often hold us back from doing the will of God. It's easy to be molded into each other's images, and difficult to be molded into the image of Christ. ... It's the response of other Christians and my own sinful need for their approval that can make me change the way I serve God."

Green (2000: 213-214)

In Luke 5, Jesus pointed out the stupidity of tearing a patch of material from a new garment just so it can be sewn as a patch onto an old one. The new garment is ruined, and the patch will look ridiculous on the old garment. Hopefully no one in their right mind would even consider doing it. We must avoid trying to patch new ways of doing things onto old institutional religious traditions. We need a clean start.

CHAPTER 43:
RELATING TO OLD-SCHOOL CLERGY WHO WANT TO JOIN YOU

In the closing chapters of this book we will look at some of the ways your effectiveness in some new outreach, might be quenched through some of the old ways that can raise their ugly heads. We have noted how church leaders sometimes have unhealthy attitudes on topics such as money, recognition, control, comfort in the familiar, and so on. These final chapters are a reminder that, having escaped from institutions with inherent problems, we are vulnerable to holding to similar practices unawares.

It's all about you and me slipping back into the old ways of our past environment. But there is one major threat we need to be wary of, and this one is the reverse. We could well have old-style leaders who want to join us in the new landscape. When they see the spontaneity, fruitfulness, and pure joy amongst you and your colleagues, they may want to join you—possibly driven by pure motives, but also possibly to bring your success into their camp and back under their control. I have seen it happen. So how might you respond to an approach by church leaders?

Strong, directive command-and-control leaders in business and sports can sometimes achieve remarkable outcomes. A sporting coach boasted of his iron-fisted approach that led to a series of successful seasons, saying *"The minute a player threatens my control … I have to take it seriously. If he's affecting results or morale or spirit he has to go. My strength has to be obvious for all to see."* Some may feel such a bullying attitude may be acceptable in the sporting arena, though I personally challenge that view. To me, sport trophies at the expense of the individual player's dignity don't seem a healthy exchange. But within the Body of Christ there is most definitely no place for bullies or those who try to control others.

Hierarchical leaders can hinder the growth of individuals in many ways. For one thing, they can push people away who might otherwise be helped. We must let God deal with the hearts of others at His pace, in His way. Alcoholics Anonymous observed,

> "... drinkers would not take pressure in any form, excepting from John Barleycorn himself [i.e. from the consequences of consuming alcohol]. They always had to be led, not pushed. They would not stand for ... aggressive evangelism ... [and] they would not accept the principle of 'team guidance' for their own personal lives. It was too authoritarian for them. In other respects, too, we found we had to make haste slowly. When first contacted, most alcoholics just wanted to find sobriety, nothing else. They clung to their other defects, letting go only little by little. They simply did not want to get 'too good too soon.' "

(AAWS, 1957: 74-75)

Another lesson learned from A.A. is that strong leaders may be a factor in the development of an unhealthy dependence. One of the early founding fathers of Alcoholics Anonymous noted,

> "Lois and I continued to find ... that if we permitted alcoholics to become too dependent on us they were apt to stay drunk."

(AAWS, 1957: 74)

Our gentle, loving God calls us to follow and depend on Him, rather than any human who wants to lead us.

We have looked earlier at the false message leaders send that we *need* them to act as a "mediator between God and man", in spite of Jesus explicitly teaching that *no* man is to take that role. Oliver and Thwaites explain how God can use many ways to teach, lead, and support us.

> "... I need to stress that there are many other areas where resources for the saints come from – prayer, family, friends, colleagues, old hymn books, walks in the country and so on. These ministry gifts sit in and among all that God has given us pertaining to life and godliness. ... As we consider the role of ministry gifts it is important to know that they are not only to be found inside local churches, they have been strategically positioned by God in the church as fullness in every sphere of creation. Our challenge is that, to date, we have not been given the sight we need to see and value them."

(Oliver & Thwaites, 2001: 146-147)

If we will just take the time to listen to God as He speaks directly to each of us, we will no longer feel a need to hear His message through human mediators.

We, the people, are moving on. But will church leaders join us?

> "For decades [the professional church leaders] have been paid from the royal treasury and have been nursing, grooming and preaching to the court. I don't doubt that they are faithful, hardworking, Godly, sacrificial men and women. But as the court changes and the bride [i.e. the Body set free] leaves the building, running in her new-found freedom, what will they do?

> *In their shock, will they let her go so far, then pull her back, because they know no other way? Will they fret and worry about losing what for so long they have held? Will they worry that they will lose all they thought they had? Will they worry that somehow their role [and] their value is less, and the voice they heard so long ago was false?*
>
> *Or will they run to keep up with her? Will they serve her on the move? Will they see new horizons of ministry unfold in spectacularly unpredictable ways? Will they see this time as more, or less? Will their hearts swell in anticipation or shrink back in fear and cowardice?*
>
> *I don't know – but the choice is there."*
>
> (Oliver & Thwaites, 2001: 211-212)

Oliver and Thwaites offer old-style church leaders the choice to hold on to the rotting traditions of the past or to join us. But do we even want them?

Earlier, the story was told of some friends who, as laity, initiated a fruitful ministry sharing leftover bread from a bakery with those in need of not only food, but friendship and support as well. If the story were to end there, it would be instructive as to the potential of any Christian taking up a challenge as God leads. But the story as it continued took a turn for the worse.

When a local pastor saw the fruitful ministry and changed lives, he decided that he would endorse the ministry, staff it, and grow it further according to *his* vision. To cut a long story short, he almost killed off the outreach. The people who started the ministry distanced themselves from the pastor because he was taking over and making changes, and the pastor fought to retain what he now considered to be "his" ministry. Thankfully, he failed in his attempt to dominate the work of others, and the original fruitful outreach started again—thankfully without him!

We must be willing to step up to the challenges God assigns, without waiting for, asking for, or desiring the blessing of church leaders to do so. And we must *never* hand over God's work to them after it has been established. It is God's work and He allows us to participate in His work for a season. It is never owned by a church or its leaders, and it is certainly *not* ours to give away, or even to permit it being taken away.

The focus has been on mobilization of the members of the Body of Christ, with the people refusing to allow church leaders to hold them back. It is interesting to note that, as members of the Body rise to take up the challenge, they become living examples of what Luther called the "priesthood of all believers". Each individual, in the eyes of God, becomes a priest.

> "But being a priest means bearing responsibility. Being a priest means separating from sin. Being a priest means intimacy with God. So ... will you be a pew-sitter or will you be a priest?"
>
> (Brown, 2002: 66)

Rinehart holds the view that the core problem of the patterns of Christendom we want to leave behind can actually be traced back to the local church leaders.

> *"I believe that if we were pressed to answer the question, 'What holds the church back?' many of us would answer from some deep, sober corner of the soul: Her leaders."*
>
> (Rinehart, 1998: 24)

This raises interesting questions: As members of Christ's true Church, do those who used to be labeled "laity" now take up their role as "priests"? And where do those who used to see themselves as "priests" in the local churches now fit? As quoted earlier,

> *"We cannot solve our problems with the same thinking we used when we created them."*
>
> (Albert Einstein)

If the leaders caused the problems in the first place, why would we think even for a moment that they will now solve any problems that might arise in any new way of ministry?!

Oliver and Thwaites tell a true life story that exemplifies the dangerous roles played by old-style leaders who want to join in the "new".

> *"A number of ministries came together and decided to work out God's plan for their nation. They spent several days together and came up with a document that contained what they said was the 'strategy'. The difficulty was that a number of individuals and other ministries were not present when the plan was formulated. So, as you might imagine, when they heard about what had happened they were somewhat miffed. Then, to add insult to miff, they were 'encouraged' to now submit their own agenda to the larger vision, to see where it fitted in to what was now 'God's plan for the nation'. It is natural for a person to think that what they are doing is central to them, but it is dysfunctional to think that it is central to everybody else. Too often, ministries looking for a following and in need of funding grasp a mandate and use it to grasp the centre, (humbly) thinking they are doing God and everybody else a favour.*
>
> *History, as well as present observation, has shown that such 'centres' usually end up, over time, becoming just another subculture, for the greater part, separate from the mainstream, kept busy maintaining their organisational existence and vested interests. Or worse, an organisation takes charge of a facet (or of the whole) of a culture/society. It is in this way that good ideas are gradually replaced by the 'rule of the good ideas'. By trying to impose its vision of what that culture should look like, these centres can become instruments that diminish or even destroy the very culture they set out to bring into being (totalitarianism, market-driven corporatism and certain church hierarchies are in view here)."*
>
> (Oliver & Thwaites, 2001: 95)

They recognized the dangers of old patterns, claiming that leaders typically

> "... surmise that nothing is happening and so resolve to go and make something happen. [They] set out to make things happen by organising this initiative and that, commissioning this group and that person to do works that will produce the results [they] envisage. Before [they] know it, [their] particular ministry, [their] new landscape 'institute' has taken to itself the mandate, as did the old (and still present) way of church leadership, and with that, moves to take charge of the people, the process and the centre yet again."
>
> (Oliver & Thwaites, 2001: 94)

and, as quoted earlier,

> "Many leaders have become convinced that nothing much can happen unless _they_ make it happen." [Emphasis mine]
>
> (Oliver & Thwaites, 2001: 94)

They note that much of this wrong thinking can be traced back to the way church-based ministers are trained:

> "We have been taught by leadership experts to get a vision and take charge ...; get a group of people to work with and under us ... ; then, as leaders, begin to break ground so that people can follow you ... As things grow you bring in more 'resources' to meet the demands now placed on you. You will now be able to keep increasing the number of church-based ministries ... that express your vision and extend your reach. As you do this, you will set up an enduring church with a strong culture ... and this will further facilitate and enable people who come in to minister in and from the base you have established ... What this ... creates is a culture that is kept inside a construct, and under a leader."
>
> (Oliver & Thwaites, 2001: 101)

The authors then go on to explain that the preferred way is

> "... a reverse of the above process [that] will lead ... to a very different outcome."
>
> (Oliver & Thwaites, 2001: 101)

To answer the question as to where the old-style leaders fit, firstly they must recognize that they are no longer in charge. They are no longer "leaders", and if they even refer to their past "leadership" role, or use phrases such as them now being "first among equals", their thinking is askew and they will not fit in to the new ministry.

There must be no trace of a hierarchical model, and they must leave behind all references to them ever having been "leaders". As quoted earlier,

> "... leaders ... must become aware, apart from the latest book on leadership [they] have read, that [they] are not in charge of the church as fullness. It has no king except Jesus and needs no king except Jesus. It does need servants, but it does not need managers pretending to be servants."
>
> (Oliver & Thwaites, 2001: 94-95)

Secondly, these old-style leaders were dangerous on their own turf. What happens when they try to join the God-led ministries of the people? Speaking to leaders in the old pattern, Oliver and Thwaites warn:

> "... so much of our patterning in the old has to do with ministries leading the way and people following them. Any ministry or movement will grow in line with the DNA laid down in the first cells of its life. ... There is a place for us [ex-leaders that represent the old ways of doing things], but it's a different place to the one we have known. Let's surrender our need to be in charge at the border crossing [where the ex-leaders in the old structures move into where God's people are already in front-line ministry], and enter the new landscape as a servant, a friend, an observer and a learner."
>
> (Oliver & Thwaites, 2001: 96)

There is a danger of bringing the old into the new. These people "in ministry" (or in fact any with "a leadership gift or propensity") may try to enter what God is doing outside the confines of the local church. But Oliver and Thwaites have a warning.

> "[If the old-style leaders] bring with them ways of leadership, thinking and structure that have been the cause of many problems in [the old style church], then they will muddy the waters for many others."
>
> (Oliver & Thwaites, 2001: 94)

Put simply, if individuals who were previously church leaders wish to join a Body-led ministry, they *must* leave behind their titles and ideas of being "the leader", or of being in any kind of leadership role. Unless they rescind their past and become simply part of the Body, they are not welcome. The Body is not rejecting them as *people*, but as long they hold on to their titles or even attempt to continue their *role* of being special and/or superior, they *cannot* and *must not* join in. To re-quote an extract,

> "The old form has to die a death: it cannot dress up in suit and tie and move its business into the [new forms of ministry]."
>
> (Oliver & Thwaites, 2001: 99)

Levine et al talk of the role of old-style commercial leaders and their role in the new, emerging market place where the community at large is now setting the rules. The common people address their old corporate leaders and say,

> "You're invited, but it's our world. Take your shoes off at the door. If you want to barter with us, get down off that camel!"
>
> (Levine, Locke, Searls and Weinberger, 2000: xvii)

If we adapt this philosophy and apply it to Christendom, we realize those who had been leaders do not have as much choice as they would like to think. In fact, any who stubbornly cling to the past and/or their status are derided.

> "Smart ... [leaders] will get out of the way and help the inevitable to happen sooner. ...

If willingness to get out of the way is taken as a measure of IQ, then very few ... have yet wised up."

(Levine, Locke, Searls and Weinberger, 2000: xvi)

They can fight against you, or they can humbly join you—not as leaders in discovery of a new way, or as spiritual super stars, but just as fellow members of the Body under *Christ's* leadership.

So be wary of leaders from the old ways stifling the new ones. The challenge will ever be for you to walk in freedom—the freedom that knowing the Truth in Jesus Christ brings. He didn't wait for, want, or need blessing from the leaders of His day before He made His move.

Once you have known freedom from traditional church constraints and dominating leadership, don't ever let them take over again.

CHAPTER 44:
NOW IT'S OVER TO YOU

A snippet from an earlier quotation is worth repeating here.

> "All over the Christian world there are chained eagles. Logs of false teaching, chains of false expectation and false doctrine are holding down some magnificent men and women who, deep down, are longing to fly. They are longing for permission, for understanding, for conviction; longing to feel the wind of the Spirit blow under outstretched wings, as they get lifted into the thermals high up in God's purpose. The [place] is here; the [time] is now. As you read, will you let the Word of God break those chains? Will you let his Spirit breathe into your faint hope, your faint faith, and let him stir you up, lift you up to something higher?"
>
> (Oliver & Thwaites, 2001: 77)

Having come this far in the book, I trust you have seen the flaws in traditional church and leadership systems, and have also been challenged by a better way. But the change will come at a price. Friends and family may misunderstand you, or even turn against you. If you believe God is calling you to freedom, are you willing to respond—or are you just going to put this book down and feel intellectually stimulated but totally unchanged in ways that count?

It is not easy to change. Often people choose to continue to live unhappily with the old, predictable ways rather than change to a better way. We have a way of freedom on offer, but will we take it? Plass defines "freedom" in a way that provides insight to this dilemma:

> "**Freedom**: a by-product of truth, and something many of us claim to desire more than anything. Only when it is actually offered, however, do we find out how much we actually want it [or don't want it], as the prisoner in the following dialogue discovers:
>
> PRISONER: (Loudly and passionately) Help! Help! Someone help me! Help! Help! Someone has to help me get out of here! (Etc.)

RESCUER: *(Armed with a large key)* It's OK! Look! I've got a key. I can let you out

P: *(After looking at his watch)* Mmm. Actually, it's very nearly lunchtime, and the food really is not at all bad here. If you came back around, say, half two?

R: *(Indicates the bag he's carrying)* I've got plenty of food for both of us. Come on! Let's get going!

P: Oh. Err, right. Okay. Right! I'll just get my stuff together.

R: *(Looking around)* Stuff? What stuff? You haven't got any stuff. Come on, let's go!

P: Right. Right. You know, it's a bit chilly at this time of the day. Maybe we'd better go in the morning after the sun has had a chance to –

R: *(Holding out a thick coat)* Here's a coat. Go on, put it on!

P: *(After putting the coat on)* Whew! It's going to be a bit jolly warm with this on. I'm already sweating and –

R: *(Impatiently offering his own coat)* Swap with me, for goodness sake! Mine's thinner. Now, let's get going before it's too late! Come on! *(They swop)*

P: Right! *(Hesitates)* You do know the way, do you?

R: *(Holds up a map)* I've got a map! I know the way!

P: Right! Right! Right! Right! Right . . .

R: Well, come on, then!

P: *(After a pause)* Look, I suppose you don't fancy moving in here with me instead, do you? It's really not that bad when you get used to it and every other Wednesday they put on a rather good sort of ...

R: No, of course I don't fancy moving in with you! ... Look – do you want to be free or not?

P: *(Rather sulkily)* Well, yes, but I think I ought to be the one to choose when I go. It doesn't seem fair to me that you just come barging in here without even making an appointment and –

R: But you were shouting about wanting to get out! I heard you! Now, come on! *(Grabs his arm)* Let's get –

P: Help! Help! I'm being kidnapped! Somebody help me! Help! Help! Rescue me! Help!

R: *(In disgust)* Oh, stay here then! *(Disappears)*

P: *(After a pause to make sure he's gone)* Help! Help! Somebody rescue me! Somebody has to get me out of here! Help! Help! *(Etc.)*"

(Plass, 2007: 57-58)

Freedom is a discovery we make for ourselves, and something we need to boldly share with others.

> *"The right to search for the truth implies also a duty; one must not conceal any part of what one has recognized to be the truth."*
>
> (Albert Einstein)

We must share with others, and we must accept that we will face opposition. But nonetheless—speak out we must.

> *"… if any of you … have a mind to make himself heard a mile off, you must make a bonfire of your reputations and a close enemy of most men who would wish you well.*
>
> *I have seen ten years of young men who rush out into the world with their messages, and when they find how deaf the world is, they think they must save their strength and wait. They believe that after a while they will be able to get up on some little eminence from which they can make themselves heard. 'In a few years,' reasons one of them, 'I shall have gained a standing, and then I will use my powers for good.' Next year comes and with it a strange discovery. The man has lost his horizon of thought. His ambition has evaporated; he has nothing to say. I give you this one rule of conduct. Do what you will, but speak out always. Be shunned, be hated, be ridiculed, be scared, be in doubt, but don't be gagged. The time of trial is always. Now is the appointed time."*
>
> (John Jay Chapman in Levine, Locke, Searls and Weinberger, 2000: 45)

Radical change can be daunting, but again Plass reminds us that, while human leaders may disappoint us, we can confidently place our trust in Jesus, and follow Him wherever He may lead, even if it is into unknown territory.

> *"Very bad beginnings [are defined as]: distorted, negative experiences of religious behaviour that can have serious long-term effects on those who start their Christian lives under the wrong leadership. …*
>
> *[In contrast,] the Son of God does not frighten children, and he is undoubtedly the leader we must follow. It can be very difficult to move on. I have seen such pain in the eyes of those who know that their master is calling them out of an environment or a set of attitudes or a point of view that is not good for them. I understand it. Human beings do so need to belong, and it can be deeply disturbing to leave even a situation in which we are being abused. At least we had a place there. We were part of it. Now the Lord is calling us out to a place where we have never been, and we have no idea where he intends to lead us. Nevertheless, if we are sure that we have heard his voice, we must go. Jesus is not like [abusive leaders], and the best place for us to be, however alien it may seem before and after we arrive, is out there on the edge with him."*
>
> (Plass, 2007: 193, 201)

Sometimes the excitement of feeling we are doing something of value can cause us to take our eyes off Jesus. We are called to live courageously, but we must still walk humbly and obediently as we follow His call.

> *"... imagination takes courage, as it involves risk.... [We need to relate to the] one who required his hearers to risk all to gain the kingdom of God and even more to advance it. This person? None other than Jesus."*
>
> (Frost & Hirsch, 2003: 189)

And of course we are not simply to be subservient like mindless robots. While there is value in God-inspired ministry, what God longs for is relationship with you. If we get so busy in enthusiastically championing a new cause that we forget our relationship with Jesus, we will have just started another "movement" that will slowly rot and die. A moment-by-moment walk with Jesus is vital, and should not be eclipsed by our busyness or trying to earn His approval.

> *"There are many books being written on the subject of church renewal. Many new ideas, new methods, new formats and new structures are being suggested as 'keys to renewal.' Many church leaders on both the left and the right are making pronouncements on the subject.*
>
> *Everyone is selling something as 'the answer.' Small groups. Charismatic experiences. Gospel rock. River or ocean baptism. Relational theology. Discovery games. Dialogue sermons. Personal evangelism. Social involvement. Conversational prayer. Depending on who it is to whom you are listening, any one of these (and more) might seem to be the 'key to church renewal.'*
>
> *Doubtless if any one of these ideas would be tried in the average church, it would be like a breath of fresh air blowing through a tomb.*
>
> *But ... is a breath of fresh air enough to raise the dead?*
>
> *In a recent magazine article, the president of a large Christian college declared that the antidote for 'dead orthodoxy' is 'evangelistic zeal.' I could almost hear the thundering chorus of 'amens' from all across the evangelical world.*
>
> *But Jesus said, 'Let the dead bury their dead' ... Nowhere did He suggest it is possible for the dead to raise the dead.*
>
> *Evangelistic zeal arising from dead orthodoxy, at best, results in a kind of walking, pressured death!*
>
> *... [What we need] more than anything else [is] to know Him!"*
>
> (Girard, 1972: 211)

It is only natural to get excited about a new "ministry" that might emerge if you break free from the constraints of the institution. But the message here is that it is not about ministry; it is about relating to Jesus. If we lose sight of our dependence on God, our "ministry" will surely lose its way. On the other hand, if we decide we are just going to meditate on loving God and live out the rest of our days in some contemplative haze, we are likely to be "so heavenly minded we are no earthly good".

In her novel, *Ruth Erskine's Crosses*, Isabella Alden describes the main character, Ruth, as a person who had put a lot of energy into helping her stepdaughters but who had a hungry soul in her relation with God, not because her efforts to help the girls were wrong but because they had dominated her priorities ahead of her relationship with God:

> *"She had surely done that which was her duty. Yes, but did a revealing Spirit whisper the words in her ear just then? – 'These ought ye to have done, and not to have left the other undone.' She had been absorbed in her labor; she had put these things first. She had risen and gone about the day, too hurried for other than a word of prayer – too hurried for any private reading. She had retired at night too wearied in mind and body for any prayer at all! She was starved! much time gone, and no bread for her hungry soul! Also, having not fed herself, how could she have been expected to feed others? … She felt like a sheep who had wandered outside, even while doing work that she surely thought was set for her – as, indeed, it was; but her eyes were just opening to the fact that one can do work that the Master has set so vigorously as to forget the resting place which he has marked for the soul to pause and commune with him and gather strength. She had been working but not resting. And then, again, it was most painfully true that, because of her lack of spiritual strength, she had done but half her work."*
>
> (Alden, 1997: 226-227)

Some teach that the Christian life is designed to be one of health, wealth and "blessing". A balanced reading of the Bible suggests otherwise. In fact, we are clearly warned that, as followers of Christ, we *will* encounter trouble.

When thinking about happy times in the pleasant home of friends, Mrs. Taylor wrote,

> *"I was almost tempted to wish myself back in that home of rest and love. But it is not for the soldier on the battlefield, however sorely pressed or wounded, to wish himself back in safety and ease."*
>
> (Taylor & Taylor, 1918: 110)

Rather than pursuing leisure, we are clearly taught by Jesus to "take up our cross".

> *"There is a needs-be for us to give ourselves for the life of the world – as He gave His flesh for the feeding of the lifeless and of living souls whose life can only be nourished by the same life-giving Bread. An easy-going non-self-denying life will never be one of power.*
>
> *Fruit-bearing involves cross-bearing. 'Accept a corn of wheat fall into the ground and die, it abideth alone.' We know how the Lord Jesus became fruitful – not by bearing His Cross merely, but by dying on it. Do we know much of fellowship with Him in this? There are not two Christs – an easy-going one for easy-going Christians, and a suffering, toiling one for exceptional believers. There is only one Christ. Are you willing to abide in Him, and thus to bear much fruit?"*
>
> (Taylor & Taylor, 1918: 626)

This theme is not an easy one, nor is it likely to ever win popularity stakes. And the price we may be called to pay may seem terribly high.

> "*The father of a dear girl in the party, Miss Susie Parker, had come over from Pittsfield, Mass., and was sitting near the platform. Seeing a wonderful light on his face, Mr. Taylor invited him to say a few words.*
>
> *'He told us with a father's feeling,' Mr. Taylor loved to recall, 'what his daughter had been in the home, to him and to her mother; what she had been in the mission-hall in which he worked, and something of what it meant to part with her now.*
>
> *' 'But I could only feel,' he said, 'that I have nothing too precious for my Lord Jesus. He has asked for my very best; and I give, with all my heart, my very best to Him.'*
>
> *'That sentence was the richest thing I got in America, and has been an untold blessing to me ever since. Sometimes when pressed with correspondence the hour has come for united prayer, and the thought has arisen, ought I not to go on with this or that matter? Then it has come back to me – 'Nothing too precious for my Lord Jesus.' The correspondence has been left to be cared for afterwards, and one has had the joy of fellowship unhindered. Sometimes waking in the morning, very weary, the hour has come for hallowed communion with the Lord alone; and there is no time like the early morning for getting the harp in tune for the music of the day. Then it has come again – 'Nothing too precious for my Lord Jesus,' and one has risen to find that there is no being tired with Him.' "*
>
> (Taylor & Taylor, 1918: 454-455)

Can we, too, with Taylor and his colleagues, agree that *no* price is too high to pay if we are to be true followers of Christ?

Some religions call upon their followers to demonstrate their willingness to suffer for their faith. I doubt I need to provide examples. For some of these people the pain is self-inflicted, to prove a point.

The way of Christ is totally different. Yes, there may be pain, but we do not foolishly look for it. Rather, just like soldiers in wartime, we are called to act in obedience, and courageously bear the consequences. A soldier does not set out to be wounded or killed, but it may happen. The focus is not on proving oneself to be a hero, or on becoming a martyr; it is very simply on obedience to the call to duty.

> "*… we do not have to be specially distinguished among our fellows in order to be useful and profoundly happy. Not many of us can be leaders of prominence, nor do we wish to be. Service, gladly rendered, obligations squarely met, troubles well accepted or solved with God's help, the knowledge that at home or in the world outside we are partners in a common effort, the well-understood fact that in God's sight all human beings are important, the proof that love freely given surely brings a full return, the certainty that we are no longer isolated and alone in self-constructed prisons, the surety that we need no longer be square pegs in round holes but can fit and belong*

> *in God's scheme of things – these are the permanent and legitimate satisfactions of right living for which no amount of pomp and circumstance, no heap of material possessions, could possibly be substitutes. True ambition is not what we thought it was. True ambition is the deep desire to live usefully and walk humbly under the grace of God."*
>
> (AAWS, 1953: 124-125) [A similar quotation provided earlier from "Bill, 1967: 254"]

Will we succeed in accomplishing all the He tasks set for us? Unless we are perfect, the clear answer is that we will fail at times. So if we know we will fall short, does that mean we should not try? Again, the answer is, "No". God knows our hearts, and it matters not if our efforts are seen by some as being heroic successes or otherwise.

> *"... God never puts a desire in our hearts, or beckons us to walk on water, unless He intends for us to step out in faith and at least make the attempt. Whether we achieve or not is almost immaterial; the passing of the test lies in whether we try, in whether we're willing to be obedient to the inner call to greatness – the onward call to spiritual adventure."*
>
> (Buckingham, 1980: 66)

The life of Caleb in the Old Testament is both inspiring and daunting. He was one of the twelve selected to check out the "Promised Land". All but himself and one of the others focused on the giants in the land, while Caleb and Joshua saw the beauty and potential under God, not the obstacles (Numbers 13). God commended Caleb as a person who followed Him wholeheartedly. That was as a forty-year-old. And when he was in his eighties, after having to wander in the desert because of the sins of others, he still had the same gutsy courage as he had four decades before (Joshua 14). The fact he achieved what God has set for him is encouraging. The fact it took decades may discourage us, but we can confidently keep our eyes on today's tasks, and let God "worry" about tomorrow.

> *"[Caleb had] no divided loyalties, [exhibited] no murmuring or complaining. Only a steady obedience to light received – and a willingness to wait 45 years to see the promise fulfilled."*
>
> (Buckingham, 1980: 71)

Neither you nor I are likely to ever be as notable as Caleb. But we can faithfully make our mark in the little corner of the world where God has placed us.

SECTION 11:

FINALLY: DON'T GO BACK TO EGYPT

You may choose to put this book down now, and launch out in freedom. I hope and pray that you do find freedom, now. And I suggest you have probably been challenged enough to make a great start.

But I would ask one thing more of you. If you don't read this following section right now, please come back and visit it later.

Throughout Scripture we find warnings to and about those who return to the folly of their old ways. The sad thing is that it is too easy to do. Proverbs warns that those who do so are like dogs who return to their vomit. Sorry about the analogy, but it's not mine. I can only assume such strong language was used to get our attention.

This part of the book looks at ways we may, even unconsciously, fall into old traps. I suggest that, as a minimum, you read it after you've traveled a bit of the journey of freedom, as a cross-check to see if you have in part "gone back to Egypt". However, I do suggest that there may be merit in reading it now, as maybe it will help avoid some of the traps.

CHAPTER 45:
MONEY CAN TRAP YOU

If you have launched out in freedom and have achieved what some might count as a measure of success, there is a danger that you may fall for the same traps that ensnared many of the old-style local church leaders.

Some have said that a set of common temptations for leaders relate to three G's—gold, glory, and girls (or to be more precise, inappropriate expressions of sexuality). Those with leadership responsibilities within Christendom are not immune to the love of money, false pride, or warped sexual relationships.

This chapter tackles our attitudes to money, and the dangers that can be associated with a ministry may potentially attract willing donors. The following chapter tackles the next temptation of "glory"—especially the dangers of gaining notoriety for heading up a "successful" ministry.

There is no chapter on the topic of sexuality. Hopefully I do not need to warn of what I hope is abundantly obvious, namely the need for self-restraint and proper boundaries for your sexuality.

Money and you

Alcoholics Anonymous learned early that it was better to have little money than abundance. Yet so many ministries standing under the banner of Christianity appear to the world as little more than organizations focused on raising money. This image is likely to be portrayed because it is true! George MacDonald, in his novel, *A Daughter's Devotion*, states,

> "Few indeed are the Christians capable of [understanding the true relations of money]. ... Those preachers and evangelists and missionaries who turn their focus toward the accumulation of money in order to 'further the gospel,' as they say, demonstrate

a profound lack of understanding of the Father's work in the life of his Son, namely, that he knows our need even before we ask. For did the Son not teach us to pray, 'Give us this day our daily bread'? Hunger itself does incomparably more to make Christ's kingdom come than ever money did, or ever will do while time lasts. Of course, money has its part, for everything has. And whoever has money is bound to use it as best he knows. But his best is generally an attempt to do saint-work by devil-proxy. And simple obedience – treating everyone you encounter as Christ would treat him, in the next five minutes, all your life long – will do more to further the coming of God's true kingdom, than all you could do with a million pounds, were it handed you to spend 'in his work' the moment you finish this sentence."

(MacDonald, 1988: 286)

The following notes on money matters focus largely on Hudson Taylor and the China Inland Mission, an outreach that stood in stark contrast to many others of its day, and perhaps even more so in today's myriad of "ministries" that seem to be clamoring for our money. As God leads you to hold out a hand of love and care to others, a look at the life and principles behind the China Inland Mission and its founder may be helpful.

We start by scrutinizing our approach to money, comparing our attitudes to those of Taylor.

On the one hand, Taylor had a deep contentedness in "travelling light". He consistently wished to make do with as little as possible. However, at one stage, the Mission had grown to the point that the modest accommodation was insufficient, and the need for larger quarters became pressing. Taylor looked around and, when he located premises that by our standards were tiny, he stated that

> *"The house seemed too large for us …"*

(Taylor & Taylor, 1918: 27)

We would probably be hesitant to occupy a property whose startling feature was that it actually had a window (but only one)!

Not only did Taylor seek to minimize mission expenditure and assets, but he also personally lived as simply as possible. Some leaders call their followers to an austere lifestyle, but choose to live extravagantly themselves. Taylor's minimalist life-style is apparent from the surprised journal of another who watched him shift into the new premises.

> *"Eighteen shillings for the transport of all their worldly belongings! And not only so: a day sufficed for packing, it would seem, and even less for settling into the new home."*

(Taylor & Taylor, 1918: 28)

In his book, *Money, Sex & Power*, Foster notes that while the love of money can destroy a person, a life that goes to the other extreme and avoids the wise and legitimate use of money is an unhealthy over-reaction. Hudson Taylor seemed to have a comfortable balance in money matters in that he was efficient and frugal in the use of funds, and lived in a very simple lifestyle, but he also did not condemn those who had money. In fact, he expressed appreciation to those who were well off and yet shared generously.

> *"[The property of some close friends], indeed, became a real oasis to all the family at Beaumont Street. How good it was to escape at times from the squalid surroundings of Whitechapel to the hills and lanes of Sussex! The fine old house and grounds, sloping down to a little lake with meadows beyond, were a paradise to the children, quite apart from the good cheer Mrs. Berger's hospitality provided."*
>
> (Taylor & Taylor, 1918: 26)

It would be easy for those living carefully within limited budgets to be judgmental towards others who had greater wealth. Taylor and his colleagues felt called to a life where they concentrated on the work at hand and trusted God for funds, while others had regular incomes and savings in bank accounts. The difference did not worry Taylor. He felt at peace about the life-style that was right *"… for them at any rate …"* and did not judge those with different values.

> *"… he was confirmed in the confidence that, <u>for them at any rate</u>, to give all their time and strength to the Lord's work and quietly wait His supplies was the right way."* [Emphasis mine]
>
> (Taylor & Taylor, 1918: 19)

It is one thing to be relaxed personally if we have little or an abundance, but how do we react when we perceive we need funds to further extend "God's work"? Again we look at Taylor's example to draw out principles in our attitude towards seeking and using money for "ministry". Taylor's way of faith is in stark contrast to so much of what we see in Christendom, from the practices of so-called televangelists down to the management of finances in local churches.

Avoid all debt

The China Inland Mission was a large affair, yet it may come as a surprise to some that it operated on a solid principle of having no debt.

> *"[Taylor] … told how the passage, 'Owe no man anything save to love one another,' had raised the question in his mind, 'Are we entitled to make exceptions in work for the Kingdom of God, and continuously to sigh under the oppression of debt?' His own conclusion had been that the words meant just what they said: that God is rich enough to supply 'all our need' as it arises, and that He likes to do so before we run into debt much better than afterwards; and he gave instances to show how, trusting Him to fulfill His own Word, and neither spending money before it was received nor making appeals for help, the seven hundred missionaries of the C.I.M. were actually sustained."*
>
> (Taylor & Taylor, 1918: 564)

For Taylor the principle of no debt, while he applied it to himself, was equally valid for the ministry as a whole.

> "... under no circumstances would he go into debt for the Mission any more than for himself."
>
> (Taylor & Taylor, 1918: 41)

Taylor believed that by taking this approach, rather than restricting God's work, it allowed God to restrict us if we were missing the mark!

> "To me it seemed that the teaching of God's Word was unmistakably clear: 'Owe no man anything.' To borrow money implied, to my mind, a contradiction of Scripture – a confession that God had withheld some good thing, and a determination to get for ourselves what He had not given. Could that which was wrong for one Christian to do be right for an association of Christians? Or could any amount of precedents make a wrong course justifiable? If the Word taught me anything, it taught me to have no connection with debt. I could not think that God was poor, that He was short of resources, or unwilling to supply any want of whatever work was really His. It seemed to me that if there were a lack of funds to carry on work, then to that degree, in that special development, or at that time, it could not be the work of God."
>
> (Taylor & Taylor, 1911: 430)

A very practical outworking of Taylor's principle was visible in the sending of further workers out to China. If there was enough money to send the willing workers, he would *send* them and trust God to *sustain* them. If there was not enough to send them, then they would not be sent by borrowing to cover travel costs. Taylor was completely relaxed in his confidence that God would supply what was needed when it was needed, if it was needed.

> "[The mission committed to] send out suitable workers as funds permitted, and keep clear of debt. ...
>
> 'It is really just as easy,' Mr. Taylor pointed out, 'for God to give beforehand; and He much prefers to do so. He is too wise to allow His purposes to be frustrated for lack of a little money; but money wrongly placed or obtained in unspiritual ways is sure to hinder blessing.
>
> And what does going into debt really mean? It means that God has not supplied your need. You trusted Him, but He has not given you the money; so you supply yourself, and borrow. If we can only wait right up to the time, God cannot lie, God cannot forget: He is pledged to supply all our need.'"
>
> (Taylor & Taylor, 1918: 54-55)

Never ask for money

Let's assume you have discovered a ministry area that you believe is important and God-ordained. Let's also assume that, like many others in such a situation, you see great potential for expansion of the good work if only you can acquire solid funding. And finally, let's assume that you have adopted Taylor's principle of avoiding debt. The challenge then may be seen as how to get more money without borrowing. And a natural strategy is to seek the financial support of those with money that might be happy to fund your ministry.

However, if we think about it, we will hopefully realize that not all "natural" responses are necessarily godly. Taylor believed the China Inland Mission was important and God-ordained. The mission had times where its expansion would apparently be hastened by more money. Yet Taylor steadfastly not only refused to borrow, but to even ask for money.

One of his motivations for refusing to give appeals, or to even allow others to pass around collection plates on his behalf, was that he did not want to benefit at the possible expense of other causes.

> *"[Hudson Taylor and his friends] saw that the faith-principles of the Mission must be carried to the point of making no appeals for money nor even taking a collection. If the Mission could be sustained by the faithful care of God in answer to prayer and prayer alone, without subscription lists or solicitation of any kind for funds, then it might grow up among the older societies without the danger of diverting gifts from their accustomed channels. It might even be helpful to other agencies by directing attention to the Great Worker, and affording a practical illustration of its underlying principle that 'God Himself, God alone, is sufficient for God's own work.'"*

(Taylor & Taylor, 1918: 52)

Another reason Taylor had for not turning to fundraising activities was so that he could focus on God and let God look after the finances.

> *"[The decision to refuse to allow an appeal for funds as part of any talk] left the speaker free in spirit, occupied with God rather than man, and more eager to give than to get."*

(Taylor & Taylor, 1918: 54)

Taylor's faith was beautiful in its simplicity. He believed that if we depend on God, we won't need to depend on appeals because God is faithful to supply.

> *"We are convinced that if there were less solicitation for money and more dependence on the power of the Holy Ghost and the deepening of the spiritual life, the experience [of not needing to appeal for money because God has abundantly supplied] would be a common one in every branch of Christian work."*

(Taylor & Taylor, 1918: 60)

A small story exemplifies the rest to be found in a life of faith.

> *"When [Hudson Taylor] was leaving next day for Rochester, N.Y., a Mr. Wilson accompanied him to the station. He felt it impressed upon him that Mr. Taylor did not have sufficient money for the tickets (a matter of about eight pounds), and upon inquiry found this to be the case.*
>
> *'Why did you not tell us?' asked Mr. Wilson, who had decided the night before to take the tickets and had come provided.*

> *'My Father knew,'* was the quiet answer; *'it was not necessary to speak to any of His children about it.'* "
>
> (Taylor & Taylor, 1918: 452)

The incidental anecdote of Taylor's dependence on God for the little needs such as a train ticket may not be well known by many. In contrast, I suspect a lot more would have heard of George Müller's grand faith that was instrumental in the establishment of a chain of orphanages in a culture where children without parents were at great risk, and where government care was negligible. Yet these two men not only lived according to common principles, but were actually close friends.

> "*[Mr. Müller spoke on] the Orphan Houses and ... hundreds of children, sheltered and provided for without a penny of endowment, without an appeal of any kind for help, or even making their wants known.*"
>
> (Taylor & Taylor, 1918: 60)

Many a time Mueller had the children sit at the empty table while he prayed for the provision of food and, lo and behold, someone would arrive at the door with enough food for everyone.

Another quite challenging story is told about Taylor, leading to the conclusion that it is better for God to speak to a person about their response than to depend on the response that might be whipped up by man-induced emotional appeals for funds.

> "*To this new friend it seemed a peculiar arrangement to have a missionary meeting without a collection, but understanding it to be Mr. Taylor's wish the announcement had been made accordingly. When the time came, however, and the speaker proved unusually interesting, Colonel Puget realised that people would give generously if only they had the opportunity.*
>
> *Rising therefore at the close of the address, he said that interpreting the feelings of the audience by his own, he took it upon himself to alter the decision about the collection. Many present were moved by the condition of things Mr. Taylor had represented, and would go away burdened unless they could express practical sympathy. Contrary therefore to previous announcements, an opportunity would now be given – But at that point Mr. Taylor interposed, asking to be allowed to add a few words.*
>
> *It was his earnest desire, he said, that his hearers should go away burdened. Money was not the chief thing in the Lord's work, especially money easily given, under the influence of emotion. Much as he appreciated their kind intention, he would far rather have each one go home to ask the Lord very definitely what He would have them do. If it were to give of their substance, they could send a contribution to their own or any other society. But in view of the appalling facts of heathenism, it might be more costly gifts the Lord was seeking; perhaps a son or daughter or one's own life-service. No amount of money could save a single soul. What was wanted was that men and women filled with the Holy Spirit should give themselves to the work in China and to the work of prayer at home. For the support of God-sent missionaries funds would never be lacking.*

> *'You made a great mistake, if I may say so,' remarked his host at supper. 'The people were really interested. We might have had a good collection.'*
>
> *In vain Mr. Taylor explained the financial basis of the Mission and his desire to avoid even the appearance of conflicting with other societies. Colonel Puget, though sympathetic, was unconvinced.*
>
> *Next morning, however, he appeared somewhat late at breakfast, explaining that he had not had a good night. In the study, after handing Mr. Taylor several contributions given for the Mission, he went on to say:*
>
> *'I felt last evening that you were wrong about the collection, but now I see things differently. Lying awake in the night, as I thought of that stream of souls in China, a thousand every hour going out into the dark, I could only cry, 'Lord, what wilt Thou have me to do?' I think I have His answer.'*
>
> *And he handed Mr. Taylor a cheque for five hundred pounds.*
>
> *'If there had been a collection I should have given a five-pound note,' he added. 'This cheque is the result of no small part of the night spent in prayer.'"*
>
> (Taylor & Taylor, 1918: 63-64)

Some within Christendom hold a different view to Taylor on the teaching "owe no man anything". For example, some teach that you do not owe money if you meet the loan payments on time.

The bottom line is that it is possible that you may feel a clear conscience in borrowing, and such a matter is between you and God. What I do suggest though, is that you check that you are not doing so to grow a ministry ahead of God's plans or for your own glory.

And whether you choose to borrow or not, much can be learned from Taylor's attitude in allowing God to prompt others to give rather than us providing the "conscience" to move people to give to us!

"Right" money, "wrong" money

Another contrast between Taylor's practices and those we so often see relates to his views on "wrong money". He believed not all money was equal. If it was given freely with right motives and at God's leading, then it would be fruitful. But if it was given, for example, through pressure to put money in a collection plate, then he would rather not have it. And he went further, stating that it might in fact be harmful to God's purposes.

> "It was no figure of speech with Mr. Taylor when he said … that he would rather have a consecrated shilling, representing real spiritual fellowship, than an unconsecrated pound; and gifts given spontaneously, apart from solicitation or the pressure even of a collection, were more likely to have that quality."
>
> (Taylor & Taylor, 1918: 53)

> "I am far more afraid of unconsecrated money than of no money at all … The Lord did not tell his disciples to carry loads of provisions into the wilderness. There was a

lad there with five barley loaves and two fishes; it was enough. The Lord wants His people to be, not rich, but in full fellowship with Him Who is rich."

(Taylor & Taylor, 1918: 429-430)

"We might indeed have had a guaranteed fund if we had wished it; but we felt it was unneeded and would do harm. Money wrongly placed and money given from wrong motives are both to be greatly dreaded. We can afford to have as little as the Lord chooses to give, but we cannot afford to have unconsecrated money, or to have money placed in the wrong position. Far better have no money at all, even to buy food with; for there are plenty of ravens in China, and the Lord could send them again with bread and flesh."

(Taylor & Taylor, 1918: 42)

Be judicious in your handling of money

We need to be careful how we use money personally. Hudson Taylor was in his late fifties and weary when it was suggested he upgrade his train ticket to a more comfortable class. Taylor responded:

"It is the Lord's money, you know; we had better be very careful about it."

(Taylor & Taylor, 1918: 476)

We also need to be careful how we handle money given by others for ministry. There have been times where local church leaders have collected money for a specific purpose, and who have publicly declared it will only be used for that purpose, yet who have used these nominated gifts for other purposes—like pastoral salaries! Taylor's ethics, thankfully, were starkly different.

"Repeatedly we have been without funds for the general requirements of the whole Mission, though for particular objects there have been balances which, of course, could not be touched."

(Taylor & Taylor, 1918: 514)

Act according to God's principles; finances are secondary

As with all aspects of our lives, one simple test on the "rightness" of our actions is to consider how we might act if it were publicly visible. But even that is not enough, for some cleverly-presented actions can mask wrong motives—but God does see our hearts. At the end of the day it is not about how much money we have (or do not have), but it is about our walk with God.

"Was money after all the chief thing, or was it really true that a walk that pleases God and ensures spiritual blessing is of more importance in His service?"

(Taylor & Taylor, 1918: 52)

If we seek first God's Kingdom and His principles, then we can and must trust Him to meet our needs.

"Depend upon it, God's work done in God's way will never lack God's supplies."

(Taylor & Taylor, 1918: 42)

God can be trusted to meet our *needs*. We need to be cautious, though. Some have followed the so-called "prosperity doctrine", but God does not promise to meet our *wishes*. If we want to look at how little might be required to meet just basic needs, we do not have to look further than the life of Jesus, who did not even have a place to lay His head.

CHAPTER 46:

SUCCESS CAN TRAP YOU

Perceived "success" can be dangerous—be it the apparent success of others that you may be tempted to copy, or the feeling that you have discovered your own strategy for success. We look at both temptations, beginning with the danger of looking to the winning ways of others.

Avoid the "success formula" of others

Some forms of "ministry" are hidden works of grace; while others, by their nature, are much more visible. The more noticeable forms can attract the attention of those who somehow are drawn to evidences of "success". As stated earlier, the "glory" in the list of common temptations—gold, glory and girls – can cause detriment if not outright downfall of an otherwise fruitful work.

Don't copy others

A subtle yet common way of being sidetracked from God's best can be searching for success strategies or formulas, and there are plenty of books on the shelves of Christian bookshops along these lines. For example, I am appalled by titles such as John Maxwell's book, *The 21 Irrefutable Laws of Leadership: Follow them and people will follow you*. How can *anyone* make claims that *their* views are irrefutable? (And as a side issue, note the subtitle—it seems to be all about getting people to follow you, rather than helping people to follow Jesus.)

We should not even be concerning ourselves as to whether or not our work is seen by others (or ourselves) as somehow being successful. And we most certainly should not be trying to copy the patterns of others to achieve such "success".

A fundamental reason to avoid copying others is the reality that we all are different even if we try to be the same. We have different needs and different callings. *No-one* can come up with a "one size fits all" approach and expect it to be appropriate to the needs of all cultures. Edward Dayton and David Fraser, in a paper titled *Strategy*, state,

> "The Standard Solution Strategy works out a particular way of doing things, then uses this same approach in every situation. ... The problem with the Standard Solution Strategy is, first, that there is a tendency not to take into account what others are doing. Because this strategy has a standard solution, it assumes that the problems are standard. Second, a standard strategy usually assumes that everyone will participate and understand what the strategy is. Obviously this does not always work. Third, a standard strategy usually grows out of one culture and has more and more difficulty as it moves into new contexts."
>
> (Dayton & Fraser, 1980: 570-571)

To try to copy what worked for one person, or in one situation, is to deny the uniqueness of the call given to you. We can and should be open to learn from others, but to mindlessly apply the style of another to your situation may be not only ineffective but dangerous, or even downright wrong.

> "While principles may be universal, practices certainly are not. Inevitably methodology carries with it the message, 'This worked for us, so it will obviously work for you,' ...
>
> ... We have occasionally tried programs that worked great elsewhere but in our particular situation seemed forced and unnatural."
>
> (Tillapaugh, 1982: 139)

> "Whenever a method is successful, the temptation arises to think it will work anywhere at any time ... Every new situation requires a new evaluation and often new, tailor-made methods."
>
> (Wagner, 1974: 579)

Rather than copying others, how much better to leave your approach to the One who knows best what is needed, in each unique situation.

Beware those who join you and try to introduce new ideas from outside

It is one error for *you* to consciously or unconsciously try to apply the "success formula" of others to your own situation. There is another danger, though. It is the *outsider* who comes into your culture and dominates, trying to enforce his or her ways. As God leads you day by day into discovery and expression of your own unique form of service, you must be on the lookout for others who may be attracted to what you are doing but who will insensitively try to get you to do things the "right" way—that is, *their* way. Watch out for this and confront it if it occurs.

In the context of missionaries building bridges to people in different cultures, McGavran suggests,

> "[Amongst groups of people] ...natural growth can be and, alas, sometimes has been, slowed down by the atmosphere and techniques of the all-pervading gathered colony approach. ... [These trends must be] recognized and renounced ..."
>
> (McGavran, 1981: 290)

Confrontation does not mean attacking the *person*. He or she may genuinely believe that the ways that were successful elsewhere must surely work here, too. Don't shoot the messenger, but do identify the attempt to colonize your work with foreign ideas.

Beware the grab for power by those outside who would be leaders

We have noted the danger of you trying to find a "success formula" and to copy it. We have looked at how others may try to do a similar thing by joining you and importing their favorite practices. Such actions may simply be a well-intentioned strategy to improve what they see you doing. We now look at another alternative motivation—it may be a controlling maneuver to gain power and to use you and your ministry to further their own ambitions.

One clear sign is any person who claims to have found the one true way. But some are less obvious in their approach. In his novel *Dawn of Liberty*, Phillips warns of the wrong motives of those who sometimes appear keen to help you in your new work.

> "They all come to start their own works, as they call them … They come to us because they think we can provide them a local base from which they can establish … what they so proudly call a work of God. … But we are nothing to them if we express hesitation. They do not see us as fellow brothers and sisters. Their only desire is to expand their own organizations. If we will join them and let them affix their label upon us, then great is their enthusiasm. …
>
> But if we try to say, 'God is at work here and we too are seeking to spread the gospel. We do not want to become part of your organization, but we do have needs that perhaps . . .,' we do not even complete such an explanation before they are gone to find some other place where they can erect their building and put up a sign to proclaim the work that has their all-important organizational name attached to it."

(Phillips, 1995: 446-447)

The attempt by some to control those who would minister for God is abundantly blatant in the following story.

> "On New Year's Eve 1868, William Booth was preparing for the Watch Night Service when he received a telegram from Henry Reed. It invited him to travel down to Dunorlan on the last train. That William accepted the invitation, at such a time and on such a night, illustrates his continued susceptibility to men of power and wealth – a weakness which grew with the years. So, abandoning the Mission's New Year observances, he travelled down to Tunbridge Wells. … [Reed was willing to buy some land for a permanent base] for £3-4,000, and would gladly spend up to £7,000 more building a hall which would accommodate a 2,000-strong congregation – as long as William Booth would agree to fill it. But it was clear that, although [William Booth] would be called Superintendent, William would not superintend in any practical sense. Reed was explicit that, unless the new mission was run in the way he chose, he would reclaim the deeds. And one of the requirements was that his resident minister would preach there and nowhere else."

(Hattersley, 2000: 165-166)

Attempts by others to control you may be less obvious than one who wants to "buy" his own private minister. Not all tactics are so blatant, but the same danger exists in many forms.

The above warnings are about those who would come and try to take over your work.

Beware of seeking the advantages of joining with a recognized force

A totally different direction, and just as wrong, is to take your work and try to hand it over to a "proper" organization. The catalyst is the reverse; the outcome is equally disastrous. An extract from an earlier quotation describes a powerful work of God in a factory that was derailed because the participants wanted to align it with the established works of others, in this case local churches. The local churches were seen (wrongly) as providing a necessary aspect to the work God had already established and blessed.

> *"We decided to send people out to churches because there were so many of us and thought we should get them to church. I suppose we were already a church in our own right, but because the church had no influence in what God was doing we started to get people into churches in the area, in the city where they lived. Unfortunately, the church didn't seem to appreciate what God had done and told us that they should have been saved at church and not at work. But we carried on trying to get people integrated into churches. This caused many problems, but that's another story."*

(Oliver & Thwaites, 2001: 143)

The authors comment that these local churches were guilty of

> *"... rebuking [Jim], trying to wrestle control of what was happening and then fighting with each other to lay hold of more congregation members ..."*

(Oliver & Thwaites, 2001: 161)

The authors also expressed the opinion that

> *"What Jim was politely saying in relation to the church as construct was that once the churches in the area began to enter into the move of God it became confused, political and over time it was stopped. God forgive us!"*

(Oliver & Thwaites, 2001: 143)

Discover your own God-given style

Tillapaugh notes that the Navigators invest in training of their staff but, subsequently, when staff members are assigned to field work, they are completely trusted to act as they see fit.

> *"[A Navigator member] is given a great degree of freedom. He is expected to remain faithful to his calling and to get the job done. He may use his house as a base or he may not; perhaps he will plan evangelistic rallies, perhaps not. He decides whether it is best to contact students on or off campus. He is not burdened with committees or a fortress mentality that expects him to use the church building as a base of operation.*

> *He is free to perform his ministry the way he feels it ought to be done. Yes, he has counsel and help but he is expected to plan and carry out his ministry in the way that is most effective for his particular target group."*
>
> (Tillapaugh, 1982: 53)

Similarly, it is noted by Beaver that the Moravians explicitly instructed those from their ranks who were moving to another location to avoid following the patterns that might have been successful in their original setting, telling them

> *"…not to apply 'the Herrnhut yardstick' (i.e., German home base standards) to other peoples and to be alert to the recognition of the God-given distinctive traits, characteristics and strong points of those people."*
>
> (Beaver, 1970: 198).

Like the Navigators and the Moravians, we too must avoid copying the apparent success patterns of others and let God guide us.

Beware the pride of your achievements

We have noted the dangers of allowing the successes of others to distract you from your own unique calling. Instead, I am trying to encourage you to discover the ways God would lead *you* that are distinctive.

But herein lies another danger. If you are pioneering a new work, it can be easy for you to take pride in its outcome rather than humbly accepting that God used a fallible person to achieve His purposes.

Too often people try to measure success in terms that can be measured on membership registers or accounting books. Rinehart warns that such thinking can be a trap:

> *"If success must be measured by numbers and size, we will forever be prisoner of those things that make us feel … successful …"*
>
> (Rinehart, 1998: 158)

One danger can be the mistaken belief that if something is deemed to be successful (according to some particular measure), it must be right.

> *"The popular assumption today is that the methods and values of the business world are right and good because, for the most part, they seem to work. Pragmatism is the guiding light."*
>
> (Rinehart, 1998: 86)

Rinehart tells the story of a church member who had written to the leadership about some concerns. In summary, the leaders responded that his concerns simply could not be valid,

> *"… because this church has grown by leaps and bounds. People write to us from all over the country wanting to know how we've done it."*
>
> (Rinehart, 1998: 53)

Rinehart then goes on to comment,

> *"This church board based its authority on the cornerstone of pragmatic effort. The church worked well, so how could it be wrong? By all visible standards, by all the eye could see and measure, there was little cause for concern. And since authority was wedded to image and performance, then the basic assumptions – the substance of the issues – didn't require a soul-searching evaluation. Who can argue with success? But now, several years later, those early concerns once addressed to the board have proven to be critical issues hindering ministry. Many of the board members have since acknowledged this."*
>
> (Rinehart, 1998: 53)

The founders of the Salvation Army achieved numerical growth, but the apparent success of their approach blinded them to seeing alternatives.

> *"... the main barrier [to possible mutually beneficial links with other local churches] ... was the indisputable fact that the Army was far too much intoxicated with its own success to lay aside its extravagances."*
>
> (Hattersley, 2000: 277)

> *"But the Booths – infatuated by their own success – were neither subtle nor sophisticated and, in consequence, saw no reason to change their ways. So, unthinking, on they charged towards the inevitable collision [between them and the church leaders in whose circuits they moved as evangelists]."*
>
> (Hattersley, 2000: 89)

When things seem to be working well, it is natural to want to formalize the formula for success, to enshrine it for perpetuity. As we venture into new initiatives we must be careful not to preserve the way we have done things that seem to have worked well so far—God may be about to radically move us to a new adventure.

> *"That which used to be a new wineskin will reject that which is a new wineskin. Or, to express it another way, once a movement becomes the establishment, its very nature, fixed and established, causes it to reject any fresh, new, spiritual movement. The establishment dislikes change. It has become too comfortable."*
>
> (Brown, 2002: 144)

As noted above, apparent success in a "ministry" can be dangerous to the whole outreach. The ministry can too easily become resistant to new thinking, and become ossified in a vain attempt to hold onto gains already made.

Perceived success can also be dangerous to the individual. Bill from Alcoholics Anonymous warns of such hazards:

> *"Disagreeable or unexpected problems are not the only ones that call for self-control. We must be quite as careful when we begin to achieve some measure of importance and material success. For no people have ever loved personal triumph more than we*

have loved them; we drank of success as of a wine which could never fail to make us feel elated. Blinded by prideful self-confidence, we were apt to play the big shot."

(Bill, 1967: 19)

And Bill's recommended solution to pride? Healthy humility, based on recognition of God's grace.

"Now that we're in A.A. and sober, winning back the esteem of our friends and business associates, we find that we still need to exercise special vigilance. As an insurance against the dangers of big-shot-ism, we can often check ourselves by remembering that we are today sober only by the grace of God and that any success we may be having is far more His success than ours."

(Bill, 1967: 19)

A moving example of willingness to serve humbly in spite of prior "success" can be seen in the life of Henri Nouwen. He was a distinguished writer and lecturer, yet gave ten years of his life to the care of severely disabled people, including one named Bill (not to be confused with "Bill" from Alcoholics Anonymous as quoted above):

"It was an awkward transition at first. Accustomed to addressing large crowds of admirers, he found it jarring to speak to people who could not understand big words, who grunted, drooled and made spastic movements during his homilies. If a resident named Bill did not like the priest's sermon, he would interrupt mass to tell him so. Nouwen found that his beautiful words and arguments had little relevance to what the residents were going through. To these damaged bodies and damaged minds, his prestigious résumé meant nothing. They couldn't even read his books. All that mattered was whether he loved them. ...

Nouwen became so attached to the people in his home, and so dependent on them, that he began taking them with him on his speaking trips. Whereas other well-known speakers might command an honorarium of five or ten thousand dollars, Nouwen would ask for just five hundred (which he would sign over to [the home for the disabled]) and a plane ticket for himself and a companion. A reporter for the Wall Street Journal remembers attending one such engagement in North Carolina. When Nouwen invited his friend Bill – the same one who interrupted mass – to the microphone to speak, the reporter thought to himself that people had come a long way to hear Henri Nouwen, not Bill.

In order to give Bill support, Nouwen stood next to him on the stage. Bill looked out over the audience, and suddenly all his words failed him. He was overcome. He simply laid his head on Nouwen's shoulder and wept. Much that Nouwen said has passed from the memory of that North Carolina audience; the memory of Bill resting his head on a priest's shoulder has not. ...

[Nouwen was assigned] one person to look after in particular: Adam. ... Adam was the weakest and most disabled person in the community. Although in his twenties, Adam could not speak, dress or undress himself, could not walk alone or eat without

help. Instead of counseling Ivy League students and juggling a busy schedule, Nouwen had to learn a new set of skills: how to feed, change and bathe Adam, how to support his glass as he drank, how to push his wheelchair over a road full of potholes. He ministered not to leaders and intellectuals but to a young man who was considered by many a vegetable, a useless person who should not have been born. Yet Nouwen gradually learned that he, not Adam, was the chief beneficiary in this strange, misfitted relationship.

From the hours spent with Adam, Nouwen gained an inner peace that made most of his other, more high-minded tasks seem boring and superficial. As he sat beside that silent child-man, he realised how obsessive, how marked with rivalry and competition, was his prior drive towards success in academia. From Adam he learned that 'what makes us human is not our mind but our heart, not our ability to think but our ability to love.'"

(Yancey, 2001: 294-296)

Don't seek for big, "important" things you can do for God. Be prepared to simply do what God calls you to do. We, like Nouwen, must be obedient and humble so that we are content performing the little acts of grace to which God leads.

"In experiences of hiddenness we learn that the ministry of small things is a necessary prerequisite to the ministry of power."

(Foster, 1985: 618)

"When the people asked John the Baptist what they should do to exhibit true repentance, he counseled, 'He who has two coats, let him share ...' The point of his teaching is its triviality – small, simple ordinary things. John was calling people to the ministry of small things."

(Foster, 1985: 618)

"The ministry of small things is among the most important ministries we are given. In some ways it is more important than the ministry of power. The work of power occurs now and again, but the work of small things occurs repeatedly throughout the course of our days. Because our daily tasks afford us constant opportunity to engage in the ministry of small things, it is through this work that we become most intimately acquainted with God."

(Foster, 1985: 618)

"... in the small corners of life, in those areas of service that will never be newsworthy or gain us any recognition, we must hammer out the meaning of obedience. Amid the obscurity of family and friends, neighbours and work associates, we find God."

(Foster, 1985: 619)

"And it is this finding of God, this intimacy with God, that is essential to the exercise of power. The ministry of small things must be prior to and more valued than the ministry of power. Without this perspective we will view power as a 'big deal'.

Make no mistake, the religion of the 'big deal' stands in opposition to the way of Christ. It is this spirit that leads to the cruelest excesses. It is one of the greatest hindrances today to a free exercise of the ministry of power."

(Foster, 1985: 619)

Not only must we be alert to the dangers of being perceived as contributing to a "successful" ministry, we must never take action that might force growth ahead of God's plans. Let Him set the agenda, let Him set the pace, let Him choose the workers, let Him choose the work. And if we happen to be chosen by Him to play some small part, let Him take the credit for any benefit or growth.

"It may seem slower ... ... to take the time to build disciples who are free to follow the Spirit and to be placed by Him where and when His program calls for it. But somehow, I believe that even if it takes longer to go that route, it is of greater eternal value to have the Spirit doing the work through the few who will let Him do it, than to have many trying to do the Spirit's work in the energy of the flesh, and then claiming God's work has been done, when in reality it has been mostly man's work."

(Girard, 1972: 167)

CHAPTER 47:
"CHANGE" CAN TRAP YOU

Give yourself permission to change

Buckingham tells the story of a coastal surf lifesaving ministry that stagnated and built themselves a fancy clubhouse, but in a safer location—further from the coast! This original group had lost the vision and gone stale. However, a new group responded to the obvious gap left by the original ministry.

> "Seeing the need, some of the people along the shore built a crude little lifesaving station. … The lifesavers were deeply committed to their task. … With no thought of themselves, they kept constant watch over the sea …"
>
> (Buckingham, 1978: 295)

But they too went soft.

> "As the years went by, I understand, the new station slowly went through the same changes that had occurred in the old."
>
> (Buckingham, 1978: 298)

There seems to be a natural tendency to sit back and take comfort in the status quo. It would appear that we have to be careful not to fall prey to the same temptation. If God directs a ministry to continue (and He may not), it should stay alive and vibrant, changing just as cells change and grow.

In the context of missionary evangelism, Taylor's life challenges us. He sought to keep pushing the frontiers rather than resting on the laurels of achievements to date and being satisfied with natural growth in established stations.

> "Spreading the knowledge of the Truth – this was indeed the aim kept in view; and though it meant deliberately forgoing the more rapid ingathering to be expected from

> *concentrating upon older work, Mr. Taylor held firmly to the principle [of seeing fruitfulness from scattering the seed widely].*"
>
> (Taylor & Taylor, 1918: 351)

It can feel not only more comfortable, but also safer, to stick with what is familiar and what seems to have "worked" so far. It requires faith to push on to new frontiers, willing to move forward even if the full, final destination is unclear.

> "*The question isn't what you may or may not believe in your head. The question is: Do you want to be a follower of Jesus? …*
>
> *[Jesus] said [to the disciples] 'Follow me.' Then he told them what to do. No long sermons about what they had to believe first. He said 'Come along with me. As we go, here's what I want you to do.' It was a pretty simple message that preachers have been making more and more complicated ever since.*"
>
> (Phillips, 1996: 219)

Some may feel that they have already "got it", and that they do not need to change. Bill from Alcoholics Anonymous shares that, in their line of work, many see themselves as different and beyond the need of applying the principles of others. But in time, they recognized that we all are needy people.

Our personal growth lies in how we face the challenge of ongoing change as God directs.

> "*In the beginning, it was four whole years before A.A. brought permanent sobriety to even one alcoholic woman. Like the 'high bottoms,' the women said they were different; A.A. couldn't be for them. But as the communication was perfected, mostly by the women themselves, the picture changed.*
>
> *This process of identification and transmission has gone on and on. The Skid-Rower said he was different. Even more loudly, the socialite (or Park Avenue stumblebum) said the same – so did the artists and the professional people, the rich, the poor, the religious, the agnostic, the Indians and the Eskimos, the veterans, and the prisoners.*
>
> *But nowadays all of these, and legions more, soberly talk about how very much alike all of us alcoholics are when we admit that the chips are finally down.*"
>
> (Bill, 1967: 24)

The alcoholic who didn't want to face the challenge of change because the other alcoholics were "different" had to realize that all of us need to change if we are to grow. There are none exempt from the need to change.

In fact, we are encouraged to be constantly open to change, even if it may go against our natural tendencies. However, we should be wary of *artificially* forcing change.

Two observed strategies to hurry along change come to mind.

The first is a clear warning against the old, hierarchical model of command-and-control. If we want to see change happen, and happen now, Oliver and Thwaites recognize that the old-style *can* force speedier change. But it comes at a price, and the irony is that the very mechanisms that can force change quickly are the same ones that will result in stagnation further down the track. That's obviously not a strategy to be recommended.

> *"When we build in line with the old front-end hierarchical leadership style, we do find that things happen more quickly. People respond more easily to things that are clear, simply and easily showcased inside a meeting, and done by others with resource and gifting. However, down the track in, say, five, ten or twenty years, these same people wake up to find that things inside the construct are slowing down. Inertia sets in as the machine now consumes more energy to keep itself going than it can get in each week. Too many movements down through history have simply collapsed under the weight of their own self-infested glory."*
>
> (Oliver & Thwaites, 2001: 103)

A second strategy to move things along more quickly is to borrow money to speed up God's work. We've already discussed this strategy, and Girard's words remind us of the folly of trying to move ahead of God's pace:

> *"I am now convinced that ways must be found to give the Lord practical 'veto power' over all ... spending. This may sound archaic in the light of modern ... business practices, but I wonder if working toward a 'cash basis' for most ... spending might not allow Him to exercise His Headship by simply not providing funds for programs and projects outside His will. In certain instances, under clear leadership of the Spirit, the Body might still decide on a step of faith that takes it beyond its visible means. But this would be the exception, not the rule."*
>
> (Girard, 1972: 205)

Taylor reinforces the views of Girard:

> *"The position of faith is incompatible with borrowing or going into debt, or forcing our way forward when the Lord closes the door before us ... If we propose a certain extension for which the Lord sees the time has not come, or which is not in accordance with His will, how can He more clearly guide us than by withholding the means? It would be a serious mistake, therefore, to refuse to listen to the Lord's 'No,' and by borrowing or going into debt do the thing to which He had objected by withholding the needed funds or facilities. All the work we are engaged in is His rather than ours; and if the Master can afford to wait, surely the servant can also."*
>
> (Taylor & Taylor, 1918: 564)

Remember that others don't need your permission to change

It is one thing for me to give myself permission to change. That takes faith and a willingness to be obedient to God's call, no matter where it may lead. Others also have the right to change, but what happens when the changes they are thinking of overlap with the ministry we are both involved in, especially if the change will impact a ministry I had founded.

There is a dilemma here. On the one hand, I need to prevent others coming in and taking over what I believe was the ministry God led me to. Yet on the other hand, there are also real dangers that I may get unnecessarily protective of "my" ministry, and may resist suggestions for change from my colleagues who in turn may believe that God has called them to open new facets of the ministry. Maybe it *is* God who wants to take the ministry to a new phase, and by "protecting" it, I may be in fact an obstacle to that God-inspired change.

So how do I discern the difference? I have individuals suggesting a change in direction, and the people involved may actually be genuine in their desire for "improvement", believing that God is leading them. I do not believe there is a simple, fool-proof answer, but unity and a reliance on God to lead will get us all through if we seek His will together.

Just as others must not force their views on me, I must not try to enforce my views on others.

One step in gaining freedom from protective practices (and "old system" ways) is to consciously refuse the temptation to even attempt to shape others to our way of thinking. By all means share our perspective, but we must not coerce others to align with us, just as we must not let others shape our way of thinking and acting—it must always come back to what we believe that God is leading us to do.

> *"Consistently, Jesus refused to use coercive power. He knowingly let one of his disciples betray him and then surrendered himself without protest to his captors. It never ceases to amaze me that Christian hope rests on a man whose message was rejected and whose love was spurned, who was condemned as a criminal and given a sentence of capital punishment.*
>
> *Despite Jesus' plain example, many of his followers have been unable to resist choosing the way of Herod over that of Jesus. The Crusaders who pillaged the Near East, the conquistadors who converted the New World at the point of a sword, the Christian explorers in Africa who cooperated with the slave trade – we are still feeling aftershocks from their mistakes. History shows that when the church uses the tools of the world's kingdom, it becomes as ineffectual, or as tyrannical, as any other power structure. And whenever the church has intermingled with the state (the Holy Roman Empire, Cromwell's England, Calvin's Geneva), the appeal of the faith suffers as well. Ironically, our respect in the world declines in proportion to how vigorously we attempt to force others to adopt our point of view."*

(Yancey, 1995: 246)

Martin Luther recognized that change could come about either by force or by peaceful means, but

> *"... the way of peace is the only sure path in the long-run. He held by this firmly, and risked his life among the infuriated peasants as readily as when he stood before the Emperor and the Diet at Worms."*

(Lindsay, 1996: 14).

Martin Luther said,

> "I will preach it, I will talk of it, I will write about it, but I will not use force or compulsion with anyone ..."
>
> (Lindsay, 1996: 122).

Under this influence, change *did* occur.

> "There was no concerted action, no plan of operation, no active incitement, but everywhere [change did occur] ... The movement was so universal in all German-speaking lands, so silent, so natural, that Ranke can compare it to nothing else save the warm rays of the spring sun quickening and making sprout the seed which has laid 'happed' in a tilled and sown field."
>
> (Lindsay, 1996: 127-128).

The message is simple. We must not try to steer God's people according to our own clever schemes. Instead, we are to trust God to lead others as He chooses. And the best way to achieve this is to draw others to God, not to us.

> "Our responsibility ... is not to change a believer's life; only the power of the Trinity can do that. Our obligation is to help believers focus on what the Father, Son, and Holy Spirit are doing in their lives, and on how to grow and minister according to God's unique design and calling. A major thrust of our equipping process is to encourage an authentic relationship and intimacy with God. Growth and ministry will then flow out of that authenticity."
>
> (Rinehart, 1998: 130-131)

Sometimes the perceived founder of an initiative will subtly (or not so subtly) convey the message that he or she is the holder of truth, and that those who fail to follow them blindly risk falling into error. I can't emphasize strongly enough that we must diligently prevent this mentality and practice creeping into our own fields of endeavor. Each follower of God is just that—a follower of God, not a follower of any human, including you or me. Maybe some will miss the mark, but we would be blatantly arrogant to deny the possibility that they may be right and we may be wrong.

And even if a particular emphasis is right at one point in time, things change. As a colleague of mine has often said, each generation must discover truth for themselves.

> "If a ministry is geared for teens, it's great while we're teenagers, but someday we all turn 20. If a ministry is geared for 18-35 year olds, what happens at 36? Perhaps the ministry is geared to street people. What happens when we go straight?"
>
> (Tillapaugh, 1982: 22)

> "While the fundamentals of the faith are indeed changeless, the external trappings and comfortable forms of conveying its truth should be in flux with every generation."
>
> (Rinehart, 1998: 158)

Of course those that work with us or branch away from us may make mistakes. But so do we. We must trust God to let others learn from their mistakes, just as we learn from ours. Bill from Alcoholics Anonymous saw suppression of such learning as a sure path to loss of usefulness:

> *"Let us always remember that any society of men and women that cannot freely correct its own faults must surely fall into decay if not into collapse. Such is the universal penalty for the failure to go on growing. Just as each A.A. must continue to take his moral inventory and act upon it, so must our whole Society if we are to survive and if we are to serve usefully and well."*
>
> (Bill, 1967: 65)

> *"Implicit throughout A.A.'s Traditions is the confession that our Fellowship has its sins. We admit that we have character defects as a society and that these defects threaten us continually."*
>
> (Bill, 1967: 149)

While others may share their vision with us, we must encourage them to develop the practice of continuously checking their vision and direction with God, and we must not control their conclusions.

> *"In the years ahead we shall, of course, make mistakes. Experience has taught us that we need have no fear of doing this, providing that we always remain willing to confess our faults and to correct them promptly. Our growth as individuals has depended upon this healthy process of trial and error. So will our growth as a fellowship."*
>
> (AAWS, 1957: 231)

This practice of continued re-evaluation reflects the reality that, while God is unchanging, we are constantly changing. If that is not the case, we stop growing.

> *"Change is the characteristic of all growth. From drinking to sobriety, from dishonesty to honesty, from conflict to serenity, from hate to love, from childish dependence to adult responsibility – all this and infinitely more represent change for the better.*
>
> *Such changes are accomplished by a belief in and a practice of sound principles. Here we must needs discard bad or ineffective principles in favor of good ones that work. Even good principles can sometimes be displaced by the discovery of still better ones.*
>
> *Only God is unchanging; only He has all the truth there is."*
>
> (Bill, 1967: 76)

Many ministries appear to be obsessed with an image of success. If they are driven by a fear of failure, they are unlikely to let newer associates loose. Stott points out the temptation to put on a show, but counters with the statement,

> *"We may be very weak. I sometimes wish we were weaker. Faced with the forces of evil, we are often tempted to put on a show of Christian strength and engage in a little evangelical saber rattling. But it is in our weakness that Christ's strength is made perfect and it is words of human weakness that the Spirit endorses with his power."*
>
> (Stott, 1980: 9)

Ministries are either organic, dynamic and fluid, or they are dead. Culture changes over time and you will surely kill it if you try to hold it back from change.

Jesus was open to all types of people. While you may start with a call to one people-group, you need to stay open to others that may arrive on your doorstep. Cymbala welcomed

> "… junkies, prostitutes, and homosexuals [as well as] … lawyers, business types, and bus drivers …"

(Cymbala, 1997: 33)

This welcoming of those on the fringe of society is contrasted with blatant rejection of those who aren't seen as being the right type. In *Seriously Funny*, Adrian Plass tells of a church from another era that carried the sign,

> "No Sailors or Prostitutes."

(Plass, 2010: 128)

The theme we are looking at here is our willingness (or otherwise) to accept the changes that God may wish to bring. If we truly make welcome those whom the rest of "nice" society rejects, you can be assured we will be challenged to change. Are we going to control the behavior within "our" ministry, or are we going to keep our hands off God's ministry and let Him make adjustments?

Openness to change means refusing to protect our own indispensability. While God *may* call a person to long-term involvement in a ministry, it is far safer to assume a transitory involvement. That way, you are less likely to get protective of "your" ministry. If God calls you to stay, fine. But assume you are on the move. That way, you will be constantly listening to Him for the next orders.

Another means of allowing for change is working to ensure that newcomers are not dependent on us. Within the traditional missions setting, Parshall states:

> "The [founder] must move on as soon as possible … Converts must not transfer their dependence onto the [founder] and away from the Lord."

(Parshall, 1979: 480)

Tied in with a refusal to demand our "ownership" of any ministry is a willingness to let newcomers help shape the future direction.

> "The strategy … is to listen to the Body and to allow the body to shape itself."

(Tillapaugh, 1982: 116)

Maintaining a heart constantly tuned to God's leading underpins our openness to change. Smalley advises that we must follow the leading of the Holy Spirit in the way ministry grows:

> "It is [the ministry] … under the leadership of the Holy Spirit which will have to determine the best ways of fostering its own growth …"

(Smalley, in Winter et. al. 1981: 499)

You and the Holy Spirit

The Holy Spirit is likened to the wind. The wind blows where it wants to blow, and cannot be controlled by you, or anyone. And you shouldn't try to control the changes the Holy Spirit may want to bring to the ministry in which He has involved you for a time, including trying to control whom He may choose to bring alongside you, or to move you on.

New Christians typically look to others for direction as to how to live. They are easily shaped by you and others. The key point is that it should be God shaping them, and no-one else.

> *"Now as a follower of Christ, the believer really wants to conform, obey and produce. He wants to cooperate with God and the church and with me, his pastor. So he allows me to press him into my mold. He conforms. He stops what I tell him to stop. He gets involved where I tell him he should get involved. He starts dutifully doing the Christian things.*
>
> *And something in him begins to die!"*
>
> (Girard, 1972: 109)

> *"[Instead, you should] dare to teach them the principle of grace, even though, humanly speaking, that is not nearly so 'safe and secure' as teaching them the law. You start teaching them that they are free from the law, and that their relationship with Christ is not dependent on their performance but on His grace and forgiveness.*
>
> *… when the dust created by 'kicking up their heels' settles, the freedom they have found in grace turns out to be freedom to follow the personal leadership of the Holy Spirit in practical ways that spell renewal and life for the church. …*
>
> *So you stop trying to 'temper' the 'risky' freedom of grace with the 'safe' bondage of law. You trust God to make His new system work."*
>
> (Girard, 1972: 117)

Girard warns against one individual trying to shape another who is young in the faith. In a similar manner, Bill of Alcoholics Anonymous warns against any central serving organization overstepping the mark and starting to direct the activities of others.

> *"A.A. world headquarters is not a giver of orders. It is, instead, our largest transmitter of the lessons of experience."*
>
> (Bill, 1967: 273)

Individually or collectively, we can share experiences; but we are not authorized to issue commands.

If we get out of the way, Rinehart suggests we could discover others flourishing in their own living relationship with God.

> *"I have discovered that living within the range of my gifts and limits fosters a deference to other members of the body that God intended all along. This type of deference*

provides others the opportunity to … develop. For example, I am not the one to manage a conference facility, but as long as I occupied that spot, someone gifted to do it would never have the chance. …

If I live according to my limits, then I won't overestimate my importance or strive to be indispensable to those I'm serving. True humility forces us to admit our limits. We can ignore this truth through sin and dysfunction, but that will only bring hurt and damage to the body."

(Rinehart, 1998: 123-124)

We have stated it several times already; it is God's ministry, not yours. The hierarchical command structures so prevalent are in complete defiance of God's desire for each individual to be led by the Holy Spirit. But how might our "letting go" work out in practice?

For one thing, we will not run discipleship training or mentoring programs so that others can look like us. And if we "hang loose", we can trust God to supply His choice of person to accomplish tasks you or others have identified, *if* He even wants them done!

"God will provide the right person exactly when that person is needed. But not before. When no one is available who is gifted or feels called to a particular needed task, we begin to pray, trusting God to provide. He does so at just the right time (which may not be our timing). Later we see God's wisdom and marvelous timing in giving us the right person in His own time."

(Rinehart, 1998: 130)

The next challenge can test our attitude as to who the ministry belongs to. Are we willing to pray that God would raise up people to take the ministry we have supported further than we ever could have?

"Perhaps the question is whether we are willing to pray that God would raise up people … who would far surpass us in their impact for Him, people whose impact might be in arenas we will never see."

(Rinehart, 1998: 129)

If we can foster the right attitude a pattern will emerge. We might initiate some ministry, have the pleasure of being part of it for a season, and then with satisfaction see others pick up the mantle and take it to its next chapter, possibly without our ongoing involvement.

"So much ministry is the repeated exercise of beginning something, watching others grow and develop, and then letting go. If we don't counteract our need to control, we will find it difficult to fulfill one of our central callings … to give away the ministry."

(Rinehart, 1998: 157)

If you are to be part of a "team" for a time, are you willing to be nothing more than "just" a team member? Jesus was not concerned about others outside His direct influence doing things differently yet 'in His name'. Alcoholics Anonymous as an organization appears to have a similar, relaxed attitude to those who might break from tradition:

> *"... in a state of great alarm [an A.A. member from Japan] said, 'Awful things are going on over there in Japan! Did you know they have two kinds of A.A.'s over there? Of course they have the Twelve Steps just as we have them here, but there is now another A.A. leader who has written Ten Steps and they are charging 100 yen to attend his meetings!'*
>
> *Once upon a time that sort of heresy would have scared us to death. Today it is only amusing [because, in the long term,] ... common sense and experience [will prevail]."*
>
> (AAWS, 1957: 82)

We have a choice. Are we going to claim ownership of a ministry, or are we going to trust God to take His outreach forward in any way He chooses?

You may or may not have had what might be classified as a supernatural calling. But all you need is to simply trust God's leading in your day-to-day decisions. Oliver and Thwaites tell the real-life story of a fisherman who

> *"... had no idea of the journey ... [but] God's hand was guiding, creating, leading, all the time. All [he] did was to respond to the prompting of God ..."*
>
> (Oliver & Thwaites, 2001: 40)

Hunt tells a story of a son who moved in the moment-to-moment flow of God's leading while his mother, Emma, was tied up in "church" responsibilities which hindered her hearing and obeying God.

> *" 'And so,' Chris continues, speaking more slowly, 'whenever I meet a person and feel the tug of the Spirit, I ask myself, 'What can I do to show God's love?' Sometimes it's something as simple as offering a glass of water. Sometimes it's as easy as buying somebody a plate of bacon and eggs.'*
>
> *'And sometimes,' [Emma's] voice clots with emotion, 'it means taking a man home with you and giving him your bed?'*
>
> *'That's right.' "*
>
> (Hunt, 2004: 257)

It was enough for Chris to hear and act. It is enough for you. And you are obliged to grant others the same freedom.

CHAPTER 48:
"GETTING ORGANIZED" CAN TRAP YOU

It seems to be a natural tendency to want to get things organized. We discover freedom, and we want to encapsulate it before it escapes, not realizing that such a statement is self-contradictory—trying to cage freedom!

Principles of anti-organization

We do *not* want to learn how to start a church, let alone actually do it, but we may learn from warnings to those who have headed down this route. Oliver and Thwaites point out that many such churches are meeting-based from the outset and hence lock in their culture:

> "When a pastor sets out to plant a church, he gathers a group of people together in a room and says 'we are going to build a church'. In that room, for the next however many number of years, they will meet to worship, fellowship, evangelise, pray, be led, hear preaching, and so on. What this does is fix the cultural coordinates for that group of people from then on in. Twenty years on, five hundred people meet in what has now become a larger room. Even though more 'out there' activities might happen, the identity of this large group has, from the start, been firmly fixed and anchored inside that meeting. The pastor, in a fit of doctrinal frustration, might declare from time to time the need to get 'out there' and win the lost, but the pulpit, the person, the giving and the affirmation that fuels this passion is, as it always has been, 'in here', inside the meeting."
>
> (Oliver & Thwaites, 2001: 175-176)

The same authors point out that we may need to be specifically warned to avoid the trap of establishing or formalizing a ministry from the outset. We must not preempt the shape of how people might work together.

> *"... I had to encourage certain people not to rush to meeting mode to fill the quiet spaces of those first <u>years</u> of new landscape life." [Emphasis mine]*
>
> (Oliver & Thwaites, 2001: 178)

We should be prepared to hold loosely to the outworking of any ministry in which we may be involved.

It is interesting to note that many refer to the early times of a collective outreach as the "formative" period. This is exactly what we wish to avoid—"forming" the rules and character into something stable and predictable. But even if we successfully resist the temptation to "get organized" at the very outset, there is still danger and temptation to *progressively* formalize the emerging traditions.

Buckingham tells a parable about a group of coastal surf lifesavers who had formed a lifesaving club some time earlier. They were now looked up to as a shining example from other similar, younger groups.

> *"Then a great argument arose [in the established group] concerning techniques. Some said the band should not be organized under leaders, but each lifesaver should walk the shore as he pleased. Others felt the lifesaving station was the last hope for those in peril on the sea, since the Inland Club was obviously not interested. Indeed, they were part of the problem. Still a third group insisted on a big, comfortable building like the Inland Club. It would provide refuge for those saved from the sea and give the band a feeling of security and respectability. Finally, there were those who said the whole principle of lifesaving was wrong. If the Inland Clubbers were foolish enough to go out in a storm, they deserved to drown. The Band (now spelled with a capital letter) should be limited only to those who were committed to the Lifesavers (also capitalized).*
>
> *The group was ready to divide. A large segment felt it was too expensive to maintain the incandescent light on the tower. The lights along the shore were enough, they maintained – citing the words from the old hymn, Let the Lower Lights Be Burning.*
>
> *The division was friendly, but final. The Incandescents (their newsletter carried the picture of a lighthouse) would continue to meet on Sunday. The Lower Lighters (their newsletter had a picture of Jesus standing at the door with a lamp in His hand) would meet on Saturday night. It made them feel spiritual to give way to their self-righteous brothers.*
>
> *The Incandescents, who had more money, built a beautiful lighthouse on the site of the old hut. It had a spacious club room on the ground floor which they rented to the Lower Lighters on Saturday night.*
>
> *As the battle between the groups raged, each side became more defensive. Fewer and fewer members were interested in going on lifesaving missions, preferring to spend their time correcting the other members of the Band. Disgruntled members returned to the Inland Club, declaring the Band had grown legalistic. The Lifesavers, they said,*

were insisting the members could not go on vacation during the monsoon season and were even demanding financial accounting from some who were slothful in paying their dues. Lifeboat crews had been hired to do the actual work of plucking the lost from the sea, which enabled the Lifesavers time to travel around the country teaching techniques.

About this time a large ship was wrecked off the coast and the hired crews brought in loads of cold, wet, half-drowned people. A great debate arose whether these outsiders should be allowed to enter the clubhouse since they had not made commitments to the Lifesavers – who were all in New Zealand teaching techniques. During the debate many of the survivors died from exposure."

(Buckingham, 1978: 296-297)

What Buckingham tells via a parable, Hattersley tells as a biographical account of William Booth and the Salvation Army:

"William Booth was gradually developing the strategy for establishing a permanent church of his own ... William Booth was so confident of his ability to redeem [the poor] that he thought it right to offer advice on the subject to other evangelists. How to Reach the Masses With the Gospel: A Sketch of the Origin, History and Present Position of the Christian Mission was advertised as 'Containing a description of the means and instrumentalities employed ... [resulting in] remarkable conversion of numbers of common people, including infidels, thieves, drunkards etc. [And all this advice on the free gift of salvation was available at a price ...] With engravings in paper 6d: cloth 1/-'."

(Hattersley, 2000: 192)

Those who joined the Salvation Army as Soldiers

"... were required to sign the 'Articles of War' ... [These were] only a beginning. The 'Orders and Regulations' followed. No one could complain that recruits were left in doubt about their duties. The Regulations for Field Officers covered 626 pages, Staff Officers 357 pages, Territorial Commissioners and Secretaries, 176 pages. The Regulations for Soldiers were compressed into a mere 164 pages. As the Army expanded its work, Regulations were also promulgated for Social Officers, Local Officers and Band and Singing Brigades."

(Hattersley, 2000: 266)

Rinehart observes this as ministries getting organized, not just coincidentally, but rather as a natural tendency:

"... there is a tendency for [ministries] ... to stagnate. Programs and infrastructures spring up to support and protect a burgeoning ministry. ... What begins as a dynamic expression of the Kingdom of God mires in the trappings of human institutionalism. ...

... we see a spiritual cycle at work in the church. Time and again, God moves in individuals' lives within the context of their own needs and culture. Then revival and *spiritual renewal break out anew, consuming the dead underbrush of institutionalism and frozen faith.*

Sinful nature, however, follows the path of least resistance, slowly replacing faith and trust with power and control, preferring to rely on the seen rather than the unseen. Eventually, the grasping chokeweeds of institutionalism and power acquire a stranglehold on the people of God."

(Rinehart, 1998: 70)

"Like the steady shifting motion of the continental shelf, every organization drifts toward perpetuating itself. Religious enterprises are no exception. What often begins as a pioneering effort, held together by faith, prayer, and a little planning, will tend toward becoming an institution, once it finds a measure of success. In the process, the real ministry agenda shifts toward maintenance."

(Rinehart, 1998: 154)

Buckingham (extending a previous quote) and Rinehart both expose an irony in the institutionalization of ministries—many vibrant works started in freedom, but end up weighed down by rules.

"The joy of adventure remains only as long as God controls. When man steps in with his reasons and fears to institutionalize and structure (or even record) that which is meant to flow free and unencumbered, life leaves. Yet it is this lack of institutionalizing which is the single factor preventing us from venturing out. How desperately the human soul wants to see a blueprint of the next step, to exert an element of control over what is about to happen. That is only our own humanity, which is afraid of the unknown, not that essence of God inside each of us. It is the essence of God which urges us to dare, to ... soar free ... toward the dwelling place of the Most High."

(Buckingham, 1980: 207-208)

"In the beginning of a new ministry, structure is largely absent. It's a situation that is both freeing and intimidating. ...

But what ... happens over time, particularly if the new ministry proves 'successful'? The structures and forms take on a life of their own. Slowly, they become the focal point ... rather than the ministry they were designed to serve."

(Rinehart, 1998: 60)

"Rather than bringing people in and helping them find a place of ministry, structures can create artificial boundaries that proclaim: 'You're not one of us. You don't do things our way.' When forms harden into traditions, they become rote and routine, losing much of their original influence. The words 'We've always done it this way' are a death knell to fresh initiative.' "

(Rinehart, 1998: 63)

Rinehart provides a direct and challenging warning—if we institutionalize, we will be repeating history's mistakes.

"GETTING ORGANIZED" CAN TRAP YOU

"Someone once said that what we learn from history is that we don't learn anything from history. ...

As we look back ... we see that in the beginning of any true spiritual movement, the Holy Spirit is released as men and women exercise faith and courage. God honors the simple stumbling efforts of His children as they step out in faith. As people move into uncharted territory toward a vision He's given them, God meets them there.

Yet, when their efforts meet with a measure of success and renewal breaks out, an insidious, counteractive process begins. The underbrush of institutionalism begins to take root. The human tendency is to build an organization around this living, dynamic thing called ministry. Then the surrounding structure becomes a heavy, cumbersome weight that cuts off spiritual light and nutrients necessary for growth. In this process of institutionalization, people come to rely on human figures at the helm. God's Spirit is quenched; freedom and innovation decline.

As leaders grow more entrenched, they invest more power and authority in their position. The priesthood of the elite increases and the priesthood of believers declines. An invisible caste system develops, making a subtle distinction between laity and clergy. Laity learn to step back out of the picture, find a comfortable place to sit, and watch the 'professionals' at work.

As any ministry takes on an organizational focus, something to protect arises. Assets, property, history, and tradition must be preserved. Eventually the light and life that produced them lie dormant, and it seems that tradition and structure are all that remain. Thus, as institutionalism takes over, reformers of almost any kind meet with resistance and suspicion. They appear to be challenging the unchallengeable."

(Rinehart, 1998: 82-83)

All Christians are by definition part of the Body of Christ. Brown notes the confusion between being a member of Christ's Body and a 'member' of some local church:

"... 'membership' ... does not mean the formal church membership that is common today, but rather being a genuine part of the Body."

(Brown, 2002: 211)

In the early days of Alcoholics Anonymous, rules started to appear for membership.

"Around 1943 or 1944, the Central Office asked the groups to list their membership rules and send them in. After they arrived we set them all down. A little reflection upon these many rules brought us to an astonishing conclusion.

If all of these edicts had been in force everywhere at once it would have been practically impossible for any alcoholic to have ever joined A.A. About nine-tenths of our oldest and best members could never have got by!"

(Bill, 1967: 41)

Having been down the route of articulating many rules, Alcoholics Anonymous swung the other way.

> *"There used to be so many membership rules out among the groups that if they were all enforced at once nobody – actually nobody – could have joined Alcoholics Anonymous. But as our fears subsided we finally said to ourselves, 'Who are we to keep anybody out? To many a desperate drunk A.A. is the court of his last appeal. How can we slam the door on anybody who stands outside?' No, we must never do that. We must always take the risk, no matter who comes in. ... Tradition Three, says, '... No matter what you have done, or still will do, you are an A.A. member as long as you say so.'"*
>
> (AAWS, 1957: 102-103)

> *"The only requirement for A.A. membership is a sincere desire to stop drinking."*
>
> (AAWS, 1957: 102)

> *"We found that the principles of tolerance and love had to be emphasized in actual practice. We can never say (or insinuate) to anyone that he must agree to our formula or be excommunicated. The atheist may stand up in an A.A. meeting still denying the Deity, yet reporting how vastly he has been changed in attitude and outlook. Much experience tells us he will presently change his mind about God, but nobody tells him he must do so.*
>
> *In order to carry the principle of inclusiveness and tolerance still further, we make no religious requirement of anyone. All people having an alcoholic problem who wish to get rid of it and so make a happy adjustment with the circumstances of their lives, become A.A. members by simply associating with us. Nothing but sincerity is needed. But we do not demand even this.*
>
> *In such an atmosphere the orthodox, the unorthodox, and the unbeliever mix happily and usefully together. An opportunity for spiritual growth is open to all."*
>
> (Bill, 1967: 158)

Many groups of Christians have rules for their people. A simple example is dress code. For some, it is very tightly defined and governed. For others it is more subtle. I attended one local church many years ago which prided itself on acceptance of all, no matter how they dressed. But the moment anyone was appointed to even as simple a task as being on a "helps" team, the expectation as to "appropriate" dress started to be communicated and was expected to be conformed to as a sign of maturity and support for the leadership.

Yancey argues that such conformance to rules is common in many religions, but should not be a dimension of Christianity:

> *"Religious systems, said Tolstoy, tend to promote external rules: Judaism did so, as did Buddhism, Hinduism and Islam. But Jesus introduced a different approach by refusing to define a set of external rules which his followers could then abide by with a sense of self-righteousness. In a pivotal passage, Tolstoy made this distinction between Christ's approach and that of all other religions:*

> *The test of observance of external religious teachings is whether or not our conduct conforms with their decrees. [Observe the Sabbath. Get circumcised. Tithe.] Such conformity is indeed possible.*
>
> *The test of observance of Christ's teachings is our consciousness of our failure to attain an ideal perfection. The degree to which we draw near this perfection cannot be seen; all we can see is the extent of our deviation.*
>
> *A man who professes an external law is like someone standing in the light of a lantern fixed to a post. It is light all round him, but there is nowhere further for him to walk. A man who professes the teaching of Christ is like a man carrying a lantern before him on a long, or not so long, pole: the light is in front of him, always lighting up fresh ground and always encouraging him to walk further."*
>
> (Yancey, 2001: 124-125)

Two of the warning signs are rules in general, and rules for "membership" in particular, whether they are written down formally or just implied.

Another danger sign for any emerging ministry is the formal appointment of some individuals to special, titled roles. But even these can be subtle—"I would like you to meet Fred, our founder." Is this an innocent statement? Maybe it might be innocent, but it is dangerous. Fred is being held up as someone who is special, set apart from the rest. Further, should not *God* be the "founder"?

Rinehart, quoting from Matthew 23:10 in the New American Standard Bible, notes the words of Jesus:

> "And do not be called leaders; for One is your Leader, that is, Christ."
>
> (Rinehart, 1998: 37)

We must never appoint leaders. Ever. And we would be advised to shun even the hint of titles to anyone.

Maybe, for legal reasons, we may have to assign people to roles such as those who manage the finances. But even there, we must work hard to avoid roles—do we even *need* a bank account? Alcoholics Anonymous learned that some organization might, in some cases, serve the group. But it was always to be the least that was absolutely required.

So what do you do if you somehow find you've got yourself organized? Oliver and Thwaites speak of a group that agreed at the outset:

> "… that if too much momentum started to build then these meetings would be stopped, so that people would not begin to think that they were in any way central to what God was doing."
>
> (Oliver & Thwaites, 2001: 186)

Put simply, if you look at the place where you have arrived, and discover traits of "organization", it may be time to deliberately disband, and let God reassign His workers as He sees fit.

A case study in the creeping cancer of getting organized

Hudson Taylor was, in many ways, a pioneer, and a man of great faith, energy and sacrifice. He also was human. It would be understandable if he followed the ways of many others and got "organized" from the outset.

The tragedy of his story is that he started with strong convictions and practices that opposed formal establishment of an organization, and yet by the end of his life had put in place so many of the aspects of "organization" that he had spoken against in his early years. If someone with such clear and outspoken principles, over a number of decades, changed so much, we must take it as a warning for ourselves.

From the very outset, the China Inland Mission had no name and no-one was appointed to nominated roles. Then, quite informally, the movement got a name.

> " 'When I decided to go forward [to China],' said Mr. Taylor of this summer,
> 'Mr. Berger undertook to represent us at home. The thing grew up gradually.
> We were much drawn together. The Mission received its name in his drawing-room.
> Neither of us asked or appointed the other; it just was so.' "

(Taylor & Taylor, 1918: 37)

This informality was not accidental. Taylor consciously recognized the need to let God shape the movement as it grew.

> "... some may think that if we had more, or more costly machinery we should do better. But oh, I feel that it is divine power we want and not machinery!"

(Taylor & Taylor, 1918: 512)

> " 'You must wait for [the ministry] to grow,' he said, ' ... First you have only a slender stem with a few leaves or shoots. Then little twigs appear. Ultimately these may become great limbs ... but it takes time and patience. If there is life, it will develop after its own order.'
>
> Thus they were content with little <u>to begin with</u> in the way of organisation. ...
> A few simple arrangements were agreed to ... that was all." [Emphasis mine]

(Taylor & Taylor, 1918: 54)

The highlighted phrase suggests that Taylor accepted that the beginnings required little organization.

On the one hand, at the outset, Taylor explicitly rejected any form of a central organization. This proved to be a significant factor in the freedom experienced by those on the front line in China. However, one small chink in the armor appeared—Taylor allows himself to be recognized as the supreme leader.

> "... much that is not said is significant by its absence. There is no mention of a Committee, no reliance upon organisation or great names. The entire direction of the Mission was to be in the hands of its founder, himself the most experienced of its

> *members, who like a General on active service would be with his forces in the field. So natural does this arrangement seem that one hardly recognises the greatness of the innovation, or that in this as in other new departures Hudson Taylor was making a contribution of exceeding value to the high politics of missions. He had simply learned from painful experience how much a missionary may have to suffer, and how the work be hampered, if not imperilled, by being under the control of those who, however well-intentioned, have no first-hand knowledge of its conditions, and are, moreover, at the other side of the world."*
>
> (Taylor & Taylor, 1918: 43)

I agree with Taylor that it would have been a flawed approach to permit even well-intentioned people back in England to "control" the actions of those on the front line in China. However, local control is not the only alternative. Taylor rejected the central committee, but allowed for a decentralized structure with the potential for a dictator to emerge. Taylor was not inclined to being a dictator, but the precedent for such a role is dangerous in any setting. And it later proved to be so for the China Inland Mission.

The manner in which Taylor retained a tight, central control over matters is apparent in his practice that all communication were to go through him.

> *"... two thousand six hundred letters [had been] attended to by Mr. Taylor personally [with Mrs. Taylor assisting] ... during a period of ten months, fully taken up with travelling and meetings."*
>
> (Taylor & Taylor, 1918: 375)

With such an enormous load, rather than encouraging others to cease looking to him as the central authority, he sought to create a structure whereby others could share the load so that he could remain as the director.

> *"... Mr. Taylor was seeking light upon how to prepare for the larger growth that was coming ... [so] he sent out a carefully considered letter to all the members of the Mission, stating what was proposed and asking their judgment."*
>
> (Taylor & Taylor, 1918: 375)

The letter proposed a 'Council' structure which was hierarchical in nature:

> *"... the members of that Council may themselves be Superintendents of districts, in which capacity they may in turn be assisted by district Councils of our missionaries. ... Many local matters can thus be locally considered and attended to without delay ..."*
>
> (Taylor & Taylor, 1918: 375)

Soon we have not only a hierarchy, with Taylor at the top, but we have designated titles and roles for those appointed by him.

> *"The older work in the province of Che-kiang was next organised, M. Meadows (the senior member of the Mission) being appointed Superintendent ...*

> *The Rev. J. W. Stevenson has, I am thankful to say, accepted the position of Director's Deputy ... He will ... represent me in my absence from China, and deal with all questions brought before him by the Superintendents requiring immediate determination"*
>
> (Taylor & Taylor, 1918: 394)

The statement that his delegate would handle issues *"requiring immediate determination"* implies that the less pressing issues would more properly be left for the real leader's return!

Not only were structures being well and truly set in place for the Mission, but Taylor was also keen to make sure the native churches were also "properly" set up. He planned a trip to inland regions so he could encourage the workers, and so that he could

> *"... confer with them about the organisation of the native church, which in some places was growing rapidly."*
>
> (Taylor & Taylor, 1918: 401)

Several danger signs were by now clearly evident, including an organizational structure and titles for appointed officers. But it continues. Firstly, there is the formalization of the structure.

> *"A Deed of Incorporation for the safeguarding of mission property was drawn up. The Council was strengthened by the addition of Mr. Robert Scott as Treasurer and several new members. An Auxiliary Council was formed in Glasgow to deal with Scottish candidates, and a Ladies' Council in London, of which Miss Soltau was appointed Secretary with entire charge of a department for the help and training of women-workers."*
>
> (Taylor & Taylor, 1918: 466)

Next, we see another warning sign of an organization heading the wrong way—the rejection of willing workers by others who have set ideas on any individual's calling from God and suitability for membership.

> *"Join us in praying for ... the right kind of labourers, also that others may be kept back or not accepted, for many are offering."*
>
> (Taylor & Taylor, 1918: 46)

This filtering of candidates who did not fit a pre-ordained shape is in stark contrast to Taylor's own life where he experienced the liberty and fruitfulness of not complying with the expectations of others. And the danger of Taylor taking the role of self-appointed selector of God's workers has been identified in the earlier story of Taylor's rejection of Henry Frost.

How much better it would have been if Taylor had just prayed for workers in the field and totally left it to God to convict, provide, train, lead and support them, just as He had done with Taylor himself—then there would have been no need at all for the China

Inland Mission and Taylor would have had much more time and energy for that to which God had called him!

Having noted the changing attitudes to formalization of the organization's structure, we go on to see the results of this shift.

One sad outcome of trying to capture the essence of a movement of God is the practice of enshrining the culture in such a manner that even God is not permitted to change it. Unfortunately, Taylor's mission assumed that, seeing God directed a particular way in one season, that must be the way for all time.

> "It is important to secure that no contingency shall alter the character of the Mission … or throw us off those lines which God has so signally owned and blessed from the commencement."
>
> (Taylor & Taylor, 1918: 375)

Protection of the traditions now becomes more important than listening for God's direction, possibly through others, about a change of tack.

> "We have our definite lines of working: we must not leave them, nor grow weary in them."
>
> (Taylor & Taylor, 1918: 358)

There emerges a subtle, controlling condemnation of those called out of his mission, particularly if they questioned his established ways of working:

> "If any leave us on account of [our established and unchangeable ways of working], they, not we, are the losers."
>
> (Taylor & Taylor, 1918: 358)

Much has been said about the difference between unity and uniformity. Unfortunately, Taylor was by now focusing on the latter, hence suppressing any richness that might come out of, as Jonathan Sacks puts it, *"The Dignity of Difference"*.

> "A little grey book … soon found its way to all the stations of the Mission …
> There were instructions for special officers, the Treasurer, the Secretary in China, and the Superintendents; instructions for senior and junior missionaries, lady evangelists and probationers, all based upon a thorough understanding of conditions in China. A course of study in the language, carefully prepared by Mr. Stevenson, Mr. Baller, and others, was adopted for use in the Training Homes; and the Principles and Practice of the mission were restated and somewhat amplified for younger workers."
>
> (Taylor & Taylor, 1918: 420-421)

This approach stands in contrast to Alcoholics Anonymous, where experiences are shared but not mandated. Their members are free to accept or reject the lessons learned by those who have gone before. It is held that many newcomers who try a different way may come to see the wisdom of the traditions. But it is also held that these traditions are open to refinement by the newcomers.

The level of Taylor's prescriptive uniformity of approach, and control of it, is highlighted by the methodology articulated for training new missionaries and their native helpers.

> *"A special Itinerant Missionary Evangelistic Band would then be required, ... [staffed by those] willing to consecrate five years of their lives to itinerant work, without thought of marriage or of settling down till their special work is accomplished. The work would be arduous, involving much self-denial, but it would bring with it much blessing and great spiritual joy, as the command, 'Preach the Gospel to every creature,' was being obeyed: in keeping of His commandments there is great reward (see Psalm xix. II).*
>
> *The workers, when ready, would go out two and two, i.e. two missionaries and two native helpers, to previously arranged districts, to sell Scriptures and Gospel tracts, and to preach the Glad Tidings. Living together in the same inns, for companionship and fellowship, they would often separate during the day, one missionary and native brother going in one direction, and the other two in another, and meeting again at night, to commend to God the work of the day, as before setting out they had unitedly sought His blessing. Two-thirds to three-quarters of their time being thus occupied, the remainder would afford opportunities for bodily and spiritual rest and refreshment, for continuing the Chinese studies of the missionaries, and the systematic Bible study of the native helpers. As the work progresses the number of these centres would need increasing."*

(Taylor & Taylor, 1918: 569)

The scourge of organized hierarchies is the practice of top-down control, taking the place of God in individually directing the actions of His people. And with all the compromises made by Taylor in the establishment of an organization, it should not be surprising that Taylor also succumbed to this practice.

Sometimes the methods of a controlling leader, such as Taylor turned out to be, are hidden behind a veneer of "religious" actions. Why shouldn't a Christian leader encourage his followers to pray? Of course, there is no harm in *encouraging* prayer. But Taylor went further than encouragement. He mandated their commitment to continued prayer until Taylor's *personal* vision of seventy new workers was realized. The prayer he was seeking was to deliver according to *his* vision rather than others seeking confirmation as to whether this was God's approach. Further, there is a veiled pressure that Taylor would take certain actions only on the condition they kept praying as agreed:

> *"All the members of the Mission present agreed to pray daily for the Seventy [new missionaries] until they should be given. ... Mr. Taylor promised to telegraph [to England] ... and ask them to receive and send out this number, if we would continue praying."* [Emphasis mine]

(Taylor & Taylor, 1918: 359)

In the account above, Taylor's controlling methods are fairly subtle. His wife is less subtle in her letter to supporters in England. The letter quoted below carries with it a message that, to not join in prayer as expected, would be a shameful thing. There is no flexibility offered that maybe the recipients of the letter may be called by God to other priorities, other ministries, or other God-given opportunities.

> *"I had wanted to ask you – when some one else rises to read the letters – to lift your hearts to God for me, and say: 'Make her a blessing to her husband: make her a blessing wherever she goes.'*
>
> *We may visit many stations. In a few weeks I hope to join the Shanghai prayer meeting, and I want to cheer them on. May I tell them that you are more in earnest for blessing than ever? If the Gospel is to be given 'To every creature,' much will depend on you, dear friends. <u>You must</u> take hold upon God for this. <u>You must</u> uphold our hands in believing, fervent prayer. The work is yours as well as ours, and so will the reward be. The Lord unite your hearts in one, and bow them before Himself in compassion for the lost. Oh, that we could have heart breakings at home over the state of the world! Dr. Pierson says, 'Prayer has turned every great crisis in the kingdom of God.' It is a solemn question for each one of us, 'What are my prayers really effecting?' Do we know that we have the petitions that we desire of Him?*
>
> *I want to carry fresh inspiration to the Training Home at Anking, and to the Sisters in Yang-chow. Will you pray that to every place we are allowed to visit, my beloved husband and I may be taken in the power of the Spirit? <u>The enemy's tactics are to divide, to discourage, to deaden. Let us realise our oneness in Christ</u>; let us be strong and of a good courage, and seek zealously and continuously the quickening influences of the Holy Spirit. God grant that the Saturday prayer meeting, which has brought such blessing in the past, may this winter be more than ever a meeting-place with God. We praise for what has been done; but when we look at what needs to be done, when we think of what might be done, we must humble ourselves before God. Time is short, opportunity great: let us be downright in earnest."* [Emphasis mine]
>
> (Taylor & Taylor, 1918: 498-499)

It is not uncommon in society to persuade others by gaining many signatures on a petition. Taylor resorted to this tactic, getting his fellow workers to sign an appeal and sending it to his colleagues in England, hoping to pressure them to act according to *his* priorities and timing.

> *"Mr. Taylor was drafting an appeal to the home churches which in due course was signed by seventy-seven members of the Mission in China."*
>
> (Taylor & Taylor, 1918: 360)

This approach is so inconsistent with Taylor's own earlier practice of taking his concerns directly to God, and not even telling others about the issues.

Finally, Taylor's organization became so rigid that any who wished to join were instructed that they *must* sign an acceptance of the 'terms and conditions' of their engagement before they could be taken on as members.

> "Mr. Taylor ... went over the Principles and Practice of the C.I.M. [that was required to be] signed by the members of the Mission before leaving England."
>
> (Taylor & Taylor, 1918: 394)

Anti-organization practices

We have seen that it is too easy to fall into the trap of "getting organized". Thankfully, there are some actions we can take to take to diminish the threat.

Have patience

One of the triggers for "getting things organized" is to try to make them happen, in our own strength and cleverness. And the simple antidote is to learn to show trust in God through patiently waiting on His time and methods.

Waiting on God will require patience, but this is God's way. Part of the waiting is to allow God to deal with old ways of thinking.

> *"It will take time for people who are accustomed to something and someone else leading them to trust their own good desire and their own discernment in taking Kingdom initiatives."*
>
> (Oliver & Thwaites, 2001: 104)

Another aspect of patience is simply waiting for God to move, rather than trying to bring *our* vision into being.

> *"Consider the example of Moses. Perhaps he was already sensing his calling to liberate his people when he killed the Egyptian who was beating the Hebrew laborer. But it was not God's time and it certainly was not God's way, so Moses had to spend forty years on the backside of the desert before he was ready to set the captives free. Man's ways are not God's ways!"*
>
> (Brown, 2002: 90-91)

Brown explains:

> *"Don't panic and say to yourself, 'Forty years! I can't wait forty years before God uses me!' Fear not. God was preparing Moses for a pretty big task, and he didn't have a worldwide body of believers to support him and work with him. Let's hope that your preparation – and mine – for full usefulness will not take forty years in the desert."*
>
> (Brown, 2002: 214)

Even if God's vision does take forty years, we must be willing to wait!

These principles are beautifully illustrated by extracts from the earlier life of Hudson Taylor. Firstly, Taylor notes that lessons are often learned as we wait:

> *"The Lord doubtless has His purpose ... and to learn any lesson He may have to teach us is more important than getting rid of the trouble."*
>
> (Taylor & Taylor, 1918: 507)

"GETTING ORGANIZED" CAN TRAP YOU

It is not always easy to wait. At times, Taylor wanted to make things happen. At one stage he had the attitude that, if the central Society's leaders would not support his vision, he would jolly-well press ahead and take action, with or without their support. However, within a few months of making this statement, Taylor's attitude had changed to that of waiting and seeing how God would arrange things.

> "It is hard … to have no settled dwelling. I have thought of buying a set of Chinese garments soon, and seeing how I get could on with them. If I could get a little place somewhere in the interior, perhaps I might settle down and be useful. …
>
> The future is in the hands of God. … There we must leave it."
>
> (Taylor & Taylor, 1911: 310)

The biographer then comments,

> "… the point specially worthy of notice is the changed attitude of [Taylor] since his last letter on the subject three months previously. Then it had been – Our plans are laid before the Society: if they do nothing, we mean to try and carry them out ourselves: if they oppose, it may become a question as to which we shall dispense with, the Society, or our plans of usefulness. Now it was – Chinese dress, a little place somewhere in the interior, and, above all, a future left in the hands of God. How great a difference! The Lord had had time to work. And as always in His providence, the moulding force came not only from outward circumstances, but from the development of His life within.
>
> Do we not need to remind ourselves in these days, especially in connection with His service, of the danger of impatience and taking things too much into our own hands? If we are really waiting on God and doing His will, hindrances that are not removed are safeguards, keeping us from mistaken courses, and bringing about the preparation of spirit necessary in ourselves before His best can be given.
>
> It does not always seem so. How little could Hudson Taylor have imagined that, even before the answer to those January letters could be received, his own outlook would be so changed that he would no longer cling to what had then seemed desirable? How little could Dr. Parker have foreseen that before summer was over he would be called to a more important and congenial sphere? And how little can we tell all we are being delivered from by our very limitations, or the wider service to which the Lord is leading in ways beyond our ken? So let us thank God from our hearts for trials that are not removed, though brought before Him in believing prayer, and praise Him for answers that seem long in coming, knowing the delay is needed to make us ready to receive them."
>
> (Taylor & Taylor, 1911: 310-311)

During the time of waiting there is no guarantee that we will see God's master plan any more clearly. We must be content to just act on the little understanding we may have.

> "[Not only in the matter of having a permanent base for settled work did Taylor seem] to have made no advance: he still had no home, no permanent work, no settled plans

ahead. Where or how he was ultimately to labour was no more clear than it had been at the beginning. But the way of faith was clearer, and he had learned to leave the future in the hands of God. One who knew the end from the beginning was guiding and would guide. So a great rest had come about it all, and he was not concerned to make everything fit in. How this visit to [a particular town] would eventuate for him personally, how it would affect his life-work he could not tell. He only knew the Lord had set before him this open door, and he was growing content to walk a step at a time."

(Taylor & Taylor, 1911: 363)

The value of waiting

An amazing story highlights the need to wait on God, as only He can see the big picture. In this case, the very lives of His workers depended on some events that at first seemed obstacles. William Burns and Hudson Taylor were working together, and both desired to minister together in a particular part of China, but they seemed to be prevented by a number of issues, not the least being a civil war in China. They could have tried to force their way by seeking political support, but they chose not to.

"It was not a question really of standing on one's rights, or claiming what it might be justifiable to claim. Why deal with second causes? Nothing could have been easier for the Master to Whom 'All power' is given than to have established His servant permanently on the island, had He so desired it. And what use was it, if He had other plans, to attempt to carry the thing through on the strength of Government help? No, 'the servant of the Lord must not strive,' but must be willing to be led by just such indications of the divine will, relying not on the help of man to accomplish a work of his own choosing, but on the unfailing guidance, resources and purposes of God.

And so, very thankfully, Hudson Taylor came to realise that all was well. A measure of trial had been allowed, over which perhaps he had felt unduly discouraged. But all was in wise and loving hands. Nothing the Lord permitted could lastingly hinder His own work."

(Taylor & Taylor, 1911: 340-341)

In hindsight, of course, we can sometimes see God's strategy. But when we are in the middle of events, all we can do is trust, even if that is not easy, and even if it stretches our faith beyond our experience to date.

"It had been a keen disappointment to them to leave the neighbourhood ... where the openings had seemed so promising ... But the Lord had other plans in view.

'He was leading us,' wrote Mr. Taylor, 'by a way that we knew not: but it was none the less His way.'

O Lord, how happy should we be
If we should cast our care on Thee,
If we from self would rest;

*And feel at heart that One above
In perfect wisdom, perfect love,
Is working for the best."*

(Taylor & Taylor, 1911: 359)

"A brief absence was all that Hudson Taylor anticipated when he parted from Mr. Burns in Swatow. He was badly needing change while the hot season lasted, and this journey to fetch his medicines fitted in very well with the plans they had in view. What was his surprise and distress, therefore, to learn upon reaching Shanghai that the premises of the London Mission had been visited by fire and that his medical outfit left there for safety was entirely destroyed.

What could it mean? Why had it been permitted? Never had he needed these belongings more. Everything in Swatow seemed to depend upon the medical work they were now in a position to undertake – and Mr. Burns was alone waiting for him.

But what was the use of returning without medicines? And where was a new supply to come from, or the means to obtain them? Purchase in Shanghai he could not, on account of the extravagantly high prices of imported articles and six or eight months might be required before they would reach him from home. It was a difficult position, and the young missionary, as he tells us, was more disposed to say with Jacob, 'All these things are against me,' than to recognise with cheerful faith that 'All things work together for good to them that love God.'

'I had not then learned,' he records, 'to think of God as the One Great Circumstance in whom we live and move and have our being, and of all lesser circumstances as necessarily the kindest, wisest, best, because either ordered or permitted by Him. Hence my disappointment and trial were very great.'

The only thing was to write and tell Mr. Burns what had happened, and to put off his return until he could go to Ning-po and see what Dr. Parker could do to help them. If he could spare a small supply of medicines to go on with, they might still be able to begin work as soon as the great heat was over. So in the hope of retrieving his losses, Hudson Taylor set out for the neighbouring city.

And then a whole set of new difficulties began. Three or four days under ordinary circumstances would have taken him to Dr. Parker, but on this occasion, he found himself three weeks after he first started no nearer his destination than at the beginning. True he had made the trip as much of an evangelistic journey as possible, preaching and distributing literature along the first part of the way. But this was not the reason of his ending up where he began, penniless and destitute, without having reached Ning-po at all or communicated with Dr. Parker.

'It is interesting to notice,' he wrote long after, 'the various events which united in the providence of God in preventing my return to Swatow and ultimately led to my settling in Ning-po and making that the centre for the development of future labours.'

> *But during this trying summer and the many unsettled months that followed, the young missionary was sorely perplexed to understand the way divine providence was taking in the ordering of his affairs. Life turns at times on a small pivot, and in looking back one is startled to realise the importance of what seemed a very little thing.*
>
> *How could Hudson Taylor have imagined, for example, that the robbery that left him in such distress upon this journey was to result in the deliverance of the entire Mission he was yet to found, during a period of financial danger? How could he suppose that the upset of all his plans and the severance of a partnership in service more precious than any he had ever known was to prove the crowning blessing of his life on the human side, bringing him into association and at last union with the one of all others most suited both to him and his work?*
>
> *But so it is God leads. His hand is on the helm. We are being guided, even when we feel it least. The closed door is as much His Providence as the open, and equally for our good and the accomplishment of His own great ends. And one learns at last that it is not what we set ourselves to do that really tells in blessing so much as what He is doing through us, when we least expect it, if only we are in abiding fellowship with Him."*
>
> (Taylor & Taylor, 1911: 387-389)

The fuller picture of what God was doing with Burns was not clear to Taylor at that time, but we have the advantage of seeing the larger picture with hindsight.

William Burns had been imprisoned—providentially, as it turned out, as a civil war would have led to his murder as a foreigner had he not been in the "safety" of the prison! Yet at the time all Taylor could see was the blocks preventing his return to work with Burns, and demands on his own time from other sources.

> *"Almost dazed, it all came over him. First one check and then another; medicines destroyed, robbery and all it had entailed, visit to Ning-po, delay in getting away, tedious return journey, and now at the last moment a closed door, – nothing but a closed door and a dear, sick brother waiting to be taken back to the city from which they had come.*
>
> *Yes, there was no question but to go. But what about Mr. Burns? Could it be that all they had looked forward to was not of the Lord?*
>
> *'Thine ears shall hear a word behind thee saying This is the way, walk ye in it' …*
>
> *But for the moment the path that had seemed so clear before them was lost in strange uncertainty."*
>
> (Taylor & Taylor, 1911: 408)

Taylor had keenly desired to support the work of Burns. But, as we have seen, not only had God's intervention saved Burns' life but, in due season, both Burns and Taylor were blessed, even though moving in separate directions.

> *"Meanwhile letters were reaching Hudson Taylor from Swatow, telling of the return of his dear and honoured friend [Burns], and the recommencement of the work there*

with many tokens of encouragement. Mr. Burns wrote with all the old affection, anticipating a renewal of their partnership in service. But while rejoicing that Swatow was again occupied, and that Dr. De la Porte had undertaken the medical side of the work, Hudson Taylor had no longer any doubt as to his own relation to it. For him that door was closed. Again and again, while making it a matter of special prayer, hindrances had been put in the way of his return, until he had come to see that it was not of the Lord. That was enough. With him a question once settled in the faith and fear of God there was no reopening it. Throughout life it was one of his outstanding characteristics that he never went back on what had once been made clear to him as Divine guidance."

(Taylor & Taylor, 1911: 418)

Taylor concluded:

"We cannot do much, but we can do a little, and God can do a great deal."

(Taylor & Taylor, 1918: 607)

*"Leave to His sovereign sway
To choose and to command;
So shalt thou wandering own His way,
How wise, how strong His hand.*

*Far, far above thy thought
His counsel shall appear,
When fully He the work hath wrought
That caused thy needless fear."*

(Taylor & Taylor, 1911: 312)

Refuse to become "civilized"

The temptations to "get organized" are many. We have looked at the desire to make things happen. But other reasons for establishing "our" organization may tempt you. Maybe it's the lure of being treated as "special", like having your name on a special car park. Or maybe you like to control the actions and beliefs of others; or one of many other reasons.

Whatever your trigger, there is a simple answer: Refuse to play the game.

"The civilized build shelters and invite God to stay with them; barbarians move with God wherever He chooses to go. The civilized Christian has a routine; the barbarian disciple has a mission. The civilized believer knows the letter of the law; the barbarian disciple lives the spirit of the law. The religiously civilized love tradition; the barbarian spirit loves challenges. The civilized are satisfied with ritual; barbarians live and thrive in the mystical. For the civilized disciple, religion provides stability and certainty; for the barbarian, a life in God is one of risk and mystery."

(McManus, 2005: 78-79)

Such words are often attractive to bold and adventurous youth (and the young-at-heart) who are willing to go beyond the systems and rituals of the status quo. But even if young people break free from the oppressive traditions of the previous generation (and I encourage them to do just that), Rinehart warns that their new-found freedom may, one generation later (if not sooner), become yet another tradition. He talks of how James and John wanted positions of honor in the kingdom that Jesus was promising, and notes that such an attitude is one that

> *"... reasserts itself with every generation."*
>
> (Rinehart, 1998: 28)

Break free. Stay free. And refuse to enslave others.

CHAPTER 49:
AVOID THE PATH TO LEADERSHIP

Throughout history, we have seen leaders who rise up and overthrow corrupt regimes, only to go on themselves to become corrupt or, at best, misled. Communists have opposed the inequity of the wealthy while they were poor, only to have a number in their ranks later become a class of wealthy privileged within the Communist party. Military coups have thrown out dictatorial leaders, only to find the new military leaders have, over time, become entrenched as dictators themselves.

Those who have been abused often turn to being abusers themselves, later playing out their hurt as perpetrators of abuse. Within Christendom, we have seen church leaders abuse their power and position. It would be tragic if some who read this book find freedom, only to use their own freedom to enslave or abuse others.

It can be frighteningly easy to unwittingly repeat the mistakes made by others from our past. The same human tendencies that we condemn in others are likely to be temptations to us, too. A few specific warnings may assist us, and remind us of the dangers.

As noted earlier in this book, Amy Carmichael simply exercised freedom from the domination of others, whether such freedom was acceptable to them or not. She was an example of an individual claiming freedom from hierarchical powers (church leaders, mission boards, etc.).

The American evangelist, Charles Finney, demonstrated the same principles, but from the standpoint of the "minister". While many in his position might seek to dominate and direct the outcomes of others, Finney apparently did not. In his presentation of the good news, he would simply state the need for repentance and forgiveness then leave the room.

"No manipulating. No emotional pitch. No pressure."

Green (2000: 37)

With no controlling manipulation, Finney saw sound results. How? By deliberately getting out of the way and letting God do the job!

> "How did [Finney] do it? He didn't. He knew the Holy Spirit would work in the hearts of people. It's not a Christian's job to bring a person to repentance and new life in Christ. Finney understood this and was careful not to rob the Spirit of his role."
>
> Green (2000: 38)

These examples challenge us to be on guard against demanding obedience from those we might feel should show us some respect.

In secular systems such as national government or the military, there are control structures to govern how its members perform their job. There are policy and procedure manuals, training programs, and forms of discipline for those who don't toe the party line. The work of the organization is well scripted, and all participants are expected to comply. Unfortunately, such approaches can also be observed amongst "ministry" programs within Christian institutions.

We must also be alert to the subtle (and not-so-subtle) practices that appear under the banner of "discipleship".

> "In the civilized view of discipleship, everything and everyone moves toward the center. Discipleship is translated into standardizing everyone into the same pattern. We have equated the promise that we would be conformed into the image of Christ with a belief that all of us will be the same. Discipleship has become the mechanism for uniformity rather than uniqueness.
>
> ... [God's] desire is not to conform us, but to transform us. Not to make us compliant, but to make us creative. His intent is never to domesticate us, but to liberate us."
>
> (McManus, 2005: 63-64)

Even if we are not part of a local church institution we must strive to give any individuals who work with us the liberty to hear what we have to say, yet ensure that they apply our experience in any way that suits them, or even let them totally reject our recommendations. That's freedom for them as well as us.

Death by leadership

In your freedom from following the visions of some church or other leader, you may have ended up following God's many calls on your life, but in a way that is hidden from the view of others. Conversely, what you are doing may be highly visible, and may be applauded by others. If this is the case, you are in danger of ending up in a leadership role, either because your eager fan club is pushing you into that role, or your own ego is pushing you. We have already looked long and hard at reasons to escape from the so-called "authority" of church leaders. A reminder is not needed that there should be no-one (including you!) who comes between God and others who seek to follow His call. But to drive the point home we'll look briefly again at how the emergence of a leader can kill off the essential life of what you are doing by allowing the ministry's ongoing outreach to depend on you.

So often people confuse their identity as a person (who they *are*) with what they *do*. In many social circumstances, one of the first questions asked of a new acquaintance is something like, "And what do you do?" Similarly, in local church settings, one may be asked what role an individual plays—the priest/pastor, or elder, or "just" (!!!) a member.

With this expectation as a background, it is easy for someone to have ambitions to be recognized as a leader, and to tie their own personal image to that ministry.

> *"When our identity … becomes fused with our ministry, then any challenge or criticism will feel quite personal – an attack on who we are. … If we are so heavily invested in the ministry, then we won't be able to let go …*
>
> *When this happens, we … begin to subtly require a blind loyalty from people, one that defers to our desires and plans, because we are 'the leader.' "*
>
> (Rinehart, 1998: 153)
>
> *"If my identity is fused with the ministry [and if I'm seen to be the leader], I will be a roadblock to the greater purposes of God."*
>
> (Rinehart, 1998: 154)

Taylor succinctly articulates a healthy relationship between us and the ministry to which we are called. We are not to become so closely aligned to a ministry that we feel it is ours, nor are we to be so detached we do not fulfil our responsibilities:

> *"It is His work, not mine nor yours: and yet it is ours – not because we are engaged in it, but because we are His, and one with Him Whose work it is."*
>
> (Taylor & Taylor, 1918: 189)

In describing the groundswell of university student interest in missionary work, and with Taylor's plans to head off to China with two ex-students just when a call came that they speak in Scotland, the biographer notes,

> *"Mr. Taylor was preparing to set out … when the unexpected happened, and God's purposes broke in upon these well-laid plans with an overflowing fullness that carried all before it.*
>
> *It came about very naturally, and apart altogether from design or effort."*
>
> (Taylor & Taylor, 1918: 380-381)

Taylor was committed to the work, but was open to God changing his priorities and plans. In a similar manner, God may call you to put in many years or even decades of faithful service, focusing on one outreach. Or He may sideline you at any time and free you up to follow Him in some totally new manner.

It is one thing to be committed to loyal service, but it is another to perform a role to meet your personal need for recognition. Our commitment has to be to God as He directs, and not to any ministry. To be more committed to the ministry or vision is to worship that ministry or vision rather than Him who gave it.

God may spotlight any such attitude by bringing new workers alongside. They may work differently to you as they may have a similar call, but with sufficient overlap to make you feel threatened if your motives are wrong. Maybe you do not go so far as to "white-ant" them, trying to lessen their influence on others. But do you feel threatened by *their* "success"? Do you try to suppress their individuality and attempt to get them to comply with the shape of ministry *you* have established?

If you have financial supporters who are called by God for that purpose, one acid test might be whether you would you are willing to introduce the new kid on the block to your financial supporters, realizing that they may now channel some of the funds that used to come to you, to the new starter? Or do you raise some pious-sounding argument as to why you need to protect the funding stream for "your" ministry?

Rinehart argues that ministries thrive if the would-be leader's ego dies, and ministries die if someone is elevated into the role of anointed leader:

> *"Wouldn't it be helpful ... [if we understood] this human digression from spiritual renewal to spiritual stagnation? Surely it is crucial to resist the human tendency to resort to strategies of power and control to bring about spiritual results.*
>
> *Suppose we see our role as servant charged with the responsibility and privilege of helping others come into the fruitful expression of God's vision for their part in the kingdom. Then we may avoid the temptation to build our own kingdoms to which we recruit others with their time and talents.*
>
> *Of course, if we continue to focus people's eyes on Christ, we will not be the 'Maypole' around which everything revolves. And that may be painful. Yet, in this way, the ministry itself will not calcify into an organizational structure that requires loyalty and protection as it moves further from the Holy Sprit's leading."*

(Rinehart, 1998: 83-84)

In spite of his many strengths, Hudson Taylor had obviously allowed his leadership style later in life to engender a dependency on him instead of God.

> *"The family feeling in the Mission had been very precious to its early workers, who were accustomed to dealing with Mr. Taylor direct about <u>every matter</u> in which advice and help were needed."* [Emphasis mine]

(Taylor & Taylor, 1918: 393)

We may wish to assume that Taylor was not conscious of the danger of having others depend on him, coming to him about *"every matter in which advice and help were needed"*. However, the danger exists whether the dependency is a conscious strategy for power, or an unconscious trend. Either way, it is the responsibility of each of us to proactively refuse to be appointed in the place of God, and to actively point others to God for His direction and wisdom.

> *"In the final analysis, allowing people to make us 'the leader' is a denial of the truth that Jesus Himself is the Head of the body. If we usurp His role, do we not become, in practice, a pseudo deity? Yet only He can lead an individual or a group of people in the way they were meant to go."*
>
> (Rinehart, 1998: 155)

We all have a role

Perhaps one of the greatest antidotes for the temptation to become a group's special "leader" is consciously maintaining a humble recognition that we each have a part to play. One person may have had the initial vision for what has subsequently become a ministry involving several people. We are trying to avoid *all* aspects of a special leadership class. For the person who instigates an outreach to set himself up as leader not only goes against this principle, but smacks of egotism.

A brief look at the examples of others may encourage us to keep our hands off the reins, and let God have His way.

Bill expresses the view that each individual has a primary responsibility for discerning their own call:

> *"… I think your choice of whether to take a particular … [ministry] job is to be found in your own conscience. No one else can tell you for certain what you ought to do at a particular time."*
>
> (Bill, 1967: 21)

Taylor experienced the necessity of looking to God for directions rather than to man. As a pioneer, he was often found to be

> *"… working without precedent in many respects …"*
>
> (Taylor & Taylor, 1918: 166)

Often God will call you to something that others do not fully understand, or may even resist. It can be lonely. But sometimes we must launch out in faith in God's ability to lead, and allow Him to direct others with a shared vision to join with us, as He sees fit.

> *"Eric Folke … deeply conscious of a call from God to [China], could find no Swedish society to send him there. Going independently, he was welcomed at the C.I.M. in Shanghai, and passed on to its training home at An-kin for the study of the language. Six months later he wrote … of his desire to work in association with the Inland Mission …"*
>
> (Taylor & Taylor, 1918: 473)

Having said that God is more than capable of joining others with us, it may not always work out that way. Sometimes we are pleasantly surprised to find fellow travelers who share a matching vision. More often, we will encounter some who have a similar vision, and we have a partial overlap. Rather than viewing only a partial alignment of calling as a disappointment, we should see this as a great encouragement—we see part of the vision, they see a different part, and God orchestrates the whole. It is He who puts the jigsaw pieces together to make the picture complete.

However, we cannot guarantee even that level of fellowship. Sometimes we must accept that others following what they believe to be their work for God may not understand us and our call. In grace, we can accept that they are fellow workers, but called to march to the beat of a different drum, or maybe a slightly different tune.

Perhaps they are missing the mark, or maybe it is we who are off track—we are all less than perfect. Or possibly it is as simple as each of us having a different calling. But whatever the reasons for our differences, we can and should work at our calling as best we understand it to be, be gracious to others who work differently, and be open to learning from them.

> *"Keenly as Mr. Taylor felt the attitude of opposition, he knew that those whose views differed most widely from his own might have just as sincere a desire for the advancement of the Kingdom of God."*
>
> (Taylor & Taylor, 1918: 293)

We need to strive for openness in working with others who have a radically different calling, or even a slightly different calling. It may be easier to write them off, but God may wish us to work together as a collection of people, complementing each other through diversity.

> *"How much easier it would have been to go on alone, independently, he may have felt. But where is there room for independence in a living organism, every part of which is bound up with the whole?"*
>
> (Taylor & Taylor, 1918: 293-294)

Taylor exhibited much of this willingness to accommodate others, going so far as to see the necessity of diversity. As quoted earlier, one of his team who often expressed different views questioned whether he should even be part of the team, but Taylor not only encouraged him to stay but also encouraged his contrary views:

> *"... Mr. Cooper possessed strong individuality and was fearless as to his convictions. Mr. Taylor's relationship ... with this beloved friend ... may be judged from an incident that took place in the early days of the China Council.*
>
> *'I do not like so often to oppose you,' said Mr. Cooper on one occasion; 'I think I had better resign.'*
>
> *'No, indeed!' was the reply, 'I value such opposition; it saves me from many a mistake.'"*
>
> (Taylor & Taylor, 1918: 554)

Hudson Taylor had a reputation for serving the needs of others.

> *"To Mr. Taylor and his companions the journey was memorable for its discomforts. Setting out toward the end of June, they found the heat intense. Flies swarmed*

> *everywhere; food was difficult to obtain; and at night the younger men, new to such conditions, were thoroughly 'played out' and often too tired to unpack their provisions or forage for a meal. More than once they were roused after hours of slumber by Mr. Taylor's cheery invitation to come and share his 'midnight chicken,' prepared as likely as not with his own hands.*
>
> *… Who that ever travelled with him could forget his unfailing care and thought for others, and the practical way in which he could turn his hand to anything. Cooking was quite in his line. 'All the way Mr. Taylor prepared food for me,' recalled Miss Murray of the journey down the Kwang-sin river, when she was recovering from her serious illness. 'He used to make omelets in the back of the boat. We would hear him beating up the eggs. He managed to get the things somehow!'"*
>
> (Taylor & Taylor, 1918: 402)

To have such a willingness to serve is a great characteristic. But Taylor's life throws us yet another challenge—when we feel called to one form of ministry, are we willing to also be supportive and a source of blessing to others who are "different" from us?

> *"When [Hudson Taylor] was speaking … he would make no plea for funds. Often I used to hear him explain, almost apologetically, that his great desire was that no funds should be diverted from other societies to the China inland Mission; and that it was for this reason he had taken up lines of working which he hoped would preclude interference with other organisations. Nothing gave him more genuine pleasure than to speak well of other missions."*
>
> (Taylor & Taylor, 1918: 374)

Bill from Alcoholics Anonymous succinctly summarizes Taylor's discovery that others who operate differently from us can still be used by God to achieve His ends and, where at all possible, we should gratefully and gladly support them:

> *"We can be grateful for every agency or method that tries to solve the problem of alcoholism – whether of medicine, religion, education, or research. We can be open-minded toward all such efforts and we can be sympathetic when the ill-advised ones fail. We can remember that A.A. itself ran for years on 'trial and error.'*
>
> *As individuals, we can and should work with those that promise success – even a little success."*
>
> (Bill, 1967: 147)

The Body of Christ has many members, and each one is vital, significant and extremely valuable. We cannot do without one another. We are all equally part of that Body and should do all that we can to keep every part working according to the purpose for which it was (or we were) designed. God has a unique and wonderful place for each of us as we live in and give out the light, life and love of Jesus Christ to those living in darkness.

He graciously gives His Spirit "shed abroad in our hearts" to direct, control and comfort us in this ministry. We have seen that there have been many, many believers struggling throughout history with the very issues of human control that we face today. We can rest in the knowledge that our loving Father knows our hearts and yearns to lead us to an ever-growing dependency on Him alone.

May we always be in tune with His voice, His leading and His ministry to those in need, in a rich and humbling awareness that we are all receivers of the grace that comes to each and every one of us so freely.

As we approach the end of this book, I wish to say "thank you" to you, the reader, for sharing this journey with me. Each of us is precious to God, and that includes you. May you discover the freedom I believe God intends for you—freedom that is based on your personal walk with God, not on another's interpretation of His purposes for your life. God bless you.

And finally, I would like to re-share the following quotation:

> *One day you and I will stand before the Judge of all the earth and give an account for our lives. What will we say when He asks us why we failed to do what we knew was right, why the affirmation of man was more important to us than the affirmation of heaven, why we willingly deceived ourselves with cheap answers rather than walk the costly path of submission to the Father's will? How will we respond?"*
>
> (Brown, 2002: 186-187)

As the author says, how will we respond?

ACKNOWLEDGMENTS

This book would not, and could not, have been shaped as it has without the courageous and insightful manner in which my wife trod the path to freedom herself. She then lovingly and gently encouraged me as I sought to discover my own path.

I have been blessed in life with many who have also invested in my journey. Sometimes they challenged me; always they demonstrated their true friendship by accepting me throughout my long and often painful journey. Some kindly reviewed the earlier emerging manuscript. Thank you, Karl, Ray and others, for such support.

If you believe in miracles of timing, then my "chance" meeting with my editor, Bronwyn Forman, was one such event. Not only is she skilled in her craft, but her own route to freedom gave her an independent and highly valuable perspective on the message of the book. She gently prodded me about the themes, and refined the content, as only an editor with passion can do.

Another "chance" meeting was with Adam Dunning. Where do I start? As a legal professional skilled in matters of copyright and defamation, he performed a thorough and insightful review of the entire manuscript. For the quality of his work, and his generosity, I cannot thank him enough. But it didn't end there. He went way beyond the call of duty, and put his heart into the review. As with Bronwyn, his astute questions and comments stretched me, and contributed enormously to the end product. He is a man with breadth and depth of diverse skills. On so many fronts he contributes to the those fortunate enough to engage with him, and to the wider community. I am most certainly grateful to have been helped on my way by this amazing man.

Behind this book is a lifetime of experiences. In my own periods of pain, I was lovingly embraced by others. They often also had aching hearts of their own, but found the strength and grace to reach out to me, and many others. The list of these people is enormous, so I dare not even try to name them all.

As you read this book, you will soon understand how I feel deeply indebted to the many authors whose works I have read, analyzed, critiqued and sometimes challenged. Some authors are identified in the bibliography; many more are to be thanked.

It might sound trite to thank my heavenly Father, too, for upholding me, and for inviting me to walk closer to Him. I'm eternally grateful for His unconditional love!

AFTERWORD

Relating to our Heavenly Father

A very quick look at the Bible seems to reveals a theme that some may find disturbing. It's this: The creator of the universe wants to relate to you and me, directly and personally.

Really? Can that be true?

Let's look at Adam and Eve. Yes, the God of the universe walked and talked with them. Even after they had sinned, God came looking for them. But they withdrew and tried to hide from Him.

We jump forward to the Israelites in the desert. After Adam and Eve, did God still want to relate to His people? Exodus 20 tells us the people said to Moses that they were willing to listen to him, but feared the outcome of God speaking to them directly. Moses was told by his father-in-law to become a go-between between God and His people.

The theme of go-betweens continues. In 1 Samuel 8, it is absolutely clear that God wants to be the King of His people. But no, they want an earthly king.

Now the point in history that changed everything. God came to us, in the form of Jesus. Again, He walked and talked with us. Importantly, he banished all forms of go-betweens, stating (in Matthew 23:8-12) beyond any form of doubt that we are to have no one claiming titles such as master / teacher / father coming between us and God. How clear can that be. And yet church traditions so often establish go-betweens, often on several levels within a hierarchy.

Jesus is our only mediator (1 Timothy 25-6), and Jesus has sent the Holy Spirit to help us. We don't need other humans to take their place.

God, our Heavenly Father, still wants to relate to us, one-on-one. Scary? Only if you don't trust Father's love. Let's embrace a relationship with Father, and walk away from church traditions that get in the way.

If you want to pursue this topic further (and I hope you do), some material you might find helpful includes the following:

- Wayne Jacobsen has shared much on the topic of relationships with God. One of his books, *He Loves Me*, presents a gentle, reasoned case for God's love and His desire to relate to each of us. The message, if embraced, has the potential to be absolutely life-changing.

- A similar them, but this time wrapped in a novel, is presented in *The Shack* by William Paul Young (with, I understand, contributions by Wayne Jacobsen, Brad Cummings and Bobby Downes). I have seen glowing praise for this book, but also concern expressed by some as to questionable theological precision in the portrayal of the Trinity. For what it's worth, I suggest that *The Shack* can be valued as a beautiful allegory, along with other timeless books such as *Pilgrim's Progress*.

- Wayne Jacobsen and Dave Coleman's book, *So You Don't Want to go to Church Anymore* might be prejudged as focusing on condemning institutional church structures. Instead, my reading of this wonderful book is that it is actually an easy-to-read novel uses fictional characters to present a delightful picture of a life lived in the freedom of trusting and following Father.

- Philip Yancey's book, *The Jesus I Never Knew*, has autobiographical elements where Yancey shares his own journey to the discovery of a very different Jesus than that presented by some churches, including his own childhood church.

- Wayne Jacobsen valued his friendship with the late Kevin Smith. Wayne's memorial words about Kevin in https://www.lifestream.org/farewell-kevin-and-thank-you/ are worth reading, as well as listening to the associated links to audio recordings of conversations with Kevin, available via https://www.thegodjourney.com/archives/archives-by-guest/#kevinsmith

Breaking free

This book has focused on dismantling the authoritative claims for "church traditions". The goal is to facilitate you walking away in freedom. I fully expect there will be many who write off this book, maybe even going so far as to claim it is heretical. Sadly, some of those that oppose your freedom may feel too threatened by the loss of control in the hierarchies that they have invested so much in. Rather than joining you in embracing their own freedom, they may get defensive, or even go out on the attack.

Don't be surprised. And don't be forced back into "slavery" to their controlling demands.

This book has referenced the works of many others. If you've found this book helpful in providing you with a new perspective, my response is to use the phrase that goes something like, "If I have seen further than some, it is because I have stood on the shoulders of giants." There are so many books that have helped me on my journey, and a tiny subset of them are noted below. You might like to read some of them for yourself

- Richard Foster's book, *Money, Sex & Power*, tackles some thorny issues in an insightful and balanced manner. The section on "power" is particularly relevant for us in light of misuse of power within institutional churches

- … and if you want to be inspired to bravery, I recommend reading *The Barbarian Way* by Erwin Raphael McManus and *No Compromise* by Keith Green.

BIBLIOGRAPHY

The material referenced in this book came from a diversity of styles and opinions. Based on my own perspective, I believe a number of books portray essential truths, while others are included as representing common but what I consider to be misguided thinking. And of course, even the "good" books may be a mixture.

The quotations included in this book are ones that helped shape my thinking. I hope you have found them insightful. And while I have tried to faithfully copy the exact wording, I apologize for any transcription errors I may have made.

ABC News. (2023) *Accused FLDS teen rapist gets slap on wrist*. Available electronically from the Internet at https://abcnews.go.com/US/accused-flds-teen-rapist-slap-wrist/story?id=12960579, extracted on 30th April, 2023.

Ackoff, R. (1991) *Ackoff's Fables*. United States of America: John Wiley & Sons.

Alcoholics Anonymous World Services, Inc. (abbreviated as AAWS within this book). (1953; quotations and page numbering from 7th Australian printing, in 2002) *Twelve Steps and Twelve Traditions*. Australia: Alcoholics Anonymous World Services, Inc.

Alcoholics Anonymous World Services, Inc. (abbreviated as AAWS within this book). (1957; quotations and page numbering from 27th reprint in 2002) *Alcoholics Anonymous Comes of Age*. New York: Alcoholics Anonymous World Services, Inc.

Alden, I. (1997) *Ruth Erskine's Crosses*. United States of America: Living Books / Tyndale House Publishers. Originally published in 1879.

Arthur, R. (1991) *Wisdom Hunter*. Oregon, USA: Multnomah Books / Questar Publishers.

Arthur, R. (1993) *Jordan's Crossing*. Oregon, USA: Multnomah Books / Questar Publishers.

Baker, P. (1997) *Weird Christians I have met*. South Australia: In Out Resources Inc.

Beaver, R. (1970) *The History of Mission Strategy*. Taken from Southwestern Journal of Theology, Vol. XII, No.2, 1970. In Winter, R. & Hawthorne, S. (Eds.) (1981) *Perspectives on the World Christian Movement*. California: William Carey Library.

Bennett, D. (1984) *Nine O'clock in the Morning*. Eastbourne, Great Britain: Kingsway Publications.

Bevere, J. (1997) *The Fear of the Lord*. Florida, USA: Charisma House.

"Bill" (anonymous co-founder of Alcoholics Anonymous). (1967) *As Bill Sees It*. New York: Alcoholics Anonymous World Services, Inc.

Brewster, E.T, E. & Brewster, E. S. *Bonding and the Missionary Task: Establishing a Sense of Belonging.* From *Bonding and the Missionary Task.* Lingua House.
In Winter, R. & Hawthorne, S. (Eds.) (1981) *Perspectives on the World Christian Movement.* California: William Carey Library.

Bridges J. (1985) *The pursuit of Holiness.* Navpress.

Brown, M. (2002) *Revolution in the Church.* Grand Rapids, Michigan: Chosen Books, a Division of Baker House Co.

Buckingham, J. (1980) *Where Eagles Soar.* Eastbourne, Great Britain: Kingsway Publications.

Buckingham, J. (1978) *The Last Word,* United States of America: Logos International.

Clarnette, D. (1967) *50 Years on Fire for God: The story of Walter Betts.* Victoria, Australia: New Life Publications.

Cymbala, J. (1997) *Fresh Wind, Fresh Fire.* Grand Rapids, Michigan: Zondervan Publishing House.

Dayton, E. & Fraser, D. (1980) *Strategy.* Excerpts from *Planning Strategies for World Evangelization.* Wm. B. Eerdman's Publishing Co., Michigan. In Winter, R. & Hawthorne, S. (Eds.) (1981) *Perspectives on the World Christian Movement.* California: William Carey Library.

Duncan, S. (2006) *Salvation Creek.* Australia & New Zealand: Bantam.

Edman, V. (1960) *They Found the Secret.* Michigan, USA: Zondervan Publishing House.

Elkins, C. (1980) *Heavenly Deception.* Illinois, USA: Tyndale House Publishers, Inc.

Foster, C. & Kennedy, P. (2010) *Hell on the way to Heaven.* Sydney, Australia: Random House Australia Pty Ltd.

Foster, R. (1985) *Money, Sex & Power.* London: Hodder & Stoughton. [Page numbers quoted from the publication of *Celebration of Discipline* and *Prayers from the Heart* jointly with *Money, Sex & Power*).

Free Indeed. (2000) *Welcome to Free Indeed.* Available electronically from the Internet at http://www.geocities.com/welcometofreeindeed, extracted on 22nd August, 2000.

Frost, M. & Hirsch, A. (2003) *The Shaping of things to Come.* Massachusetts, USA: Hendrikson Publishers, Inc.

Gilley, G. (2005) *This Little Church Went to Market.* Darlington, England: Evangelical Press.

Girard, R. (1972) *Brethren, Hang Loose.* Michigan, USA: The Zondervan Corporation.

Glasser, A. (1976) *Crucial Dimensions in World Evangelization.* Nashville: Broadman Press. In Winter, R. & Hawthorne, S. (Eds.) (1981) *Perspectives on the World Christian Movement.* California: William Carey Library.

Goerner, H. (1979) *All Nations in God's Purpose*. California: William Carey Library. In Winter, R. & Hawthorne, S. (Eds.) (1981) *Perspectives on the World Christian Movement*. California: William Carey Library.

Grant, C. (1976) *Europe's Moravians: A Pioneer Missionary Church*. Evangelical Missions Quarterly, Vol. 12, #4. In Winter, R. & Hawthorne, S. (Eds.) (1981) *Perspectives on the World Christian Movement*. California: William Carey Library.

Green, K. (2000) *If you Love the Lord*. Oregon: Harvest House Publishers.

Green, M. & Hazard, D. (1989) *No Compromise*. Great Britain: Word Publishing.

Gulley, P. (1997) *Front Porch Tales*. Oregon, USA: Multnomah Books.

Hatcher, L. (2005) *I'm Not Crazy, I'm Just A Little Unwell*. Sydney, Australia: Strand Publishing.

Hattersley, R. (2000) *Blood & Fire*. London, Great Britain: Abacus.

Hayford, J. (1997) *Pastors of Promise*. California, USA: Regal Books.

Henke, D. (2000) *Spiritual Abuse*. Available electronically from the Internet at http://www.watchman.org/profile/abusepro.htm, extracted on 14th October, 2000.

Herman, N. (circa 1666) *The Practice of the Presence of God*. Collected by Revell, F. (1958) *The Practice of the Presence of God, with Spiritual Maxims*. Grand Rapids, Michigan, USA: Spire Books.

Hesselgrave, D. (1978) *The Role of Culture in Communication, and World-view and Contextualization*. From *Communicating Christ Cross-Culturally*. Zondervan Publishing House. In Winter, R. & Hawthorne, S. (Eds.) (1981) *Perspectives on the World Christian Movement*. California: William Carey Library.

Hiebert, P. *Culture and Cross-Cultural Differences, and Social Structure and Church Growth*. In Winter, R. & Hawthorne, S. (Eds.) (1981) *Perspectives on the World Christian Movement*. California: William Carey Library.

Hunt, A. (2004) *The Debt*. Nashville, USA: Westbow Press.

Jacobsen, W. & Coleman, D. (2006) *So You Don't Want to go to Church Anymore*. CA, USA: Windblown Media.

Joyner, R. (1996) *The Final Quest*. USA: Whitaker House.

Kane, J. (1980) *The Work of Evangelism*. From *Life and Work on the Mission Field*. Baker Book House. In Winter, R. & Hawthorne, S. (Eds.) (1981) *Perspectives on the World Christian Movement*. California: William Carey Library.

Kim, E. (1977) *If I Perish*. Chicago, USA: Moody Press.

Kwast, L. *Understanding Culture*. In Winter, R. & Hawthorne, S. (Eds.) (1981) *Perspectives on the world Christian movement*. California: William Carey Library.

Latourette, K. (1953) *A History of Christianity*. Harper and Row, Publishers, Inc.. In Winter, R. & Hawthorne, S. (Eds.) (1981) *Perspectives on the World Christian Movement*. California: William Carey Library.

Lausanne Committee for World Evangelization, the.(1978) *The Willowbank Report*. The Lausanne Committee for World Evangelization. In Winter, R. & Hawthorne, S. (Eds.) (1981) *Perspectives on the World Christian Movement*. California: William Carey Library.

Lausanne Committee for World Evangelization, the (1980) *Christian Witness to the Chinese People*. Excerpts from the series of Lausanne Occasional Papers emerging from the Consultation on World Evangelization, Thailand, 1980. In Winter, R. & Hawthorne, S. (Eds.) (1981) *Perspectives on the World Christian Movement*. California: William Carey Library.

Levin, T. (2007) *People in Glass Houses*. Melbourne, Australia: Black Inc.

Levine, R., Locke, C., Searls, D. and Weinberger, D. (2000) *The Cluetrain Manifesto*. Cambridge, Massachusetts: Perseus Books.

Lindsay, T. (1996) *Martin Luther: The man who started the Reformation*. Great Britain: Christian Focus Publications. An updated version of Thomas Lindsay's 1900 book, *Luther and the German Reformation*.

Lucado, M. (1994) *When God Whispers Your Name*. Dallas, Texas: Word Incorporated.

MacArthur, J. (1997) *The Power of Integrity*. Illinois, USA: Crossway Books, a division of Good News Publishers.

MacDonald, G. (1983(a)) – Edited by Phillips, M. *The Poet and the Pauper: The Baronet's Song*. Minnesota, USA: Bethany House Publishers. Original published in 1879 under the title *Sir Gibbie*.

MacDonald, G. (1983(b)) – Edited by Phillips, M. *The Poet and the Pauper: The Shepherd's Castle*. Minnesota, USA: Bethany House Publishers. Original published in 1883 under the title *Donal Grant*.

MacDonald, G. (1988) – Edited by Phillips, M. *A Daughter's Devotion*. Minnesota, USA: Bethany House Publishers. Original published in 1881 under the title *Mary Marston*.

McDowell, J. (1999) *The New Evidence That Demands a Verdict*. Nashville, USA: Thomas Nelson Publishers.

McGavran, D. (1981) *The Bridges of God*. Excerpts from *The Bridges of God*. In Winter, R. & Hawthorne, S. (Eds.) (1981) *Perspectives on the World Christian Movement*. California: William Carey Library.

McManus, E. (2005) *The Barbarian Way*. Nashville, USA: Thomas Nelson Publishers.

Moffett, S. *Evangelism: The Leading Partner*. In Winter, R. & Hawthorne, S. (Eds.) (1981) *Perspectives on the World Christian Movement*. California: William Carey Library.

Moody, D.L. (circa 1890) *The Faith Which Overcomes*. London: Morgan & Scott.

Mott, J. (1901) *The Responsibility of the Young People for the Evangelization of the World*. Excerpts from *Missionary Issues of the Twentieth Century*. In Winter, R. & Hawthorne, S. (Eds.) (1981) *Perspectives on the World Christian Movement*. California: William Carey Library.

NBC News. (2023) *Ex-teen bride winds $16 million case against polygamous group*. Available electronically from the Internet at https://www.nbcnews.com/news/us-news/ex-teen-bride-wins-16-million-case-against-polygamous-group-n799286, extracted on 30th April, 2023.

Nee, W. (1967) *Changed into His Likeness*. Eastbourne, Great Britain: Kingsway Publications. In Nee, W. *Classics from Watchman Nee*, Eastbourne, Great Britain: Kingsway Publications.

Nida, E. (1972) *Communication and Social Structure*. Reprinted from *Message and Mission*. William Carey Library Publishers. In Winter, R. & Hawthorne, S. (Eds.) (1981) *Perspectives on the World Christian Movement*. California: William Carey Library.

Noble, J. (2002) *The Shaking*. London, UK: Monarch Books.

Nouwen, H. (1972) *The Wounded Healer: Ministry in Contemporary Society*. New York, USA: Doubleday.

Nouwen, H. (1989) *In the Name of Jesus: Reflections on Christian Leadership*. New York: Crossroads. In Rinehart, S. (1998) *Upside Down: The paradox of servant leadership* United States of America: Navpress

Oliver, D. & Thwaites, J. (2001) *Church that Works*. Milton Keynes, England: Word Publishing.

Ortiz, J. (1975) *Disciple*. Illinois, USA: Creation House.

Parshall, P. (1979) *God's Communicator in the 80's*. Reprinted from *Evangelical Mission Quarterly*. Evangelical Missions Information Service, Illinois. In Winter, R. & Hawthorne, S. (Eds.) (1981) *Perspectives on the World Christian Movement*. California: William Carey Library.

Patterson, G. (1981) *The Spontaneous Multiplication of Churches*. In Winter, R. & Hawthorne, S. (Eds.) (1981) *Perspectives on the World Christian Movement*. California: William Carey Library.

Pawson, D. (1984) *God is Calling the Church to Change*. Adelaide, Australia: Excerpts from an audio-taped presentation to the United Charismatic Convention, 1984, sponsored by the House of Tabor.

Pearse, G. (1800s) *Thoughts on Holiness*. London: R & R Clark, Edinburgh.

Peretti, F. (1999) *The Visitation*. Nashville, Tennessee, USA: Word Publishing.

Peretti, F. (2000) *The Wounded Spirit*. Nashville, Tennessee, USA: Word Publishing.

Phillips, M. (1995) *The Secret of the Rose (4) – Dawn of Liberty*. Illinois: Tyndale House Publishers, Inc.

Phillips, M. (1996) *Mercy and Eagleflight*. USA: Christian Family Book Club.

Phillips, M. (1998) *The Garden at the Edge of Beyond*. Minnesota: Bethany House Publishers.

Plass, A. (1991) *View From A Bouncy Castle*. Great Britain: Fount Paperbacks.

Plass, A. (1995) *Stress Family Robinson*. Great Britain: Marshall Pickering.

Plass, A. (1999) *The Visit*. Michigan, Great Britain: Harper Collins.

Plass, A. (2006) *Jesus – Safe, Tender, Extreme*. Michigan, USA: Zondervan.

Plass, A. (2007) *Bacon Sandwiches and Salvation*. United Kingdom: Authentic Media.

Plass, A. (2010) *Seriously Funny*. United Kingdom: Authentic Media.

Poitier, S. (2001) *The Measure of a Man*. UK: Pocket Books.

Reagan, M. (2004) *Twice Adopted*. Tennesse, USA: Broadman & Holman Publishers.

Richardson, D. (1981) *The Hidden Message of 'Acts'*. (Taken from *Eternity in Their Hearts*. California: Regal Books.) In Winter, R. & Hawthorne, S. (Eds.) (1981) *Perspectives on the World Christian Movement*. California: William Carey Library.

Rinehart, S. (1998) *Upside Down: The Paradox of Servant Leadership*. United States of America: Navpress.

Robinson, G. (2007) *Confronting Power and Sex in the Catholic Church*. Mulgrave, Victoria, Australia: John Garratt Publishing.

Robinson, M. & Smith, D. (2003) *Invading Secular Space*. London, UK: Monarch Books.

Sacks, J. (2003) *The Dignity of Difference*. London, United Kingdom: Continuum.

Safa, R. (1990) *Blood of the Sword - Blood of the Cross*. England: Joint publication by Sovereign World and STL Books.

Sheldon, C. (1984) *In His Steps*. New Jersey: Spire Books. Originally published in the Chicago Advance, 1896.

Sheldon, C. (1999) *Jesus Is Here*. Ohio, United States of America: Barbour Publishing, Inc. Originally published in the Chicago Advance, 1896.

Smalley, W. *Cultural Implications of an Indigenous Church*. From *Readings in Missionary Anthropology II*. William Carey Library Publishers. In Winter, R. & Hawthorne, S. (Eds.) (1981) *Perspectives on the World Christian Movement*. California: William Carey Library.

Snyder, H. (1975) *The Problem of Wineskins*. IL: Inter-Varsity Press. Quoted in Tillapaugh, F. (1982) *Unleashing the Church*. California: Regal Books.

Snyder, H. (1977) *The Church in God's Plan*. Excerpts from *Community of the King*. USA: Inter-Varsity Press. In Winter, R. & Hawthorne, S. (Eds.) (1981) *Perspectives on the World Christian Movement*. California: William Carey Library.

Snyder, H. (1983) *Liberating the Church: The Ecology of Church and Kingdom*. Downers Grove: InterVarsity. In Rinehart, S. (1998) *Upside Down: The paradox of servant leadership*. United States of America: Navpress

Snyder, H. (1989) *Signs of the Spirit: How God Reshapes the Church*. Grand Rapids: Academic Books. In Rinehart, S. (1998) *Upside Down: The paradox of servant leadership*. United States of America: Navpress

Stott, J. (1980) *The Bible in World Evangelization*. Adapted from an address delivered in a plenary session of the *Consultation on World Evangelization*. Thailand. In Winter, R. & Hawthorne, S. (Eds.) (1981) *Perspectives on the World Christian Movement*. California: William Carey Library.

Taylor, H and Taylor, G. (1911) *Hudson Taylor in early years—The Growth of a Soul*. Singapore: Overseas Missionary Fellowship (IHQ) Ltd.

Taylor, H and Taylor, G. (1918) *Hudson Taylor and the China Inland Mission—The Growth of a Work of God*. Singapore: Overseas Missionary Fellowship (IHQ) Ltd.

Taylor, J. [Hudson] (circa 1865) *The Call to Service*. Excerpts from *A Retrospect*, Overseas Missionary Fellowship. In Winter, R. & Hawthorne, S. (Eds.) (1981) *Perspectives on the World Christian Movement*. California: William Carey Library.

Taylor, J. (1975) *Enough is Enough*. London: SCM Press.

Telchin, S. (1981) *Betrayed*. UK: Marshalls Paperbacks.

Tillapaugh, F. (1982) *Unleashing the Church*. California: Regal Books.

Tippett, A. (1975) *The Evangelization of Animists*. From *Let the Earth Hear His Voice*. World Wide Publications, Minneapolis. In Winter, R. & Hawthorne, S. (Eds.) (1981) *Perspectives on the World Christian Movement*. California: William Carey Library.

Wagner, C. Peter. (1974) *The Fourth Dimension of Missions: Strategy*. From *Stop the World, I Want to Get On*. William Carey Library Publishers, Pasedena. In Winter, R. & Hawthorne, S. (Eds.) (1981) *Perspectives on the World Christian Movement*. California: William Carey Library.

Wall, E. (2008) *Stolen Innocence*. New York, USA: HarperCollins.

Winter, R. (1973) *The Two Structures of God's Redemptive Mission.* Excerpts from an address to the All-Asia Mission Consultation in Seoul, Korea. In Winter, R. & Hawthorne, S. (Eds.) (1981) *Perspectives on the World Christian Movement.* California: William Carey Library.

Winter, R. (1974) *The New Macedonia: A Revolutionary New Era in Mission Begins.* Text of an address to the July 1974 Lausanne Congress, also reprinted by William Carey Library Publishers in 1975. In Winter, R. & Hawthorne, S. (Eds.) (1981) *Perspectives on the World Christian Movement.* California: William Carey Library.

Winter, R. & Hawthorne, S. (Eds.) (1981) *Perspectives on the World Christian Movement.* California: William Carey Library.

Yancey, P. (1988) *Disappointment with God.* (In joint publication with *Where is God when it hurts?*) Michigan, USA: Zondervan Publishing House.

Yancey, P. (1995) *The Jesus I Never Knew.* Michigan, USA: Zondervan Publishing House.

Yancey, P. (1997) *What's So Amazing about Grace?* Michigan, USA: Zondervan Publishing House.

Yancey, P. (2001) *Soul Survivor: How My Faith Survived the Church.* London, England: Hodder & Stoughton.

Yancey, P. (2006) *Prayer.* London, England: Hodder & Stoughton.

www.ingramcontent.com/pod-product-compliance
Lightning Source LLC
Chambersburg PA
CBHW082147070526
44585CB00020B/2121